BRITISH IMPERIALISM:
INNOVATION AND EXPANSION 1688–1914

Also available

British Imperialism: Crisis and Deconstruction 1914–1990

P.J. CAIN and A.G. HOPKINS

British Imperialism: Innovation and Expansion 1688–1914

P.J. Cain and A.G. Hopkins

Longman
London and New York

Longman Group UK Limited,
Longman House, Burnt Mill,
Harlow, Essex, CM20 2JE, England
and Associated Companies throughout the world.

Published in the United States of America
by Longman Publishing, New York

First published 1993
Second impression 1993

ISBN 0 582 49175 4 (CSD)
ISBN 0 582 49176 2 (PPR)

British Library Cataloguing-in-Publication Data

A catalogue record for this book is
available from the British Library

Library of Congress Cataloging in Publication Data

Cain, P. J., 1941–
    British imperialism : innovation and expansion, 1688–1914 / P.J.
Cain and A. G. Hopkins.
        p.   cm.
    Includes bibliographical references and index.
    ISBN 0–582–49175–4. – ISBN 0–582–49176–2 (pbk.)
    1. Great Britain – Colonies – History. I. Hopkins, A. G. (Antony
G.) II. Title
JV1011.C17 1993
325′.241′09 – dc20   92–21715
                                                      CIP

Set by 9 in Bembo
Produced by Longman Singapore Publishers (Pte) Ltd.
Printed in Singapore

Contents

List of Tables and Maps

TABLES

MAPS

Preface

The origins, scope and argument of this study are set out in some detail in Chapter 1. We have also acknowledged specific debts to enlisted scholars at appropriate points throughout the text. It remains for us to express here our appreciation of those who have done so much, in different ways, to keep the whole enterprise afloat. We should like to record our gratitude to the Social Science Research Council for Personal Research Grants in 1980–81 and 1983, to colleagues in the University of Birmingham and the Graduate Institute of International Studies for their advice and tolerance of our various impositions, to our students, whose exposure to several versions of our interpretation helped to educate their teachers, and to libraries and librarians, especially in the University of Birmingham and the University of California, Los Angeles, for their resourcefulness in supplying the wide range of materials needed for this study. We also owe a special debt to Sue Kennedy and Diane Martin whose secretarial help has been invaluable. Finally, and most important of all, we must pay tribute to our families, who have borne the deprivations imposed by slow-moving authors with unwavering fortitude and whose limitless support has finally been rewarded by an event that is as surprising as it has been long-promised: this time, the book really is finished.

P.J.C.
University of Birmingham
A.G.H.
The Graduate Institute of International Studies, Geneva.
May 1992

Note on Sources

Since our text makes judgements that rest upon a wide range of detailed research, we have placed our notes at the foot of the page so that our sources can be easily recognised and traced. We hope that this arrangement will give prominence, and hence acknowledgement, to the many scholars whose work has made our own study possible, and that it will be helpful to readers who wish to pursue particular topics or lines of enquiry of their own. In the text and notes the two books which comprise this study are referred to, for the sake of simplicity, as Volume I and Volume II. Books and articles are cited in full on first mention in each chapter, are referred to subsequently by short titles, and should therefore be readily identifiable. The place of publication of books is London unless another location is given. Presenting our citations in this way removes the need to produce a separate bibliography; had we added a consolidated list of references we would also have required a third volume – a prospect that neither the authors nor even their accommodating publishers could have faced.

Acknowledgements

The publishers would like to thank the following for permission to reproduce copyright material: Cambridge University Press for table 3.2 from *British Regional Employment Statistics, 1841–1971*, C.H. Lee (1979), table 5.6 from *Abstract of British Historical Statistics*, B.R. Mitchell and P. Deane (1962), tables 6.1 and 6.2 from *Mammon and the Pursuit of Empire: The Political Economy of British Imperialism, 1860–1912*, Lance E. Davis and Robert A. Huttenback (1987); Harvard University Press for table 5.7 from *Economic Elements in the Pax Britannica*, A.H. Imlah (1958); Oxford University Press for table 5.8 from *British Economic Growth, 1856–1973*, R.C.O. Matthews, C.H. Feinstein and J.C. Odling-Smee (1983); Gage Educational Publishing Company for table 8.2 from *Canada: An Economic History*, W.L. Marr and D.G. Paterson (1980).

Whilst every effort has been made to trace the owners of copyright material in one case this has proved impossible, and we take this opportunity to offer our apologies to any copyright holders whose rights we may have unwittingly infringed.

Abbreviations

African Econ. Hist.	African Economic History
Am. Hist. Rev.	American Historical Review
Am. Pol. Sci. Rev.	American Political Science Review
Austral. Econ. Hist. Rev.	Australian Economic History Review
Brit. Jour. Internat. Stud.	British Journal of International Studies
Brit. Jour. Pol. Sci.	British Journal of Political Science
Brit. Jour. Soc.	British Journal of Sociology
Bull. Bus. Hist. Soc.	Bulletin of the Business History Society
Bull. Inst. Hist. Research	Bulletin of the Institute of Historical Research
Bull. Inst. Mod. Hist.	Bulletin of the Institute of Modern History
Bus. Hist.	Business History
Bus. Hist. Rev.	Business History Review
Canadian Hist. Rev	Canadian Historical Review
Canadian Jour. Econ.	Canadian Journal of Economics
Canadian Jour. Econ. and Pol. Sci.	Canadian Journal of Economics and Political Science
Canadian Jour. Pol.	Canadian Journal of Politics
Comp. Stud. in Soc. and Hist.	Comparative Studies in Society and History
Econ. Hist. Rev.	Economic History Review
Econ. Jour.	Economic Journal
Eng. Hist. Rev.	English Historical Review
Expl. Econ. Hist.	Explorations in Economic History
Geog. Jour.	Geographical Journal
Hisp. Am. Hist. Rev.	Hispanic American Historical Review
Hist. Jour	Historical Journal
Hist. Pol. Econ.	History of Political Economy
Hist. Research	Historical Research

Indian Econ. and Soc. Hist. Rev.	*Indian Economic and Social History Review*
Indian Hist. Rev.	*Indian Historical Review*
Internat. Hist. Rev.	*International History Review*
Int. Jour. African Hist. Stud.	*International Journal of African Historical Studies*
Int. Jour. Middle East Stud.	*International Journal of Middle East Studies*
Jour. African Hist.	*Journal of African History*
Jour. Brit. Stud.	*Journal of British Studies*
Jour. Contemp. Hist.	*Journal of Contemporary History*
Jour. Econ. Hist.	*Journal of Economic History*
Jour. Eur. Econ. Hist.	*Journal of European Economic History*
Jour. Hist. Geog	*Journal of Historical Geography*
Jour. Hist. Soc. Nigeria	*Journal of the Historical Society of Nigeria*
Jour. Imp. and Comm. Hist.	*Journal of Imperial and Commonwealth History*
Jour. Indian Hist.	*Journal of Indian History*
Jour. Interdisc. Hist.	*Journal of Interdisciplinary History*
Jour. Latin Am. Stud.	*Journal of Latin American Studies*
Jour. Mod. Hist.	*Journal of Modern History*
Jour. Transport Hist.	*Journal of Transport History, 3rd Series*
Jour. Southern African Stud.	*Journal of Southern African Studies*
Latin Am. Research Rev.	*Latin American Research Review*
Midd. East. Stud.	*Middle Eastern Studies*
Mod. Asian Stud.	*Modern Asian Studies*
PP	Parliamentary Papers
Pacific Hist. Rev.	*Pacific Historical Review*
Scottish Econ. and Soc. Hist.	*Scottish Economic and Social History*
Soc. Rev.	*Sociological Review*
South Afr. Hist. Jour.	*South African Historical Journal*
Trans. Royal Hist. Soc.	*Transactions of the Royal Historical Society*

PART ONE
Introduction

CHAPTER ONE
The Problem and the Context

In a decolonised world the empire no longer strikes back, but there is a sense in which it lives on after its demise. The present generation, the first in Britain for some 300 years to survey a world without prominent imperial landmarks, has seen a remarkable increase of interest in the empire, as witness the formidably impressive volume of historical research published since the 1950s and the growth of public nostalgia for a world we have lost and, in some respects, may never have had. Given that the explosion of research can intimidate as well as aid further scholarship and that the imperial content of novels and television programmes may be approaching saturation level, the appearance of yet another book on British imperialism needs an explicit justification beyond that provided by the enduring importance of the subject itself. In the case of a general work, such as this one, good cause can be shown either by updating previous surveys or by venturing a new interpretation. It is difficult to say which is the more hazardous enterprise: the former threatens to bury the surveyor alive under an avalanche of specialised research which descends faster than it can be moved; the latter offers the prospect of ordeal by public exposure, a fate reserved for those who suppose that they have something new to say on a topic which, being so vast, has absorbed novelties from more ingenious minds in the course of the past century.

Well might prospective authors pause before setting course for a journey which harbours such irreducible risks. Our own route follows the high road in search of novelty but also scans the alternatives by synthesising a good deal of detailed research. Whether this decision provides insurance against disaster, or compounds the risk by inviting two fates instead of one, is for readers to judge. Our aspiration developed, not out of a sense of superior vision, but from a need to address some basic anomalies in existing explanations of the impulse towards imperial expansion; our commitment took shape when our lectures on this subject, having reached the high point of exegesis so readily inspired by criticism of others, were eventually brought down to earth by the formidable and protracted task of constructing an alternative. This sobering experience has enhanced our appreciation of the contribution made by our predecessors, even where we disagree with them. Indeed, the fact that there have been so few attempts to offer a fundamental reappraisal of the causes of British imperialism during the century which has passed since Sir John Seeley published *The Expansion of England* suggests just how extraordinarily difficult it is to devise an interpretation which combines an awareness of the detailed literature with a measure of independence from existing approaches, whether marked out by apologists or by enemies of empire.[1]

The discussion which follows seeks to place our own contribution in its wider analytical framework. We begin by setting the issue we have chosen to address, that of the causes of imperialism, in its historiographical context and by outlining the evolution of our own views on the subject. Any interpretation of a problem as vast as this one necessarily involves the use of correspondingly large terms which, if left undefined, may confuse the reader and which, if improperly defined, may also prejudice the argument. The rest of the chapter is therefore devoted to laying out for inspection the assumptions and concepts which underpin our interpretation. We continue by defining our use of the term 'capitalism' and by drawing attention to its hitherto underemphasised non-industrial forms. This discussion leads to a consideration of the social agents of capitalist enterprise, and here we lay stress on the concept of gentility and its relationship to economic activity and political authority. The implication of this approach, that manufacturing interests had less influence on the formulation of economic and international policy than has usually been assumed, is then made explicit, though this conclusion is not to be read as an attempt to minimise the importance of the process of industrialisation. We next examine the overseas manifestations of what we term 'gentlemanly capitalism' by looking specifically at the concept of imperialism and at its various guises. Finally, since the

1. Seeley's book, first published in 1883, is generally taken to mark the beginning of the modern, professional study of the subject. See J.G. Greenlee, 'A "Succession of Seeleys": the "Old School" Re-examined', *Jour. Imp. and Comm. Hist.*, 4 (1976).

whole of this discussion rests upon a view of what constitutes historical explanation, we conclude with a brief statement of our methodology, not to promote the claims we make but to enable readers to evaluate them.

THE HISTORIOGRAPHICAL SETTING

The difficulty of making an effective case for looking at the causes of British imperialism afresh may suggest that the answers are already known, or at least that one interpretation has come to dominate the subject to the extent of threatening to make its rivals redundant. There have certainly been times when a particularly illuminating thesis has gained majority support among liberals or radicals (though never among both). But no solution has proved to be permanent, and if there is one judgement that scholars of different persuasions can agree on today it is that no such certainties exist at present. Specialists will have their own explanations of why the growth of knowledge should have brought less, and not more, coherence to historical understanding. Our own argument will be that the central weakness in existing accounts of overseas expansion and imperialism is that they underplay or misjudge the relationship between the British economy and Britain's presence abroad. Putting the metropolitan economy back at the centre of the analysis, we suggest, makes it possible to establish a new framework for interpreting Britain's historic role as a world power.

Writers in the Marxist tradition cannot, of course, be accused of underplaying this relationship, but in our view they often misjudge both the development of the British economy and its links with overseas expansion. The classical theories of Marxist imperialism will be considered later, but it is clear that their modern successors have allotted a crucial role to industrialisation in precipitating imperialism[2] and that this position, as we shall try to demonstrate, is ill-founded. Neo-Marxist analyses of imperialism suffer from other serious weaknesses. Key terms such as 'capitalism' are insufficiently defined and are applied with too much generality to retain their explanatory

2. See, for example, Immanuel Wallerstein, *The Modern World System, II, Mercantilism and the Consolidation of the European World Economy, 1600–1750* (New York, 1980), p. 258.

5

power;[3] the use made of historical evidence is at times quixotic;[4] and a primary concern with the underdevelopment of regions outside Europe has led to a stereotyped view of the 'exploiting metropole'.[5] Although these interpretations have achieved considerable popularity in recent years, it is perhaps worth noting that their greatest influence has been on social scientists other than historians.

The large number of scholars who deny the existence of a close relationship between the development of the home economy and imperialist forms of expansion draw on two influential traditions. The first, which prevailed down to the 1950s, confined the study of imperialist impulses to the creation and evolution of colonies which made up the constitutional empire.[6] This definition gave the presentation of imperial history a political and legal bias, and this was reinforced by the fact that economic history was still in its infancy. In a world of shifting concepts the formal empire, the area painted red on the map, had a reassuringly solid physical presence. On inspection, however, its limitations readily became apparent. In the first place, the constitutional standing of the member-countries was neither identical nor fixed. Some parts of the empire rose to dominion status and acquired considerable formal control over their own affairs; others remained crown colonies, governed from London and subordinated in all significant matters of policy to decisions made in Westminster; and in between were various intermediate categories, such as protectorates, mandates and condominiums.[7] Historians usually deal with this problem by sorting the empire into different constitutional groups. This strategy serves for narrative purposes, but it leaves untouched the central issue of the degree of control exercised

3. This is particularly the case in the work of Andre Gunder Frank, *Latin America: Underdevelopment or Revolution* (1969), but there are also difficulties of usage in Immanuel Wallerstein, *The Capitalist World-Economy* (1979).

4. Andre Gunder Frank argues that the Industrial Revolution 'began with the year 1760' and was based on 'Bengal Plunder'. See his *Dependent Accumulation and Underdevelopment* (1978), pp. 72–3.

5. Ibid. Ch. 4; Wallerstein, *Capitalist World-Economy*, p. viii. An excellent recent study of neo-Marxist theories of imperialism can be found in Anthony Brewer, *Marxist Theories of Imperialism: A Critical Survey* (2nd edn 1990), Chs. 7–11.

6. In its original meaning a colony was a place of settlement and on this definition a number of British possessions would not be classified as colonies. However, we follow here conventional usage whereby the term refers to parts of the formal empire. For a discussion of neglected nineteenth-century terminology, from which so much present-day debate springs see M.I. Finley, 'Colonies: an Attempt at a Typology', *Trans. Royal Hist. Soc.*, 26 (1976).

7. And others: see Martin Wight, *British Colonial Constitutions, 1947* (Oxford, 1952), pp. 1–5.

by the centre, for this is not necessarily measured by an index of constitutional standing.

The second important influence stems from the work of Robinson and Gallagher, which has set the agenda for the study of imperial history during the last forty years. Robinson and Gallagher were the first historians to give prominence to the distinction between the formal empire of legal control and the 'informal' empire of influence and were also the progenitors of the 'peripheral' or 'excentric' theory of imperialism.[8] The concept of informality has helped to define imperial history in terms of the various frontiers and peripheries which were created or touched by the foreign presence. In doing so, it has greatly enlarged the earlier orthodoxy, with its narrow focus on political formalities. According to Robinson and Gallagher, the formal empire was the tip of an iceberg: submerged below the waterline lurked the invisible or informal empire, which at times was larger than the area under sovereign control. Members of the informal empire saw neither colonial governors nor colonial tax-gatherers, but they remained, nevertheless, under London's economic, cultural or diplomatic dominion. The notion of informal empire has prompted a long-running debate between its advocates, for whom the invisible has indeed materialised, and the sceptics, who question the validity of elevating an informal presence to imperial status. The controversy has flagged in recent years, not least because of the admitted difficulty of giving precision to such a broad concept;[9] but the debate has been invaluable in underlining the importance of considering shades of influence, degrees of effective control and measures of diminished sovereignty. In theory at least, it is now hard, though not impossible, to write a naive history of British imperialism.

8. J. Gallagher and R.E. Robinson, 'The Imperialism of Free Trade', *Econ. Hist. Rev.*, 2nd ser. VI (1953). Although Gallagher and Robinson were the first to employ the concept of informality in an analytically important way, they did not invent it. They borrowed the term 'informal empire' from C.R. Fay, *Imperial Economy and its Place in the Foundation of Economic Doctrine, 1600–1932* (Oxford, 1934). The phrase was also employed by H.S. Ferns in his pioneering article, 'Britain's Informal Empire in Argentina, 1806–1914', *Past and Present*, 4 (1953). The idea, if not the precise terminology, has a long history. Lenin, for example, referred to Persia, China and Turkey as 'semi-colonial countries' as early as 1916. See V.I. Lenin, *Collected Works*, XXII (Moscow, 1964), p. 257. Leland H. Jenks used the term 'invisible empire' in his famous study *The Migration of British Capital to 1875* (1927), and it is echoed in W.K. Hancock, *Survey of British Commonwealth Affairs*, II, Pt. I (Oxford, 1940), p. 27. Hancock also used Fay's phrase, 'informal empire', though without acknowledgement.

9. The most determined recent attempt to define informal empire can be found in Jürgen Osterhammel, 'Semi-Colonialism and Informal Empire in Twentieth-Century China: Towards a Framework of Analysis', in Wolfgang J. Mommsen and Jürgen Osterhammel, eds. *Imperialism and After: Continuities and Discontinuities* (1986).

The coverage offered by the present study examines the central issue of the exercise of power in international relations by considering both regions which were brought into the formal empire and those which remained outside it. We accept, of course, the need to give prominence to the constitutional empire because of its collective importance, whatever measure is chosen, in the history of British imperial expansion. Accordingly, we have examined the leading constituents, Canada, Australia, New Zealand, India and Africa, in some detail, though our survey of the empire is not fully comprehensive.[10] Outside the formal empire, we have chosen as case studies South America, China and the Ottoman Empire, regions where Britain's presence was both prominent and subject to keen rivalry from other foreign powers. Following our previous discussion, we do not assume that effective influence within the empire can be easily inferred from the constitutional status of the territory concerned; nor do we begin by supposing that Britain's informal influence automatically gave her an informal empire. Our procedure, in both cases, is to consider what Britain's interests were, how they were represented, and with what results in terms of limiting the independence of other countries. This involves an assessment, where the evidence permits, of different levels of influence – from the 'rules of the game' governing international relations to business pressures and domestic political decisions.

According to Robinson and Gallagher, the extension of informal empire was the outstanding feature of Britain's expansion overseas after 1815. They linked the spread of informal control to Britain's growing need for new markets and sources of supply as industrialisation proceeded, though without specifying the precise relation between the changing economy and the informally dominated frontier. On this view, informal empire was preferred to formal rule largely because it was cheap; but informal control could be exercised only if the frontier territory was both willing and able to cope with the impact of Britain's invading influence by throwing up local collaborators. However, despite linking the expansion of both formal

10. The principal omissions are the West Indies, Burma and south-east Asia (Singapore and Malaya). In an ideal world these areas would be included: they have been omitted purely for pragmatic reasons of space and time, as has a study of Siam (Thailand), which is a fascinating example of informal empire. We have also left aside the problem of Ireland. Anglo-Irish relations, besides being of daunting complexity, raise the wider question of Britain's ties with the so-called 'Celtic Fringe' as a whole, and this issue opens up, in turn, the problem of internal colonialism. For a schematic account see Michael Hechter, *Internal Colonialism: the Celtic Fringe in British National Development, 1536–1966* (1975).

and informal empire before 1870 to the process of economic development, and especially to industrialisation, Robinson and Gallagher
claimed that economic or social change in Britain was of insufficient
importance thereafter to account for the rapid expansion of formal
empire in Africa and Asia at the close of the century. Instead, they
directed attention to the periphery and, in particular, to the collapse
of the collaborative regimes which had sustained Britain's informal
presence, to the activities of independent (or at least semi-independent) sub-imperialists on the frontiers, and to Britain's need to counter
the expansive tendencies of other industrialising nations which established themselves as world powers for the first time after 1870. One
clear implication of this analysis was that the growth of the formal
empire was a product of Britain's relative decline as a great power:
the extension of sovereignty in Africa was only a poor recompense
for the shrinkage of the informal economic empire elsewhere. This
'peripheral' theory of imperialism has informed many of the major
recent studies of both European and British expansion overseas in the
late nineteenth and early twentieth centuries.[11]

The peripheral interpretation was an understandable and appropriate response to two powerful contemporary influences. The first, the
intellectual climate created by the Cold War, produced an awareness
of Britain's own subordination to the United States and provoked a
reaction to Marxist theories, and especially to their metropolitan-
based determinism and often cavalier treatment of evidence. The
second influence sprang from decolonisation, which encouraged a
shift away from traditional imperial history and created a new interest
in the history of former colonial territories. By combining opposition
to the intellectual dirigisme of Marxism with the fruits of fresh
research on and beyond the frontiers of empire, the peripheral thesis
offered an appealing way of updating liberal interpretations of imperialism. Any analysis of imperialism advanced today undoubtedly needs
to demonstrate an awareness of the now considerable literature
connecting European interests and indigenous societies.

To accept this point, however, is not necessarily to accept the
peripheral thesis, any more than to establish a metropolitan economic

11. The principal contributions to the peripheral thesis are: Ronald Robinson,
'Non-European Foundations of European Imperialism: Sketch for a Theory of Collaboration', in Roger Owen and Bob Sutcliffe, eds. *Studies in the Theory of Imperialism*
(1972); and idem, 'The Excentric Idea of Imperialism with or without Empire', in
Mommsen and Osterhammel, *Imperialism and After*. J.S. Galbraith, 'The "Turbulent
Frontier" as a Factor in British Expansion', *Comparative Studies in Society and History*, II
(1960), is an early contribution of lasting value. For a broad survey emphasising the
periphery, see D.K. Fieldhouse, *Economics and Empire, 1880–1914* (1973).

basis for imperialism is to embrace Marxism. Precise judgement on this issue depends on the exact weight attributed to the periphery as a cause of imperialism, and on this matter proponents of the thesis speak with different inflections. Dilute versions amount to a plea for incorporating new evidence on the turbulent frontier by making space for the part played by sub-imperialists and by indigenous societies themselves in resisting imperialist forces or negotiating with them. This is a welcome and, in principle, an uncontroversial corrective to older approaches.

The strong version of the thesis, however, makes the far larger claim that the fundamental cause of imperialism is to be found on the periphery itself. This claim runs into serious objections stemming from a degree of analytical imprecision underlying the thesis. One problem is that the peripheral approach cannot account for the fact that local crises occurred in identifiable chronological clusters in parts of the world often far removed from each other, except by appealing to a law of coincidence which itself is an admission of weakness. A further problem arises from the failure to distinguish symptoms from causes. To identify crises on the periphery is not necessarily to prove that they had their origins there. The strongest version of the thesis ought to be able to demonstrate not only that there was friction on the frontier (in itself a commonplace finding), but also that its origins lay in independent developments within the local society concerned. In theory, this is perfectly possible: the ideal case would hold the European presence constant and show that the local crisis which drew foreign interests (reluctantly) inland emerged from deep-seated demographic, religious or other causes which had not been provoked or significantly altered by previous external influences.

As it happens, however, the leading advocates of the peripheral thesis have yet to make this case. They focus on local crises at points where European and indigenous interests intersect, and attribute the cause to the locality and personalities involved. But, as we have just suggested, this perspective may focus on the symptoms rather than the cause, and it certainly mistakes part of the cause for the totality. It seems reasonable to conclude that, from the perspective adopted here, the peripheral thesis is as valuable but also as modest as its name implies: it examines aspects of causation which are restricted to the periphery. It is not, in principle, in conflict with a view from the metropolis which aims to show how the frontier came into being and to identify the underlying causes of turbulence which expressed themselves in local crises.

The attempt to downplay the role of economic change in the

metropole and to shift causation to the periphery has not passed unchallenged. Inspired initially by the work of D.C.M. Platt,[12] some imperial historians have emphasised the importance of the 'Great Depression' in the late nineteenth century in rousing British business pressure groups to agitate for safe markets in an expanded empire and to demand government backing in their search for new openings for commodity exports and capital investment in hitherto marginal areas, like China.[13] The pressure exerted by Chambers of Commerce and other influential groups representing business to extend the boundaries of formal empire in tropical Africa when trade was depressed has also been thoroughly documented;[14] a host of monographs and articles on the background to specific imperialist episodes has suggested that the crises on the periphery which led to extensions of British control were often triggered by economic changes originating in the metropolitan economy. In 1980, our own dissatisfaction with the peripheral thesis led us to try to synthesise this growing body of research and to relate its findings more closely to the evolution of the British economy as revealed by the recent work of economic historians.[15]

The resulting essay indicated that there was a correlation between changes in economic structure and in the nature and pace of growth of Britain's overseas trade on the one hand, and the extension of informal and formal control abroad on the other. But the argument suffered from two important defects. In the first place, although the article gave some prominence to the importance of invisible income and foreign investment after 1850, and endeavoured to connect this with imperialism, it gave industry, and provincial manufacturers and merchants, too much space in the story and did not pay the service sector enough attention. Secondly, it proved impossible, except in

12. D.C.M. Platt, *Finance, Trade and Politics in British Foreign Policy, 1815–1914* (1968).

13. See especially Platt's article 'British Policy During the New Imperialism', *Past and Present*, 39 (1968). Surveys of the literature which include discussions of this question are: W.Roger Louis, ed. *Imperialism: The Robinson and Gallagher Controversy* (1976); P.J. Cain, *Economic Foundations of British Expansion Overseas, 1815–1914* (1980); C.C. Eldridge, ed. *British Imperialism in the Nineteenth Century* (1984). A fine textbook by Bernard Porter, *The Lion's Share: A Short History of British Imperialism, 1850–1970* (2nd edn 1984), employs a theoretical structure derived from Robinson and Gallagher but gives greater emphasis to the role of economic anxiety in creating a climate for imperialist action after 1870.

14. See, for example, W.G. Hynes, 'British Mercantile Attitudes Towards Imperial Expansion', *Hist. Jour.*, XIX (1976).

15. P.J. Cain and A.G. Hopkins, 'The Political Economy of British Expansion Overseas, 1750–1914', *Econ. Hist. Rev.*, 2nd ser. XXXIII (1980).

one or two exceptional cases, to establish that the business agitation which was so clearly apparent in times of crisis, both in Britain and on the frontier, actually influenced the decisions of the policy-makers. Robinson and Gallagher assumed that what they called the 'official mind' was separate from business, free of its influence and capable of acting in the national interest rather than merely responding to the narrow prejudices of the market-place. Subsequent research, pointing to the social gulf between gentlemanly governing elites and 'trade', seemed to magnify this particular problem.[16] In the circumstances, it was quite reasonable for the supporters of the peripheral thesis to claim that, even when British interests on the frontier were purely economic, governments would act to extend British authority only when some political problem on that frontier, arising from the local situation – for example a breakdown in law and order – appeared to affect the national interest.[17]

In 1986 we tried to remedy these defects by developing a clearer line of argument based on the evolution of what we called 'gentlemanly capitalism'.[18] This advance was greatly helped by the publication of new research on the service sector and the City of London. The evidence now available makes it possible to argue that the rapid growth of services after 1850 is the key to a better understanding of the peculiar nature of British overseas expansion and imperialism. If commerce and finance were the most dynamic element in the nation's economic thrust overseas, then concentrating on the rise of services rather than upon the decline of industry inevitably changes perspectives on imperialism, down-grading to some extent the importance of formal acquisitions, including the Scramble for Africa, while bringing into better focus a vigorous and expanding informal presence, notably in areas of white settlement.

Furthermore, our reading of the literature on services and finance led us to conclude that the periodisation of British imperialism needed to be recast. It became clear that our analysis ought to be pushed back to cover the financial revolution and the rise of the 'moneyed interest' at the close of the eighteenth century, and extended well beyond 1914, which is the conventional halting point for studies of Britain's

16. See Platt, *Finance, Trade and Politics*, Pt. I.

17. For an astute presentation of this approach see Fieldhouse, *Economics and Empire*, Ch. 13.

18. Our first attempts to express our new position were made in 'Gentlemanly Capitalism and British Expansion Overseas, I: the Old Colonial System, 1688–1850', *Econ. Hist. Rev.* 2nd ser. XXXIX (1986); and II. 'New Imperialism, 1850–1945', ibid. XL (1987).

imperial expansion, and, accordingly, for the debate over the existence of informal empire too. However, in 1986 we were concerned principally to suggest a way of looking at British history afresh, and our treatment of the imperial dimension was necessarily and deliberately abbreviated. In the present study, and with more space at our disposal, we hope to substantiate claims on both fronts. Even so, it has proved impossible to analyse all three centuries of British and world history with the degree of detail needed to engage fully with the specialised literature. We have dealt with the resulting problem of emphasis by outlining our argument for the period as a whole in this chapter and in our general Conclusion (which appears in Volume II), by treating the eighteenth century and the period after 1939 in more schematic fashion in Chapter 2 and in the penultimate chapter of Volume II, and by concentrating on the sizeable period in between. This has enabled us to focus on the principal debates about British imperialism at the time when the empire was at its greatest extent, and to reappraise the period after World War I, when discussion of colonial nationalism and imperial decline gathers pace. The alternative would have been to have begun in 1815 or 1850 and to have ended in 1914 or 1939 without incorporating previous or subsequent events, except perhaps as part of a brief sketch of the general historical context. Our compromise, imperfect though it is, ought to make it possible for readers to see how our interpretation applies to the whole period and should enable specialists to enlarge the argument should they wish to do so.

Examining service-sector capitalism also provides the crucial link between the economy and the process of decision-making, since senior officials were recruited from the service sector and were inevitably infected by its perspectives and its values. In other words, we would now argue with some confidence that it is impossible to separate the world of 'acceptable' business from that of elite politicians and from their perceptions of the national interest. If leading politicians were invariably gentlemen, they were also products of the most successful part of British capitalism; some of them were major participants in non-industrial enterprise at home and abroad. Hence our conviction that a fuller understanding of the connections between British economy and society and British imperialism requires a close acquaintance with gentlemanly capitalism.

In reaching this position we must acknowledge our indebtedness to some of the classic contributions to the understanding of the emergence of modern imperialism. In emphasising finance, services and other non-industrial sources of wealth and power in our own inquiries we are returning, to some extent, to the preoccupations of the classical theorists of imperialism whose ideas were formulated in the first 30 years of the century. Most of the early theories, including the Marxist variants associated with writers such as Hilferding and Lenin, were attempts to understand continental economies whose history and structures were different in crucial respects from those of Britain. Moreover, the most popular version of the original thesis of finance or monopoly capitalism, that put forward by Lenin in *Imperialism: The Highest Stage of Capitalism* (1916), suffers from serious analytical flaws, as even sympathetic critics now acknowledge.[19] Nonetheless, these theories have proved useful in helping us to put British imperialism in a global context.

We must also recognise how much we have learned from those early theorists who claimed that imperialism could be understood only by attending, not to modern capitalism itself, but to the fact that capitalism was under the social and political direction of older elites. Joseph Schumpeter, writing in 1919 with the recent industrialisation of the European continent in mind, felt that there was still a marked distinction between the aristocracy and the bourgeoisie: 'the social pyramid of the present age has been formed, not by the substance and laws of capitalism alone, but by two different social substances and the laws of two different epochs'.[20] The bourgeoisie were the main creators of wealth and the great driving force behind economic and social change; but ideologically and politically they were dependent upon the prestige of the landed and military classes who could use the power of capitalism to further their own, profoundly anti–capitalist, ends. Heirs to an age-old tradition of warfare and conquest, the dominant elites of Europe had bent capitalism to their will, and the rampant imperialism of the recent past, like World War I itself, was the outcome. Had the capitalists managed to sweep away feudal power or had the traditional force 'changed its profession and function and become the ruling class of the capitalist world',[21] then, Schumpeter believed, the cultural life of modern Europe would have been profoundly different. In this case, imperialism (which he seems to have equated with the extension of formal empires) might never have

19. For critiques of Marxist theories of imperialism see Brewer, *Marxist Theories of Imperialism*; Norman Etherington, *Theories of Imperialism: War, Conquest and Capital* (1984), Chs. 6 and 7; Bill Warren, *Imperialism: Pioneer of Capitalism* (1980); and V.G. Kiernan, *Marxism and Imperialism* (1974), Chs. 1–3, 5 and 6.

20. Joseph Schumpeter, 'The Sociology of Imperialism', in idem, *Imperialism and Social Classes* (1951), p. 92.

21. Ibid.

existed because capitalism, if left to develop freely, would have laid the foundations for international peace by bringing about economic interdependence among nations. As the European country which had industrialised first and moved furthest from feudalism, Britain seemed to Schumpeter less prone to imperialist aggression than her neighbours and nearer the ultimate (and historically inevitable) goal of pacific internationalism.

Schumpeter's pure and pacific capitalism has yet to make an appearance and is not now expected. On the other hand, his insight that the capitalist system's development was significantly affected by the non-capitalist environment from which it sprang and that imperialism cannot be understood simply as a manifestation of modern economic forces, is a profound one. But, whereas Schumpeter stressed the gulf between traditional elites and the modern economy, our own emphasis is placed on the extent to which capitalism and tradition came to terms with each other to create a unique domestic 'substance' and, as a result, to produce a unique form of overseas expansion and imperialism. We argue that the rulers of Britain in the seventeenth and eighteenth centuries changed their 'profession and function' to a considerable degree, and that out of the union between land and the market emerged what we have called gentlemanly capitalism. As we have already suggested (and will demonstrate in detail later), gentlemanly capitalism then developed in ways which emphasised the distance between land, high finance and the upper reaches of the service sector on the one side, and mechanical industry on the other. There was no sharp, Schumpeterian antithesis between aristocracy and capitalism in Britain after 1850, but there was a distinction to be drawn between gentlemanly and industrial capital. The former set the cultural tone, was closer to the centre of power and was the dominant influence upon the expression of that power overseas. In this connection, we should also point out that Schumpeter's concern was to show how ruling elites distorted and used an alien force, capitalism, which would eventually destroy them. In our own account, capitalism is actually absorbed by the elites and adapted to suit their needs; from this perspective, imperialism becomes one of the methods by which that elite can prosper and continually renew itself.

In this particular context, we should mention also the work of Thorstein Veblen, the most neglected of the classical writers on the subject of modern imperialism. Like Schumpeter, Veblen saw imperialism as being driven mainly by the needs of old-fashioned, dynastic power structures which harnessed capitalist wealth to their own purposes. At the same time, he recognised the inevitability of the development of big business and worked out a theory of 'business enterprise' which had strong similarities to Hilferding's finance capitalism. Most of Veblen's reasoning was based upon a close study of American capitalism and of the evolving relationship between new forms of business enterprise and traditional landed hierarchies in Wilhelmine Germany. Nonetheless, Veblen was well aware that British capitalism had followed a different historical course and that traditional elites in Britain had come to terms with the market to an unusual degree. Hence his description of British policy-makers as 'gentlemanly investors' and his recognition of the fact that they were the key actors in the drama of British imperialism.[22]

J.A. Hobson's writings have been a further valuable source of inspiration. Hobson's claim that 'finance is . . . the governor of the imperial engine'[23] led him far too frequently to assume that politicians were in the pockets of the most powerful men in the City, and his tendency to resort to conspiracy theories, perhaps exacerbated by his occasional employment as a journalist on sensitive imperial frontiers, has often discredited him in the eyes of modern historians. Moreover, unlike his Marxist contemporaries, Hobson tended, as did Schumpeter, to identify imperialism with the subjugation of 'backward nations' in Africa and Asia, and he never offered an analysis of imperialism that accounted for the vast flows of capital to the emerging Dominions and to South America. He also shared with Schumpeter the naive idea that it was possible to find a form of capitalism that would bring peace and prosperity to all.

Despite these flaws, Hobson sometimes showed a better understanding of the unique nature of the British economy and its international ramifications than his contemporaries or many of his later critics. He drew a distinction between the industrial north and the service-sector south which, though crude by modern standards and somewhat disfigured by his own political prejudices, we can now see to have been basically valid and important. Hobson was sure that this division was vital to a true understanding of imperialism, since the foreign investment which lay behind it emanated largely from the

---

22. See Thorstein Veblen, *The Theory of Business Enterprise* (1904); *Imperial Germany and the Industrial Revolution* (1915); and *An Inquiry into the Nature of Peace and the Terms of Its Perpetuation* (New York, 1919), pp. 249, 288, 290. Neither Schumpeter nor Veblen has attracted much attention from scholars in recent years in their role as imperial theorists. Veblen in particular is virtually an untapped source in this regard. An exception to this neglect can be found in Etherington, *Theories of Imperialism*, Ch. 8. There is also a useful chapter in Tom Kemp, *Theories of Imperialism* (1967).

23. J.A. Hobson, *Imperialism: A Study* (1988 edn), p. 59.

south of England. And he was aware, too, of the extent to which the prestige accompanying Britain's particular brand of imperialism derived from the links between modern finance and traditional sources of power. Hobson was not foolish enough to believe that British export manufacturers were free of the taint of imperialism or that they did not benefit from it materially, but he always felt that industrialists were contained within a power system they neither directed nor controlled. The most interesting of Hobson's ideas from our vantage point do not figure prominently in his most famous work, *Imperialism: A Study*, first published in 1902, and his other writings on imperialism have only recently received some of the scholarly attention they deserve.[24] But his British version of the theory of finance capital has been important in helping us to put together our own picture of the domestic origins of imperialism, to which we now turn.

THE ARGUMENT

The detailed argument we wish to advance begins with the observation that modern British history is bound up with the evolution of several separate but interacting forms of capitalist enterprise – agricultural, commercial, and financial, as well as industrial. This initial statement is not designed to point towards a naive, multicausal interpretation of imperialism which includes everything and explains very little; nor is it intended to promote a new, albeit broadly-based form of economic determinism. But it does involve some reconsideration of capitalism both as a concept and in its historical application; it also requires a reappraisal of the social agents of capitalist enterprise, particularly, as we shall see, the role of that elusive creature, the English gentleman.

Historians approach the definition of large terms with a degree of caution which suggests their keen awareness of the prospect of failure. Short definitions are inadequate and long definitions are rarely practicable, while the absence of definitions lays a trap for others to

24. For an introduction to Hobson as an imperial theorist see Brewer, *Marxist Theories of Imperialism*, Ch. 4; Etherington, *Theories of Imperialism*, Chs. 3 and 4; Peter J. Cain, 'J.A. Hobson, Financial Capitalism and Imperialism in Late Victorian and Edwardian England', *Jour. Imp. and Comm. Hist.*, XIII (1985); and idem, 'Variations on a Famous Theme: Hobson, International Trade and Imperialism, 1902–38', in Michael Freeden, ed. *Reappraising J.A. Hobson: Humanism and Welfare* (1990).

spring. In the case of the much-discussed concept of capitalism, our main purpose is to clarify the usage adopted here rather than to tilt at the impossible by trying to establish a universal and eternal meaning. Evidently, if the definition is too broad it will explain everything and therefore nothing; if it is drawn too narrowly it will fail by excluding phenomena that need to be explained.

Some attributes of capitalism are uncontroversial: profit-seeking, individualism, specialisation, a market economy, rational calculation and the postponement of present consumption for the sake of future returns are characteristics that enter most definitions, if in varying proportions and combinations. Other features, however, are sometimes implied or even omitted. To take just one example, Braudel and Wallerstein, in their different ways, use the term to refer to exchange relationships generally without linking them to productivity gains or to the commercialisation of factors of production.[25] This definition is adequate for the purpose of contrasting exchange with subsistence, but it misses the cumulative element in capitalist enterprise, which in turn provides the key to its ability to transform as well as to expand economic structures. Marx and Weber both distinguished between mercantile or trading capitalism and other forms, especially those which held out the prospect of continuous accumulation by the application of capital (and, for Weber, capital accounting) to the production of manufactures.

Considering capitalism as an abstract construction opens the way to further, virtually boundless, theoretical discussion. Our aim at this point, however, is simply to list the ingredients of an uncontentious definition in order to avoid prefabricating its historical forms and stages. In fact, nearly all historical discussion has followed the classic evolutionary route, beginning with hunting and gathering and moving on to agriculture, commerce and industry, and has focused on the transition from pre-capitalist structures to industrial capitalism – with an optional extension to post-industrial society. Economists have traditionally endorsed this progression, which they have seen as a transition in three stages: from primary to secondary and finally to tertiary activity.[26] As a generalisation at the highest level, this conception of history has considerable merit. When tailored to specific events and periods, however, it can misconstrue the history of capitalism by minimising or misplacing activities which, though

25. Fernand Braudel, *Capitalism and Material Life, 1400–1800* (1973); Wallerstein, *The Modern World System* (New York, 1974).

26. The seminal modern statement, now neglected but still well worth reading, is Allen G.B. Fisher, 'Capital and the Growth of Knowledge', *Econ. Jour.*, 43 (1933).

meeting the criteria listed above, do not fit into accepted categories or phases. Established approaches to modern British economic history, for example, concentrate on explaining one central problem, the cause and course of the Industrial Revolution. One consequence of this focus is to rank developments in the eighteenth century according to their function in promoting or retarding future industrialisation; another is to underplay the role of important non-industrial activities in the nineteenth century; and a third is to treat events in the twentieth century as the outcome of Britain's decline as an industrial power.

This focus has an evident and powerful justification: Britain did create the world's first Industrial Revolution, and the process of industrialisation is undoubtedly central to modern British history. To accept these propositions, however, is not necessarily to agree that the emphasis has been correctly placed or that the connections with antecedent and subsequent events have been well joined. We shall argue here that non-industrial forms of capitalist enterprise, particularly those in finance and commercial services, have not received the historical recognition they deserve, and that they were in fact much more important in terms of output and employment before, during, and after the Industrial Revolution than standard interpretations of British economic history allow. They also had a greater degree of independence than has been acknowledged: their role in history was not merely to serve as minor contributors to the industrial revolution before being subsumed by it; nor were they simply offshoots of one of its subsequent development stages. The prosperity of the financial and service sector was derived from land and from trade in goods other than British manufactured exports, as well as from the products of the Industrial Revolution. Productivity gains in the transactions sector played a part in keeping staple exports competitive in overseas markets after manufacturing had entered a less innovative phase.[27]

This interpretation runs against both an older, heroic conception of the Industrial Revolution and a newer, growth-oriented historiography which tends to equate development with industrialisation. As we shall try to show, however, our argument is consistent with specialised, if still fragmented, research on British history which has begun to appear in recent years. It draws support, too, from the work of economists whose interest in the service sector has been stimulated

27. See, for example, C.H. Lee, 'The Service Sector, Regional Specialisation, and Economic Growth in the Victorian Economy', *Jour. Hist. Geog.*, 10, (1984); Clyde G. Reed, 'Transactions Costs and Differential Growth in Seventeenth-Century Western Europe', *Jour. Econ. Hist.*, 33 (1973); and Douglass North, 'Ocean Freight Rates and Economic Development, 1750–1913', *Jour. Econ. Hist.*, 18 (1958).

by the problem of deindustrialisation, by the emergence of post-industrial societies, and by development prospects in the Third World.[28]

No satisfactory definition of services has yet been devised.[29] At the most general level, and often for purposes of national accounting, services are treated as a vast residual, the sum of all activities which are neither primary nor secondary. This approach has the minor merit of tidiness, but its inherently negative quality and its presumption that the definition of primary and secondary activities is unproblematic severely limit its value. More positively, efforts have been made to classify services from the perspectives of production and consumption. This approach yields two slightly different lists, the former being the larger because it includes intermediate services, whereas the latter is restricted to services intended for final demand. Both have their uses, but they obviously carry different implications for the analysis and measurement of the service sector as a whole. Attempts to identify characteristics which are common to all services have concentrated on the fact that they supply a demand but are not physical commodities. In Adam Smith's phrase, they 'perish in the very instant of their performance'; that is to say, a service is acquired as it is produced and cannot be stocked. Moving and selling goods are services because they connect points of supply and demand by acts of transport and exchange which are not, in themselves, storable

---

28. The standard texts on modern British economic history tend to treat services as being incidental to other more important activities and rarely discuss the role of the service sector. This is true even of the two capacious volumes edited by Roderick C. Floud and Donald N. McCloskey, *The Economic History of Britain Since 1700* (Cambridge, 1981). Pioneering studies of the service sector have been made by Clive Lee, whose detailed research has been brought together in *The British Economy Since 1700* (Cambridge, 1986). See also P.K. O'Brien, 'The Analysis and Measurement of the Service Economy in European Economic History', in R. Fremdling and P.K. O'Brien, eds. *Productivity in the Economies of Europe* (Stuttgart, 1983). The importance of traded services in boosting per capita incomes in Britain (as opposed to France) is emphasised by Patrick O'Brien and Caglar Keyder, *Economic Growth in Britain and France, 1780–1914* (1978), pp. 63, 66, 75–6, 163–4, 197.

29. For example: T.P. Hill, 'On Goods and Services', *Review of Income and Wealth*, 23 (1977); Irving B. Kravis, *Services in the Domestic Economy and in World Transactions* (Geneva, 1983); and Ronald K. Shelp, *Beyond Industrialisation: Ascendancy of the Global Service Economy* (New York, 1981). In view of the general argument advanced in the present study, it is particularly interesting to note that economists now place considerable emphasis on the potential for developing traded services in Third World countries. Introductions to the recent literature include: Andre Sapir, 'North–South Issues in Trade and Services', *World Economy*, 8 (1985); Jagdish Bhagwati, 'Splintering and Disembodiment of Services and Developing Nations', in idem, *Essays in Development Economics*, Vol. I (Oxford, 1985), and Gary Sampson and Richard Snape, 'Issues in Trade in Services', *World Economy*, 8 (1985).

commodities. This definition produces a substantial list of activities, notably in banking, insurance, the professions, communications, distribution, transport, public service and a multiplicity of personal services. It is in this sense and with these occupations in mind that we refer, in general terms, to the service sector.

It is apparent from this list of occupations that the service sector is closely linked with other sectors, and that part of the problem of definition (and measurement) stems from the intimacy of the connection. As we have noted, the conventional assumption, though one which has attracted little historical research, is that services were the junior, dependent partner of manufacturing during the classic phase of industrialisation and achieved a sizeable degree of importance and independence only at a late stage, uncertainly dated but clearly identified as post-industrialism; it is easy to see how this belief, together with the somewhat intangible quality of service activities, has led to the view that services are essentially derivative from and even parasitic on the anterior and superior process of producing goods, and do not themselves create 'real' value.[30]

A full consideration of these complex issues would involve a lengthy detour from our intended course; but some brief comments on the role of the service sector are required to underpin the historical discussion which follows. Our argument treats services as being dynamic rather than passive: it sees the service sector as being characterised by a process, referred to by Bhagwati as splintering, which allows services to be derived from goods but also enables goods to be derived from services.[31] This process involves specialisation, productivity gains, and the transformation of production. Specialisation, as we shall see, took place through the more or less continuous creation of new employments in the service sector, beginning, as far as this study is concerned, with the rise of the new moneyed interest in the eighteenth century. Productivity gains arose from innovations such as bills of exchange, actuarial tables, transport improvements, company law, the financial press, and the submarine cable – to cite just a few varied examples from an extensive list. The transformation of production occurred most obviously through the creation of export economies in many parts of the world beyond Europe, where British finance, transport and allied commercial services were much in evidence. The relationship between finance

30. This is a prominent theme in the writings of economists from Smith to Kaldor (whose influence was partly responsible for the introduction of Selective Employment Tax, which was designed to halve the growth of service employment).
31. Bhagwati, 'Splintering and Disembodiment'.

and domestic production, especially manufacturing, is a complex matter which will be referred to later in this study. For the present, it can be said that the City of London (and to a large extent the banking system in general) played a much greater part in financing the distribution of manufactured goods than it did in their production. Whether or not the City's separation from manufacturing retarded Britain's industrial progress is an important and controversial subject in its own right. It is not, however, one that we propose to explore fully here because the outcome does not affect the substance of our argument, which is to relate the City and associated activities to an understanding of Britain's presence abroad rather than to the debate over the timing and causes of Britain's decline as an industrial power.

One crucial characteristic of the service sector needs special emphasis in the context of the present argument: in its higher reaches it provided suitable occupations for gentlemen. However, before taking our argument further, we must first define what we mean by gentility and explain the nature of the relationship between the gentleman and the market.

GENTILITY AND THE MARKET

The English gentleman was made as well as born.[32] Gentle birth conferred an unmatched advantage, the lustre of time; but gentle status could also be acquired by initiation. The history of the English gentleman is therefore one of continuous evolution accompanied by social tension, as established gentlemen, whose rank was burnished by age, were confronted by aspirants whose time had not quite come. The fact that definitions of gentlemanly status were constantly shifting, albeit subtly and slowly, undoubtedly presents problems for historical generalisation; equally, however, changes in the meaning of the term provide a way of plotting the moving contours of English social history over a long period of time.

In their ideal form, however, the main qualities of gentility

32. Unlike the French *gentilhomme*, whose status was determined solely by birth or royal appointment. The definitive historical study of the English gentleman has yet to be written. Introductions include: Philip Mason, *The English Gentleman: The Rise and Fall of an Ideal* (1982); and David Castronovo, *The English Gentleman: Images and Ideals in Literature and Society* (New York, 1987).

remained fixed points of reference from Chaucer to Waugh.[33] The perfect gentleman adhered to a code of honour which placed duty before self-advancement. His rules of conduct were Christian as well as feudal in inspiration, and his rank entitled him to a place in the vanguard of Christ's army, though with the knights and officers rather than among the infantry. Young gentlemen passed through a long process of education designed to meld these social and religious values; subsequently, they commanded positions in society which provided them with sufficient leisure to practise the gentlemanly arts, namely leadership, light administration and competitive sports. A gentleman required income, and preferably sizeable wealth, but he was not to be sullied by the acquisitive process any more than he was to be corrupted by the power which leadership entailed.

In an order dominated by gentlemanly norms, production was held in low repute. Working directly for money, as opposed to making it from a distance, was associated with dependence and cultural inferiority. Writing well after machine industry had become an accepted feature of life in Europe and America, Veblen observed that

> there are few of the better class who are not possessed of an instinctive repugnance for the vulgar forms of labour . . . . Vulgar surroundings . . . and vulgarly productive occupations are unhesitatingly condemned and avoided . . . . From the days of the Greek philosophers to the present, a degree of leisure and of exemption from contact with such industrial processes as serve the immediate everyday purposes of human life has ever been recognised by thoughtful men as a pre-requisite to a worthy or beautiful, or even a blameless, human life.[34]

The problem of living in the world while also rising above its sordid realities was negotiated by a process of delicate social diplomacy. Gentlemen bridged the gap between their need for income and their disdain for work by participating in approved activities, the most favoured of which interposed an appropriately wide distance between the mundane world of producing commodities and the higher calling of directing others, and enabled wealth to be accumulated in ways that were consistent with a gentlemanly life-style.

In this particular, as in most others, the tone of gentlemanly life was set by the ambivalent attitude to capitalism expressed by the

33. On this subject, and particularly on its nineteenth-century manifestations, see the outstanding and underused study by Mark Girouard, *The Return to Camelot: Chivalry and the English Gentleman* (New Haven, Conn., 1981). We have also made much use of John Scott, *The Upper Classes: Property and Privilege in Britain* (1982).

34. Thorstein Veblen, *The Theory of the Leisure Class: An Economic Study of Institutions* (1924 edn), pp. 37–8.

landed aristocracy, the dominant social force in Britain until the late nineteenth century. It is easily forgotten that, initially, the most important form of capitalist wealth in Britain was the rentier capitalism which arose from the ownership of land by a numerically small elite. By the close of the seventeenth century the landed magnates had ceased to be a feudal aristocracy and were ready to embrace a market philosophy. Nonetheless, they were still the heirs of a feudal tradition: the landed capitalism which evolved in Britain after the Stuarts was heavily influenced by pre-capitalist notions of order, authority and status. Hence the emphasis which continued to be placed on land as an inalienable asset to be passed on intact, as far as possible, through the generations; the assumed primacy of relations, even economic ones, based upon personal loyalties and family connections; the 'studied opposition to the matter-of-fact attitude and business routine';[35] the contempt for the everyday world of wealth creation and of the profit motive as the chief goal of activity; and the stress laid on the link between heredity and leadership. Since the prestige of birth, together with independent means, allowed an unusual degree of freedom of action, the landed elite also had an authority 'beyond any precise professional or functional limits'. The 'cult of the amateur', so familiar until recent times in every sphere of life from sport to politics, had its origins in this 'distinctive – because innate, hereditary and hence general – character of aristocratic power'.[36]

The peculiar character of the modern British aristocracy was shaped by merging its pre-capitalist heritage with incomes derived from commercial agriculture. The landed class not only controlled the traditional levers of authority but also was the most successful element within emergent capitalism. The more a career or a source of income allowed for a life-style similar to that of the landed class, the higher the prestige it carried and the greater the power it conferred. Because of their remoteness from the world of daily work, some traditional service occupations proved compatible with the gentlemanly ideal. Indeed, gentlemen could use the weapon of social exclusion, reinforced by their political influence, to colonise and monopolise acceptable occupations, such as the higher reaches of the law, the upper echelons of the established church, and the officer class of the armed services, ensuring, as a result, that they afforded suitably

---

35. R. Bendix, *Max Weber* (1966 edn), p. 366.
36. The quotations are taken from Jonathan Powis, *Aristocracy* (1984), pp. 88–9. See also the powerful essay by Joseph Schumpeter, 'The Rise and Fall of Whole Classes', in his *Imperialism and Social Classes*.

high incomes.[37] Intermediate levels were filled by semi-gentlemen in the same manner; among the lower ranks were included gentlemen's gentlemen whose status – and income – reflected the prestige of those they served.

This division between gentlemanly and ungentlemanly occupations and forms of wealth is similar to Weber's distinction between 'propertied' wealth on the one hand and 'acquisitive' or 'entrepreneurial' wealth on the other.[38] The first implies a rentier interest, not just in land but in other forms of property, while the second involves active participation in the market and in the creation of goods and services. Weber recognised the generally higher status accorded to propertied wealth and the greater power and authority which it commanded.[39] In the present context, however, Weber's categories need modifying to allow for the fact that some forms of 'entrepreneurial' wealth were closer to the gentlemanly ideal than others. A line has to be drawn not just between rentiers and businessmen but also, among the latter, between those whose relationship with the productive process was direct and those whose involvement was only indirect. Manufacturing was less eligible than the service sector: even at the highest levels, captains of industry did not command as much prestige as bankers in the City.[40]

In view of the prominent position occupied by the financial and commercial activities of the City of London in the ensuing argument, it is important for us to stress that, although the City was a centre of 'entrepreneurial' activity in Weber's sense, it eventually became, in its

37. Randall Collins, *Weberian Sociological Theory* (Cambridge, 1986), pp. 129ff.
38. Max Weber, *Economy and Society: An Outline of Interpretive Sociology* (ed. G. Roth and C. Wittich, 1978), Ch. IV: 'Status Groups and Classes'. The word 'acquisitive' is used instead of 'entrepreneurial' or 'commercial' in A.M. Henderson and Talcott Parsons' translation of Max Weber, *The Theory of Social and Economic Organization* (New York, 1947). Helpful interpretations of Weber's sociology include: Frank Parkin, *Max Weber* (1982): Reinhart Bendix, *Max Weber: An Intellectual Portrait* (1959); Seymour Martin Lipset, 'Social Stratification and Social Class', *International Encyclopaedia of the Social Sciences* (1968), and idem, 'Values, Patterns, Class and the Democratic Polity: the United States and Great Britain', in Reinhart Bendix and Seymour Martin Lipset, eds. *Class, Status and Power: Social Stratification in Comparative Perspective* (2nd edn 1967); Talcott Parsons, 'The Professions and Social Structure', in *Essays in Sociological Theory: Pure and Applied* (Glencoe, Ill., 1949); John Rex, 'Capitalism, Elites and the Ruling Class', in Philip Stanworth and Antony Giddens, eds. *Elites and Power in British Society* (Cambridge, 1974).
39. Weber, *Economy and Society*, p. 307.
40. This idea is, to some extent, the result of reading David Lockwood, *The Black Coated Worker: A Study in Class Consciousness* (1958), esp. pp. 202ff; and W.G. Runciman, *Social Science and Political Theory* (Cambridge, 1965), pp. 137–8. There are also some suggestive comments in Geoffrey Ingham, *Capitalism Divided? The City and Industry in British Social Development* (1984), pp. 240–3.

higher reaches, a branch of gentlemanly capitalism and, as such, exercised a disproportionate influence on British economic life and economic policy. Bankers and financiers often rose to prominence in societies dominated by aristocrats because the aristocracy's propensity for 'generosity' promoted indebtedness.[41] And, as will become clear in the next chapter, the fate of the City was entwined with that of the aristocracy in Britain after 1688 – with all the expected consequences in terms of wealth, prestige and incorporation into the body politic. Before the twentieth century, the great businesses of the City generated fortunes that were much larger than those acquired in industry and they were conducted upon principles that were much closer to the ideals of gentlemanly capitalism fostered by the landed class and their supporters than to the mores of manufacturing, even before mechanisation. Merchant bankers and merchant princes, for example, could possess great wealth without at the same time having a means of support that was wholly visible. More positively, gentlemanly ideals were vital to the success of the activities discussed here because they provided a shared code, based on honour and obligation, which acted as a blueprint for conduct in occupations whose primary function was to manage men rather than machines. The greatest bankers and merchants were located in the City, close to the centres of political power, and the nature of their occupation gave them sufficient leisure to enjoy a gentlemanly life-style while enabling them to cultivate the social connections which were, at the same time, a vital source of their success in business.[42] Their activities fitted the definition of capitalism offered earlier, and they were also capitalists in the direct sense of owning, mobilising and controlling capital.

In addition, capitalists at the top of the gentlemanly hierarchy created or commanded an invaluable scarce resource which was a form of capital in itself: information. The most eminent figures in the Square Mile were those who had access to information which was either denied to others, including fellow members of the City fraternity, or which reached them at a later date. Privileged information, from which large fortunes and high standing flowed, came principally from contact with those who controlled the machinery of state. Once in the charmed circles of power, bankers gained both immediate profit and entry to a network of contacts and information that opened up additional prospects; as their connections multiplied,

41. Powis, *Aristocracy*, pp. 28–9.
42. For an engaging introduction to City life from an early-twentieth-century perspective see Ronald Palin, *Rothschild Relish* (1971).

so too did their prestige and authority. As confidence in selected bankers grew, they were entrusted with the savings of the elite, and this advantage gave them a position in financial markets which less favoured competitors could not match. The greatest bankers were able to amass huge fortunes without having to mobilise vast stocks of their own resources because they were able to channel the capital of others. A banker's chief asset was not his immediate reserve of capital but his prestige, which depended in turn on his standing as a key agent of elite groups whose leadership was universally acknowledged. For these reasons, the relations formed between the upper reaches of the financial world on the one hand and high society and high politics on the other were rooted more in face-to-face contact and personal understandings than in perfect market competition or in the cold rationality which Weber associated with modern bureaucracy and with modernisation itself.[43]

This is not to say that all capitalists were in the service sector or that all gentlemen were capitalists. Landed wealth was the product of capitalist enterprise, even if it also produced rentier incomes, but it clearly lay outside the service sector. As our argument suggests, however, landed wealth steadily gave way to wealth generated in the service sector in the course of the nineteenth century, which is when our subject and our study begin to expand. Some other occupations, however, present more complex problems of classification. Senior military officers, clerics and civil servants were unquestionably gentlemen and their occupations can be allocated firmly to the service sector, but they scarcely qualified as capitalists. The resolution of this conundrum lies in recognising that capitalist activities in the service sector were accompanied by services which were not in themselves capitalistic. In fact, all forms of capitalism attach services and servants to themselves and may also be subject to rulers who are not capitalists either. However, it is worth remarking here that, like the landed class, gentlemen in both the private and public parts of the non-business sector became increasingly infected with the capitalist ethic. The move to meritocratic recruitment in the professions in the nineteenth century was intended both as a device to maintain and enhance gentlemanly status and as a method of rigging the market effectively once patronage had ceased to be a socially acceptable means

---

43. There is no study of the relations between high finance and high politics in Britain to compare with Fritz Stern, *Gold and Iron: Bismarck, Bleichröder, and the Building of the German Empire* (1977), from which we have learned a great deal. On this theme, see also the interesting comment on financial power in Collins, *Weberian Sociological Theory*, p. 137.

of rationing. In this manner, the burgeoning market system in the service sector was captured and used by the forces of tradition, providing one further instance of the axiom that capitalism 'is less active than acted upon by existing forms of social stratification'.[44] Moreover, insofar as the elites in the professions and in government had any direct contact with the world of business, it was much more likely that they would meet and take advice from City financiers than from men of industry, of whom they were often both ignorant and suspicious.

Nonetheless, there is a valid distinction to be drawn between capitalism as a broadly encompassing structure and the capitalists whose activities give the structure its particular cast and colour. This distinction raises a further set of analytical issues, the most important of which, in the present context, concerns the relationship between economics and politics. It would be naive, though scarcely novel, to assume that economic wealth automatically confers political power or that government is simply the executive arm of particular class interests. On the other hand, in rejecting this view we do not feel obliged to join the esoteric (and inconclusive) discussion over the 'relative autonomy' of the state or to try to define the precise degree of 'semi-independence' enjoyed by the agents of government.[45] For our purposes, it is sufficient to accept that non-capitalist elements can and often do play an important part in a capitalist system and to outline the nature of the relationship which pertained in the historical case under review.[46]

In essence, we shall argue that the gentlemanly ethic formed a tight bond between capitalist and non-capitalist elements within service capitalism with the result that the gentlemanly elite had a common view of the world and how it should be ordered. This degree of coherence or like-mindedness explains why, at the top of the gentlemanly order, the barriers between business and government were no more than mobile Chinese walls. This is not of course to suggest that unity meant unanimity: disagreements of priority and perspective were not only possible but also common, both between the City and

44. Parkin, *Max Weber*, p. 96.
45. The modern formulation of this debate is associated with the work of Ralph Miliband, *The State and Capitalist Society* (1969) and Nicos Poulantzas, *Political Power and Social Classes* (1973) and subsequent discussion, especially in the *New Left Review*. For further references see Poulantzas, 'The Capitalist State: a Reply to Miliband and Laclau', *New Left Review*, 95 (1976).
46. John Goldthorpe, 'On the Service Class, its Formation and Future', in Antony Giddens and G. Mackenzie, eds. *Social Class and the Division of Labour* (Cambridge, 1982).

Whitehall and among banking houses and government departments. The point to emphasise, however, is that disputes occurred within the family. Disagreements were expressed freely because the values underlying them were not in question and because both sides were aware that they were arguing about the precise route to be taken rather than about the general direction of policy.

Given the importance of this common world view in understanding the link between economic and political dimensions of international policy, it is worth stressing at this point that the most senior British officials, at home and abroad, were drawn largely from the ranks of those whose ties were with landed, rentier or service-sector wealth rather than with industry. In the post-imperial era, members of the home civil service still exhibit an extraordinarily high degree of cohesion, which continues to flow from shared social and educational experience and is focused on London.[47] Even today, in a world increasingly characterised by impersonal relations, it is possible to speak of 'family life in the Treasury or village life in Whitehall', where 'mutual trust is a pervasive bond' and where business is transacted 'in the market place exchange of an agreed culture' – albeit a culture distanced from industrial capitalism and often hostile to it.[48]

THE EVOLUTION OF THE GENTLEMANLY ORDER

While the sociology of the gentleman, and more generally of what Veblen called the leisure class, merit further exploration, our interest lies in the historical shape taken by the gentlemanly ideal.[49] The

47. As it remains today: 'British political administration is concentrated spatially as well as numerically . . . if you are not in (or within easy reach of) London, you are politically nowhere. Success in political administration depends upon judgements of your fellows and to be judged you must get to London. In a hundred different ways, the provincial can reveal that he is not intimately acquainted with current wisdom.' See H. Heclo and A. Wildavsky, *The Private Government of Public Money* (2nd edn 1981), pp. 7–8.

48. Ibid. pp. 2–3.

49. Although we shall refer to gentlemen as a group which shared certain defining characteristics, we recognise of course that a full social history would pay more attention to intra-group differences as well as to the distinction between gentlemen and others. Here, it is sufficient for us to make the point that gentlemen were not identical. In principle, it was possible to be a gentleman by living up to the moral code of gentility; hence the phrase 'one of nature's gentlemen' and its attendant hope that shared rules of conduct would bind the nation as one. In practice, being a gentleman (and being accepted as a gentleman) was a matter of bearing as well as behaviour, and this was a quality bought at considerable cost in both time and money through informal

original heraldic definition of a gentleman was one who had been granted the right to possess a coat of arms. The symbolic power of this usage outlived its practical application: a gentleman continued to be identified by his bearing even though he carried a furled umbrella instead of a sword; he remained closely associated with military and civil authority; and he subscribed to the values of the landed interest long after land had ceased to be the main source of national wealth. What changed, amidst these continuities, was the social form assumed by gentlemanly rank.

The Glorious Revolution of 1688 was an important moment in this transformation because it entrenched the landed interest in the countryside and consolidated its hold on the polity. As the gentry celebrated their deliverance from the tyrannies imposed or threatened during the seventeenth century in conspicuous consumption and the revitalised pleasures of the chase,[50] so too they were reminded by commentators such as Richardson, Addison and Steele that the moral basis of privilege lay in meeting the social obligations of rank.[51] If this contest proved somewhat one-sided, it was also enlivened by claims for gentlemanly status from those whose origins lay outside the land. At the close of the seventeenth century, Locke noted that trade was 'wholly inconsistent with a gentleman's calling',[52] and early in the eighteenth century Bolingbroke campaigned to keep the new 'mon-eyed interest' at bay.[53] By the end of the century, however, leading financiers and merchants in the City had been accorded gentlemanly status.[54] Their promotion rewarded their support of the landed order and reflected subtle changes in the concept of property which further defined and improved the status of financial instruments and move-

---

and formal education. Even so, there were intangible but instantly recognisable gradations of gentility among those who had succeeded in embellishing nature: Asquith, who qualified by most criteria as being a gentleman above the majority of gentlemen, was nevertheless regarded for many years as being 'not quite a gentleman' by those who felt that his education at the City of London School was not fully redeemed by his sojourn at Balliol. See Girouard, *Return to Camelot*, p. 263.

50. See, for example, N. McKendrick, J. Brewer and J.H. Plumb, *The Birth of a Consumer Society* (1982), and P.B. Munsche, *Gentlemen and Poachers: The English Game Laws, 1671–1831* (Cambridge, 1981).

51. This theme is pursued by Homai J. Shroff, *The Eighteenth-Century Novel: The Idea of the Gentleman* (New Delhi, 1978).

52. Quoted in Harold Nicolson, *Good Behaviour* (Gloucester, Mass., 1955), p. 194.

53. Cain and Hopkins, 'Gentlemanly Capitalism and British Expansion Overseas, I: the Old Colonial System, 1688–1850', pp. 512–13.

54. And some had defined themselves. See Ralph Strauss, *Lloyds': The Gentlemen at the Coffee House* (New York, 1938), pp. 69, 73.

able goods.[55] Lower down the commercial hierarchy, Locke's dictum still applied, and newcomers who made wealth in unacceptable ways or with unacceptable speed remained beyond the pale. Nabobs could buy property and favours, but they had difficulty purchasing social status and they remained, in Burke's view, 'animated with all the avarice of the age'.[56]

The process of redefinition gathered pace from the late eighteenth century, and was decisively altered during the Victorian era, when gentlemen were produced on an unprecedented scale.[57] The public schools, reformed and greatly expanded, were the crucial agents of this transformation, creating gentlemen out of those who lacked property by educating them in country houses set in broad acres, emphasising individual effort within a context of communal endeavour, and instilling the values of order, duty and loyalty. If the content of education still emphasised the heritage from Greece and Rome, it was partly because the classical model provided a blueprint for training an elite cadre dedicated to the service of the state. The higher reaches of education were similarly infused: in the course of the century Oxford and Cambridge turned seriously to the task of equipping the new guardians with the principles of good government, while developments in political economy fashioned a new vision of progress, a complex fusion of Benthamite utilities and Tory virtues which offered a programme of moral and material advancement set within a cautious evolutionary context.[58] These developments were accompanied by a renewed reverence for royalty.[59] The panoply of state occasions was reinvented and much elaborated, the honours system was enlarged and refined by the introduction of arcane gradations, and the upper echelons of the social hierarchy were swollen by the entry of new nobles and knights.

A spirit of chivalrous medievalism left its imprint on virtually every facet of Victorian high culture – from the artistic influence of

55. John Brewer, 'English Radicalism in the Age of George III', in J.G.A. Pocock, ed. *Three British Revolutions: 1641, 1688, 1776* (Princeton, NJ, 1980).

56. Quoted in Nicolson, *Good Behaviour*, p. 195.

57. The authoritative source is Girouard, *Return to Camelot*.

58. Two recent valuable contributions to this theme are: David Eastwood, 'Robert Southey and the Intellectual Origins of Romantic Conservatism', *Eng. Hist. Rev.*, CIV (1989); and Peter Mandler, 'Tories and Paupers: Christian Political Economy and the Making of the New Poor Law', *Hist. Jour.*, 33 (1990).

59. See David Cannadine, 'The Context, Performance and Meaning of Ritual: the British Monarchy and the "Invention of Tradition", c.1820–1977', in Eric Hobsbawm and Terance Ranger, eds. *The Invention of Tradition* (Cambridge, 1983). The comment by W.L. Arnstein, 'Queen Victoria Opens Parliament: the Disinvention of Tradition', *Hist. Research*, 63 (1990), is interesting but does not disturb the point made here.

the pre-Raphaelites and the enthusiastic construction of medieval castles and gothic churches to the elaboration of a complex etiquette of deportment and manners devised to separate gentlemen from players and calculated to subdue, by the ordeal of social humiliation, those who attempted to rise above their station without first completing a long and costly *rite de passage*. In these and many other ways, Victorian England was looking back, not merely in nostalgia but with creative intent, at the same time as its technological inventiveness was opening up new economic and geographical frontiers. As the Industrial Revolution gathered pace, so too the demand for ramparts and armour rose.

A full explanation of this phenomenon falls beyond the scope of these pages, and in any case does not yet lie readily to hand. The interpretation offered here will focus on two particularly important developments. The first was the creation in the late eighteenth century of a form of new conservatism as the propertied order closed ranks against the threat of radical criticism at home and republican invasion from abroad.[60] While this conservatism carried a strong die-hard element into and through the nineteenth century, it also contained a growing and ultimately preponderant reformist strand.[61] Liberal Tories were never quite the same as progressive Whigs, but their differences were contained within a common framework of understanding. As Edward Collins's marquis explained to his attentive listener, a Manchester manufacturer: 'A Tory is a man who believes England should be governed by gentlemen. A Liberal is a man who believes any Englishman may become a gentleman if he likes'.[62] During the French Wars, political opposition at home was muted by checks on civil liberties and by a spirit of solidarity produced by the needs of national defence, and the economy was placed on a war footing funded by the continued expansion of the national debt. After 1815, however, it was clear that fundamental changes were needed to restore the health of the economy, to meet criticism of Old Corruption, and ultimately to keep civil order. The first step in meeting this challenge was to redefine the role and purpose of the ruling class; the price of survival was the introduction of far-reaching, if gradual,

60. P. Langford, 'Old Whigs, Old Tories and the American Revolution', in P. Marshall and G. Williams, eds. *The British Atlantic Empire Before the American Revolution* (1980).

61. See Boyd Hilton, *Corn, Cash and Commerce* (Oxford, 1977); and idem, 'Peel: a Reappraisal', *Hist. Jour.*, 22 (1979).

62. Edward Collins, *Marquis and Merchant*, Vol. I, p. 171; Quoted in Ivan Melada, *The Captain of Industry in English Fiction, 1821–1871* (Albuquerque, 1970), p. 186.

reforms of the constitution, of the patronage system, of social legislation and of economic policy – culminating in the shift to free trade in the middle of the century.

The second development centred on claims for gentlemanly status from a new set of aspirants in the burgeoning service sector in London and the Home Counties. From the 1820s Whigs and reforming Tories recognised the need for allies if the landed interest was to survive the reforms it had set in train. At the point where this realisation met the social and political ambitions of service interests, an alliance was struck which strengthened and greatly enlarged established ties between the land and the merchant princes and bankers of the City, and added representatives from the professions and from newer branches of tertiary employment. These claimants coveted gentility but lacked the acres and rural background needed to gain access to it. The problem was overcome in the course of the century by allowing gentlemen to be fashioned by the public schools. This compromise caused much heart-searching and moralising among social commentators, especially novelists, over the definition of gentility and the consequences of allowing the true aristocracy of birth to mingle with the pseudo-aristocracy of wealth.[63] By the late nineteenth century, however, the amalgamation had taken place and the landed interest, once the senior partner, had come to lean heavily on money made in the service sector, especially in the City of London.

The nineteenth-century gentleman was therefore a compromise between the needs of the landed interest whose power was in decline and the aspirations of the expanding service sector. In return for social recognition, the middle-class urban gentleman was co-opted into the struggle against radicalism and its looming consequence, democracy, and assigned a leading role in introducing an alternative programme of improvement. He was also seen as a counterpoise to the claims of provincial manufacturing industry, which threatened to elevate the provinces over the centre by means of money made in unacceptable ways. Finance and the service sector were vital in this regard in that they provided capitalism with an acceptable face by generating income streams that were invisible or indirect. Moreover, the gentleman's code of government purported to rise above class and rank, and to serve the interests of the nation as a whole. By exercising authority in a manner that exemplified selfless dedication to duty, the gentleman

---

63. See Robin Gilmore, *The Idea of the Gentleman in the Victorian Novel* (1981), and Norman Russell, *The Novelist and Mammon: Literary Responses to the World of Commerce in the Nineteenth Century* (Oxford, 1986).

was able to justify his continued right to rule, while also defending property and privilege. It is easy to dismiss gentlemanly claims of service to the community as being rhetorical devices which were useful chiefly in protecting a privileged position in society. If this had been the case, it is hard to see how the gentleman could have survived the upheavals of nineteenth-century British society. In practice, gentlemen were often active in the community and offered leadership on terms which were generally acceptable. Hippolyte Taine, who visited Britain in the 1860s, was sure that gentlemen of 'independent fortune' were not simply 'privileged persons, ornamental parasites' or even a 'tolerated memorial', but 'an effective moving power'. Taine was equally convinced that they were 'the most enlightened, the most independent, the most useful citizens in the country' and that, at his very best, 'a real gentleman is a real noble . . . capable . . . of sacrificing himself for those whom he leads'.[64]

The imperial mission was the export version of the gentlemanly order. In some respects, indeed, the gentlemanly code appeared in bolder format abroad in order to counter the lure of an alien environment. Roman discipline had not prevented Mark Antony from 'going native'; lesser mortals needed uncompromising values and unwavering control, injections of Spartan spirit which the costly deprivations of the public school environment readily supplied.[65] When confronted with the challenge of new frontiers, gentlemen assumed proportions that were larger than life and at times became heroic figures. The empire was a superb arena for gentlemanly endeavour, the ultimate testing ground for the idea of responsible progress, for the battle against evil, for the performance of duty, and for the achievement of honour.[66]

Individual endeavour, however, has to be placed in its social context: the refurbished gentlemen who played the game overseas both expressed and reinforced the new forces emerging at home during a period of profound transformation. Not surprisingly, Britain's representatives abroad shared the social origins and values of their counterparts in the metropole. They took to paternalism as squires to the manner born, and they tried to recreate abroad the

---

64. H.A. Taine, *Notes on England* (8th edn 1885), pp. 174–5.

65. J.A. Mangan, *The Games Ethic and Imperialism* (1985).

66. See, for example, Alan Sandison, *The Wheel of Empire* (1967), and G.D. Killam, *Africa in English Fiction* (1968). It is interesting to find that the celebrated French colonial administrator, Lyautey, had a high regard for the qualities of the English gentleman as a ruler of alien people; and the *Ecole coloniale* was founded in 1899 to raise the standards of French administrators to similar levels. See Louis Hubert Lyautey, *Lettres du Tonkin et de Madagascar, 1894–1899* (Paris, 1920), pp. 71–2.

hierarchy which they were familiar with at home. British diplomacy sought to identify gentlemen abroad, to create them where they did not exist, and to decide, in the case of societies which resisted acculturation, whether to invoke the 'forbearing use of power' which Samuel Smiles regarded as being 'one of the surest attributes of the true gentleman'.[67] At the same time, the reforming principles of political economy were eagerly applied to distant lands: approved property rights, individualism, free markets, sound money and public frugality provided discipline and purpose for both moral and material life, underpinned good government and produced congenial allies. The Anglican version of the Christian message, closely entwined with economic orthodoxy, was transmitted by like-minded missionaries: the Bible accompanied the plough; spiritual rectitude marched with fiscal prudence. Utilitarians treated the empire as a vast laboratory for experimenting with scientific principles of human betterment; missionaries came to see it as a crusading vehicle for collective salvation. Together, they created a new international order in the nineteenth century by devising and implementing the world's first comprehensive development programme.

World War I decimated the gentlemanly ranks and knocked more than the edges off notions of chivalry and honour. Thereafter, commentators were more inclined to see the weaknesses in the gentlemanly ideal, to parody gentlemanly amateurs and privileged drones, and to explore, whether with regret or approval, the decline of the gentlemanly order.[68] There seems little doubt that the gentlemanly code was diluted by becoming generalised and secularised, and that democracy cost the gentleman some of his exclusiveness and respect. As W.S. Gilbert observed: 'when everybody's someone then no one's anybody'. Yet the gentlemanly ideal was not replaced by an alternative, and the widening use of the term was a measure of the spread of gentlemanly values, even if, at the fringes of rank, there was often more form than substance. At the centre, however, the upper reaches of the gentlemanly order were untroubled and to some extent reinforced by their unplanned democratic success, which increased the number of those who recognised their betters and were still willing to defer to them. The established educational routes to gentility lost none of their vitality, and the extension of gentlemanly status to top industrialists (principally those who directed large firms

67. Quoted in Mason, *The English Gentleman*, p. 214.
68. These are well-known themes in the novels of Waugh and Wodehouse, and they were pursued by social commentators such as Harold Laski, *The Danger of Being a Gentleman and Other Essays* (1939), and Simon Raven, *The English Gentleman* (1961).

with headquarters in London) was less of a take-over by industry than its final absorption. Overseas, the gentlemanly code, like the gentlemanly spirit, was kept alive by the challenges of Bolshevism, nationalism and war, and was applied, after 1945, to new problems: managing the Labour Party at home, and development and decolonisation abroad.

The genius of the English, in Burke's judgement, was to infuse tradition with modernity, thereby preserving it. Gentlemanly capitalism was a formidable mix of the venerable and the new: it combined inherited and invented traditions with profitable enterprise in occupations which were compatible with gentility. The gentlemanly capitalist had a clear understanding of the market economy and how to benefit from it: at the same time he kept his distance from the ordinary and demeaning world of work. In his own sphere he was also highly efficient. Tom Paine's jibe that the nobility were men of no ability is not lacking in illustrious examples;[69] but the feudal remnants, and the tendency for aristocrats and gentlemen to behave in an 'economically irrational' manner,[70] could be useful assets in occupations which placed a premium on organising men and information rather than on processing raw materials. High finance, like high farming, called for leadership from 'opinion-makers' and trust from associates and dependants. A gentleman possessed the qualities needed to inspire confidence; and because his word was his bond transactions were both informal and efficient. Shared values, nurtured by a common education and religion, provided a blueprint for social and business behaviour. The country house led to the counting house; the public school fed the service sector; the London club supported the City. Gentlemanly enterprise was strongly personal, and was sustained by a social network which, in turn, was held together by the leisure needed to cultivate it. The predominance of in-group marriage, like the elaboration of techniques of heirship to entail property, was not a gesture to traditionalism, but a strategy to reinforce group solidarity, to create economic efficiency and political stability, and to take out an option on the future by ensuring dynastic continuity. Social proximity was aided by geographical concentration; both came together in London, the focal point of the gentleman and his activities. In this world conspicuous consumption was not merely wasteful; it was a public manifestation of substance, a refined adver-

69. Tom Paine, *Rights of Man*, in *The Political and Miscellaneous Works of Thomas Paine* (1819), I, p. 75.
70. Weber, *Economy and Society*, p. 307.

tisement which used hospitality to sustain goodwill, to generate new connections and to exclude those of low income or low repute.[71]

In describing how ethics fit actions, our aim has been to establish the characteristics of gentlemanly capitalism, not to pass judgement on it. We have deliberately avoided adopting the radical distinction between productive and unproductive labour, for instance, not only because it is hedged with difficulties of definition but also because it fails to recognise the capitalist qualities of the activities we have identified.[72] What can be said, however, is that the bias of incomes and status favoured gentlemanly occupations to a much greater extent than standard accounts of British economic history allow, and that the attributes of the leisured amateur, though highly effective in his own sphere of enterprise, were less well suited to the needs of industry in an age of 'scientific rationalism'.[73]

THE MANUFACTURING INTEREST

Cobdenite entrepreneurial ideologies which stressed the need for a social revolution to place the industrial bourgeoisie at the centre of the social and political stage faced formidable barriers, even at the high point of the Industrial Revolution. The impressive success of gentlemanly capitalism in its landed form until 1850 and the growing wealth and power of service capitalism after that date meant that manufacturers who sought prestige and authority often had to adapt to gentlemanly ideals. And players could become gentlemen only by abandoning the attitudes or even the occupations which had brought them their original success.[74] The Industrial Revolution emerged from an already highly successful capitalist system, and it took place without any fundamental transformation in the nature of property ownership or in the disposition of social or political power. The

71. For an attempt to employ Veblen's concept of conspicuous consumption in an historical context see Roger S. Mason, *Conspicuous Consumption: A Study of Exceptional Consumer Behaviour* (1981). Conspicuous consumption and group intermarriage, like exclusive education, are means towards what Weber calls 'social closure', a phenomenon examined by Frank Parkin, *Marxism and Class Theory: A Bourgeois Critique* (1979).

72. The distinction originates with Adam Smith, *An Inquiry into the Nature and Causes of the Wealth of Nations* (eds. R.H. Campbell, A.S. Skinner and W.B. Todd, Oxford, 1976), Bk. II, Ch. III.

73. This theme is discussed in Douglass C. North, *Structure and Change in Economic History* (Toronto, 1981), Chs. 12–13.

74. D.C. Coleman, 'Gentlemen and Players', *Econ. Hist. Rev.*, 2nd ser. XXVI (1973).

benefits of the dynamic growth of manufacturing, whether via the division of labour or through the advent of machinery, were bound to lead, in these circumstances, to a large proportion of the gains accruing to non-industrial forms of property. One result of this development was that, in a society which was only slowly becoming democratic, even in the early twentieth century,[75] and where power was concentrated in the hands of wealthy elites, manufacturers neither owned enough 'top wealth' nor made it in a sufficiently acceptable way to be able to impose their will on the political system. In the nineteenth century the industrial bourgeoisie in Britain was forced to come to terms with gentlemanly capitalism: it modified rather than superseded it, and in turn felt the weight of its compelling influence. Marx's assumption that industrial capitalism was the dominant force after 1850 and that the 'moneyed interests' were subservient to it is overdrawn, as we shall see.[76]

Industrialists who traced their descent from yeomen and small gentry might refer to themselves as 'gentleman manufacturers',[77] but the claim, however authentic, was also contradictory because full-time involvement in the 'vile and mechanical' world of industry,[78] with its long hours and need for unremitting attention to detail, was incompatible with the freedom necessary to gentlemanly status.[79] Some prominent manufacturers were only too eager to use their wealth to lift their families into the landed and gentlemanly sphere, and the prestige of the gentlemanly life continued to exert a powerful influence: even Samuel Smiles, the leading ideologist of the provincial business class, held the status of an independent Christian gentleman to be the desired end of the pursuit of self-help, and it must have been difficult for his readers to dissociate this position from the life-style of the more benevolent and public-spirited of the existing gentlemanly class.[80] Radicals like Richard Cobden, who dedicated their lives to the abolition of aristocratic power and wealth in Britain, failed badly,

75. In 1914 Britain was the only European country, save Hungary, not to have manhood suffrage. See H.C.G. Matthew, R.I. McKibbin and J.A. Kay, 'The Franchise Factor in the Rise of the Labour Party', *Eng. Hist. Rev.*, XCI (1976), pp. 723–6.

76. 'The complete rule of industrial capital was not acknowledged by English merchant's capital and moneyed interests until after the abolition of the duties on corn etc'. Karl Marx, *Capital*, III (1909 edn), p. 385, n. 47. Ch. 38 and pp. 385ff are also of interest in this context.

77. François Crouzet, *The First Industrialists: The Problem of Origins* (Cambridge, 1985), p. 44.

78. Powis, *Aristocracy*, p. 10.

79. Crouzet, *The First Industrialists*, p. 81.

80. Samuel Smiles, *Self Help* (ed. A. Briggs, 1958), p. 29 and Ch. XIII.

partly because the gentlemanly ideal was so attractive; but even when industrialists were profoundly antagonistic to the landed interest and their associates, they were often forced by the pressures of working-class discontent to come to terms with the existing social order. Industrialists were the shock troops of capitalism; the hostility that they generated, especially after 1815, undermined some of the authority which growing wealth might otherwise have offered them. Given their indirect relationship to the productive process and the more fragmented and less class-conscious work-force they employed, gentlemanly capitalists could present themselves more easily as natural leaders capable of offering disinterested advice, whilst also deriving substantial benefits from developments in which industrialists were the most visible agents of change.[81] British industrialists were thus trapped between a gentlemanly culture which flourished on capitalist wealth but derided technology, and trades unionists and socialists who exalted production but were deeply suspicious of the profit motive.

From this perspective, the Industrial Revolution can be seen as a new phase in what was already a highly successful and broad-based process of economic development. Britain was the most advanced economic power in Europe long before the onset of mechanisation or the beginning of the factory system. Given aristocratic adaptation to capitalism and Britain's early achievements as a commercial and financial nation, it is hardly surprising that, in 1850, power remained largely in traditional hands or that the elite proved capable of adapting its policies to suit changing times. The re-adoption of the gold standard, the rigorous discipline exercised over government expenditure and even the initial moves towards free trade had more to do with the elite's recognition of Britain's status as an international service centre than with her position as the world's workshop. The growth of provincial manufacturing appears also to have been accompanied by a progressive withdrawal of the landed classes from contact with industry and by a re-emphasis on class and status differences, including, as we have seen, a revamping of the idea and ideal of the gentleman. It is noticeable, too, that few recruits to industry came from well-connected merchants in London and the outports, and that on the occasions when industrialisation forced merchants 'to take a

---

81. This point is made by Weber in *Economy and Society*, pp. 931–2. We are aware of the fact that some services, notably transport, were heavily unionised by the late nineteenth century and subject to the same pressures as mechanical industry. But finance and the professions were much less affected by this problem.

new look at their prospects' they went into shipping, banking and financial services in preference to industry.[82]

Despite the growth of organisations such as the Anti-Corn Law League in the 1840s, provincial manufacturing interests were not in the political mainstream in the nineteenth century. In a fiercely competitive business world, few manufacturers felt wealthy enough or secure enough to turn their attention from work to politics or to the social activities which were indispensable to political success at national level. From the standpoint of policy-makers in London, provincial manufacturers were regarded as outsiders who might become a dangerous and destabilising radical force if squeezed too hard by economic crises. In these circumstances they would have to be bought off. But there was a difference between accommodation and assimilation. Palmerston's aggressive imperialism during the severe depression of the late 1830s and early 1840s provides a perfect example of a policy designed to keep industry content but also at arm's length.

If provincial manufacturers had not found their way to the centres of power by 1850, they were unlikely to do so thereafter, despite the steady decline in the importance of agriculture and of the landed interest. Before 1850 the great staple industries were the single most important driving force in economic development; after this date the epicentre of dynamic economic change began to shift back from north to south, from export industries in the provinces to the combination of services and industries characteristic of the south-east, where the newly evolving forms of gentlemanly capitalism were most in evidence. Despite a considerable growth in the numbers of rich manufacturers, wealth derived from heavy industry did not become of overmastering importance in Britain nor did the prestige of manufacturing improve markedly, given the impressive success of non-industrial forms of capitalism, especially finance. The wealth of most manufacturing capitalists remained limited and their interests local. Before the appearance of the large firm in the twentieth century, manufacturers inhabited a world in which atomistic competition prevailed, and this had the further consequence of making political cohesion more difficult.[83] Moreover, the minority who amassed

82. Crouzet, *The First Industrialists*, Chs. 5 and 7.
83. On this problem see Mancur Olsen, *The Logic of Collective Action*, (Cambridge, Mass., 1965). Growing concentration in finance and distribution, on the other hand, was not only a rational response to economic opportunity, but also politically efficient. For a discussion of the relationship between economic fragmentation and political influence in a contemporary setting see Robert H. Bates, *Markets and States in Tropical Africa* (Berkeley, Calif., 1981).

fortunes on a par with those made from land or in the City often adopted gentlemanly life-styles and attitudes, becoming incorporated into a system created by others rather than devising a distinctive and prestigious social presence of their own. As a result, economic policy continued to be the preserve of the gentlemanly elites who controlled the machinery of central government. Manchester, Leeds and Birmingham were heard of only at times when a particular event or crisis compelled them to present their case in London, where finance and commerce achieved overwhelming dominance.

The distance which separated the gentlemen of power from the bulk of the manufacturing class was graphically illustrated in the late nineteenth century, when the former grappled with the agonising problem of how and when to introduce the latter to the benefits of the honours system, the great status-conferring machine of the gentlemanly order, a system which many industrialists were only too ready to accept on terms set by the traditional holders of power and prestige.[84] It is, of course, true that heavy industry and services were interdependent and that the City and provincial exporters co-operated to their mutual benefit.[85] But, as we shall try to show, both the domestic and the international economies evolved in ways which advanced the cause of services more than the cause of export industries. This was the case after 1850, and it applied even more forcefully after 1914: when free trade cosmopolitanism came under threat, policy-makers almost automatically assumed that their chief priority was to retain Britain's status as an international financial power.

In suggesting that the influence of the manufacturing sector was relatively limited, even in the early twentieth century, it needs to be emphasised that we are attacking a presumption and a prejudice that the opposite must, somehow, have been the case, rather than adopting a paradoxical stance in the face of a substantial body of research supporting an interpretation that conflicts with our own. Historians who recognise the fact that the political elite rarely contained an industrial element often fall back on the argument that these elites maintained their position only because they were willing to carry out

84. It is instructive to find that, even in 1990, the 'most an industrialist can usually hope for is to become a baron, the lowliest form of peer', and that industrialists 'generally receive the lowliest form of knighthood too – the knight bachelor, a title awarded in medieval times to those knights too young or too poor to display their own banners', *Financial Times*, 29 December 1990.

85. A point made strongly by M. Daunton, 'Gentlemanly Capitalism and British Industry, 1820–1914', *Past and Present*, 122 (1989), pp. 137–40.

the wishes of their supposed masters; but, in the nature of things, this is almost impossible to prove. Direct evidence of successful industrial pressure is even harder to come by, and the number of empirical studies of the influence of manufacturers on imperial policy is very limited. Indeed, few scholars take care to differentiate between manufacturers and businessmen in general; but what little information there is tends to suggest that, although provincial industry could often make an immense amount of noise, its substantive achievements in influencing imperial policy were small.

THE TERMS OF THE TRADE: EXPANSION AND IMPERIALISM

Specialists in imperial history well understand the frustration which prompted Sir Keith Hancock's much-quoted remark that 'imperialism is no word for scholars', and they may even sympathise with his plan for consigning it to the dustbin.[86] Disposing of the term, however, does not dispose of the problem, and any substitute is likely to come with the ideological accoutrements which Hancock rightly wished to jettison. The fact is that historians need holistic terms, even if they also need to be wary of them.[87] Their principal obligation in this regard is to declare the contents of their baggage and to avoid smuggling bias under the cover of objectivity.

The term 'imperialism' is used here to refer to a species of the genus expansion. States commonly sponsor or permit pacific expansion beyond their own borders, typically through trade, cultural exchange and the movement of peoples. International relations arise from these contacts, and diplomatic ties follow where they are not already present. Such forms of expansion are not necessarily imperialist: they may be too slight to impinge significantly on the host country or, if weighty, they may be counterbalanced by inflows of comparable magnitude, in which case the result is a set of more or less mutually agreed arrangements between approximately equal partners. These characteristics of external expansion are noted here in schematic fashion simply to make the point that imperialism is a branch of international relations and not its totality. The distinguish-

86. W.K. Hancock, *Wealth of Colonies* (Cambridge, 1950), p. 1.
87. The case is neatly put by Robert C. Stalnaker, 'Events, Periods and Institutions in Historians' Language', *History and Theory*, 6 (1967).

ing feature of imperialism is not that it takes a specific economic, cultural or political form, but that it involves an incursion, or an attempted incursion, into the sovereignty of another state. Whether this impulse is resisted or welcomed and whether it produces costs or benefits are important but separate questions. What matters for purposes of definition is that one power has the will, and, if it is to succeed, the capacity to shape the affairs of another by imposing upon it. The relations established by imperialism are therefore based upon inequality and not upon mutual compromises of the kind which characterise states of interdependence.

Since most attention is usually paid to cases which illustrate the success of imperialist ambitions, it is worth recording that there were also failures. The difference between knocking on the door and opening it can be regarded, conceptually, as marking a distinction between an imperialism of intent and an imperialism of result. Britain's relations with the world beyond Europe before the mid-nineteenth century can easily be misread unless this difference is borne in mind. The notion of an imperialism of intent also underlines the fact that imperialist impulses express a conscious act of will: the agents of imperialism normally believe that they represent a superior power, ideologically as well as materially, and their actions are driven on by a sense of mission which embraces, legitimises and uplifts their private ambitions.

Emphasising the conscious intentions of the actors concerned makes appropriate allowance for the role of individual agency in imperialism; but it lends little support to the view that the events and episodes normally included in the history of imperialism were no more than idiosyncratic or random occurrences. The fact that the individuals concerned had a sense of wider purpose, which they shared with like-minded compatriots beached on other shores, itself casts doubt on the thesis that imperialism was a big accident caused by a 'fit of absence of mind'.[88] Such judgements represent understandable reactions to brands of history which claim to foretell the future by offering a partial reading of the past, but the suggestion that an essentially chaotic view of history is preferable to an excessively regimented one simply substitutes one doubtful view of the past for another. Accidents of course happen, but when they occur in clusters and on a global scale some thought needs to be given to the possibility that they had underlying causes which, while still being man-made, were not, in themselves, accidental.

88. J.R. Seeley, *The Expansion of England* (1883), p. 8.

Consequently, we need also to think of imperialism as a process transmitting impulses from a particular source of energy. The definition needs to be kept open at this point to encompass types of domination which are not confined to a single brand of assertiveness or to a specific historical stage. One of the major problems of assigning imperialism to a particular phase in the evolution of capitalism, for instance, is the presumption that the 'normal' course of capitalism is known and that its future can therefore be predicted. If imperialism is indeed the highest stage of capitalism, as Lenin thought, it becomes difficult to see how to relate it to subsequent episodes which ought not to exist. Historians with an inventive turn of mind may reach for terms such as late capitalism, but if the terminus continues to recede even sympathetic observers may come to suspect that the truth lies less in the prediction than in supposed deviations from it. This cautionary example shows how interpretations which begin as spacious and illuminating insights can easily make historians hostages in cells of their own choosing. Imperialism can be linked to a distinctive form of capitalism, but this can be done without excluding causes which may carry more weight in explaining forms of imperialism other than those dealt with here, and without presuming that the historic path of capitalism is known and predictable.

Gentlemanly capitalism undoubtedly helped to promote expansionist forces of investment, commerce and migration throughout the world, including Europe and the United States. Its main dynamic was the drive to create an international trading system centred on London and mediated by sterling. World trade was to be financed by short-term credits (principally bills on London); world development was to be promoted initially by long-term loans to foreign governments and subsequently through direct overseas investments. The whole package was to be tied together by a regime of international free trade, which would encourage specialisation, cut transaction costs and create an interlocking system of multilateral payments. The resulting expansion of global commerce was to be handled, transported and insured by British firms. British manufactured exports were a very visible part of this panorama, but the design was not drawn by industrialists and, as we have already noted, their interests were not paramount.

This vision was not inevitably imperialistic; nor were its imperialist forms invariably militaristic.[89] Nevertheless, there was a tendency for

89. We make this point to avoid misunderstandings of the kind expressed in

expansionist impulses to become imperialist, especially where they came up against societies which needed reforming or restructuring before expansionist ambitions could be realised, and which also seemed to be either amenable to change or incapable of resisting it. If industrialists were the shock troops who took the brunt of the class struggle at home, representatives of the service sector formed the advance guard of capitalism abroad. In promoting their interests, they necessarily came into direct contact with potential clients, customers and producers in distant parts of the world in ways that British manufacturers (and consumers) did not.[90] Not surprisingly, officers in the front line gathered much of the reconnaissance reaching London, passed on judgements about the suitability of foreign countries for the role assigned to them, and made recommendations about how they might be aligned to fit Britain's international purpose.

The marriage of private and public interests was readily arranged, partly because of the increasing importance of invisible earnings and income from foreign investment in settling Britain's balance of payments, and partly because the gentlemen at the top of the banking and service hierarchy shared the values and spoke the language of the political decision-makers. But the resulting alliance was much more than a narrow sectional deal between segments of the elite. Put simply, overseas expansion and the imperialism which accompanied it played a vital role in maintaining property and privilege at home in an age of social upheaval and revolution. The alliance was equally involved in promoting abroad sets of like-minded rulers and congenial states which were designed to be dependable allies in a global campaign to subdue republicanism and democracy by demonstrating the superiority of the liberal ideal of improvement. The link between the domestic and overseas parts of this strategy was forged by the gentlemanly diaspora, which was also perfectly placed to ease the transition from expansion to imperialism by extending the ideology of mission and rendering it patriotic. It is no coincidence that the most pervasive images of imperialism and empire were those which projected gentility rather than industry. The public portrait of the

---

Andrew Porter's article, 'The South African War (1899–1902): Context and Motive Reconsidered', *Jour. African Hist.*, 31 (1990), p. 51, which would have gained from using Peter Cain, 'Capitalism, War and Internationalism in the Thought of Richard Cobden', *Brit. Jour. Internat. Stud.*, 5 (1979).

90. This observation is both obvious and neglected; its conceptual ramifications have only recently attracted the attention of economists. See, for example, Jagdish N. Bhagwati, 'Trade in Services and the Multinational Trade Negotiations', *World Bank Economic Review*, 1 (1987).

imperial world was framed by civic virtues and depicted manly exploits, country life on estates and plantations, and social gatherings under tropical verandahs.[91] By stretching a point, it was possible to speak of the 'romance of the steamship'; but the chivalry of empire never embraced Birmingham or Manchester.

Imperialism, then, was neither an adjunct to British history nor an expression of a particular phase of its industrial development but an integral part of the configuration of British society, which it both reinforced and expressed. It is a telling comment on the power of scholarly specialisation that the principal debates on the evolution of British history during the past three centuries have managed, nevertheless, to marginalise the study of imperialism and empire.[92] At the same time, imperialist enterprise was enfolded in a grand development strategy designed by Britain to reshape the world in her own image. It was spearheaded, not by manufacturing interests, but by gentlemanly elites who saw in empire a means of generating income flows in ways that were compatible with the high ideals of honour and duty, and it remained a dynamic, expanding force long after decline, as measured by British comparative industrial performance, is conventionally thought to have set in.

IDEOLOGY AND METHODOLOGY

As is now abundantly clear, the subject of this study requires the use of terms which have powerful ideological connotations. Accordingly, we ought not to venture further into the history of imperialism without offering an explicit statement of our own perspective and its

91. Manifested separately or in combination. Imperial eccentrics, it might be said, were those who took one aspect of the empire-building role to hitherto unknown extremes. Lawrence, for example, was gripped by medieval legends and crusading fantasies which were topped up by reading the *Morte d'Arthur* during his desert campaigns and personified by his loyal Arab 'knights' and 'squires'. His ability to represent the world in terms of his idea of it made him a master of legendary truth as well as, eventually, a legend himself. See Lawrence James, *The Golden Warrior: The Life and Legend of Lawrence of Arabia* (1990). For a fascinating French perspective see Maurice Larès, *T.E. Lawrence, la France et les français* (Paris, 1980). Lawrence studied in France between 1907 and 1910 and wrote a dissertation on the castles of the crusaders.

92. The empire is, of course, wheeled on stage from time to time, especially at moments of crisis. But it has neither a permanent nor a central place in the major debates on the evolution of modern British history and its exclusion, usually without explicit justification, is characteristic of both right- and left-wing approaches to the past.

attendant methodology.[93] Our principal aim here is to understand the causes of British imperialism, not to pass judgement on them. Some readers may seek to connect our account of causation to their own views of the costs or benefits of imperialism, at home and abroad; but of course the merits of this exercise cannot be evaluated in advance of its execution. To avoid misunderstanding, however, we ought to note that our neutrality on this important subject is prompted by pragmatic considerations rather than by a concern to steer clear of controversy or to claim a special immunity for our own argument.[94] Quite simply, the problem of causation is itself so vast and so fiercely contested that to attempt an account of equal substance on its wide-ranging consequences would have led to congestion and to a loss of focus.

This reasoning suggests that the consequences of imperialism are not simply entailed by its causes; had they been similar in time and place, it might have been feasible to have squeezed extra answers from the evidence we had already consulted. But, even when the moral aspects of imperialism have been separated from its material impact (an operation which itself requires micro-surgery), it is still not possible to 'read off' results from axioms of causation. This does

93. We should note at this point that we have decided against aligning our interpretation with any one of the contending possibilities offered by international relations theory. We are greatly indebted to this source for helping to clarify the assumptions and connections of our argument. In the end, however, we came to the conclusion that our thesis could be made to fit all or none of the approaches currently on offer, and that to engage in a dialogue with what is now a voluminous literature while also trying to control our main historical theme would create more difficulties than it would solve. The extent of these difficulties cannot be laid out fully here. In the present context, we must confine ourselves to observing that there is first of all a problem as to what constitutes international relations theory, the answers being different in the United States, Britain and France – the three leading producers. Secondly, the most influential body of work, that generated in the United States, is itself divided between realist, neo-realist and other schools, and deploys a terminology respecting regimes, hegemons and other entities which needs to be considered carefully and therefore at some length. Finally, since international relations theory is culturally specific (though aiming at universality), potential users are perhaps justified in exercising caution before adopting a viewpoint that may be more parochial than its advocates imagine. The current debate over the decline of the United States as a world power, for example, is beginning to reveal that many supposedly timeless and objective notions were in fact the product of a brief period of global dominance and were fashioned for the purpose, albeit by an art that concealed art, even from the artificers. Isabelle Grunberg, 'Exploring the "Myth" of Hegemonic Stability', *International Organization*, 44 (1990), provides a penetrating analysis which can be compared to the critiques that brought down modernisation theory in the early 1970s.

94. The question of the costs and benefits of imperialism has been assessed by Lance E. Davis and Robert A. Huttenback, *Mammon and the Pursuit of Empire: The Political Economy of British Imperialism, 1860–1912* (Cambridge, 1986).

not diminish the relevance of the history presented here to the study of the present day; it is still possible to make a case for treating history as a practical art needed, as Ibn Khaldun put it, 'for the acquisition of excellence in ruling'. But it does mean that the appeal of simple theories of a complex world is likely to exceed their accuracy, and that the first step for those who seek to change or conserve the present is to understand how it came to be fashioned.

We do not suppose that the results of our inquiry are value-free in the naive sense of standing apart from assumptions and priorities which all authors necessarily carry with them. But we have tried to distinguish between our presuppositions and the testable propositions derived from them. Our interpretation therefore has no privileged status: it stands or falls by normal tests of evidence and inference. We do not invoke iron laws or appeal to an 'inner logic' of history; nor do we suppose that the terms we use or the forces we identify have lives of their own which are independent of the human beings who create them.[95] But, since there is no fruitful empiricism without hypotheses, we have constructed a central proposition, based on gentlemanly capitalism and its impulses, and tested it against various case studies. In doing so, we have attempted to steer a course between excessively broad arguments, which subsume the world under the most generalised conceptions of capitalism, nationalism or racism, and readily become tautological, and an excessively narrow preoccupation with the particularities of place and time, which either rules out the possibility of generalisation or tries to infer too much from too little. Our examples have not been pre-selected to serve our particular line of inquiry, but have been chosen because they are generally agreed to be the most important cases which any theory of British imperialism has to encompass. At the same time – to borrow an analogy from statistics - our analysis has tried to find a measure of central tendency which provides the best fit for the evidence rather than to explain every single observation. Contrary facts inevitably arise, and it is open to others to decide whether these are qualifications and exceptions which do not disturb our main hypothesis or whether they are fatal to it. If the possibility of refutation is disquieting for the authors concerned, they can take comfort from the fact that the principle of falsification can be applied to science but not to necromancy.

The chief aim of our interpretation is to establish the context

95. A. Arato, 'Lucacs' Theory of Reification', *Telos*, 11 (1972) provides a valuable discussion of this problem.

within which actions took place; that is, to understand why actors of a certain kind were where they were when they were, and why their views of the world inclined them to act in the way they did. Translated into historical practice, this task involves the description of two contexts, one at home and one abroad, and of the links between them. We address this problem primarily by organising the evidence to identify the processes of which individuals were a part.[96] This procedure involves the selection and emphasis of some facts rather than others and the use of hindsight to bring out aspects of causation which may not have been stated or perceived clearly by participants at the time. To this extent, we accept that we are seeking to explain trends and events in terms of causes rather than trying to understand individual actions in terms of motives. Thus, we are concerned less with anatomising the biographical entrails of a Dilke or a Rhodes than with explaining why Dilke-like and Rhodes-like figures arose in the first place.

This approach to historical method does not imply a preference for types of causal explanations which infer individual actions from general 'covering laws', still less that our argument has been suborned by the tempting simplicities of determinism. On the contrary, our account of historical context is based on the interplay between process and agency; and if we focus on the former rather than on the latter it is because it is more appropriate to the purpose and scale of our particular inquiry, and not because of a belief in its inherent superiority. In this matter we follow Weber, who distinguished between causal explanation and empathy without suggesting that the two were incompatible, and also more recent philosophical opinion, which has moved away from earlier overstatements of the opposition between naturalistic and other forms of historical explanation.[97] Accordingly, we have attempted to read out of the evidence rather than to read into it, and to use contemporary opinion to check that our retrospective vantage point has not imposed unacceptable anachronisms on the past – even though much illustrative detail has had to be compressed and some of it has had to be omitted.

At the same time, reconstructing the historical context provides a measure for explanations which assign priority to individual motiv-

96. Along the lines set out by W.H. Walsh, 'Colligatory Concepts in History', in W.H. Burston and D. Thompson, eds. *Studies in the Nature and Teaching of History* (1967).
97. Two helpful summaries of the issues are: W. Outhwaite, *Understanding Social Life: The Method Called Verstehen* (1975), and Patrick Gardiner, ed. *The Philosophy of History* (Oxford, 1974).

ation, and it helps, too, to distinguish between reasons for action and causes of action, which may or may not be the same. Historians who feel that explanations of imperialism fail if they do not trace the man with the smoking gun may be disappointed with an account that concentrates on locating the stance of the combatants at the point of the draw; but they should also bear in mind that identifying the finger on the trigger provides an incomplete reconstruction of the causes of conflict.[98] The appropriate test of our interpretation, we suggest, is not whether it puts the case beyond all doubt but whether it offers an account which is both plausible and illuminating. In some respects, this is the more difficult examination, for being right about small issues is easier than shedding light on large ones.

The fact that our interpretation emphasises economic consider-ations and also traces the direction of causation from centre to periphery may give rise to doubts over the claims made so far about its neutral and non–deterministic character. While there is a great deal to be said on the problems of monocausality and bias in historical explanation, we shall confine ourselves here to two observations which have particular relevance to our analysis. In the first place, the stress laid on economic aspects of imperialism does not imply a commitment to the belief that economic forces are, *a priori*, more important than other considerations. It means only that the extent of their significance is to be determined by empirical investigation. In principle, there is no reason why the emphasis of causation should not be found elsewhere: the fact that we could not see how to do this does not mean that it cannot be done. At the same time, it will become clear that our own interpretation draws on political and ideological considerations without treating them as superstructures built on an economic base, and that we have attempted to point to interconnections without also losing the main thread of the argument. Secondly, and similarly, drawing a line of causation from the centre to the periphery is not to be seen as the product of a Euro-centric bias complemented by a dated disregard for the internal history of countries outside Europe. If we have restricted ourselves in this regard, it is because our concern is with the causes of imperialism and not with its consequences or with the domestic history of colonialism. Aspects of causation are of course to be found on the periphery, and these will be dealt with. Within these limits, we hope that our case studies show some understanding of the spirit as well as of the

98. Appearances can also deceive, as readers of Agatha Christie know well.

empirical findings of recent research on the various frontiers we have covered. But the generic causes, in our view, have their origins at the centre. This judgement accounts for the focus of our work; once again, however, it owes its status to empirical evidence and not to assumptions about the immanence of the European destiny.

This defence, even if extended, will not reassure historians who invoke the principle of multicausality. Nevertheless, it is worth noting that this position contains its own, often unacknowledged, difficulties. We can all agree that complex events are likely to have complex causes. By drawing up an impressive list of candidates, historians can readily display their scholarship, and by including everything they can protect themselves from hungry critics on the prowl for omissions. The trouble with this procedure is that it can easily redefine the problem instead of solving it. To accept the infinite complexity of historical events is not to acquire immunity from the obligation to select some segments of evidence rather than others and to judge their relative importance. The appeal to multicausality can easily degenerate into an attempt to duck this challenge by referring to the need to avoid the errors of monocausality and determinism. This is a sleight of hand that succeeds more often than it deserves: the exercise of selectivity and judgement may produce monocausal and determinist arguments, but this is just one of several more desirable possible outcomes.

Multicausal accounts of historical problems frequently culminate in the verdict that the truth lies somewhere between two extremes. The claim sounds judicious; but it may also reflect the predicament of those who wish to reach a conclusion while also expressing their determination, in Burke's phrase, 'to die in the last dyke of prevarication'. The truth may indeed lie somewhere between two extremes, but, then again, it may not. Clio has not laid down a law to this effect, and even if she had we might reasonably appeal for directions as to where, even approximately, the somewhere in question might be found.

CONCLUSION

Judgement on the originality of the thesis advanced here must be left to others. Our obligation at this point is simply to summarise the nature of the claims we wish to make in this regard. These can be placed under two headings. The first centres on our account of the origins of imperial impulses, and is based on a reinterpretation of the character and course of modern British history. Our argument draws particularly on research into economic history, but it has implications for social and political history and is therefore not confined solely to one specialised branch of historical studies. The second claim follows the first and takes the form of a historiographical revision of standard approaches to the study of British imperialism in order to reunite the history of the centre and of its diverse peripheries and to suggest adjustments to the accepted chronology of the subject.

Although these are substantial claims, they have also to be related to a modest definition of historical originality. Historical knowledge and understanding advance incrementally rather than seismically, and even the most original interpretations shift the emphasis rather than rewrite the script. This is why Thucydides remains highly relevant to the study of international relations, whereas Ptolemy has no part to play in contemporary astronomy.[99] Put another way, it can be said that most of the cards of historical interpretation have long been dealt; professional scholars can hope, at best, to reshuffle the pack. The point is clearly illustrated by the study of British imperialism, which has been the subject of serious and detailed scrutiny for over a century, and it is underlined by the present work, which rests on the backs of other scholars, as our copious references readily acknowledge. Once found, moreover, originality can turn out to be a qualified merit. One scholar, for example, might be original in his discovery of evidence but unoriginal in his use of it; another might have an original idea but a limited mastery of historical sources. The former contributes knowledge but not understanding; the latter offers understanding without knowledge. Our attempt to move some of the accepted boundary stones of the vast subject we have chosen to address has to be placed in this cautionary context. We have ourselves kept in mind the fact that Sisyphus laboured in vain.

---

99. See, for example, Michael W. Doyle, 'Thucydidean Realism', *Review of International Studies*, 16 (1990), and Steven Forde, *The Ambition to Rule: Alcibiades and the Politics of Imperialism in Thucydides* (Ithaca, NY, 1989).

CHAPTER TWO

Prospective: Aristocracy, Finance and Empire, 1688–1850

Starting points have origins which lie beyond the antecedents chosen to define them. A plausible case could be made for beginning this study in the late sixteenth century, as this would encompass the Elizabethan explorers, the foundation of the East India Company, and the establishment of the first colonies in the New World. In taking the Glorious Revolution as our point of departure instead, we do not intend to minimise the importance of these events, to suggest that our argument is incompatible with them, or indeed to claim that 1688 was itself a cataclysmic year in the making of imperial history. We do, however, wish to argue that the Revolution brought together and lent impetus to forces that left a deep imprint not only on domestic history, as is well known, but also on the character and course of colonial development – a proposition that is less well appreciated. By taking this additional step, we hope to establish a systematic connection between British and imperial history from the outset of our study; by tracing the evolution of this relationship, we hope to show how one phase in the history of the empire dissolved into another in the nineteenth century.

HISTORIOGRAPHICAL PERSPECTIVES

To reach this point we need first to define our position with respect to the existing historiography. As far as Britain is concerned, this means choosing between interpretations which emphasise the persistence of an *ancien régime* dominated by an oligarchy of landowners from 1688, or even from 1660, down to 1832 or even beyond, and those which emphasise evidence of change as demonstrated, variously, by the Revolution of 1688, the Hanoverian succession, the rise of a 'polite and commercial' middle class, the growth of an impolite radicalism, the American and French Revolutions and, finally, industrialisation.[1] Our contribution to this wide-ranging but also highly specialised debate can be only a modest one. It appears to us that the boundaries of discussion have been drawn too narrowly around political, constitutional and ideological issues and have not fully incorporated the results of recent research into economic history, even where reference is made to the Industrial Revolution. Our purpose in including this dimension, however, is not to renovate an argument about industrialisation but to emphasise the continuing importance of agriculture and the significance of innovations in finance and commercial services. In claiming that these innovations made headway because they were compatible with the 'traditional' social order, we shall indicate how an argument for change can be combined with one emphasising continuity without, we hope, collapsing the case into generalities.

The imperial perspective also needs to be brought into focus. At present, the mainland colonies are the only part of the empire to appear either prominently or regularly in the controversy over the direction taken by eighteenth-century Britain, principally because constitutional issues carried contemporary debate over political rights and duties across the Atlantic. The empire as a whole, however, does not feature systematically in the discussion, and its role is often pared down to the point at which near-sighted observers might begin to doubt its existence.[2] This anomaly has persisted despite the fact that Britain's presence abroad was substantially enlarged in the course of the eighteenth century. Territorial advances were made in India and in the North American settlements that were to become Canada; the West Indies rose to head the list of Britain's trading partners; commercial ties with the mainland colonies increased down to the War of Independence, survived the creation of the United States, and prospered thereafter. Imperial assertiveness was neither dimmed by the loss of the American colonies nor extinguished by the resumption

1. The continuity thesis has been restated by J.C.D. Clark, *English Society, 1688–1832: Ideology, Social Structure and Political Practice during the Ancien Regime* (Cambridge, 1985). Statements of the alternative view are too numerous to be listed, but for the one quoted here (and for further references) see Paul Langford, *A Polite and Commercial People: England, 1727–1783* (Oxford, 1989).

2. See Philip Lawson, 'The Missing Link: the Imperial Dimension in Understanding Hanoverian Britain', *Hist. Jour.*, 29 (1986), and the agenda drawn up by J.G.A. Pocock, 'British History: a Plea for a New Subject', *Am. Hist. Rev.*, 87 (1982).

of peace in 1815 after the long war with France. Colonies of settlement were promoted in New South Wales from the 1780s, in the Cape after the turn of the century, and in New Zealand from the 1840s. During and after the French Wars a chain of naval bases, some within the empire and others outside it, was established to police the ocean routes and to create points of entry into tropical Africa, South America, the Persian Gulf, south-east Asia and the Far East. Forceful diplomacy, occasionally accompanied by house-breaking, continued to be used to bend the world overseas to Britain's will and reached a new peak of intensity with the exercise of Palmerston's muscular authority during the 1830s and 1840s.

The omission of these sizeable developments from serious consideration of the course of British history after 1688 is to some extent the result of an excess of specialisation that affects all fields of historical study. But it can also be explained by the fact that imperial historians themselves have long been unsure about what role to assign the empire in the evolution of the mother country. Despite the creation of what is now a voluminous and impressive body of literature, no general interpretation of the eighteenth-century empire has succeeded either in commanding acceptance or in generating the creative dissent needed to inspire a superior alternative.[3] Imperial historians have themselves become divided by a common empire: specialists on North America have devised one set of controversies and dates; those working on India have evolved another. The outcome of these separate inquiries, valuable though it is, has contributed more to an understanding of the history of the states that arose from the debris of empire, whether British or Mughal, than to an awareness of a common imperial purpose. In these circumstances, it is easy to draw the conclusion that no common purpose and no significant unity existed, and thereby to make a virtue out of what, on closer inspection, might be a weakness in historical analysis.

There was a time when this problem appeared to have a satisfactory solution. On the assumption that the history of the empire was defined by events affecting its constitutional standing, it was acceptable for the *Cambridge History of the British Empire* to regard the creation of the United States as marking the termination of the 'old'

---

3. See the judgements of I.K. Steele, 'The Empire and Provincial Elites: an Interpretation of Some Recent Writings on the English Atlantic, 1675–1740', in Peter Marshall and Glyn Williams, eds. *The British Atlantic Empire Before the American Revolution* (1980), p. 2, and Peter Marshall, 'The British Empire in the Age of the American Revolution', in William M. Fowler and Wallace Coyle, eds. *The American Revolution: Changing Perspectives* (Boston, Mass., 1979), p. 193.

empire.[4] However, as it became apparent that this criterion excluded too much that was relevant to an understanding of the realities of imperial relations and international power alike, increasing attention was paid to influences other than those defined by constitutional considerations. The weightiest statement of the revisionist case was presented in Vincent Harlow's *The Founding of the Second British Empire, 1763–1793,* which sought to reduce the importance attached to 1783 and to suggest that the real turning point in Britain's imperial relations occurred with the successful conclusion of the Seven Years' War 20 years earlier in 1763.[5] This date symbolised both the achievement of British naval supremacy and the emergence of new expansionist forces based on incipient industrialisation and characterised by a quest for markets and raw materials rather than for territorial possession. Harlow's argument thus contained elements of the idea of informal empire that Gallagher and Robinson applied to the mid-Victorian period.[6] In effect, Harlow's interpretation created what might be called the long nineteenth century, whereby 1763 became the starting point for the industrial-based, free-trading imperialism that was to prevail until the neo-mercantilist policies of rival powers disrupted it at the close of the nineteenth century.

Had this interpretation held, historians of empire would have a thesis to offer the wider world. However, it is generally accepted that Harlow's argument created more difficulties than it could resolve. Important though it was, Britain's success in 1763 signified neither her ascendancy as a naval power nor the elimination of the French challenge. Harlow's emphasis on the part played by the process of industrialisation is also at variance with current assessments of the chronology of the Industrial Revolution, which have moved the turning point forward to the close of the eighteenth century rather than back to 1763. Similarly, in underlining the significance of early experiments with free trade, Harlow was left with the problem that protectionism remained in place until well into the nineteenth century.

4. J. Holland Rose, A.P. Newton and E.A. Benians, eds. *The Old Empire From the Beginnings to 1783* (Cambridge, 1929). See also Sir Reginald Coupland, *The British Empire After the American Revolution* (1930).

5. Vol. I, *Discovery and Revolution* (Oxford, 1952), and Vol. II, *New Continents and Changing Values* (Oxford, 1964). The discussion that follows draws especially on Vol. I, pp. 1–11, 147–8, 154, 158 and 647, and Vol. II, pp. 1–3, 259, 782–6 and 792–3, and on two valuable guides: Peter Marshall, 'The First and Second Empires: a Question of Demarcation', *History*, 44 (1964), and Ronald Hyam, 'British Imperial Expansion in the Late Eighteenth Century', *Hist. Jour.*, 10 (1967). There is also a perceptive review of Vol. I by Richard Pares in *Eng. Hist. Rev.*, LXVIII (1953).

6. J. Gallagher and R.E. Robinson, 'The Imperialism of Free Trade', *Econ. Hist. Rev.*, 2nd ser., VI (1953).

This difficulty entailed another: in stressing the shift of policy towards trade rather than dominion, Harlow was unable to account adequately for Britain's continuing expansion within the formal empire in British North America, the West Indies and India, while his idea that there was a 'swing to the east' following the loss of the mainland colonies minimised the enduring importance of economic ties with the United States as well as with the Atlantic economy generally.

These weaknesses have yet to be overcome either within the liberal tradition of scholarship or outside it.[7] Indeed, as far as imperial history is concerned, the contribution made by those opposed to 'bourgeois' scholarship has proved to be disappointingly conventional. Andre Gunder Frank, for example, claimed that the Industrial Revolution 'began with the year 1760', and that the last quarter of the eighteenth century marked the transition from mercantile to industrial capitalism.[8] Wallerstein's treatment is far more detailed, but the result falls into a familiar pattern. He, too, distinguishes between mercantile capitalism, which occupied the 'long' seventeenth century (1600–1750), and industrial capitalism, which predominated thereafter. The point of transition is symbolised by the year 1763, which saw 'the victory of certain segments of the world bourgeoisie, who were rooted in England, with the aid of the British state'.[9] But this date, as we have seen, had already been selected by Harlow and been criticised subsequently, and Wallerstein is unable to substantiate his additional claim that the bourgeoisie rose (finally) to power in the mid-eighteenth century. If, today, historians of all persuasions are more likely to halt in 1776 or 1783, it is not because the conventional case for doing so is convincing but because the alternatives are even less persuasive; and one result of this decision is that the period between 1783 and 1815 is covered imperfectly or not at all.[10]

It should be evident by now that we cannot simply present a summary of an acceptable interpretation of eighteenth-century

---

7. Starting points other than that advanced by Harlow have been put forward: 1748 is one; the 'middle of the eighteenth century' is another. But these suggestions have not been accompanied by a thesis encompassing the 'first' empire as a whole. Harlow's argument therefore deserves to retain its place in the historiography of the eighteenth-century empire, despite the fact that it now has few advocates.

8. *Dependent Accumulation and Underdevelopment* (1978), pp. 72–3 and the discussion of periodisation on pp. 7–10.

9. Immanuel Wallerstein, *The Modern World System*, Vol. II, *Mercantilism and the Consolidation of the European World Economy, 1600–1750* (New York, 1980), p. 258 and the discussion of periodisation on pp. 2–9.

10. A recent exception, which should encourage imperial historians to look more closely at this neglected period, is C.A. Bayly, *Imperial Meridian: The British Empire and the World, 1780–1830* (Cambridge, 1989).

imperialism because it does not lie readily to hand; if we adopt any of the existing approaches we are likely to drive through signs warning of the hazards surrounding concepts such as mercantilism, free trade and the Industrial Revolution. The problem is to devise a route that offers a plausible way of connecting the history of Britain to the history of the empire. There are, no doubt, a number of possibilities. But the one that appears to us to have the greatest explanatory power is that which begins by focusing on the structure of authority installed by the Revolution of 1688 and its attendant property rights, rewards and sanctions, and views imperialism as an attempt to export the Revolution Settlement (and hence to entrench it at home) by creating compliant satellites overseas. Domestic and imperial developments were joined in various ways, but none was more pervasive than the bond created by finance. As the financial revolution underwrote the new regime at home, so it helped to fund settlement, export-production and trade overseas: the evolution of the credit and revenue-raising system provides a means of tracing not only the fortunes of the revolution settlement itself but of the empire as well.

THE FINANCIAL REVOLUTION: PRIVATE INTERESTS AND PUBLIC VIRTUES

The period 1688–1850 owes its unity to the economic and political dominance of a reconstructed and commercially progressive aristocracy which derived its power from land. Agriculture remained the most important economic activity for the greater part of the period, whether measured by its share of national income, its contribution to employment, or by its ability to generate large fortunes.[11] In 1790, no less than three-quarters of all agricultural land was owned by no more than 4,000–5,000 aristocrats and gentry, who presided over a series of innovations which raised productivity, increased incomes from rents, and helped to lift land values.[12] Down to the 1760s the

11. We follow here N.F.R. Crafts, 'British Economic Growth, 1700–1831: a Review of the Evidence', *Econ. Hist. Rev.*, 2nd ser. XXXVI (1983); idem, 'British Industrialization in an International Context', *Jour. Interdisc. Hist.*, 19 (1989); and C.H. Feinstein, 'Capital Formation in Great Britain', in Peter Mathias and N.M. Postan, eds. *The Cambridge Economic History of Europe* (Cambridge, 1978), VII, Pt. 1.

12. J.V. Beckett, 'The Pattern of Landownership in England and Wales, 1660–1880', *Econ. Hist. Rev.*, 2nd ser. XXXVII (1984); J.R. Wordie, 'Rent Movements and the English Tenant Farmer, 1700–1839', *Research in Economic History*, 6 (1981); P.K. O'Brien, 'Quelle a été exactement la contribution de l'aristocratie britannique au progrès de l'agriculture entre 1688 et 1789?', *Annales*, 42 (1987).

prosperity of agriculture, especially in the south-east, was boosted by foreign demand, which drew grain exports out of the country; thereafter, the growth of the domestic market ensured that investment in agriculture remained high and that farm incomes stayed buoyant.[13] Throughout the eighteenth century, purchasing power derived from agricultural rents and wages formed the basis of consumer demand for both domestic manufactures and imports, including colonial products.[14] As we shall see, the dominance of agriculture was not seriously questioned until the 1820s; even so, its decline was pro-tracted and became irreversible only with the measures opening Britain to free trade at the close of the 1840s.

As the landed interest threw off the last traces of feudalism, eliminating the threat not of a rising bourgeoisie but of conservative farmers, so too its representatives increased their grip on the levers of power in the aftermath of the Civil War. Following the Revolution of 1688, the magnates consolidated their political authority as they consolidated their estates.[15] These 'great oaks', as Burke called them, shaded the country because they possessed, in land, a form of wealth that also carried the supreme badge of authority, being permanent, prestigious and allowing time for the affairs of state. In dominating parliament, the landed interest also gathered together the main lines of authority, notably the legal system, public expenditure, and defence, which joined the seat of government in London to the most distant provinces. The control exercised by the peerage over the House of Commons remained undisturbed before 1832 and was only slowly eroded thereafter, while its dominance of the executive lasted well beyond 1850.[16] Social exclusiveness was maintained by in-group marriage, ideological cohesion was demonstrated by a commitment to the Church of England, and cultural homogeneity was shaped by

13. A.H. John, 'The Course of Agricultural Change, 1660–1760', in L.S. Pressnell, ed. *Studies in the Industrial Revolution Presented to T.S. Ashton* (1960), pp. 125, 130–2; and for the stimulus provided by the corn bounties, idem, 'English Agricultural Improvement and Grain Exports, 1660–1765', in D.C. Coleman and A.H. John, eds. *Trade, Government and Economy in Pre-Industrial England: Essays Presented to F.J. Fisher* (1976), pp. 48–50.

14. Patrick O'Brien, 'Agriculture and the Home Market for English Industry', *Eng. Hist. Rev.*, C (1985).

15. See, for example, Geoffrey Cannon, ed. *The Whig Ascendancy* (1981); G.E. Mingay, *English Landed Society in the Eighteenth Century* (1963), pp. 10–11, 111–13.

16. M.W. McCahil, *Order and Equipoise: The Peerage and the House of Lords, 1783–1806* (1978); J. Slack, 'The House of Lords and Parliamentary Patronage in Great Britain, 1802–32', *Hist. Jour.*, 23 (1980); John Cannon, *Aristocratic Century: The Peerage of Eighteenth-Century England* (Cambridge, 1984); Ellis Archer Wasson, 'The House of Commons, 1660–1945: Parliamentary Families and the Political Elite', *Eng. Hist. Rev.*, CVI (1991).

the public schools, whose pupils, 'the glory of their country' in Defoe's judgement, were set apart from their contemporaries, 'the mere outsides of gentlemen', who were educated by other means.[17] None of this is to suggest, even in a summary as compressed as this, that the country was run by an oligarchy which became somnolent because it was allowed to rest undisturbed: opposition sprang from different quarters and was sometimes powerful enough to trouble the repose of the most complacent members of the government. But opposition that was Tory or urban middle class in origin remained within constitutional limits, at least after 1745; and, when radical protest broke the bounds of law and convention, it was brought under control.[18] At such moments, the instinct of self-preservation sharpened the quality of political judgement and caused property-owners to sink their differences in their common interest.

The most important development outside agriculture in the eighteenth century was the financial revolution of the 1690s centred on the foundation of the Bank of England and the creation of the national debt.[19] These innovations were linked to wider developments within the financial sector: the recoinage of 1697 and the establishment, thereafter, of a *de facto* gold standard; the evolution of specialised merchant banks in the City; the growth of a market in mortgages; the increasing use of bills of exchange to settle domestic and international obligations; the rise of the stock exchange; the development of marine and fire insurance; and the appearance of a financial press.[20] The early

17. Quoted in Cannon, *Aristocratic Century*, p. 39.
18. See, for example, Linda Colley, *In Defiance of Oligarchy: The Tory Party, 1714–60* (Cambridge, 1982); idem, 'Eighteenth-Century Radicalism Before Wilkes', *Royal Hist. Soc. Trans.*, 31 (1981); John Stevenson, *Popular Disturbances in England, 1700–1870* (1979); and John Brewer, 'English Radicalism in the Reign of George III', in J.G.A. Pocock, ed. *Three British Revolutions* (Princeton, NJ, 1980). The constituencies and the towns are dealt with by Frank O'Gorman, *Voters, Patrons and Parties: The Unreformed Electorate of Hanoverian England, 1734–1832* (Oxford, 1989); and Nicholas Rogers, *Whigs and Cities: Popular Politics in the Age of Walpole and Pitt* (Oxford, 1989).
19. Our thinking on this subject, and on the period as a whole, owes a great deal to two very different but complementary books: P.G.M. Dickson, *The Financial Revolution in England: A Study in the Development of Public Credit, 1688–1756* (1967), and J.G.A. Pocock, *The Machiavellian Moment: The Florentine Contribution to the Atlantic Republican Tradition* (Princeton, NJ, 1975). See also idem, 'The Machiavellian Moment Revisited: a Study in History and Ideology', *Jour. Mod. Hist.*, 53 (1981); idem, *Virtue, Commerce, and History* (Cambridge, 1985); and Julian Hoppit, 'Attitudes to Credit in Britain, 1680–1790', *Hist. Jour.*, 33 (1990).
20. A.E. Feaveryear, *The Pound Sterling: A History of English Money* (2nd edn 1963), pp. 154–7; J. Sperling, 'The International Payments Mechanism in the Seventeenth and Eighteenth Centuries', *Econ. Hist. Rev.*, 2nd ser. XIV (1962); D.M. Joslin, 'London Private Bankers, 1720–1785', *Econ. Hist. Rev.*, 2nd ser. VII (1954), pp. 175–9, 184; Dickson, *Financial Revolution*, pp. 225–8, 493, 505–6, and Ch. 20; Larry Neal, 'The

eighteenth century saw the expansion of the East India Company and the South Sea Company, the two great companies whose shares formed a sizeable part of the stock market, the growth of Lloyds as the international centre of underwriting, and the formation of new insurance companies, such as the Sun Fire Office (1708) and the Exchange Assurance Company (1720).[21] The external effects of these innovations were felt, in turn, on other activities in the service sector. Improvements in credit and commercial services boosted the shipping industry, promoted overseas trade and assisted the balance of payments by generating invisible earnings.[22] The expansion of overseas commerce encouraged the rise of large mercantile firms whose size enabled them to mobilise the capital and credit needed for long-distance trade.[23] As the eighteenth century witnessed the consolidation of large estates and their perpetuation through the male line, so it saw the growth of a merchant oligarchy and its 'entailment' through commercial dynasties. It was during this period, too, that non-commercial branches of the service sector were expanded and defined. Official employment, especially in new or reformed departments, such as the Board of Trade and the Treasury, became associated with a concept of public duty that was the hallmark of gentility and was handed on, often from father to son, while in the private sector a number of prominent occupations acquired the status of professions and their members became acknowledged as gentlemen.[24]

All of these developments came together in London, and gave further impetus to the growth of what was already a large and

Rise of a Financial Press: London and Amsterdam, 1681–1810', *Bus. Hist.*, 30 (1988). Recent research drawing attention to the importance of the service sector in the eighteenth century is summarised by N.F.R. Crafts, *British Economic Growth during the Industrial Revolution* (Oxford, 1985), pp. 12–13, 16–17.

21. Dickson, *Financial Revolution*, Ch. 16; P.G.M. Dickson, *The Sun Insurance Office, 1710–1960* (1960); B.E. Supple, *The Royal Exchange Assurance: A History of British Insurance, 1720–1970* (Cambridge, 1970); A.H. John, 'Insurance Investment and the London Money Market of the Eighteenth Century', *Economica*, 20 (1953).

22. Ralph Davis, *The Rise of the English Shipping Industry in the Seventeenth and Eighteenth Centuries* (2nd edn. 1972), pp. 389–90; Simon Ville, 'Michael Henley and Son, London Shipowners, 1775–1830: With Special Reference to War Experience', (Ph.D. thesis, London University, 1983).

23. Jacob M. Price, 'What Did Merchants Do? Reflections on British Overseas Trade, 1660–1790', *Jour. Econ. Hist.*, 49 (1989), pp. 273, 278–82.

24. John Brewer, *The Sinews of Power: War, Money and the English State, 1688–1783* (1989), Ch. 3 (which also discusses the relationship between public service and patronage); Geoffrey Holmes, *Augustan England: Professions, State, and Society, 1680–1730* (1982). Our formulation (see also Chapter 1) suggests that some occupations in the private sector were compatible with gentlemanly status and therefore refines the contrast drawn by Brewer, *Sinews of Power*, p. 206.

expanding urban centre.[25] The great institutions which supported the financial revolution, and indeed the Glorious Revolution too, were based in the City, where they benefited from the externalities generated by geographical proximity and overlapping functions. As the leading port, London itself was already distinguished by the wealth and cosmopolitan character of its merchant community, and was well placed to launch new ventures overseas. London's manufactures also came to reflect the expansion of the financial and service sector: older industries, such as silk and cloth, lost ground to foreign and provincial competitors, but new industries, ranging from sugar-processing to the production of high-quality furniture, arose to meet the needs of the country's most important concentration of wealthy consumers as well as its largest mass market.[26] No other town experienced such a striking development of consumer-oriented industries that relied so heavily on wealth derived ultimately from overseas trade and government expenditure; and no other town evolved such refined gradations of status as were found among London's service class of gentlemen's gentlemen, superior shopkeepers, clerks and the semi-employed attendants of the great and the pretenders to greatness.

This is not to say that London was unique: recent work on provincial towns as well as the long-established record of outports, such as Liverpool, Bristol and Glasgow, indicates that both the financial revolution and the elite-consumer tastes that accompanied it spread beyond the metropolis in the course of the eighteenth century.[27] But imitation flattered the power of the centre rather than diluted it: London remained outstanding not only in its size but also

25. E.A. Wrigley, 'A Simple Model of London's Importance in Changing English Society and Economy, 1650–1750', *Past and Present*, 37 (1967), and the pioneering studies by F.J. Fisher now gathered together in *London and the English Economy, 1500–1800* (1990). For the concentration of wealth and service-sector employments see James Alexander, 'The Economic Structure of the City of London at the End of the Seventeenth Century', *Urban History Yearbook* (1989); L.D. Schwartz, 'Social Class and Social Geography: the Middle Class in London at the End of the Eighteenth Century', *Social History* , 7 (1982); and John A. James, 'Personal Wealth Distribution in Late Eighteenth-Century Britain', *Econ. Hist. Rev.*, 2nd ser. XLI (1988).

26. A.E. Musson, 'The British Industrial Revolution', *History*, 67 (1982), pp. 257–8. See also Neil McKendrick, John Brewer and J.H. Plumb, *The Birth of a Consumer Society* (1982), though the precise date of birth is open to discussion, as the title of Joan Thirsk's study of the seventeenth century suggests: *Economy, Policy and Projects: The Development of a Consumer Society in Early Modern England* (Oxford, 1978).

27. See, for example, P.J. Corfield, *The Impact of English Towns, 1700–1800* (Oxford, 1982); Peter Borsay, *The English Urban Renaissance: Culture and Society in the Provincial Town, 1660–1770* (Oxford, 1989); and the important essay by J.A. Chartres, 'Cities and Towns, Farmers and Economic Change in the Eighteenth Century', *Hist. Research*, 64 (1991).

in the qualitative differences that separated so many of its functions from those of even the largest provincial towns. There was only one Bank of England, one Lloyds and one national debt, and they were all found in London. Moreover, the City was distinguished from the outset by its close involvement with government finance and by its pronounced overseas orientation. The long-term capital market, as it emerged in London, was already separated from the rest of the country; provincial needs were met by local credit networks.[28] If the supremacy of the metropole was underpinned by powerful economic causes, it owed much of its distinction to the fact that London was the capital as well as the main port. The proximity of the City to parliament, to the departments of state and to the court provided opportunities for gaining access to information and for influencing policy that simply did not exist elsewhere. Provincial business could compete at the same level only by relocating its headquarters in London, as happened increasingly after 1850.

The causes of the financial revolution cannot be examined here in any detail. But it is clear that the pre-conditions had long been present in the shape of the City's merchants and goldsmiths, its cosmopolitan connections and its already extensive international trade. By the late seventeenth century, it was apparent, too, that dear money had placed Britain at a disadvantage in her struggle with the Dutch, and that improved credit was a vital part of her defence strategy – which included overseas expansion.[29] A further perception, which was to be realised fully in the course of the next three centuries, was that invisible earnings had an important contribution to make to the balance of payments, especially at a time when commodity exports (in this case woollen textiles) were experiencing difficulties in overseas markets.[30] However, no fundamental revolution was possible before 1688 because James II's pro-French and pro-Catholic policies frightened the predominantly Protestant bankers and investors whose support it required. The gentlemanly revolution of 1688 removed this fear by installing not just a new monarch but a new type of monarchy. The financial independence of the crown was destroyed: to secure an

---

28. Peter Mathias, *The Transformation of England* (1979), pp. 91–4; B.L. Anderson, 'Provincial Aspects of the Financial Revolution of the Eighteenth Century', *Bus. Hist.*, 11 (1969), pp. 11–12; and idem, 'Money and the Structure of Credit in the Eighteenth Century', *Bus. Hist.*, 12 (1970).

29. Dickson, *Financial Revolution*, pp. 4–6, 304–5.

30. Davis, *Rise of the English Shipping Industry*, p. 300; Dickson, *Financial Revolution*, pp. 304–5. It ought to be noted here that 'mercantilist' writers were well aware of the importance of invisible items in the balance of payments: see Jacob Viner, *Studies in the Theory of International Trade* (1937), pp. 13–15.

adequate income the king was compelled to govern through parliament and thus to acknowledge the political dominance of the landed interest.[31] The price that had to be paid was participation in the continental wars of the new ruler and his successors, and it was the demand for war finance after 1688 that precipitated the expansion of the national debt.

The distinctiveness of these innovations also needs to be emphasised. The extensive literature on economic growth defines 'early start' and 'late start' countries almost exclusively with reference to the development and spread of industry. What has still to be fully appreciated is the extent of Britain's lead in the area of finance and commercial services and the degree to which it set her apart from her rivals, as well as the role of these activities in the history of economic development.[32] The suggestion that Britain was about a century ahead of France in evolving modern financial institutions[33] is supported by recent detailed research on public finance and monetary policy.[34] Both the form taken by the public debt and its management were far more advanced in Britain than they were in France. During the final conflict between the two powers from 1793 to 1815, Britain was able to borrow extensively and efficiently because investors had confidence that their money would be returned, whereas France was forced to rely much more heavily on taxation because creditors were unimpressed by the government's record in honouring its obligations. Moreover, confidence in sterling enabled Britain to leave the gold standard in 1797 and adopt an emergency monetary policy without provoking a flight from the currency. What part this difference played in the outcome of the wars is impossible to say, but its existence needs to be stressed, not least because superior credit facilities, in

31. Clayton Roberts, 'The Constitutional Significance of the Financial Settlement of 1690', *Hist. Jour.*, 20 (1977).

32. This subject has been put on the agenda of historical inquiry by Patrick O'Brien and Caglar Keyder, *Economic Growth in Britain and France, 1780–1914* (1978). Contemporaries were well aware of the disparity: François Crouzet, 'The Sources of England's Wealth: Some French Views in the Eighteenth Century', in P.L. Cottrell and D.H. Aldcroft, eds. *Shipping, Trade and Commerce: Essays in Memory of Ralph Davis* (Leicester, 1981), pp. 71–2.

33. Charles P. Kindleberger, 'Financial Institutions and Economic Development: a Comparison of Great Britain and France in the Eighteenth and Nineteenth Centuries', *Expl. Econ. Hist.*, 21 (1984).

34. D. Weir, 'Tontines, Public Finance and Revolution in France and England, 1688–1789', *Jour. Econ. Hist.*, 49 (1989); Michael D. Border and Eugene N. White, 'A Tale of Two Currencies: British and French Finance During the Napoleonic Wars', *Jour. Econ. Hist.*, 51 (1991); and a source that might easily be overlooked in this connection, Gilbert Faccarello and Philippe Steiner, eds. 'La pensée économique pendant la révolution française', *Economies et sociétés*, 13 (1990), Pt. 4.

helping to make Britain an international power, had given her a considerable stake to defend, as well as the means of doing so.

If the developments that flowed from the financial revolution seem recognisably modern, so they were. Contemporaries were universally impressed and often greatly disturbed by the far-reaching implications of the financial revolution, and their reactions gave rise to a debate that still echoes today in discussions of Britain's economic problems. Swift's alarm at the rise of the moneyed interest led him to argue that financiers had encouraged the flow of capital abroad to the detriment of the country's real interests, which lay in preserving the value of productive investments in agriculture:

> I have known some People such ill Computers as to imagine the many Millions in Stocks and Annuities are so much real Wealth in the Nation; whereas every Farthing of it is entirely lost to us, scattered in Holland, Germany and Spain.[35]

Defoe drew attention to another recurring feature of the debate, one that also struck Hobson nearly two centuries later: the division between a highland, pastoral and industrial north and west and a lowland, arable and commercial south and east.[36] In making this distinction, Defoe also underlined London's special function as a centre of finance and commercial services. His aim, however, was not to attack the capital, but rather to defend the role of services in maximising employment and adding value to economic activities.

As these contrasting interpretations suggest, the rise of the moneyed interest was the subject of one of the principal controversies of the eighteenth century.[37] To some observers, the new financiers were patriots whose expertise in organising low-cost credit funded the defence of the realm, overseas expansion and domestic employment. To others, they were upstarts who threatened to undermine the established social order by importing 'avarice' into a world that depended on 'virtue' to guarantee good government. As Bolingbroke, the most eminent of the City's critics in the early eighteenth century, put it: 'the landed men are the true owners of our political vessel; the

---

35. *The Conduct of the Allies* (1711), quoted in Dickson, *Financial Revolution*, p. 26.

36. Peter Earle, 'The Economics of Stability: the Views of Daniel Defoe', in Coleman and John, *Trade, Government and Economy*, pp. 277–8; and idem, *The World of Daniel Defoe* (1976), Pt. 3.

37. In addition to the references given in n. 19, there is a particularly valuable set of essays in J.G.A. Pocock, ed. *Three British Revolutions: 1641, 1688, 1776* (Princeton, NJ, 1980).

moneyed men, as such are but passengers in it'.[38] The question of ownership was indeed central because the activities of the moneyed interest created new forms of property, essentially paper instruments representing financial claims and obligations, that appeared to be insubstantial but were in practice powerful and invasive. The national debt became a particular focus of attention partly because it was readily identifiable and partly because it continued to expand through-out the century. On one view, the debt saved Britain from defeat at the hands of France; on another, it subverted the kingdom from within by attracting capital away from agriculture, by advancing representatives of the City to positions of privilege previously held exclusively by the landed interest, and by threatening the nation with bankruptcy. Not surprisingly, the debate joined by Swift and Defoe was carried on by Hume, Smith and Burke later in the century and by Southey and his contemporaries in the 1820s.[39]

However, the debate was being resolved even as it was being continued. As the eighteenth century advanced, the new financial institutions and services took root, and leading members of the moneyed interest were accepted into the inner circles of political and social influence.[40] The economic argument for incorporating the City was compelling because its expertise was vital to financing the wars that were the price of upholding the Revolution Settlement.[41] The national debt was also directly profitable to the small minority who could afford to invest in it – mainly substantial bankers, merchants and landowners, most of whom lived in London or the Home Counties (or had a residence there).[42] The growing integration of land and finance was symbolised by the action of the Earl of Bath, reputedly one of the wealthiest magnates in the country, who lent his weight in 1737 to a successful move to prevent a reduction in the

38. Quoted in Donald Winch, *Adam Smith's Politics* (Cambridge, 1978), p. 123. Isaac Kramnick, *Bolingbroke and his Circle* (Cambridge, Mass., 1968), has provoked methodological criticism but remains the classic statement.

39. Pocock, *Virtue, Commerce, and History*; Winch, *Adam Smith's Politics*; David Eastwood, 'Robert Southey and the Intellectual Origins of Romantic Conservatism', *Eng. Hist. Rev.*, CIV (1989).

40. For a broad survey of these tendencies see P.J. Corfield, 'Class by Name and Number in Eighteenth-Century Britain', *History*, 72 (1987).

41. For one example see Larry Neal, 'Interpreting Power and Profit in Economic History: a Case Study of the Seven Years War', *Jour. Econ. Hist.*, 37 (1977).

42. This remained the case right down to 1815. See Dickson, *Financial Revolution*, pp. 58–9, 285, 295, 297–8, 302; Alice Carter, *Getting, Spending and Investing in Early Modern Times* (Assen, The Netherlands, 1975), pp. 19, 66–75, 136–7; also J.R. Ward, *The Finance of Canal Building in Eighteenth-Century England* (Oxford, 1974), pp. 140–2, 171–2. For the very similar composition of the original subscribers to the Bank of England, see Dickson, *Financial Revolution*, p. 256.

interest paid on the national debt because his wife's considerable capital was invested in government stock.[43] In addition, the debt helped to fund the patronage system, which gave light work to many potentially idle hands, especially younger sons of landed families. In 1726 about one-quarter of the peerage held government or court office, and in the second half of the century it became increasingly acceptable for the younger sons of aristocrats to take posts in the colonies, including placements arranged by the East India Company.[44] Outside the national debt, important connections between the country's large landowners and the City were formed by apprenticing younger sons to the leading merchant houses, especially those involved in the prestigious import and export trades,[45] and by the growth of the mortgage market, which developed rapidly as mortgages became the recognised means of obtaining credit on the security of land.[46] In these ways, the fortunes of the magnates who made the Revolution of 1688 and the merchant bankers who underwrote it became increasingly entwined both in the definition of the national interest and in matters of personal finance.

Social integration was necessarily a gradual process, but it was greatly helped by affinities in the life-styles of leading City figures and magnates at their meeting points in London, and by the subsequent gentrification of new money through the purchase of land, inter-marriage and the acquisition of titles.[47] This process led to the assimilation of recent immigrants, such as Jacob Houblon, who founded a City dynasty, bought a country estate, and finally entered

43. R.S. Neale, 'The Bourgeoisie, Historically, has Played a Most Important Part', in Eugene Kamenka and R.S. Neale, eds. *Feudalism, Capitalism and Beyond* (1975), p. 90.

44. Mingay, *English Landed Society*, pp. 71–6; P.J. Marshall, *East India Fortunes: The British in Bengal in the Eighteenth Century* (1976), pp. 9–14.

45. Richard Grassby, 'Social Mobility and Business Enterprise in Seventeenth-Century England', in Donald Pennington and Keith Thomas, eds. *Puritans and Revolutionaries: Essays in Seventeenth-Century History Presented to Christopher Hill* (Oxford, 1978), pp. 355–7, 365–6, 378–9. The direct connection with trade may have declined in the course of the eighteenth century as more attractive openings arose in public service, but at the highest levels ties between land and trade remained close, especially in London: Nicholas Rogers, 'Money, Land and Lineage: the Big Bourgeoisie of Hanoverian London', *Soc. Hist.*, 4 (1970), pp. 444–5.

46. Dickson, *Financial Revolution*, pp. 5–7; Neale, 'The Bourgeoisie', p. 98.

47. Dickson, *Financial Revolution*, p. 282; Carter, *Getting, Spending*, p. 106; Rogers, 'Money, Land and Lineage', pp. 444–7; G.C.A. Clay, 'The English Land Market, 1660–1770: the Role of the Moneyed Purchasers'. We are grateful to Dr Clay for allowing us to cite his unpublished paper. As F.M.L. Thompson points out, the purchase of a country estate did not necessarily mean that the new owner left the town or his business: 'Desirable Properties: the Town and Country Connection in British Society Since the Late Eighteenth Century', *Hist. Research*, 64 (1991).

parliament during the reign of George II – who was also, of course, a member of a successful immigrant family.[48] It assisted established banking families, too, such as the Hoares, who gained impetus from the financial revolution, married into the English and Irish peerage, and thereafter combined broad acres with service to the City and to the crown.[49] Old money also prospered from new opportunities: Henry Lascelles came from a family of Yorkshire landowners but he made his own fortune from colonial trade (principally imports from Barbados), entered parliament, and at his death in 1753 was worth an estimated £284,000 in land, the national debt, and loans to planters in the West Indies.[50] His son, Edwin, became a baron in 1796, and his grandson became Earl (and Viscount) Harewood in 1812.[51] By the close of the eighteenth century, the principle of the national debt had won general acceptance, though there was continuing concern about its size, and the avarice that Bolingbroke had associated with the moneyed interest had become virtuous in public service and in enhancing the private wealth of the magnates who managed the country. Bankers became gentlemen not least because gentlemen needed bankers.

Manufacturers were already important and familiar figures on the landscape in 1688, and their role expanded thereafter, as is well known. The woollen industry made a sizeable contribution to domestic employment, export earnings and state revenues in the eighteenth century, and the cotton industry performed a similar function, on an even larger scale, in the nineteenth century. At the same time, it must also be acknowledged, in the light of recent research, that industrialisation was a much slower process than was once thought: it now seems unlikely that there was a marked upward shift in the contribution made by manufacturing to national output in the 1740s; the spurt of the 1780s was confined largely to cotton goods; it was not until the 1820s that the quantitative weight of new industries imposed itself on the

48. Derek Jarrett, 'The Myth of "Patriotism" in Eighteenth-Century English Politics', in J.H. Bromley and E.H. Kossman, eds. *Britain and the Netherlands*, Vol. 5 (The Hague, 1975), p. 124. For the background see Daniel Statt, 'The City of London and the Controversy over Immigration, 1660–1722', *Hist. Jour.*, 33 (1990).

49. G.C.A. Clay, 'Henry Hoare, Banker, and the Building of the Stourhead Estate'. We are grateful to Dr Clay for allowing us to cite his unpublished paper on this subject.

50. Richard Pares, 'A London West India Merchant House', in idem, *The Historian's Business* (Oxford, 1961).

51. Thereafter, the family was prominent in public service, especially the army. Its eminence was crowned in 1922, when the 6th earl married Princess Mary, the only daughter of George V.

economy as a whole.[52] Only then did investment in industry become significantly larger than in agriculture; even so, the greater part of manufacturing output still came from small-scale, traditional (often household) units of production. Given the persistence of low productivity in so much of the manufacturing sector, it ought not to be surprising to find that industrial producers were content to shelter behind protectionist barriers for most of the period under review.[53] Even in branches of industry where productivity was growing impressively, such as cotton goods, the risks associated with new manufacturing techniques inspired a high degree of caution with respect to free trade.[54] Moreover, productivity gains in manufacturing still had to be realised in rising sales; and, as the home market became saturated, manufacturers found themselves relying increasingly on the world-wide system of distribution organised and financed from London.[55]

The success of the new industrial forces was therefore highly qualified, even in 1850. The number of large fortunes amassed by industrialists did not compare with those derived from land and from the financial and service sector.[56] Moreover, manufacturers did not make money in acceptable ways, and were not considered to be suitable candidates for entry into what Hume called 'that middling rank of men who are the best and finest basis of public liberty.'[57] In the eighteenth century, members of the banking and mercantile elite gained a degree of social approval for their activities that was 'not accorded to the captains of industry, whose profit-making inhibited

52. Crafts, *British Economic Growth*; idem, 'British Industrialization'; C.K. Harley, 'British Industrialisation Before 1841: Evidence of Slower Growth during the Industrial Revolution', *Jour. Econ. Hist.*, 42 (1982). Peter H. Lindert, 'Remodelling British Economic History', *Jour. Econ. Hist.*, 43 (1983).

53. Contemporary views are discussed by Michael Kammen, *Empire and Interest: The American Colonies and the Politics of Mercantilism* (Philadelphia, Pa, 1970).

54. Mathias, *Transformation*, pp. 23, 31; D.J. Jeremy, 'Damming the Flood: British Government Attempts to Check the Outflow of Technicians and Machinery, 1780–1843', *Bus. Hist. Rev.*, 51 (1977); Douglas Farnie, *The English Cotton Industry and the World Market, 1815–96* (Oxford, 1979), p. 97. On the benefits of protection to special interests see, for example, N.B. Harte, 'The Rise of Protection and the English Linen Industry, 1690–1790', in N.B. Harte and K.G. Ponting, eds. *Textile History and Economic History* (Manchester, 1973).

55. S.D. Chapman, 'British Marketing Enterprise: the Changing Role of Merchants, Manufacturers and Financiers, 1700–1860', *Bus. Hist. Rev.*, 53 (1979).

56. W.D. Rubinstein, 'The Victorian Middle Classes: Wealth, Occupation, and Geography', *Econ. Hist. Rev.*, 2nd ser. XXX (1977); idem, 'Wealth, Elites, and the Class Structure of Modern Britain', *Past and Present*, 76 (1977). Information on the eighteenth century is less systematic, but see, for example, Brewer, *Sinews of Power*, pp. 208–9.

57. Quoted in Thomas A. Horne, *The Social Thought of Bernard Mandeville* (1978), p. 95. See also Winch, *Adam Smith's Politics*, p. 99.

the pursuit of pleasure, and whose petty bourgeois origins created formidable social barriers'.[58] It is true that sections of the landed interest benefited as producers from connections with industry, most obviously by supplying wool to textile manufacturers or by leasing mineral rights; but in general they used the capital they raised in London to improve their estates, and few landed magnates derived much of their income from investment in manufacturing, even in the nineteenth century.[59] Successful bankers and merchants were also disinclined to involve themselves in manufacturing, and showed a consistent preference for investments in urban property and country estates.[60] Indeed, there is evidence to suggest that landowners responded to the rise of the new industries by distancing themselves from them at the close of the eighteenth century, while merchants who expanded their operations were more likely to move into banking, shipping and allied services than into manufacturing.[61]

Industry's direct political influence also remained limited, even after the constitutional reforms of 1832. This was partly because the Bounderbys of the Midlands and the north of England (as they were increasingly portrayed by spokesmen in the south) had neither the time nor the social connections to shape national policy, and partly because they were rarely able to present a united front when they decided to make the attempt. A General Chamber of Manufacturers was formed in 1785, but its one great success – aborting Pitt's Anglo-Irish treaty – was motivated by timid protectionism rather than bourgeois self-confidence; and divisions among manufacturers on the issue of freer trade destroyed their unity in the following year, when the Anglo-French commercial treaty was negotiated, and led to the demise of the Chamber in 1787.[62] Thereafter, it proved impossible to

58. Rogers, 'Money, Land, and Lineage', p. 453.

59. Dickson, *Financial Revolution*, p. 203; Mingay, *English Landed Society*, pp. 197–8; David Spring, 'English Landowners and Nineteenth-Century Industrialisation', in J.T. Ward and R.G. Wilson, eds. *Land and Industry: The Landed Estate and the Industrial Revolution* (Newton Abbot, 1971), pp. 39–42, 51–3.

60. See n. 44. Also John, 'Insurance Investment', p. 157; Joslin, 'London Private Bankers', p. 185; Thompson, 'Desirable Properties'.

61. François Crouzet, *The First Industrialists: The Problem of Origins,* (Cambridge, 1985), pp. 68, 77, 80–4; Michael W. McCahill, 'Peers, Patronage and the Industrial Revolution, 1760–1800', *Jour. Brit. Stud.,* 16 (1976); David Spring, 'English Landowners', pp. 51–2.

62. On the General Chamber see Donald Read, *The English Provinces, 1760–1960: A Study in Influence* (1964), pp. 22–33. However, in scoring their success it seems likely that the manufacturers were manipulated by Pitt's opponents, who supplied the Chamber with alarming and possibly misleading information about the proposed Irish treaty. See J. Ehrman, *The Younger Pitt: The Years of Acclaim* (1969), pp. 207–9; and Harlow, *Founding of the Second British Empire*, I, p. 608.

pull the manufacturing interest together, except on an *ad hoc* basis, until the 1830s, and even then unity tended to follow the business cycle in emerging at times of slump and dissolving with the return of prosperity.

An alliance between land and money was firmly in place well before the economic and political consequences of industrialisation compelled attention. When the new industries eventually made their presence felt, their importance in generating income from overseas trade and in creating employment was widely acknowledged in government circles. But their representatives never took control of policy: they were claimants among others whose interests had to be balanced and mediated, not a force whose time had finally come; and, as far as international policy was concerned, their claims fitted into government priorities rather than challenged them. To adapt a phrase, the industrial bourgeosie played an evolutionary part, at least in the period down to 1850.

THE EVOLUTION OF THE MILITARY-FISCAL STATE

At the centre of the state that emerged from the Revolution of 1688 stood a strong government which proved itself capable of greatly increasing the funds at its disposal, of sustaining warfare for long periods, and of maintaining political unity. The alarms were many and real, from the Jacobite threat at home to the Jacobin threat from abroad, and fissures opened at moments of crisis; but the galleon of state sailed on, leaving the loss of the mainland colonies to one side, moving steadily, if also anxiously, through the French Wars, negotiating the transition to free trade and avoiding revolution in 1848, Europe's year of universal upheaval. Property rights, especially land and financial claims, were defended by the law, as enacted by a parliament dominated by landed interests, by financial inducements, notably patronage, and by a powerful military presence based on an expanded army and navy and bolstered by substantial subsidies to continental allies. If legal measures were relatively costless, patronage was less so, and the military presence was an insatiable consumer of resources. Consequently, it ought not to be surprising to find that the fastest growing sector in the eighteenth century as a whole was probably government and defence rather agriculture or manufacturing.[63] Increased public expenditure imposed revenue demands which, in turn, ensured that high priority was given to managing public credit efficiently, to expanding the tax base, and to improving its administration, from the Treasury down to the excise collection. The result was a state characterised by a form of military-fiscalism, but one that sought to create additional revenues by market-oriented policies and not merely by diverting them from other sources.[64]

This enterprise, as we have seen, was launched on a raft of credit, and it was kept afloat by maintaining a judicious, if often uncertain, balance between revenue and expenditure. This balance, in turn, depended upon matching the needs of the Treasury with those of political stability, which set the ultimate limit to fiscal demands. If taxation provoked civil unrest, property values would be placed at risk and investors would lose confidence in the government and sterling. The financial revolution undoubtedly created opportunities for speculation, and these could easily produce crises and instability. But the longer-term interest of the managers of the financial system lay in curbing these tendencies, and their efforts eventually led to the emergence of what subsequently became an orthodoxy: the idea that sound money and sound government stood together.

The necessary balancing act was achieved by striking a series of bargains with key pressure groups. One set of bargains took the form of buying in or incorporating a limited number of powerful interests, principally the City and the country gentry. The City, which was tied into the regime through its investment in the national debt, began to exert considerable influence on policy at the point where public borrowing requirements met foreign policy, and was assimilated in the course of the eighteenth century in ways that we have touched

63. Crafts, 'British Economic Growth, 1700–1831: A Review of the Evidence', *Econ. Hist. Rev.*, 2nd ser. XXXVI (1983), Table 5, p. 187. We have phrased our comment to take account of R.V. Jackson, 'Government Expenditure and British Economic Growth in the Eighteenth Century: Some Problems of Measurement', *Econ. Hist. Rev.*, 2nd ser. XLIII (1990). Given that the problems of data and definition are so formidable, we have not attempted to tie our argument closely to one particular set of figures.

64. We refer here to an idea mentioned in our article, 'Gentlemanly Capitalism and British Expansion Overseas, I: the Old Colonial System, 1688–1850', *Econ. Hist. Rev.*, 2nd ser. XXXIX (1986), p. 521 and n. 112, and developed independently and with greater authority by Brewer, *Sinews of Power*, and Burton Stein, 'State Formation and Economy Reconsidered', *Mod. Asian Stud.*, 19 (1985). Brewer's point of reference is continental Europe; Stein's is eighteenth-century India. There would appear to be scope for putting the two together in order to define the term more closely and to explore its historical exemplars more fully.

upon.[65] Members of the provincial gentry who had Tory sympathies were encouraged to keep their hostility to the national debt within bounds by being offered rewards that were already available to Whig loyalists. The land tax was held at low levels, efforts were made to bring defence expenditure under control following the Peace of Utrecht in 1713, and steps were taken to curb excesses of financial speculation after the South Sea Bubble in 1720.[66] Finally, from the middle of the century increasing numbers of Tories were readmitted to public office, and thus had their independence compromised by the comforts of patronage.[67] Out of these measures emerged a highly regressive system of taxation, a growing commitment to financial orthodoxy, and a renewed sense of solidarity among the landed interest.

A second set of bargains bought off or accommodated particular interests by offering concessions that were designed to keep them content but also at arm's length. Manufacturers, for example, wanted import tariffs fixed at levels that would protect domestic industry. Given the general importance of manufacturing to the economy, their request was listened to: no government wished to damage wealth-creating activities, and members of parliament were sensitive to the fact that increased unemployment had consequences for local rates (which would have had to rise to pay for poor relief) and civil order.[68] In this case, however, a high-tariff regime was already favoured as a means of generating revenue to service the national debt, and manufacturers were thus able to benefit from policies that were devised for a wider purpose.[69] Out of concessions of this kind emerged a complex

65. For examples of the City's influence (a subject that needs looking at in greater detail) see Lucy S. Sutherland, 'The City of London in Eighteenth-Century Politics', in R. Pares and A.J.P. Taylor, eds. *Essays Presented to Sir Louis Namier* (Oxford, 1956); Dickson, *Financial Revolution*, pp. 228–33, 239; H.T. Dickinson, *Walpole and the Whig Supremacy* (1973), pp. 108–9.
66. The best account of the South Sea Bubble is in Dickson, *Financial Revolution*, Chs. 5–8. It is important to note, though we cannot pursue the point, that the South Sea Bubble was also the first international financial crisis of modern times. On the progressive integration of financial markets see E.S. Schubert, 'Innovations, Debts and Bubbles: International Integration of Financial Markets in Western Europe, 1688–1720', *Jour. Econ. Hist.* 48 (1988), and the further references given there. The evolution of financial crises in England is charted by Julian Hoppitt, 'Financial Crises in Eighteenth-Century England', *Hist. Jour.*, 39 (1986).
67. Jarrett, 'The Myth of "Patriotism"', pp. 124–34, 138–40.
68. Joyce Oldham Appleby, *Economic Thought and Ideology in Seventeenth-Century England* (Princeton, NJ, 1978), pp. 127–8, 166–7; Stevenson, *Popular Disturbances*, pp. 70–2, 113–16, 118–19.
69. Ralph Davis, 'The Rise of Protection in England, 1669–1786', *Econ. Hist. Rev.*, 2nd ser. XIX (1966).

of commercial regulations that entered into what can be termed 'mercantilism' – providing this is thought of less as a coherent 'system' than as an accretion of separate deals, albeit one with a degree of hard-headed logic behind it.[70]

There is no simple way of charting the evolution of this military-fiscal system because the study of some of its main ingredients, especially credit and taxation, has only recently begun to attract detailed research.[71] The most obvious and most important theme is that joining public expenditure and war: expenditure increased rapidly during the major wars of the eighteenth century and did so on a rising trend which culminated in the massive costs of the French Wars between 1793 and 1815.[72] In 1700 the national debt stood at £14m.; in 1748 it was £78m.; by 1763 it had jumped to £133m.; by 1783 it had grown to £245m.; and in 1815 it reached £700m.[73] Interest payments on the national debt swallowed more than 50 per cent of public expenditure in peace time and in consequence assumed massive proportions: one calculation suggests that they were equivalent to about half the value of total exports in the eighteenth century.[74] It is now apparent that the real burden of taxation was heavier in England than in France both on a per capita basis and as a share of national income, and that it increased as the century advanced.[75] It is also clear that the bulk of the tax burden was borne by the mass of consumers, principally in the form of excise and customs duties, while the land tax supplied a small and diminishing proportion of the total.[76] The

70. The pragmatic aspects are emphasised by D.C. Coleman, 'Mercantilism Revisited', *Hist. Jour.*, 23 (1980), and the logic by Cosimo Perrotta, 'Is the Mercantilist Theory of the Favourable Balance of Trade Really Erroneous?', *Hist. Pol. Econ.*, 23 (1991).

71. The pioneering study is Peter Mathias and Patrick O'Brien, 'Taxation in Britain and France, 1715–1810: a Comparison of the Social and Economic Incidence of Taxes Collected for the Central Governments', *Jour. Eur. Econ. Hist.*, 5 (1976). Important recent contributions are: Patrick O'Brien, 'The Political Economy of British Taxation, 1660–1815', *Econ. Hist. Rev.*, 2nd ser. XLI (1988); and J.V. Beckett and Michael Turner, 'Taxation and Economic Growth in Eighteenth-Century England', *Econ. Hist. Rev.*, 2nd ser. XLIII (1990).

72. The clearest guide (given in constant prices) is in Jackson, 'Government Expenditure', Figs. 1–2, pp. 222–3.

73. Brewer, *Sinews of Power*, pp. 114–16, provides a convenient summary.

74. Peter Mathias, *The First Industrial Nation: An Economic History of Britain, 1700–1914* (2nd edn. 1983), p. 38.

75. Mathias and O'Brien, 'Taxation in Britain and France'; Beckett and Turner, 'Taxation and Economic Growth', pp. 388–91; Brewer, *Sinews of Power*, pp. 126–34.

76. Although excise duties became the chief source of tax revenue, they cannot be distinguished readily from customs duties because excise duty was also levied on a number of imports and not just on goods produced at home. See J.V. Beckett, 'Land Tax or Excise: the Levying of Taxation in Seventeenth- and Eighteenth-Century England', *Eng. Hist. Rev.*, C (1985).

social incidence of taxation identifies the chief beneficiaries of the Revolution Settlement: the landed interest, which voted itself valuable tax benefits; the bond-holders in London and the Home Counties, who gained from transfers made by taxpayers in the country as a whole; and the merchants trading overseas (in association with shipowners, contractors and members of the armed services), who profited from the drive to increase earnings and revenues from the colonies.[77]

Although the principle of the national debt gradually became accepted, its size preoccupied commentators to an increasing extent as the century advanced. After the Seven Years' War (1756–63) in particular, concern about Britain's ability to service the debt prompted successive governments to take steps to improve the efficiency of tax-gathering at home and to search for new sources of revenue abroad.[78] The fact that revenue was raised mainly by indirect taxes made payment marginally less painful than it would otherwise have been, and opposition to the growing weight of taxation was generally held within constitutional limits. Nevertheless, the tax burden fuelled the radical movements that developed from the 1760s: it had a place in the spontaneous protests that appeared at moments of crisis, when it merged with more immediate problems, such as unemployment (often arising out of credit failures) and food shortages; it entered the organised radicalism of Wilkes in the 1760s and 1770s and of Wyvill in the early 1780s.[79] The regional and social bases of the movements led by Wilkes and Wyvill were very different, but between them they mounted a comprehensive attack on the unrepresentative character of the legislature, the power of the executive and the operation of the patronage system, and they had in common demands for greater accountability and efficiency in public affairs. The eighteenth-century

77. Mathias, *Transformation of England*, p. 126. Some interesting comparisons are made by Hilton L. Root, 'The Redistributive Role of Government: Economic Regulation in Old Regime France and England', *Comp. Stud. in Soc. and Hist.*, 33 (1991). The most obvious comparison, however, is with the broadly similar distribution of gains suggested for the nineteenth century (after the introduction of income tax) by Lance E. Davis and Robert A. Huttenback, *Mammon and the Pursuit of Empire: The Political Economy of British Imperialism, 1860–1912* (Cambridge, 1987), Chs.7–8.

78. Brewer, *Sinews of Power*, Ch. 4 and p. 124; James C. Riley, *International Government Finance and the Amsterdam Capital Market, 1740–1815* (Cambridge, 1980), pp. 103–8.

79. John Brewer, 'English Radicalism in the Reign of George III', in Pocock, ed. *Three British Revolutions*; John Torrance, 'Social Class and Bureaucratic Innovation: the Commissioners for Examining the Public Accounts, 1780–87', *Past and Present*, 78 (1978). A related facet of popular dissent during this period has been revealed by James E. Bradley, *Popular Politics and the American Revolution in England: Petitions, the Crown and Public Opinion* (Macon, Ga, 1986).

amalgam of patronage and protection was also criticised at this time by commentators who perceived that expanding commercial services and new industries could gain from measures that promoted more competitiveness in the market and less interference from the state. Pitt's tentative moves towards 'economical reform' and freer trade in the 1780s were a response to these criticisms. In taking these steps, however, Pitt was not preparing to launch a bourgeois revolution but trying to reinforce an oligarchic order by increasing revenues from customs duties, curbing the growth of the national debt, and placating irate taxpayers.[80]

Reformers failed at the point where the prospect of success appeared to threaten property values or, in the case of Pitt's experiments, when the outbreak of the French Wars created a state of emergency. The revolt of the American colonies had already caused property-owners to draw together in defence of established authority. The conflict with France raised the prospect of invasion by republicans and Jacobins, and greatly magnified the danger to order and property. These challenges, both at home and from abroad, were met by elaborating a brand of 'new conservatism' which brought property-owners together in defence of the status quo.[81] By the close of the century the defenders had become a formidable group: the landed interest had already been strengthened by the readmission of Tory sympathisers, and holders of new forms of property in paper credits and commercial wealth had also won acceptability, with the result that they took up positions inside the castle rather than with the besiegers. In the event, the need to place the economy on a war-footing postponed reform, and the immense cost of the French Wars carried the national debt to new heights. In 1815 the structure of Old

80. John Ehrman, *The British Government and Commercial Negotiations with Europe, 1783–93* (Cambridge, 1962), p. 193. For the pragmatic and selective use made of Adam Smith see C.R. Ritcheson, 'The Earl of Shelbourne and Peace with America, 1782–1783: Vision and Reality', *Internat. Hist. Rev.*, 5 (1983); and John E. Crowley, 'Neo-Mercantilism and *The Wealth of Nations*: British Commercial Policy after the American Revolution', *Hist. Jour.*, 33 (1990). N.54 refers to the reluctance of the industrial bourgeoisie to play the heroic role so often assigned to them by subsequent commentators.

81. Paul Langford, 'Old Whigs, Old Tories and the American Revolution', in Peter Marshall and Glyn Williams, eds. *The British Atlantic Empire Before the American Revolution* (1980); Linda Colley, 'The Apotheosis of George III: Loyalty, Royalty and the British Nation, 1760–1820', *Past and Present*, 102 (1984); Thomas Philip Schofield, 'Conservative Political Thought in Britain in Response to the French Revolution', *Hist. Jour.*, 29 (1986). The expansion of the concept and content of what constituted acceptable forms of property is considered by Paul Langford, *Public Life and the Propertied Englishman, 1689–1798* (Oxford, 1991).

Corruption not only was still in place but also had been considerably enlarged.

Radical criticism was countered partly by suppressing it and partly by appealing to the solidifying forces of patriotism – a step that also involved elevating the dignity of the monarchy.[82] These moves were accompanied by an ideological refurbishment that helped to guide the propertied interest into and through the nineteenth century. Burke, among others if also above them, elaborated a political philosophy that defended inequalities in the ownership of property, justified the right of a minority to determine the government of the country and emphasised the importance of manners (and hence deference) in establishing rules of conduct.[83] But it was left to a revitalised Christianity to undertake the moral rearmament of the nation by anchoring behaviour to standards set by enduring biblical principles, thus insulating society from the wayward novelties propagated by those whom Burke referred to, disapprovingly, as the 'enterprising talents' of the country. The message advertising spiritual equality was also designed to produce social solidarity, which in turn formed a line of defence against the spread of subversive ideas proclaimed in France. It is interesting to find that only one reform of note, the celebrated measure outlawing the slave trade in 1807, was passed in Britain during the period of the French Wars.[84] This Act, promoted chiefly by evangelicals and humanitarians, rallied public opinion behind the Godly notion of the equality of man. It held out the promise of improvement for those who were denied minimal human rights, but it also preserved the principle of social inequality among all free men, and any disturbance caused by its enactment affected societies outside

82. Clive Emsley, *British Society and the French Wars, 1793–1815* (1979); Ian R. Christie, *Stress and Stability in Late-Eighteenth-Century Britain: Reflections on the British Avoidance of Revolution* (Oxford, 1984); H.T. Dickinson, *British Radicalism and the French Revolution, 1789–1815* (1985); Colley, 'The Apotheosis of George III'. There was also, of course, the exit option – emigration.

83. J.G.A. Pocock, 'The Political Economy of Burke's Analysis of the French Revolution', *Hist. Jour.*, 25 (1982); Schofield, 'Conservative Political Thought'. If manners maketh man, their further refinement into politeness helped to make gentlemen. For a study of this process (at an earlier point in the century) see Lawrence E. Klein, 'Liberty, Manners and Politeness in Early Eighteenth-Century England', *Hist. Jour.*, 32 (1989); and on an allied subject, Frank O'Gorman, 'Electoral Deference in "Unreformed" England, 1760–1830', *Jour. Mod. Hist.*, 56 (1984).

84. The massive literature which this subject has now generated can be approached through Barbara L. Solow and Stanley L. Engerman, eds. *British Capitalism and Caribbean Slavery* (Cambridge, 1987), and the references given there. The important point to note from the present perspective is that abolition was not promoted by a rising industrial bourgeoisie seeking to reach the goals of liberty and free trade set for it by a later generation of Whig historians.

Britain. At home, the classical precept still marked the way forward: justice was knowing one's place; temperance was keeping it.

Nevertheless, even as 'Old Corruption' continued to expand, important changes were taking place, some of them behind the scenes, and these created acute tensions between supporters of the status quo and those who saw the need to reshape policy both to deal with the size of the national debt and to cope with the new forces released by rapid economic change. After about 1800, there was a growing awareness in government circles that Britain's ability to defend herself against larger powers depended critically on the pace of economic development; and it was recognised, too, that development had indeed been taking place over a long period, though no special emphasis was attached at the time to the new mechanised industries.[85] Moreover, it was generally agreed that this process was a result of the considerable degree of freedom enjoyed by the domestic economy, and that this was one of the liberties guaranteed by the Glorious Revolution.[86] In the eyes of those who discussed and determined policy, Britain's strength and stability relied on continuing capitalist development, which was held to be in the interest of the poor, the 'middling orders' and the rich alike. The brand of capitalism in question was thought to rest upon a foundation of law and custom which the gentlemanly elite could fairly claim to have created and sustained. As the French Wars drew to a close, the central issue was not whether the gentlemanly order would have to yield to a rising industrial bourgeoisie, but what direction policy would have to take to carry that order into the nineteenth century.

It was at this point that uncertainties about the shape of future economic policy came to the surface. The debate over the renewal of the East India Company's charter in 1813, for example, provides a rare insight into the split within the City at this time between those who supported the Company and the regulative system in general, and those who were eager to abolish restrictions and to open up new opportunities.[87] The Corn Law of 1815, on the other hand, was a wholly conservative measure that reflected the assumption that agriculture and the landed interest remained central to the economy and

85. J.E. Cookson, 'Political Arithmetic and War in Britain, 1785–1815', *War and Society*, 1 (1983).

86. Idem, 'British Society and the French Wars, 1783–1815', *Australian Journal of Politics and History,* 31 (1985).

87. Anthony Webster, 'The Political Economy of Trade Liberalization: the East India Company Charter Act of 1813', *Econ. Hist. Rev.*, 2nd ser. XLIII (1990).

society.[88] In the event, the direction of policy as a whole came to be determined by the forward-looking members of the post-war Tory government who realised that the burden of the national debt, which consumed nearly 80 per cent of public revenue in the immediate post-war years, the weight of taxation entailed by debt service, and the persistence of monopoly endangered Britain's prospects for both economic growth and social stability.[89] The deep cuts in public spending after 1815, the return to the gold standard in 1819, the reductions in tariff rates in the 1820s and the progressive withdrawal of the government from direct participation in the economic process were all initiated by the gentlemanly elite. Their central purpose was to restore the confidence of investors and other property-holders in the credit system and hence in the credibility of the government. From one point of view, these moves can be seen as a reaction to the fiscal excesses imposed by the French Wars. In a longer perspective, they also represented an extension of the pressures for accountability, efficiency and 'economical reform' that had manifested themselves before the outbreak of the wars but had been postponed by them. The difference was that, after 1815, reform ceased to be associated mainly with radical and 'country' outsiders and acquired the general support of the propertied interest, and it did so for the compelling reason that it was seen to be necessary to the preservation of the gentlemanly order.[90]

Yet these acts of self-preservation should not be treated as if they were merely mechanical reactions to unpleasant stimuli. In engineering a sizeable shift in economic policy, progressive Tories and Whigs both sought to establish an ideological link between commercial society and improvement and between improvement and the advance of civilisation. By occupying the moral high ground, the reformers showed their awareness of the need to establish a legitimising ideology that would validate the changes they sponsored and also attract new supporters. The details of how this was achieved have still to be fully understood, though it is apparent that the problem can no longer be cast in terms of simple dualities, whether between Whigs and Tories

88. Boyd Hilton, *Corn, Cash and Commerce: The Economic Policies of the Tory Governments, 1815–1830* (Oxford, 1977), Ch. 1.

89. On these themes see Hilton, *Corn, Cash and Commerce*.

90. Hilton, *Corn, Cash and Commerce*, Chs. 4–7, and pp. 305–6; Norman Gash, 'After Waterloo: British Society and the Legacy of the Napoleonic Wars', *Trans. Royal Hist. Soc.*, 5th ser. 28 (1978); and A.D. Harvey, *Britain in the Early Nineteenth Century* (1978), p. 312.

or between free trade and mercantilism.[91] Burke's defence of property and privilege had to be refurbished in the light of the defeat of France, the diminished fear of Jacobinism, and the increasingly visible presence of manufacturing industry. Above all, there was a need to demonstrate that the brand of capitalism that had carried Britain through the eighteenth century retained its vitality, and that changes in economic policy were not only natural but also authorised adjustments to its trajectory. Only in this way was it possible for the landed interest to distance itself from Old Corruption while still keeping one step ahead of critics who wanted more radical reform. This was done partly by updating the eighteenth-century debate over the means of reconciling private interests with civic virtue, and partly by adding new elements, drawn, to take two very different examples, from the Scottish Enlightenment and from evangelical Anglicanism. In repositioning itself to direct a form of economic change that offered, so it seemed, the best chance of maintaining those elements of inequality that Burke wished to preserve, the gentlemanly order took account of the rise of industry but stopped short of embracing it. Industry was to be harnessed and therefore controlled; and, as we have seen, early in the nineteenth century a new generation of urban gentlemen began to be fashioned, principally from the service sector, to assist in the management process.[92]

Only an elite whose gentlemanly traditions were permeated by capitalist assumptions could have attempted such a dramatic shift in policy and could have responded so flexibly to pressures from below. Only an elite with these qualities, moreover, could have recognised in the 1820s that the looming imbalance between population growth and domestic sources of food supply was weakening the dominance of agriculture and increasing the need to move towards a more open economy.[93] At the same time, Britain's policy-makers also realised that there was a growing need to provide new industries, especially cotton goods, with overseas markets to deal with problems of foreign

91. Recent work has opened up some important new lines of inquiry: Eastwood, 'Robert Southey'; Peter Mandler, 'Tories and Paupers: Christian Political Economy and the Making of the New Poor Law', *Hist. Jour.*, 33 (1990); J.W. Burrow, *Whigs and Liberals: Continuity and Change in English Political Thought* (Oxford, 1988); and Boyd Hilton, *The Age of Atonement: The Influence of Evangelicalism on Social and Economic Thought, 1795–1865* (Oxford, 1988). Norman Gash (*Eng. Hist. Rev.*, CIV (1989), pp. 136–40) offers a perceptive review of the issues raised by Hilton's study. For an assessment of economic opinion in 1820 see William D. Grampp, 'Economic Opinion When Britain Turned to Free Trade', *Hist. Pol. Econ.*, 14 (1982).

92. See Chapter 1, pp. 31–4.

93. Hilton, *Corn, Cash and Commerce*, Ch. 4.

competition and domestic unemployment.[94] The link between the difficulties experienced by both agriculture and industry was provided by the City and its associated international services: if tariffs were reduced, imported corn would solve the problem of food supply, suppliers would have the purchasing power to buy British manufactures, and the ensuing expansion of trade would be financed, insured and transported principally by London. Increased trade would generate additional revenues, thus allowing the tax burden to be eased and the national debt to be reduced to manageable proportions. The policy changes which followed from this analysis, like the political concessions made in 1832, were astute moves to prevent the erosion of landed power by placating and partly incorporating the most successful representatives of the new wealth produced by economic development.[95] In implementing reform, the landed interest was thus responding to the results of economic advance on a broad front and not just to the rise of mechanised industry, important though that was. The Reform Act of 1832, for example, put the seal of political acceptance on new property in the south of England as well as on that created by the Industrial Revolution in the provinces.

The legislation of 1840–60, which finally installed free trade, established 'Gladstonian orthodoxy' in public finance, and ended the reign of the last chartered companies, was the logical outcome of the measures introduced by Lord Liverpool's government after 1815.[96] At the same time, it is evident that the assertiveness of provincial industry, spearheaded by the Anti-Corn Law League, increased dramatically in the final stages of this process.[97] However, industry's commitment to reform is to be read less as an expression of its triumphant advance than as an indication of its gathering difficulties.

94. The difficulties of the cotton industry in the 1820s are dealt with by S.D. Chapman, 'Financial Restraints on the Growth of Firms in the Cotton Industry, 1790–1850', *Econ. Hist. Rev.*, 2nd ser. XXXII (1979), pp. 55–8. On government perceptions of the importance of international services see Hilton, *Corn, Cash and Commerce*, p. 63.

95. M. Brock, *The Great Reform Act* (1973) remains the standard work. See also O'Gorman, 'Electoral Deference'.

96. Hilton argues that the Whigs could not afford to make concessions on economic policy 'because the only hope of winning office was by economic bribes to the country gentry'. Consequently, economic reform was postponed during the 1830s. The Tories, on the other hand, tried to stave off political reform in the 1820s and again in the 1840s by making economic concessions to the enemies of the landed interest. Hilton, *Corn, Cash and Commerce*, pp. 306–7.

97. William D. Grampp, *The Manchester School of Economics* (Stanford, Calif., 1960), Ch. 5; Lucy Brown, *The Board of Trade and the Free Trade Movement, 1830–42* (Oxford, 1958), pp. 108–10, 121–3, 132–3. For a recent view see T.J. McKeown, 'The Politics of Corn Law Repeal and Theory of Commercial Policy', *Brit. Jour. Pol. Sci.*, 19 (1989).

Fierce competition and falling prices, both at home and abroad, meant that rapid economic growth, in boosting the importance of mechanised industry in the economy, also contributed to a continuing crisis of excess capacity and low profitability.[98] This crisis was at its worst in the depression of 1837–42, when a sharp rise in urban unemployment fuelled the unrest which expressed itself in the Chartist movement.[99] The failure to solve these problems by assertive imperialist actions served only to encourage industry's interest in free trade as a means of creating markets and cutting costs.[100] Consequently, free trade was pushed further and faster than was thought expedient by the bulk of the landed interest. The budgets of 1842 and 1845 introduced additional modifications to what remained very largely a protectionist system, and as late as 1843 Peel was still trying to expand overseas trade by adjusting tariff preferences.[101] But the repeal of the Corn Laws in 1846 was a surrender to free trade which, a generation later and despite Peel's hopes, began to erode the profitability of agriculture and with it the particular form of gentlemanly capitalism, based on the wealth and power of the landed interest, which had arisen out of the Revolution Settlement of 1688.[102]

Even at this point, however, the decline of the landed interest did not deliver economic policy into the hands of the representatives of

98. R.A. Church, ed. *The Dynamics of Victorian Business* (1980), Ch. 1; J.K.J. Thompson, 'British Industrialization and the External World: A Unique Experience or Archetypal Model?', in M. Bienefeld and M. Godfrey, eds. *National Strategies in an International Context* (1982).

99. The cyclical crises of the period are still best described by R.C.O. Matthews, *A Study in Trade Cycle History, 1833–1842* (Cambridge, 1954), esp. pp. 209–17.

100. See pp. 99–100.

101. By increasing the preferences allowed to Canadian wheat, for example. See R.L. Schuyler, *The Fall of the Old Colonial System* (1945), pp. 142–4.

102. D.C. Moore, 'The Corn Laws and High Farming', *Econ. Hist. Rev.*, 2nd ser. XVIII (1965). Peel believed that arable farming could survive if it became more responsive to market forces. As it happened, domestic cereal prices were seriously affected by foreign competition before the 1860s, as Wray Vamplew has shown: 'The Protection of English Cereal Producers: the Corn Laws Reassessed', *Econ. Hist. Rev.*, 2nd ser. XXXIII (1980). However, it cannot be assumed that protection would have helped the landed interest to retain power for very long. Protection would have retarded economic growth, reduced real wages and, by intensifying social conflict, might have brought demands for sweeping changes to property relations. On the connection between free trade and economic growth see Donald N. McCloskey, 'Magnanimous Albion: Free Trade and British National Income, 1841–1881', *Expl. Econ. Hist.*, 17 (1980); P.J. Cain, 'Professor McCloskey on British Free Trade, 1841–1881: Some Comments', ibid., 19 (1982); and McCloskey's reply, ibid. The repeal of the Corn Laws was followed, in 1849, by the repeal of the Navigation Acts. This was a significant but also a symbolic measure because the Acts had already been modified in the 1820s. On this subject see Sara Palmer, *Politics, Shipping and the Repeal of the Navigation Laws* (Manchester, 1991).

British industry, though in the 1840s this must have seemed a strong possibility. Ultimately, the chief beneficiaries of the strategy based on free trade, the gold standard and balanced budgets were the City of London and its associates in the service sector, though this outcome could not have been predicted with certainty even as late as 1850. Down to 1815, the City had tied much of its fortunes to the national debt and, indirectly, to the network of patronage which radicals labelled Old Corruption. Cutting these profitable ties was unwelcome and painful. Lord Liverpool's reform programme was designed partly to emancipate governments from excessive dependence on the City and was deeply resented there.[103] As noted earlier, the debate over the East India Company's charter in 1813 revealed that the City was uncertain whether to support the old order or to anticipate the new one, and its ambivalence weakened its influence with the government.[104] Attacks on the chartered companies also threw an unwelcome degree of light on the role of the Bank of England in directing monetary policy, and led to checks upon its powers.[105] In 1850, the City appeared to be less certain than industry of the road to follow.[106]

Nevertheless, the City, as the centre of a dynamic service economy, became the leading beneficiary of the reforms initiated after 1815. The return to gold and the moves towards freer trade were designed to turn Britain into the warehouse of the world rather than its workshop. The skills developed in domestic finance early in the eighteenth century helped to launch sterling on its international career at the close of the century, when invisible earnings began to assume importance in the balance of payments. Impetus was given to this development by the decline of Amsterdam, which enabled London to emerge as the world's leading financial centre from the 1790s, by the influx during the French Wars of refugee bankers, who enhanced the City's international expertise, and by Britain's role as chief paymaster of the allies.[107] In the 1820s, overseas finance assisted the post-war reconstruction of Europe and began to fund development projects

103. Hilton, *Corn, Cash and Commerce*, pp. 56f.
104. See n. 87 and R.W. Hidy, *The House of Baring in American Trade and Finance* (Cambridge, Mass., 1949), pp. 17–20.
105. See pp. 143–8.
106. For Rothschild's views see B. Davis, *The Rothschilds* (1983), pp. 68–9. The exact role of the City in the debates of the 1830s and 1840s needs further investigation. Meanwhile, we have adopted a cautious position to avoid reading into the past more than the evidence currently justifies.
107. Riley, *International Government Finance*, pp. 195–200; S.D. Chapman, 'The International Houses: the Continental Contribution to British Economic Development, 1800–1860', *Jour. Eur. Econ. Hist.*, 6 (1977); J.M. Sherwig, *Guineas and Gunpowder: British Foreign Aid in the Wars with France, 1793–1815* (1969).

further afield. Thereafter, foreign investment, combined with new domestic opportunities, such as railway construction, provided the basis of rentier fortunes as the eighteenth-century edifice of public debt and patronage was gradually dismantled.[108] Free trade also benefited the City by transforming London into a great entrepôt for world trade in foodstuffs and raw materials, thus boosting shipping services, marine insurance, specialised commodity exchanges, and wholesaling and commission agencies. In the course of this transformation, many prominent export industries became dependent on City credits to finance their operations; and in the case of cotton textiles the degree of dependence seriously impaired the industry's profits.[109]

By the mid-Victorian period, free trade and overseas investment were propelling the City towards the leadership of a global economy instead of merely a colonial one. The Bank of England, the pivotal instititution in the Square Mile, took on a new lease of life as the accepted regulator of the intricate network of international payments that arose to meet the needs of specialised, multilateral trading ties. Moreover, once committed to a world role, the gentlemen of the City were well placed, by virtue of social and physical proximity, to carry their interests into the corridors of power in London, unlike British industry, which suffered from being heterogeneous, small scale and provincial. Later in the century, as Britain's overseas investments reached unprecedented heights and as her export industries began to feel the pressure of foreign competition, the City's international dominance gave it an authority in the economic affairs of the nation that was second to none.

EXPORTING THE REVOLUTION SETTLEMENT

In the most general terms, the empire created before the mid-nineteenth century represented the extension abroad of the institutions and principles entrenched at home by the Revolution of 1688. The export version of the new order was compelled to adjust to the

108. See W.D. Rubinstein, 'The End of "Old Corruption" in Britain, 1780–1860', *Past and Present*, 101 (1983); and, for a case study, James Raven, 'The Abolition of the English State Lotteries', *Hist. Jour.*, 34 (1991).

109. S.D. Chapman, 'British Marketing Enterprise', pp. 321–3; idem, 'Financial Restraints on the Growth of Firms', p. 58. There is some evidence that industrialists were already putting their savings into safe foreign and home investments marketed in the City. See Mary B. Rose, 'Diversification of Investment by the Greg Family, 1800–1914', *Bus. Hist.*, 21 (1979), p. 89.

conditions it encountered overseas, but it remained a recognisable reflection of its domestic self. Indeed, the various crises of empire helped to define the profile of the gentlemanly order in Britain more clearly both by revealing and by determining the limits of its flexibility.

The imprint of the landed interest was felt most obviously in the colonies of settlement, especially in the New World, which was the most important growth area for British trade and influence in the eighteenth century. The planters in the West Indies and the gentry in the mainland colonies saw themselves as being Britons and wanted to remain so.[110] If they distanced themselves from some aspects of the emerging British way of life, they also espoused gentlemanly ideals, succumbed to the 'irresistible lure' of London,[111] and employed the rhetoric of the 'country' opposition to express their dissent and their preferences.[112] Even in regions where white settlement was unimportant, such as India, extensions of imperial control were accompanied by systematic attempts to establish property rights in land, and the new rulers instinctively looked to indigenous landholders to provide steady support for civil order.[113] In settled and non-settled parts of the empire alike, the patronage system provided employment for the younger sons of magnates and gentry, and endowed authority with a military bearing and a paternal style that survived long after 1850.[114] The influence of the City and the newer forces thrown up by the financial revolution was very evident too, especially in the impetus given to overseas trade by improved credit facilities, by the expansion of the mercantile marine, powerfully supported by the Navigation Acts, and by advanced forms of commercial capitalism, such as the

110. See Nicholas Canny and Anthony Pagden, eds. *Colonial Identity in the Atlantic World, 1500–1800* (Princeton, NJ, 1987); Carl Bridge, P.J. Marshall and Glyndwr Williams, ' Introduction': a "British" Empire', *Internat. Hist. Rev.*, 12 (1990).

111. Richard L. Bushman, 'American High-Style and Vernacular Cultures', in Jack P. Greene and J.R. Pole, eds. *Colonial British America: Essays in the New History of the Early Modern Era* (Baltimore, Md, 1984), p. 367.

112. Richard Pares, *A West India Fortune* (1950); idem, *Merchants and Planters* (Cambridge, 1960); Tamara P. Thornton, *Cultivating Gentlemen: The Meaning of Country Life Among the Boston Elite, 1785–1860* (New Haven, Conn., 1989); and Pocock, *Three British Revolutions*, 'Introduction', and Chs. 8, 10 and 11.

113. For two contrasting cases see Rajat Roy and Ratna Roy, 'Zamindars and Jotedars: a Study of Rural Politics in Bengal', *Mod. Asian Stud.*, 9 (1975); and Neil Rabitoy, 'System v Expediency: the Reality of Land Revenue Administration in the Bombay Presidency, 1812–1820', *Mod. Asian Stud.*, 9 (1975).

114. Stephen S. Webb, *The Governors-General: The English Army and the Definition of Empire, 1569–1681* (Chapel Hill, NC, 1979); Paul David Nelson, *William Tryon and the Course of Empire: A Life in British Imperial Service* (Chapel Hill, NC, 1990); Marshall, *East India Fortunes*, pp. 9–14; Bayly, *Imperial Meridian*, pp. 133–6.

East India Company, with its close links with Westminster and its predominantly City-based investors.[115] Overseas expansion was backed by other important interest groups: manufacturers who needed a vent for their surplus products, export merchants who handled their goods, and import merchants and their associates who dealt with the re-export trades.[116] Expansion abroad also conferred indirect benefits on the home government, which gained from enlarged customs revenues, on the landed interest, which in consequence enjoyed favourable tax treatment, and on investors in the national debt, whose returns rose when borrowing and interest rates increased.[117]

The pursuit of what Adam Smith termed 'opulence' merged with the interests of defence to produce Britain's long-serving 'Blue Water' policy.[118] Since Britain could not hope to control continental Europe

115. The Navigation Acts were reinforced in 1696 and the East India Company, founded in 1600, was restructured in 1708. On the capitalist qualities of the Company see K.N. Chaudhuri, *The Trading World of Asia and the English East India Company, 1660–1760* (Cambridge, 1978), and Hoh-cheung Mui and Lorna H. Mui, *The Management of Monopoly: A Study of the English East India Company's Conduct of its Tea Monopoly, 1784–1833* (Vancouver, 1984). Complementary views are expressed in Leonard Blusse and Femme Gastra, eds. *Companies and Trade: Essays in Overseas Trading Companies During the Ancien Regime* (The Hague, 1981). The investors have been analysed by H.V. Bowen, 'Investment and Empire in the Later Eighteenth Century: East India Stockholding, 1756–1791', *Econ. Hist. Rev.*, 2nd ser. XLII (1989). While Dr Bowen is in agreement with the main direction of our argument, he questions (pp. 195–6) our claim that gentlemanly capitalism was a 'formidable mixture of the venerable and the new' on the grounds that there were few landowners among the East India Company's stockholders. We accept his evidence but not his conclusion. Our claim does not depend on showing that landowners were stockholders in the Company but on a broader set of connections arising from the financial revolution and the increased degree of social integration that it encouraged – as we have suggested earlier in this chapter.

116. On mercantile lobbies see Brewer, *Sinews of Power*, pp. 169, 231–49. We acknowledge that there is a gap in the literature at this point: there is no study of the eighteenth century to match the detailed work undertaken on the seventeenth century by Robert Brenner, *Merchants and Revolution: Commercial Change and Political Conflict in the London Merchant Community, 1550–1660* (Princeton, NJ, 1992), and on the turn of the century by D.W. Jones, *War and Economy in the Age of William III and Marlborough* (Oxford, 1988).

117. Consumers, especially but not exclusively in London and the south-east, also benefited from the increased availability (at steadily falling prices) of imports of colonial products.

118. See Richard Pares, 'American Versus Continental Warfare, 1739–63', in idem, *The Historian's Business* (Oxford, 1961); W.A. Speck, 'The International and Imperial Context', in Jack P. Greene and J.R. Pole, eds. *Colonial British America: Essays in the New History of the Early Modern Era* (Baltimore, Md, 1984); Daniel A. Baugh, 'Great Britain's "Blue Water" Policy', *Internat. Hist. Rev.*, 10 (1988); and, for a view that extends beyond strategic considerations, J.S. Bromley, 'Britain and Europe in the Eighteenth Century', *History*, 66 (1981).

and felt herself to be threatened by the emergence of any large single power there, she capitalised on her geographical location and her comparative advantage in services by building up her naval power instead. The Navigation Acts, as we have seen, boosted British shipping, which in turn fostered both trade and defence. This policy commended itself because it was cheap, and hence kept taxation within acceptable bounds and avoided the need for a standing army, which was a highly sensitive option on political grounds as well as a costly one. By commanding the seas, Britain hoped to prevent France from blockading her trade with the continent and to frustrate any attempt at invasion. By the middle of the eighteenth century, these calculations had already been made and acted on. In the 1750s, Pitt was well aware that the threat of invasion endangered both financial and political stability. He observed that 'paper credit may be invaded in Kent', and anticipated the 'consternation that would spread through the City, when the noble, artificial yet vulnerable fabric of public credit should crumble in their hands'.[119] However, Britain's focus on naval defence did not mean that she was isolated from the continent. On the contrary, both diplomacy and money were devoted to the task of creating allies in Europe, especially among the smaller states that were conscious of their vulnerability in the face of larger neighbours. But the balance of advantage lay in the blue water and overseas; and one of the consequences of this decision was to elevate the standing of those who supported it, so that in time they became defenders of the national interest and not merely advocates of sectional advantage.

The most striking commercial results of the Blue Water strategy in the eighteenth century can be seen in the changing direction of British trade.[120] Continental Europe's share of Britain's home-produced exports fell from 82 per cent in 1700–1 to 40 per cent in 1772–3, while imports from Europe declined from 68 per cent of the

119. Quoted in Pares, 'American Versus Continental Warfare', p. 144. See also ibid. pp. 140–3.

120. The trade data summarised in the following five paragraphs derive principally from: Ralph Davis, 'English Foreign Trade, 1700–1774', in W.E. Minchinton, ed. *The Growth of English Overseas Trade in the Seventeenth and Eighteenth Centuries* (1969); idem, *The Industrial Revolution and British Overseas Trade* (Leicester, 1979); François Crouzet, 'Toward an Export Economy: British Exports during the Industrial Revolution', *Expl. in Econ. Hist.*, 17 (1980); Jacob M. Price, 'New Time Series for Scotland's and Britain's Trade with the Thirteen Colonies and States, 1740–1791', *William & Mary Quarterly*, 32 (1975); and Crafts, 'British Economic Growth'. A slightly fuller commentary is given in P.J. Cain and A.G. Hopkins, 'The Political Economy of British Expansion Overseas, 1750–1914', *Econ. Hist. Rev.*, 2nd ser. XXXIII (1980), pp. 470–8. Additional references will therefore be given selectively.

total to 47 per cent during the same period. Over a rather longer term, Europe's share of Britain's total overseas trade dropped from 74 per cent in 1713–17 to 33 per cent in 1803–7.[121] This fundamental reorientation of British commerce was prompted by two considerations. In the first place, it seems likely that down to the third quarter of the century Britain's foreign trade was propelled primarily by import-led demand, especially for new colonial products, such as sugar, tea and tobacco, and was driven by rising incomes in London and south-east England, which in turn derived from wealth generated from arable farming and from finance and services.[122] The second influence was the difficulty of increasing sales of manufactured goods (chiefly woollens) in Europe and the need, consequently, to prise open new markets elsewhere. These were found chiefly in the mainland colonies, where competition was limited, rather than in Asia, where British goods were unable to make headway against local substitutes.[123]

The import bill was met partly by pushing manufactures into new corners of the world, and partly by capturing the re-export trade, that is by selling colonial products in continental Europe. The re-export trades made a notable additional to Britain's own exports: they accounted for about one-third of the value of all exports during the first three-quarters of the eighteenth century and played a vital part in closing the gap that would otherwise have opened up in Britain's visible trade balance. Britain's competitive advantage in the transactions sector thus made it possible for her to solve the formidable problems posed by the limited competitiveness of woollen textiles and by the array of protectionist barriers that hampered access to the major markets on her door-step in continental Europe, and also to dominate the rapidly expanding trade in overseas products. In doing so, she forged a chain of multilateral links that spanned the world and enabled a system of compensating balances to function long before the better-known settlements pattern of the nineteenth century came into being.[124] Even as the Industrial Revolution was beginning,

121. Seymour Drescher, *Econocide: British Slavery in the Era of Abolition* (Pittsburgh, Pa, 1977), p. 20.

122. On import-led growth see F.J. Fisher, 'London as an Engine of Growth', in J.S. Bromley and E.H. Kossmann, eds. *Britain and the Netherlands*, 6 (1971); and Davis, 'English Foreign Trade', p. 108.

123. Chaudhuri, *Trading World*, Chs.10–11.

124. See Davis, *Industrial Revolution*, pp. 53–61, 73, 85; and the neglected study by C.J. French, 'The Trade and Shipping of the Port of London, 1700–1776', (Ph.D. thesis, Exeter University, 1980), Ch. 2. By the middle of the eighteenth century contemporary writers had distinguished between the balance of trade and the balance

Britain was already becoming the warehouse and shop-window of the world.

With the development of the cotton industry from the 1780s, Britain finally had a product that gave her a competitive edge in major markets, and exports became a powerful 'engine of growth' of national income for the first time.[125] The rate of export expansion rose steeply, and the ratio of exports to national income doubled between 1783 and 1801, when it reached 18 per cent. Cotton products accounted for about 53 per cent of the increase in total export values between 1784–6 and 1814–16. By 1804–6, cotton goods were responsible for no less than 42 per cent of the value of total exports, and in 1805–7 more than two-thirds of the value of the cotton industry's output was exported. The main markets were found outside the empire, in Western Europe and the United States, and after 1806 (when Napoleon's blockade closed much of Europe to British exports) in Latin America. However, these impressive developments did not signal the 'triumph of industry' or even the triumph of one particular industry. By the close of the eighteenth century, Europe and the United States had already reached the peak of their relative importance as markets for British cotton goods, and early in the new century manufacturers were again seeking new outlets for their products.

After 1815, despite the resumption of peace, exports failed to act as an engine of growth, as they had done after 1780. The volume of exports increased rapidly between 1815 and 1850, but values grew much more slowly as productivity gains reduced manufacturing costs and cut export prices. But falling prices did not enable Britain to hold on to her share of major markets: exports of cotton goods lost ground in Europe and the United States, where import-substitution aided by protection severely limited the prospects of foreign suppliers. Consequently, as we noted earlier, the cotton industry suffered from bouts of excess capacity and from reduced profit margins during the 1820s and 1830s.[126] Exports of other finished goods, notably woollens and

---

of payments, and soon afterwards David Hume published his celebrated analysis, 'Of the Balance of Trade', in his *Essays and Treatises on Several Subjects*, Vol. I (1772). At the close of the century, Paine made a characteristically scathing reference to the 'motley amphibious-charactered thing called the balance of trade', which, he said, was deployed to deceive members of parliament whose understanding of 'fox-hunting and the game laws' was somewhat ahead of their knowledge of economics. See Paine, *Complete Works*, p. 492.

125. Crouzet, 'Toward an Export Economy'.

126. See pp. 80–4.

metal products, did increase in Europe and the United States; but the overall tendency, even at this early date, was for Britain to become a supplier of semi-finished manufactures, such as yarn, to her rivals (especially those in Europe), thus aiding their industrialisation.

The inadequate rate of growth of exports, combined with rising demand for imports (fuelled by increased population), caused the trade gap to widen, especially in the late 1830s and early 1840s. Since income from shipping services increased only slowly, a trade-plus-services gap also appeared.[127] From the mid–1820s Britain depended upon rapidly increasing returns on foreign investments in Europe, North America and the Middle East to provide a small current-account surplus and to hold imports of raw materials at a level that would maintain domestic employment. In the period after 1815 the City therefore began to assume a fully international role and to perform a key function in balancing Britain's payments. During this period, too, London's finance and commercial services continued to play a vital part in creating markets for Britain's staple exports and in securing the resources needed as inputs into industry. In the case of exports, for example, no less than four-fifths of the increase in values that occurred between 1816–20 and 1838–42 arose from sales to new markets in Asia, Latin America and Africa.[128]

We turn, finally, to the ways in which the impulses we have described so far, in shaping British history and the course of overseas trade, also shaped the history of the empire. The installation in 1688 of a cohesive government, whose supporters had seen instability and were determined to avoid it, expressed itself in centralising tendencies that aimed at bringing all of the outer provinces under closer central control. Scotland was incorporated by the Act of Union in 1707, the Welsh, who were already incorporated, were subjected to renewed Anglicising influences, and Ireland was placed under the management of an Anglo-Irish, protestant gentry.[129] Further afield, the mainland colonies came under firmer direction from the Board of Trade and from a new generation of military governors, and were integrated more closely with the developing Atlantic economy managed from London.[130]

127. Cain and Hopkins, 'Political Economy', p. 475.

128. Calculated from A.H. Imlah, *Economic Elements in the Pax Britannica: Studies in British Foreign Trade in the Nineteenth Century* (New York, 1958), Table 12.

129. For a recent survey see J.C.D. Clark, 'English History's Forgotten Context: Scotland, Ireland, Wales', *Hist. Jour.*, 32 (1989).

130. I.K. Steele, *The Politics of Colonial Policy: The Board of Trade in Colonial Administration, 1696–1720* (Oxford, 1968); Webb, *The Governors-General*; and, for colonial reactions to first royal absolutism and then Whig oligarchy, the essays by Murrin and Lovejoy in Pocock, *The British Revolutions*.

Whether or not this flurry of activity was followed by a period of 'salutory neglect' is a matter of dispute.[131] It is equally plausible to suggest that, once the initial institutional changes had been made, Britain's main interest lay in developing trade and increasing revenues, and that this priority is not captured by measures of administrative activity. However, the failure of overseas trade to grow at a pace that met the expectations of powerful mercantile lobbies in London helped to push Walpole into war with Spain between 1739 and 1748; and the Seven Years' War that followed in 1756 witnessed the further development of an ideology of aggressive commercial expansion.[132] When the war came to an end in 1763, France had been driven out of Canada and India, and Britain had emerged as a major colonial and commercial power. In the course of this struggle, Britain had tightened her hold on the colonies in order to secure her defences. After the war, as the costs of victory began to be counted, she extended her grip in searching for ways of balancing the budget and servicing the national debt. This quest led to increased revenue demands both at home, as we have seen, and in the colonies, where it was accompanied by a spirit of assertiveness that was one of the legacies of military success.[133] Since Britain's fiscal problems were not offset by domestic economic growth or by foreign trade during the 1760s and 1770s,[134] there was some anxiety about her ability to maintain the level of re-exports needed to settle the import bill, and at moments of crisis doubts were also expressed about her creditworthiness.[135] It is against this background that Britain's changing relations with India and her mainland colonies in the third quarter of the century can best be approached.

Until the mid-eighteenth century, Britain's interests in India were represented by the East India Company and associated private traders,

131. James A. Henretta, *'Salutory Neglect': Colonial Administration Under the Duke of Newcastle* (Princeton, NJ, 1972); and the commentary in Speck, 'The International and Imperial Context'.

132. For a summary and further references see Brewer, *Sinews of Power*, pp. 173–8, and H.T. Dickinson, *Walpole and the Whig Supremacy* (1973), Ch. 6 and pp. 105–6, 135–7.

133. On the mood of assertiveness that took hold in the 1760s see P.J. Marshall, 'Empire and Authority in the Later Eighteenth Century', *Jour. Imp. and Comm. Hist.*, 15 (1987); and for the perception (by others) that Britain was the main threat to peace and stability after 1763 see H.M. Scott, *British Foreign Policy in the Age of the American Revolution* (Oxford, 1990).

134. For the abysmal performance of Britain's exports during this period see Crouzet, 'Toward an Export Economy', p. 52.

135. For example, Riley, *International Government Finance*, pp. 123–5.

and were almost exclusively commercial.[136] From the 1720s, however, the Company's trade in its main spheres of activity in western India and Bengal began to run into difficulties. The problem stemmed principally from the dislocation caused by the break-up of the Mughal empire, but was compounded by competition from French companies and by military costs incurred during the conflict with France in the middle of the century. The attempt to resolve these problems, by restructuring trade relations to improve profitability and by using local revenues to subsidise the Company's activities, produced two important initiatives. The first, prompted by Clive's enterprise, led in 1756 to the Battle of Plassey, which delivered Bengal into British hands and a fortune into his own.[137] The second resulted in 1759 in the capture of Surat, which gave Britain a commanding position on the west coast.[138] The British government's interest in these advances was aroused by a desire to annex some of the Company's gains for its own budgetary needs:[139] 'Plassey plunder' did not fund the Industrial Revolution, as was once supposed, but it did enable Britain to indigenise the national debt by purchasing foreign (especially Dutch) holdings.[140] Thereafter, the quest for revenues to pay for military costs became a permanent one, and it greatly distorted the Company's commercial operations. As the East India Company began to generate debts and not just revenues in the 1770s, the British government found itself drawn further into the task of controlling the Company's administration and, in this way, of managing India too.[141]

136. The detailed literature has now been brought together in two complementary studies: P.J. Marshall, *Bengal: The British Bridgehead. Eastern India, 1740–1828* (Cambridge, 1987), and C.A. Bayly, *Indian Society and the Making of the British Empire* (Cambridge, 1988). We should like to express our debt to Prof. Marshall for the comments and advice he has generously supplied over many years on the subject of British interests in India in the eighteenth century.

137. We are aware that we are over-compressing an episode that began rather than ended with Plassey, which was more of a coup than a battle. Subsequent developments culminated in the more important military engagement at Buxar in 1764. On Clive see Huw V. Bowen, 'Lord Clive and Speculation in East India Company Stock, 1766', *Hist. Jour.*, 30 (1987). We are grateful to Dr Bowen for discussing these and related issues; we hope that any differences that remain are those of perspective rather than of substance.

138. Lakshmi Subramanian, 'Capital and Crowd in a Declining Asian Port City: the Anglo-Bania Order and the Surat Riots of 1795', *Mod. Asian Stud.*, 19 (1985), relates the problems of the 1790s to commercial and financial difficulties that first surfaced in the middle of the century. On the subsequent shift of influence from Surat to Bombay see Pamela Nightingale, *Trade and Empire in Western India, 1784–1806* (Cambridge, 1970).

139. Huw V. Bowen, 'A Question of Sovereignty: the Bengal Land Revenue Issue, 1765–67', *Jour. Imp. and Comm. Hist.*, 16 (1988).

140. Marshall, *East India Fortunes*, p. 256; Davis, *The Industrial Revolution*, pp. 55–6.

141. The principal measures were the Regulating Act of 1773, Pitt's India Act of

Britain was not pulled into India simply by a breakdown of 'law and order'. The decline of central authority disrupted existing relations, but it did not lead to anarchy and it spawned a cluster of independent and semi-independent states whose ambitions sometimes cut across Britain's own purposes. Nor was Britain's advance the product of new industrial forces at home. The role of private traders expanded in the second half of the century, but their interest lay in selling Indian rather than British manufactures.[142] It is more plausible, we suggest, to view the move into India as being the result of competition between two military-fiscal organisations, one represented by the Mughals and their successor states and the other by the Company and the British government.[143] Both sides sought revenues to bolster trading profits, and both became involved in territorial expansion as a result. The outcome was strongly influenced by the military resources that the two were able to mobilise, and this in turn depended largely upon finance. The key decisions in this respect were made by local merchant bankers, who stood at the point of intersection between British and Indian commercial and political systems. In the end, the British were able to present themselves as the side likely to succeed, if not deserving of success: they won the support of the 'great moneyed men' of Surat before capturing the port;[144] and the balance of advantage in Bengal tilted in the Company's direction when local financiers deserted the nawab in 1756 and jeopardised his control of provincial treasuries.[145] Clive's actions were not directed

---

1784, and the Charter Act of 1793. The political background to the first of these measures has now been reappraised by H.V. Bowen, *Revenue and Reform: the Indian Problem in British Politics, 1757–1773* (Cambridge, 1991).

142. See, for example, P.J. Marshall, 'Economic and Political Expansion: the Case of Oudh', *Mod. Asian Stud.*, 9 (1975); and Anthony Webster, 'British Export Interests in Bengal and Imperial Expansion in South-East Asia, 1780–1824: the Origins of the Straits Settlements', in Barbara Ingham and Colin Simmons, eds. *Development Studies and Colonial Policy* (1987).

143. On the Mughal empire as a patronage state that was ceasing to deliver, see Richard B. Barnett, *North India Between Empires: Awadh, The Mughals and the British, 1720–1801* (Berkeley, Calif., 1980).

144. The relative power of the Company and the banias (and much else of consequence) is debated by Lakshmi Subramanian, 'Banias and the British: The Role of Indigenous Credit in the Process of Imperial Expansion in Western India in the Second Half of the Eighteenth Century', *Mod. Asian Stud.*, 21 (1987), and Michelguglielmo Torri, 'Trapped Inside the Colonial Order: the Hindu Bankers of Surat and their Business World during the Second Half of the Eighteenth Century', *Mod. Asian Stud.*, 25 (1991). See also Subramanian's reply in ibid.

145. We base ourselves here on J.D. Nichol's important study, 'The British in India, 1740–1763: a Study in Imperial Expansion into Bengal', (Ph.D. thesis, Cambridge University, 1976), pp. 62–75, Chs.3–4, and pp. 163–71. There is a published

from London; but they cannot be understood unless they are placed in the broader context of the financial revolution, the expansionist forces that it generated, and the problems these forces experienced on distant frontiers, where credit lines were fully stretched and where the junctions made with representatives of indigenous financial and fiscal systems were a necessary precondition of commercial success.

Similar influences – the search for revenue and the extension of commercial credit – were at work in the New World too, the main difference being that in North America they ran into young states that were being built up, whereas in India they were entangled with an ancient empire that was breaking down.[146] Just as the war with France had heightened an awareness of the importance of the empire, so the coming of peace in 1763 was accompanied by a determination to strengthen Britain's grasp on the mainland colonies. Mercantilist regulations were tightened by a battery of controls designed to raise revenues and to limit the independent economic development of the colonies.[147] As Charles Jenkinson, the Secretary of the Treasury, put it in 1765, the idea was to administer the colonies 'in such a manner as will keep them useful to the Mother Country'.[148] Exactly how burdensome Britain's demands proved to be is a matter of debate; but the point to emphasise in the present context is that they were resented partly because they disappointed the expectations of the colonists, who anticipated being rewarded for their loyalty during the war with France, and partly because they were perceived to be unjust on grounds of principle. At the same time, key interest groups in the mainland colonies also found themselves subjected to pressures arising from developments in the private sector. The massive expansion of overseas trade that had occurred in the course of the century had been

---

discussion of these issues, but it is at a rather general level and does not include an assessment of Nichol's research: Karen Leonard, 'The Great Firm Theory of the Decline of the Mughal Empire', *Comp. Stud. in Soc. and Hist.*, 21 (1979); J.F. Richards, 'Mughal State Finance and the Pre-Modern World Economy', ibid. 73 (1981); and Leonard's reply in ibid.

146. We have benefited particularly from Greene and Pole, *Colonial British America*; Peter Marshall and Glyn Williams, eds. *The British Atlantic Empire before the American Revolution* (1980); and Pocock, ed. *Three British Revolutions*. J. McAllister, 'Colonial America, 1607–1776', *Econ. Hist. Rev.*, XLII (1989), surveys the economic history of the period.

147. Summarised by Jack P. Greene, 'The Seven Years' War and the American Revolution: the Causal Relationship Reconsidered', in Marshall and Williams, *British Atlantic Empire*, pp. 90–5. For a case study see Thomas C. Barrow, *Trade and Empire: The British Customs Service in Colonial America, 1760–1775* (Cambridge, Mass., 1967).

148. Quoted in Greene, 'The Seven Years' War', p. 90.

financed largely by advances made by merchant bankers in London.[149] When trading conditions deteriorated in the 1760s and 1770s (and especially after the financial crisis of 1772), relations between creditors and debtors came under very considerable strain, not least because the colonists felt that indebtedness limited their sense of personal independence as well as their profits. These pressures were imprinted particularly strongly on Massachusetts and Virginia, the two colonies that were in the forefront of opposition to Britain's impositions. Merchants in Boston who jibbed at the demands made upon them became advocates of a less regulated market system;[150] planters in Virginia mounted what was, in effect, an agrarian revolt in defence of their gentlemanly status and against attempts to tax them and to call in outstanding debts.[151]

As a result of these developments, Britain lost the allegiance of vital sections of the colonial elite in the mainland colonies. Lack of patronage contributed to this outcome by limiting the number of loyalist supporters, and so did a progressive break-down in communications, which deprived the elite of effective representation in London.[152] Much more important, however, was the fact that the mainland colonies were developing aspirations of their own which were neither readily diluted by patronage nor easily contained within a regulated colonial system.[153] The colonists were becoming more confident of being able to manage their own affairs, though independence was not their first choice until it was, in a sense, thrust upon them. Population and wealth were expanding, and there were signs that trade relations could be diversified.[154] Furthermore, segments of

149. On these topics see Jacob M. Price, 'The Transatlantic Economy', in Greene and Pole, *Colonial British America*; idem, *Capital and Credit in British Overseas Trade: The View from the Chesapeake, 1700–1776* (Cambridge, 1980); and Mira Wilkins, *The History of Foreign Investment in the United States to 1914* (Cambridge, Mass. 1989), pp. 14–15.

150. John W. Tyler, *Smugglers and Patriots: Boston Merchants and the Advent of the American Revolution* (Boston, Mass., 1986); William Pencak, 'Warfare and Political Change in Mid-Eighteenth-Century Massachusetts', in Marshall and Williams, *British Atlantic Empire*.

151. T.H. Breen, *Tobacco Culture: The Mentality of the Great Tidewater Planters on the Eve of Revolution* (Princeton, NJ, 1985).

152. Alison, G. Olson, 'The Board of Trade and London-American Interest Groups in the Eighteenth Century', in Marshall and Williams, *British Atlantic Empire*.

153. Jack. P. Greene, *Peripheries and Center: Constitutional Development in the Extended Polities of the British Empire and the United States, 1607–1788* (Athens, Ga, 1986); Pocock, *Three British Revolutions*.

154. Marc Egnal, 'The Economic Development of the Thirteen Continental Colonies, 1720–1775', *William & Mary Quarterly*, 32 (1975); James F. Shepherd, 'British America and the Atlantic Economy', in Ronald Hoffman, et al. eds. *The Economy of Early America: The Revolutionary Period, 1763–90* (Charlottesville, Va, 1988); Peter A.

the elite were acquiring expansionist ideas of their own which were further encouraged after 1763 by the removal of the threat from France.[155] In Massachusetts, Virginia and Carolina, these aspirations were hurried into political shape by the need to take control of a more radical strain of opposition which, in representing the discontents of poor whites, also posed a threat to property and privilege in the colonies.[156] A comparison with the West Indies is instructive, for there the planters did not rebel, even though they suffered many of the same frustrations.[157] The difference was that Jamaica and Barbados were truly dependent. The planters there were few in number and many of them were absentees. They relied heavily on British finance and totally on the British navy, and could envisage no alternative to either. In the West Indies, independence was simply not possible, even if it had been conceived.

The assertiveness which characterised imperial policy in the 1760s and 1770s not only survived the loss of the mainland colonies but also was reaffirmed after the event and then further reinforced by the French Wars. Lord North's government fell in 1782 not because its policies towards the mainland colonies were unpopular but because they failed.[158] Thereafter, the consolidation of 'new conservatism' in Britain combined with the need to put the economy on a war footing were translated directly into imperial policy. The aristocratic, military element placed itself in the vanguard of the imperial presence, colonial patronage was greatly extended, and the empire acquired a Christian purpose as an instrument of moral defence against Jacobinism. Extensions of authority in British North America, Australia, the Cape, Ireland, the West Indies, India and south-east Asia reinforced the empire and strengthened Britain's defence against foreign aggressors. No more colonies were to be lost through the error, as Lord Thurlow saw it, of allowing them too much 'political liberty'.[159] The

Coclanis, 'The Wealth of British America on the Eve of the Revolution', *Jour. Interdisc. Hist.*, 21 (1990); Julian Gwyn, 'British Government Spending and the North American Colonies, 1740–1775', in Marshall and Williams, *British Atlantic Empire*, pp. 82–3.

155. Marc Egnal, *A Mighty Empire: The Origins of the American Revolution* (Ithaca, NY, 1988).

156. T.R. Clayton, 'Sophistry, Security and Socio-Political Structures in the American Revolution: Or Why Jamaica did not Rebel', *Hist. Jour.*, 29 (1986); Gary Nash, *The Urban Crucible: Social Change, Political Consciousness and the Origins of the American Revolution* (Cambridge, Mass., 1979).

157. Clayton, 'Sophistry, Security'.

158. Marshall, 'Empire and Authority', pp. 114, 119–20.

159. Thurlow to Grenville, 1–10 Sept. 1789. Quoted in David Milobar, 'Conservative Ideology, Metropolitan Government and the Reform of Quebec, 1782–1791', *Internat. Hist. Rev.*, 12 (1990), p. 51.

Canada Act of 1791 imposed a conservative constitution on Quebec; unruly colonists in New South Wales and the Cape were disciplined by a succession of authoritarian governors; and insurrection in Ireland in 1798 was first forcefully put down and then dealt with by the Act of Union in 1801.[160] The West Indies were marked out as suppliers of cotton to replace the United States, India was to become a bastion of landed values and a model of agrarian improvement, and the Straits Settlements were to guarantee free passage for the resulting exports from Bengal and for imports from China.[161]

As far as commercial policy was concerned, the immediate reaction to the loss of the American colonies was to repair the breach in the protectionist wall by means of the Navigation Act of 1786. The French Wars which followed in 1793 emphasised the continuing importance of colonial supplies to national security. Shifts in the direction of exports to Europe and North America from the 1780s undoubtedly helped to bring about some liberalisation of trade with the United States, and in 1794 the Jay Treaty acknowledged the significance of extra-colonial ties by according ships from the United States the same rights as British vessels in trade with the West Indies.[162] However, this was a matter of making a virtue out of necessity: it was a grudging modification to a system which remained resolutely protectionist in intent, rather than an early sign of a confident move towards free trade. Similarly, the modification of the East India Company's monopoly of Indian trade in 1793 and its abolition in 1813 were aimed at developing trade with the Far East so that India could improve its contribution to the imperial system, not at assisting foreign traders to gain entry to regions opened by British enterprise.[163] Down to 1815, policy-makers in Britain were as much agreed on the need to maintain protected colonial outlets for goods

160. Milobar, 'Conservative Ideology'; Alan Atkinson, 'The Little Revolution in New South Wales, 1808', *Internat. Hist. Rev.*, 12 (1990); Stanley Trapido, 'From Paternalism to Liberalism: the Cape Colony, 1800–1834', *Internat. Hist. Rev.* 12 (1990); R.B. McDowell, *Ireland in the Age of Imperialism and Revolution, 1760–1800* (Oxford, 1979); Thomas Bartlett, '"A People Made Rather for Copies than Originals": the Anglo-Irish, 1760–1800', *Internat. Hist. Rev.*, 12 (1990).

161. Drescher, *Econocide*, pp. 56–60; Bayly, *Imperial Meridian*, pp. 121–6, 155–60, 209–11; Marshall, *Bengal*, pp. 140–58; Webster, 'British Export Interests in Bengal', pp. 166–7.

162. D.L. Mackay, 'Direction and Purpose in British Imperial Policy, 1793–1801', *Hist. Jour.*, 17 (1974). On the effort made to incorporate the trade of the United States into the system see Gerald S. Graham, *Sea Power and British North America, 1783–1820* (Harvard, Mass., 1941); and S.G. Checkland, 'American Versus West Indian Traders in Liverpool, 1793–1815', *Jour. Econ. Hist.*, 17 (1958).

163. P.J. Marshall, *Problems of Empire: Britain and India, 1757–1813* (1968), pp. 95–101. This question is referred to in Chapter 10 of the present study.

and services as they were on the importance of liberalising the home market.

After 1815, the role of the empire was adjusted, slowly and hesitantly, to fit the changing priorities of the metropole. Having helped the war effort, the empire was mobilised – not for the last time – in the cause of winning the peace. The reforms set in train at home left their mark on the empire too as Britain set about designing an international regime that would make the world safe for the monarchical, propertied, gentlemanly order that had survived, providentially, the threats of republicanism and secularism. The empire was to be adapted, not abandoned, to meet this new challenge, above all by putting in place a set of 'like-minded', co-operative elites who would demonstrate that the British view of the world could and should be reproduced elsewhere, and that economic progress was compatible with, indeed required, individual liberty, differential property rights, and political stability. As Goderich, the Colonial Secretary, declared in 1833, Britain's aim was 'to transfer to distant regions the greatest possible amount both of the spirit of civil liberty and of the forms of social order to which Great Britain is chiefly indebted for the rank she holds among the civilised nations'.[164] India was the most prominent illustration of this policy, despite the fact that 'improvement' was imposed by paternal rather than liberal means.[165] The colonies of settlement, though still at an early stage of development, also had an important place in this design.[166] They offered openings for migrants as well as for capital and commerce, and were thought to be the most promising launching points for the 'Anglicising' mission.[167] In the 1820s the Colonial Office planned to 'create and uphold an opulent gentry' in Australia, as in the other colonies of white settlement;[168] in the troubled 1830s and 1840s considerable interest was shown in the possibility of taking government action to promote factor flows to the colonies, and especially to

---

164. Quoted in J.J. Eddy, *Britain and the Australian Colonies, 1818–31* (1969), p. xiii.

165. For the emergence of the idea that sound money, free markets and good government marched together see Neil Rabitoy's study of Bombay, 'The Control of Fate and Fortune: the Origins of the Market Mentality in British Administrative Thought in South Asia', *Mod. Asian Stud.*, 25 (1991).

166. A.G.L. Shaw, 'British Attitudes to the Colonies, c.1820–1850', *Jour. Brit. Stud.*, 9 (1969).

167. This term came into use in the late eighteenth century, when it was applied principally to French Canadians and Afrikaners. See James Sturgis, 'Anglicisation at the Cape of Good Hope in the Early Nineteenth Century', *Jour. Imp. and Comm. Hist.*, 11 (1982).

168. Eddy, *Britain and the Australian Colonies*, p. 224.

widen the 'field of employment' for the middle class as the apparatus of state contracted at home.[169]

These changes occurred within a structure that was still based on colonial preferences, even though these were being modified from the 1820s. Indeed, the vigorous protectionist policies adopted in Europe and the United States after 1815 appeared to confirm the wisdom, or at least the necessity, of adhering to Britain's traditional policy. By limiting access to major markets, the new mercantilism adopted by foreign powers also prompted Britain to take an interest in extending trade to underdeveloped areas that lay outside her formal control. The extension of informal influence after 1815 is best understood, not as an alternative to the old colonial system, but as an addition to it which reflected the increasingly cosmopolitan character of Britain's trade and finance and the growing ambivalence of her commercial policy during the period of transition to free trade. This means of expansion was made possible by the elimination of the French naval threat, which greatly reduced the need for direct British political influence abroad and made the pursuit of new markets compatible with the drive for cheap government.[170] Castlereagh and Canning believed that the steady liberalisation of trade with new partners, especially in Latin America, would naturally promote British influence, and that this would extend beyond commerce: British experts were at hand to supply appropriate constitutions for new states; British missionaries stood ready to convert the heathen; and the City was beginning to explore the prospects of funding this programme of world development.[171]

By the 1830s, Canning's successor as Foreign Secretary, Lord Palmerston, was more aware of the obstacles to achieving this desirable state of affairs as a result of the growth of competition from Europe and the United States and the urgent need to find new markets for industry and commerce in the underdeveloped world. Palmerston's almost instinctive commitment to free-market economics ought not to be surprising, given that he inherited beliefs espoused by the gentlemanly elite at the beginning of the century. But the effort he put into extending Britain's trade and influence in

169. Wakefield's list of possible beneficiaries of a policy of systematic colonisation makes interesting reading. See 'A Letter from Sydney', in E. Lloyd Prichard, ed. *Collected Works of E.G. Wakefield* (Glasgow, 1968), p. 165.

170. The naval aspects are dealt with by Gerald S. Graham, *Tides of Empire: Discursions on the Expansion of Britain Overseas* (1972), pp. 80f.

171. C.J. Bartlett, *Castlereagh* (1966), pp. 235f; P.J.V. Rolo, *George Canning: Three Biographical Studies* (1965), pp. 254–8.

the extra-European world needs to be emphasised because it is still underplayed by diplomatic historians. Palmerston was determined to 'export abroad the same self-regulating system which was transforming British society'.[172] To this end, he was willing to impose free trade on reluctant rulers, to evict recalcitrant ones, and to advance 'legitimate commerce' by putting down the African slave trade.[173] Behind this grand design, which aimed at creating a cluster of economic satellites managed by foreign beneficiaries of English culture, stood Palmerston's persistent concern about the possibility of social breakdown in the 1830s and 1840s, when industry was severely depressed and Chartism was at its height.[174] It is no coincidence that Palmerston's interventionist policy reached new levels of intensity during this period. The war against China, the bombardment of slave ports on the west coast of Africa, the treaties with Turkey and Egypt and the attack on Argentina's protectionist policies,[175] all reflected his concern to find overseas solutions to domestic problems and his particular belief that 'it is the business of government to open and secure the roads for the merchant'.[176]

Palmerston carried into the mid-nineteenth century the peculiarly British mixture of economic liberty and gentlemanly paternalism that had its origins in the late seventeenth century. He also infused these ideas with a renewed sense of mission: the belief that the British model of development could be exported overseas and the conviction that it had to be exported if it were to be preserved at home. Unfortunately for Britain, this strategy ran into serious difficulties. The colonies of settlement made slow and disappointing progress, India resisted or frustrated modernisers as much as she was bent to

172. See R.J. Gavin's important and unfortunately still unpublished study, 'Palmerston's Policy Towards East and West Africa, 1830–1865', (Ph.D. thesis, Cambridge University, 1958), pp. 16–48.
173. This is the theme of Sir Thomas Fowell Buxton's *The African Slave Trade and its Remedy* (1840). The best study of these developments remains Jack Gallagher, 'Fowell Buxton and the "New African Policy", 1838–1842', *Cambridge Historical Journal*, 10 (1950). See also A.G. Hopkins, 'Property Rights and Empire Building: Britain's Annexation of Lagos, 1861', *Jour. Econ. Hist.*, 40 (1980).
174. R.J. Gavin, 'Palmerston and Africa', *Jour. Hist. Soc. Nigeria*, 6 (1971), p. 94. Palmerston was particularly upset by French expansion in north Africa. There was also a close connection between the difficulties experienced by British exports, unemployment and social unrest, and the aggressive stance taken towards Argentina during the Uruguayan dispute in 1841–5. See H.S. Ferns, *Britain and Argentina in the Nineteenth Century* (Oxford, 1960), Ch. IX; Peter Winn, 'British Informal Empire in Uruguay in the Nineteenth Century', *Past and Present*, 73 (1976), pp. 104–8; and V.G. Kiernan, 'Britain's First Contacts with Paraguay', *Atlante*, 3 (1955).
175. These matters are dealt within greater detail in Chapters 9 and 11–13.
176. C.K. Webster, *The Foreign Policy of Palmerston*, II (1951), pp. 750–1.

their will, and the penetration of other underdeveloped countries was confined very largely to coastal regions.[177] The abortive attempt to integrate the Latin American republics more firmly into the international economy in the 1820s was indicative of the problems Britain faced, and the losses suffered then remained as a warning for a generation of City bankers. Development and influence alike awaited the coming of the railway and the opening of the interior during the second half of the century. Meanwhile, the failure to extend Britain's economic reach by these informal, if also forceful, means increased the pressure to adopt complete free trade in the 1840s, and brought nearer the demise of the particular brand of gentlemanly capitalism that Palmerston so aptly represented.

CONCLUSION

The dominance of the landed interest and its aristocratic leaders provides a unifying theme for the years between 1688 and 1850 and points to an underlying continuity covering a period of one and a half centuries. But this claim does not lend support to the 'continuity thesis', if that is taken to mean the perpetuation into the nineteenth century of an *ancien régime*. On the contrary, our interpretation suggests that the regime founded in 1688 was substantially new and that much of its innovative character stemmed from the financial revolution it helped to sponsor. The result, as we have described it, was the creation of a form of capitalism headed by improving landlords in association with improving financiers who served as their junior partners. This joint enterprise established a tradition of modernisation and was itself the product of a modernisation of tradition that both conserved gentlemanly values and carried them forward into a changing world.

The various challenges made and encountered by the new regime indicate subdivisions which break the continuity of the period, though they do not destroy its unity at a much higher level of historical generalisation. In particular, we have tried to show how the historical contours of the gentlemanly order were shaped by the need to service the national debt, to fund patronage and to manage the political system in ways that preserved privilege, civil peace and the constitution. These imperatives drove the machinery of state through the

177. See Chapters 9–13.

eighteenth century and into the era of reform. In turn, they go far towards explaining the gentlemanly elite's commitment to economic growth and its interest first in constructing a system of commercial protection and national credit, and then in moving towards free trade and a wider role for British finance. This transformation was bound up with a complex realignment of cultural values which involved legitimising new activities by converting private interests into public virtues, harnessing the monarchy to buttress political stability, and calling upon the Church to stiffen the moral fibre of the nation.[178] By distinguishing in these ways between changes within a social system and changes to the system itself, it becomes possible to see how the former contribute to the latter and thus to devise an analysis that takes account of both continuity and change.

We have also tried to demonstrate how the constellation of forces that was entrenched and released by the Glorious Revolution found expression in Britain's international policy and overseas presence. From this perspective, imperialism was a means of defending the Revolution Settlement by building a strong navy and by creating satellites that gave Britain a measure of independence from powerful neighbours on the continent of Europe. Equally, it was a means of exporting the Revolution Settlement by promoting a propertied interest abroad and by capitalising on Britain's comparative advantage in finance and commercial services to supply credit, carriage and insurance, and thus to capture an increasing share of world trade. Aside from our particular argument on this subject, we have also put a general case for reintegrating the history of the empire with that of the metropole during this period. In doing so, we are returning to a perspective which contemporaries regarded as being uncontroversial, though it has now been diminished by the specialisation required of modern scholarship. Tom Paine, among many others, was well aware of these global connections. He had a shrewd appreciation of the relationship between the national credit and political order, and he saw, too, that there was a link between the fortunes of empire in Asia and in the New World. As he observed of the government's attempt to rescue the East India Company's declining fortunes in 1773 by giving it a monopoly of tea: 'it is somewhat remarkable that the produce of that ruined country, transported to America, should there

178. We take this opportunity to express our broad agreement with Bayly, *Imperial Meridian*, p. 253, and to add that we had insufficient space to examine the cultural aspects of gentlemanly capitalism in the article to which he refers: Cain and Hopkins, 'Gentlemanly Capitalism'. We hope that we have gone some way towards remedying this defect in the present study.

kindle up a war to punish their destroyer'.[179] It is not necessary to accept Paine's interpretation of the causes of the revolt of the mainland colonies to agree with him on the wisdom of keeping in view the relationship between the parts and the whole.

Successful expansion, reinforced by colonial acquisitions, generated profits and revenues, helped to service the national debt, and contributed to employment and political stability. In this guise, imperialism was expansive and often aggressive. The extension of credit and the search for revenue led to collisions on diverse peripheries, while the contest for colonies and for control of world trade played its part in causing the large-scale wars that began in 1739 and culminated in 1815. By that date the costs of war had expanded the national debt to the point where it was threatening to topple the structure it was supposed to support. Once France had been defeated, a new campaign had to be mounted to bring public expenditure under control, to generate extra revenue and to create employment at home. This exercise committed Britain to a new overseas development drive which sought to mobilise the empire while also adding a cosmopolitan element to it by moving progressively towards free trade. The aim in both cases was to secure resource pools, to open markets and to put in place a set of allies who would ensure that the values defended by war were reinforced by a lasting peace.

The survival of mercantilism in the nineteenth century was therefore not the result of its success in meeting Britain's needs. Platt's argument that the imperial system was more or less self-sufficient down to the 1840s underestimates both the acute difficulties experienced by the export industries during this period and the growing urgency of problems arising on the domestic front.[180] As we have suggested, it was the inadequacy of the regulated system inherited from the eighteenth century that prompted renewed overseas expansion and the accompanying moves to reduce protectionism after 1815. But this does not mean, either, that the period saw the creation of a form of free-trading imperialism arising out of the expansive and confident forces generated by new industries and technology.[181] Britain's intentions in seeking to extend her informal influence were perfectly clear, but the results were very limited down to the middle of the nineteenth century. As we have seen, it was Britain's inability

179. Paine, *Complete Works*, p. 98.
180. D.C.M. Platt, 'The National Economy and British Imperial Expansion Before 1914', *Jour. Imp. and Comm. Hist.*, 2 (1973/4). See also the more extended comment in Cain and Hopkins, 'Political Economy', p. 476.
181. Gallagher and Robinson, 'Imperialism of Free Trade'.

to solve her problems either within the existing empire or by informal means that provoked Palmerston's final burst of bellicosity and impelled Peel's risky lunge towards free trade.

After 1850, free trade destroyed the old colonial system and, in combination with the rise of new wealth, ensured the gradual demise of the landed aristocracy, thus bringing one phase of gentlemanly capitalism to an end. But the new economic and political structures that arose – and the imperialism that flowed from them – were still not dominated by industrial capitalism. From the middle of the nineteenth century, the main area of growth was the service sector, and the most rapidly developing region in Britain was the south-east. The City was at the heart of both. London stood at the centre of a well-developed network of international services, and these were destined to expand rapidly as world trade increased in the second half of the century. Even before 1850, financial flows from the City were an important determinant of the rhythm of development in the colonies.[182] Beyond formal empire, London's influence as the main source of long-term finance had begun to spread to Europe and North America after 1815, and was poised to increase dramatically after 1850, as the age of the steamship and railway began.[183] The City and the service sector overcame their hesitations, supported the introduction of free trade and proved, down to 1914, to be its chief beneficiaries. They also carried into free-trading Britain many of the cultural values acquired in the course of their long apprenticeship to the landed aristocracy. After 1850, as one form of gentlemanly capitalism began to fail, another arose to take its place.

---

182. For examples of networks of trade and factor movements connecting the City with the colonies during this period see Frank J.A. Broeze, 'Private Enterprise and the Peopling of Australia, 1831–50', *Econ. Hist. Rev.*, 2nd ser. XXXV (1982); and W.E. Cheong, *Mandarins and Merchants: Jardine Matheson & Co., a China Agency of the Early Nineteenth Century* (Malmo, 1978), Chs. 6–7.

183. Insights into the growth of British overseas credit operations and investments can be found in D.C.M. Platt, *Foreign Finance in Continental Europe and the U.S.A., 1815–70: Quantities, Origins, Functions and Distribution* (1984).

PART TWO

The Gentlemanly Order

'Something Peculiar to England': The Service Sector, Wealth and Power, 1850–1914[1]

When historians of British imperialism have taken any serious note of the work of economic historians, they have concentrated mainly upon the slowing rate of growth of the British economy in general, and of industrial growth in particular, after 1870 and the more rapid growth of other industrialising nations. Generally speaking, these trends are well attested in the literature, although some of the implications of the growth figures for overseas expansion have not been drawn out.

ECONOMIC GROWTH

Contemporaries were apt to divide the period 1850–1914 into three parts: a 'Great Victorian Boom' between 1850 and 1873; a succeeding Great Depression until the mid-1890s; and then a return to prosperity culminating in a vigorous full-employment boom between 1910 and 1913. These labels were attached on the basis of limited knowledge of the movement of prices and profits, and are often misleading. In their pioneering work, Deane and Cole found that, apart from one or two short exceptional periods, rates of growth of GNP and national income in the United Kingdom accelerated until the 1890s and then fell off markedly.[2] Deane's later estimates of GNP modified this, arguing for a peak in growth rates in 1858–73 followed by a sharp

1. The quotation in the title is taken from Robert Henry Super, ed. *The Complete Prose Works of Matthew Arnold* (Ann Arbor, Mich., 1965), Vol. II, p. 88.
2. Phyllis Deane and W.A. Cole, *British Economic Growth, 1688–1959: Trends and Structure* (Cambridge, 1964), pp. 282–4, 311.

deceleration and interrupted by a brief revival in the 1890s.[3] Feinstein's early work also indicated a slow-down in growth in the 1870s and an equally sharp dip at the end of the century.[4] The latest available estimates are much more emphatic in placing the decisive break in the growth of domestic product around 1900, and reveal no obvious turning point in 1870. Evidence about productivity trends is much more tentative but the indications are that total factor productivity (the share of growth which cannot be accounted for simply by additional labour and capital inputs) fell off decisively only around the turn of the century (Table 3.1). If the most recent work on earlier periods is included, the picture that emerges is of a steady acceleration in the growth of both productivity and output between the late eighteenth century and about 1870, at which point there is some evidence of deceleration, a partial upsurge in the 1890s and a more decisive fall after 1900.[5] The relative decline of the economy is also marked, at least for the period after 1870. Growth rates in the United States and Germany were bound to be higher than in Britain because of considerably higher rates of growth of population. But the evidence of international productivity comparisons also shows that Britain was lagging after 1890, and the lag is only partly explained by the ability of the late-starters to call on a much larger pool of low-productivity agricultural labour than was available at the time in Great Britain.[6]

Sectorally, the most dramatic event was the decline of agriculture, where output actually fell between 1865–82 and 1889–99.[7] The

3. Phyllis Deane, 'New Estimates of Gross National Product for the United Kingdom, 1830–1914', *Review of Income and Wealth*, XIV (1968), esp. Table 2, p. 98.

4. C.H. Feinstein, *National Income, Expenditure and Output of the United Kingdom, 1955–1965* (Cambridge, 1972), Table 7, p. 19; see also D.N. McCloskey, 'Did Victorian Britain Fail?', *Econ. Hist. Rev.*. 2nd ser. XXIII (1970); D.H. Aldcroft, 'McCloskey on Victorian Growth: a Comment', *Econ. Hist. Rev.*, 2nd ser. XXVII (1974), pp. 272–3; and McCloskey, 'Victorian Growth: a Rejoinder', ibid. pp. 275–7. The last three articles are reproduced in Donald N. McCloskey, *Enterprise and Trade in Victorian Britain: Essays in Historical Economics* (1981). An early essay stressing the importance of 1900 as a turning point is R.C.O. Matthews, 'Some Aspects of Post-War Growth in the British Economy in Relation to Historical Experience', *Transactions of the Manchester Statistical Society* (1964–5) and reprinted in Derek H. Aldcroft and Peter Fearon, eds. *Economic Growth in Twentieth-Century Britain* (1969).

5. N.F.R. Crafts, *British Economic Growth during the Industrial Revolution* (Oxford, 1985), p. 45. See also C.H. Lee, *The British Economy Since 1700: A Macro-Economic Perspective* (1986), Ch. I.

6. Angus Maddison, *Economic Growth in the West: Comparative Experience in Europe and North America* (1964), esp. Table 1.1, p. 28, and Table 1.3, p. 30.

7. C.H. Feinstein, R.C.O. Matthews and J.C. Odling-Smee, 'The Timing of the Climacteric and its Sectoral Incidence in the United Kingdom, 1873–1913', in Charles P. Kindleberger and Guido di Tella, eds. *Economics in the Long View: Essays in Honour of W.W. Rostow*, Vol. 2, Pt. I (1982), Table 8.4, p. 178.

Table 3.1 Rates of growth of output and productivity, cyclical peak to cyclical peak: United Kingdom; 1856–1913 (per cent per year)

	GNP	GDP[b]	TFP[a](GDP)	Manufacturing output	TFP[a](Manuf)
1856–60	1.6	1.7	0.4	2.5	1.2
1860–65	3.0	2.0	0.6	1.7	−0.1
1865–73	2.7	2.4	1.1	3.2	1.3
1873–82	1.6	1.9	0.6	2.3	1.1
1882–89	1.9	2.2	0.9	1.9	0.4
1889–99	2.3	2.2	0.8	2.3	1.1
1899–1907	1.8	1.2	−0.3	1.6	0.1
1907–13	1.6	1.6	0.3	1.0	0.3
1856–73	2.5	2.2	0.8	2.6	0.9
1873–99	2.0	2.1	0.7	2.2	0.9
1899–1913	1.7	1.4	0.0	1.4	0.3

Sources: First column (GNP): P. Deane, 'New Estimates of Gross National Product for the United Kingdom, 1830–1914', *Review of Income and Wealth*, XIV (1968), pp. 106–7. Rest of table: C.H. Feinstein, R.C.O. Matthews and J.C. Odling-Smee, 'The Timing of the Climacteric and its Sectoral Incidence in the United Kingdom, 1873–1913', in C.P. Kindleberger and Guido di Tella eds. *Economics in the Long View: Essays in Honour of W.W. Rostow*, Vol. II, Pt I, (Basingstoke, 1982), pp. 175, 178; R.C.O. Matthews, C.H. Feinstein and J.C. Odling-Smee, *British Economic Growth, 1856–1973* (Oxford, 1982), App. L, pp. 606–7.

Notes: [a] Total Factor Productivity (see p. 108).
   [b] Composite figures based on a number of different estimates.

movement of manufacturing output was closer to that of output as a whole. The Hoffman-Lomax index of industrial production shows a break below 3 per cent per annum growth in the 1870s with a significant revival in the 1890s.[8] Another series, which removes cotton textile production from the total in order to eliminate the distortions introduced by the cotton famine in 1861–5, dates the deceleration in growth from the 1860s: but figures for industrial production per head show a downturn after 1900 as well as 40 years earlier.[9] The latest figures also suggest a decline in the rate of growth of output after 1875, a revival after 1890 and a decisive fall in the Edwardian period, though the productivity figure points to 1900 as being the climacteric

8. K.S. Lomax, 'Growth and Productivity in the United Kingdom', in Aldcroft and Fearon, *Economic Growth*, Table 2, p. 12.
9. D.J. Coppock, 'The Climacteric of the 1890s: a Critical Note', *Manchester School*, XXIV (1956), pp. 7–8.

(see Table 3.1).[10] What is more important from our perspective is the extent of the growth of services after 1850. The growth rate of commerce (weighted by its share in Gross Domestic Product) was on a par with that of manufacturing over the period as a whole and its contribution to productivity was broadly similar. Transport and communications and public and professional services also made contributions to growth which were as significant as that made by mining.[11]

AGRICULTURAL DECLINE

Despite Peel's optimistic assumption, free trade was a sentence of execution on British agriculture; but the sentence was not carried out immediately. Before world-wide rail and steamship links were established, domestic farming enjoyed a degree of natural protection and flourished in the generation after the repeal of the Corn Laws as income and output in Britain grew rapidly.[12] Even so, imports of cereals were sufficiently high to keep prices down and encouraged a steady shift from arable to pasture.[13] From the 1860s the effects of the world-wide application of new transport technology began to be felt, and cheap cereals poured in from Russia, Eastern Europe and the United States. The price of wheat fell by about half in 30 years and other grain prices were almost as badly affected because the intensity of competition was aggravated by the slow growth of demand.[14] Farmers and landlords who were dependent on arable saw their incomes and rents tumble. The gross value of arable output fell from

10. For general discussion of nineteenth- and early-twentieth-century growth patterns see R.A. Church, *The Great Victorian Boom, 1850–1873* (1975); S.B. Saul, *The Myth of the Great Depression, 1873–1896* (1969); François Crouzet, *The Victorian Economy* (1982), Chs. 2 and 3; Sidney Pollard, *Britain's Prime and Britain's Decline: The British Economy, 1870–1914* (1989), pp. 1–17.

11. R.C.O. Matthews, C.H. Feinstein, and J.C. Odling-Smee, *British Economic Growth, 1856–1973* (Oxford, 1982), pp. 222–3, 288–9, App. L., pp. 606–7; Lee, *The British Economy since 1700*, Table 1.4, p. 12.

12. See E.L. Jones, *The Development of English Agriculture, 1815–73* (1968), pp. 17–30. For an overview of the agricultural industry within the context of landed society see F.M.L. Thompson, *English Landed Society in the Nineteenth Century* (1963).

13. Wray Vamplew, 'The Protection of English Cereal Producers: the Corn Laws Reassessed', *Econ. Hist. Rev.*, 2nd ser. XXXIII (1980), esp. p. 391; Church, *The Great Victorian Boom*, pp. 60–1; E.L. Jones, *Agriculture and the Industrial Revolution* (1975), Ch. 9.

14. M. Tracy, *Agriculture and Western Europe* (1964), Table 10, p. 49.

£104m. in 1867–9 to £62m. in 1894–1903 and much land went out of cultivation or reverted to pasture.[15] Most of the strain was taken up by the landed interest itself since rents fell more rapidly than overall income.[16] Even so, the pastoral sector continued to prosper, despite growing foreign competition, largely because of rapidly increasing demand for meat and dairy produce in the expanding cities and towns. Income from pastoral farming actually rose between 1870 and 1900, signalling a shift in the locus of agricultural power from the wheat-growing south to the pastures of the north.[17] While arable landlords suffered sharp falls in income, large owners of pastoral land, like the Earl of Derby, improved their positions. Overall, though, the decline in arable marked the end of agriculture's crucial role in the economy. Its share of national income declined from about one-fifth in 1850 to one-sixteenth in 1900; and income from farm ownership fell from roughly one-fifth of all property income in 1856 to one-twentieth by 1913.[18]

Britain also moved, in the same space of half a century, from practical self-sufficiency in basic foodstuffs to a dependence on imports for roughly half her annual consumption. This represented at one and the same time a sublime faith in her ability to export enough to pay for this additional import burden and to protect her overseas commerce through naval supremacy. Arable agriculture was the first outstanding victim of Britain's mid-century commitment to the international division of labour, one momentous consequence of which was the decline in the wealth and influence of the landed aristocracy who had hitherto been the dominant component of gentlemanly capitalism.

INDUSTRY AFTER 1850

If arable agriculture was the first significant casualty of Britain's economic internationalism after 1850, some segments of manufacturing industry also began to show signs of difficulty in coping with free

15. T.W. Fletcher, 'The Great Depression of English Agriculture, 1873–96', *Econ. Hist. Rev.*, 2nd ser. XIII (1960–1), reprinted in P.J. Perry ed. *British Agriculture, 1875–1914* (1973). See Appendix, p. 54.
16. Tracy, *Agriculture and Western Europe*, Table 9, p. 48.
17. Fletcher, 'The Great Depression', passim.
18. Deane and Cole, *British Economic Growth, 1688–1959*, Table 76, p. 291; Matthews, Feinstein and Odling-Smee, *British Economic Growth*, Table 6.1, p. 164.

trade. Throughout the period, industrialists remained chronically pessimistic about profit margins and markets, except in brief periods of breakneck boom, such as 1849–53, 1869–73 and 1910–13. The pessimism before 1880 was grounded in the fierceness of domestic competition[19] and, after that, confirmed by the growing threat posed to both domestic and foreign markets by industrialising rivals.[20] As industrialisation spread abroad, often behind protectionist barriers, the transformation of industry in Britain was steady rather than dramatic. Textiles, iron, steel and other metals, coal and engineering dominated industry in 1914 as they had in 1850. Though textiles had declined in relative importance, steel output had outpaced iron and Britain had developed the world's most efficient shipbuilding industry. Also, despite the rapid spread of steam technology across industry in the late nineteenth century[21] and the rise of the joint-stock form of enterprise, big business was slow to appear in Britain and the typical firm in 1914 was still small by the standards of Germany or the USA. When compared with these developing rivals, British industry was showing disturbing signs of technological and organisational backwardness in some key industries like steel by the 1890s, and the take-up of innovative technology in new fields – chemicals and electricals, for example – was slow.

Some of the statistical research on manufacturing suggests that overall rates of growth of output and productivity did not decline until after 1900, though the rate of growth of both should have risen rather than stagnated in the late nineteenth century, given the extent to which Britain could import technology from others after 1870.[22] However, there is little doubt that the downturn in the performance of many of the older, export-oriented staples of provincial England occurred much sooner. Rates of growth of output and productivity in textiles, for example, declined precipitately in the 1870s and revived only very modestly in the great export boom before 1913;[23] the metal

19. Roy A. Church, ed. *The Dynamics of Victorian Business*, (1980), Ch. 1.

20. There is some evidence that the share of profits in GNP at current prices rose in the period 1850–70 and fell thereafter. See Matthews, Feinstein and Odling-Smee, *British Economic Growth*, Table 6: 1, p. 164. The influence of foreign competition in squeezing profits is discussed in ibid. p. 196.

21. A.E. Musson, 'Industrial Motive Power in the United Kingdom, 1800–70', *Econ. Hist. Rev.*, 2nd ser. XXIX (1976), esp. p. 436.

22. Matthews, Feinstein and Odling-Smee, *British Economic Growth*, pp. 535–7.

23. Crouzet, *The Victorian Economy*, pp. 191, 197; D.A. Farnie, *The English Cotton Industry and the World Market, 1815–1896*, (Oxford, 1979), Table 9, p. 199, argues for sharp declines in productivity in the industry from the 1850s. Matthews, Feinstein and Odling-Smee, in *British Economic Growth*, also suggest a sharp fall in productivity growth in textiles as a whole, *c*. 1860 (p. 450).

trades, especially iron, showed similar trends.[24] Relative decline must also be dated at least as far as back as 1870 and probably before. In 1870 Britain still produced one-third of world manufacturing output, but her share had fallen to one-seventh at the outbreak of World War I.[25] In steel production, one of the key activities of the time, the relative decline was more alarming. Britain's share of output fell from just over one-third in the late 1870s to one-tenth by 1909–13, at which point Germany produced twice as much as Britain, and the United States twice as much again.[26]

THE SERVICE SECTOR

Even though British industrialism had passed its zenith in world terms late in the nineteenth century, it is still taken for granted that industry dominated British economic life after 1850 and provided the main economic dynamic before World War I. This judgement would be unexceptionable if it were applied to, say, southern Scotland and Wales, north and north-west England, the West Riding and the west Midlands, but it is difficult to sustain if applied to the whole country. The share of mining, manufacturing and building in national income rose from 34 per cent to 40 per cent of the total between 1841 and 1911 but most of that expansion was accounted for by mining, especially coal, and manufacturing's share was stagnant. The manufacturing sector's share of total employment was also stable, at around one-third of the total, after 1841.[27] The chief compensation for agricultural decline after 1840 came not from industry but from services.[28]

24. See, for example, the data on iron and steel production in Crouzet, *The Victorian Economy*, p. 246.
25. League of Nations, *Industrialization and World Trade* (New York, 1945), p. 13.
26. P.L. Payne, 'Iron and Steel Manufactures', in D.H. Aldcroft, ed. *The Development of British Industry and Foreign Competition, 1875–1914: Studies in Industrial Enterprise* (1968), p. 72.
27. Deane and Cole, *British Economic Growth, 1688–1959*, Table 31, p. 143, and Table 37, p. 166.
28. The latest statistical work indicates that 'during the second half of the 19th century, structural change in Britain involved principally a shift of resources from agriculture to services, rather than to manufacturing'. See N. Gemmell and P. Wardley, 'The Contribution of Services to British Economic Growth, 1856–1913', *Explorations in Economic History*, 27 (1990), p. 302. Crouzet, while recognising the importance of service growth for both employment and income after 1840, still tends to see this growth as being subservient to that of the industrial sector, which is assumed to be the dominant force in economic life. In this he reflects received opinion: *The Victorian Economy*, pp. 68–71, 188.

The share of services in employment was higher in Britain in the nineteenth century and early twentieth centuries than anywhere else save the Netherlands,[29] and, as Table 3.2 shows, that share was increasing steadily from the mid-nineteenth century. The table also makes clear the concentration of service employment in the south-east of England: that region alone accounted for one-third of all service employment in Britain in 1841 and two-fifths in 1911.

Table 3.2 Share of services in employment, 1841–1911 (per cent)

Region	1841	1881	1911
North-west	20.0	24.9	26.9
South-east	35.8	41.8	45.8
Great Britain	26.3	30.2	33.1

Source: C.H. Lee, *British Regional Employment Statistics, 1841–1971* (Cambridge, 1979), Series A, employment categories 22–27: transport; distribution; insurance, banking, financial and business services; professional and scientific; miscellaneous; public administration and defence.

Looking at manufacturing and service employment in isolation from each other does not give a true picture of the complex nature of development in Britain after 1850 or of the importance of the south-east. Lee has recently identified three crucial areas of growth in terms of output and employment: those connected with mining; the staple export trades and heavy industries; and a third group in which a complex of services and linked consumer-good industries was the dominant form, and of which London and its environs was the greatest exemplar.[30] This third group was growing more rapidly than the others as early as the 1840s. At that date, it was dominant only in London, Middlesex and Surrey but its influence grew thereafter until, by the outbreak of war in 1914, it had encompassed all of what we now call the Home Counties, as the agricultural frontier in the south-east of England retreated.[31] The pre-eminent position of the south-east within this service-consumer industry complex was very marked. The whole group accounted for 55 per cent of British employment in 1841

29. P.K. O'Brien, 'The Analysis and Measurement of the Service Sector in European Economic History', in R. Fremdling and P.K. O'Brien, eds. *Productivity in the Economies of Europe* (Stuttgart, 1983), p. 82. For further analysis of the differences in structure between Britain and other European countries see Gemmill and Wardley, 'The Contribution of Services', pp. 300–2.

30. C.H. Lee, 'Regional Growth and Structural Change in Victorian Britain', *Econ. Hist. Rev.*, 2nd ser. XXXIV (1981).

31. Ibid. pp. 442–3.

and 65 per cent 70 years later. Of the employment in the south-east, 71 per cent fell into this category at the first date and 85 per cent at the second, at which point the region was responsible for 37 per cent of all employment in the group.[32] Not only was employment rising faster in the south-east than elsewhere but also the London-centred area was more closely integrated economically than the others, which were more dependent on exports either to other regions or abroad.

Moreover, although the development of services was often an adjunct of industrial development in the provinces, the reverse was true in the south-east. There, the growth of consumer manufactures was often stimulated directly by the growth of service income and employment.[33] A case in point was the engineering sector, an area of rapid technological change: nearly half of all the new jobs created in instrument engineering in this period, and over two-fifths of those in electrical engineering, were found in the south-east.[34] Also, under the stimulus of rising real wages after 1870, consumer industries and services offered some of the most impressive examples of dynamic entrepreneurship in Britain,[35] including the massive transformation which took place in retail trading and the rapid development – much of it involving complex technical change – of the finance and banking sector.[36]

At the heart of this highly successful service economy was London, a city which, while shedding many of its old-established industries (like shipbuilding) under pressure from the provinces,[37] was as much a magnet for people, wealth and power in 1900 as it had been in 1750. In 1801 London contained 12 per cent of the population of England and Wales; by 1901 the figure had risen to 20 per cent. It grew faster than any other conurbation in Great Britain after 1850 and, by 1911, its

32. The calculations are based on material in C.H. Lee, *British Regional Employment Statistics, 1841–1971*, (Cambridge, 1979).

33. Lee, 'Regional Growth and Structural Change in Victorian Britain', pp. 449–50; Pollard, *Britain's Prime and Britain's Decline*, pp. 51–2.

34. Lee, *The British Economy since 1700*, p. 135.

35. There is much evidence for this in Charles Wilson, 'Economy and Society in Late Victorian Britain', *Econ. Hist. Rev.*, 2nd ser. XXIII (1965).

36. A distinguished modern economist has recently highlighted these two sectors in an attempt to overcome the view of most of his colleagues that services are not technically progressive and are inevitably areas of low productivity. Jagdish Bhagwati, 'Splintering and Disembodiment of Services and Developing Nations', in Bhagwati, *Essays in Development Economics*, I (Oxford, 1985), pp. 98–9. For a positive, if tentative, view of the importance of services to productivity growth after 1870 see Gemmell and Wardley, 'The Contribution of Services to British Economic Growth', pp. 307, 317.

37. This is one of the themes of Gareth Stedman Jones's now classic account, *Outcast London: A Study in the Relationship between Classes in Victorian Society* (Oxford, 1971), pp. 152–5.

population was equivalent to the six other great centres of population combined.[38] Indeed, London's growth after 1850, like the growth of the south-east region itself, was a reassertion of an ancient dominance rather than a novel force in British life. As Dyos expresses it, 'the shift of resources into the exploitation of the northern provinces, and others, in the eighteenth and nineteenth centuries might be represented simply as an interlude in a much larger historical trend'.[39] If, between 1750 and 1850, the economic tide had run in favour of the industrial provinces it swung decisively back again, to the traditional centre of wealth and power, in the Victorian and Edwardian epoch.

THE NEW GENTLEMANLY CAPITALISTS

Before 1914, aristocratic ideals and life-styles retained a powerful appeal in Britain despite the relative decline of land as an economic force. The peerage was still highly visible and active, culturally and socially, and landed gentlemen played a leading role in high politics until the outbreak of war. Even in 1900, members of parliament with landed backgrounds had a disproportionate share of government posts and Lord Salisbury's last administration was known as the 'Hotel Cecil', so strong was the imprint of his own family upon it.[40] It was not so obvious, however, that this pervasive aristocratic presence betokened real power and influence. In recent years, both Marxist and 'liberal' historians have disagreed among themselves and with each other about whether the continued prominence of the landed elite reflected a real aristocratic dominance or whether aristocratic government and cultural norms were merely convenient veils behind which the 'bourgeoisie' could work its will undisturbed.[41]

---

38. H.J. Dyos, 'Greater and Greater London: Notes on Metropolis and Provinces in the Nineteenth and Twentieth Centuries', in J.S. Bromley and E.H. Kossman eds. *Britain and the Netherlands*, Vol. IV, *Dominion and Provinces* (The Hague, 1971), pp. 100–1. Also Crouzet, *The Victorian Economy*, pp. 95–8; Francis Sheppard, 'London and the Nation in the Nineteenth Century', *Trans. Royal Hist. Soc.*, 5th ser. 35 (1985), pp. 54–5; Pollard, *Britain's Prime and Britain's Decline*, p. 52.

39. Dyos, 'Greater and Greater London', pp. 91–2.

40. J.P. Cornford, 'The Parliamentary Foundations of the Hotel Cecil', in R. Robson, ed. *Ideas and Institutions of Victorian Britain* (1968); see also F.M.L. Thompson, 'Britain', in D. Spring ed. *European Landed Elites in the Nineteenth Century* (Baltimore, 1977). The changing fortunes of the landed classes have now received authoritative treatment in David Cannadine, *The Decline and Fall of the British Aristocracy* (1990).

41. The importance of the continued existence of a landed aristocracy and the culture derived from it has been a matter of lively debate in Britain during the last

Our argument will be that aristocratic power was in clear decline but that power and prestige devolved more upon a new gentlemanly class arising from the service sector than it did upon the industrial bourgeoisie. The landed aristocracy could mitigate their economic difficulties after 1870 only by reaching an accommodation with other forms of wealth, but the links they made were largely with non-industrial rather than industrial sources, as we shall see. And, insofar as their political and social power was on the wane, their successors were gentlemen from the service sector or from finance rather than manufacturers from the industrial provinces.

As the basis of Britain's economic fortunes shifted from the land and agriculture to urban-based manufacturing and service activities, the transformation was registered unambiguously in the sources of top wealth holding (Table 3.3). From our perspective what is important is that, as land declined as the chief source of great fortunes, especially after 1880 when arable agriculture felt the full force of foreign competition, commerce and finance more than held their own, with industry, as replacements. The predominance of non-landed wealth over land was not apparent until the end of the century; but since the statistics are for fortunes declared at death it can usually be assumed that the greater part of this wealth had been accumulated a generation earlier and that 1880 is roughly the point at which land ceased to be the outstanding source of great wealth in Britain. Working on the same generational principle, it is also apparent that there was a strong surge in the growth of large fortunes made in manufacturing, if the food, drink and tobacco industries are included, but that these sectors did not make further relative gains during the next 30 years. Moreover, if account is taken of all the industrial regions of the provinces, then their share of peak wealth-holding

---

twenty years. Without attributing our own views to any single historian, we can say that we have found the following very stimulating: Perry Anderson, 'Origins of the Present Crisis', *New Left Review*, 33 (1964); E.P. Thompson, 'The Peculiarities of the English', *The Socialist Register*, 11 (1965) and reprinted in *The Poverty of Theory and Other Essays* (1978); J.R.B. Johnson, 'Peculiarities of the English Route: Barrington Moore, Perry Anderson and English Social Development', (University of Birmingham, Centre for Contemporary Cultural Studies, Occasional Paper, History Series, 26, 1975); Tom Nairn, *The Break-up of Britain*, (2nd edn, 1981), Ch. 1; Martin J. Weiner, *English Culture and the Decline of the Industrial Spirit, 1850–1980* (Cambridge, 1981); David Cannadine, *Lands and Landlords: The Aristocracy and the Towns* (Leicester, 1980); Arno Mayer, *The Persistence of the Old Regime: Europe to the Great War* (1981); and, most recently, Perry Anderson, 'The Figures of Descent', *New Left Review*, 161 (1987). For a useful discussion of the debate see also Paul Warwick, 'Did Britain Change? An Inquiry into the Causes of National Decline', *Journal of Contemporary History*, 20 (1985).

Table 3.3 Non-landed fortunes at death, 1860–1919 (£0.5m. or more)

	1860–79	%	1880–99	%	1900–19	%
Manufacturing and mining	44	35.7	82	36.7	124	34.2
Food, drink and tobacco	3	2.4	36	16.1	48	13.2
Finance	40	32.5	47	21.1	79	21.9
Commerce	29	23.5	47	21.1	101	27.9
Other	7	5.6	11	4.9	10	2.8
Total (non-landed)	123		223		362	
(Land)	(280)		(174)		(140)	

Source: W.D. Rubinstein, *Men of Property: The Very Wealthy in Great Britain Since the Industrial Revolution* (London, 1981), Tables 3.3, 3.4, pp. 60–6.

Notes: A small percentage of landed fortunes covers the period 1858–79 but not enough to change the total in column 1 significantly.

It must be emphasised here that Rubinstein's statistics do not include the value of the land of those whose property was subject to legal settlements forbidding sale and in which any particular owner had only a life interest.

The compilation of the groups is as follows: Manufacturing and mining comprise columns 1–11 of the tables; Food, drink and tobacco, columns 12–15; Finance, columns 16–18 and 22–3; Commerce, columns 19–21 and 24–5; Other, columns 26–32.

stayed at around three-tenths of the total throughout the period 1850–1914, with the rise of fortunes in areas like South Wales in the late nineteenth century being compensated by the declining importance of the Manchester region (Table 3.4). The fact that the industrial regions did not perform more strongly overall probably reflects not only the growing strength of trades unionism, which cut into profits, but also the persistence of the small firm and the growth of the foreign challenge both at home and in markets overseas after 1880. Where some form of monopoly did exist, the manufacturing wealthy multiplied. No fewer than six of the sixteen millionaire fortunes declared at death in Scotland between 1873 and 1913 came from members of the J.P. Coats sewing-thread combine; twenty of the thirty-four millionaire fortunes made in food, drink and tobacco between 1860 and 1919 came from that traditional big business, brewing. They were the exceptions, and textiles were more typical of manufacturing as a whole. Only fifteen millionaires and twenty-five half-millionaires were produced by the whole of cotton manufacturing in Britain between 1860 and 1919.[42]

42. R. Britton, 'Wealthy Scots, 1876–1913', *Bull. Inst. Hist. Research*, LVIII (1985). W.D. Rubinstein, *Men of Property: The Very Wealthy in Britain Since the Industrial Revolution* (1981), Table 3.3, pp. 62–3, and Table 3.4, pp. 64–5.

Table 3.4 Geographical origins of non-landed fortunes, 1858–1919 (£0.5m. or more)

	1858–79	%	1880–99	%	1900–19	%
City	51	41.5	51	22.9	82	22.7
Other London	12	9.8	32	14.3	47	13.0
Lancashire	13		22		24	
Yorkshire	9		8		25	
North-east	6		11		26	
Midlands	6		20		25	
Northern Ireland	–		1		3	
South Wales	4		2		7	
Total, industrial	38	30.9	64	28.7	110	30.5
Clydeside[a]	8⎫	15.5	15⎫	13.9	28⎫	15.8
Merseyside[a]	11⎭		16⎭		29⎭	
Others	3		45		66	
Grand total	123		223		362	

Source: Rubinstein, *Men of Property*, Tables 3.11 and 3.12.

Note: [a] Merseyside and Clydeside have been listed separately from the industrial areas because of the predominance there of commercial fortunes.

Commerce and finance were traditional sources of non-landed wealth and declined sharply in relative importance in the third quarter of the century (Table 3.3). The City of London, the centre of these activities,[43] suffered from this trend, its relative share falling from two-fifths to just over one-fifth (Table 3.4). At the same time, fortunes made in the rest of London became more prominent, partly because of its association with the food, drink and tobacco industries, especially brewing,[44] which were an important part of the consumer goods sector so strongly associated with the south-east of England. In the late nineteenth and early twentieth centuries, commerce and finance more than held their own as producers of great wealth and London, and the City, retained their relative shares: in terms of millionaire fortunes alone the City actually made important relative gains at the latter end of the period. The concentration of wealth within the City is indicated by the fact that merchant banking alone produced 22 millionaire and 29 half-millionaire fortunes between 1860 and 1919, a better record than the vast cotton textile industry could boast. The preponderance of the City is even more marked if attention

43. Rubinstein, *Men of Property*, Table 3.10, p. 88.
44. Ibid. pp. 62–5.

is focused on the tax statistics. Of incomes over £5,000 per annum assessed for tax under schedule D in 1879–80, the number originating in Metropolitan Middlesex and London was 1,210 as against 730 for the three major English industrial areas – Lancashire, Yorkshire and Warwickshire/Staffordshire – combined. The City alone accounted for 630 of the metropolitan incomes or just over one-half of the total. Furthermore, at over £41 m., the total income assessed for tax in the City was four times as high as in Manchester and ten times greater than in Birmingham.[45]

One reason for this concentration of wealth was London's dominance of the international side of the service economy and, within that, the pronounced importance of a few major institutions. Joint-stock banking amalgamations put power into the hands of no more than a dozen leading companies by 1914,[46] a degree of concentration unparalleled in Britain outside of transport. Moreover, a large share both of the market for short-term credit and of the far more lucrative loan flotation business was controlled by a handful of merchant banks. Although competition from the joint-stock banks was increasing by 1914, seven of the major merchant banks were responsible for about one-third of all the acceptance credits in the market in 1913[47] and many of the old established houses had a dominant role in the issue business for particular countries: for example, the Rothschilds held first place in regard to Brazil and Chile, while Barings were the predominant force in Argentina and Canada.[48] The confidence inspired by the outstanding merchant banks and merchant houses gave them a virtual monopoly of the business of many of their clients. As Bagehot put it: 'an old established bank has a "prestige" which amounts to a "privileged opportunity"; though no exclusive right is given it by law, peculiar power is given it by opinion'; and he went on to emphasise that 'the "credit" of a person – that is the reliance which may be placed on his pecuniary fidelity – is a different thing

---

45. W.D. Rubinstein, 'Wealth, Elites and the Class Structure of Modern Britain', *Past and Present*, 76 (1977), p. 110.

46. On bank amalgamations see Joseph Sykes, *The Amalgamation Movement in English Banking, 1825–1924* (1926). The clearing banks, which earned high profits before the war, were mostly controlled by the elite of merchant banks in the City via directorships. On clearing-bank profits see Youssef Cassis, 'Profits and Profitability in English Banking, 1870–1914', *Revue internationale d'histoire de la banque*, 34–5 (1987).

47. Stanley Chapman, *The Rise of Merchant Banking* (1984), App. 4, p. 209. In accepting bills, merchant banks were guaranteeing them and thus making them more saleable. For further details on the international money market see Chapter 5.

48. Ibid. pp. 86–7.

from his property'.[49] Consequently, the most prestigious financiers were able to handle vast amounts of other people's money while putting relatively small amounts into the business as capital, with the result that the most successful could earn profits which were immense by the standards of most industrial capitalists.[50]

The City was the point at which the international economy intersected with the service capitalism of the south-east. It is fairly certain that the south-east always had a higher per capita income than other parts of the country but its lead had probably narrowed in the early nineteenth century, only to widen again towards 1900.[51] Schedule D income tax per capita averaged £16.41 in Britain in 1879–80 but £22.49 in the south-east,[52] an indicator not only of the vast fortunes to be made in the City but also of the large number of the 'servant-keeping classes'[53] living in the Home Counties in late Victorian England. One-third of all adult males in London in 1860 paid tax as opposed to about 10 per cent in northern industrial towns, and the middle-class share of London's population grew significantly later in the century.[54]

Just as the south-east was the most dynamic sector of the economy in the late nineteenth century, so too it was the region where an invigorated elite adapted aristocratic cultural norms to suit more modern conditions. One fundamental blow to aristocratic power was loss of control over the gentlemanly professions in government, Church and army as a result of reforms in the recruitment system and the beginning of meritocratic selection between 1850 and 1870.[55] Nonetheless, the final collapse of the old patronage system did not

49. Walter Bagehot, 'Lombard Street', in *Collected Works* (ed. Norman St J. Stevas, 1978), IX, pp. 171, 191.

50. Ibid. pp. 171–2. On banking profits and fortunes see also Youssef Cassis, *Les Banquiers de la City à l'époque eduardienne (1890–1914)*, (Geneva, 1984), Ch. V.

51. Lee, *The British Economy Since 1700*, pp. 130–2.

52. Lee, 'The Service Sector, Regional Specialization and Economic Growth', *Journal of Historical Geography*, 10 (1984), Table 7, p. 149.

53. H. Pelling, *Social Geography of British Elections, 1885–1910* (1967), p. 83.

54. W.D. Rubinstein, 'The Size and Distribution of the English Middle Class in 1860', *Historical Research*, 144 (1988), esp. pp. 79–80. By 1911–12 London had 14 per cent of the population of Britain but contained 44 per cent of its taxable income. The corresponding figures for 1848–9 are 12 per cent and 29 per cent respectively. See W.D. Rubinstein, 'Education and the Social Origins of British Elites, 1800–1970', *Past and Present*, 112 (1987), pp. 199–200.

55. For the army and the Church see P. Razzel, 'Social Origins of Officers in the Indian and British Home Armies, 1758–1962', *British Journal of Sociology*, 14 (1963); C.B. Ottley, 'The Social Origins of British Officers', *Sociological Review*, new series XVIII (1970); D.N.J. Morgan, 'The Social and Educational Background of Anglican Bishops: Continuity and Change', *Brit. Jour. Soc.*, 20 (1969).

provoke a social revolution but merely handed over power to a large, non-industrial middle class which was mainly resident in the London region[56] and eager to secure genteel employment. The examination system acted as a rationing device for this class, which had already benefited considerably from patronage.[57] The reconstruction of these traditional professions was accompanied by the transformation of others, such as medicine and engineering, all of which were reorganised in such a way as to restrict supply and increase income.[58]

Despite this capitalist exploitation of their own intellectual property rights,[59] the professions as a whole saw themselves as gentlemen, or at least aspired to be such, and assumed the possession, in Matthew Arnold's words, of 'fine and governing qualities'.[60] In order to meet these new needs the leading public schools and the ancient universities became manufactories for the creation of public servants and professionals who blended the aristocratic ideal of leadership and service with the new administrative abilities and techniques demanded by a complex urban society[61] to produce that characteristic mixture of amateurism and efficiency which was the mark of the English establishment well into the twentieth century.[62] This newly formed

56. Rubinstein, 'Education and the Social Origins of British Elites', pp. 197–8.

57. J.M. Bourne, *Patronage and Society in Nineteenth-Century England* (1986), esp. Ch. II.

58. On the development of service professionalism in general see W.J. Reader, *Professional Men: The Rise of the Professional Class in Nineteenth Century England* (1966), esp. pp. 185ff; Harold Perkin, *The Rise of Professional Society: England Since 1880* (1989), Chs. 3 and 4; T.R. Gourvish, 'The Rise of the Professions', in T.R. Gourvish and Alan O'Day eds. *Later Victorian Britain* (1988). On engineering as a profession see R.A. Buchanan, 'Gentlemen Engineers: the Making of a Profession', *Victorian Studies*, 26 (1982–3).

59. Perkin, *The Rise of Professional Society*, p. 123.

60. Arnold was speaking in evidence to the Taunton Commission on public schools in 1868: Perkin, *Rise of Professional Society*, pp. 83, 529. In this context see also H.B. Thomson, 'The Choice of a Profession', in B. Dennis and D. Skilton, eds. *Reform and Intellectual Debate in Victorian England* (1987), pp. 67, 70–1; and T.W. Heyck, *The Transformation in Intellectual Life in Victorian England* (1982), pp. 20–2.

61. Rupert Wilkinson, *The Prefects. British Leadership and the Public School Tradition: A Comparative Study* (1964). For the connection between professions and public schools see also Rupert Wilkinson and Thomas Bishop, *Winchester and the Public School Elite: A Statistical Analysis* (1967), and T.W. Bamford, *The Rise of the Public Schools* (1967). For Oxbridge in this context see especially, Sheldon Rothblatt, *The Revolution of the Dons: Cambridge and Society in Victorian England* (Cambridge, 1981), and for universities in a more general framework, Heyck, *The Transformation of Intellectual Life*. A pioneering attempt to see the professional classes as a new gentry can be found in G. Kitson Clark, *The Making of Victorian England* (1962), pp. 251–74.

62. See in particular here W.L. Burn, *The Age of Equipoise* (1964), pp. 253ff and esp. p. 264; and Geoffrey Best, *Mid-Victorian Britain, 1851–1875* (2nd edn 1973), pp. 168–78.

gentlemanly class, paternalist in its assumptions and held together by the club-like spirit which resulted from a common educational and social background, was deeply suspicious both of landed indolence and of the world of trade and everyday work.[63] But, though they had to break free of aristocratic control in order to develop, both the ideology[64] and the practice of these service-based professions were much closer to aristocratic ideals than they were to those of industry,[65] especially as regards their control over their own time, their ability to charge fees rather than to depend upon salaries or wages,[66] their contempt for mere money-making and the personal rather than mechanical nature of their work. They also acted as the transmitters of gentlemanly cultural norms to the lower levels of service capitalism inhabited by the likes of Pooter[67] and the clerking heroes of H.G. Wells, who combined an ethic of extreme economic individualism with an almost desperate desire for a status untainted by 'Trade'.[68]

The connection went deeper than the mere cultural influence of the great upon the small. Although most recruits into the highest ranks of the public service, the Church and other professions were from families in the south of England already connected with the service sector, they were frequently drawn from the lower income end of the taxpaying spectrum, finding their way to the top through a combination of parental determination to pay for public school education and their own ability to exploit the Oxbridge scholarship system.[69]

Gentlemanliness was, therefore, a marked feature of those parts of the 'official mind' which were closely concerned either with the management of government finances, such as the Treasury,[70] or with

63. Perkin, *The Rise of Professional Society*, pp. 119–121.

64. Perkin (ibid., p. 119) appears to argue that the professional ideal was often mistakenly associated with pre-industrial ideas, but he does not emphasise sufficiently the extent to which the professional ethic in society owed its power to the fact that it was an updated version of traditional gentlemanly attributes. See also Gourvish, 'The Rise of the Professions', pp. 34–5.

65. They were also better paid than most industrial or mining managers. See Reader, *Professional Men*, p. 202. As Reader points out, the pay of many professionals had less to do with their actual skills than with their status as gentlemen (p. 203).

66. L.H. Gann and P. Duignan, *The Rulers of British Africa, 1870–1914* (1978), p. 200.

67. As in George and Weedon Grossmith's *Diary of a Nobody*, first published in 1892.

68. See Geoffrey Crossick, ed. *The Lower Middle Class in Britain, 1870–1914* (1977), esp. Crossick's overview essay, pp. 39–46.

69. Rubinstein, 'Education and the Social Origin of British Elites', passim; Perkin, *The Rise of Professional Society*, pp. 87–92.

70. Henry Roseveare, *The Treasury: The Evolution of a British Institution* (1969), Ch. 6. For a view of the whole process see Peter Gowan, 'The Origins of the Administrative Elite', *New Left Review*, 162 (1987).

Britain's overseas responsibilities and possessions. The Foreign Office, and more particularly the diplomatic service, retained thoughout the period a much more aristocratic flavour then other sections of government: applicants for the diplomatic service, for example, had to have private means.[71] The Foreign Office also retained a wider patronage network than was available elsewhere, especially through the consular service which, even in the twentieth century, remained 'a harbour of refuge for retired army officers and for failures whose only recommendation was aristocratic, official or personal influences'.[72]

The gentlemanly class formed the backbone of the Colonial Office[73] and of the administration which ruled India after 1850 and then spread its influence into south-east Asia and into Africa after partition. Most British colonial governors, for instance, 'came from the south-eastern part of England or were educated there' at public school and then perhaps went on to Oxbridge; and they were, generally speaking, the sons of other civil servants, professional men, army officers or – most frequently – clergymen.[74] Their narrow educational background and social origins offered them a code of honour which ensured that governors were 'gentlemen both in the sociological and ethical meaning of the word'.[75] The ordinary district officers were of similar social and cultural backgrounds and, like their leaders, saw their roles as bringing 'law and order' and endowing local elites with the same leadership qualities – and the same educational institutions – as they possessed themselves. They were vigorous proponents of the telegraph, the railway and all the other infrastructual investments without which civilisation – and good careers for the 'sons of gentlemen' – could not be advanced, but they tended to despise business and modern urban life.[76] Their natural

71. Zara S. Steiner, *The Foreign Office and Foreign Policy, 1898–1914* (Cambridge, 1969), p. 21. On the Foreign Office in general see Valerie Cromwell and Zara S. Steiner, 'The Foreign Office Before 1914', in Gillian Sutherland, ed. *Studies in the Growth of Nineteenth-Century Government* (1972); and R.T. Nightingale, 'The Personnel of the British Foreign Office and Diplomatic Service, 1851–1929', *American Political Science Review*, 24 (1930).

72. D.C.M. Platt, *The Cinderella Service* (1971), p. 22.

73. Richard M. Kesner, *Economic Control and Colonial Development: Crown Colony Financial Management in the Age of Joseph Chamberlain* (Oxford, 1981), pp. 53ff.

74. Gann and Duignan, *The Rulers of British Africa*, pp. 174–5. Also, C.A. Hughes and J.F. Nicholson, 'A Provenance of Pro-Consuls: British Colonial Governors, 1900–60', *Jour. Imp. and Comm. Hist.*, 4 (1975).

75. Gann and Duignan, *The Rulers of British Africa*, p. 181.

76. Ibid. pp. 199–200 and p. 53; Cyril Erlich, 'Building and Caretaking: Economic Policy in British Tropical Africa, 1890–1960', *Econ. Hist. Rev.*, 2nd ser. XXVI (1973), pp. 650–1; R.C. Bridges, 'Europeans and East Africans in the Age of Exploration', *Geographical Journal*, CXXXIX (1973), pp. 227–9.

economic links were with the City rather than industry. The Crown Agents, for example, who handled most of the economic transactions between Britain and the colonies on capital account, belonged 'to the social universe of the universities, the great government departments and the clubs', and they operated via an informal, even secretive, network of financial institutions in the City 'on the basis of trust of a kind that could only exist in a society where private business and public administration were linked by informal ties of school, class and clubland.'[77]

THE CITY OF LONDON AND GENTLEMANLY CAPITALISM

Links between the Crown Agents and the City provided one small instance of the fact that, in the evolving world of gentlemanly culture focused on London, in which aristocracy was still an important element, finance – or at least City finance – had a place while industry still lacked one. The City of London had a traditional importance as the financier of aristocratic governments in Britain, with the Bank of England acting as chief intermediary between the two; and the bonds between the world of finance and of politics and power were strengthened by daily contact in the metropolis. As the power of the land declined and gentlemanly capitalism established itself anew, the City maintained its position as banker to governments while evolving in ways which made it the financial headquarters of elite wealth and elevated a part of the City itself into the gentlemanly capitalist sphere.

The gentlemanly capitalist City was to a large extent dominated by the great merchant banking houses which, having acquired vast wealth in commerce, had then graduated to become financiers of British and overseas governments. It was the link with governments which brought the leading houses into the world of power and diplomacy. Through their dealings with government, they also moved into the overlapping world of superior social connections, becoming bankers to the aristocracy and personal friends and intimate advisers of the politically powerful. This position at the centre of elite society was the basis of the prestige Bagehot pointed to as being the hallmark of the most successful banking organisations, a prestige that made them, to some degree, the arbiters of what was or was not

77. Gann and Duignan, *The Rulers of British Africa*, p. 69.

acceptable in the City. Many, though not all, of these great houses were represented on the Court of the Bank of England, the official channel of communication between governments and City, which supplemented the more informal relationships that existed between merchant banker and politician.

At its most fruitful, City life combined great wealth with freedom from continuous work. 'Banking', as Bagehot put it, 'is a watchful, but it is not a laborious trade'; it allowed, he thought, for the 'educated refinement' which had characterised the life of many London private bankers.[78] The private banks were dying fast after 1870, swallowed by the joint stocks: but their leaders often lived on as directors of the larger banks[79] and Bagehot's observation was true also of the great merchant banking families like the Rothschilds, Barings and Grenfells. Peerages came to many of these City dynasties much sooner than to industrialists and they often lived, and worked, in a style appropriate to great landed wealth.[80] The leading figures in the banking world were not idle but they operated in a world where leisure was often difficult to distinguish from work. A new recruit to the London house of Morgan wrote to tell Alfred Milner that 'the City does not involve long hours or much fatigue. But it means incessant presence and attention. You never know when you may be called upon'.[81] He was describing a world which, like that of high politics, depended as heavily upon networks of social intercourse as it did upon formal structures. The City magnate operated in an intricate world where business, social life and political intrigue all over-lapped,[82] one where these activities were so entwined that the members of great City families who were not involved directly in the business could nonetheless bring great benefits to it because of the information they gathered and the connections they forged.

78. Bagehot, 'Lombard St.', pp. 183–4 For an insight into the business of a private bank, Williams, Deacon & Co., which survived into the late nineteenth century see E.J.T. Ancaster, '20 Birchin Lane, London. Mr. Newman's Entrance, 1883', *The Royal Bank of Scotland Review*, No. 155 (1987).

79. Y. Cassis, 'Management and Strategy in the English Joint-Stock Banks, 1890–1914', *Bus. Hist.*, XXVII (1985), pp. 302–4.

80. Ronald Palin, *Rothschild Relish*, (1970), pp. 40–2, 63.

81. The writer was Dawkins, fresh from the colonial service. See Kathleen Burk, *Morgan Grenfell: The Biography of a Merchant Bank, 1838–1988* (Oxford, 1989), p. 58.

82. The friendship between Natty Rothschild and Lord Randolph Churchill, although unusually intense, is illustrative of the intimacy of some of these relationships. R.F. Foster, *Lord Randolph Churchill: A Political Life* (Oxford, 1981), pp. 30, 194–5, 277, 290–1, 331, 375, 395. This is a good point at which to say how much our understanding of the interrelations between finance and politics has been illuminated by Fritz Stern, *Gold and Iron: Bismarck, Bleichröder and the Building of the German Empire* (New York, 1977).

Many of the leading City figures were Jewish in origin, members of families which had been attracted to London because of its pivotal position in world finance. The extended families of the Jewish bankers stretched across the globe, giving them a superb information network and also providing them, *in extremis*, with extensive lines of credit. The City was, simultaneously, both a British institution and a cosmopolitan one. The great Jewish families epitomised this duality, combining country houses, sons at Eton and Harrow, and outspoken loyalty to the crown and the empire with a global spread of personal and economic connections which stretched well beyond the limits of formal British influence. In addition, close relationships among the ramifying cousinhood meant that there was a better chance of finding the new entrepreneurial talent necessary to the vitality of the houses across the generations. This left others free to devote themselves to the artistic life, to politics or to sport, or to keeping the family in the social swim by entertaining royalty.[83]

The employees of the great were frequently gentlemen themselves, and their working hours could be even shorter than Hilaire Belloc's celebrated Peter Giles who toiled

> All day long from 10 till 4;
> For half the year or even more;
> With but an hour or two to spend;
> At luncheon with a city friend.[84]

Leisure came not simply from the wealth generated by the principal bankers but from the nature of their business in the City, which was conducted among a small, close-knit group of people who shared a similar public-school education and life-style,[85] and whose gentlemanly code allowed transactions to be entered into and honoured, informally, without the need for elaborate bureaucracy.[86] Like the

83. The Rothschilds obviously fit this pattern to some degree, but a more spectacular example is provided by the Sassoon dynasty. See Stanley Jackson, *The Sassoons: Portrait of a Dynasty* (1989).

84. From *Cautionary Verses*, first published together in 1940 but written before World War I. Compare this with George Littlehales, a senior manager at Rothschilds in the 1920s, who lived too far away to be expected to come in regularly: 'When he did turn up it was usually about noon. He would spend the next hour prodding his men into greater diligence, at one o'clock he went to lunch and at 2.30 he caught his train home from Liverpool St.'. Palin, *Rothschild Relish*, p. 91. See also Chapman, *The Rise of Merchant Banking*, p. 169.

85. Youssef Cassis, *La City de Londres, 1870–1914* (Paris, 1987), pp. 154ff; also idem, *Les Banquiers de la City*, Ch. VII.

86. See the shrewd comments of Palin, *Rothschild Relish*, on Colonel Scott of the cashier's department at Rothschild's (p. 49). For a wider viewpoint see also Michael Lisle-Williams, 'Beyond the Market: the Survival of Family Capitalism in English Merchant Banks', *Brit. Jour. Soc.*, XXXV (1984).

higher professions, the nature of much City business at this level was personal rather than mechanical and it allowed the amateur spirit full play.[87]

At the beginning of the period, although land and City could even then be seen as 'dividing . . . the social empire of the kingdom between them',[88] the aristocracy still thought of intermarriage as an occasional irksome necessity.[89] By the 1890s, the great merchant bankers not only shared a similar educational background with aristocrats and leading professionals but also were regularly intermarrying with the landed interest and, at the highest social levels, the great financiers and the aristocrats had begun to merge.[90] There is considerable truth in the contemporary view that

> 'The great merchant banker of today is an English gentleman of the finished type. He is possibly a peer, and an active partner in a great City firm: if he is not a peer, the chances are he is a member of the House of Commons. He is a man of wide culture . . . . There is in fact but one standard of 'social position' in England and it is that which is formed by the blending of the plutocratic and the aristocratic element.[91]

Certainly, 'Society', which acted as an upper-class information network as well as conferring social distinction on its members, had widened considerably beyond its original aristocratic limits by 1880, and the weightier City men were by then an intrinsic part of the system.[92]

87. For an example see Arncaster, '20 Birchin Lane, London', p. 41.

88. The quotation is from *The Book of Snobs*, first printed in Punch in the late 1840s. See *The Works of William Makepeace Thackeray*, Vol. XIV (1884), p. 41.

89. 'It used to be the custom of some very old-fashioned clubs in this city, when a gentleman asked for change for a guinea, always to bring it to him in washed silver: that which had passed immediately out of the hands of the vulgar being considered 'as too coarse to soil a gentleman's fingers'. So, when the City Snob's money has been washed during a generation or so; has been washed into estates, and woods, and castles, and town-mansions, it is allowed to pass current as real aristocratic coin' (ibid. pp. 42–3).

90. Y. Cassis, 'Bankers and English Society in the Late Nineteenth Century', *Econ. Hist. Rev.*, 2nd ser. XXXVIII (1985); idem, *Les Banquiers de la City*, Ch. VI.

91. T.H.S. Escott, *England: Its People, Polity and Pursuits* (1885), pp. 314–5.

92. On the importance of Society see the excellent book by Leonore Davidoff, *The Best Circles: Society, Etiquette and the Season*, (1973), pp. 36–7 and Ch. V. Society's constituents in the 1880s were listed by a contemporary as royalty, the aristocracy, diplomats, the representatives of high finance, 'Turf and Stock Exchange', judges, lawyers and other eminent professional men including politicians and artists. The only figure with any direct contact with industry who received a mention was Joseph Chamberlain. See [T.H.S. Escott], *Society in London: By a Foreign Resident* (5th edn, 1885). Escott made particular note of the importance of financial wealth and the links between City figures such as the Rothschilds and senior politicians (pp. 86–7, 90).

The great majority of those who worked in the City were not a part of the web of gentlemanly connection any more than the majority of those who worked in the professions were a part of it. The Stock Exchange, run by former public schoolboys in a club-like atmosphere and ruled by gentlemanly codes of behaviour, was rising in the social scale by this time. Its prestige was enhanced by the informality of its proceedings and by the fact that business could be discussed 'effectively and lucratively round dinner tables or at a shoot'.[93] On the other hand, even such an important group as the managers of the large and growing joint-stock banks, whose work was characterised as bureaucratic and time-consuming, failed to qualify as gentlemen at all and this was emphasised by their exclusion from the Court of the Bank of England, which was dominated by the merchant bankers.[94] Even the latter were not an homogeneous or unchanging group by any means. Among those who established a permanent presence in the later nineteenth century were new firms, such as Kleinworts and Schroders, whose business ethics and life-style had more in common with northern industrialists than with the banking aristocracy and who disliked the Bank of England and its coteries. This new wave of immigrants from the continent made large inroads into the bill-acceptance business of the established merchant bankers though, unlike the Anglo-American invaders, Morgans, they made little impact on the much more lucrative and prestigious business of issuing stocks and bonds.[95]

The rise of new wealth is a reminder of the dynamic nature of the Victorian and Edwardian City, which had to change continuously in order to retain London's leading position in the world economy.[96] City wealth was often precarious: firms with an established reputation

93. W.J. Reader, *A House in the City: A Study of the City and the Stock Exchange based on Records of Foster and Braithwaite, 1825–1975* (1979) p. 82; Cassis, *La City de Londres*, pp. 167–70.

94. Cassis, 'Management and Strategy', pp. 309–10. It should be noted that, the Rothschilds apart, only three firms of Jewish origin which had been thoroughly anglicised had representatives on the Bank of England's directorate.

95. Chapman, *The Rise of Merchant Banking*, pp. 121–4 and Ch. 10; idem, 'Aristocracy and Meritocracy in Merchant Banking', *Brit. Jour. Soc.*, XXXVII (1986); Stephanie Diaper, 'Merchant Banking Growth in the Second Half of the Nineteenth Century', *Revue internationale d'histoire de la banque*, 34–5 (1987). On Morgan's see Burk, *Morgan Grenfell*, Ch. 2. Chapman makes much of the fact that Kleinworts had far more capital in the business by 1900 than, for example, Rothschilds. The acceptance business depended crucially upon capital, but issues depended on prestige. The fact that firms like Rothschilds and Morgans could do so much business on so little capital is a sign of their key role as gentlemanly capitalists. See Burk, *Morgan Grenfell*, pp. 67–8, 71–2.

96. R.C. Michie, 'Dunn, Fischer and Co. in the City of London', *Bus. Hist.*, XXX (1988).

and great prestige in the Square Mile could falter or even fail suddenly if a partner decided to withdraw his capital, if the business fell into the hands of ineffective or uninterested sons, or if there was no one to inherit.[97] Even the mighty could stumble, as the Baring Crisis of 1890 clearly demonstrates. The same process of change also raised new wealth and could catapult individuals or firms into great prominence with amazing speed. The City was so much a part of the life of London's elites by the late nineteenth century that it was easy for spectacular wealth to make an impact socially.[98] But to move into the highest circles, where society and politics overlapped, it was insufficient simply to consume conspicuously in the style of Julius Wernher, the South African mining magnate.[99] Needed also were friends in high places and the willingness and the ability to do the state some service, perhaps by using influence or lending money in politically sensitive arenas like the Middle East, when the usual intermediaries, like the Rothschilds, did not care to involve themselves – both outstanding factors in the meteoric rise of Ernest Cassell and the Sassoons to prestige and authority around the turn of the century.[100]

Taking the City as a whole, it would be fair to describe it in 1850 as 'an intimate club of familiar people undertaking easily recognisable tasks', whereas by 1900 it had grown spectacularly and was populated mainly by 'hordes of specialists each making out their own peculiar contribution to an increasingly complex process' that few understood in the round.[101] Most of the 40,000 firms which populated the City around the turn of the century had a short life, and they and their 350,000 employees worked and lived in an atmosphere with which

97. M.J. Daunton, 'Inheritance and Succession in the City of London in the Nineteenth Century', *Bus. Hist.*, XXX (1988), and idem, 'Firm and Family in the City of London in the Nineteenth Century: the Case of F.G. Dalgety', *Historical Research*, 148 (1989).

98. Escott pointed to the link in Society between sport, gambling and the City: 'When it is not the Turf, it is the Stock Exchange, and perhaps this is one reason why the City plays so large a part in the arrangements of the West End'. See *Society in London*, pp. 117–18.

99. Prof. Perkin argues as if all forms of new wealth were equally conspicuous in society, though his own evidence shows how important finance was. He also does not distinguish between those, like Wernher, who were noticeable and those who were powerful. See *The Rise of Professional Society*, esp. pp. 63–76. For an interesting study of new wealth in Edwardian Britain see Jamie Camplin, *The Rise of the Plutocrats: Wealth and Power in Edwardian England* (1978).

100. Pat Thane, 'Financiers and the British State: the Case of Sir Ernest Cassell', *Bus. Hist.*, XXVII (1986). See also Jackson, *The Sassoons*, pp. 90–1.

101. Michie, 'Dunn, Fischer and Co.', esp. p. 196.

any small industrialist would have been familiar. These were not conditions which conduced to a gentlemanly life or which attracted social honours and prestige. But the wide range of occupations did mean that the City of London housed a broad spectrum of society from aristocrats at one end to £100-a-year clerks at the other; through its vast chain of institutions, it linked the powerful with the marginal and even with the shady and dishonourable.[102] Moreover, through its enormous commercial sector, the City provided a connection between domestic and international economic life and between high finance on the one side and industry on the other. It was this diversity of institutions, practices and ideas which allowed the few who could speak for the City to claim, with some plausibility, that it was representative of national interests and that what was good for the Square Mile was necessarily good for Britain.

Although the composition of the City changed over time and the complexity of its operations increased, at the end of the period it was still led by a small cohesive elite, centred on the Bank of England, which was wedged firmly into the British 'establishment' in the late nineteenth century.[103] The power of this elite was also growing. Before the last quarter of the nineteenth century the bankers were an adjunct to aristocratic control; after 1914 financial power was clearly more potent than that of the land. The period 1880 to 1914 was one of precarious equipose, when the power of finance, growing increasingly cosmopolitan, reached a transitory equality with that of land, whose agricultural base was being slowly undermined by the free trade internationalism on which the City flourished.[104]

102. On this theme see, Dilwyn Porter, '"A Trusted Guide to the Investing Public": Harry Marks and the *Financial News*, 1884–1916', *Bus. Hist.*, XXVII (1986). City corruption, involving minor members of the aristocracy, was a major theme in Anthony Trollope's novel, *The Way We Live Now*, first published in 1875. Overseas finance was sometimes raised by eccentric aristocrats who could coax money from the gentlemanly classes to invest in companies run by characters whom the well-bred would never acknowledge socially. Richard Davenport-Hines and Jean Jacques van-Helten, 'Edgar Vincent, Viscount D'Abernon, and the Eastern Investment Company in London, Constantinople and Johannesburg', *Bus. Hist.*, XXVII (1986).

103. For further interesting light on the social role of the City in the late nineteenth and early twentieth centuries, see Y. Cassis, 'Merchant Banks and City Aristocracy', *British Journal of Sociology*, XXXIX (1988), pp. 114–19; S.D. Chapman, 'Reply to Youssef Cassis', ibid. pp. 121–5; and S.D. Chapman, *Merchant Enterprise in Britain: From the Industrial Revolution to World War I* (Cambridge, 1992).

104. José Harris and Pat Thane, 'British and European Bankers, 1880–1914: an "Aristocratic Bourgeoisie"?', in Pat Thane, Geoffrey Crossick and Roderick Floud, eds. *The Power of the Past: Essays for Eric Hobsbawm* (1984), p. 228.

INDUSTRY, PROVINCIALISM AND POWER

The representatives of industry did not achieve the same degree of prestige and power in the period before World War I.[105] Although the number of 'self-made men' was diminishing and there was a strong hereditary element in business by 1914, the average manufacturer was too small and too provincial (at a time when power was beginning to focus even more strongly on London)[106] to make an impact at the centre.[107] Among this class in the regions there could still be found a strong tradition of hostility to the established Church, landed monopoly and royalty, and grave misgivings about London-based finance. Even in these circles mere 'money-grubbing' was frowned upon and there was a growing emphasis upon the importance of service to the community and of the value of cultural achievement, which provided a bridge between industrialists and gentlemanly life-styles.[108] Among the wealthiest manufacturers, the tendency to conform to gentlemanly norms of conduct was stronger. Where firms were bigger than average, as in steel, wealth was more concentrated and the public school and Oxbridge influence was felt early:[109] indeed, some large firms began to acquire gentlemanly directors in the manner of joint-stock banks.[110] It has been claimed that if manufacturers often bought land they usually acquired only enough to establish themselves in a good house with a decent park. However, new evidence shows that the wealthiest at least bought substantial quantities of land with the idea of improving their status or founding a dynasty: only the childless seemed uninterested in land purchase.[111] But, even among the super-

105. Donald Coleman and Christine McLeod, 'Attitudes to New Techniques: British Businessmen, 1800–1850', *Econ. Hist. Rev.*, 2nd ser. XXXIX (1986), p. 609.

106. David J. Jeremy, 'Anatomy of the British Business Élite, 1860–1980', *Bus. Hist.*, XXVI (1984), Table 9, p. 19.

107. For example, hosiers, who were in a small-scale, extremely competitive business, were less likely to have privileged backgrounds or to obtain the 'right' education. See Charlotte Erikson, *British Industrialists: Steel and Hosiery, 1850–1950* (Cambridge, 1959), Ch. IV.

108. Business success was often linked with nobility of character by Smiles. In her famous novel, *The Manchester Man* (1876), Mrs Linnaeus Banks went further than this. The hero, Jabez Clegg, although self-made, turns out to be a lost member of a business family with long-standing gentlemanly connections who remind him that there is more to life than work.

109. Erikson, *British Industrialists*, Ch. II.

110. D.C. Coleman, 'Gentlemen and Players', *Econ. Hist. Rev.*, 2nd ser. XXVI (1973).

111. Nineteenth-century land purchases by non-aristocratic buyers is a complex subject. W.D. Rubinstein, 'New Men of Wealth and the Purchase of Land in the Nineteenth Century', *Past and Present*, 92 (1981), argues that land was too expensive for most non-landed wealthy to buy in quantity. Lawrence Stone and Jeanne C.

rich, most had no wider ambitions than to concentrate their political and social talents on their localities.[112] So provincial were they – even the far from negligible number who were Anglican, Tory and deeply respectful of aristocracy – [113] that when manufacturing wealth did begin to multiply rapidly after 1860 and to become more politically visible, gentlemanly governments found it hard to assimilate them. When the question of honours for industrialists was seriously broached in the 1880s, the Liberal government of the day reacted 'almost as if they were talking about some remote, foreign tribe which they believed to be important but of whose intentions they were suspicious and which they were uncertain how to treat'[114].

Gladstone's hesitations about granting peerages to cotton capitalists reflected the assumption that what was quintessentially 'English', what was nationally regarded as significant or otherwise, was something that gentlemen had a right and duty to define.[115] Matthew Arnold's famous proposal for a common public-school education for

---

Fawtier Stone go further in *An Open Elite? England, 1540–1880* (abridged edn, Oxford, 1986), and claim that industrialists did not buy land because the status of industry was so low and they knew that they would not be accepted in 'society'. They also admit, however, that industrialists may not have wished to enter 'society' (pp. 195–6). The contrary case has recently been put by F.M.L. Thompson, 'Life after Death: How Successful Nineteenth-Century Businessmen Disposed of their Fortunes', *Econ. Hist. Rev.*, 2nd ser. XLIII, (1990). For further insights see idem, 'English Landed Society in the Nineteenth Century', in Thane, Crossick and Floud, *The Power of the Past*, pp. 209–11; David Spring and Eileen Spring, 'Social Mobility and the English Landed Elite', *Canadian Journal of History*, XXI, 3 (1986); and R.C. Michie, 'Income, Expenditure and Investment of a Victorian Millionaire: Lord Overstone, 1823–1883', *Bull. Inst. Hist. Research*, LVII (1985), pp. 67–8. Rubinstein's latest views on this question can be found in 'Gentlemen, Capitalism and British Industry, 1820–1914', *Past and Present*, 132 (1991). pp. 159–64. For a good example of localism see Anthony Howe, *The Cotton Masters, 1830–1860* (Oxford 1984), pp. 252–4.

112. For some insight into provincial industrial culture and political life see A.J. Kidd and K.W. Roberts, eds. *City, Class and Culture: Studies of Cultural Production and Social Policy in Victorian Manchester* (Manchester, 1985); D. Smith, *Conflict and Compromise: Class Formation in English Society, 1830–1914* (1982); also John Garrard, *Leadership and Power in Victorian Industrial Towns, 1830–80* (Manchester, 1983). Some of the differences between provincial industrialism and gentlemanly culture were expressed through the creation of the 'redbrick' universities at the turn of the century. The best introduction to this development is M. Sanderson, 'The English Civic Universities and the 'Industrial Spirit', 1870–1914', *Historical Research*, 144 (1988).

113. There was a startlingly high proportion of men of Anglican religious faith among the very wealthy. See Rubinstein, *Men of Property*, Ch. V. For Tory paternalism among cotton manufacturers see Patrick Joyce, *Work, Society and Politics: The Culture of the Factory in Later Victorian England* (1980), Ch. 6, and n.52 above.

114. Bourne, *Patronage and Society*, p. 46. See also H.J. Hanham, 'The Sale of Honours in Late Victorian England', *Victorian Studies*, III (1960).

115. Phillip Dodd, 'Englishness and the National Culture', in Robert Colls and Phillip Dodd, eds. *Englishness: Politics and Culture, 1880–1920* (1986).

the children of both gentlemen and the industrially wealthy was a serious attempt to create a unified bourgeois elite in the face of aristocratic decline. However, his greatest fear was that power would fall into the hands of the 'Philistines' of industrialism, and his proposals were intended to ensure that the cultural norms of industrialism would give way to gentlemanly ones. Gentlemen ought to learn some science and be given some understanding of the world of trade, but industrialists were expected to embrace 'sweetness and light', as currently defined in the public schools and ancient universities, and, more importantly, to learn that leadership was a different and far more elevated art than that of mere money-making.[116]

GENTLEMANLY CAPITALISM AND POLITICS

Direct aristocratic influence upon high politics also declined before 1914. In mid-century, the aristocracy's command of the House of Commons was still overwhelming: even among the Liberals, the party in which radicalism found a home, nearly half of all the members of parliament (MPs) who sat in the House between 1859 and 1874 were either large landowners or 'gentlemen of leisure'.[117] But, by 1914, the number of MPs with non-landed economic *interests* had risen very rapidly. Landowning ceased to be the majority interest in the House among both parties, as is illustrated by the figures available for the *occupations* of members in 1914 and by the prominence of professional men (mainly lawyers), manufacturers and other businessmen by that time (see Tables 3.5 and 3.6).

116. Reader, *Professional Men*, p. 113. In many ways, Arnold's ideal type was the new professional class of the south-east of England. He was aware of the development of 'a large class of gentlemen in the professions, the services, literature, politics – and a good contingent is now added from business also. This large class, not of the nobility but with the accomplishments and taste of an upper class, is something peculiar to England'. Arnold was speaking at the time at the Royal Institution in London and felt that, 'of this class I may probably assume that my present audience is in large manner composed'. Super, *The Complete Prose Works of Matthew Arnold*, Vol. II, pp. 88–9. See also F.G. Walcott, *The Origins of Culture and Anarchy: Matthew Arnold and Popular Education in England* (1970), esp. p. 45.

117. John Vincent, *The Formation of the British Liberal Party, 1857–68* (1976), p. 3. When Lord Derby joined the Cabinet in 1882, he noted that nearly all his colleagues were 'large' or 'moderate-sized landowners' or 'connected with the Whig aristocracy' or with the 'landowning class'; he was satisfied that 'it would be difficult to find a Cabinet with less admixture of anything that in France would be called democracy'. Quoted in Marvin Swartz, *The Politics of British Foreign Policy in the Age of Disraeli and Gladstone* (1985), p. 145.

Even in mid-century, the Tory Party had a greater share of aristocratic MPs than the Liberals, and the landed interest's adherence to the right in British politics became stronger over time. Simultaneously, the south, and especially the south-east, of England hardened its support for Conservatism.[118] The large, non-industrial middle class in London and the Home Counties, much of it directly connected with City finance, had a dominating influence over its non-unionised and more deferential workforce; it was their brand of gentlemanly capitalism which shaped the Conservative Party and ensured that the aristocracy still had a prominent role to play at the highest levels of politics.[119] Liberal strength increased the further north one travelled[120] and rested to a large degree on the industrial towns, where provincial manufacturers and workers often shared a hostility to gentlemanly culture and the status quo it represented. Not surprisingly, manufacturing interests were always larger among Liberal MPs than among Tories (Appendix One).

There is no doubt, though, that after 1870 there was some drift of all business interests, not just landed ones, towards the Conservative Party. The extension of the franchise in 1867 and 1884 roused fears for property in general and these were confirmed by the growth of trade unionism and of anti-capitalist, as well as anti-aristocratic, ideas

---

118. On the emergence of regional voting patterns and the growing Conservatism of the south-east see Pelling, *Social Geography*, Chs. 2 and 3; Hanham, *Elections and Party Management*, pp. 225–7; T.J. Nossiter, *Influence, Opinion, and Political Idioms in Reformed England: Case Studies from the North-East, 1832–74* (Brighton, 1975), pp. 185–92; J.P.D. Dunbabin, 'British Elections in the Nineteenth and Twentieth Centuries: a Regional Approach', *Eng. Hist. Rev.*, XCV (1980); Martin Pugh, *The Making of Modern British Politics, 1867–1939* (1982), Chs. 3 and Table 3:1, p. 43.

119. Lord Salisbury was impressed by the power of what he called 'Villa Toryism'. Peter Marsh, *The Discipline of Popular Government: Lord Salisbury's Domestic Statecraft, 1881–1902* (Brighton, 1978), p. 36.

120. This is clear from the work of Nossiter, Dunbabin and Pelling cited in n. 118, and from Pugh, *The Making of Modern Politics, 1867–1939*, p. 64. The two anomalies as far as the Liberals were concerned were the west Midlands after 1886 – largely explained in relation to Joseph Chamberlain – and Lancashire, where a working-class electorate showed a surprisingly strong tendency to vote Conservative until, as one might expect, the free trade issue pushed them towards Liberalism in 1906. Lancashire Toryism was greatly influenced by the reaction of Protestant locals to Irish Catholic immigrants. This was in part an economic issue since the Irish were seen to be a threat to wages and employment in the indigenous community. In addition, Joyce has recently emphasised the extent to which Toryism might reflect the politics of a particularly dominant cotton master who often had the same paternalist relationship towards his workforce as the landed aristocracy had, and who also received the same kind of loyal support. On Lancashire politics in general see Pelling, *Social Geography*, Ch. 12, and P.F. Clarke, *Lancashire and the New Liberalism*, (Cambridge, 1971). On the influence of employers on political choice in certain areas see Patrick Joyce, 'The Factory Politics of Lancashire in the Later Nineteenth Century', *Hist. Jour.*, XVIII (1975).

among working men. Gladstone's Irish legislation in the 1880s and his subsequent conversion to Home Rule[121] also offended the remaining Whig aristocrats within the Liberal Party and alarmed business interests, which feared the disintegration of the empire and a wholesale attack on property rights. Among MPs with City credentials, Liberalism finally went out of favour in the 1880s (Table 3.6); those with financial interests who still adhered to Liberalism after this time tended to have their economic roots in the provinces rather than in London.[122] The drift of business and landed interests away from Liberalism forced the party into a more radical stance in order to appeal to the new mass electorate in the provinces.[123] The sharpness of the attack on land and the 'unearned increment' in Chamberlain's Unauthorised Programme of the 1880s – which was aimed at City wealth as well as at the aristocracy[124] – and in the Newcastle Programme a decade later reflects this. It also represents a determined attempt to focus on non-industrial targets in order to keep the Liberal electorate united, and to divert attention from direct conflicts between workers and manufacturing interests in the Liberal Party's provincial strongholds.[125]

Although the Liberals remained the favoured party of the manufacturing interest up to 1914, the drift to Conservatism among them was quite marked (Table 3.6) and was accentuated by the disputes over protectionism after 1880, as we shall see. The spread of economic interests across the parties by 1914 was such that it was impossible to

121. For the effects of Irish policy on English political economy see T.W. Heyck, 'Home Rule, Radicalism and the Liberal Party, 1886–95', *Jour. Brit. Stud.*, XXIII (1974); and Pugh, *The Making of Modern Politics*, pp. 33–9.

122. Cassis, *La City de Londres*, Table 18, p. 171, for the political affiliations of banker MPs after 1892; also G.R. Searle, 'The Edwardian Liberal Party and Business', *Eng. Hist. Rev.*, XCVIII (1983), pp. 44–6.

123. The substantial literature on the anti-privilege elements in liberalism and the character of its electorate and policies includes: Nossiter, *Influence, Opinion and Political Idioms in Reformed England*, esp. Ch. 10; J.R. Vincent, *Pollbooks: How Victorians Voted* (Cambridge 1967), esp. pp. 15ff; J. Chamberlain, et al., *The Radical Programme* (ed. D. Hamer, Brighton, 1971), esp. the introduction; Michael Barker, *Gladstone and Radicalism: The Reconstruction of Liberal Policy in Britain, 1885–94* (Brighton, 1975); Harold Perkin, 'Land Reform and Class Conflict in Victorian Britain', in his *The Structured Crowd: Essays in English Social History* (Brighton, 1981), Ch. 7; Bentley B. Gilbert, 'David Lloyd George: Land, the Budget and Social Reform', *American Historical Review*, LXXXI (1976); idem, 'David Lloyd George: the Reform of British Landholding and the Budget of 1914', *Hist. Jour.*, XXI (1978); Avner Offer, *Property and Politics: 1870–1914, Landownership, Law, Ideology and Urban Development in England* (Cambridge, 1981), Chs. 20–3; Searle, 'The Edwardian Liberal Party and Business', pp. 47–8. On the economic theory behind the anti-land movement after 1870 see Avner Offer, 'Ricardo's Paradox and the Movement of Rent in England, c. 1870–1910', *Econ. Hist. Rev.*, 2nd ser. XXXIII (1980).

124. Perkin, *The Structured Crowd*, 117–18.

125. Pugh, *The Making of Modern Politics*, p. 32.

speak of either as 'representing' industry. Moreover, MPs from constituencies in manufacturing areas often saw themselves as representing their locality rather than attempting to make a mark on the national stage. Even in the Liberal Party, leadership almost automatically devolved on the remaining gentlemanly capitalists and the professional politicians, and the direct influence of the business element was limited.[126] Liberalism had not become identified with industry to quite the extent that the Conservative Party had become the political arm of the aristocracy, the City and the gentlemanly capitalism of the south-east.

Aristocratic power was in steady decline during this period,[127] and what authority it still exerted in 1914 was dependent upon its role within a wider gentlemanly capitalist culture which had grown dramatically over the previous 50 years. Industry and industrialists did not play starring roles in the evolution of this new ideology of gentlemanliness, nor did they have the same degree of control over political power which the aristocrats, the City financiers and the professional classes of London and the Home Counties possessed. This is not to say that they had been suborned by some aristocratic ideal of ruralism and leisure, as has been claimed.[128] Small scale and indelibly provincial as they were, most industrialists in Britain were untouched by the aristocratic ideal. As Rubinstein has expressed it:

> In Britain, the net effect of the industrial revolution was systematically to advantage the older and more conservative, rather than the newer and most radical, sectors of the British wealth structure – above all the great landowners and the bankers and merchants of the City of London, rather than the manufacturers and industrialists, a circumstance which had the most profound effects on the evolution of British society and its class system.[129]

126. Searle, 'The Edwardian Liberal Party and Business', p. 46. Also Douglas Farnie, 'The Structure of the British Cotton Textile Industry, 1846–1914', in Akio Okochi and Shin-Ichi Yonekawa, eds. *The Textile Industry and Its Business Climate* (Tokyo, 1982), p. 71.

127. The loss of aristocratic power over local government in industrial areas was more marked than at the national level. On local government, see J.M. Lee, *Social Leaders and Public Persons: A Study of County Government since 1888* (Oxford, 1963), Pts. I and II. Aristocrats sometimes made spirited attempts to retain influence in urban areas where they were extensive property owners. See Cannadine, *Lands and Landlords*, passim.

128. By Weiner, in *English Culture and the Decline of the Industrial Spirit*, passim.

129. W.D. Rubinstein, 'Entrepreneurial Effort and Entrepreneurial Success: Peak Wealth-Holding in Three Societies, 1850–1930', *Bus. Hist.*, XXV (1983), p. 17. See also Sidney Pollard, *Britain's Prime and Britain's Decline: The British Economy, 1870–1914* (1989), pp. 227–35.

Cobden had thought of the coming of Free Trade as the prelude to the triumph of industrialism in Britain. But Cobdenite ideologies could not prevail because his chosen people did not have sufficient wealth and influence to make them dominant either economically or ideologically. Suitably modified, the aristocratic ideal survived because it was adopted and supported by the gentlemanly class which arose from the service sector in the nineteenth century and proved to be the most successful and dynamic element in British economic life between 1850 and 1914.[130]

APPENDIX ONE: ECONOMIC INTERESTS AND OCCUPATIONS OF MEMBERS OF PARLIAMENT, 1868–1914

The economic interests of MPs on both sides of the House are given in Table 3.5. 'Professional service' consists mainly of lawyers but also newspaper proprietors. Brewing is subsumed under manufacturing; merchants are included with commerce and finance. The shift from landed (and military) interests is marked.

MPs could, and often did, have more than one economic interest, so the number of interests is greater than the numbers of MPs.

One way of gauging the extent to which a particular economic interest was stronger in one party than in another is by using the 'associative index' developed by Perkin, which counteracts the influences of electoral swing upon the share of different interests in parliament. An index of the strength of particular interests in the Liberal Party can be found by using the following formula:

130. Rubinstein's methods of assessing wealth-holding and the conclusions he has drawn from his evidence have been sharply criticised recently by N.J. Morgan and M.S. Moss, 'Listing the Wealthy in Scotland', *Bull. Inst. Hist. Research*, LIX (1986), and by B. English, 'Probate Valuations and the Death Duty Registers', ibid. LVIII (1984). Their reservations are summarised in M.J. Daunton, ' "Gentlemanly Capitalism" and British Industry 1820–1914', *Past and Present*, 122 (1989), pp. 128–9. Rubinstein's response, reasserting his position in debate with Daunton, is in *Past and Present*, 132 (1991). In reply, Daunton argues that, even if Rubinstein is correct about wealth distribution, he assumes too easily that wealth confers power. 'It does not necessarily follow that the financial and commercial middle classes dominated the formation of economic policy because they left large fortunes and paid more income tax' (ibid. p. 182). We entirely agree that wealth, power and status are related in complex ways: it is precisely for this reason that we have suggested the concept of gentlemanly capitalism to explain why some forms of capitalist wealth confer more prestige and authority on their owners than do others.

$$\frac{\text{Liberal members of interest}}{\text{Conservative members of interest}} \times \frac{\text{Conservative MPs}}{\text{Liberal MPs}}$$

Any resulting number above 1.0, for example, would indicate that, at any particular time, the Liberal share of the interest was greater than the Liberal share of the MPs of the two parties and vice versa. This formula produces the result shown in Table 3.6.

Table 3.5 Economic interests of MPs; 1868–1910 (per cent for each party)

	1868		1892		1910 (Jan)	
	Lib	Con	Lib	Con	Lib	Con
Landowning	26.1	45.9	9.0	24.1	7.2	21.6
Military service	6.9	13.6	1.8	8.6	2.6	9.5
Finance, commerce	16.4	10.3	16.5	22.5	16.9	20.9
Professional service	17.3	9.4	29.5	18.3	28.5	16.1
Manufacturing	12.0	4.4	24.8	12.1	27.3	20.1
Transport	13.0	13.6	8.9	10.5	9.5	8.7

Sources: J.A. Thomas, *The House of Commons, 1832–1901: A Study of its Economic and Financial Character* (Cardiff, 1939); idem, *The House of Commons, 1906–1911: An Analysis of its Economic and Social Character* (Cardiff, 1958).

Table 3.6 Liberal MPs: associative index, 1868–1910

	1868	1880	1892	1900	1906	1910*
Landowners	0.66	0.54	0.36	0.44	0.48	0.30
Military service	0.59	0.46	0.20	0.27	0.32	0.25
Finance and commerce	1.86	0.92	0.71	0.58	0.75	0.73
Transport services	1.11	1.06	0.81	0.97	0.66	0.99
Merchants	3.57	2.45	2.26	1.42	2.22	2.02
Professional services	2.14	1.99	1.58	1.61	1.97	1.52
Manufacturing	3.19	2.10	1.97	1.69	1.25	1.22

* The election of January 1910 only.

Sources: As Table 3.5, and Harold Perkin, *The Structured Crowd: Essays in English Social History* (Brighton, 1981), pp. 128–31.

Table 3.6 clearly shows the predominance of Conservatism among landowners, those with military interests, and in finance and commerce as early as 1880. It also illustrates the drift of manufacturing interests and merchants towards Conservatism after 1868.

Interests are unsatisfactory as indices of economic alignment because they are not weighted: landowners with £10,000 per annum in farm rents and £500 in an investment trust would register two interests but they are hardly comparable. So it is useful to supplement the interest tables with information on occupations. Unfortunately, this information is scarce: the only usable table, for 1914, is reproduced as Table 3.7.

Table 3.7 Occupations of members of parliament, 1914 (per cent share in each party)

	Unionist	Liberal
Landowning	22.1	6.1
Military and government service	20.8	9.1
Professional services	34.0	42.1
(of which, lawyers)	(26.7)	(26.9)
Commerce and finance	13.2	15.5
Industry	9.9	24.2
Working men	–	3.0

Source: J. Ramsden, *The Age of Balfour and Baldwin, 1902–1940* (1978), Table 5.1, pp. 98–9. The table does not include the occupations of all MPs, some of which are unknown. Merchants are included in Commerce and finance. Industry includes building and brewing.

Table 3.7 does show the concentrations of landed wealth and of military personnel in the Conservative and Unionist Party and also the continued prominence of manufacturers among the Liberals. But if the table of economic interests perhaps overstresses the importance of finance, the occupational table probably underrates it. Few MPs were financiers but very many had substantial financial holdings.

CHAPTER FOUR

Gentlemanly Capitalism and Economic Policy: City, Government and the 'National Interest', 1850–1914

In previous chapters we have tried to show that, as the wealth, cultural standing and political authority of the aristocracy diminished, the reformed gentlemanly class that arose in the course of the nineteenth century achieved greater wealth and social status than the manufacturers who were associated with the major staple industries of Britain. It remains for us to demonstrate that this economic and social superiority was reflected in the making of economic policy after 1850, and in its chief modifications after 1880.

GLADSTONIAN FINANCE

The great cry for a generation after 1850 – as it had been for over a generation before – was for a small state and 'cheap government'.[1] The demand is inexplicable unless placed in the context of the unprecedented success and dynamism of the private economy in Britain over nearly 200 years. The tremendous buoyancy of 'natural society' and the widespread 'middling' wealth which it entailed discredited government as an economic agent. Government was unnecessary because it diverted income and savings from their 'natural' channels, and it was corrupt because it spent the taxpayer's money lavishly and on behalf of those with political influence. The desire for freedom of individual economic choice merged readily into a general hostility to aristocratic government, the national debt and

1. Norman Gash, *Pillars of Government and Other Essays in State and Society, c. 1770–c. 1880* (1986), pp. 43–54.

'Old Corruption', providing a common anti-aristocratic focus for both middle-class and working-class radicals which occasionally overrode their own mutual antagonisms and appeared as a common element in the works of thinkers as far apart as Tom Paine and J.S. Mill.[2] It was this broadly-based consensus which lay behind the drastic cuts in expenditure at the end of the Napoleonic Wars, established the view that government expenditure should be low and budgets balanced, and led to the return to the gold standard in 1819 on the assumption that the need to maintain convertibility into gold would force inflation out of the system and make financial discipline at the centre unavoidable. Government expenditure (including central funds allocated to local authorities) fell from an equivalent of 29 per cent of GNP in 1814 to 11 per cent in 1841 and 9 per cent in 1870.[3] The share of national debt repayment as a percentage of total expenditure also fell sharply over this period.[4]

Agreement among the non-aristocratic properties classes and a large section of the working population on a limited role for the state helps to explain Gladstone's extraordinary success as Chancellor and Prime Minister in mid-century and beyond. In keeping such a tight hold on expenditure, and in completing the transition to free trade begun in the 1820s, Gladstone believed that he was releasing the economy from unnatural restraint and allowing, at one and the same time, the maximum degree of liberty for individuals and the most rapid and widespread economic growth, as well as eliminating the chief source of corruption in public life.[5] As a result, his popularity transcended class divisions, and he became the 'People's William' – the man who epitomised a liberal consensus centred on middle-class property, both industrial and non-industrial, but who also respected aristocratic and gentlemanly values and appealed to the artisan classes with their deep hostility to the state as an engine of repression and as a 'tax-eater'.[6] Gladstone, with his gentlemanly background, thus had

2. Some aspects of this issue are dealt with in Peter J. Cain, 'Hobson, Wilshire and the Capitalist Theory of Capitalist Imperialism', *History of Political Economy*, 17 (1985), pp. 457–8.

3. A.T. Peacock and J. Wiseman with J. Veverka, *The Growth of Public Expenditure in the United Kingdom* (Princeton, 1961), Table 1, p. 37.

4. J. Veverka, 'The Growth of Government Expenditure in the United Kingdom since 1790', *Scottish Journal of Political Economy*, X (1963), Table 3, p. 119.

5. John Morley, *The Life of William Ewart Gladstone* (1908 edn) Vol. I, Bk. V, Ch. IV: 'The Spirit of Gladstonian Finance'.

6. Gladstone's attempt to maintain a balance between direct and indirect taxes was a crucial element here. See H.C.G. Matthew, *Gladstone, 1809–74* (Oxford, 1986), pp. 121–8. For a short but useful summary of the principles of Gladstonianism see S.G. Checkland, *The Gladstones: A Family Biography, 1764–1851* (Cambridge, 1971),

an authority and a following denied to Cobden and other radical industrialists who, despite their association with free trade and cheap government, were isolated, on the one hand, by the depth of their antipathy to aristocracy and, on the other, by the class bitterness which separated them from the working masses.

Free trade and cheap government had different origins. But it is clear that, after 1840, both Peel and Gladstone accepted the view that free trade, like low taxation, was vital to stamp out corrupt vested interests, to remove politics from the contaminating influence of commerce and to confer a benefit – cheap food – which, being seen as universal, would damp down social conflict and lead to class reconciliation. Free trade also narrowed the sources of taxation and led to the reintroduction of income tax in 1842. From then on, the propertied interest had an incentive to try to curb public spending. Extravagance might mean either higher direct taxes or the reintroduction of protection. The first posed a threat to the cardinal virtue of thrift; the second could be construed as an attack on the 'poor man's breakfast table', and was popularly associated with a profligate attitude to government expenditure.[7] Once it was clear that the revocation of free trade was equivalent to political suicide, the aristocrats of the Conservative Party recognised that they had to curb expenditure or face tax increases which would hurt them badly. Although Disraeli and Salisbury were less stringent than Gladstone in the application of the principles of 'sound' finance, they felt obliged to follow the same general policy.[8]

GLADSTONIANISM, THE BANK OF ENGLAND AND THE GOLD STANDARD

Gladstonianism gave a considerable boost to the power of two emerging gentlemanly institutions, the Treasury, the supervisor of

---

pp. 398–9. For a more detailed account see H. Roseveare, *The Treasury: The Evolution of a British Institution* (1968), Ch. 7. There is also an interesting comment from a modern perspective by Barry Baysinger and Robert Tollison, 'Chaining Leviathan: the Case of Gladstonian Finance', *Hist. Pol. Econ.*, 12 (1980).

7. For the link between free trade and budgetary restraint see Roseveare, *The Treasury*, p. 187.

8. A.N. Porter, 'Lord Salisbury, Foreign Policy and Domestic Finance, 1860–1900', in Lord Blake and Hugh Cecil, eds. *Salisbury: The Man and his Policies* (1987), pp. 155–9; also P.R. Ghosh, 'Disraelian Conservatism: a Financial Approach', *Eng. Hist. Rev.*, XCIX (1984).

government spending, and the Bank of England which, as guardian of the gold standard, was the most important element in determining the money supply in Britain. Gladstone ruthlessly centralised the process of budgetary decision-making, and encouraged the newly meritocratic Treasury to exercise and extend its dominance over individual departments of state which often had an easy attitude to spending the nation's revenues.[9] The Bank's progress towards modernity was less simple.[10] It attracted a great deal of hostility from industrialists and middling property-owners because of its historic role as the financier of Old Corruption, and its power and privileges were under constant attack after 1815. The return to gold in 1819 was undertaken partly to curb the influence of the government's banker by reducing expenditure; and, after a bitter struggle, the Bank lost its monopoly of joint-stock status in the legislation of 1825 and 1833. Governments thus showed some sympathy with the argument that the Old Lady's monopoly had been responsible on occasion for an oversupply of money and for inflation.

Yet the Bank survived. Governments could accept the demise of other chartered monopolies, such as the East India Company, because they had ceased to have an interest in influencing commerce and could happily leave it to the mercy of the market. In contrast, no government was prepared to relinquish ultimate control of the money supply, and not all the considerable force and propaganda of the 'free banking' school could make headway against this conviction. Given the Bank's size and importance in the money market, and their own intimate relations with it, governments had to decide whether to utilise the Bank as an instrument of public policy in a more formal manner than hitherto or whether to replace it with new institutions. But throughout the 1820s and 1830s the Bank remained in an awkward position as a private institution with important but ill-defined public responsibilities, while governments alternated between complaining about its discretionary power and exhorting it to use those powers to help the system out of crisis.

One solution, popular with elements in the industrial provinces who distrusted the Bank's freedom of action, was to create a new

---

9. Roseveare, *The Treasury*, pp. 183–6; Matthew, *Gladstone*, pp. 110–11.

10. The main sources of information on the Bank are Boyd Hilton, *Corn, Cash and Commerce: The Economic Policies of the Tory Governments, 1815–1830* (Oxford, 1977); Frank W. Fetter, *The Development of British Monetary Orthodoxy, 1797–1875* (Cambridge, Mass. 1965); Lawrence H. White, *Free Banking in Britain: Theory, Experience and Debate, 1800–1845* (Cambridge, 1984); Michael Collins, *Money and Banking in the United Kingdom: A History* (1988).

central bank with purely administrative control over a money supply mechanically related to gold holdings, leaving the Bank of England to operate purely as a private concern. Peel was sympathetic to the aims of these reformers but felt that he could achieve them by an easier route. In the Bank Charter Act of 1844, he adapted the structures of the Bank in order to eliminate its schizoid tendencies. Working on the bullionist assumption that gold and notes were the key factors in money supply, Peel set up a rigidly controlled Issue Department within the Bank while also ensuring that, in due time, the note-issuing powers of other banks in England would cease. On the other hand, the Banking Department was left to act freely in the market. Unfortunately, the bullionist definition of money was too limiting in leaving aside bank deposits and in ignoring the rapid development of the cheque system. In these circumstances, the commercial activities of the Banking Department had an important influence upon the money supply, interest rates and flows of gold. Having reluctantly given up its influence over the issue of currency, the Bank could still exercise a profound authority in the market by different means; the intricate and confused argument about where its private role ended and its public one began continued unabated.

The Bank remained for a time an object of suspicion outside its own circle of intimates in the City. Those hostile to it often perceived the Bank as being no more than 'a relic of feudalism',[11] and this hostility was shared by Gladstone, who was deeply suspicious of traditional 'money power'.[12] His creation of a Post Office Savings Bank in 1861 was expressly designed to give the Treasury access to funds independent of the Bank. At one point, he even considered amending the Bank Charter Act to allow the Treasury to create bonds in financial crises, thus loosening the Bank's grip on the money supply and on interest rates.[13]

The Act of 1844 largely absolved the Bank from the obligation to manage the nation's money and, after 1850, its interventions in the market were dictated largely by a concern for profit rather than by any sense of wider public duty.[14] As the biggest player in the London

11. On this see Fetter, *The Development of British Monetary Orthodoxy*, pp. 253–5.

12. Morley, *Life of Gladstone*, I, pp. 608–9.

13. Ibid. pp. 386, 512–13; Matthew, *Gladstone*, pp. 117–18; Richard Shannon, *Gladstone, Vol. I, 1809–65* (1982), pp. 287–9, 296, 319, 332, 417, 425, 431–2.

14. M. de Cecco, *Money and Empire: The International Gold Standard, 1890–1914* (Oxford, 1974), p. 83. See also Deiter Ziegler, *Central Bank, Peripheral Industry: The Bank of England in the Provinces, 1826–1914* (Leicester, 1990). The standard accounts of the Bank's development are Sir John Clapham's highly readable study, *The Bank of England: A History*, Vol. II (Cambridge, 1944), and R.S. Sayers, *The Bank of England, 1891–1944*, 2 vols (Cambridge, 1976).

market, the Bank's chief general interest was the retention of the gold standard on which City cosmopolitanism and Britain's rising invisible income depended. Gold was the basis of the credit system, and London's ability to supply gold at all times at fixed rates of exchange was the foundation of confidence in City credit and vital to its business. In theory, the system worked automatically: changes in foreign trade and payments induced inflows and outflows of gold which led in turn to rises or falls in money supply and interest rates. In fact, the Bank never had enough gold to allow for automaticity, mainly because it was a competitive animal with no desire to hoard large stocks of non-earning metal. Also, leaving the market completely to its own devices might have led to devastating credit crises: a heavy drain of gold and a sharp contraction in money supply could have brought the whole system down or rendered it politically unacceptable.[15] The Bank had to intervene on occasion and it learned to do so pragmatically. Faced with a drain of gold, the Bank could raise its interest rate, Bank Rate, and use its power over the commercial banks' reserves to force a restriction of credit, thus deflating the economy, discouraging imports, correcting the balance of payments and stopping the drain. In these conditions the joint-stock banks would usually call in their own short-term loans to the discount houses, the chief actors in the commercial bill market, forcing a contraction of activity there and also ensuring that the discount houses would have to borrow from the Bank of England at Bank Rate, thus making the new, higher rates effective.

In the early years of the period the strategy did not work well. A dispute with one of the leading bill acceptors, Overend and Gurney, in 1858 caused the Bank to withdraw its facility of rediscounting for the market in a crisis, and this made it difficult to use Bank Rate as a disciplinary measure. The Bank was also extremely reluctant to accept the classic central banker's role as lender of last resort. The market was bailed out in the 1866 crisis because the Bank recognised that a complete collapse of confidence would have undermined London's position in the world. But there was little general confidence that the Bank would act in this way again, and the joint-stock banks were left to assume that the Bank might not accept the ultimate responsibility. This concern forced them to remain highly liquid, to eschew long-term lending to industry and to keep a large percentage of their assets

15. This was *the* central concern of Walter Bagehot's famous *Lombard Street*, first published in 1873.

on call in the London market, thus adding to the internationalist bias of the monetary system.

Uncertainty about Bank policy also played its part in galvanising amalgamations among the joint-stock banks, for banks with nation-wide networks of branches were less liable to large fluctuations in business and to crises of confidence. Indeed, by the 1890s the biggest joint-stock banks were much larger than the Bank of England. The latter still competed strenuously for business, and thus kept its gold stocks low. The result was that, when drains occurred, the Bank had to take swift action which could disrupt credit and anger the clearers. After the shock of the Baring Crisis in 1890, the Bank made more strenuous efforts at control by competing less and restoring its discounting function in the bill market. Besides exhorting the joint-stock banks to keep adequate reserves, the Bank also evolved new management techniques designed to protect its gold reserves without too great a restriction upon domestic credit. A number of strategies were tried over the years: among the most prominent were the 'gold devices' whereby the Bank raised its gold price in order to attract the metal to London and offset drains, both internal and external. This was superseded, around the turn of the century, by a much more sophisticated use of the Bank Rate, not so much to discipline domestic credit as to attract holders of surplus funds in Europe into sterling in time of need.[16] London's power to attract funds in this way reflected the unique nature of the bill market there and the ability, aided by the growth of foreign banks in London, to draw easily upon the short-term capital of the continent. De Cecco has claimed that the system was moving towards breakdown after 1900 because Britain's ability to command gold was threatened as other nations absorbed it in vast quantities and refused to allow it to circulate freely.[17] But this does not really come to terms with the evidence that the monetary authorities did discover increasingly sophisticated ways of defending

16. On the working of the gold standard system see R.S. Sayers, *Central Banking After Bagehot* (Oxford, 1957), pp. 8–19; idem, 'The Bank in the Gold Market, 1890–1914,' in R.S. Sayers and T.S. Ashton, eds. *Papers in English Monetary History* (1953), pp. 132–50; W.M. Scammell, 'The Working of the Gold Standard', *Yorkshire Bulletin of Economic and Social Research*, XVII (1975); C.E.A. Goodhart, *The Business of Banking, 1890–1914* (1972), pp. 218–19; I.A. Bloomfield, *Short Term Capital Movements Under the Pre–1914 Gold Standard, 1900–1913* (Princeton Studies in International Finance, No. 24, 1969), pp. 42–57; B. Eichengreen, *The Gold Standard in Theory and History* (1985), pp. 3–19; and Ian M. Drummond, *The Gold Standard and the International Monetary System, 1900–1939* (1987), Ch. 1.

17. de Cecco, *Money and Empire*, Chs. 5 and 6.

the reserves and attracting gold without drastic effects on domestic credit.[18]

Dissent over the priority given to external criteria (that is, the maintenance of London's international financial position) in deciding economic policy never disappeared entirely. The joint-stock banks' resentment at London's control of monetary policy and the Bank's monopoly of the gold reserve was one aspect of the implicit difficulty involved in reconciling the needs of the domestic economy with those of sterling viewed as an international asset and as a medium of exchange. The conflict was made worse by the social distance which, before 1914, separated the largely provincial joint-stock bankers from the public-school gentlemen who ran the merchant banks and accepting houses and provided the bulk of the Bank's directors. The chief antagonist of the Bank of England was the Midland Bank, which would have liked to redistribute financial power by holding its own gold reserve; the Midland was the only one of the great joint-stock banks which could fairly claim to have close links with industry. Anything like a showdown was deferred until the outbreak of war in 1914, when a very sharp increase in Bank Rate led the joint-stock banks to question the whole basis of financial authority.[19] The Bank's instinctive defence of the international role of sterling in the war crisis of 1914 foreshadowed its stance in the 1920s, when convertibility became an issue for the first time in a century.[20]

THE CITY OF LONDON AND THE NATIONAL INTEREST

The success of Gladstonianism rested upon policies that took management of the economy out of the hands of party politicians and transferred it to the Treasury and the Bank of England, which could be said to be beyond the reach of everyday political conflict. This new alignment, together with the esoteric nature of financial management,

18. In this context we should also emphasise that the development of a sophisticated credit mechanism in London meant not only an extension of the importance of sterling but also a considerable economy in gold use and in gold flows, except in times of crisis. This point has recently been emphasised by R.C. Michie, 'The Myth of the Gold Standard: an Historian's Approach', *Revue internationale d'histoire de la banque*, 32–3 (1986).

19. de Cecco, *Money and Empire*, pp. 100–2 and Ch. 7.

20. For interesting recent discussions of the role of the Bank see Sidney Pollard, *Britain's Prime and Britain's Decline: The British Economy, 1870–1914* (1989), pp. 245–50, and Zeigler, *Central Bank, Peripheral Industry*, pp. 129–37.

gave these gentlemanly institutions a certain political invisibility. There were, of course, disputes about policy and who should control it, as we have seen, but most of these took place behind closed doors in the small space between Whitehall and Threadneedle Street.[21]

Government and industry were not totally separated, as the Factory Acts and a host of other legislative enactments show. Interference increased as the century progressed, and sometimes to good effect, though there is little sign that gentlemen in Whitehall had any real understanding of what industry was about.[22] Everyday contacts with the private market were made through the City of London, whose major institutions became increasingly entwined in gentlemanly culture after 1850. The main intermediary between the politically powerful and finance came via the Bank of England, whose directorate, as we have seen, was dominated by the leading city merchant banks and merchant houses. And it was the City, as the financial fulcrum of the service sector, which benefited most obviously from Gladstonian policies. Although the end of Old Corruption lost the City a great deal of business, it also forced its members further into the international financial arena, where they scored their greatest success. Although paradoxical, this transformation was not altogether unintended by policy-makers: in the 1820s Huskisson had expected invisible trade to be the chief beneficiary of tariff revision and, by the 1850s, it seems to have been taken for granted that free trade was important not just for the sake of manufacturing but because Britain was 'the great Emporium of the commerce of the World'.[23]

Nonetheless, the City's success owed far more to the gold standard and to stern control of public expenditure than it did to free trade. As Goschen, Chancellor of the Exchequer and a leading figure in the City, put it in 1891, London's position as an international service centre rested on the fact that 'it is known that any obligations held payable in England mean absolutely and safely so much gold'. This confidence gave the City 'the command of capital from abroad' and made it possible 'to tap the continent for cheap money'.[24] Without convertibility at a fixed rate, the use of sterling in world trade would have been much reduced by uncertainty. With it, traders and investors

21. On this theme see Geoffrey Ingham, *Capitalism Divided? The City and Industry in British Social Development* (1984), esp. Chs. 5 and 6.

22. Pollard, *Britain's Prime and Britain's Decline*, pp. 250–1.

23. Sir John Graham quoted in Olive Anderson, *A Liberal State at War: English Politics and Economics During the Crimean War* (1967), p. 252.

24. G.J. Goschen, *Speech at Leeds on the Insufficiency of Our Cash Reserves and of Our Central Stock of Gold* (1891), quoted in S. Ambirajan, *Political Economy and Monetary Management: India, 1766–1914* (New Delhi, 1984), p. 120.

had an incentive not only to use sterling but also to hold sterling assets, which had the advantage of yielding a rate of return related to Bank Rate, while gold did not.[25] Next to convertibility, low direct taxation was of prime importance. After 1850, Britain was lightly taxed compared with her European neighbours,[26] and capital came to Britain for that reason as well as to find the security guaranteed by the navy and by the stability of her political and social structure.[27]

In its success, the City developed a strong sense of self-esteem and, not surprisingly, assumed that its own interests were those of the nation's. So fundamental was this belief that it was only rarely expressed as, for example, during the budgetary crisis of 1909, when the head of Barings, Lord Revelstoke, lamented that the Liberal government was ignoring 'the extent to which the prosperity of the nation has been due to its great capital resources, its heritage of financial supremacy, its unshaken credit'.[28] Lord Rothschild was even blunter: without the City, he claimed, 'England could not exist'.[29] In less apocalyptic terms, financier-politicians like Goschen could take it for granted that the City's international success was bound to be for the good of the whole domestic economy.[30]

Industrialists often made similar claims for their own activities. But, despite Gladstone's early doubts, it was the City which became accepted in governing circles at its own valuation. The City possessed a coherence, a concentration and a geographic centrality which industry could not match. Moreover, as the century progressed, the leading bankers in the City became integrated into elite culture. All this, together with the City's freedom from the class hostility which so reduced the ability of industrialists to appear as credible political leaders and made City advice seem comparatively disinterested,

25. On the use of sterling as international money see H. van B. Cleveland, 'The International Monetary System in the Inter-War Period', in B.M. Rowland, ed. *Balance of Power or Hegemony: The Inter-War Monetary System* (New York, 1976), pp. 18–22.

26. Gash, *Pillars of Government*, p. 53.

27. In 1909 Lord Rosebery, a City man as well as an aristocrat, based his opposition to Lloyd George's supertax proposals on the proposition that it would scare foreign capital away from Britain. *Parliamentary Debates* (Lords), IV, 1909 cc. 947–9, 24 Nov. 1909.

28. Ibid. c. 799, 22 Nov. 1909. It was this, he said, which had made Britain 'the Bank and the workshop of the world', which itself is revealing about his order of priorities.

29. Ibid. c. 1153, 29 Nov. 1909.

30. Ibid. c. 1277, 29 Nov. 1909. The City's image of its own importance comes out strongly in a valuable recent thesis by S.R. Smith, 'British Nationalism, Imperialism and the City of London, 1880–1900' (unpublished Ph.D. thesis, London University, 1985).

explains why governments in need of counsel turned instinctively to the City rather than to the industrial provinces.[31]

The bimetallic controversy of the 1880s and 1890s provides an excellent insight into the nature and extent of City influence, and is worth close examination in this context, even though it cannot be dramatised simply as a battle between 'producers' and 'rentiers'.[32] The demand for a bimetallic standard was provoked by the slide in silver prices as silver production increased after 1880 and as a growing number of countries abandoned silver and adopted the gold standard. One effect of the collapse of silver prices was to revalue sterling against silver-based currencies, making it harder to export to silver-standard countries and easier to buy imports from them.[33] The obvious remedy, according to the supporters of bimetallism, was to reach an international agreement which would fix the ratio of gold to silver prices, thus halting the steady devaluation of silver-based currencies.

Those who championed the retention of the existing gold standard stressed the fact that Britain's commerce had flourished under it. They also pointed out that sterling's revaluation against non-gold currencies increased Britain's invisible income (since payments for invisibles had to be made in sterling) and helped to raise real incomes and living standards by lowering import prices.[34] On the other side, alarm was widespread among agriculturalists, who were already suffering acutely from foreign competition;[35] but it is more difficult to detect a 'producers' alliance' of manufacturers and trade unionists who were united in opposition to the gold standard. The main centre of provincial hostility to gold was Lancashire, where fears for the future of the cotton export trade with India became acute as the silver rupee began to fall steadily against sterling; many ferocious attacks upon the evils of London's money power and the rentier mentality emanated from there, especially during the depression of the early 1890s.[36] The intensity of support from other industrial areas is more problematic; even within Lancashire itself, the most voluble critics of orthodoxy

31. S.G. Checkland, 'The Mind of the City, 1870–1914', *Oxford Economic Papers*, new ser., IX (1957).

32. The best introduction to the controversy is by E.H.H. Green, 'Rentiers versus Producers? The Political Economy of the Bimetallic Controversy', *Eng. Hist. Rev.*, CIII (1988). See also Checkland, 'The Mind of the City', pp. 262, 276; Y. Cassis, *La City de Londres, 1870–1914* (Paris, 1987), pp. 177–81; Ambirajan, *Political Economy and Monetary Management*, p. 121; Pollard, *Britain's Prime and Britain's Decline*, pp. 237–8.

33. Michael Collins, 'Sterling Exchange Rates, 1847–1880', *Jour. Eur. Econ. Hist.*, 15 (1986), pp. 521ff.

34. Green, 'Rentiers versus Producers?', p. 595.

35. Ibid. pp. 598–9.

36. Ibid. pp. 595–602.

were merchants and local bankers with interests in the cotton trade. Some manufacturers did join with trade unionists to condemn the gold standard, but just as many thought that Lancashire's problems were more likely to be solved by cutting wages than by raising prices.[37] There was also support for bimetallism in the City, especially among businesses dependent on trade with the Far East.[38] There was, therefore, no consensus for bimetallism among producers and not all men of commerce and finance were adamant for the gold standard. On the other hand, while industry proved to be a 'babel of voices'[39] on this issue as on many others, opinion in the City was heavily weighted in favour of orthodoxy, and this was probably the crucial reason why there was never any realistic chance that the bimetallists would win the day.

Bimetallism was important because it raised in acute form the question of 'the relative worth of productive and service interests to the economy'.[40] By adhering to the gold standard, governments were assenting, sometimes explicitly, to the City view that it was vital to Britain's command of international commerce and finance, which were the central activities of the economy and the key to the prosperity of the domestic economy as a whole. Despite the presence of a bimetallist element in the Liberal Party, mainly Lancastrian in origin, the party was convinced that the gold standard was the 'sheet anchor' of the British economy. The true political home of monetary radicalism was the Conservative Party, where there was considerable support for bimetallism among its leaders, including Salisbury and Balfour. Nonetheless, Conservative Chancellors proved as impeccably orthodox as their Liberal counterparts, and this reflected City pressures. Defence of orthodoxy among the most influential City figures was so strong that Hamilton, the Gladstonian Under-Secretary at the Treasury, thought that it would be impossible for any politician with bimetallic sympathies to be Chancellor. As he noted, a crucial qualification for the post, which involved working closely with the City, was a belief that the prosperity of the country depended above

37. A.C. Howe, 'Bimetallism, c. 1880–1898: a Controversy Re-opened', *Eng. Hist. Rev.*, CV (1990), pp. 381–2; Edward R. Wilson, 'Lancashire Cotton and the Bimetallic Controversy of the 1890s', (M. Soc. Sci. Diss., University of Birmingham, 1990), pp. 162, 178–80, 191–4. Wilson does not believe that bimetallism was a popular cause in other industrial centres (pp. 180–1).

38. Daunton, 'Gentlemanly Capitalism and British Industry, 1820–1914', *Past and Present*, 122 (1989); Wilson, 'Lancashire Cotton', pp. 196–8.

39. E.E.H. Green, 'The Bimetallic Controversy: Empiricism Belimed or the Case for the Issues', *Eng. Hist. Rev.*, CV (1990), pp. 672–4.

40. Ibid. pp. 679–80.

all on Britain's commercial supremacy and on the banking system which supported that commerce. A Chancellor who was a bimetallist would be seen as challenging this position and would be unable to gain the City's confidence.[41]

Gentlemanly elites in the City could also rely on the support of the official class: a large number of the permanent officials at the Treasury and at the Board of Trade gave their blessing to the powerful, City-based Gold Standard Defence Association because they saw clearly that bimetallism was an attack on the internationalism and openness which had been the hallmark of British economic policy for over half a century.[42] In fact, the influence of the City and its administrative allies was so pervasive that it is doubtful if bimetallism would have surfaced as an issue at national level had there not been elements within the Square Mile who were dissatisfied with gold.[43] Nonetheless, if the City's claim to represent the nation was somewhat exaggerated, the victory of the supporters of the gold standard cannot be represented as some kind of Hobsonian financial conspiracy. By the 1890s, when the bimetallic agitation was at its height, the City was the financial hub of the most dynamic part of the economy. Moreover, the cosmopolitan economic policy which the City favoured also suited the interests of large sections of Britain's export industries. Gentlemanly finance had political influence not only because it was embedded within elite decision-making structures but also because it represented enormous economic strength.

THE BARING CRISIS AND ITS RESOLUTION

The bimetallic controversy illustrates, among other things, the informality of the relationship between City elites and government and the 'empathy' between them. But the swift and decisive way in which the Baring Crisis of 1890 was handled is, perhaps, the best illustration both of the City's capacity for coherent action and of the strength of its connection with political power.

In 1890, the firm of Baring Bros, one of the most prestigious in the City, found itself in great difficulties. The firm had underwritten several loans to Argentina during the previous few years and was

41. Cassis, *La City de Londres*, p. 181. For the political alignment see Howe, 'Bimetallism', p. 389; Wilson, 'Lancashire Cotton', pp. 165–72.
42. Green, 'Rentiers versus Producers?', p. 611.
43. Howe, 'Bimetallism', p. 383–4.

unable to meet its obligations. Had Barings failed, the consequence for international credit would have been extensive and a world liquidity crisis, with ramifications impossible to foresee or to control, might have been inevitable. The crisis was aborted, however, by the swift action of the Bank of England, in conjunction with the leading acceptance houses in the City, and with government approval. Before Barings' plight became known outside the intimate circle within the City, a guarantee fund to cover their obligations, totalling £17m., was subscribed, and knowledge of this fund was sufficient to prevent either Barings' failure or a widespread collapse of credit when their difficulties became common knowledge.[44]

The Baring Crisis offers perhaps the most revealing picture of the close relationship between government, the Bank of England and the City elite in the pre–1914 period. The increasing intimacy of the connection becomes clear when the crisis of 1890 is compared with that of 1866. The crucial difference between the two crises appears to be that, while Overend and Gurney were insolvent, Barings were merely illiquid. Overend's insolvency was the result of dishonesty as well as stupidity, whereas Barings had simply been imprudent. Nonetheless, once the 'lock up' had occurred, and before Barings were forced to consult the Bank, *The Economist* did not think that they had acted very honourably, and Clapham seems to agree.[45]

Secondly, Overend and Gurney were one, albeit the biggest, of a number of joint-stock finance companies in trouble in 1866: in 1890, Barings were the only major house with a critical problem. In 1866, the Bank was faced with the very difficult task of how to handle a whole spate of dubious financiers and found it easier to do this by letting them default, meeting the subsequent panic by acting as 'lender

44. The most authoritative account of the crisis can be found in L.S. Pressnell, 'Gold Reserves, Banking Reserves and the Baring Crisis of 1890', in C.R. Whittesley and J.S.G. Wilson, eds. *Essays in Money and Banking in Honour of R.S. Sayers* (Oxford, 1968), pp. 192–207. See also Roy A. Batchelor, 'The Avoidance of Catastrophe: Two Nineteenth-Century Banking Crises', in Forrest Capie and Geoffrey E. Wood, eds. *Financial Crises and the World Banking System* (1986); and Philip Zeigler, *The Sixth Great Power: Barings, 1762–1929* (1988), pp. 244–66. We would also like to thank Prof. Pressnell for causing us to rethink our position on this issue. What follows amplifies and modifies our previous highly compressed statement, which followed de Cecco's analysis rather too closely. See P.J. Cain and A.G. Hopkins, 'Gentlemanly Capitalism and British Expansion Overseas, II: New Imperialism, 1850–1945', p. 5; de Cecco, *Money and Empire*, pp. 80–2, 89–95. Batchelor, 'The Avoidance of Catastrophe', pp. 43, 71, lends credence to this view. The Argentine aspects of the crisis are dealt with in Chapter 9, pp. 292–7.

45. *The Economist* thought some of Barings' dealings in Argentina were 'of doubtful character' (22 Nov. 1890, p. 1465) and 'shady' (13 June 1891, p. 757). Clapham, *The Bank of England*, II, p. 325.

of last resort' and obtaining government approval to suspend the 1844 Act, which restricted the Bank's ability to lend. In 1890, they could nip the crisis in the bud by helping out one company.[46]

On this evidence, it appears that the 1866 and the 1890 crises were not, as De Cecco implies, similar and that there was a prima facie case for the Bank to react to them in very different ways. Nonetheless, the Bank's instinctive response to both crises was not quite as impartial as its leading officials no doubt believed that it was.

The Bank not only was prepared for the 1866 crash (its reserves were built up in advance) but also was quietly pleased to see Overend fail. This reflected both a reasonable distaste for Overend's activities between 1860 and 1866 and the long-standing rivalry between the Bank and the Corner House: the bitterness left behind by the Bank's decision on rediscounting in 1858 and Overend's retaliatory action in 1860 was very marked.[47] *The Economist*'s argument, that one reason why Overend's went down and Barings survived was that the former did not approach the Bank for help in time, rather glosses over the problem of Overend's bad relations with the Bank and fails to emphasise the fact that Barings enjoyed much closer ties with authority.[48]

The closeness between Barings and the Bank raises the wider question of the intimate nature of crisis management in 1890. The almost automatic, informal intercourse between government, Treasury, Bank and merchant houses, and the great speed with which decisions were taken, does give the impression of a gentleman's club at work.[49] Goschen, the Chancellor of the Exchequer, was put in the

---

46. E.T. Powell, *The Evolution of the Money Market, 1385–1915: An Historical and Analytical Study of the Rise and Development of Finance as a Centralized, Co-ordinated Force* (1915: 1966), pp. 400–7, 523–31; W.T.C. King, *History of the London Discount Market* (1936), pp. 242–55, 307–9; J.H. Clapham, *The Bank of England*, II, pp. 260–9, 325–36; R.G. Hawtrey, *A Century of Bank Rate* (1938), pp. 109–110; *The Economist*, 22 Nov. 1890, p. 1465.

47. Clapham, *Bank of England*, II, pp. 242–6; King, *History of the London Discount Market*, pp. 193, 213–15.

48. *The Economist*, 22 Nov. 1890, p. 1466. It is worth noting that one of the emissaries sent by the Bank to assess whether or not Barings could be helped, agreed with 'some reluctance' that they could, since he knew that if he withheld his assent 'the Governor would be unable to take further action': Zeigler, *The Sixth Great Power*, p. 249. A well-informed, if anonymous, writer later claimed that 'The Great House was supported because it was a Great House'. See 'The Recent Criticism of the Bank of England', *Econ. Jour.*, IV (1894), p. 348.

49. The best indications of this are the accounts in Pressnell, 'Gold Reserves, Banking Reserves and the Baring Crisis of 1890', pp. 200–4; Hon. A.D. Elliot, *The Life of George Joachim Goschen, First Viscount Goschen*, II (1911), pp. 170–2 and pp. 183–4; Clapham, *Bank of England*, II, pp. 328–33; Roger Fulford, *Glyn's, 1753–1953: Six Generations in Lombard St.* (1953), pp. 207–17.

picture immediately the Bank became aware of Barings' plight. He, and other members of the Cabinet, resisted the Bank's initial demand for direct financial assistance, partly because this would have involved parliament and precipitated the financial panic that the authorities and the City both wished to avoid.[50] Instead, Goschen urged the Bank to organise a guarantee fund with which to pay Barings' creditors and maintain faith in the City. If this was done then 'the government would help the Bank with the difference between what it could raise and what it needed to give Barings if this proved necessary'.[51] All the initial negotiations on the guarantees involved only that part of the City most closely associated with the Bank. The clearing banks were brought in very late and more or less confronted with a *fait accompli*; when, not surprisingly, there were murmurs of dissent they were suppressed by Lidderdale, the Governor of the Bank, with what in banking terms was brute force since he threatened to close the accounts at the Bank of England of those banks which felt that Barings should be left to their own devices. Powell was right to claim that the Baring Crisis was met by a new spirit of cooperation, but some of that co-operation – or rather the form which it took – was forced on those outside the Bank's immediate circle.[52]

It was said by Clapham that the problem in 1866 was a domestic one[53] while most authorities on the Baring Crisis assume that the matter was international in scope and, by implication, one requiring more drastic intervention. Kindleberger, at least, does not think that Clapham was right about 1866,[54] but it is probably true that the 1890 crisis, had it broken, would have had more serious repercussions on London's world role. It is possible, given Barings' enormous international reputation, that their fall could have triggered a global panic of unprecedented proportions, especially since the foreign banking presence in London was much greater in 1890 than in 1866.[55] The elite merchant banking fraternity was certainly aware that the 1890 crisis posed a direct threat to them; the hysteria which Goschen detected on

50. Elliot, *The Life of George Joachim Goschen*, II, p. 172; Zeigler, *The Sixth Great Power*, p. 249.

51. Pressnell, 'Gold Reserves, Banking Reserves and the Baring Crisis of 1890', p. 201.

52. Powell, *The Evolution of the Money Market*, pp. 526–8; Joseph Wechsberg, *The Merchant Bankers* (1967), p. 141.

53. Clapham, *Bank of England*, II, p. 268.

54. Charles P. Kindleberger, *Keynesianism v. Monetarism and Other Essays* (1985), p. 199.

55. L.S. Pressnell, 'Comment', in Capie and Wood, *Financial Crises and the World Banking System*, p. 76.

his visit to the City at the beginning of crisis week[56] reflected the very real fear of people like Rothschild that their own businesses would be permanently damaged.[57]

What was at stake in 1890 was the position of London as an international financial centre: the Bank of England's swift, even ruthless, reaction reflected its instinctive recognition of this weighty fact. The Bank's moves, while clearly intended to prevent a general conflagration hurtful to the whole international business community, also seem to have maximised the advantages of the international houses closely associated with it. The feeling that the Bank's solution to the crisis had benefited some interests more than others was fairly widespread once the first shock was past. The joint-stock banks in particular felt that the Bank was using the crisis as a way of both increasing its power over them and of enhancing its position as a competitor. There was also a great deal of resentment about how well Barings had done out of the resolution of the crisis and a general feeling that no one could be expected to be bailed out in the same way again.[58] Also, the solution to the Argentine debt crisis, reached in 1891, appears to have been heavily influenced by the Rothschild Committee's, and the Bank's, determination to get the best deal for Barings and the guarantors rather than to find a solution which treated all Argentina's creditors equitably.[59] This involved the Bank in some rather 'indelicate' activity[60] clearly related to the illiquidity problems which beset it as a result of its quick action to save Barings.[61]

There was no Marxist inevitability about the solution found: with a weaker governor than Lidderdale in charge the crisis might have

56. Elliot, *Life of J.G. Goschen*, II, pp. 170–1.

57. Pressnell, 'Gold Reserves, Bank Reserves and the Baring Crisis of 1890', pp. 200, 202. When the Bank asked for a contribution to the guarantee fund, Rothschild complied reluctantly, perhaps because he felt that locking up more of his firm's capital might make his own position even more difficult. See Fulford, *Glyn's, 1753–1953*, p. 210. In persuading him to help, his City colleagues emphasised that by saving Barings he was saving himself: Zeigler, *The Sixth Great Power*, p. 253. Also Pressnell, 'Gold Reserves, Banking Reserves and the Baring Crisis of 1890', pp. 217–19; Clapham, *Bank of England*, II, p. 336; Fulford, *Glyn's, 1853–1953*, p. 211; Anon, 'The Recent Criticism of the Bank of England', p. 348; *The Economist*, 22 Nov. 1890, p. 1,466, 13 June 1891, p. 757, 12 Jan. 1895, p. 44.

58. It should be noted that, though Barings were saved, they did suffer considerable capital loss; although they eventually re-established themselves in the international loan business they never had quite the same predominance as before. On Latin American and other loans, they often had to share the spoils with Morgans. See Zeigler, *The Sixth Great Power*, pp. 260–3, 294–319; Kathleen Burk, *Morgan Grenfell: The Biography of a Merchant Bank, 1838–1988* (Oxford, 1989), pp. 54–7.

59. *The Economist*, 17 June 1893, pp. 721–2.

60. Ibid. 15 Sept. 1894, p. 1,126.

61. A. Crump, 'The Baring Financial Crisis', *Econ. Jour.*, I (1891), pp. 393–4.

engulfed the City and changed its history. Again, we are not saying that the Bank ought necessarily to have allowed the crisis to develop and then met it by suspending the Bank Charter Act, as in 1866. Rather, our argument is that, given Lidderdale's outstanding abilities, the Bank was able to find a solution to the crisis which not only prevented an international panic, but also helped to reinforce existing structures of power and influence within the City. The Bank's actions were not conspiratorial: the governor genuinely believed that the best way of meeting the crisis was by building up the strength of the informal networks which made gentlemanly capitalist control of finance possible.

INDUSTRY AND ECONOMIC POLICY

Industrialists were not at the centre of economic policy-making before 1914, nor did they aspire to be, as Cobden and Bright were reluctantly forced to admit. Manufacturing interests made themselves felt at the centre in the form of 'pressure from without', either on specific issues which affected them directly or at times of acute economic crisis, when fears of social upheaval inspired a hunger for new markets and brought Chamber of Commerce delegates down to London to importune the gentlemanly statesmen of the day. The Victorian economy lurched erratically between periods of high boom and deep depression, and there were severe slumps in economic activity every seven to ten years on average, with troughs in 1858, 1868, 1879, 1886, 1893, 1903–4 and 1908–9.[62] The crises from the 1870s onwards were felt more severely than earlier ones because of falling prices and the dramatic increase in the pressure of foreign competition. At these times of slack demand and unused capacity, industrialists were especially fearful of the penetration of 'backward areas' by foreign countries which would then use protection to exclude British trade. There is strong evidence that pressure in times of economic crisis for an extension of British authority in Asia and Africa to safeguard markets for British traders influenced the shaping of policy in these areas, as we shall see.[63]

Nonetheless, this success needs to be put in perspective. First, the process required the provinces to seek the attention of governments

62. R.S. Sayers, *A History of Economic Change in England, 1880–1939* (1969), Ch. 3.
63. W.G. Hynes, 'British Mercantile Attitudes Towards Imperial Expansion', *Hist. Jour.*, XIX (1976).

and highlights the extent to which they were generally outside the normal circles of power. Second, the pressure from the provinces for action in Africa and Asia was frequently supplemented by pressure from the City, which often shared the enthusiasm for imperial expansion in these circumstances.[64] Third, and more important, in the traditional empire of the white colonies and India, in Latin America, Egypt and South Africa, where the potential economic benefits were considerably greater than those in the new territories of tropical Africa, industry was not the dominant economic force behind the British presence. In these regions, and in the ageing and fragile empires of Turkey and China, British financial and commercial penetration were the foundations of her expanding power, as we shall see.

CITY AND GOVERNMENT IN THE NINETEENTH CENTURY

In the eighteenth century the British state was, to adapt a Marxist phrase, little more than a managing agency for the aristocracy; the City of London and the Bank of England found their rationale as the commercial and financial agents of the landed order. In the early part of the nineteenth century this order was challenged by new social and economic pressures, forcing the aristocracy and its allies on to the defensive; and the battle was complicated by the fact that existing elites not only were under attack from outside but were themselves split between the supporters of tradition and others willing, and even eager, to allow the fresh winds of economic change to fill their sails. In the City, this tension between conservative elements surrounding the chartered companies and more liberal ones moving in the direction of free trade, occasionally led to paralysis. In these circumstances, as competing interests clashed and became deadlocked, there were many openings for forceful governments to act independently of the great interests and to determine policy. It was by no means inevitable that this would occur; but the elites who controlled the state apparatus did, on the whole, accept the need for change and acted with decision, coming to terms with modernity as the aristocratic order gave way slowly to a more widely based gentlemanly one, accommodating the new industrialism on the way. The leading financial institutions of the

64. On this see Smith, 'British Nationalism, Imperialism and the City of London, 1880–1914', passim.

nation were similarly renewed rather than replaced. In 1815, the City was still a centre of traditional money, closely identified with chartered monopolies and the financing of an extravagant state, but it responded remarkably to new opportunities offered by the growth of the international economy.

If the state stood against a divided City to some degree after 1815 and forced it to accept the disciplines of the gold standard and parsimonious government and to adjust to competition, the adaptation had taken place completely by 1880. Legislation which had been seen initially as a burdensome interference in Liverpool and Peel's time was, by then, regarded as the foundation stone of the prosperity of both the City and the nation; no clear line could be drawn between gentlemanly governments and a united gentlemanly City over matters of fundamental importance in economic and financial policy, as the authority of the Bank of England over monetary policy, the failure of the bimetallist agitation and the inter-party consensus on budgetary matters all indicate.

CHAPTER FIVE
'The Great Emporium': Foreign Trade and Invisible Earnings, 1850–1914[1]

COMMODITY TRADE AND FOREIGN COMPETITION

The steady shift in the epicentre of British economic activity after 1850 from north to south, and from the traditional staples of the Industrial Revolution to services, is reflected in the changing composition of British foreign trade. The period witnessed a steady increase in the importance of 'invisible' income from trade in services and from the returns on overseas investments, while 'visible' exports suffered from increased competition and the slow pace of transformation of Britain's industrial base.

Between 1850 and the early 1870s exports grew with great speed both in volume (except for a brief pause during the cotton famine of 1861–5) and value. Growth in values was sharply halted in the late 1870s and remained low until the end of the century. The decline in the rate of growth of volumes was less precipitous but still fell to very low levels in the 1890s. After 1900, however, there was a return to growth rates of pre-1870 dimensions (Table 5.1). Exports grew at a faster rate than income between 1840 and 1870 and after 1900, and at a slower rate between 1870 and 1900: the ratio of exports to Gross National Product at current prices rose from 10 in 1841 to 20 in 1870, fell to 15 in 1901 and then rose again to 21 in 1912.[2] Changes in the

1. The phrase is Sir John Graham's, when First Lord of the Admiralty during the Crimean conflict in 1854. Quoted in O. Anderson, *A Liberal State at War: British Politics and Economics During the Crimean Conflict* (1967), p. 252.
2. François Crouzet, *The Victorian Economy* (1982), p. 112. For selected figures see Paul Bairoch, *Commerce extérieur et développement économique de l'Europe au XIXe siècle* (Paris, 1976), pp. 193, 209.

pace of growth of exports closely followed those in world trade as a whole.[3]

Table 5.1 British domestic exports: growth between cyclical peaks, 1856–1913 (per cent per year)

	By value	*By volume*[a]
1856–60	4.1	3.6
1860–65	4.1	0.0
1865–73	5.3	5.6
1873–82	0.7	3.0
1882–89	0.4	2.5
1889–99	0.7	1.0
1899–1907	6.1	4.0
1907–13	3.6	2.9
1856–73	4.7	2.7
1873–99	0.1	2.1
1899–1913	5.1	3.6

Sources: B.R. Mitchell and P. Deane, *Abstract of British Historical Statistics* (Cambridge, 1962); A.H. Imlah, *Economic Elements in the Pax Britannia* (New York, 1958).

Note: [a] Volumes have been calculated from Imlah's export price index with 1880 as the base year.

In the third quarter of the century growth was rapid and also evenly spread. European demand for British products increased at a faster than average rate between 1846–50 and 1871–5. The most rapid growth area of all was north and north-eastern Europe (mainly Scandinavia and Denmark), which became increasingly dependent upon the British market for primary exports; but the growth of exports to industrial Europe was also high. This was a period of 'take off' in Western Europe, and Britain benefited by being able to supply the 'inputs for industrialization'[4] – semi-finished manufactures such as yarns and pig-iron rather than finished manufactures – at a time when, albeit often for political reasons, the trend in Europe was towards freer trade.[5] The United States was at a similar stage of development as the railway system pushed out from the eastern states, but export growth was muted by continued high protection and by

3. William Ashworth, *An Economic History of England, 1870–1939* (1960), p. 148.

4. Ralph Davis, *The Industrial Revolution and British Overseas Trade* (Leicester, 1979), p. 34. Albert H. Imlah, *Economic Elements in the Pax Britannica: Studies in British Foreign Trade in the Nineteenth Century* (New York, 1958), Table 9.

5. Charles P. Kindleberger, 'The Rise of Free Trade in Western Europe', *Jour. of Econ. Hist.*, XXXV (1975), pp. 36ff.

the effects of the Civil War in the early 1860s (Table 5.2).[6] Despite the buoyancy of industrial markets, Britain's chief manufactured export, cotton piece-goods, was increasingly being driven out of Europe and America. Exports of piece goods to these areas fell from 29 per cent of the total in 1840 to only 12 per cent in 1870,[7] and, by the latter date, the cotton trade had become extremely dependent on markets in newly settled countries and the underdeveloped world: two-thirds of Britain's exports to India and Turkey in 1871–5 were cotton manufactures.[8] Nonetheless, in this period, the overall growth of markets in underdeveloped countries (including those within the empire) was slower than the average. The development of the white colonies, on the other hand, was rapid (Tables 5.2 and 5.3).

Table 5.2 Exports of British produce by region, 1846–1913 (quinquennial averages, per cent)

	1846–50	1871–75	1881–85	1896–1900	1909–13
North and north-east					
Europe	3.9	5.9	4.7	7.8	6.8
Industrial Europe[a]	23.0	28.1	23.3	24.2	21.8
United States	17.9	13.2	11.6	7.4	6.5
Newly settled countries[b]	18.7	21.2	25.0	24.4	28.5
Underdeveloped countries	35.6	31.6	35.4	36.2	36.2

Sources: Mitchell and Deane, *Abstracts; Statistical Abstract of the United Kingdom* (HMSO).

Notes: [a] Industrial Europe consists of the 'North-west Europe' and 'Central and South-east Europe' groups in Mitchell and Deane.

[b] Includes South Africa, Australia, Canada, New Zealand and Central and South America.

Between 1875 and 1900 the growth of international trade was much slower and export values increased very sluggishly as prices fell. It is probable that the enormous boom of 1869–73 created considerable excess capacity in world industry and that this increased competition, lowered prices and inhibited investment.[9] The development of Western Europe and the United States had reached the point where Britain was subject to fierce competition in neutral markets and, by 1900, in

6. On British trade with the United States see Jim Potter, 'The Atlantic Economy, 1815–60', in L.S. Pressnell, ed. *Studies in the Industrial Revolution Presented to T.S. Ashton* (1960).

7. Thomas Ellison, *The Cotton Industry of Great Britain* (1886), p. 64.

8. These figures are derived from the *Annual Statement of Trade and Navigation*.

9. This was the view of the *Majority Report of the Royal Commission on Depression in Trade and Industry*, PP 1886, C 4893.

Table 5.3 Exports of British produce to the empire, 1846–1913 (quinquennial averages, per cent)

	1846–50	1871–75	1881–85	1896–1900	1909–13
British settlement colonies[a]	8.7	12.0	16.2	16.7	17.5
India and Burma	9.4	8.9	12.9	11.8	11.9
Rest of empire	9.2	5.9	5.9	5.6	5.6
British empire	27.3	26.8	35.0	34.1	35.0

Source: Mitchell and Deane, *Abstract; Statistical Abstract of the United Kingdom* (HMSO).

Note: [a] Includes South Africa.

some cases, such as iron and steel, even in her own market and in the empire. Her problems were aggravated by the growth of protectionism in other industrial countries and by the steady fall in primary produce prices as the first phase of world railway building in mid-century came to fruition. Since primary produce prices fell faster than the price of manufactured imports, the terms of trade moved in Britain's favour; but this advantage may have been more than offset by the reduction in the demand for British exports from the primary exporters whose incomes were squeezed as prices fell.

As industrialism spread, British exports to other developed countries fell in value quite sharply. Markets in north and north-east Europe kept up well, but they were mainly primary producers dependent on the British market and on British capital and financial institutions. Loss of position in the American market and in industrial Europe was marked. Compensation was found in increased exports to the newly settled parts of the white empire (except Canada, where growth was relatively slow and United States' competition keen) and India. Textiles were still the key to growth in Indian markets, though that growth itself was alarmingly slow in the world trade crises of the late 1870s and the early 1890s. The increased importance of India is the chief reason for the rising share of underdeveloped countries in Britain's export economy after 1870 (Table 5.1). Most of the increase in the share of India and the white settlement colonies took place in the late 1870s, when the share of the empire as a whole rose from just over one-quarter to more than one-third; but the empire's relative significance did not increase much further before World War I (Table 5.3).

By contrast, industrial Europe and the United States took 41 per cent of British exports in 1871–5 and only 32.2 per cent in 1896–1900. The fall in exports to Europe would undoubtedly have been greater had it not been for the demand for British coal. Coal provided only 2 per cent of exports in 1851, rising to 9 per cent by 1910;[10] coal exports to European industrial countries were crucial in offsetting the effects of competition and rising protectionism on British industrial exports. In the case of Germany, for example, exports of coal accounted for 42 per cent of all the increase in the value of exports from Britain between 1872 and 1913; the corresponding figures for France and Italy were 57 per cent and 80 per cent respectively.[11] But the dependence of the world's first industrial nation upon exports of coal by 1900 was a serious worry to contemporaries. Britain's share of world trade in manufactures declined markedly after 1870;[12] it is possible that, by strengthening the balance of payments and keeping up the price level, coal exports may have speeded the process.[13]

This relative decline was the result of a heavy commitment of resources to commodities whose growth rates were slowing down.[14] When, in 1850, over half of British exports were textiles this was a sign of modernity; the fact that textiles still represented a quarter of the total in 1910 was a cause for concern, as was Britain's under-representation in high growth areas such as chemicals and electrical goods in comparison with Germany and the United States.[15] The basis of export strength was also extremely narrow: 14 per cent of British exports in 1913 were textiles destined for India and the Dominions.[16] The empire also supplied a bolt-hole for a number of industrial exports which were finding competition in Europe and elsewhere too difficult to meet;[17] several other extra-European markets which were dependent upon Britain economically and fell within the orbit of her informal control served the same purpose. Britain's problems were eased by a rapid increase in the growth of exports after 1900; but this was the result of a boom in world trade, and

10. Phyllis Deane and W.A. Cole, *British Economic Growth, 1688–1959* (Cambridge, 1962), Table 9, p. 31.

11. These figures have been calculated from the statistics in the *Annual Statement of Trade and Navigation*.

12. W. Arthur Lewis, 'International Competition in Manufactures', *American Economic Review: Papers and Proceedings*, XLVII (1957), p. 579; S.B. Saul, 'The Export Economy, 1870–1914', *Yorkshire Bulletin of Economic and Social Research*, XVII (1965), p. 12; R.C.O. Matthews, C.H. Feinstein and J.C. Odling-Smee, *British Economic Growth, 1856–1973* (Oxford, 1982), Table 14.5, p. 435.

13. Matthews, Feinstein and Odling-Smee, *British Economic Growth*, p. 455.

14. H. Tysinski, 'World Trade in Manufactured Commodities, 1899–1950', *Manchester School*, XIX (1951).

15. See Deane and Cole, *British Economic Growth, 1688–1959*, Table 9, p. 31.

16. Werner Schlote, *British Overseas Trade From 1700 to the 1930s* (Oxford, 1952), pp. 154, 172–3.

17. Ibid. pp. 166–7.

Britain's share of world trade in manufactured goods continued to fall. The recovery of exports also took place within an economy suffering from low growth and stagnant productivity.

The relationship between the changing fortunes of British manufacturing output and the output of the economy as a whole is complex and will be given detailed treatment later. But it is clear that the fortunes of exports were of crucial significance to many of the traditional industrial areas and were intimately bound up with their decline. The fall in growth rates of cotton textile exports after 1860 was particularly sharp. In the main, this problem was the result of the fact that the industry was fully mechanised by this time, had few openings for further increases in productivity without radical technological change, and its comparative advantage was beginning to slip away as industrialisation spread. Even by 1870, the loss of markets in other industrial countries was severe and the dependence on exports to underdeveloped lands very marked. In the face of chronic overproduction after 1890 – a condition aggravated by the smallness of the average firm and the fiercely competitive nature of the industry – the importance of empire markets, especially India, and the eagerness for new ones, whether in Africa or China, can hardly be overemphasised.[18] Other traditional industries, like metals, also suffered seriously from the decline in export growth after 1870. In their case, the decline was the result of an emerging lack of competitiveness which kept costs at too high a level; their uncompetitiveness was a threat to their possession of both the domestic market and that in the empire, so much so that their leaders often became devotees of protection and imperial preference.

Import volumes rose a little faster than export volumes before 1875 but much faster from then until 1900, though the effect was mitigated by a favourable shift in the terms of trade. Imports of 'manufactures and miscellaneous goods' actually rose from just over 3 per cent of the total in 1860 to 25 per cent by 1900.[19] At constant prices, manufactured imports were equivalent to 10 per cent of manufactured exports in 1854 rising to one-third in 1913, and the growth of imports

18. R.E. Tyson, 'The Cotton Industry', in D.H. Aldcroft, ed. *British Industries and Foreign Competition*; L.G. Sandberg, *Lancashire in Decline: A Study in Entrepreneurship, Technology and International Trade* (Columbus, Ohio, 1974); D.A. Farnie, *The English Cotton Industry and the World Market, 1815–96*, (Oxford, 1979), pp. 171ff; J. Nicholson, 'Popular Imperialism and the Provincial Press: Manchester Evening Newspapers, 1895–1902', *Victorian Periodicals Review*, XII (1980), pp. 85, 89–90.

19. Deane and Cole, *British Economic Growth, 1688–1959*, p. 33.

was so rapid that, between 1870 and 1913, *net* manufactured exports (exports minus imports) grew at only 0.4 per cent per annum.[20]

Net exports of manufactures to foreign countries rose in the 1860s but then fell with alarming rapidity until the turn of the century, apart from a brief recovery in the 1880s. In 1902, according to contemporary Board of Trade figures, they fell to their lowest point of slightly less than £20m.; and, at that time, Britain was actually in deficit to foreign countries in trade in the most highly finished goods. There was a recovery from 1903 onwards; but despite the hectic boom in world trade just before the war, net exports showed a tendency to stagnate after 1906 and, in 1913, the recovery had taken Britain back only to the position she held in 1870. By contrast, net exports to the empire increased steadily until the 1880s, marked time in the following decade, and then rose to previously unrecorded heights just before World War I (Table 5.4).

Table 5.4 Net exports of British manufactures; 1860–1913 (£m.)

| | Foreign countries | | British empire | |
	(a)	(b)	(a)	(b)
1860	68.5		34.8	
1870	94.4		41.3	
1880	72.0		72.1	
1890	80.9		70.0	
1900	40.5		68.1	
1901	25.3		79.4	
1902	19.3		84.1	
1903	26.3		87.2	
1904	35.3		87.6	
1905	54.0		88.1	
1906	64.0	80.9	92.5	93.6
1907	98.0	84.9	106.1	108.7
1908	68.8	76.3	97.6	100.5
1909		71.1		102.6
1910		93.7		119.6
1911		88.1		127.9
1912		85.8		142.8
1913		88.6		157.6

Sources: Figures for (a) 1860–1908 are from Board of Trade, *Statistical Tables and Charts Relating to British and Foreign Trade and Industry* PP. 1909, Cd4954, and for (b) 1906–13 are from the *Statistical Abstract of the United Kingdom* (HMSO).

20. W. Arthur Lewis, *Growth and Fluctuations, 1870–1913* (1978), pp. 118–19.

Nonetheless, a crude division between the fate of manufacturing trade with foreign countries and with the empire gives a misleading impression of the importance of the latter since most of Britain's imports of manufactured goods came from a handful of newly industrialising and developing countries. In 1913, when manufactured imports accounted for 25 per cent of all imports, two-thirds of the total (£112.3m.) came from four European countries with which Britain had heavy deficits on manufacturing trade (Table 5.5). Only £58m. came from other foreign countries, and the United States accounted for nearly one-half of that (£26.4m.). Britain also exported nearly as much to 'other foreign countries' as she did to the empire and her net export position with them was nearly as healthy as it was with her own possessions. Part of this surplus on manufactured trade was with other advanced countries, including The Netherlands and the United States – to which Britain sold £6.7m. more than she bought in 1913 – but most of it was gained in trade with the non-industrial periphery including Latin America and the Middle and Far East. This is another way of emphasising how much Britain had come to depend upon exports not just to the empire but to a wide range of what Arthur Lewis has called 'semi-industrial' countries in this period. By 1913, Germany sold more manufactured goods in Europe than did

Table 5.5 British Trade in manufactures, 1913 (£m.)

	Imports	Exports and re-exports	Net exports[a]
Germany	−56.1	+30.2	−25.9
Belgium	−17.4	+9.0	−8.4
France	−29.6	+19.2	−10.4
Switzerland	−9.2	+4.4	−4.8
Total[b]	−112.3	+62.8	−49.5
Other foreign countries	−58.0	+196.0	+138.0
All foreign countries[c]	−170.3	+258.8	+88.5
British empire	−23.4	+181.0	+157.6
Total[d]	−193.7	+439.8	+246.1

Source: *Annual Statement of Trade and Navigation.*

Notes: [a] Difference between imports and exports/re-exports.
[b] Total for Germany, Belgium, France and Switzerland
[c] Total for Germany, Belgium, France, Switzerland and other foreign countries.
[d] Total for all foreign countries plus British empire.

Britain – $925m. worth as opposed to $624m. – and matched Britain's performance in sales to the very poorest of non-industrial countries. However, to the semi-industrial group – which included Australia, New Zealand, South Africa, India, Brazil, Argentina, Chile, Colombia, Mexico and Turkey – Britain sold $810m. worth of manufactures, nearly four times as much as Germany, and equivalent to two-fifths of all her manufactured exports.[21] This reflected a cosmopolitanism which no other trading nations of the time could match or even seriously challenge;[22] it also formed an important element in an economic imperialism which ranged far beyond a concern with the Scramble for Africa and even with 'formal' empire as a whole.

Table 5.6 Visible trade balance: Britain, 1851–1913 (annual averages, £m.)

	Exports and re-exports	Imports	Balance of trade[a]	%[b]
1851–75	195	−246	−51	−26.2
1876–1900	291	−411	−120	−41.2
1901–13	483	−631	−153	−31.2

Source: Mitchell and Deane, *Abstract*.

Notes: [a] Difference between exports/re-exports and imports.
[b] Balance of trade divided by sum of exports and re-exports.

The rise in manufactured imports was one of the principal influences on the size of the balance of trade deficit which the British ran during this period. The trade gap was partly filled by re-exports, which ran at between 12 per cent and 16 per cent of gross imports between 1850 and 1913, but the gap remained considerable, as Table 5.6 shows. It widened markedly during the period 1875–1900, as export growth slowed down and manufactured imports began to rise sharply, before narrowing again after 1900 when, for the first time since the boom of 1868–73, exports rose faster than imports. This gap was more than filled by 'invisible' exports, or exports of services, which were the international expression of the growing importance of the service sector whose structures we have already described.

21. Ibid. p. 121.
22. Two-thirds of all British exports went to extra-European destinations in 1909–11. The corresponding figure for Germany was 26 per cent. See Paul Bairoch, 'Geographical Structure and Trade Balances of European Foreign Trade from 1800 to 1970', *Jour. Eur. Econ. Hist.*, III (1974), p. 566.

TRADE IN SERVICES

There are few generalisations about Victorian and Edwardian Britain which are more firmly based than the assertion that, as Britain's manufacturing industries began to decline in relative importance and exports became less competitive, a more than adequate compensation was found through the growth in 'invisible' exports. As Arthur Lewis put the matter over 30 years ago: 'having ceased to be able to command an abnormal share of world trade in manufactures, Britain temporarily maintained her balance of payments by achieving an abnormal share of the world's shipping, insurance, and, other commercial services', which 'developed so considerably that a large surplus was still left to finance a growing export of capital, the accumulated stores of which themselves provided Britain with an ever growing income from interest and dividends'.[23] The sources of, and broad movements in, Britain's invisible income are summarised in Table 5.7.

Table 5.7 Invisible trade and balance of payments: Britain, 1851–1913

	1851–75	*1876–1900*	*1901–13*
Balance of trade	−51	−120	−153
Business services[a]	+24	+35	+49
Shipping	+35	+58	+87
Balance of services[b]	+59	+93	+136
Overseas investment income	+26	+80	+151
Balance of payments[c]	+34	+53	+134

Source: Imlah, *Economic Elements in the Pax Britannica*. We have preferred Imlah's figures to those produced by C.H. Feinstein, *Statistical Tables of National Income, Expenditure and Output, 1855–1965* (Cambridge, 1972), because Feinstein's series begins only in 1870 and does not distinguish shipping from other services.

Notes: [a] Business services include insurance and are net of some miscellaneous expenditure on services, including government spending abroad.
[b] Business services plus shipping.
[c] Balance of trade plus balance of services plus overseas investment income.

Shipping income rose steadily throughout the period 1850 to 1914 (Table 5.7). In the wake of the repeal of the Navigation Acts, competition from the American and Scandinavian merchant marines was acute – the British proportion of the tonnage of shipping cleared

23. W. Arthur Lewis, *Economic Survey, 1919–39* (1949), p. 77.

in cargo through British ports fell from 70 per cent in 1848 to 60 per cent in 1858 – although in absolute terms tonnage grew rapidly. The rise of the iron ship, in which the British had a competitive edge, and the adverse effects of the Civil War on American shipping gave Britain a relative advantage over other shipping nations, and her share of the tonnage using British ports rose to over 70 per cent again by the late 1890s. Britain's share began to decline towards World War I, as did her share in the world's steam tonnage. This had risen steadily from 26 per cent in 1860 to around 60 per cent in 1890 before falling off sharply to just over 40 per cent in 1914. The steeper fall in Britain's share of steam tonnage than in her share of tonnage in British ports probably indicates the unsurprising fact that Britain was losing out more in non-British trade than she was in her own. In the British trade, too, shipping felt the benefits of empire. Britain's share in shipping services with British possessions trading in British ports actually rose from 87 per cent in 1880–4 to 96 per cent in 1905–9.[24] The growth of shipping income was, of course, intimately related to the growth of other forms of invisible income, such as re-exports, which came mainly from the empire, where British shipping was dominant, and the shipping insurance business, of which London was the world centre.

Britain's income from shipping was large because her trade was large: the value of her net imports in 1860 was about 30 per cent of the rest of the world's exports and her share was still 17 per cent in 1913.[25] This high share was partly the result of free trade: the openness of the British market encouraged the growth of Britain as a re-export centre. But it is also evident from the size of the merchant marine that Britain's shipping was extensively used for non-British trade, and the same was true of 'foreign trade services' (Table 5.7).

As Britain was the world's outstanding international trader and the greatest free market in the world, the main British ports, and especially London, became great warehouses for the primary commodity trade of the world, the chief centres for the buying and selling of everything from precious stones to basic foodstuffs. This immense traffic was the source of the business in international short-term credits for which the City of London was justly famed.[26] After 1860,

---

24. These figures are taken from Board of Trade, *Memoranda on Foreign Trade*, Cd 4954 (1909).

25. Imlah, *Economic Elements in the Pax Britannica*, p. 191.

26. An overdue reminder of the *commercial* basis of the City of London's financial operations has recently been provided by Geoffrey Ingham, *Capitalism Divided? The City and Industry in British Social Development* (1984), p. 5.

there was a decline in the use of the internal bill of exchange as a means of trade payment, and it was superseded by the use of the cheque system provided by the rapidly developing joint-stock banking network.[27] The discount houses in the London market, which had hitherto dealt mainly in domestic paper, shifted their attention to international credit, the 'bill on London'. Many of the leading merchant bankers, whose more prestigious activities included the issue of foreign loans, nonetheless made a good living in 'acceptance' business, that is in guaranteeing bills which could then be more easily placed in the discount market. The latter was dependent on using funds provided by the joint-stock banks, which regarded the money laid out in the London market as an ideal pool of near-liquid but profitable assets.[28] This market in short-term credit was the City of London's most unique feature. Its power is indicated by the extent to which foreign merchants, trading between their own countries and Britain, often found it profitable to operate from London, where they could more easily utilise the sterling credits that trade depended upon: the City was constantly absorbing foreign firms and foreign talent in this way. Many other foreign banking institutions, lacking the same local facilities where money was both easily available and also earning a return, found London an ideal place for their spare assets, which then formed part of the vast pool of liquidity keeping world trade on the move.

One very important source of overseas funds for the market was provided by the international and imperial banks, which had their headquarters in the City. These banks first became prominent in the white colonies in the 1830s and had become global in scope by the 1860s. The spread of joint-stock banks at home was paralleled by an enormous extension of their influence abroad. After various legislative hindrances were removed in the late 1850s and early 1860s, their orbit became world-wide. George Goschen, gentlemanly banker and Chancellor of the Exchequer during the Baring Crisis of 1891, could claim in the 1880s

> that English and French banking principles are on a crusading tour throughout the world. . . . Banks abound whose familiar names in every variety suggest the one pervading fact of the marriage of English capital with foreign demand. There is the Anglo–Austrian Bank, the Anglo–Italian Bank, the Anglo–Egyptian Bank. There is the English and

27. S. Nishimura, *The Decline of Inland Bills of Exchange in the London Money Market, 1855–1913* (Cambridge, 1971).
28. M. de Cecco, *Money and Empire: The International Gold Standard, 1890–1914* (Oxford, 1974), Ch. 5.

Swedish Bank; there is the British and Californian Bank, there is the London and Hamburg Continental Exchange Bank; there is the London and Brazilian Bank, the London Buenos Ayres and River Plate Bank, and even a London and South American Bank. [29]

These banks, raising their capital in Britain and their deposits locally and using them as a basis to extend trade credit, were extremely important in spreading British trade and finance, and British influence, around the globe and in integrating large parts of the world into the international economy under Britain's leadership.[30] This trade credit was supplemented by the creation of 'finance' or 'accommodation' bills, based upon no particular trading transaction, but important in extending liquidity in many smaller countries, including some in Europe, like Denmark, which relied heavily on trade with Britain.

FOREIGN INVESTMENTS

Despite considerable growth, the returns on invisible services and shipping were insufficient, after the mid-1870s, to fill entirely the deficit on visible trade (Table 5.7), and Britain's ability to generate a balance of payments surplus came to depend increasingly upon the returns on investments abroad.

Britain was at the centre of the market for international finance after 1850. Numerous attempts have been made to estimate the accumulated total of British assets abroad since the pioneering work of Paish undertaken before World War I. Until recently, assessments by different methods had led to a broad agreement that British investments overseas were worth £195m.–230m. in the mid–1850s, rising to about £700m. in 1870, over £2,000m. by 1900 and to between £3,500m. and £4,000m. by 1913. The periods of most rapid growth were 1869–73, the late 1880s and 1909–13, with low points in the late 1870s and the 1890s. By 1913, these assets are said to have produced an income of roughly £200m., equivalent to about one-

29. G.J. Goschen, *Essays and Addresses* (1905), p. 23.

30. A.S.J. Baster, *The Imperial Banks* (1929) and idem, *The International Banks* (1934) are still extremely valuable studies. See also Youssef Cassis, *La City de Londres* (Paris, 1987), pp. 37–40, and idem, 'Competition Advantage in British Multinational Banking since 1890', in Geoffrey Jones, ed. *Banks as Multinationals* (1990). On investment banks, which were often explicitly designed to transfer capital abroad, see P.L. Cottrell, 'London Financiers and Austria, 1863–75: the Anglo-Austrian Bank', *Bus. Hist.*, XI (1969), and idem, 'The Financial Sector and Economic Growth: England in the Nineteenth Century', *Revue internationale d'histoire de la banque*, 4 (1971).

tenth of the national income.[31] These figures have been strongly challenged by D.C.M. Platt. His argument is that because Britain marketed foreign securities it should not be taken for granted that British investors either bought them or, if they did buy them, that they held on to them for long periods, and that all previous estimates are exaggerated because, like Paish's, they fail to recognise this. So, whereas Paish's estimate just before the war was for an accumulated holding of about £4,000m., Platt argues that this figure should be reduced to £3,100m. or just over three-quarters of the generally accepted total.[32]

In some ways, Platt's claims are a sophisticated modern version of criticisms of Paish's estimates voiced by contemporaries such as Keynes, and there is some substance in them.[33] The most recent survey of shareholdings of companies which raised money in London for overseas ventures shows that, on average, nearly 17 per cent of the shares of firms operating in foreign countries were held abroad. Moreover, although only about 3 per cent of the shares of firms located in the empire were so held, 8 per cent of shares in firms located in the empire were held in the empire itself.[34] The importance of foreign participation in loans raised in the City of London is also clear from the detailed records of particular issues. Of the £1.5m. raised in 1888 for the Argentine North-Eastern railway company, around two-fifths at least were raised in Paris and Berlin, though the syndicate underwriting the loan was organised by the London merchant bankers, Antony Gibbs and Son.[35] Similarly, when Barings

31. On the rise of British foreign investments overseas see P.L. Cottrell, *British Overseas Investment in the Nineteenth Century* (1975), and M. Simon, 'The Pattern of New British Portfolio Foreign Investment, 1865–1914', in J.H. Adler, ed. *Capital Movements and Economic Development* (1967), reprinted in A.R. Hall, *The Export of Capital from Britain, 1870–1914* (1968); and, most recently, Lance E. Davis and Robert A. Huttenback, *Mammon and the Pursuit of Empire: The Political Economy of British Imperialism, 1860–1912* (Cambridge, 1987), Table 2.1, pp. 40–1. For George Paish's original estimates of overseas investment see: 'Great Britain's Capital Investments in Other Lands', *Journal of the Royal Statistical Society*, LXXII (1909); and 'Great Britain's Capital Investments in Individual Colonies and Foreign Countries', ibid. LXXV (1911).

32. D.C.M. Platt, *Britain's Investment Overseas on the Eve of the First World War* (1986), Table 2.3, p. 60. For similar argument see idem, 'British Portfolio Investment Overseas Before 1870: Some Doubts', *Econ. Hist. Rev.*, 2nd ser. XXXIII (1980).

33. J.M. Keynes, 'Great Britain's Foreign Investment (1910)', in *Collected Works of John Maynard Keynes*, XV (Cambridge, 1971); pp. 57–8; E. Crammond, 'International Finance in Times of War', *Quarterly Review*, 425 (1910), p. 317; also B.R. Tomlinson, 'The Contraction of England: National Decline and the Loss of Empire', *Jour. of Imp. and Comm. Hist.*, XI (1982), pp. 63–4.

34. Davis and Huttenback, *Mammon and the Pursuit of Empire*, Table 7.5, p. 209.

35. Stanley Chapman, *The Rise of Merchant Banking*, p. 159.

organised a loan for the Argentine government in 1907, only 43 per cent of the money was raised in London: 31 per cent came from France and 26 per cent from Germany.[36] It is also true that foreign loans originally purchased by Britons were often repatriated: many of the stocks of American railroads bought in Britain in the 1880s found their way back to the United States over the next 30 years.[37]

On the other hand, Platt may have underestimated the extent to which British investors subscribed to loans raised in foreign centres such as Paris. But a more important difficulty with his position is that he assumes that the bulk of the capital raised on the London Stock Exchange before 1913 was portfolio investment – that is, loans issued by foreign or imperial firms or governments over which the British buyer of stock had no control. Platt estimates that a total of £2,600m. of portfolio investment was outstanding in 1913 compared with only £500m. worth of direct investments resulting from the creation of British-owned companies overseas. Of other recent global estimates, however, one suggests that direct investments were around 35 per cent and another that they were between 44 per cent and 60 per cent of the total of accumulated assets by 1913: a similarly high proportion of direct investment has been found in a detailed analysis of British investments in Argentina.[38] If these estimates are correct, then the likelihood that the bulk of the capital would be owned and retained by British nationals is strong. Beside this, Platt's revisions of the direct estimates of foreign investment made by Paish and others conflict with the indirect one made by Imlah. The latter was based upon the accumulated balance of payments surpluses calculated from his revision of British visible and invisible trade income. Platt is critical of Imlah's figures,[39] but offers no alternative to them.

Platt's achievement is to cast doubt on the legitimacy of all estimates, including his own. This is evident from Davis and Hutten-back's recent work. They concentrate on the export of finance raised

---

36. Cassis, *La City de Londres*, p. 119.

37. Platt, *British Investments Overseas*, pp. 116–26. A considerable turnover in assets is indicated by research on British investments in overseas land and on the dealings of the British Assets Trust. See A.J. Christopher, 'Patterns of British Overseas Investment in Land, 1885–1913', *Institute of British Geographers Transactions*, 10 (1985); and R.C. Michie, 'Crisis and Opportunity: the Formation and Operation of the British Assets Trust, 1897–1914', *Bus. Hist.*, XXVI (1983).

38. Peter Svedberg, 'The Portfolio-Direct Composition of Private Foreign Investment in 1914 Revisited', *Econ. Jour.*, LXXXVII (1978); Mira Wilkins, 'The Free-Standing Company, 1870–1914: an Important Type of British Foreign Direct Investment', *Econ. Hist. Rev.* 2nd ser. XLI (1988); Irving Stone, 'British Long Term Investment in Latin America, 1865–1913', *Bus. Hist. Rev.*, XLII (1968).

39. Platt, *British Overseas Investments*, pp. 17–21.

in London, and deliberately avoid the problem of how much of this finance represented long-term foreign investment. Yet they still manage to offer three different sets of estimates: a minimum one based on issues taken up entirely in the United Kingdom plus two others which allow for, *inter alia*, calls on capital made in foreign countries. As a result, Davis and Huttenback produce estimates ranging from a low of £3,165m. to a maximum of £4,779m.; all three estimates carry the proviso that 'the actual totals are almost certainly higher than the figures reported' in their main source, the financial press.[40] For all these reasons, it is difficult to accept that the original estimates should be replaced without further detailed research,[41] although Platt's emphasis on Britain as an international service centre as well as a lender is a salutary one.

Recent disputes over the size of Britain's foreign investments have not really disturbed conventional judgements on their geographical location or their composition by enterprise.[42] Before about 1870, loans to central governments were predominant and were mainly placed in Europe and the Middle East, though even at that stage railway investments in Europe, North America and India were significant. After 1870, as capitalism spread across the globe, communications improved steadily and a truly international economy came into being. Vast infrastructural investments were made in South America, Australasia and Asia as well as the United States. By 1913, 65 per cent of British investments were in newly settled countries, including the white settled colonies, but ranging far beyond them: over the period 1865–1914, roughly three-fifths of all the money raised in London went to foreign countries and two-fifths to the empire, with the centre of gravity in the latter area shifting steadily from India to the white colonies.[43] In addition, whereas half of the money raised in Britain for foreign or empire activities in 1865–72 went to governments, two-thirds of new funds in 1909–13 were

40. Davis and Huttenback, *Mammon and the Pursuit of Empire*, pp. 35–6 and Table 2.1, p. 40.

41. See, in addition, W.P. Kennedy's review of Platt in *Econ. Hist. Rev.*, 2nd ser. XL (1987); and, more recently, the criticisms of Platt's estimates in Charles Feinstein, 'Britain's Overseas Investments in 1913', *Econ. Hist. Rev.*, 2nd ser. XLIII (1990).

42. The best discussion of the geographical and institutional distribution of overseas investments remains Simon's 'The Pattern of New British Portfolio Foreign Investment', cited above and idem, 'The Enterprise and Industrial Composition of New British Portfolio Investment, 1865–1914', *Journal of Development Studies*, III (1967). His overall picture is not seriously disturbed by the new surveys by Davis and Huttenback, *Mammon and the Pursuit of Empire*, Ch. II, and Platt, *British Overseas Investments*, Chs. V and VI.

43. Davis and Huttenback, *Mammon and the Pursuit of Empire*, Table 2.1, pp. 40–1.

raised for private concerns; of the reduced government portion, much more was issued by municipalities and provincial authorities in 1913 than in 1870, a sign in particular of the growing strength and complexity of capitalist organisation on the newly settled frontier. Railways remained the first preference of British investors placing money abroad. Only about 15 per cent of investments went directly into mining or manufacturing industry just before the war.[44]

The increased predominance of British loans abroad and of Britain as a market for international funds, was part of the rapid internationalisation of the economy after 1850. And, as the free-trade regime established itself, Britain grew in importance as banker, moneylender, insurer, shipper and wholesaler to the world at large. As a result, the demand for Britain's currency, sterling, was widespread. Sterling developed into the most important international currency, and circulated in the world, or at least outside Europe, almost as freely as it did at home. Confidence in sterling was maintained by its convertibility into gold or other currencies at a fixed ratio, which made it easy to hold and to use; sterling also benefited from the fact that the British navy secured the safety of British trade and protected the island from invasion, making Britain 'the strong box and the safe of Europe'.[45] In addition, foreigners could be induced to hold sterling because it earned interest if it was held in British financial institutions, whereas gold itself, the basis of the system, was sterile. Sterling's use was further enhanced by strong links between the markets for short-term credits and those for bonds. Funds in London for trading or similar purposes, if temporarily unemployed, could find a home in some safe, easily saleable stock marketed on the Stock Exchange,[46] which had a range and a liquidity unmatched in the world at that time. Hence, it is reasonable to argue that, before 1914, there was a sterling standard in operation rather than a gold standard;[47] and confidence in sterling clearly increased the desire to buy British goods and British services.

44. Simon, 'Enterprise and Industrial Composition', p. 289. Davis and Huttenback, *Mammon and the Pursuit of Empire*, pp. 53ff, indicate a considerable interest in agriculture, mainly plantations, in the empire. See also Platt, *British Overseas Investments*, Table 6.2, p. 114.

45. The words of Lord Rosebery in *Parliamentary Debates* (Lords), 1909, IV, 22 Nov. 1909, c. 947–8.

46. R.C. Michie, 'Options, Concessions, Syndicates and the Provision of Venture Capital, 1880–1913', *Bus. Hist.*, XXIII (1981), pp. 158–9; also idem, 'Different in Name Only? The London Stock Exchange and Foreign Bourses, c. 1850–1914', *Bus. Hist.*, XXX (1988).

47. W.M. Scammell, 'The Working of the Gold Standard', *Yorkshire Bulletin of Economic and Social Research*, XVII (1965).

The openness of the economy encouraged the growth of the service economy, and the continuance of free trade was important to its success. Free trade meant that all those who had payments to make in Britain, whether in return for British exports or in payment for loans or services, could earn sterling by selling commodities in the British market. Britain's deficit on her visible trading account was a necessary function of the part which she played as an international mart and banker.[48] In turn, the service sector generated an increasingly large invisible income which filled the visible trade gap, left a surplus on the current account of the balance of payments and thus provided the means to swell British assets abroad and increase rentier incomes. This is clear from Table 5.6 and also from Table 5.8, which looks at foreign trade in the context of the growth of gross domestic product.

Table 5.8 Balance of payments on current account: ratios to GDP, 1856–1913 (per cent)

	1856–73	*1874–90*	*1899–1913*
Exports of goods	17.9	18.4	17.7
Imports of goods	−20.9	−23.9	−23.8
Balance of trade[a]	−3.0	−5.5	−6.1
Net services income	4.7	5.1	4.3
Balance of trade and services[b]	1.7	−0.4	−1.8
Net income for abroad	2.8	5.4	6.8
Balance of payments on current account[c]	4.5	5.0	5.0

Source: R.C.O. Matthews, C.H. Feinstein and J.C. Odling-Smee, *British Economic Growth, 1856–1973* (Oxford, 1983) p. 442

Notes: [a] Difference between exports and imports.
  [b] Balance of trade plus net services income.
  [c] Balance of trade and services plus net income for abroad.

Table 5.8 demonstrates both the inability of services alone – at between 4 per cent and 5 per cent of GDP – to fill the widening trade gap, and the growing dependence on income from foreign assets, which had reached the equivalent of almost 7 per cent of GDP in the 20 years before the war. Using Feinstein's figures, we can look at this from a different angle. Between 1870 and 1913 income from trade in services usually bought about one-sixth of gross imports; at the same time, income from assets owned abroad rose from around 15 per cent

48. S.B. Saul, *Studies in Overseas Trade, 1870–1914* (Liverpool, 1960), Chs. 3–4; R. Skidelsky, 'Retreat from Leadership: the Evolution of British Economic Foreign Policy', in B.M. Rowland, ed. *Balance of Power or Hegemony* (New York, 1976).

of gross imports in 1871–5 to 27 per cent in 1909–11.[49] The income from services may be underestimated,[50] and that from foreign investment exaggerated, as we have seen; but the growing importance of invisible income, at a time when industrial exports were weakening and manufactured imports rising, cannot be in doubt.

COMMERCE, FINANCE AND FREE TRADE

Finally, it is worth emphasising that the interconnections between the 'invisible' elements in the account and between invisible and visible trade were highly complex and important. As we have already seen, the use of sterling encouraged the role of London as a banking centre and as a 'strongbox' for world saving, and this in turn enhanced London's ability to lend abroad. Overseas loans also encouraged the use of British banking and commercial facilities abroad[51] and British shipping and insurance. The re-export trade, which was equivalent to between 12 and 16 per cent of gross imports, depended on Britain's position as an international wholesale market and on her credit and financial network. It was London's pre-eminent role as an entrepôt for trade – a result of Britain's unique economic development and her policy of free trade – which made her the outstanding centre for trade credit and insurance. The vast commerce of London was the solid base on which the 'bill on London', and sterling's supremacy, rested. The outcome was a short-term credit market which was unique in the world and capable of attracting money from many other foreign banking centres on the look-out for safe but highly liquid openings for their spare funds.[52]

Britain's shipping was also tied in with her function as a financial centre: it was a testimony to the extent and ramification of the monetary network that between one-fifth and one-quarter of all British-owned ships rarely entered British ports.[53] Links with industry were close as well, since even Britain's greatest industrial success story of the post–1850 period, shipbuilding, was in many ways a

49. These calculations are derived from C.H. Feinstein, *Statistical Tables of National Income, Expenditure and Output of the U.K., 1855–1965* (Cambridge, 1973), Table 15.

50. Saul, 'The Export Economy', p. 10.

51. For imperial and international banks as conduits for overseas investment see Goschen, *Essays and Addresses*, pp. 22–3.

52. R.J. Truptil, *British Banks and the London Money Market* (1936), pp. 125–6.

53. Crouzet, *The Victorian Economy*, p. 313.

function of the creation of her invisible empire of commerce and the demand for her mercantile marine that this helped to stimulate. The size of the market was a factor in British technological superiority: it allowed 'different yards to specialize in certain types of ships, to apply mass production methods to some processes and to use their capital assets to the maximum'.[54]

The relationship between the overall flows of British foreign investment and the movement of British commodity exports was more complex.[55] British loans were never tied: exports and loans came, as we shall see in Chapter 6, from two different income streams, two different regional economies. But British governments in the dependent empire often used loans to finance projects in which the purchase of British goods and services was taken for granted. And exports sometimes followed in the slipstream of foreign investment elsewhere because of close kinship relations – as in the white colonies – or because of Britain's overall dominance of the financial and trading network, as occurred in some parts of Latin America. But the relationship between capital export and commodity exports weakened over time as competition increased. This fact raises the wider question (which we shall address in Chapter 6) of whether Britain's extensive foreign investments were of overall benefit to the economy.

54. Ibid. pp. 253–4.
55. Bairoch, *Commerce extérieur et développement économique*, pp. 110–111, and 199–200, argues for a correlation between merchandise exports and capital export; but compare this claim with Sidney Pollard, 'Capital Exports – Harmful or Beneficial?', *Econ. Hist. Rev.*, 2nd ser. XXXVIII (1985), p. 508. See also idem, *Britain's Prime and Britain's Decline: The British Economy, 1870–1914* (1989), pp. 103–4.

CHAPTER SIX

Two Nations? Foreign Investment and the Domestic Economy, 1850–1914

The sharp increase in the share of British savings going abroad after 1850 was a response both to new demands created by a growing world economy and to the pressures of increased supply. Edelstein's comprehensive survey of fluctuations in British investment overseas suggests, firstly, that the upward trend in foreign investment from 1850 to the 1870s was due, in the main, to the demands of countries such as the United States who were embarking on heavy infrastructural investments and lacked adequate savings of their own. Foreign investment in the early part of the period was, therefore, the result of the 'pull' of attractively high interest rates abroad. This influence was still felt after 1870: Australia, Argentina and the United States played the most prominent role in the foreign investment boom of the 1880s and Canada proved to be the most important market for British capital just before World War I. After 1870, though, the pull of foreign demand was supplemented increasingly by changes in the structure and the growth of the British economy which tended to 'push' savings out into foreign fields. The general tendency was for the weight of savings to push down the rate of interest in Britain and drive investors to look for more profitable opportunities abroad, as the economy adjusted after 1870 to a permanently lower rate of growth. This latter phenomenon flowed from the convergence of a number of major influences, including the secular decline in the birthrate and the consequent slower growth in the demand for major population-sensitive investments such as housing.[1] It was also very obviously connected with the fact that, as savings rose rapidly after

1. Michael Edelstein, *Overseas Investment in the Age of High Imperialism, 1850–1914* (New York, 1982), passim. There is a convenient summary of his principal findings on pp. 288–311.

1870, industry did not change in ways that created a sizeable demand for new investment.

THE CITY AND FOREIGN INVESTMENT

The role of the City, in this context, was to act as a channel through which savings that would once have gone into the national debt or into railways in Britain now found their way into similar investments offering a steady return abroad. The bulk of these savings came from the gentlemanly capitalist class and from the service sector of the south-east. This is borne out by the most recent evidence, Davis and Huttenback's analysis of 80,000 shareholders in 260 firms, operating both in Britain and abroad between 1883 and 1907, which at some time raised money in the City.[2] One particularly striking finding of their research is that investors with a background in business much preferred home to foreign investments and, perhaps even more surprising, foreign stocks to imperial ones (Table 6.1).

Table 6.1 Relative holdings of overseas stocks (by occupation), 1865–1914 (UK = 100)

Occupation	Foreign firms	Empire firms
Merchants	173	76
Manufacturers	24	13
Professional and Management	66	64
Miscellaneous Business	100	41
All business	86	45
Financiers	228	97
Military	63	76
Miscellaneous Elites	200	260
Peers and Gentlemen	97	166
All Elites	115	153

Source: Lance E. Davis and Robert A. Huttenback, *Mammon and the Pursuit of Empire: The Political Economy of British Imperialism, 1860–1912* (Cambridge, 1987), Table 7.6, p. 212.

The only exceptions to this generalisation were merchant investors, who showed a greater interest in foreign companies: for every £100

2. Lance E. Davis and Robert A. Huttenback, *Mammon and the Pursuit of Empire: The Political Economy of British Imperialism, 1860–1912* (Cambridge, 1987), pp. 195–6.

they invested in domestic securities, they put £173 into foreign concerns. Nonetheless, they, too, preferred domestic investments to those available in the empire. Manufacturers, for their part, were four times more likely to invest in a British-based company than one in a foreign land and seven times more interested in domestic than in imperial firms. Overall, the business class (which includes the professions – law, management, medicine, education, etc.) was responsible for one-half of the investment in British-based companies but rather less than one-third of those in foreign countries or the empire. Investors with a background in manufacturing accounted for less than 6 per cent of Britain's overseas loans.[3]

In contrast, Davis and Huttenback's 'elite' category – which corresponds roughly to our gentlemanly capitalist class, though it omits some of the professional groups we would include in this class – had a much greater predeliction for cosmopolitan investments. The financiers among them were indifferent between domestic and imperial outlets but had a massive preference for foreign investments over both. 'Peers and gents', on the other hand, were marginally more favourable to domestic than to foreign investment but preferred empire investments to both by a very wide margin. 'Miscellaneous elites', including ecclesiastics, government officials and some parliamentarians, had a decided preference for both foreign and empire stocks over domestic ones; among elites, only military men showed an inclination to favour domestic stocks (Table 6.1).

Although there was some overlap between the groups, the kinds of investments chosen by businessmen and elites were often sharply different. Business investors, especially manufacturers, insofar as they ventured abroad at all, were much more inclined than elites to favour firms working in agriculture, mining or industry, thus making investments abroad similar to those they chose at home. Elites preferred banks, public utilities, transport and other infrastructural investments as well as government paper – again searching outside Europe for the kinds of investments they tended to favour in Britain.[4] Among elite groups, 'peers and gents' were dominant, accounting for around one-fifth of all investors in British-based companies in Davis and Huttenback's sample and no fewer than one-quarter of the stockholders in both foreign and empire-based firms.[5] Investors in this sociological category were also among the largest stockholders.

3. Ibid. Table 7.33, p. 204.
4. Ibid. Table 7.7, p. 213.
5. Ibid. Table 7.33, p. 204.

Of the 35 largest identified by Davis and Huttenback, 22 were peers or gentlemen, 10 were merchants and 3 were bankers.[6]

The importance of this group as overseas investors dovetails neatly with evidence from other sources concerning the business behaviour of the aristocracy in response to the decline in rents from arable agricultural land which set in after 1870. The 8th Duke of Devonshire shifted assets out of both agriculture and industry after 1890 and invested heavily in overseas railways and government stocks, which provided a considerable part of his income before 1914, and the major part of it by the 1920s.[7] Similarly, the Earl of Leicester, also one of the top 50 income-earners in Britain in the late nineteenth century, offset falling rent rolls by putting a large amount of his surplus income into railways both at home and in the empire after 1870.[8] There are other examples of adjustments to rural adversity which involved foreign investment,[9] and some of them were doubtless inspired by the new educational and social ties which brought landed gentlemen into close touch with gentlemanly City bankers. Earls Grey and Wantage benefited in this way from connections in the Square Mile;[10] and the funding of many of the investment trusts, formed at the end of the century and spearheaded by merchant banks and merchant houses, came from the traditionally wealthy.[11] The preference which peers and gentlemen showed for empire was probably a result of their social connections since many of them had relations or friends in government or colonial administration or had served abroad themselves. As Michie notes,

> the Empire found it easier and less expensive to borrow in Britain than foreign countries, as the British investor was more inclined to trust those who belonged to the wider British community, though the actual security offered might be identical.[12]

6. Ibid. p. 206.

7. David Cannadine, 'Landowner as Millionaire: the Finances of the Dukes of Devonshire, c. 1800- c.1926', *Agricultural History Review*, CCV (1977).

8. Susan W. Martins, *A Great Estate at Work: The Holkham Estate and its Inhabitants in the Nineteenth Century* (1980), pp. 58–65 and App. II.

9. David Spring, 'Land and Politics in Edwardian England', *Agricultural History*, 58 (1984), pp. 22–6. It was still the case in 1914 that the majority of the landed aristocracy depended mainly upon these rentals for survival and reacted to the depression by selling land and by introducing economies. See Andrew Adonis, 'Aristocracy, Agriculture and Liberalism: The Politics, Finance and Estates of the Third Lord Carrington', *Hist. Jour.*, 31 (1988), pp. 881–3.

10. R.C. Michie, 'The Social Web of Investment in the Nineteenth Century', *Revue internationale d'histoire de la banque*, 18–19 (1979), pp. 164–8.

11. S.D. Chapman, 'British-Based Investment Groups before 1914', *Econ. Hist. Rev.*, 2nd ser. XXXVIII (1985).

12. Michie, 'The Social Web of Investment', p. 173.

That trust must have been much increased through the intimate contacts between members of the gentlemanly class, who were the 'natural leaders' in both Britain and large parts of the empire.

Table 6.2 Geographical distribution of stockholders, 1865–1914 (per cent of value held)

| Residence of stockholders | Location of firms | | |
	UK	Foreign	Empire
Foreign	0.4	16.7	2.6
Empire	0.1	0.1	8.5
London	20.8	50.9	58.5
Non-metropolitan England	59.1	25.8	21.2
Scotland, Wales and Ireland	19.5	6.2	9.1
Unknown	—	0.3	0.1
	100	100	100

Source: Davis and Huttenback, *Mammon and the Pursuit of Empire*, Table 7.5, p. 209.

The non-industrial basis of most overseas investments is revealed with equal clarity through an examination of the geographical spread of stockholding (Table 6.2). Shares in domestic firms were widespread, but London dominated overseas investment. London investors took one-fifth of the shares of the domestic companies but over one-half of those operating overseas. For every £100 invested at home, provincial English and Celtic investors were prepared to place only £50 abroad, whereas Londoners put £156 and £161 in foreign or imperial companies respectively. Most of the direct investment overseas of the late Victorian age flowed from the metropolis. One emerging trend after 1870 among City firms which had long been engaged in the finance of trade in primary products from the furthest corners of the globe, was to react to the challenge of falling mercantile profits (caused by the telegraph and other technical innovations) by investing in the production of the commodities they serviced. This investment in mines, plantations and similar activities abroad involved the creation of firms which were organised and managed at the point of production, but their direction remained firmly in London hands.[13]

13. Mira Wilkins, 'The Free Standing Company 1870–1914: an Important Type of British Foreign Investment', *Econ. Hist. Rev.*, 2nd ser. XLI (1988), passim. On this theme see also Chapman, 'British-Based Investment Groups'. For a good regional example see R.T. Stillson, 'The Financing of Malayan Rubber', *Econ. Hist. Rev.*, 2nd ser. XXIV (1971). See also Charles Harvey and Jon Press, 'Overseas Investment and the Professional Advance of British Metal Mining Engineers, 1851–1914', *Econ. Hist.*

London's cosmopolitanism was such that even its resident manufacturing class was heavily biased in favour of overseas investment, as were its professional investors. It is also noticeable that regions close to London were more inclined to invest overseas than were the provinces, while the Home Counties themselves had a very positive leaning in favour of imperial investments.[14]

Overseas investment did not offer very high average returns either in foreign lands or the empire. Edelstein concluded that, during the whole period from 1870 to 1913, returns on foreign investment were higher than on domestic investment but by only a small margin: domestic securities in Britain brought in 4.6 per cent on average, the equivalent foreign stocks 5.72 per cent. Furthermore, domestic investment was a better financial bet in 1870–6, 1887–96 and 1910–13.[15] Davis and Huttenback, on the other hand, argue that foreign and empire stocks did better than domestic stocks before 1880, but from then until Edwardian times domestic returns were higher. For the whole period 1860–1914 they conclude that foreign investment was slightly less fruitful than domestic. Empire investments performed marginally better than both, but the big benefits from imperial investment were gained before 1880 and before the Scramble for Africa had really got under way.[16]

It could be inferred from this evidence that overseas investment, after 1880 at any rate, was simply irrational or misguided;[17] but in view of what has already been said about the lack of interest among industrialists and other provincial businessmen in new sources of

----

Rev., 2nd ser. XLII (1989). It has recently been emphasised that, in the case of overseas mining investment, the initiative came mainly from the periphery and that 'the pull from the periphery was at its strongest in territories of increasing British influence', Charles Harvey and Jon Press, 'The City and International Mining, 1870–1914', *Bus. Hist.*, XXXII (1990), p. 113.

14. Davis and Huttenback, *Mammon and the Pursuit of Empire*, Table 7.8, pp. 214–15 and p. 215.

15. Michael Edelstein, 'Realized Rates of Return on U.K. Home and Overseas Portfolio Investment in the Age of High Imperialism', *Expl. Econ. Hist.*, 13 (1976), Table 7, p. 314; and idem. *Overseas Investment in the Age of High Imperialism*, Ch. 5.

16. Davis and Huttenback, *Mammon and the Pursuit of Empire*, Ch. 3, esp. p. 107, and App. 3.2, p. 117. On this topic see also Sidney Pollard, 'Capital Exports, 1870–1914: Harmful or Beneficial?', *Econ. Hist. Rev.*, 2nd ser. XXXVIII (1985), pp. 495–8.

17. One consequence of Davis and Huttenback's work has been a renewal of interest in the old question of whether the empire paid. On this see, especially, P.K. O'Brien, 'The Costs and Benefits of British Imperialism, 1846–1914', *Past and Present*, 120 (1988); A.G. Hopkins, 'Accounting for the British Empire', *Jour. Imp. and Comm. Hist.*, XVI (1988), and Andrew Porter, 'The Balance Sheet of Empire, 1850–1914', *Hist. Jour.*, 31 (1988).

finance, this would be too hasty a judgement. Elites were enmeshed in one 'social web of investment' centred upon London, provincial businessmen in others.[18] Elites were looking for investments which were compatible with a gentlemanly life-style and found them abroad when they ceased to be available in sufficient quantity at home; provincial businessmen, on the whole, found their own domestic network satisfactory before 1914 without needing to invade, on a large scale, those dominated by their social betters. As Davis and Huttenback express it, 'Britain was not one capital market but two'.[19]

Given this social segregation of investment opportunities, it is hardly surprising that non-industrial investors needed to look abroad in the late nineteenth century to find outlets for their surplus capital. As well as the traditional gentlemanly classes already discussed, institutional investors, such as banks and insurance companies, were faced by serious problems which more or less forced them to look abroad to maintain income, especially after 1890. Agricultural mortgages were a losing game after the decline of arable agriculture under the stress of foreign competition; 'Gladstonian' government finance limited severely the amount of new government paper on the market and helped to push down the rate of interest on government stock;[20] new issues by those traditional favourites, domestic railway companies, were in short supply after 1870, and the profitability of the companies was also under severe pressure from the 1890s.[21] The obvious response, in the absence of any dynamic industrial demand at home, was to find similar investments abroad.[22] The shift towards overseas government stocks and foreign and imperial railway company bonds and shares is very marked, for example, in the records of the leading insurance companies, whose overseas holdings often increased from under 10 per cent of total assets in 1870 to 40 per cent

18. Michie, 'The Social Web of Investment', passim.

19. Davis and Huttenback, *Mammon and the Pursuit of Empire*, p. 211. They also argue that elites benefited in particular because they paid a disproportionately small amount of the taxes necessary to defend overseas investment while receiving a larger share of the gains. Ibid. pp. 244–52.

20. Thus allowing the conversion of consols in the 1880s. C.K. Harley, 'Goschen's Conversion of the National Debt and the Yield on Consols', *Econ. Hist. Rev.*, 2nd ser. XXIX (1976). Government stocks accounted for 38 per cent of the value of all stocks quoted on the Exchange in 1873 and for only 9 per cent by 1913. Youssef Cassis, *La City de Londres, 1870–1914* (Paris, 1987), Table 5, p. 49.

21. The major companies did not experience difficulties in raising money until after 1900. See R.J. Irving, 'British Railway Investment and Innovation, 1900–14: an Analysis with Special Reference to the North Eastern and London and North Western Railway Companies', *Bus. Hist.*, XIII (1971).

22. W.P. Kennedy, *Industrial Structure, Capital Markets and the Origins of British Economic Decline* (Cambridge, 1989), pp. 145, 148–9.

or more by 1913.[23] The joint-stock banks, too, became considerably more adventurous in their investment policies especially in the 1890s, when the rate of return on traditionally secure investment at home began to fall rapidly, and by 1913 'bonds of all kinds came to be grist to the banker's mills'.[24]

Had the share of savings going abroad not increased, returns on some domestic investments – government stock for instance – might have fallen to starvation levels. It is also possible that, given the barriers to industrial investment, a lack of foreign outlets might have produced severe crises of oversaving. Although Edelstein's analysis of overseas investment flows is principally based on neo-classical assumptions about the downward tendency of the rate of interest on domestic investment in response to limited home opportunities and a rising supply of savings, he does pinpoint two short periods, in the late 1870s and in 1901–3, when 'desired' savings overshot 'desired' domestic investment opportunities considerably. In his judgement, these bouts of Hobsonian oversaving may have triggered off the great overseas investment booms of the 1880s and 1905–13.[25] Without foreign outlets, these savings might have lain in idle balances and caused severe depressions.

The extension of foreign investment often involved an increase in risk-taking as the emphasis shifted over time from government-backed loans to investment in private railway companies in an ever-widening range of countries.[26] But it would be wrong to overemphasise the risks associated with many of Britain's foreign investments after 1850, for these were often ideally suited to the needs of a growing body of landed and other rentier and gentlemanly investors

23. B. Supple, *The Royal Exchange Assurance* (Cambridge, 1970), pp. 330–48; B.L. Anderson, 'Institutional Investment Before the First World War: the Union Marine Insurance Company 1897–1915', in S. Marriner ed. *Business and Businessmen: Studies in Business, Economic and Accounting History* (Liverpool, 1978); J.H. Treble, 'The Pattern of Investment in the Standard Life Assurance Company, 1875–1914', *Bus. Hist.*, XXII (1980).

24. C.A.E. Goodhart, *The Business of Banking, 1891–1914* (1972), pp. 127–41. The flurry of interest in overseas investment after 1909 may have had some connection with the fears of swingeing increases in taxation threatened by the Liberal Chancellor of the Exchequer, Lloyd George: Hartley Withers, *Stocks and Shares* (2nd edn 1917), pp. 295–9. See also *Parliamentary Debates* (Lords), IV (1909), cols. 745 (Lansdowne), 796–8 (Revelstoke), 1,155 (Rothschild). Joint-stock banks became increasingly interested in direct participation in overseas loan flotations before 1914. See A.R. Hall, *The British Capital Market and Australia, 1870–1914* (Canberra, 1963), p. 72; Cassis, *La City de Londres*, Table 10, p. 115.

25. Edelstein, *Overseas Investment in the Age of High Imperialism*, pp. 177–95.

26. R.C. Michie, 'Options, Concessions, Syndicates and the Provision of Venture Capital, 1880–1913', *Bus. Hist.*, XXIII (1981), pp. 149–50.

looking for safe, fixed interest securities.[27] Their incomes might have fallen to alarmingly low levels without a marked movement into foreign stocks, especially after 1870.[28] As Vincent has pointed out, a great deal of wealth in mid-nineteenth-century England was concentrated 'not in the hands of entrepreneurs and captains of industry, but in the hands of widows, spinsters, rich farmers, clergymen, academics, squires and rentiers claiming gentility',[29] that is, the cast of characters who populate the pages of Mrs Gaskell's *Cranford* rather than the philistine industrialists of *Hard Times*, or those with whom Karl Marx was obsessed. These gentlemanly investors, like the landed aristocracy, inhabited a cultural universe very different from that of industrialists and had few openings for secure investment outside land, railways and the national debt before 1870.[30] The shift to safe foreign investments was one way of maintaining both the income and the status of the non-industrial wealthy and their supporters. Foreign investments were important, too, along with directorships of companies, mining royalties and ground rents, in extending the power and influence of the landed interest longer than would otherwise have been possible.[31] Foreign investments also gave new life to a commercial and financial middle class centred on the City, which transformed itself between 1850 and 1914 into the centre of an international service economy. And it was landed wealth, together with returns on overseas investments, which provided the foundation for the rapid growth of the service economy in London and the south-east and gave the region pre-eminence before 1914.[32]

27. On the rentier character of British overseas investment after 1870 see W.P. Kennedy, 'Foreign Investment, Trade and Growth in the United Kingdom, 1870–1913', *Explorations in Economic History*, II (1974) pp. 425–39; D.R. Adler, *British Investment in American Railways, 1834–98* (Charlottesville, Va, 1970), pp. 197–8; H.W. Richardson, 'British Emigration and Overseas Investment, 1870–1914', *Econ. Hist. Rev.*, 2nd ser. XXV (1972), pp. 109–10.

28. Supple, *Royal Exchange Assurance*, p. 335.

29. John Vincent, *Pollbooks: How Victorians Voted* (Cambridge, 1967), p. 41.

30. An excellent illustration of the narrow nature of investments considered suitable for gentlemen is provided by R.C. Michie, 'Income, Expenditure and Investment of a Victorian Millionaire: Lord Overstone, 1823–1883', *Bulletin of the Institute of Historical Research*, LVII (1985). Overstone, however, was rather more conservative than the average in his later years. It is interesting to note that by Edwardian times E.M. Forster's middle-class, cultivated, rentier heroines were heavily into 'Foreign Things'. See *Howards End* (1910), p. 11.

31. G.D. Phillips, *The Diehards: Aristocratic Society and Politics in Edwardian England* (Cambridge, Mass, 1979), pp. 39–44; C.H. Lee, *The British Economy Since 1700: A Macro-Economic Perspective*, (Cambridge, 1986), pp. 36–7. Some landowners also developed interests of an industrial kind. See Harold Perkin, *The Rise of Professional Society: England since 1800*, (1989), pp. 67–9.

32. C.H. Lee, 'The Service Sector, Regional Specialization and Economic Growth in the Victorian Economy', *Journal of Historical Geography*, 10 (1984), p. 154.

FOREIGN INVESTMENT AND INDUSTRY

Whether foreign investment was a positive force in British economic development or whether it was merely a symptom of economic decline has been a matter of controversy for some years. The simplest response to the problem is to assume that markets behaved optimally and that, since resources were fully employed in Britain, capital going abroad was merely seeking a higher return than that available locally.[33] But the assumption of a fully employed economy after 1850 is probably unrealistic; if it is removed, the problem becomes much more difficult to determine, even when it is allowed that capital export, besides bringing in a direct return of around 5 or 6 per cent annually, stimulated commodity exports, lowered the cost of imports and also increased national income by making the terms of trade more favourable.[34] Given potentially very high rates of return on domestic investment,[35] some modern historians have claimed that, if Britain had employed the capital and labour which left her shores after 1850 at home, the growth rate after 1870 could have been as high or higher than that achieved during the 'Mid-Victorian Boom'.[36] It is tempting to conclude that the reason for Britain's relatively poor performance after 1870 was not so much that her savings were lower than those of her rivals but that, whereas Germany and the United States invested about 12 per cent of their annual income domestically, Great Britain put only 7 per cent of hers back into the national economy and sent another 4 or 5 per cent abroad.[37]

One reason frequently alleged for this low rate of domestic investment was the failure of the financial establishment to adjust to new industrial circumstances. It is certainly true that the major

33. This is assumed, for example, by D.N. McCloskey, 'Did Victorian Britain Fail?' *Econ. Hist. Rev.*, 2nd ser. XXIII (1970). See also idem, 'No It Did Not: A Reply to Crafts', in ibid. XXXII (1979).

34. Michael Edelstein, 'Foreign Investment and Empire, 1860–1914', in Roderick Floud and Donald McCloskey, eds. *The Economic History of Britain since 1700. Vol II: 1860 to the 1970s* (Cambridge, 1981), pp. 84–7.

35. If there was less than full employment then the upper limits on returns to domestic investment would be determined by the capital-output ratio, which is estimated at 4:1. R.C.O. Matthews, C.H. Feinstein and J.C. Odling-Smee, *British Economic Growth, 1856–1973* (Oxford, 1982), pp. 135–7. This would allow for average returns of up to 25 per cent.

36. See especially here Kennedy, 'Foreign Investment, Trade and Growth in the United Kingdom, 1870–1913'; and idem, 'Economic Growth and Structural Change in the United Kingdom, 1870–1914', *Jour. Econ. Hist.*, XLII (1982).

37. Pollard, 'Capital Exports 1870–1914, p. 489; B.J. Eichengreen, 'The Proximate Determinants of Domestic Investment in Victorian Britain', *Jour. Econ. Hist.*, XLII (1982).

banking and financial institutions did not develop as a part of an emerging finance capitalism in the style of the United States or Germany; there was no welding of the joint-stock banks, money markets and Stock Exchange with provincial manufacturing industry.[38] Banks with a primary interest in long-term industrial investment did appear in the 1860s and 1870s, but their lives were brief. As Kennedy puts it:

> a point had been reached where the entire system had either to be re-organized to withstand the greater risks of steadily enlarging industrial requirements or the system had to withdraw from long-term industrial involvement. The system withdrew.[39]

After 1870, the major joint-stock banks preferred the liquidity brought by increasing contact with the London money market to long-term involvement with industry. At the outbreak of war in 1914, they were not holders of industrial equity;[40] neither they nor the merchant banks of the City of London had concerned themselves much with the issue of securities for manufacturing companies. As for their impact on the Stock Exchange, only 600 of the 5,000 stocks quoted in 1910 were of industrial and commercial origin and a good many of those were overseas-based concerns.[41] The share of British-based companies in the money raised in London was, indeed, falling before 1914. Davis and Huttenback's survey found that one-third of domestic and foreign finance went to British-based companies or home governments between 1865 and 1914, but the proportion was 47 per cent in 1865–9 and it fell to just over one-fifth in 1909–13.[42] Of the money raised for British-based projects, only about 18 per cent went into manufacturing on average during the years 1865 to 1914, or about £29m. per annum. This represented roughly 6 per cent of all the finance raised in London in these years. In sharp contrast, something like one-quarter went into railway companies operating in the empire or foreign countries.[43] It is not surprising that this disparity has been seen as a failure on the City's part. Even the leading historian

38. The classical description of finance capitalism is, of course, Rudolf Hilferding, *Finance Capital: A Study of the Latest Phase of Capitalist Development*, (English edn 1982).
39. W.P. Kennedy, *Industrial Structure, Capital Markets and the Origins of British Economic Decline*, p. 122. See also idem, 'Institutional Response to Economic Growth: Capital Markets in Britain to 1914', in L. Hannah, ed. *Management Strategy and Business Development: An Historical and Comparative Study* (1976), p. 160.
40. Goodhart, *The Business of Banking, 1891–1914*, p. 135.
41. Cassis, *La City de Londres*, p. 48.
42. Davis and Huttenback, *Mammon and the Pursuit of Empire*, Table 2.1, p. 40.
43. Ibid. Table 2.6, p. 54.

of Britain's merchant banks believes that they, like other financial intermediaries, were 'incredibly slow' to react to opportunities offered by industry before 1914.[44]

But were these opportunities actually available? Is it correct to speak, in Kennedy's words, of 'steadily enlarging industrial requirements' and to argue that the bias of the capital market towards overseas investments meant that potential investors had only scanty knowledge of 'new industries' and were unable to assess them adequately?[45] The financial needs of provincial industry continued to be met, as in the early and mid-nineteenth century, not by London but by a complex of methods including provincial stock exchanges and a host of private, local sources so widespread and so informal that contemporaries found it hard even to guess at the level of investment in domestic industry before 1914.[46] No great changes, either geographical or technical and organisational, occurred among the traditional staple industries after 1870 sufficient to disturb these financial relationships seriously or to render them obsolete. Capital remained abundant in areas of well-established industrial strength such as Lancashire.[47] Indeed, the ease and cheapness with which capital could be raised for established industrial concerns by traditional methods was probably one of the chief reasons for the maintenance of a high degree of competition in British industry and the persistence of the small firm.[48] Severe competition meant that the need to produce high dividends for shareholders lowered the incentive to plough back profits and increase investment ratios, and inhibited the growth of the large firm.[49]

As a result, the joint-stock banks, for example, were given no great incentive to offer anything other than their time-honoured services to industry - principally overdraft facilities and short-term credit[50] - and the City and the Stock Exchange remained similarly

44. Chapman, *The Rise of Merchant Banking*, p. 103.

45. Kennedy, *Industrial Structure, Capital Markets and the Origins of British Economic Decline*, Ch. 5.

46. Keynes, 'Great Britain's Foreign Investment', p. 58.

47. Farnie, 'The Structure of the British Cotton Industry, 1846–1914', in Akio Okochi and Shin-Ichi Yonekawa, eds. *The Textile Industry and its Business Climate* (Tokyo, 1982), p. 55.

48. Lance Davis, 'The Capital Market and Industrial Concentration: the U.S. and the U.K., a Comparative Survey', *Econ. Hist. Rev.*, 2nd ser, XIX (1966).

49. For an example see Wayne Lewchuk, 'The Return to Capital in the British Motor Vehicle Industry, 1896–1939', *Bus. Hist.*, 27 (1985).

50. P.L. Cottrell, *Industrial Finance, 1830–1914: The Finance and Organization of English Manufacturing Industry* (1980), pp. 210–44.

remote from industrial investment. It is true that merchant bankers and other City financiers were often unjustifiably suspicious of limited liability industrial companies, but this was a prejudice they shared with many industrialists.[51] They and their partners on the Exchange were clearly better fitted to handling the large loans floated by national and municipal governments or large corporations than to raising the small sums required by the typical British firm. They usually came into contact with home industry only on those relatively rare occasions when a substantial loan was floated as part of a company's conversion from partnership to joint-stock status.[52] Even joint-stock flotation was used more as a way of preserving the individuality of particular firms than as a means of promoting rationalisation or creating a corporate structure.[53]

In other words, it is difficult to blame the City for failing to adapt to industry when the industry it was supposed to serve did not put forth radical new demands for its services.[54] This lack of demand for new sources of finance was one result of the slowness of the evolution of Britain's industrial structure, explanations of which are legion. Britain's difficulties can be ascribed to the peculiar strength of trade unionism, which inhibited the replacement of labour by capital and led to overmanning in many industries.[55] Alternatively, they may be attributed to her 'early start' as an industrial power and her 'overcommitment' to the labour-intensive phase of economic development

51. Stanley Chapman, *The Rise of Merchant Banking* (1984), p. 99; Michael H. Best and Jane Humphries, 'The City and Industrial Decline', in Bernard Elbaum and William Lazonick, eds. *The Decline of the British Economy* (Oxford, 1986), p. 227. It should be noted, however, that for the aristocratic merchant bankers, like Barings, acceptances were the 'bread and butter' business and issuing foreign loans the 'jam'; and 'the financing of British industry was fare for the servants' hall or, worse still, fit only for the dogs', Philip Zeigler, *The Sixth Great Power: Barings, 1762–1929* (1988), p. 290.

52. Keynes, 'Great Britain's Foreign Investments', p. 58; Hall, *The London Capital Market and Australia*, esp. Ch. 1; Ranald C. Michie, *Money, Mania and Markets: Investment Company Formation and the Stock Exchange in the Nineteenth Century* (Edinburgh, 1981), esp. Pt. V; Edelstein, *Overseas Investment in the Age of High Imperialism*, Ch. III.

53. Best and Humphries, 'The City and Industrial Decline', p. 226; Farnie, 'The Structure of the British Cotton Industry, 1846–1914', p. 74. For a more detailed study of the joint-stock movement in Lancashire see D.A. Farnie, *The English Cotton Industry and the World Market, 1815–1896* (Oxford, 1979), Chs. 6 and 7.

54. For other surveys of the vast literature on this topic see Best and Humphries, 'The City and Industrial Decline', pp. 223–9; Pollard, 'Capital Exports, 1870–1914', and idem, *Britain's Prime and Britain's Decline: The British Economy, 1870–1914* (1989), Ch. 2.

55. D. Coleman and C. MacLeod, 'Attitudes to New Techniques: British Businessmen, 1800–1950', *Econ. Hist. Rev.*, 2nd ser. XXXIX (1986), pp. 605–9, for a critical survey of the relevant literature.

based on textiles, steam-power and the small firm,[56] a phase much lengthened by the ease with which the staple industries could continue to find markets in the empire and other parts of the globe subject to British influence. Relative decline can also be explained in terms of entrepreneurial failure:[57] the steel industry provides some excellent examples.[58] But whatever explanation is offered (and some of the more complex ones include all the approaches noted here and more besides),[59] it is obvious that Britain's industrial crisis after 1870 can be understood as a series of events largely uninfluenced, for good or ill, by the City and its institutions. There are some instances of new industries finding it hard to raise money in London or being forced to raise it in a non-optimal manner because they could not penetrate conventional financial barriers;[60] but there is little evidence of any general shortage of funds. New industries in Britain before 1914 often found it difficult to raise capital, not because London financiers were unwilling to open their doors to them but because demand for their services was small and their prospects were often uninviting – a

56. See especially, H.W. Richardson, 'Retardation in Britain's Industrial Growth, 1870–1913', *Scottish Journal of Political Economy*, XII (1965), and idem, 'Over-Commitment in Britain before 1930', *Oxford Economic Papers*, XVII (1965). Both are reprinted in Derek H. Aldcroft and Harry W. Richardson, eds. *The British Economy, 1870–1939* (1969). Also: William Ashworth, 'The Late Victorian Economy', *Economica*, new ser. XXXIII (1966); Bernard Elbaum and William Lazonick, 'The Decline of the British Economy: an Institutional Perspective', *Jour. Econ. Hist.*, XLIV (1984). For a discussion of similar themes in a wider perspective see Mancur Olsen, *The Rise and Decline of Nations* (1982).

57. There is a vast literature on this theme, and for a thorough survey a reader should consult P.L. Payne, *British Entrepreneurship in the Nineteenth Century* (1988). See also A.L. Levine, *Industrial Retardation in Britain, 1880–1914* (1967) and Coleman and McLeod, 'Attitudes to New Techniques', passim. The comments of Matthews, Feinstein and Odling-Smee, *British Economic Growth*, also show some agreement with an entrepreneurial interpretation on pp. 381–2, 539–40. For a spirited contrary argument see Donald McCloskey and Lars Sandberg, 'From Damnation to Redemption: Judgements on the Late Victorian Entrepreneur', *Explorations in Economic History*, IX (1971).

58. On the steel industry, see Donald McCloskey, *Economic Maturity and Entrepreneurial Decline* (Cambridge, 1974), and, especially, Robert Allen, 'Entrepreneurship and Technical Progress in the North-East Coast Pig-Iron Industry: 1850–1913', in Paul Uselding, ed. *Research in Economic History*, 6 (1981).

59. See, for example, the comprehensive surveys by François Crouzet, *The Victorian Economy* (1982), Ch. 12, and P. Mathias, *The First Industrial Nation: An Economic History of Britain, 1700–1914* (2nd edn. 1983), pp. 369–93; also Pollard, *Britain's Prime and Britain's Decline*, passim, and the *Oxford Review of Economic Policy*, 4 (1988).

60. For example: A.E. Harrison, 'F. Hopper and Co. – The Problems of Capital Supply in the Cycle Manufacturing Industry, 1891–1914', *Bus. Hist.*, 24 (1982); Kennedy, 'Institutional Response to Economic Growth'; John Armstrong, 'Hooley and the Bovril Company' *Bus. Hist.*, XXVIII (1986).

consequence perhaps, of the massive commitment to the older industries and traditional sources of energy in Britain after 1870.

In an ideal world, new industry might have prospered on long-term finance backed by the state, but this was out of the question, politically and ideologically, in Britain before 1914. Had British industrial growth been faster, then the City and the banks would have been faced with the challenge of transforming themselves to meet new opportunities. Whether they could or would have done so cannot be known; but it is idle to complain that no finance capitalism on a German model developed in Britain in the late nineteenth century when British industry did not grow and change as rapidly as it did on the continent. Finance capitalism arose in response to a crisis of industrial funding in Germany: in Britain this crisis never developed, at least before 1914.[61]

FOREIGN INVESTMENT AND ECONOMIC GROWTH

That the bias in London financial markets was a natural one in the circumstances and reflected, in a very real sense, the configuration of the economy does not, of course, necessarily mean that heavy overseas investment did not have long-run deleterious effects. The very ease with which capital could be sent abroad and the virtual certainty of the returns probably had an influence in tempering entrepreneurial drive[62] by creating a level of prosperity which put off the need for fundamental industrial change. It is possible, too, that an oversavings crisis, however painful, might have been the prelude to dynamic industrial growth had not overseas investment provided relief from the need to change.

The most recent statistical work does provide some evidence that, after 1870, high foreign investment was inimical to overall industrial growth. Before 1870, home and foreign investment fluctuated more or less in unison and in conformity with the familiar seven-to-nine-year trade cycle. After that date, the paths of home and foreign investment diverged, each setting into a pattern of swings approxi-

---

61. Lee, *British Economic Growth since 1700*, pp. 66–70, is worth consulting here. For a comprehensive survey of the literature on finance and industry in Britain see Michael Collins, *Banks and Industrial Finance in Britain, 1800–1939* (1991).

62. Matthews, Feinstein and Odling-Smee, *British Economic Growth*, p. 355; Pollard, 'Capital Exports, 1870–1914', p. 512.

mately 20 years in length which were inverse to each other.[63] The peaks of capital export in the late 1880s and in 1909–13 were periods of low domestic investment, while troughs in foreign investment in the late 1870s and the 1890s were accompanied by a strong upsurge in capital formation at home.[64] When foreign investment was high, exports and the export regions boomed,[65] but domestic investment as a whole and, it appears, manufacturing investment as well were low, and total output grew more slowly. The overall growth of manufacturing output and investment was far more dependent upon changes in domestic activity than it was on changes in exports.[66] The sharp fall in foreign demand in the downswing after 1873 affected overall manufacturing growth only slightly: the temporary cessation of foreign investment and the miserably slow growth of exports in the 1890s were accompanied by a revival of the rate of growth of manufacturing, of productivity and of growth as a whole.

If bursts of foreign investment had short-run beneficial effects on exports, they may have retarded the development of export industries in the longer term by cushioning them against the need for technical and organizational change. If, for whatever reason, there had been less foreign investment, then staple export industries might have been forced to adapt themselves more quickly and investors would have had a greater interest in other domestic opportunities – with radical effects on the structure of capital markets and financial institutions.[67] Foreign investment, like formal empire, proved to be a considerable force in favour of conservatism in industry, not only by keeping up overseas sales of traditional manufactures from a number of export-producing regions but also by offering easy alternatives to new and risky domestic ventures.

Despite provincial industrialists' general aversion to overseas

63. The best explanation of the emergence of the twenty-year cycle is given by H.J. Habakkuk, 'Fluctuations in Housebuilding in Britain and the United States in the Nineteenth Century', *Jour. Econ. Hist.*, XXII, (1962), reprinted in A.R. Hall, *The Export of Capital from Britain, 1870–1914* (1968).

64. The best introduction to the vast literature on this subject is P.L. Cottrell, *British Overseas Investment in the Nineteenth Century* (1975), pp. 35ff.

65. There is a detailed examination of the relationship between long swings in investment and exports in A.G. Ford, 'The Transfer of British Foreign Lending, 1870–1913', *Econ. Hist. Rev.*, 2nd ser. XI (1958–9), and idem, 'Overseas Lending and Internal Fluctuations, 1870–1914', *Yorkshire Bulletin of Economic and Social Research*, XVII (1965). On the alternation in the level of activity between export regions and other parts of the economy see J. Parry Lewis, *Building Cycles and Britain's Growth* (1965), esp. Chs. 5–7.

66. Matthews, Feinstein and Odling-Smee, *Britain's Economic Growth*, Table 9:10, and p. 282.

67. Ibid. pp. 254–6.

opportunities, capital export was a significant feature of investment decisions in Lancashire and industrial Scotland. While growth was slowing and the textile industry was losing its technological lead,[68] Lancashire was producing a surplus of capital, some of which flowed abroad. Lancashire capitalists provided 8 per cent of the capital placed in the foreign-based firms in Davis and Huttenback's sample, and the region had a greater taste for foreign than for home investment after 1880.[69] Slower growth after 1870, low industrial investment and a high rate of foreign investment also coexisted in lowland Scotland. Between 1870 and 1914, the Clyde was the most important location for shipbuilding and heavy engineering in Britain. But, as profits fell under the stress of competition after 1870, the tendency was for manufacturers to put more of their savings abroad. An estimated 10 per cent of Scotland's national income went abroad every year. Scottish capitalists were particularly interested in the empire, for which they provided about 8 per cent of the capital in this period.[70] In both Lancashire and industrial Scotland it is probable that capital export reinforced the natural tendency to technological conservatism that was further encouraged by the maintenance of export demand, especially in empire markets. By 1914, the whole set of relationships must have posed a formidable barrier to change.[71]

Britain's initial success, both as a provider of the new industrial commodities and of services like shipping, credit and insurance produced a large balance of payments surplus in the latter half of the nineteenth century. This surplus was the basis for her extensive capital exports. As the value of assets held abroad increased, the stream of dividend and interest payments increased likewise. Until the 1870s, the flow of new investment abroad exceeded the value of

68. On this question see William Lazonick, 'Industrial Organization and Technological Change: the Decline of the British Cotton Industry', *Bus. Hist. Rev.*, 57 (1983).

69. Davis and Huttenback, *Mammon and the Pursuit of Empire*, Table 7.5, p. 209, and Table 7.8, p. 214. An example of Lancastrian overseas investment is provided by M. Rose, 'Diversification of Investment by the Greg Family', *Bus. Hist.*, XX (1979), esp. p. 91.

70. Davis and Huttenback's figures are for the whole of Scotland rather than just industrial Scotland, and some of the overseas investment must have come from non-industrial, mainly landed, sources. Roughly one-third of all those who died worth £100,000 or more in Scotland in this period were landowners, but the bulk of the wealthy came from manufacturing origins. R. Britton, 'Wealthy Scots, 1873–1913', *Bull. Inst. Hist. Res.*, LVIII (1985), pp. 79, 81–2.

71. For the Scottish example see Tony Dickson, ed. *Scottish Capitalism: Class, State and Nation from Before the Union to the Present* (1980), esp. pp. 248–55; B. Lenman, *An Economic History of Modern Scotland, 1660–1976* (1977), esp. pp. 192–3; and B. Lenman and K. Donaldson, 'Partner's Income, Investment and Diversification in the Scottish Linen Area, 1850–1921', *Bus. Hist.*, XII (1971).

in-payments. After that date, save for the late 1880s and the few years before World War I, when overseas flows were exceptionally high, the position was decisively reversed. Over the whole period 1870–1913, incoming payments exceeded capital exports by roughly £1 billion.[72]

To accommodate this massive inflow, Britain had to allow a high and rising level of imports since this was the only way in which the borrowers could meet their debt obligations. Free trade was a necessary adjunct to the repayment of foreign debts, but, in allowing increasing levels of primary produce to enter Britain, free trade also exposed her to competition from her industrial rivals. This reduced industrial profitability, investment and growth, especially in those new industries which could not compete in world markets as easily as cottons or other more traditional exports. However, in reducing the rate of growth of British exports, foreign competition performed the same function as rising imports in helping Britain to solve her invisible repayments problem because a decelerating rate of growth of exports decreased the demand for sterling and improved the ability of overseas debtors to meet payments on accumulated loans. Had the rate of growth of exports been higher, Britain's balance of payments surplus would have been larger and, in lieu of higher foreign investment (which, in the long term, would only have made the repayment problems worse), might have led to a grand international liquidity crisis as the world ran out of sterling.

This economy, founded on free trade, capital export and high imports, was not best fitted to the needs of export manufacturers. Foreign investment booms undoubtedly produced benefits for traditional export industries such as textiles, but in doing so they reinforced Britain's commitment to industries which were no longer at the forefront of world industrial change. At the same time, the free-trade policy inevitably subjected the newer industries to the full blast of competition from Germany, the United States and elsewhere, retarded their progress and inhibited investment. Britain's export sector was not well prepared to meet the needs of the second industrial revolution, whose transforming power after the 1870s was to be far greater than that of the first.[73] A low rate of industrial investment contributed to technological and organisational backwardness in key areas, such as chemicals and engineering, and to an excessive commitment to the time-honoured and the traditional – something for which

72. Pollard, *Britain's Prime and Britain's Decline*, Table 2.6, p. 69.
73. Douglass C. North, *Structure and Change in Economic History* (New York, 1981), Chs. 12 and 13.

the British eventually paid a heavy price after 1945, when the international economy, held back by two world wars and an intervening Great Depression, finally took off and left Britain behind.[74]

On the other hand, this open economy was entirely compatible with the rise of the complex of services and consumer industries we have already described. These activities developed particularly rapidly in London and the south-east region and gained perhaps their greatest stimulus from the income generated by foreign investment. The open economy was also entirely supportive of the commercial and financial sector, and especially of the City of London, since the huge inflow of imports under free trade and the large outflows of capital, which were characteristic of the British economy in this period, were the basis of its success after 1850.[75]

FOREIGN INVESTMENT AND GENTLEMANLY CAPITALISM

There was a considerable degree of overlap between the world of services and consumer goods in the south-east and that of the heavily industrialised provinces, and it is undoubtedly true that the City of London and the northern export staples had a common dependence on international trade. Nonetheless, Davis and Huttenback felt constrained to argue, as we have seen, that in terms of investment preferences Britain was sociologically divided; and it is important for us to emphasise, at this juncture, that the gentlemen who were the chief overseas investors were also the leading lights in the service economy which was, in many ways, culturally as well as economically, distinct from provincial, industrial Britain. Despite his obvious animus against gentlemanly elites, his rather too clear-cut distinction between north and south, and his failure to recognise the dynamic nature of the development of south-eastern England, J.A. Hobson caught something of the flavour of the division. He distinguished

74. For two ways of generalising this experience see W. Arthur Lewis, *Growth and Fluctuations, 1870–1913* (1978), Ch. 5, and Michael Beenstock, *The World Economy in Transition* (1983 edn), Ch. 6.
75. The last two paragraphs have been greatly aided by the work of Pollard, *Britain's Prime and Britain's Decline*, pp. 108–10; and by Kennedy, *Industrial Structure*, pp. 153–63, which also offers a Hobsonian-type demand-deficiency argument for slow industrial growth not utilised here, as does idem, 'Notes on Economic Efficiency in Historical Perspective the case of Britain, 1870–1914', in Paul Uselding, ed. *Research in Economic History*, 9 (1984).

between 'Producers England', where industry set the tone of life and 'Consumers England', which he described in the following manner:

> The Home Counties, the numerous seaside and other residential towns, the cathedral and University towns, and in general terms, the South are full of well-to-do and leisured families whose incomes, dissociated from any present exertion of their recipients, are derived from industries conducted in the North or in some oversea country. A very large share, probably the major part, of the income spent by these well-to-do residential classes in the South, is drawn from investments of this nature. The expenditure of these incomes calls into existence and maintains large classes of professional men, producers and purveyors of luxuries, tradesmen, servants and retainers, who are more or less conscious of their dependence upon the goodwill and patronage of people 'living on their means'. This class of 'ostentatious leisure' and 'conspicuous waste' is subordinated in the North to earnest industry: in the South it directs a large proportion of the occupations, sets the social tone, imposes valuation and opinions. . . . Most persons living in the South certainly have to work for a living, but much of their work is closely and even consciously directed by the will and demands of the moneyed class.[76]

The society led by the 'moneyed class' had evolved over the previous 50 years of high overseas investment. The mid-century squads of genteel investors listed by Vincent were an elite of that part of British society still agricultural at base, still dominated by landed capitalism and cut off from the industrialism that was transforming a large part of provincial England and the Celtic fringes. Trapped within the cultural norms of this rural and small town society, the only acceptable and accessible investment outlets open to this elite were land and government stock. As the world economy expanded and opportunities for foreign investment grew, the numbers of socially acceptable investment outlets multiplied and the vast flows of returning income which resulted helped first to reproduce this gentlemanly elite and then, slowly, to recreate it in a new form. In other words, the nature of the new economic society which emerged in London and the south-east in the latter half of the nineteenth century was moulded by the social and cultural preferences of a gentlemanly class which was itself changed by the process.

The City of London was the economic powerhouse of this service sector and of the gentlemanly order which dominated it. As such, it was a part of gentlemanly capitalism itself. There have been some fascinating debates between Marxists in recent years about the extent and nature of the power of the City of London. Despite many marked

76. J.A. Hobson, 'The General Election: a Sociological Interpretation', *Sociological Review*, 3 (1910), p. 113.

disagreements among them, they all begin with the assumption that the City's position depended entirely upon its wealth, and they fail to investigate the extent to which that wealth was created in a particular social context that set the limit upon both its nature and its extent.[77] In practice, after 1850, City wealth was determined to a large degree by the continuing weight of landed wealth and by the size of gentlemanly investment abroad, which were the two chief driving forces behind the evolution of the distinctive Victorian and Edwardian economy already described in this chapter.

The peculiar path of development adopted by the British had, therefore, more than mere economic significance. The growth and predominance within Britain of the service sector and of wealth based on foreign investment meant also the continued dominance of a non-industrial elite. The older gentlemanly elite based on land was losing its power, though this loss was slowed down by the transference of assets from land into services and abroad. From the late nineteenth century the landed interest was forced to share this power, with industrialists to some degree, but more often with the bankers, financiers and professionals who rose to influence and prestige as the service sector grew in importance. Out of this union of land and service wealth the new gentlemanly capitalist class was born.

---

77. For a good example see Geoffrey Ingham, *Capital Divided: The City and Industry in British Social Development* (1984) passim and the recent controversy between Ingham and Barratt Brown, on which see Michael Barratt Brown, 'Away with all the Great Arches: Anderson's History of British Capitalism', *New Left Review*, 167 (1988), and Ingham's 'Commercial Capital and British Development : A Reply to Michael Barratt Brown', ibid. 172 (1988). There is also an interesting contribution to this debate from D. Nicholls, 'Fractions of Capital: the Aristocracy, the City and Industry in the Development of Modern British Capitalism', *Social History*, 13 (1988).

CHAPTER SEVEN

Challenging Cosmopolitanism: The Tariff Problem and Imperial Unity, 1880–1914

What eventually undermined the Gladstonian consensus and threatened the ability of governing elites to keep economic policy out of the public eye were rising defence costs and the new demands made upon civil expenditure by policies designed to meet the needs of the more democratic electorate created by the 1867 and 1884 Reform Acts. Gladstone's great budgetary feats were made possible by neglecting defence spending and by the luck which enabled Britain, given the state of Europe, to enjoy naval supremacy on the cheap.[1] The extent of the luck was made plain during brief periods of adversity like the Crimean War, when soaring military expenditure pushed up direct taxation sharply, Bank Rate rose steeply to stem a drain of gold, governments were forced to add to the national debt and even free trade was threatened before the war came abruptly and unexpectedly to an end in 1856.[2] Half a century later, the Boer War also triggered off a similar financial crisis, which threatened orthodoxy and the City's supremacy.[3] Like the earlier conflict, it also led to sharp criticism of the amateurism and inefficiency of Britain's

---

1. C.J. Bartlett, ed. *Britain Pre-eminent: Studies in British World Influence in the Nineteenth Century* (1969), p. 173; Gerald S. Graham, *Tides of Empire: Discursions on the Expansion of Britain Overseas* (1972), p. 82. A survey of British naval history, placing it within the context of a changing economy, is Paul Kennedy, *The Rise and Fall of British Naval Mastery* (1976). See also Bernard Semmel, *Liberalism and Naval Strategy: Ideology, Interest and Sea Power during the Pax Britannica* (Boston, Mass., 1986).

2. Olive Anderson, *A Liberal State at War: English Politics and Economics During the Crimean War* (1967), Chs. 6–8.

3. Clive Trebilcock, 'War and the Failure of Industrial Mobilization, 1899–1914', in J.M. Winter, ed. *War and Economic Development: Essays in Memory of David Joslin* (Cambridge, 1975), pp. 141, 143. See also the important new study by Aaron L. Friedberg, *The Weary Titan: Britain and the Experience of Relative Decline, 1895–1905* (Princeton, NJ, 1988), Ch. 3.

governing institutions.[4] The Crimean conflict was a set-back to Gladstonianism soon retrieved: by 1900 the Boer conflict only exacerbated the tendency for defence, especially naval expenditure, to grow in response to the threat posed to the Pax Britannica by first French and Russian and, later, German expansion.

When faced with rising bills for defence and a growing demand for welfare expenditure, the Liberals remained strong in their free-trade faith and thus had to rely on increases in direct taxation. But in order to maintain their middle-class vote in the industrial provinces they tried to avoid penalising income from foreign investment and kept income tax increases down by directing most of their fire at the landed aristocracy.[5] Lloyd George's 1909 budget, the House of Lords crises of 1909–11 and the Liberal land campaign that followed were a direct outcome of the attempt by Gladstone's successors to wrestle with the new problems of rising public spending – problems that could be resolved only by reducing even further the Liberal connection with the landed interest.

As defenders of aristocracy and the status quo, the Conservatives, faced with the need to improve Britain's defences, resisted direct tax increases. But they were forced in return to resort to tariffs, a commitment clearly made by 1910.[6] The City, as part of the Conservative interest, moved in the same direction. City influence on naval rearmament – a necessary 'insurance premium' to safeguard British commerce and finance – was impressive,[7] but the City did not relish paying for what was so clearly in the nation's interest as well as its

---

4. Anderson, *A Liberal State at War*, Chs. 3 and 4; G.R. Searle, *The Quest for National Efficiency, 1899–1914: A Study in British Politics and National Thought* (Oxford, 1971).

5. There is a wide literature on these aspects of the political economy of Liberalism in Edwardian England. Particularly useful in this context are H.V. Emy, 'The Impact of Financial Policy on English Party Politics Before 1914', *Hist. Jour.*, XV (1972); Bentley B. Gilbert, 'David Lloyd George: Land, the Budget and Social Reform', *Am. Hist. Rev.*, LXXXI (1976); idem, 'The Reform of British Landowning and the Budget of 1914', *Hist. Jour.*, XXI (1978); B.K. Murray, *The People's Budget, 1909–1910: Lloyd George and Liberal Politics* (Oxford, 1980); Avner Offer, *Property and Politics, 1870–1914: Landownership, Law, Ideology and Urban Development in England* (Cambridge, 1981); and idem, 'Empire and Social Reform: British Overseas Investment and Domestic Politics, 1908–1914', *Hist. Jour.*, XXVI (1983).

6. See Emy, 'The Impact of Financial Policy on English Party Politics'.

7. This is one of the major themes of S.R. Smith, 'British Nationalism, Imperialism and the City of London, 1880–1900' (unpublished Ph.D., Univ. of London, 1985), pp. 169–97, 314–56. See also Peter Stansky, *Ambitions and Strategies: The Struggle for Leadership of the Liberal Party in the 1890s* (Oxford, 1964), pp. 24, 34. The fact that Gladstone resigned as Prime Minister over the question of the naval estimates in 1894 is symbolic of the transformation of the economic basis of politics and of the City's decisive shift away from Liberalism.

own and, when forced to choose, preferred to spread the burden by accepting increased indirect taxation. If the choice was between maintaining free trade or suffering higher direct taxation, which might scare capital away from London, the City by 1910 was clear about its priorities.[8]

FREE TRADE AND EMPIRE UNITY

Given that the Conservatives had always been less committed to free trade than the Liberals and that, by the turn of the century, the temptation to raise indirect taxes was becoming almost irresistible, it seems surprising that Chamberlain's Tariff Reform campaign, launched in 1903, should have split the party and allowed the Liberals their first real taste of power for 20 years. The failure of Chamberlain's campaign may seem the more puzzling in that it was based on a passionate desire for imperial economic unity. Since Disraeli's time, the Conservatives had always been the party identified both with the desire for closer unity with the white empire and with a more aggressive line on expansion in Africa and Asia than the Liberals, many of whom were infected with 'little Englandism', inherited from Cobden and Gladstone.

Although he was by no means a 'no foreign policy' man, Gladstone did lean more towards Cobden's view of the universe than he did to the 'free trade imperialism' of Palmerston.[9] This stance was probably reflective of northern, urban Liberalism which, before the 1880s, was relatively confident in Britain's ability to sell its wares world-wide. Gladstone tended to take Britain's power for granted. He once argued that if all Britain's overseas possessions and means of influence abroad were suddenly removed we should, simply because of the physical and mental powers of the British people, soon re-establish ourselves as world leaders. In his view, Britain's strength lay in Britain, not in her empire, and his superb confidence in Britain's intrinsic power meant that he had very little sympathy for those who worried about military and naval security. He did not believe, for instance, that the possession of formal empire was important. India, he argued, was

8. On City pragmatism in the matter of tariffs see below, pp. 217–8.
9. For Cobden's views see Peter Cain, 'Capitalism, War and Internationalism in the Thought of Richard Cobden', *British Journal of International Studies*, V (1979); and Oliver McDonagh, 'The Anti-Imperialism of Free Trade', *Econ. Hist. Rev.*, 2nd ser. XIV (1961–2).

not a source of strength and profit to Britain and our presence there could be justified only if we could show that we were leading the Indians towards civilisation. His attitude to the white colonies was that they should grow up and shoulder their own responsibilities as soon as possible though, at the same time, he hoped that a close but informal affinity would continue to bind Britain and her 'children' together.[10] Gladstone did not, of course, propose to leave India and, like most other radicals, he assumed that the economic dependence of the white colonies would continue irrespective of the nature of the political tie. Nonetheless, his determined attempt to cut expenditure on colonial defence after 1868 provoked a great uproar, not at first in the Conservative Party itself, which was slow to react, but among colonial intellectuals, journalists and professional men, many of whom resided in London and were not always representative of their homelands.[11] It is useful to look at the main ideas spawned by the agitation of 1869–71 because a number of them endured and became part of the stock-in-trade of imperialists before 1914.

Many of those who opposed Gladstone's policies were struck by the rapid growth of other 'empires', especially the federated states of Germany (created in 1870) and the United States. They were impressed by the large populations and geographical spread of these youthful great powers and fearful of their potential for future growth. It was clearly an article of faith among many Conservatives after 1870 that Britain might be dwarfed by these nations in the future. Hence, Britain needed the strength given by her empire and in particular should look to unification with the white colonies. The growth potential of the white colonies was expected to be similar to that of the United States, and many observers clearly believed that, together with Great Britain, they would one day provide a level of population and wealth sufficient to maintain the empire's position as a great power. Another emphasis of the time was that the ideal of universal free trade was no longer realisable, that protectionism was increasing again and that the white colonies would become critically important as markets before long. If they were cut adrift abruptly they might easily be absorbed by other powers.[12]

There is no doubt that rising fear of the might of other great powers - illustrated by the power of the North in the American Civil

---

10. W.E. Gladstone, 'England's Mission' *The Nineteenth Century*, IV (1878).
11. C.C. Eldridge, *England's Mission: The Imperial Idea in the Age of Gladstone and Disraeli, 1868–80* (1973), Ch. 4.
12. Ibid. Ch. 5. See also C.A. Bodelsen, *Studies in Mid-Victorian Imperialism* (1960), Pts. II and III.

War and by Germany's defeat of France in 1870 – had much to do
with the reaction to Liberal colonial policy in 1869–71. There is no
doubt, either, that Gladstone's own vision of the world depended
crucially upon Britain's ability to maintain her economic supremacy
over all her rivals. But, 'once doubt had been cast on the Manchester
School's prophecy of an era of universal peace and free trade,
dominated industrially by Great Britain, the value of overseas possessions once again became a completely open question'.[13] If Britain's
security was threatened, it began to seem madness to some commentators for her to acquiesce in a colonial policy which allowed the
empire slowly to fragment. Froude's conception of the empire,
surrounded by a tariff wall, self-subsisting, strong in population and
wealth and with the flow of migrants to her potential enemy, the
United States, diverted to the empty lands within the Queen's
jurisdiction, began to have a wide appeal at this juncture.[14] Modern
communications, it was felt, made such a united empire a possibility
and offered a shelter against a hostile world, which was increasingly
seen in social Darwinist terms.[15]

Disraeli, astute politician that he was, sensed this change in the
political wind earlier than most of his colleagues and, as leader of the
Conservative Party, turned on the Liberals and accused them of
weakening the empire and sapping the strength of Britain. His strident
imperialism at this time has often been seen as a typically cynical piece
of political manoeuvring, merely a convenient way of discrediting
Gladstone and winning the election of 1873. It has also been claimed
that much of Disraeli's imperialism was designed to provide a political
sideshow which would keep the minds of the newly enfranchised
masses off their domestic woes rather than to achieve specific goals
overseas.[16] But, if proponents of imperial unity before 1870 were

13. Eldridge, *England's Mission*, p. 126.

14. J.A. Froude, 'England and her Colonies', and 'The Colonies Once More', in
Short Studies on Great Subjects (1871).

15. On the changing ideological background see John Roach, 'Liberalism and the
Victorian Intelligentsia', *Cambridge Historical Journal*, XIII (1957); and, for a contemporary example, E. Dicey, 'Our Route to India', *The Nineteenth Century*, I (1877).

16. On Disraeli's supposed cynicism about the white Empire see Robert Blake,
Disraeli (1966), pp. 455, 523–4. A 'social imperialist' streak in Disraelian imperialism
has been detected by Freda Harcourt, 'Disraeli's Imperialism, 1866–68: a Question of
Timing', *Hist. Jour.*, 23 (1980), and to a lesser extent by P.J. Durrans, 'A Two-Edged
Sword: the Liberal Attack on Disraelian Imperialism', *Jour. Imp. and Comm. Hist.*, X
(1982), esp. pp. 267, 277–9. Harcourt's position is similar to that taken up by Joseph
Schumpeter in Ch. 2 of his famous *Imperialism* (1951), which sees imperialism as 'the
catch phrase of domestic politics'. For a criticism of Harcourt's analysis of Disraeli see
Nini Rodgers, 'The Abbyssinian Expedition of 1867–8: Disraeli's Imperialism or John
Murray's War?', *Hist. Jour.*, 27 (1984).

unfashionable, they still existed, and Disraeli was prominent among them. His advocacy of empire unity had often been vague but it was consistent.[17] The popularity of his views after 1870 probably had something to do with the changing nature of the Conservative Party itself, whose southern British base was increasingly connected with empire through colonial employment and investment in empire railways and governments.

In his famous Crystal Palace speech of 1872, Disraeli offered the Conservative Party as the repository of tradition and national honour and the true home of gentlemanly capitalism, while the Liberals were damned as upholders of 'cosmopolitan principles imported from the Continent'. The Conservatives had three aims: to uphold the traditional institutions of the country such as the established Church and the landed aristocracy; to elevate the conditions of the mass of the people; and 'to uphold the Empire of England' which, Disraeli claimed, Liberalism had tried to destroy.

Deftly ignoring the convergence of policy of both Tory and Liberal administrations over the previous 20 years, Disraeli argued that self-government for the white colonies was obviously right but that it ought to have been associated with

> a great policy of Imperial consolidation, it ought to have been accompanied by an Imperial tariff, by securities for the people of England for the enjoyment of the unappropriated lands which belong to the sovereign as their trustee and by a military code which shall have precisely defined the means and responsibilities by which, if necessary, the country should call for aid for the colonies themselves. It ought further to have been accompanied by the institution of some representative council in the metropolis which should have brought the colonies into constant and continuous communications with the Home Government.[18]

Leaving aside the question of the disposal of colonial lands, the main items on the agenda in the discussions between Britain and the white colonies over the next 40 years are all here.

If, as we have seen, there was a strong convergence between the parties on economic policy, it was also the case that something like a consensus on imperial questions began to emerge, at least at Cabinet level. Liberals remained wedded to free trade and were thus deeply suspicious of any attempts at uniting the empire economically. The

17. Stanley R. Stembridge, 'Disraeli and the Millstones', *Journal of British Studies*, 5 (1965).

18. T.E. Kebbel, ed. *Selected Speeches of the late Rt. Hon. The Earl of Beaconsfield* (1882), Vol. II, pp. 523–35.

party also retained its Cobdenite wing, which was hostile to any extension of the boundaries of empire and ready to pillory the interests, political or economic, they believed were conspiring to force on the nation a policy of imperial aggression. Nonetheless, Gladstone's lofty disdain for empire clearly stopped short of any desire to dismember it. Moreover, denunciations of expansion helped to disguise a partly subconscious acceptance of Britain's economic leadership and of her informal influence, and thus failed to confront the awkward question of what might have to be done should such relationships begin to collapse. The financial crisis of the early 1880s in Egypt – to whose stocks, marketed in the City, Gladstone was an enthusiastic subscriber – and its resolution by military force followed by occupation, was notable in bringing this implicit Liberal imperialism into the political light.[19] And Gladstone's successor, Rosebery, whose City affiliations were more direct, was happy enough to pursue a forward policy in Africa in the 1890s, despite misgivings among his political colleagues.

On the Conservative side, it has recently been claimed that the fear of high taxation, aimed at landed wealth, among the party's aristocratic leadership was so great that they were driven to oppose high-cost enterprises like imperial expansion.[20] As we have already seen, however, Gladstonian financial rectitude was no real barrier to painting more corners of the world red. The argument also ignores the extent to which the Tory leadership, of which Salisbury was a prime example, had been emancipated from a dependence on income from agriculture and had come to see itself as the protector of a wide band of propertied interests, many of them involving overseas income and the extension of British power abroad.[21] Furthermore, just as the Liberals provided a traditional home for anti-imperialist sentiment, so the Conservative Party acted as a time-honoured refuge for imperial enthusiasts. Conservatives were the main force behind bodies like the Imperial Federation League in the 1880s;[22] they showed the most

19. H.G.C. Matthew, ed. *The Gladstone Diaries*, Vols. X and XI, (Oxford, 1990), pp. lxxi–lxxii. See also below, pp. 362–9.

20. A.N. Porter, 'Lord Salisbury, Foreign Policy and Domestic Finance, 1860–1900', in Lord Blake and Hugh Cecil, eds. *Salisbury: The Man and his Policies* (1987).

21. John France, 'Salisbury and the Unionist Alliance', and F.M.L. Thompson, 'Private Property and Public Policy', in Blake and Cecil, *Salisbury: The Man and his Policies*.

22. On the imperial unity movement as a whole see J.E. Tyler, *The Struggle for Imperial Unity, 1868–95* (1938); Nicholas Mansergh, *The Commonwealth Experience*, Vol. 1, (2nd edn 1981); W.D. McIntyre, *The Commonwealth of Nations: Origin and Impact, 1869–1971* (Oxford, 1977); and W.K. Hancock, *Survey of British Commonwealth Affairs*, Vol. I (Oxford, 1937), Ch. 1.

alarm at the rise of continental tariffs from the late 1870s;[23] and they were the first to consider seriously the possibility of bringing in imperial preference.[24] But they could not unite behind Chamberlain to oppose the New Liberalism which was replacing Gladstonianism. On the fiscal question the leadership had anyway to manoeuvre with great delicacy since a frontal attack on free trade could spell political disaster. Despite his hostility to Peel and his strong views on imperial unity, Disraeli had led the Conservatives away from protectionism as early as 1852 for electoral reasons. Salisbury also kept the issue out of the public gaze as far as possible when anti-free trade sentiment began to arise in the 1880s and for similar reasons, as we shall see. Chamberlain broke with tradition in making tariffs a matter of central concern in 1903 and, in so doing, he split the party, which had long ceased to depend either upon land or protection. Indeed, what made Chamberlain's initiative so devastating to the Conservatives was that it could easily be construed as an attack on the complex of gentlemanly economic forces which were in control of the party by the turn of the century.

CHAMBERLAIN AND PROTECTIONISM

The two periods when anti-free trade movements became important politically – the early 1880s and after 1903 – both followed rapid increases in manufactured imports in the previous decade and falls in net exports of manufactures. Both movements, the National Fair Trade League in the 1880s and early 1890s and then the Tariff Reform campaign, voiced strong criticisms of existing economic policy and of the economic structures they believed this policy helped to produce. The League was extremely critical of the effects of a high level of British foreign investment on manufacturing industry:

> An important effect of the combined influence of foreign tariffs and free imports is to discourage and lessen the investment of capital in the development of our agriculture and manufactures and to stimulate and increase its investment in foreign land and securities and foreign industrial enterprises: the inevitable consequence being that a large and increasing amount of food, clothing and other commodities is imported in payment

23. J. Gastan, 'The Free Trade Diplomacy Debate and the Victorian European Common Market Initiative', *Canadian Journal of History*, XXII (1987).
24. L. Trainor, 'The British Government and Imperial Economic Unity, 1890–5', *Hist. Jour.*, XIII (1970).

of income due to owners of foreign investments here resident, and therefore without a corresponding export of the production of our own industry. This directly operates to limit the employment of labour in the country. We think that this important feature of our economic position has not hitherto received the attention it deserves.[25]

Fair Traders were wrong to assume that much British foreign investment went into industrial enterprises abroad; but they were correct in thinking that the effect of the returning income, in connection with the policy of free trade, was to increase competitive pressures on both agriculture and industry in Britain. The main thrust of the campaign in the 1880s was for tariffs to be used as diplomatic weapons in the struggle to reduce the protective barriers erected by Britain's rivals in the depression of the late 1870s. This reflected both the conviction that Britain could compete easily in a free-trade universe and the belief that protection in Germany and other industrial countries prevented British exports from penetrating their markets and, at the same time, allowed foreign rivals to dump their surplus produce in Britain below cost price without fear of retaliation.[26]

Chamberlain and the Tariff Reformers also stressed the link between free trade, low domestic investment and a high rate of capital export. But they did so with a greater sense of urgency and with wider industrial support since, by 1900, the erosion of Britain's industrial superiority had gone further and the demand for protection, as well as for retaliatory tariffs, had become distinctly stronger. The Tariff Reformers raised the spectre of a de-industrialised Britain, where crucial industries like steel, vital for defence and for great power status as well as for wealth creation, were lost; they pointed to the time when Britain could no longer maintain her position in the world and would be faced with a breakdown in social order as industry disintegrated.[27] The campaign of 1903–6 was, in fact, a

25. *Minority Report of the Royal Commission on Depression in Trade and Industry*, PP 1886, C 4893, para 59. See also Sidney Pollard, *Britain's Prime and Britain's Decline: The British Empire, 1870–1914* (1989), p. 236.

26. The most useful studies of the Fair Trade movement are: Tyler, *The Struggle for Imperial Unity*, which places Fair Trade in the context of the wider movement for imperial unity at the time; J.H. Zebel, 'Fair Trade: an English Reaction to the Breakdown of the Cobden Treaty System', *Journal of Modern History*, XII (1940); and Benjamin H. Brown, *The Tariff Reform Movement in Great Britain, 1881–95* (1943). There is an excellent regional study by Roger J. Ward, 'The Tariff Reform Movement in Birmingham, 1877–1906', (Unpublished MA thesis, London University, 1971).

27. For a brief discussion of the Tariff Reform case see Peter Cain, 'Political Economy in Edwardian England: The Tariff Reform Controversy', in Alan O'Day, ed. *The Edwardian Age: Conflict and Stability, 1900–1914* (1979), pp. 41–4. A wider and still very readable discussion of the politics and economics of Tariff Reform is Bernard Semmel, *Imperialism and Social Reform: English Social Imperialism, 1895–1914* (1960).

concerted attack on the whole drift of economic policy in Britain after 1850, since the Tariff Reformers argued that the ultimate result of a policy of free trade would be the creation of a rentier-dominated service economy which would be impotent in the face of its enemies. As Chamberlain put it in 1904

> whereas at one time England was the greatest manufacturing country now its people are more and more employed in finance, in distribution, in domestic service and in other occupations of the same kind. That state of things is consistent with ever increasing wealth. It may mean more money but it means less men. It may mean more wealth but it means less welfare; and I think it worthwhile to consider – whatever its immediate effects may be – whether this state of things may not be the destruction ultimately of all that is best in England, all that has made us what we are, all that has given us our power and prestige in the world; whether it will not be bad for these qualities if we sink into the position of Holland which is rich – richer than it ever was before – but still an inconsiderable factor in the world.[28]

In the 1880s the Fair Traders wanted a small duty on manufactured imports and they put some emphasis on the need for closer links with the empire, suggesting small preferential duties in favour of the white colonies.[29] Chamberlain was more empire-minded than his predecessors because he was even more convinced that the industrial future lay with great empires and federations, such as Russia and the United States, with their huge populations and vast natural resources. Many Tariff Reformers firmly believed that it was only by uniting Britain with her white colonies – whose populations were expected to expand enormously in the twentieth century – and by using their joint power to exploit the underdeveloped parts of empire, that industrial leadership and great-power status could be retained. Chamberlain himself constantly claimed that a system of imperial tariffs would be crucial in

---

The most recent survey is by Friedberg, *The Weary Titan*, Ch. 2. Imports of steel in 1913 were equivalent to 45 per cent of exports by value. P.L. Payne, 'Iron and Steel Manufacturers', in D.H. Aldcroft, ed. *British Industry and Foreign Competition, 1870–1914* (1968), p. 75.

28. Joseph Chamberlain, *Speeches* (ed. C.W. Boyd, 1914), Vol. II, pp. 267–8. For another speech in a similar vein, Jim Tomlinson, *Problems of British Economic Policy, 1870–1945* (1981), p. 54; for similar sentiments see W.J. Ashley, *The Tariff Problem* (1903), pp. 112–13. Ashley was by no means the only intellectual interested in the growth of services and concerned with the problems which we now call 'de-industrialisation'. For other contributions which contain material germane to this theme see H.J. Mackinder, 'The Great Trade Routes', *Journal of the Institute of Bankers*, XXI (1900), and W.S. Hewins, *Apologia of An Imperialist: Forty Years of Empire Policy*, I (1929), pp. 56ff.

29. *Minority Report of the Royal Commission on Depression in Trade and Industry*, Paras 129, 137.

linking Britain's destiny with those parts of the empire whose growth potential was far greater than that of the motherland.[30] When Colonial Secretary in the late 1890s, he demonstrated his interest in imperial economic integration by trying to increase state economic involvement in the development of the dependent empire in order to encourage a more secure supply of imports and better markets for British goods.[31] In 1896, the same reasoning prompted him to suggest creating a free-trade empire with a common tariff against foreign countries, which he hoped would form the economic basis for greater unity.

The *Zollverein* idea fell foul of free-trade opinion in Britain and also offended the white colonies, which feared that their recently won economic independence would be infringed. Instead, the colonies advocated a system of mutual preferences which would allow them to protect their own industry. Chamberlain and his supporters fell back upon their proposals as being the most politically plausible. The hope was that, if the electorate could be persuaded to accept them, a united empire would eventually arise which would compensate for Britain's own economic decline.[32] In 1903, when he began his campaign, Chamberlain was convinced that the empire issue ought to be the paramount one in British politics; but he soon became aware that domestic protection had a broader popular appeal than empire preference. His campaign was designed to educate the electorate, but, not surprisingly, as it developed Chamberlain's speeches also began to reflect the protectionist concerns of those who rallied to Tariff Reform, even though empire economic unity remained his primary aim.[33]

The National Fair Trade League had considerable support within

30. Julian Amery, *Life of Joseph Chamberlain*, Vol. VI (1968), p. 540; Chamberlain, *Speeches*, Vol. II, pp. 231–2.

31. S.B. Saul, 'The Economic Significance of "Constructive Imperialism"', *Jour. Econ. Hist.*, XVII (1959); R.M. Kesner, *Economic Control and Colonial Development: Crown Colony Financial Management in the Age of Joseph Chamberlain* (Westport, Conn., 1981); Robert V. Kubicek, *The Administration of Imperialism: Joseph Chamberlain at the Colonial Office*, (Durham, NC, 1969).

32. For the background of Chamberlain's 'conversion' to a preferential policy see Amery, *Life of Joseph Chamberlain*, Vol. V (1951), and Vol. VI (1968); Peter Fraser, *Joseph Chamberlain* (1966), esp. Chs. 10–12; Elie Halévy, *History of The English People in the Nineteeth Century*, Vol. V (1961 edn), pp. 285–331; J.H. Zebel, 'Joseph Chamberlain and the Genesis of the Tariff Reform Campaign', *Jour. Brit. Stud.*, VII (1967); W.K. Hancock, *Survey of British Commonwealth Affairs*, Vol. II, Pt. I (Oxford, 1940), pp. 72ff; and, more recently, Richard Jay, *Joseph Chamberlain: A Political Study* (Oxford, 1981), Chs. 8 and 9.

33. A.J. Marrison, 'The Development of a Tariff Reform Policy during Joseph Chamberlain's First Campaign, May 1903 – February 1904', in B.M. Ratcliffe, ed. *Trade and Transport : Essays in Economic History in Honour of T.S. Willan* (Manchester, 1977). For Chamberlain's views see Amery, *Life of Joseph Chamberlain*, V, pp. 409–10, 415; VI, p. 473. For his shifting views by 1905 see ibid. VI, p. 725.

the Conservative Party in the 1880s and its policy could possibly have become established as the Tory answer to urban Liberalism. This did not happen partly because industry was hopelessly split over the protectionist issue and partly because the Home Rule crisis brought a large draft of Liberal Unionists, most of them solidly free trade in sympathy, into alliance with the Conservatives after 1886. Conservative leaders were also keen to marginalise the Fair Trade campaign for fear of its electoral implications.[34] Chamberlain's attempt to overturn economic orthodoxy and to change the nature of the political debate after 1903 was more challenging since, as one of the leading politicians of his day, he had the power to put the tariff question at the centre of political controversy. The tariff campaign gave the Conservative Party a modern 'cry', a new way of attracting the votes of the working men enfranchised in 1884.[35] It offered a programme of 'social imperialism' designed to unite property with labour in the cause of empire and to head off the formation of a mass party dedicated to socialism. But, had Chamberlain achieved his ambition, he might have overturned the existing heirarchy in the Conservative Party and threatened gentlemanly leadership in general.[36]

Chamberlain had begun his career as a radical industrialist hostile to the landed class. He combined his radicalism with a strong sense of the need for empire and empire markets: his opposition to Irish Home Rule in 1886 forced him out of the Liberal Party and compelled him, if only to maintain his influence, to take his Midlands support into an alliance with the Conservative Party, which at least shared his enthusiasm for empire. The hostility which his unorthodox attitudes to state spending as Colonial Secretary provoked within the Conservative Party,[37] and its indifference to industrial concerns, convinced him that the party, like the Liberals, was not an ideal

34. Ward, 'The Tariff Reform Movement in Birmingham', pp. 296–7; Tyler, *The Struggle for Imperial Unity*, Ch. 6.

35. E.H.H. Green, 'Radical Conservatism: the Electoral Genesis of Tariff Reform', *Hist. Jour.*, XXVIII (1985); Amery, *Life of Joseph Chamberlain*, V, p. 311.

36. This wider aspect of the Tariff Reform campaign has not been considered in any depth. The most thorough political account of the movement, Alan Sykes, *Tariff Reform in British Politics, 1903–13* (Oxford, 1979) deals mainly with Westminster infighting, and Semmel's *Imperialism and Social Reform*, despite its many virtues, does not really explore this theme either. There are some suggestive hints in Peter Fraser, 'Unionism and Tariff Reform: the Crisis of 1906', *Hist. Jour.* V (1962), and in the interesting review of Sykes' book by Dilwyn Porter, 'Fiscalitis: a Suitable Case for Treatment', *Moirae*, 6 (1981). See also Pollard, *Britain's Prime and Britain's Decline*, pp. 241–2.

37. This comes out most clearly in a particular case study, that by R.E. Dumett, 'Joseph Chamberlain, Imperial Finance and Railway Policy in British West Africa in the Late Nineteenth Century', *Eng. Hist. Rev.*, XC (1975).

vehicle for his views or for the interests he represented. It is doubtful if the Tariff Reform campaign[38] was expressly designed to overthrow the existing leadership of the Conservative Party, but it was nevertheless a danger to it. The campaign could have succeeded only if the Conservatives had made large electoral gains in provincial industrial areas at the expense of the Liberals. Had they done so on the basis of a programme which put industrial concerns at the forefront of politics, the centre of gravity of Tory politics would have shifted from the south to the north, from services to industry. More important, success for Tariff Reform would have transformed the party's ideological stance from one based on gentlemanly capitalism to another inspired by an aggressive, industrial radicalism. Like his famous brand of municipal socialism in the 1870s and his 'Unauthorised Programme' of the early 1880s, Chamberlain's tariff campaign was an attempt to create a 'producers' alliance' of industrial capitalists and their workforce which, besides muting industrial class conflict, was also expressly designed to encourage industry to assert itself and to take the nation's destinies out of the hands of the gentlemanly class. Since Chamberlain was making a direct assault on gentlemanly culture, it was inevitable that he would be condemned, in similar terms, by traditional leaders on both sides of the political divide. Almost instinctively, his attempt to place industrial wealth creation and its problems at the head of the political agenda was condemned as 'utterly sordid'[39] because it catered for the 'ignoble passions' of 'vulgarity and cupidity'.[40]

INDUSTRY, THE CITY AND FREE TRADE

Although Tariff Reformers were often determined to dramatise a split between industry and the service sector from which gentlemanly

38. Apart from the sources mentioned already, there is a wide literature upon the political development of the Tariff Reform campaign including: Richard A. Rempel, *Unionists Divided: Arthur Balfour, Joseph Chamberlain and the Unionist Free Traders* (Newton Abbot, 1972); A.K. Russell, *Liberal Landslide: The General Election of 1906* (Newton Abbot, 1973), pp. 65–73, 80, 83–91, 172f; K.D. Brown, 'The Trade Union Tariff Reform Association', *Jour. Brit. Stud.*, XI (1970); Neal B. Blewett, *The Peers, The Parties and the People: The General Elections of 1910* (1972); Richard J. Scally, *The Origins of the Lloyd George Coalition: The Politics of Social Imperialism, 1900–18* (Princeton, NJ, 1975).

39. Robert Cecil, quoted in Dennis Judd, *Balfour and the Empire: A Study in Imperial Evolution, 1874–1932* (1968), p. 93.

40. The sentiments of Campbell-Bannerman in a letter to Bryce, quoted in Amery, *Life of Joseph Chamberlain*, VI, p. 541.

capitalism drew much of its strength, they did not succeed in doing so. As we have already seen, support for tariffs often came from traditional sources in the Conservative Party who saw them as a better way of raising revenue than increasing direct taxation. On the other side, faced with preferences on food, many industrial workers were more impressed by the danger of the 'dear loaf' than they were by promises of more employment and better wages in an imperial economy. The representatives of industrial capital were almost as divided about Tariff Reform as they had been by Fair Trade. There were strong pockets of support for tariffs in iron, steel and engineering, for example, where foreign competition was keenly felt. Cotton textiles, on the other hand, faced little challenge either at home or abroad and stood by free trade, while shipbuilding prospered on the cheap imports which the steel masters wanted to check.[41]

Similarly, although some industrialists were deeply frustrated by traditional methods of raising finance and were critical of the City's role in channelling British savings abroad, the tariff campaign did not reveal any fundamental rift between London finance and provincial industry. Industrial critics of the City were few and the extent of foreign investment became a national issue in 1909 only because discontented aristocrats and leading City men on the Conservative side combined to complain that the Liberals' proposals for supertax were driving capital abroad and hurting the domestic economy. The implication of this argument, however, was that without such an unnecessary stimulus – and even with a tariff to raise revenue instead – the natural balance between foreign and home investment would be found again with only 'surplus' capital continuing to flow abroad. Liberals, in their turn, dismissed the claims about the effects of taxation on capital export. They emphasised that industrial investment was raised largely outside the City and underlined the importance of capital export to the health of British foreign trade.[42]

In the election campaign of 1910, Churchill rallied Lancashire's industry behind free-trade Liberalism by vigorously denying protectionist claims that foreign investment harmed home industry.[43] Mindful, perhaps, of the large local commitment to foreign investments, he ridiculed the idea that capital for domestic industry was difficult to

41. For the split in industry see the interesting article by A.J. Marrison, 'Businessmen, Industries and Tariff Reform in Britain, 1903–30', *Bus. Hist.*, 25 (1983). For the reaction of the workers see Brown, 'The Trade Union Tariff Reform Association'.
42. See the fascinating debate in the House of Lords in *Parliamentary Debates* (Lords), Vol. IV, 1909, Cols. 745–904, 22 Nov., and Cols. 947–1328, 24 Nov.
43. W.S. Churchill, *The People's Rights* (1909, 1970), pp. 104ff.

find and claimed that, in Lancashire at least, foreign investment was an important method of diffusing surplus capital. He argued that capital sent abroad encouraged the development of cheap imports of food and raw materials rather than fostered foreign industrial competition, as protectionists believed, and also that it left Britain 'almost entirely in the form of British exports'. In conclusion, Churchill clearly identified the interest of foreign investment with the interests of industry and with the nation as a whole, claiming that

> foreign investment and its returns are a powerful stimulus to the industrial system of Great Britain, that they give to the capital of the country a share in the new wealth of the whole world which is gradually coming under the control of scientific development, and that they sensibly enlarge the resources on which the state can rely for peaceful development and war-like need. [44]

Not a great many Conservatives would have objected to this: as one Liberal leader put it in 1909, the beneficial nature of foreign investment was 'a ground of common agreement'[45] between the parties. Chamberlain himself, when speaking in the City in 1904, came as one who saw 'the future of the country as a country of production, as a creator of new wealth and not merely the hoarder of invested securities',[46] but he did not suggest that there was any fundamental antagonism between the City and industry. Rather, he linked the fortunes of City and industry together and then claimed that both depended on the future development of the empire under a regime of tariffs. He admitted that some firms in the City took a cosmopolitan view of economic affairs and that to these, 'the fate of our manufacturers therefore is a secondary consideration: that provided the City of London remains, as it is at present, the clearing house of the world, any other nation may be its workshop'. But he felt he could appeal to a larger group in the City who would recognise a symbiotic relationship between finance and industry and between these two and empire development:

> You are the clearing-house of the world. Why? Why is banking prosperous among you? Why is a bill of exchange on London the standard currency of all commercial transactions? Is it not because of the productive energy and capacity which is behind it? Is it not because we have hitherto, at any rate, been constantly creating new wealth? Is it not because of the multiplicity, the variety, and the extent of our transactions? If any one of these things suffers even a check, do you suppose that you will not feel it? Do you imagine that you can in that

44. Ibid. p. 110.
45. Lord Crewe's words. See *Parl. Deb.* (Lords), IV (1909), c. 1327.
46. Amery, *Life of Chamberlain*, VI, p. 535.

case sustain the position of which you are justly proud? Suppose – if such a supposition is permissible – you no longer had the relations which you have at present with our great Colonies and dependencies, with India, with the neutral countries of the world, would you then be its clearing-house? No, gentlemen. At least we can recognize this – that the prosperity of London is intimately connected with the prosperity and greatness of the Empire of which it is the centre. Banking is not the creator of our prosperity, but is the creation of it. It is not the cause of our wealth, but it is the consequence of our wealth; and if the industrial energy and development which has been going on for so many years in this country were to be hindered or relaxed, then finance, and all that finance means, will follow trade to the countries which are more successful than ourselves.[47]

He went on from this to argue that, since the development of industry depended upon the empire, and the development of empire upon the abandonment of free trade, the City had good reason to support his campaign.

Chamberlain's audience would hardly have accepted his assumption that industry was the central source of national wealth. But Chamberlain was right to believe that there were those in the City who were sympathetic to the view that finance and industry were interdependent and that the empire had a special part to play in maintaining Britain's economic position in the world. City men had been interested in the question of imperial federation and imperial unity from the 1880s and had put their weight enthusiastically behind imperial expansion at the time of the Scramble for Africa.[48] Some of the leading figures remained passionately in favour of free trade after 1903, convinced that tariffs would undermine City cosmopolitanism and threaten invisible earnings;[49] however, there were others who saw no such danger and some who were behind Chamberlain's campaign because they, too, felt that industrial decline was occurring and that it would inevitably undermine the City's position in the world economy.[50] Most fell between these extremes. Balfour's elec-

47. Ibid. p. 536. For Chamberlain's London associations and his own links with the City see Ronald Quinault, 'Joseph Chamberlain: a Reassessment', in T.R. Gourvish and Alan O'Day eds. *Later Victorian Britain* (1988).

48. Smith, 'British Nationalism, Imperialism and the City of London, 1880–1900', pp. 209ff.

49. See, for example, F. Huth Jackson, 'The "Draft on London" and Tariff Reform', *Econ. Jour.*, XV (1904).

50. R.H. Inglis Palgrave, 'The Economic Condition of the Country', *National Review*, 42 (1903–4); idem, 'The Industrial Condition of the Country', ibid. 45 (1905). For some shrewd general comments on the City's attitude to the tariff campaign see Youssef Cassis, *La City de Londres, 1870–1914* (Paris, 1987), pp. 181–3, and idem, *Les Banquiers de la City à l'époque edouardienne, 1890–1914* (Geneva, 1984), pp. 357–64.

tion as a City MP in 1906 suggests a cautious approach to the question because the Conservative leader deliberately adopted a stance halfway between the free-trade and Chamberlainite wings of the party when he argued that tariffs could be used as a retaliatory device.[51] The City's pragmatism no doubt indicates a degree of uncertainty about the merits of the contending parties. It also reflects the fact that the issue was not regarded as one of outstanding importance by most prominent men in the City: the movement away from free trade proposed by the Tariff Reformers was probably too small to change either the pattern or the volume of world commerce very much and, in any case, the City was far more interested in keeping the gold standard than in maintaining free trade.

Chamberlain and other prominent Tariff Reform supporters insisted that City wealth depended, in the final analysis, upon the prosperity of British industry; but they never succeeded in convincing either educated opinion or the electorate in general that free trade and a high level of foreign investment were harmful to the industrial structure. Many of their Conservative opponents and a large section of the electorally victorious Liberal Party denied that there was any fundamental industrial problem, while even those who shared Chamberlain's misgivings about Britain's future often refused to accept the argument that preferences and protection were the key to industrial revival. Some of his antagonists also went out of their way to stress the importance of overseas investment to exports and, by extension, to industrial development. Indeed, the overall effect of the debate on free trade was to highlight the significance of the City to the whole economy and to strengthen its perceived position as the rock upon which British economic strength was built. In so doing, it reinforced the tendency of governments to rely on the City for advice and left the policies upon which the City depended most, notably the gold standard, untouched except for behind-the-scenes criticism from some of the joint-stock bankers.

The Tariff Reform campaign of 1903–6 failed because the Chamberlainites, despite adding a protectionist layer to the original argument about preferences for the empire, could not unite industry and the industrial workforce. The spread of interests, both industrial and non-industrial, which favoured free trade and internationalism was too great to make the policy electorally successful. The campaign

51. For Balfour's views, which were based on the notion that tariffs were acceptable as retaliatory devices, see his *Economic Notes on Insular Free Trade* (1903). There are extracts from this in W.H.B. Court, *British Economic History, 1870–1914: Commentary and Documents* (Cambridge, 1965), pp. 452–9.

split the Conservatives in 1903–6, led to their disastrous defeat in the 1906 election and contributed to further defeats in the two elections of 1910. One of its effects, for example, was to rally free-trade business interests to the side of Liberalism and to halt, to some extent, the drift of industrialists to the political right (see Appendix Two).

The Fair Trade movement and the Tariff Reform campaign were, in their way, cries of alarm about the drift of the British economy in the direction of services and the implications of this drift for the domestic economy and Britain's world position. Had Chamberlain managed to unite industry behind him, his campaign might have succeeded. His failure to do so, like that of the Fair Traders before him, illustrates both the power of the perceived connection between free trade, foreign investment and industrial strength and also the fragmented nature of industry in Britain, which could never speak on any major issue with one voice. Tariff Reform gathered considerable support from the 'newer' end of British industry, that most hurt by German competition and impressed by German success. Many of the entrepreneurs in this sector argued not just for protection, but for greater state involvement in business on continental lines. They were also deeply frustrated by traditional methods of raising finance and by the exclusion of industrialists from policy-making.[52] Ideologically, however, they were far apart from traditional industrialists, like those in cotton textiles, where free-trade sentiment was still strong, where worries about City finance of domestic industry were an irrelevance and where government was still viewed with deep suspicion (see Appendix Two). Since a large section of industry was content with the status quo, gentlemanly hegemony over economic policy was unlikely to be seriously threatened.[53] Had industrial imports con-

52. For a good example of a Tariff Reform businessman and his background, see R.P.T. Davenport-Hines, *Dudley Docker: The Life and Times of a Trade Warrior* (Cambridge, 1985), Chs. 3 and 4. For other examples of aggrieved manufacturers see Scott Newton and Dilwyn Porter, *Modernization Frustrated: The Politics of Industrial Decline in Britain since 1900* (1988), pp. 11–12, 37, and D. Porter, 'The Unionist Tariff Reformers, 1903–14' (Unpublished Ph.D. thesis, Manchester University, 1976), pp. 19–36, 206–8.

53. There were some highly tentative negotiations involving Lloyd George and the successors of Chamberlain, such as Milner, in 1910 about the possibilities of combining the 'progressive' sections of both parties to form a new social imperialist political force in Britain. Had it succeeded, such a combination could well have brought industrialists nearer to the forefront of British politics; but the chances of success, given the bitterness of the party disputes of the time, were always extremely small. See Scally, *Origins of the Lloyd George Coalition*, especially the introduction and pp. 375–86. Nonetheless, under the hammer of Lloyd George's 'socialism', many traditional Liberal businessmen were beginning to wonder by 1913 whether modest protection from the Conservative Party was not better than free trade and increased direct taxation under the Liberals. See P.F. Clarke, 'The End of Laissez-Faire and the Politics of Cotton', *Hist. Jour.*, XV (1972).

tinued to flood in after 1903 at the rate of the previous ten years, the anti-free-trade forces might have gained more momentum; but Chamberlain had the ill-luck to begin his attack just as exports recovered and began to grow at a rate higher than any time since the early 1870s.[54]

After the 1906 election, the Tariff Reformers briefly dominated the Conservative Party, controlling two-thirds of the remaining 157 MPs.[55] Nonetheless, in the longer term, the 1903–6 campaign failed to change the nature of the Conservative Party. This became clear from 1909 onwards when the Liberals, faced with rising expenditure, decided to introduce higher taxation. As Chancellor of the Exchequer, Lloyd George was keen not to alienate his own middle-class support and he was also made aware of the link between Britain's high levels of foreign investment, the buoyancy of foreign trade and the customs revenue which gave him the leeway both to pay for social reform and to build Dreadnoughts as the German naval threat grew.[56] He concentrated his attack mainly on unearned income, especially land, provoking the great budgetary crisis of 1909 and the constitutional crisis of 1909–11. The Conservatives failed to head off the Liberal attack, which reduced the power of the House of Lords, losing both elections in 1910. But they made a strong recovery from the débâcle of 1906, rallying their southern vote in defence of the status quo rather than winning more of the northern vote, as the Tariff Reformers had hoped. After 1910, the cry of industrial regeneration and protection was almost drowned in the noises emanating from opponents of Irish Home Rule, from discontented aristocrats and gentry (who, like the City and other financial interests, feared Liberal tax policies), and from the rising anti-plutocratic and militaristic radical right – many of them forces which Chamberlain would have liked to eject from the party or subject to the will of industry.[57]

The fact that, by 1910, most Conservatives, including those in the City, were advocating tariffs meant only that they recognised the need for new sources of revenue: it certainly did not mean either that they were converted to a strategy of industrial regeneration or that a cosmopolitan view of economic policy was seriously threatened.

---

54. This was recognised by contemporaries. See Amery, *Life of Joseph Chamberlain*, V, p. 320.

55. Ibid. Vol. VI, p. 789.

56. On this important theme see Offer, 'Empire and Social Reform: British Overseas Investment and Domestic Politics, 1908–1914'.

57. Sykes, *Tariff Reform in British Politics, 1903–13*, Ch. 13; G.R. Searle, 'Critics of Edwardian Society: the Case of the Radical Right', in O'Day, *Edwardian England*.

Imperial preference, Chamberlain's pet idea, fell from prominence. It was obvious to the Conservatives after 1910 that, if they were to win another election and safeguard the status quo from future Liberal attack, they had to gain a bigger share of the northern urban vote. They set out to do this in 1913 by abandoning imperial preference because the 'dear loaf' cry raised against them by the Liberals in 1906 and again in 1910 had been so successful.[58] In 1914, the two main parties still represented a solid wall of opposition to any fundamental changes in Britain's internationalist economic policy. It was a wall which the Tariff Reformers could neither scale nor demolish.

COSMOPOLITANISM AND INDUSTRIAL DECLINE

It would be difficult to argue that the protectionists represented the national interest more faithfully than did the advocates of economic orthodoxy; but, as the Tariff Reformers foretold, sticking to orthodoxy had some grim consequences for Britain's position as an industrial and world power. This does not mean that the Tariff Reform solution to Britain's industrial plight would necessarily have worked. Many of the more intelligent free-trade critics were quick to point out that protection and preference might simply provide bolt-holes for uncompetitive firms, slowing down rather than increasing the pace of technical change.[59] This was a charge that the Fair Traders and Tariff Reformers found hard to repudiate at the time, and empire markets certainly provided a home for an uncomfortably large share of the exports of many of Britain's staple industries. It is true, too, that policies of protection and preference would have been assured of success only had they been combined with a more wide-ranging attack on economic policy and with radical measures of state intervention in industry. These were steps which most Tariff Reformers, as good capitalist businessmen, were unwilling to contemplate. Nonetheless, complaints by Tariff Reform and Fair Trade supporters that domestic industry had been starved of funds by excessive foreign investment were, as we have seen, not altogether misleading.

A protectionist strategy might also have raised the rate of profit in the more important capital-intensive industries such as steel and

58. Semmel, *Imperialism and Social Reform*, pp. 124–7.
59. For a summary of the argument on the free trade side see Cain, 'Political Economy in Edwardian England: the Tariff Reform Controversy', pp. 44–5.

helped to bring about some shift in the relative proportions of domestic and foreign investment, and in the balance between services and heavy industry in Britain.[60] In addition, Chamberlain's campaign had the merit of highlighting the extent to which, in an economy dedicated to cosmopolitanism, the fate of arable agriculture could eventually be shared by important sectors of industry, posing grave problems for employment and for Britain's ability to sustain an empire and a world role. Perhaps only the defeat of so many of her industrial rivals in the two world wars saved Britain from the consequences of openness for so long: much of what the protectionists predicted has come to pass since 1945.

The beginnings of the industrial decline which worried the Tariff Reformers also posed a threat to Britain's financial empire, though in ways that were not really appreciated by contemporaries. It has recently been argued that the use of sterling as a reserve asset in place of gold after 1900 was a sign of growing weakness. Britain's overseas loans were not entirely matched by her current surplus on the balance of payments so that her 'basic balance' (current account surplus less spending on capital account) was in deficit. This deficit exceeded Britain's small reserves of gold. According to Lindert, the problem was solved by inducing other countries, especially those within the empire, to hold sterling assets rather than gold, a solution which cannot be explained 'without reference to the familiar story of Britain's loss of export markets and the steady advance of imports'.[61] The rise of sterling reserve assets after 1900 probably did cushion the country against the need for internal adjustment in crises, and the size of the reserves was partly a function of Britain's imperial power; but their existence was not in itself a sign of weakness. A comparison between the outflows of portfolio investment and the current account surplus in the 1890s and after 1900 suggests that the basic balance was stronger in the latter period, when sterling reserves were accumulating;[62] large sterling holdings may have arisen, not from any

---

60. Michael Edelstein, *Overseas Investment in the Age of High Imperialism: The United Kingdom, 1850–1914* (1982), p. 222.

61. P.H. Lindert, *Key Currencies and Gold, 1900–1913* (Princeton Studies in International Finance, No. 24, 1969), p. 75.

62.

	Money Calls (£m. annual av.)	Current Account Surplus (annual av.)	2 as % 1
1891–1900	60.7	45.5	82.2
1901–1913	134.5	124.4	92.5

The figures for money calls are from M. Simon, 'The Pattern of New British Portfolio Investment, 1865–1914', in J.H. Adler, ed. *Capital Movements and Economic Development*

discernible weakness in the balance of payments, but from growing confidence in sterling as London refined its techniques of international monetary management and became increasingly accepted as a repository for other nations' spare international assets.

Table 7.1 British balance of trade surpluses (+) and deficits (−): by Region, 1871–1913 (£m.)

	1871–5	*1896–1900*	*1913*
Industrial and developed countries	−32	−156	−157
Newly settled countries	− 3	− 18	− 29
Underdeveloped countries	−28	+ 13	+ 52
World total	−63	−161	−134
British white colonies	0	− 18	− 12
Rest of empire	−11	+ 11	+ 29
British empire	−11	− 7	+ 17

Sources: B.R. Mitchell and P. Deane, *Abstract of British Historical Statistics* (Cambridge, 1962); and *Statistical Abstracts of the United Kingdom* (HMSO).
Note: South Africa is included in British white colonies and newly settled countries.

If sterling was under threat by 1914, the threat certainly had an industrial origin but it was of a more obscure and complex kind than Lindert considers. In the 1870s, Britain's balance of trade deficits were fairly evenly spread between developed and underdeveloped countries alike, and her account with the countries of recent settlement (including the white colonies) was more or less in balance (Table 7.1). Since Britain had a considerable surplus on invisibles with nearly all her trading partners, she had no acute settlement problems with any country or group of countries. After 1870, her balance of trade deficit with industrial Europe and the United States grew very rapidly. Imports of food and manufactures from these countries leapt up while her own exports faltered because of uncompetitiveness and protectionism. Britain paid off these huge deficits with her industrial competitors partly through her invisibles and partly via a complex system of multilateral settlements. Industrial Europe and the United

(1967), Table II, and the current account surplus is from C.H. Feinstein, *Statistical Tables of National Income Expenditure and Output in the UK, 1855–1865* (Cambridge, 1973). Lindert himself recognises the force of this argument to some extent in *Key Currencies and Gold*, p. 74.

States had deficits with the underdeveloped and newly settled worlds and, since Britain had surpluses there, she could pay off her debts to her industrial rivals by settling their debts with her underdeveloped creditors. Towards 1914, many of Britain's surpluses with countries in the newly settled world began to diminish as their exports of primary produce to Britain swelled and as her exports grew less competitive in their markets. Britain's ability to meet her deficit with Europe and the United States thus came to depend more and more upon the invisible surplus as a whole and on her ability to export manufactured commodities, mainly textiles, to a limited range of underdeveloped countries many of which, like India, were within the empire (Table 7.1). Insofar as Britain's traditional exports were growing slowly in world trade and competition was increasing, the multilateral settlement pattern was under threat and, had it broken down, confidence in the whole sterling-based system could have been undermined.[63] As Chamberlain had claimed, the fate of the City and of British industry were closely connected, but in ways which neither he nor most of his contemporaries understood.

APPENDIX TWO: MANUFACTURING INTERESTS IN PARLIAMENT, 1868–1910

Some indication of the impact of the Tariff Reform campaign on industrial opinion can be gathered from data on the political affiliations of MPs with a background in manufacturing. In Table 7.2, numbers above 1.0 indicate that the Liberal share of the manufacturing interests concerned was greater than the Liberal share of the total number of Liberal and Conservative MPs. Numbers below 1.0 show that the Conservative share of the interest was greater than the Conservative share of the total number of Liberal and Conservative MPs (see Appendix One, pp. 138–40).

The table indicates that, over the whole period, manufacturing interests in Parliament were shifting steadily away from the over-whelming adherence to Liberalism evident in the 1860s. However,

63. For the classic account of this multilateral mechanism see S.B. Saul, *Studies in British Overseas Trade, 1870–1914* (1960), Chs. 3 and 4. There is also a concise summary of the major themes in François Crouzet, 'Trade and Empire: the British Experience from the Establishment of Free Trade until the First World War', in B.M. Ratcliffe, ed. *Great Britain and her World, 1750–1914: Essays in Honour of W.O. Henderson* (Manchester, 1975).

Table 7.2 Liberal MPs associative index: manufacturing interests, 1868–1910

	1868	1880	1892	1900	1906	1910*
Heavy industry	3.96	2.23	2.04	1.75	0.96	0.87
Textiles	5.40	1.72	2.89	2.33	4.78	5.04
Other manufacturing	4.66	5.56	1.90	2.01	1.22	1.27
All manufacturing	3.19	2.10	1.97	1.69	1.29	1.22

* The election of January 1910 only.

Sources: Harold Perkin, *The Structured Crowd: Essays in English Social History* (Brighton, 1981); J.A. Thomas, *The House of Commons, 1832–1901: A Study of its Economic and Financial Character* (Cardiff, 1939); idem, *The House of Commons, 1906–1911: An Analysis of its Economic and Social Character* (Cardiff, 1958).

the most decisive movement towards Conservatism occurred among businessmen connected with heavy industry, including metal manufacture and engineering, and the Tariff Reform movement appears to have accentuated this drift. In contrast, Chamberlain's campaign appears to have reversed the decline in allegiance to the Liberals among those MPs with an interest in textiles, as it also did among those MPs with a background in merchanting. In both these cases, the threat to free trade reinforced a commitment to liberalism.

PART THREE

The Wider World

'An Extension of the Old Society': Britain and the Colonies of Settlement, 1850–1914[1]

One of the outstanding features of the economic history of the second half of the nineteenth century was the enormous increase in international trade and international specialisation which took place principally under Britain's leadership. The rapid growth of world trade was part of a much wider process of change in the international economy involving a great movement of factors of production – capital and labour – across the globe. In Europe, the decline of agriculture and the shift to industry and services in the towns led to a vast displacement of peoples both within the continent and overseas; the latter movement brought the 'new world' of America, Australasia and southern Africa firmly into the capitalist net, settling them with emigrants from Europe and shaping them into centres of primary produce for export to the industrialising world.

THE INTERNATIONAL ECONOMY AND THE NEW WORLD

If we look at this complex extension of capitalism from Britain's angle, its main elements can easily be identified. Britain was a country with a shortage of land and, therefore, primary produce had a high price. She also had an abundance of labour, both skilled and unskilled, and of capital too by world standards; but she faced the Ricardian-Malthusian nightmare that, in the long run, her development might be choked off by a shortage of agricultural land. On the other hand,

1. The quotation is taken from E.G. Wakefield, 'A Letter from Sydney', in E. Lloyd Prichard, ed. *The Collected Works of Edward Gibbon Wakefield* (Glasgow, 1968), p. 165.

the newly colonised areas had such an abundance of land that it was often practically a free good, but they lacked the labour and capital needed to bring their natural resources into full production. Imports of primary produce by Britain under free trade were the equivalent of extending her own land area; in the newly settled country, imports of manufactured commodities and of services embodied the capital and labour in short supply domestically. But without a massive shift of capital and labour from Britain (and other parts of Europe) to these new lands, the process of trade interaction could not have taken place so rapidly; and a network of transport and utilities had to be built in these areas before they were equipped to play their part.[2] It was the extension of railway and shipping networks, embodying many technological improvements over half a century, which brought the price of transport tumbling down and made it possible, by the 1890s, for wheat to be brought thousands of miles from the newly settled frontier to Britain and sold at a price which was half that ruling in the British market 20 years earlier.

The place occupied by the newly settled countries in this global upheaval in economic relations, and their importance to Britain, must not be overstated. The 35 million people who left Europe for the new world after 1870 still represented only about two-fifths of its total population increase.[3] Vast quantities of the capital exported from European countries found other European homes, as was the case particularly with French loans which poured into Eastern Europe and Russia.[4] Besides this, the factor movements out of Europe were, on a global scale, only a part of a wider movement which also distributed

2. This 'factor endowment' approach to international trade, found in the work of Adam Smith, is expounded succinctly by D.P. O'Brien, *The Classical Economists* (Oxford, 1975), pp. 170–2. It is also at the heart of the Wakefieldian argument for colonisation, on which see Donald Winch, 'Classical Economics and the Case for Colonization', *Economica*, new ser. 30 (1963). A factor endowment approach is much more realistic in this context than one based on Ricardian or orthodox neo-classical theory, since the latter cannot account for the importance of international factor movements. The best exposition of the contrast between the two positions remains J.H. Williams, 'The Theory of International Trade Reconsidered', *Economic Journal*, 39 (1929).

3. Frank Thistlethwaite, 'Migration from Europe Overseas in the 19th and 20th Centuries', in Herbert Moller, ed. *Population Movements in Modern European History* (1964). See also I. Ferenczi, 'A Historical Study of Migration Statistics', *International Labour Review*, XX (1929). There is now a comprehensive review of English and Welsh experience in Dudley Baines, *Migration in a Mature Economy: Emigration and Internal Migration in England and Wales, 1861–1901* (Cambridge, 1985).

4. On the distribution of French overseas investment in 1900 and 1914 see Herbert Feis, *Europe, The World's Banker, 1870–1914* (Clifton, NJ, 1974), p. 51. French investment in Europe is dealt with by René Girault, *Emprunts russes et investissements français en Russie, 1887–1914* (Paris, 1973), and Raymond Poidevin, *Les relations économiques et financières entre la France et L'Allemagne de 1898 à 1914* (Paris, 1969).

millions of Indians, Chinese and other non-Europeans throughout Asia.[5] New sources of primary products in the world economy were also manifold, including a range of commodities from the tropics and significant contributions from Europe. Britain herself became the world's most important exporter of coal in the second half of the century and she took in large supplies of Russian wheat, German sugar beet, Scandinavian iron and timber and Danish dairy produce – to mention only a few of the most prominent European items. Denmark's development in this context is particularly interesting in that, as a small country, she was crucially dependent for growth on British demand for her agro-industrial products. Britain took 38 per cent of Denmark's exports in 1873 and three-fifths at the end of the century and, by 1913, Denmark was Britain's biggest food supplier after the United States and Argentina. She was also part of the sterling system, and British investors were important in funding Denmark's railways – all of which suggests that Denmark was just as much within the orbit of Britain's overseas economic influence as were the smaller, newly settled countries.[6]

Britain provided about two-fifths of the world's total of exported capital between 1870 and 1914,[7] and most of that went to the new lands, as did the bulk of her migrants. Some areas – the white colonies of Australia, New Zealand, Canada and South Africa as well as the United States – took both migrants and capital from Britain; but Britain's capital exports to Argentina and Brazil went along with migrants from Southern Europe, and, in the case of Chile, substantial investment by Britain and other European nations induced hardly any migrant flow at all.

In the case of the largest newly settled country, the United States, there was no question of her economic relationship with Great Britain involving any form of economic subordination. In the late nineteenth century the United States already had a population equivalent to that of the great European powers and a large and rapidly growing industrial sector based on the home market. The capital which she borrowed from Britain provided her with only a small portion of her investment needs. Britain's position *vis-à-vis* the United States is best illustrated by her tactical retreat over Canada, which we shall examine later in this chapter, and by her inability to give any substantial aid to

5. W. Arthur Lewis, *Growth and Fluctuations, 1870–1913*, (1978) pp. 185–8.

6. B. N. Thomsen and B. Thomas, *Anglo-Danish Trade, 1661–1963* (Aarhus, 1963), pp. 175–6, 297–8, 344.

7. Brinley Thomas, 'The Historical Record of International Capital Movements to 1913', in J.H. Adler, ed. *Capital Movements and Economic Development* (1967), p. 10.

the free-trade, cotton-growing South in the American Civil War. In the smaller new countries, however, the impact of Britain, via factor movements and trade, was often a decisive element in their development. Some idea of this can be gauged from the fact that the four principal countries with which we deal – Australia, New Zealand, Canada and Argentina – together accounted for about 17 per cent of both Britain's exports and imports in 1913, while their trade dependence on Britain was altogether greater.

All the small, newly-settled countries had high ratios of trade to national income, and this is a clear indication of the importance of the international economy in their development – an importance emphasised from the time of Gibbon Wakefield to the so-called 'staple' theorists of modern times.[8] Australia's development, for example, has recently been described in terms of a succession of staple exports – from whaling in the early nineteenth century, wool after 1820, gold at mid-century and dairy produce in the 20 years before World War I – which created internal demand linkages and attracted foreign capital and migrants.[9] Export-led growth does not, of course, tell the whole story of the development of new countries. It gives little clue, for example, to the reasons for economic progress in the French Canadian province of Quebec, which was much less affected by Canadian links with the international economy than were other provinces;[10] generally speaking, too heavy a concentration on external stimuli can obscure important domestic sources of growth and change. An emphasis on the crucial role of exports may also invert the process of economic development. In Canada, during the wheat boom of 1900–14, it

8. For an introduction to the staple theory of economic growth see Douglass C. North, 'Location Theory and Regional Economic Growth', *Journal of Political Economy*, LXIII (1955); Albert O. Hirschmann, *The Strategy of Economic Development* (New Haven, Conn., 1958), Ch. VI; Melville H. Watkin, 'The Staple Theory of Economic Growth', *Canadian Journal of Economics and Political Science*, XXIX (1963).

9. There is an abundance of material on Australian growth which adopts the staple approach. The pioneering work was by J.W. McCarty, 'The Staple Approach in Australian Economic History', *Business Archives and History*, IV (1964) and Geoffrey Blainey, 'Technology in Australian History', ibid. V (1965). See also McCarty's, 'Australia as a Region of Recent Settlement in the Nineteenth Century', *Australian Economic History Review*, 12–13 (1972–3). A widely used textbook which adopts this approach is W.H. Sinclair, *The Process of Economic Development in Australia* (Melbourne, 1976), esp. Ch. 1. For Canada see Watkins, 'The Staple Theory of Economic Growth'; R.E. Caves and R.H. Holton, *The Canadian Economy* (Cambridge, Mass., 1961); Richard Pomfret, *The Economic Development of Canada* (Toronto, 1984), Ch. 3; and William L. Marr and Donald G. Paterson, *Canada: An Economic History* (Toronto, 1980), pp. 10–18.

10. Kenneth A.H. Buckley, 'The Role of Staple Industries in Canada's Economic Development', *Jour. Econ. Hist.*, XVIII (1958).

would be hard to argue that grain exports were the key to growth. Britain was by far the largest purchaser of wheat internationally, but her imports accounted for only 10 per cent of the total production of all the wheat-exporting countries in the late 1880s and 5 per cent in 1909–13. Britain's demand for Canadian wheat could not have added more than 2 per cent to Canada's per capita income at the time, and the boom, like other phases of rapid development in new countries, must be explained in terms of its domestic origins.[11]

Nevertheless, if export to Britain was not the immediate cause of growth, Britain still had a decisive part to play. Rapid internal growth in new countries soon ran up against ceilings imposed by capital and labour shortages and an inability to meet domestic requirements without a soaring import bill. Development had to be sustained by immigration and financed by borrowing which, on a per capita basis, was often massive by European standards. The capital inflow, most of it from London sources, was crucial in sustaining booms; but it had to be paid for eventually by the creation of export income. In the long term, therefore, the pace and extent of economic growth in new countries depended upon immigration, the ability to borrow extensively in Europe and success in finding exports to finance the loans.[12] In the Canadian case, much of what she borrowed from Britain between 1900 and 1914 was paid for by exporting wheat and other commodities to Britain during World War I and in the 1920s.

Whether growth was export-led or whether it occurred as a result of the roundabout process described above, rapid change in many small, newly settled countries could be achieved only at the cost of dependence on British capital and, ultimately, conformity to the rules of the economic game as set in London. This was as true of the emergent Dominions as it was of Argentina or Chile,[13] despite the

11. See Mancur Olson, 'The U.K. and the World Market in Wheat and Other Primary Products', *Explorations in Economic History*, XI (1973–4).

12. An early example of this is described by Douglas McCalla, 'The Wheat Staple and Upper Canadian Development', in J.M. Bumstead, ed. *Interpreting Canada's Past*, Vol. I, *Before Confederation* (Toronto, 1986). An emphasis on the complexity of development on new frontiers in the later nineteenth century can be found in Richard Pomfret, 'The Staple Theory as an Approach to Canadian and Australian Economic Development', *Austral. Econ. Hist. Rev.*, 21 (1981).

13. The only major work which looks at newly settled countries in a comparative context is Donald Denoon, *Settler Capitalism: The Dynamics of Dependent Development in the Southern Hemisphere* (Oxford, 1983), which covers Australia, New Zealand, South Africa, Argentina, Uruguay and Chile. Denoon's general views on the relationship between the settlement countries and Great Britain seem to be compatible with our own. We would also like to direct attention to C.B. Schedvin, 'Staples and Regions of Pax Britannica', *Econ. Hist. Rev.*, 2nd ser. XLIII (1990), which appeared too late to be incorporated into our arguments.

fact that the former were making steady progress towards political independence from Britain from the 1840s. What we must first show is that the constitutional freedom of the emerging white Dominions was gained at the same time as their economic development bound them more closely to the financial system based on London and that, in this sense, the white colonies exchanged a position of political dependence for a place in a wider and looser framework of 'free-trade imperialism' – even if the latter was only apparent clearly in times of economic crisis.

POLITICAL LIBERTY AND FINANCIAL DEPENDENCE

In recent years there has been a considerable revision of historical opinion concerning British attitudes to colonies of new settlement in the mid-nineteenth century. Most of the participants in the debate have been political historians, and the economic dimension of Anglo-colonial relationships after 1850 has been somewhat neglected. The trade dependence of many white colonies has been noted, of course, but the implications of this dependence within the context of an evolving system of 'responsible government' have not been seriously considered in Britain for many years. Our intention here is to spell out some of the consequences of colonial dependence on capital supply from Britain from mid-century, first in general terms, and then by looking briefly at two specific issues: the economic evolution of Australasia and the creation of a Canadian state independent of the United States.

The assumption that there was a simple connection between the form taken by Anglo-colonial economic relations at any one time and the kind of governmental authority exercised by Britain in the settlement colonies has a long history. Adam Smith's opinion was that political control of the colonies from London was essential to force the mercantilist system upon them. 'The maintenance of this monopoly', he wrote, 'has hitherto been the principal, or more properly perhaps, the sole end and purpose of the dominion which Great Britain assumes over her colonies'.[14] Similarly, until quite recently it was generally believed that the abandonment of the

14. Adam Smith, *The Wealth of Nations*, ed. R.H. Campbell, A.J. Skinner and W.B. Todd (Oxford, 1976), II, p. 614.

preferential system between 1846 and 1860 led logically to the ending of Britain's interest in controlling colonial destinies.[15] It has now become apparent, however, as a result of extensive research undertaken on the background to the granting of responsible government, that those who expressed strong anti-imperial sentiment in mid-century were mainly vociferous, but unrepresentative, free-trade radicals. Indeed, in 1953 Gallagher and Robinson went so far as to claim that the granting of political liberty represented merely a transition from formal to informal methods of controlling settlement colonies and that

> responsible government, far from being a separatist device, was simply a change from direct to indirect methods of maintaining British interests. By slackening the formal political bond at the appropriate time, it was possible to rely on economic dependence and mutual good feeling to keep the colonies bound to Britain while still using them as agents for further British expansion.[16]

Gallagher and Robinson believed, therefore, that free trade and responsible government were simply the economic and the political aspects of the same policy, though one which marked a decisive shift, not from imperialism to colonial freedom, as their predecessors had believed, but from one form of imperialism to another.

There is no doubt that some contemporary statesmen clearly felt that responsible government was compatible with maintaining, even strengthening, the colonial tie. Earl Grey, for example, did not see responsible government as a step on the road to imperial fragmentation. He gloried in 'the global union which linked the mother country with her children in the colonies', and took it for granted that Britain would continue to exercise authority within the empire of settlement even after political liberty had been granted, partly to ensure that free trade would be maintained.[17] But Grey's clarity of vision was unusual. Most of the statesmen and officials who took the decisions were more hesitant and often held a bewildering variety of opinions on colonial

---

15. The classic accounts here are C.A. Bodelsen, *Studies in Mid-Victorian Imperialism* (1960), and R.L. Schuyler, *The Fall of the Old Colonial System: A Study in British Free Trade, 1770–1870* (New York, 1945).

16. J. Gallagher and R.E. Robinson, 'The Imperialism of Free Trade, 1815–1914', *Econ. Hist. Rev.*, 2nd ser. VI (1953), p. 4.

17. Earl Grey, *The Colonial Policy of Lord John Russell's Administration* (2nd edn 1853), I, pp. 281–2. See also Peter Burroughs, 'The Determinants of Local Self-Government', *Jour. Imp. and Comm. Hist.*, VI (1978), pp. 321–2; and A.G.L. Shaw, 'British Attitudes to the Colonies ca. 1820–50', *Jour. Brit. Stud.*, IX (1969), pp. 84–85.

subjects.[18] A good many took refuge in the image of Britain as the 'mother country' whose 'children' would eventually grow up, leaving open the question of how rapid the process of growth might be and how colonies which had achieved adult status might relate to their parent.[19] Very few observers had a clear idea of the future of Anglo-colonial relations: in retrospect, the granting of responsible government, like political reform at home, was something of a leap into the unknown.

Under the old system of colonial administration, power rested with the governor and with councils which, although partly elected, were mainly composed of officials supported by patronage and by the wealthiest elements in the local colonial society who, whether representing land or commerce, were dependent upon the British connection. This elite was, in every sense, 'an extension of the old society' and only too well aware of the importance of imperial power and imperial favour.[20] As the colonies grew in size and complexity so did the desire for greater freedom from direct British control. This was enhanced, after 1815, by the decline of British patronage as Parliament became more critical of expenditure on colonies: the plea for greater local autonomy grew commensurately with rising levels of local taxation. The great catalyst for change here was the Canadian rebellion of 1837–8, which inspired the famous Durham Report of 1840. However, Durham proposed only a very limited form of local control: in his plan, Britain would have retained the final say not only in foreign affairs but also in the disposal of colonial lands and in tariff policy, both of which local politicians were eager to control.[21] Had Durham's views prevailed, the colonies could have expected little

18. The pioneer studies included J.S. Galbraith, 'Myths of the "Little England" Era', *Am. Hist. Rev.*, LXVII (1961–2), and Richard Koebner and Helmut Dan Schmidt, *Imperialism: The Story and Significance of a Political Word* (Cambridge, 1964). The latest survey is Stanley R. Stembridge, *Parliament, the Press and the Colonies, 1846–1880* (1982). See also Ged Martin, *The Durham Report and British Policy* (Cambridge, 1972).

19. Koebner and Schmidt, *Imperialism*, p. 76; Ged Martin, 'Anti-Imperialism in the Mid-Nineteenth Century and the Nature of the British Empire, 1820–1870', in Ronald Hyam and Ged Martin, *Reappraisals in British Imperial History* (1975), pp. 101–06.

20. Peter Burroughs, *The Canadian Crisis and British Colonial Policy, 1828–1841* (1971), pp. 20–21. For a good example of a colonial elite, see Robert E. Saunders, 'What was the Family Compact?', in J.K. Johnson, ed. *Historical Essays on Upper Canada* (Toronto, 1975).

21. For the substance of Durham's recommendations see A.B. Keith, ed. *Speeches and Documents on British Colonial Policy, 1763–1917* (Oxford, 1961 edn), I, pp. 113–72. The best modern commentary is Martin, *The Durham Report*. See also the latest scholarly summation in respect of North America: Philip A. Buckner, *The Transition to Responsible Government: British Policy in British North America* (Westport, Conn., 1985).

more than what Wakefield termed 'municipal self-government',[22] and tension between London and the periphery would have grown more acute.

In practice, from the late 1840s the British bowed to local pressures and, in line with observed constitutional changes taking place in Britain herself, accepted the idea that, in mature colonies, governors should in future form ministries from the majority elements in elected legislatures. In doing so, they moved faster and further than traditional colonial elites wished to travel. In Australia in the early 1850s, for example, a concerted effort was made by the old, wool-rich rural elite – the 'squattocracy' – to fashion a constitution which would allow an hereditary upper chamber, modelled on the House of Lords, to check the democratic excesses of the more popular lower house. This failed, less because of local opposition which, in the turmoil of the gold rush era, hardly had time to cohere, than because the British determined on a swift move to the kind of institutional arrangements already emerging in Canada. These allowed for a conservative second chamber but of a more moderate variety than envisaged by vested economic interests in the colonies themselves.[23] As in the Canadian provinces, the movement to self-government could be achieved only at the cost of reducing both the power of the traditional sources of British influence in the colonies, which adhered to the land, to government and to administration, and the economic activities which had flourished under the protectionist system.

Gallagher and Robinson's belief that the granting of political liberties made no essential difference to Britain's imperial power in the colonies needs careful qualification. Responsible government did mean a devolution of power to the periphery, 'comparable in its way with the decolonization of Africa a century later'.[24] The tacit acceptance, around this time, of the colonists' right to dispose of their land even though, in legal terms, it was often under the authority of the British crown, is evidence enough of this. Ward argues, additionally, that the British 'did not expect the liberties granted with full responsible government to be offset by colonies of settlement becoming

22. Martin, *The Durham Report*, p. 61.

23. John M. Ward, *Empire in the Antipodes: The British in Australasia, 1840–1860* (1966), Ch. 7; Ged Martin, *Bunyip Aristocracy: The New South Wales Constitutional Debate of 1853 and Hereditary Institutions in the British Colonies* (1986). For an interesting comment on the failure to establish a colonial aristocracy on the English model see G.C. Bolton, 'The Idea of a Colonial Gentry', *Historical Studies: Australia and New Zealand*, 13 (1967–9).

24. Peter Burroughs, 'Colonial Self-Government', in C.C. Eldridge, ed. *British Imperialism in the Nineteenth Century* (1984), p. 62.

increasingly dependent on the mother country for money, markets or men'.[25] This is undoubtedly correct; but there is a danger that emphasising it may obscure how economically dependent the white colonies were and how much their dependence was already taken for granted in Britain. Britain's economic superiority and leadership were simply assumed, and expected to endure, even by radicals.[26]

Metropolitan assumptions about colonial economies certainly helped to shape perceptions of when and where to grant political liberty. One important point which has emerged from the modern debate, for example, is that the coming of colonial self-government followed the recognition, by Britain, that many of the white colonial societies were reaching levels of maturity that were incompatible with direct rule. Burroughs, writing of the Canadian colonies, claims that Grey, then Colonial Secretary, had realised by 1846 that 'circumstances now imperatively demanded the acceptance of self-government in communities with adequate population, wealth, social stability and political experience'.[27] Similarly, Ward argues in more general terms that responsible government came to be seen 'as an evolutionary process of constitutional change, in which Britain shared the advanced conventions of her own political life with colonies that became substantial British communities overseas'.[28] Statesmen who had already learned that domestic political adjustments, like the 1832 Reform Act, were necessary to accommodate widespread social and economic change were also capable of appreciating the need for similar moves in mature colonies of settlement and of recognising that withholding political freedoms at this point would only have provoked resentment and unrest. But what 'maturity' meant to the British, among other things, was that some of the colonies in Canada and Australia had developed into well-ordered capitalist societies capable of functioning as satellite economies without direct intervention.

Responsible government certainly brought with it a remarkable degree of freedom, and quickly too. Within three years of achieving self-government the Australian states of New South Wales and Victoria had decided upon a democratic voting system, despite

25. John M. Ward, *Colonial Self-Government: The British Experience, 1759–1856* (1976), p. 289.

26. Martin, 'Anti-Imperialism in the Mid-Nineteenth Century', pp. 111–14.

27. Burroughs, 'The Determinants of Local Self Government', p. 241. For a similar line of argument see B.A. Knox, 'Reconsidering Mid-Victorian Imperialism', *Jour. Imp. and Comm. Hist.*, I (1972–3).

28. Ward, *Colonial Self-Government*, p. 289.

Britain's disapproval of a measure which could only reduce her direct influence; by 1859, the province of Canada had adopted protection, despite the hostile incredulity of statesmen in the metropolis, where free trade was assuming the status of natural law.[29] Nor did any British government seriously attempt to influence policy on colonial land sales, despite the fact that, legally speaking, colonial land was at the disposal of the crown.[30] Interference at this level would have been counter-productive as British statesmen, remembering the revolt of the 13 American colonies, were quick to recognise.

Britain retained considerable power over the white colonies, including the right to veto discriminatory tariffs and to supervise colonial legislation on immigration and shipping,[31] but her most important sphere of direct authority was international relations, a dimension of political life which the colonists were happy to ignore, partly out of ignorance and incapacity and partly because the implication of Britain's supremacy here was that she would pay the costs of imperial defence. Despite drastic pruning of expenditure by Gladstone's Liberal government in the early 1870s,[32] Britain's defence expenditure remained high by the standards of other industrial countries. Between 1860 and 1912 the British spent an average of £1.14p per capita on defence, which amounted to 37 per cent of central government expenditure. By contrast, colonies which either already had responsible government or achieved it in this period, spent around 12p per head on defence, a mere 3 or 4 per cent of their annual budgets.[33]

Britain's assumption of the defence burden meant that the colonies could devote the bulk of their own savings to social and economic development.[34] High levels of domestic investment were pushed even higher by the colonies' ability to borrow in London cheaply. Empire investments, including those in the white colonies, were much sought

29. For the correspondence between the colonies and Britain on this issue see Keith, *Speeches and Documents*, II, pp. 51–83.

30. Martin, *The Durham Report*, pp. 59–69.

31. Beverly Kingston, *The Oxford History of Australia, 1860–1900*: Vol. III, *Glad, Confident Morning* (Oxford, 1988), pp. 295–6.

32. C.C. Eldridge, *England's Mission: The Imperial Idea in the Age of Gladstone and Disraeli, 1868–80* (1973), Ch. 3.

33. Lance E. Davis and Robert A. Huttenback, *Mammon and the Pursuit of Empire: The Political Economy of British Imperialism, 1860–1912* (Cambridge, 1987), Table 5.1, p. 161. Britain's average expenditure per capita over the whole period was almost double that of France and Germany (Table 5.2, p. 164). For an interesting general discussion of the (usually vain) attempts to persuade colonists to contribute to imperial defence see ibid. pp. 145–160.

34. Ibid. p. 163.

after by British investors though, as we shall see, at different times one or other of the colonies might be out of favour with the London market. Capital could be borrowed cheaply by comparison with the rates of interest offered to even the most eligible foreign borrowers; and it was made cheaper still by various legislative enactments, especially the Colonial Stocks Act of 1900, which allowed trustees, who had hitherto been restricted in their purchase of investments on their clients' behalf to certain British and Indian stocks, to add some colonial securities to their portfolios.[35]

The British preference for empire stocks, especially those of the white empire, may have owed something to patriotism rather than to pure market forces. Returns on private capital placed in the empire, including private railway investments, were higher than returns on corresponding investments in Britain or in foreign countries before the mid–1880s, but performed less well over the succeeding 30 years.[36] Nonetheless, the somewhat fragmentary evidence which exists does indicate that returns on stocks issued by public authorities in the empire were better than on corresponding British securities.[37] Nearly three-fifths of the borrowings of colonies of responsible government between 1865 and 1914 were on public account,[38] and they provided an ideal vehicle for investors looking for safe outlets abroad. Default was unheard of in these British territories, whether directly controlled or not. This is one of the key reasons why the colonies could borrow cheaply: they offered almost complete safety at a rate of return higher than that on standard British investments, such as consols.[39]

With the British to protect them and to supply them with migrants and with capital, it is not surprising that the white colonies should have grown rapidly, in terms of both population and output, or that they should have achieved average living standards which were well

35. David Jessop, 'The Colonial Stocks Act of 1900: a Symptom of the New Imperialism?', *Jour. Imp. and Comm. Hist.*, IV (1976); Davis and Huttenback, *Mammon and the Pursuit of Empire*, pp. 168–9.

36. Davis and Huttenback, *Mammon and the Pursuit of Empire*, pp. 104–10 and esp. Table 2.15, p. 107, and their comments on p. 171. Also, L.S. Pressnell, 'The Sterling System and Financial Crisis before 1914', in Charles P. Kindleberger and Jean-Pierre Laffargue, eds. *Financial Crises: Theory, History and Policy* (Cambridge, 1982), p. 150.

37. A.K. Cairncross, *Home and Foreign Investment, 1870–1913* (Cambridge, 1953), pp. 217–30; Michael Edelstein, 'Realized Rates of Return on U.K. Home and Overseas Portfolio Investment in the Age of High Imperialism', *Explorations in Economic History*, 13 (1976), p. 319.

38. Davis and Huttenback, *Mammon and the Pursuit of Empire*, Table 2.6, p. 54.

39. Ibid. p. 171. Australian state bonds were known in the nineteenth century as 'colonial Consols'. N.G. Butlin, Alan Barnard and J.J. Pincus, *Government and Capitalism: Public and Private Choice in Twentieth-Century Australia* (Sydney, 1982), p. 16.

in advance of those in the parent country in the late nineteenth century. At the same time, and inevitably, the nature of this development was such as to bring them into a close economic and financial dependence upon Britain. In a very real sense, the colonies became part of the 'invisible' financial and commercial empire which had its centre in the City of London.[40]

Ward is right to maintain that politicians did not anticipate any strengthening of economic ties between metropole and frontier after responsible government was granted, but it is still the case that, although there was little awareness of it in higher political circles, the economic bonds between metropole and colonies were tightening just as the political ones were slackening. Habakkuk is one of the few British historians to have recognised this.[41] Free trade, he claimed, came about partly because the old, restrictive colonial system had failed to satisfy fully Britain's international needs as her economy expanded; but British possessions, including settlement colonies, did find a more important niche as markets and sources of supply in the cosmopolitan structure which arose after 1850. Major shifts in the economic relations between the imperial centre and the colonies of settlement were early examples of that great transformation of the world economy in which the industrialising countries became locked into a much more complex international division of labour with the agricultural periphery than hitherto. Growing links between Britain and the newly settled world, including the white colonies, were one of the most dynamic features of this development, which involved not only a greatly extended trade but also the export of British capital and labour.[42] Britain's ability to supply the colonies with development finance, either from home sources, or through London's position as a channel for European savings, was a crucial element in the chain of connection and often indispensable to colonial growth. With the capital came new forms of control, as Habakkuk recognised:

> Down to the 'fifties, and while the export of capital to the colonies was still unimportant, the colonies were economically dependent upon the United Kingdom, but their economic activity was not directly controlled by it. This applies in large measure even to India. But when in the 'fifties the colonies drew largely on British capital supply, they found they had neither the means nor the administrative capacity to redeem and carry on with ease the public works which they desired. England had to supply

40. The phrase 'invisible empire' is in Leland H. Jenks, *The Migration of British Capital to 1875* (1927; 1963), p. 1.
41. H.J. Habakkuk, 'Free Trade and Commercial Expansion, 1853–70', *Cambridge History of the British Empire*, II (Cambridge, 1940).
42. See Denoon, *Settler Capitalism*, passim, for this process.

not merely the original capital but the permanent direction. The companies formed to build railways, found banks and cultivate tea had their headquarters in London and worked their properties from England. The Empire had become in a new sense an integral part of the British economic system.[43]

The white colonies could have chosen a different future for themselves, one which relied less on exports and less on imported capital and migrants. Had they done so, they would have enjoyed greater autonomy but growth would have been markedly slower. In practice, neither the 'staple' approach to rapid development, nor the need for British markets and factors of production which this development entailed, was ever seriously brought into question. Australasia and Canada were dominated by 'ideal prefabricated collaborators' who were concerned, above all else, 'to keep export markets open and capital flowing'.[44] Local politics often involved little more than faction fighting, based on regional differences or disputes over tariff policy between groups otherwise unquestioningly committed to the export economy: 'formal political life became a contest between those groups who accepted the logic of export-led development'.[45] Given this almost instinctive commitment, white colonial growth was limited by the need to conform to the expectations of British financiers and by the need to play the game by London's rules, even though colonial economies emerged from the tutelage described by Habakkuk to a large extent, and the British preference for portfolio investment gave colonial recipients a greater control over capital flows than more direct investment would have done.[46]

The influence of British finance was pervasive. Sometimes, as in Australasia, it took the very obvious form of the large Anglo-colonial banks; but, even in Canada, where the influence of the Anglo-banks was much more limited, the banking system was created on British lines and was geared mainly to the needs of primary production, transport and foreign trade. Moreover, in both Australasia and Canada, economic power rested on urban rather than rural bases after 1850 and was in the hands of commercial and financial groups centred

43. Habakkuk, 'Free Trade and Commercial Expansion', pp. 798–9.
44. Ronald Robinson, 'Non-European Foundations of European Imperialism', in Roger Owen and Bob Sutcliffe, eds. *Studies in the Theory of Imperialism* (Oxford, 1972).
45. Denoon, *Settler Capitalism*, p. 223; Cf. Geoffrey Bolton, *Britain's Legacy Overseas* (Oxford, 1973), p. 128.
46. R.T. Naylor, 'The Rise and Fall of the Third Commercial Empire of the St. Lawrence', in Gary Teeple, ed. *Capitalism and the National Question in Canada* (Toronto, 1972).

on the foreign trade sector, rather than those of manufacturers or agriculturalists, as was the case in Britain itself.[47] The acceptance of conservative English financial practices, especially as regards long-term lending, made dependence on imported capital greater.[48] It was the predominant influence of the export sector in these countries which ensured that budgetary orthodoxy on British lines was adhered to and fostered an 'internationalist' approach to economic management.

After 1850, the old ruling groups, based on imperial patronage and mercantilist commerce lost influence. However, the new elite which flourished under free trade, although shorn of the gentlemanly accoutrements which were out of tune with the brash democratic certainties of colonial life, remained dependent upon the financial favours of gentlemanly capitalists in London; and local economic ideologies were shaped to British standards, particularly City ones. This explains why default was unthinkable and why, in consequence, colonial securities were seen as such good investments in Britain. The extent of this practical and ideological dependence upon the British economy in general, and upon the City of London in particular, is best understood by taking a brief look at the economic history of the Australian colonies and of New Zealand, especially during those periods of financial stringency when dependence was more starkly demonstrated.

AUSTRALASIA

The first Australian colony of New South Wales was formed in 1788 as a penal settlement and its development was for many years

47. W. Armstrong, 'The Social Origins of Industrial Growth: Canada, Argentina and Australia, 1870–1913', in D.C.M. Platt and Guido di Tella, eds. *Argentina, Australia, Canada: Studies in Comparative Development, 1870–1965* (1985), pp. 87–91. Throughout the pre–1914 period, pastoral and agricultural occupations were dominant among peak wealth-holdings in Australia. But after 1860, when free land-selection policies were introduced, many of the rural wealthy became dependent on the banks because they were forced to bid higher for land; and through the banks they became more directly dependent both upon urban, commercial Australia and upon the City of London. See W.D. Rubinstein, 'The Top Wealth Holders of New South Wales, 1817–1939', *Australian Economic History Review*, XX (1980), esp. Table 5, p. 148; and Kingston, *Oxford History of Australia*, pp. 263–5.

48. R.T. Naylor, *The History of Canadian Business, 1867–1914, I: The Banks and Finance Capital* (Toronto, 1975), p. 68.

propelled by direct British subsidy.[49] As late as 1831 the subsidy added a quarter to the Australian national income.[50] While transportation and emancipated convicts were the dominant force, the growth of domestic agriculture was rapid[51] and it was only in the 1830s that wool, and the export of wool, became a major galvanising force in the economy. It was the wool industry which first attracted private British capital to Australia in large quantities and brought enthusiastic City of London support for the various land-sale and emigration schemes promoted both by individuals and by governments striving to foster local economic development.[52] The establishment of British-based banks in Australia in the 1830s was also a 'response to the desire of the British investor for a larger share in and more direct control over the golden fleece'.[53] Their successful competition with local banks provoked hostility in Australia, where it was feared that the remittance of profits to Britain would drain Australia of investible funds. In the crisis of the early 1840s, when many local banks went under, the Anglo-banks became the dominant financial force on the continent.[54] Australian banks made a vigorous comeback after 1850 and this meant that the share of commercial bank assets held by

49. The best modern introductions to Australian history which put economic developments in the context of wider currents of historical change are Kingston, *Oxford History of Australia*, Vol. III; Stuart McIntyre, *Oxford History of Australia*, Vol. IV, *1901–1942* (Oxford, 1986), Chs. 1–6, and M. Dunn, *Australia and the Empire: From 1788 to the Present* (Sydney, 1984). An interpretation of Australian economic development based on neo-Marxist under-development theory is provided by Philip McMichael, *Settlers and the Agrarian Question: Capitalism and Colonialism in Australia* (Cambridge, 1984). A similar treatment is provided by Peter Cochrane, *Industrialization and Dependence: Australia's Road to Economic Development, 1870–1939* (St Lucia, 1980). See also J.D.B. Miller, ed. *Australians and British: Social and Political Connexions* (North Ryde, 1987) and A.F. Madden and W.H. Morris-Jones, eds. *Australia and Britain: Studies in a Changing Relationship* (1980). On New Zealand, the best general introduction remains K. Sinclair, *A History of New Zealand* (1980 edn). There is also useful coverage of Australasian history in Ronald Hyam, *Britain's Imperial Century, 1815–1914: A Study of Empire and Expansion* (1976), Ch. 11.

50. N.G. Butlin, 'Contours of the Australian Economy, 1788–1860', *Austral. Econ. Hist. Rev.*, XXVI (1986), pp. 101–4. For the estimates on which this conclusion is based see N.G. Butlin and W.A. Sinclair, 'Australian Gross Domestic Product, 1788–1860: Estimates, Sources and Methods', in the same issue of the *Review*.

51. Butlin, 'Contours of the Australian Economy, 1788–1860', p. 118.

52. On the City of London connection see Frank J.A. Broeze, 'Private Enterprise and the Peopling of Australia, 1831–50', *Econ. Hist. Rev.*, 2nd ser. XXXV (1982). The role of government in economic development is considered in J.J. Eddy, *Britain and the Australian Colonies, 1818–1831: The Technique of Government* (Oxford, 1969), and Peter Burroughs, *Britain and Australia, 1831–55* (Oxford, 1967).

53. S.J. Butlin, *The Foundations of the Australian Monetary System, 1788–1851* (Melbourne, 1953), p. 258. The principal British banks are discussed on pp. 259–68.

54. Ibid. pp. 264–5, 345–55, 378.

British-owned banks fell from two-thirds of the total in 1851 to two-fifths in 1890. The British banks retained their competitive edge in financing Anglo-Australian trade; it is noticeable that the most successful Australian-owned banks were the 17 which opened offices in London in order to obtain direct access to City finance, expertise and business connections.[55]

The dependence of Australian prosperity after 1850 upon the international economy, and upon links with Britain in particular, was very marked. Australia was a trade-dependent nation: foreign trade per head of population in 1912 was nearly £34, slightly higher than Britain's but over twice as large as Germany's and four times as large as that of the United States. In 1912, Britain took 40 per cent of Australia's exports and supplied half of her imports. Although Britain's share had declined since the early 1860s, when she had taken 60 per cent of Australia's exports and supplied 75 per cent of her imports, the mother country was still overwhelmingly important to Australia's international success.[56]

Of more fundamental significance, though less generally appreciated, was the fact that, like New Zealand's, Australia's money supply and, therefore, her long-run growth was determined by her economic relations with Britain. Banks in Australia, whether local or imperial, regulated credit according to the level of their London balances. When these balances rose, the banks in Australia expanded credit, and when they fell, the money supply was contracted. In other words, the level of Australian credit depended upon the state of the balance of payments; this was chiefly a function of Australia's trade and payment relations with Britain.[57]

On this basis, it is tempting to reduce Australian economic history to a crude description of her staple exports and to see prosperity purely as a function of success in selling gold, other minerals and wool on London markets. But the links between colony and parent were more subtle. Had Australia relied entirely on exports for her success, Britain's cyclical fluctuations would have been transmitted to her more directly via the mother country's fluctuating demands for

55. D.T. Merrett, ' "Paradise Lost?" British Banks in Australia', in G. Jones, ed. *Banks as Multinationals* (1990), pp. 63–71.

56. D.C.M. Platt, *Latin America and British Trade, 1806–1914* (1972), pp. 107, 111; N.G. Butlin, *Investment in Australian Economic Development, 1861–1900* (Cambridge, 1964), p. 28. An excellent introduction to Australian experience in foreign trade can now be found in Barrie Dyster and David Meredith, *Australia in the International Economy in the Twentieth Century* (Cambridge, 1990).

57. A.H. Tocker, 'The Monetary Standards of Australia and New Zealand', *Economic Journal*, 34 (1924).

Australian exports. Yet Australian growth, a few minor interruptions apart, was almost continuous between 1850 and 1890 and, at an average of about 5 per cent per annum, was considerably higher than in Britain.[58] Moreover, when Australia fell into deep depression in the 1890s, exports from Australia to Britain were rising rapidly after stagnating in the previous decade (Table 8.1). Australia's ability or inability to borrow in London was as crucial to the pace and the stability of her economic growth as were the changing fortunes of her export industries.

The gold rushes of the 1850s – classic export-led booms – had a weighty influence upon the future of Australia. Population in the colonies rose from less than 500,000 in 1850 to 1.2 million ten years later.[59] Together with the very high levels of per capita income created in gold mining, this increase triggered off a demand for infrastructural investment, construction and services. It also led to a marked growth in some sectors of manufacturing industry since Australia's remoteness from Europe gave her a degree of natural protection.[60] The gold era had a strong influence on the economy well into the 1880s, when the 'echo' effect of the population explosion of the 1850s underlay a sharp increase in the demand for 'population-sensitive' investment and helped to propel the economy into another boom.[61]

From our perspective, it is important to recognise that the hectic pace of development between 1860 and 1890 could not have been sustained without a large inflow of labour and capital. Immigration, mainly from Britain and Ireland, accounted for roughly one-third of the population increase in these 30 years.[62] Capital exports from Britain were of even greater proportional significance. Accustomed to prosperity in the gold decade and determined to preserve living

58. Butlin, *Investment in Australian Economic Development*, p. 16. For a good overview of Australian economic growth in the late nineteenth century see W.A. Sinclair, *The Process of Economic Development in Australia* (Melbourne, 1976).

59. For the gold rush period the best accounts remain Geoffrey Blainey, *The Rush That Never Ended: Mining in Australia* (Melbourne, 1963), and E.V. Portus, 'The Gold Discoveries of 1850–60', in the *Cambridge History of the British Empire*, VII, Pt. I, (Cambridge, 1933).

60. N.G. Butlin, 'Some Perspectives on Australian Economic Development, 1890–1965', in Colin Forster, ed. *Australian Economic Development in the Twentieth Century* (1970), p. 299.

61. Alan C. Kelley, 'Demographic Change and Economic Growth in Australia, 1861–1911', *Explorations in Entrepreneurial History*, V (1967–8); A.R. Hall, 'Some Long Period Effects of the Kinked Age-Distribution of the Population of Australia, 1861–1961', *Economic Record*, XXXIX (1963).

62. Butlin, 'Some Perspectives on Australian Economic Development', Table 6.8, p. 289.

Table 8.1 Balance of payments and net capital imports: Australia, 1881–1900 (quinquennial averages, £m.)

	1	2	3	4	5	6	7	8	9
	GDP at factor cost	Exports	Imports	Interest and dividend payments	Bullion and specie movement	Balance of payment (net capital import) (2−3−4+5)	Col. 4 as % of Col. 2	Col. 2 as % of Col. 1	Col. 3 as % of Col. 1
1881–85	158.2	28.8	36.9	6.7	0.2	−14.6	23.3	18.2	23.3
1886–90	194.1	27.9	37.3	10.0	−0.1	−19.5	35.8	14.4	19.2
1891–95	163.1	35.8	28.6	12.7	−0.8	− 6.3	35.5	22.0	17.5
1896–1900	172.4	42.2	36.0	12.1	0.6	− 5.4	28.7	24.5	20.8

Sources: Column 1: N. G. Butlin, *Australian Domestic Product: Investment and Foreign Borrowing, 1861–1900*. (Cambridge, 1962), Table 1, p. 6; Columns 2–6: E. A. Boehm, *Prosperity and Depression in Australia, 1887–97* (Oxford, 1971), Table 7, p. 15.

standards which were probably higher than anywhere else save the United States, Australian voters expected the state to supplement private initiatives by investing heavily in public utilities and transport to open up the continent. The resulting high levels of growth created a demand for imports which could be met only by borrowing, especially in the 1860s and 1880s. During the 1870s, when wool exports were buoyant, capital imports could be kept at low levels, but in other decades capital flows from Britain were heavy. Borrowings in the 1860s and 1880s were equivalent to half of the gross investment made in Australia and most of the capital imported was on public account.[63] Sterling-standard constraints were rarely felt because borrowings kept balances in London healthy.

For more than 30 years after the gold bonanza, the colonists found it relatively easy to borrow. Gold gave the continent an Eldorado image; kinship offered the British a sense of security about Australian investment which meant that the colonies could often borrow when foreign supplicants were frowned upon. In the late 1870s, for example, when the British economy was in depression and imports were falling, Australia could have been severely affected but was rescued, in part, by British interest in Australian securities as a refuge in a troubled world.[64] In the 1880s, when 'push' factors began to operate in Britain,[65] borrowing became even easier for the Australians. It was in the latter part of this decade that clear signs of over-borrowing began to show themselves as pastoral stations were pushed into marginal territory, construction activity began to shade off into frenetic land speculation, and railway-building failed to stimulate external economies.[66] Heavy borrowing in the 1860s was paid for by

63. See N.G. Butlin, 'Colonial Socialism in Australia', in H.G.J. Aitken, ed. *The State and Economic Growth* (New York, 1959); idem, *Investment in Australian Economic Development*, p. 29. See also Dyster and Meredith, *Australia in the International Economy*, Table 2.6, p. 34. The average amount borrowed by the Australian colonies between 1865 and 1914 was roughly £7m. per year of which £5.6m. was by public authorities. See Davis and Huttenback, *Mammon and the Pursuit of Empire*, Table 2.4, p. 48. For a detailed study of one state's borrowings in Britain, see P.N. Lamb, 'Early Overseas Borrowing by the New South Wales Government', *Business Archives and History*, IV (1964). Between 1856 and 1868 £6.6m. was raised in London as against £2.3m. in Sydney (p. 61). For further details on Australia and the London money market see R.S. Gilbert, 'London Financial Intermediaries and Australian Overseas Borrowing', *Austral. Econ. Hist. Rev.*, XI (1971), esp. pp. 41–5.

64. J.D. Bailey, *Growth and Depression: Contrasts in the Australian and British Economies, 1870–1880* (Canberra, 1956), Ch. V and pp. 123–36.

65. M. Edelstein, *Overseas Investment in the Age of High Imperialism: The United Kingdom, 1850–1914* (1982), Ch. XI.

66. Butlin, *Investment in Australian Economic Development*, p. 37 and pp. 407–24. On the problems of the pastoral companies see the articles by Neville Cain, 'Capital

rapid export growth, but investment in the 1880s failed to generate the exports needed to pay for Australia's loans. In the wool industry, the chief source of export income between 1860 and 1890, costs rose as marginal land was pressed into service at the same time as world wool prices were falling. Exports were about 27 per cent of GDP by value in 1861–5, but only 14 per cent in 1886–90.[67] Overseas debt payments, on the other hand, were equal to 19 per cent of the value of exports in 1881 and 39 per cent in 1891 (Table 8.1).[68] Given the ease with which money could be borrowed, an irrational air of high expectations in Sydney and Melbourne, and the downward trend in primary produce prices as a whole in the 1880s, it was perhaps inevitable that a great deal of investment should go into areas remote from the export sector and that the process should end eventually in a balance of payments crisis – just as it did in Argentina and Brazil.[69]

There is no doubt that the initial downturn in activity in the key construction sector was triggered off by purely Australian problems;[70] but the crisis entered its most acute phase after 1891 when, in the wake of the Baring Crisis, the British lost interest in new investments in Australia. Even in the late 1880s, Australian exports were moving so slowly that, given the accumulating interest on debt which had to be paid annually, increasing amounts of British capital were needed merely to maintain the high level of imports reached in the early part of the decade (Table 8.1). After 1891, the Australians were faced with the need to finance the import bill, on which the level of domestic activity crucially depended, entirely from export earnings already

---

Structure and Financial Disequilibrium: Pastoral Companies in Australia, 1880–93', and 'Pastoral Expansion and Crisis in New South Wales, 1880–93: the Lending View', both in *Australian Economic Papers*, II (1963).

67. Butlin, *Investment in Australian Economic Development*, Table 7, p. 28 for the 1861–5 figures; the 1886–90 estimates are Butlin's figures as revised by E.A. Boehm, *Prosperity and Depression in Australia, 1887–1897* (Oxford, 1971), Table 43, p. 187. See also H. Coombs, 'Balance of Payments Problems: Old and New Style', in N.H. Drohan and J.H. Day, eds. *Readings in Australian Economics* (Melbourne, 1966), pp. 72–3.

68. Calculated from Boehm, *Prosperity and Depression in Australia*, Table 7, p. 15.

69. A.R. Hall, *Australia and the London Capital Market, 1870–1914* (Canberra, 1963), Ch. VIII. See also B.L. Bentick, 'Foreign Borrowing, Wealth, and Consumption: Victoria, 1873–93', *Economic Record*, 45 (1969).

70. Emphasis on the domestic roots of the depression can be found in Butlin, *Investment in Australian Economic Development*, Ch. VI; and in W.A. Sinclair, 'The Depression of the 1980s and the 1890s in Australia: a Comparison', in Drohan and Day, *Readings in Australian Economics*, pp. 85–90. Modern interpretations of the crisis are discussed in Dyster and Meredith, *Australia in the International Economy*, pp. 44–9.

deeply bitten into by the need to service existing debt.[71] Exports did rise in the early 1890s, bolstered by the output of newly discovered gold-mines in Western Australia; but the effects of this were partly cancelled out in the latter part of the decade by the long drought which affected wool production and exports.[72] Consequently, a large part of the adjustment forced by reduced capital imports had to be achieved by cutting commodity imports, which fell by roughly a quarter between 1886–90 and 1891–5. Capital imports dropped from an average of £19m. a year in the late 1880s to about £5m. at the turn of the century (much of it placed in Western Australian gold) while debt repayments, which were only £5m. in 1881, rose to over £12m. per annum in the 1890s (Table 8.1).

By the late 1890s, the Australians not only had to manage without large scale capital imports but also were using a portion of their own savings on debt repayments. Reduced sterling balances in London led inevitably to a severe squeeze on domestic credit. GDP fell sharply in the 1890s and did not reach its 1890 level again until 1903.[73] What helped incomes to recover after this experience was industrial growth based on import substitution and the opening up of the market for refrigerated meat and dairy produce in Britain and Europe.[74] Exports also rose rapidly enough between 1900 and 1910 for the Australians to finance capital formation and to service debts without importing capital; but imports leapt up again after 1910 and the rise in borrowing from Britain just before the World War I indicated that Australia was still dependent on access to the London capital market when her economic activity approached full employment levels.[75]

The Australian depression was intensified in the mid- and

71. On the balance of payments crisis see Coombs, 'Balance of Payment Problems', pp. 75–6, and Boehm, *Prosperity and Depression in Australia*, Ch. VII.

72. A vivid picture of the crisis produced by drought and over-capitalisation of marginal stations is given in Neville Cain, 'Companies and Squatting in the Western Division of New South Wales, 1896–1905', in Alan Barnard, ed. *The Simple Fleece: Studies in the Australian Wool Industry*, (Parkville, Victoria 1962).

73. N.G. Butlin, *Australian Domestic Product, Investment and Foreign Borrowing, 1861–1938/39* (Cambridge, 1962), Table 1, p. 6.

74. W.A. Sinclair, 'Aspects of Economic Growth, 1900–1930', in A.H. Boxer, ed. *Aspects of the Australian Economy* (Melbourne 1965). See also Dyster and Meredith, *Australia in the International Economy*, pp. 49–59.

75. Butlin, *Australian Domestic Product, Investment and Foreign Borrowing*, Table 265, p. 444. The figures suggest that, just before World War I, Australia was about to feel the effects of another steep upswing in population growth of the kind experienced in the 1880s. Kelley, 'Demographic Change and Economic Growth', Table 1, p. 214. In 1914, when national income was roughly £80 per head, Australian borrowings from Britain were equivalent to £75 per person. McIntyre, *Oxford History of Australia*, 4, p. 42.

late–1890s by the loss of liquidity following the banking crisis of 1893. Confidence in the system was lost because too many institutions had locked up money, borrowed on short loan, in real assets such as land, which proved unsaleable after 1890. Numerous land and mortgage companies collapsed after 1891 and many of the banks which had financed them were also brought down. It was once believed that the banking crisis was precipitated by the withdrawal of British-held banking deposits – which had increased dramatically in the 1880s – but there is little evidence of this.[76] It is interesting, however, that those banks which raised their capital in London came out of the crisis in better shape than those which raised funds locally. Of the twenty-eight joint-stock banks existing in 1890, only four were British but two of these, the Australasia and the Union Bank, were of particular importance, accounting for one-fifth of all bank deposits in Australia. In 1893, nineteen of the twenty-eight banks were forced to close their doors at least temporarily. Of these nineteen, two were the smaller British-owned banks and, of the nine survivors, only three were large banks and two of them were the Australasia and the Union.[77]

We have already seen that London-based banks played an important role in Australian finance from the 1830s onwards and that, although they raised their deposits locally, they provoked resentment in Australia, as elsewhere, because they repatriated their profits. Local banks often established themselves, from the 1850s onwards, by taking advantage of this antagonism.[78] But all the Australian banks, like other colonial banks, were British in one sense, whether they raised their capital in London or not, because they owed their origins to regulations laid down by the British Treasury, and the most important of them had opened London offices. Also, as already noted, their domestic role was constrained by the sterling system and the cosmopolitanism this forced upon them.

As in Britain, the banks were mainly concerned with the short-term finance of commerce and trade. But, although they eschewed long-term lending to industry, the major Australian banks were tempted into accepting land and other fixed assets as security against advances, although this practice had been frowned upon initially by

---

76. Boehm, *Prosperity and Depression in Australia*, pp. 302–12.

77. S.J. Butlin, *The Australia and New Zealand Bank: The Bank of Australasia and the Union Bank of Australia Ltd., 1828–1951* (1961), p. 279; and Boehm, *Prosperity and Depression in Australia*, Table 65, pp. 272–3.

78. A.J.S. Baster, *The Imperial Banks* (1929), pp. 59–60, 138–40; Geoffrey Blainey, *Gold and Paper* (Melbourne, 1958), pp. 5–7.

officialdom in Britain.[79] One reason for the survival of the Anglo-banks was their conservatism in lending in this way, and, ironically enough, their prudence in refusing to accept a great many deposits from British sources when many local banks used them to extend credit to a dangerous extent after 1885. Another vital element in their survival was their more extensive links, often via interlocking directorships, with the City of London, which offered them credit lines right up to the Bank of England itself.[80]

Bank reconstruction (paying off depositors, including the British, over an extended period of time) locked up a great deal of capital in Australia in the 1890s and both deepened and prolonged the depression. The financial crash had even wider ramifications. It gave a strong impetus to the federation movement, from which the Commonwealth of Australia emerged in 1901, since it convinced business interests of the need to unify and extend the internal market.[81] It was also a decisive moment in the evolution of the Australian labour movement, helping to create not only its structures but also its ideological stance, by focusing attention on the 'soulless money-bags', both indigenous and British, who had shattered the working man's dream.[82] This labourite *cri de coeur* reflected the plain fact that the bankers, merchants and other businessmen who dominated Australian economic policy saw no way out of the crisis other than to play the game London's way. Angered by rumours, some emanating from Britain, of possible default, the Chief Secretary of New South Wales claimed in 1893 that

> The abhorrence which any suggestion of repudiation always provokes here need not be dwelt upon. Time will prove that no such word shall ever with justice be applied to any Australian Colony.[83]

Foreigners might threaten not to pay, but repudiation was out of the question as far as the politically powerful in Australia were concerned.

79. Baster, *The Imperial Banks*, p. 40; Butlin, *The Australia and New Zealand Bank*, pp. 249–51.

80. Butlin, *The Australia and New Zealand Bank*, p. 281.

81. C.M.H. Clark, *A Short History of Australia* (Sydney, 1963), p. 173. Before Federation in 1901, the economic links between the colonies were small compared with their contacts with Britain. See Kingston, *Oxford History of Australia*, III, p. 298. An important collection of essays on this topic is A.W. Martin, ed. *Essays in Australian Federation* (Melbourne, 1969). See also H. M. Schwartz, *In the Dominions of Debt: Historical Perspectives on Dependent Development* (Ithaca, NY, 1989), Ch. 3; and Dyster and Meredith, *Australia in the International Economy*, pp. 60–4.

82. Richard Jebb, *Studies in Colonial Nationalism* (1905), pp. 203–8; C.M.H. Clark, ed. *Select Documents in Australian History, 1851–1900* (Sydney, 1955), pp. 305–10. See also Peter Love, *Labour and the Money Power* (Melbourne, 1984).

83. Sir E. Dibbs, quoted in Clark, *Select Documents in Australian History*, p. 311.

Gladstonianism was practically a reflex action in the crisis.[84] Australian governments were anxious not only to demonstrate their monetary orthodoxy but also to trim their tariffs in the 1890s to please Britain and they even made some grudging concessions on contributions to imperial naval defence – all with the aim of improving their credit in London and re-opening the possibilities for further borrowing.[85]

The debt burden affected Australian attitudes towards closer relations with Britain in another direction. As in Canada, political independence was asserted and tariff autonomy realised as early as 1870.[86] Tariffs were imposed mainly for revenue purposes, but they did have some impact in encouraging manufacturing employment, especially in Victoria, and the manufacturing base was economically and politically significant by the 1890s.[87] The need to economise on imports in the 1890s reinforced this interest and, by the time that the Commonwealth of Australia was founded in 1901, it had become axiomatic that protection (along with the exclusion of cheap labour through the white Australia policy) was vital to create jobs and maintain traditionally high living standards.[88] Australia objected strongly to political unity in the empire and to a free-trade empire which would expose her industries to greater British competition. After 1895, though, the Australian appetite for a system of preferential tariffs within the Empire grew, since a privileged position in the British market would have supported export income and eased the problem of debt repayment. As Richard Jebb, the Chamberlainite propagandist, put it in 1905:

84. Boehm, *Prosperity and Depression in Australia*, pp. 178, 190, 207.

85. Luke Trainor, 'The Economics of the Imperial Connexion: Britain and the Australian Colonies, 1886–96' (Institute of Commonwealth Studies, Seminar Paper, University of London, 1979). It is worth noticing, too, that the Act of the British Parliament which created the Australian Commonwealth in 1901 was shaped in important particulars by the need to soothe the fears of British investors. See B.K. de Garis, 'The Colonial Office and the Commonwealth Constitution Bill', in Martin, *Essays in Australian Federation*.

86. W.A. Sinclair, 'The Tariff and Manufacturing Employment in Victoria, 1860–1900', *Economic Record*, XXXI (1955); idem, 'The Tariff and Economic Growth in Pre-Federation Victoria', ibid. XLVII (1971).

87. On manufacturing industry see A. Thompson, 'The Enigma of Australian Manufacturing, 1851–1901', *Australian Economic Papers*, IX (1970).

88. Ian Turner, *Industrial Labour and Politics: The Labour Movement in Eastern Australia* (Cambridge, 1965), Chs. I and II; Robin Gollan, *Radical and Working Class Politics: A Study of Eastern Australia, 1850–1910*, (Parkville, 1965), Ch. 9. A recent study of white nationalism is Avner Offer, 'Pacific Rim Societies: Asian Labour and White Nationalism', in John Eddy and Deryck Schreuder, eds. *The Rise of Colonial Nationalism* (Sydney, 1988).

In Australia the object is financial independence of the British bondholder. The reduction and ultimate liquidation of the Australian public debt, whatever the means adopted to effect it, obviously will be facilitated by the development of direct trade with the creditor country. . . . Hence the preferential system, if it helps to retain the major portion of Australia's foreign trade in the channel through which interest and principal find their nearest way to the British bondholder, naturally commends itself to those who desire the financial emancipation of their country.[89]

Preferences were also important to the colonies as a whole because it was only by generating export income that they could keep the level of internal demand high enough to sustain a market for locally produced manufactures.[90] Maintaining local industry was vital to both living standards and employment in a continent where, despite its dependence on primary exports, the bulk of the population lived in urban areas. The most industrialised state, Victoria, protected its manufacturing sector in the late nineteenth century and, after 1901, the Commonwealth government did likewise. British exporters thus had to face the irritant of a colonial tariff as well as increasing competition from third countries in Antipodean markets.[91] One result of this was a growing interest in the possibility of mutual preferences within the empire, with colonial privileges in the British market being offset by discriminating favours for British exports in the white empire.

New Zealand provides a further dramatic instance of growth shaped by British economic dominance. The islands' dependence on trade with Britain actually increased in the period under review. In the 1860s, trade with Australia was more important than trade with Britain: economically, New Zealand was merely an offshoot of her larger neighbour. Rapid growth was accompanied by a more direct commercial and financial relationship with Britain, which accounted for 40 per cent of New Zealand's trade in the early 1860s, rising to around 80 per cent from the early 1880s to World War I.[92]

Like Australia, New Zealand had its gold bonanza and its spectacular immigrant rush in the 1860s; here again, the enormous boom in

---

89. Jebb, *Studies in Colonial Nationalism*, pp. 230–1.

90. Ibid. Australia tried to stimulate British interest in preferences by offering her own from 1906. See Dyster and Meredith, *Australia in the International Economy*, pp. 65–6.

91. For increased foreign competition in the Australian market see I.W. McLean, 'Anglo-American Engineering Competition, 1870–1914: Some Third Market Evidence', *Econ. Hist. Rev.*, 2nd ser. XXIX (1976).

92. G.R. Hawke, *The Making of New Zealand: An Economic History* (Cambridge, 1985), Fig. 3.4, p. 58.

public investment after 1870, funded to a large extent by London, was an attempt to build up an infrastructure to cope with rapidly rising numbers and to maintain high living standards in a country where voters expected politicians actively to promote their economic welfare.[93] As in the Australian case, New Zealand's desire to borrow and Britain's willingness to lend were only tenuously related to any immediate criterion of market efficiency, though there was never any question of default.[94] Public debt increased from about £9m. in 1870 to £39m. in 1893, or from £44 per head to over £60, much of it borrowed when the price of wool, the principal export, was falling: exports per head fell from £22 to £12 between 1863 and the early 1880s.[95] In the mid–1880s Britain turned her attention to Australia and Argentina, and New Zealand found borrowing more difficult. The outcome was a prolonged economic depression ending in a banking crisis in the mid–1890s similar to that already described for Australia.[96] The scale of New Zealand's debt was so great by the 1890s that even a large surplus of exports over imports of £55m. between 1887 and 1914 covered only about one-half of the country's external debt obligations and outward flows of private capital, and the gap had to be plugged by further borrowing.[97] As in Australia's case, the problem of debt repayment forced New Zealand to adopt a deflationary policy which kept down imports.[98] New Zealand also benefited from import substitution; and the rapid rise in exports, once refrigeration was established in the 1890s, made it possible for the country to grow and at the same time to become less dependent on capital imports.

Both Australia and New Zealand were vulnerable because of their

93. The best accounts of New Zealand's economic history from our perspective are Hawke, *The Making of New Zealand*; C.G.F. Simkin, *The Instability of a Dependent Economy: Economic Fluctuations in New Zealand, 1840–1914*, (Oxford, 1951); and R.C.J. Stone, *Makers of Fortune: A Colonial Business Community and its Fall* (Auckland, 1973). See also Schwartz, *In the Dominions of Debt*, Ch. 5.

94. J.A. Dowie, 'Business Politicians in Action: the New Zealand Railway Boom of the 1870s', *Business Archives and History*, V (1965); F. Capie and K.A. Tucker, 'Foreign Investment in New Zealand, 1870–1914' (unpublished MS, 1976).

95. Simkin, '*The Instability of a Dependent Economy*', p. 24.

96. Hawke, *The Making of New Zealand*, pp. 71–83. The New Zealand banking system was heavily influenced by both British and Australian institutions. Ibid. pp. 60–4.

97. W. Rosenberg, 'Capital Imports and Growth, the Case of New Zealand: Foreign Investment in New Zealand, 1840–1958', *Econ. Jour.*, LXXI (1961), Tables III and IV, pp. 95–6. New Zealand earned a persistent surplus on her balance of trade from the late 1880s onwards. Details can be found in J.B. Condliffe, 'The External Trade of New Zealand', *New Zealand Official Year Book* (1915), pp. 875–6.

98. Rosenberg, 'Capital Imports and Growth', pp. 107–8.

smallness and their commercial and financial dependence. The political autonomy which responsible government gave them has to be weighed against their status as economic, and especially financial, satellites of Britain when assessing the degrees of freedom achieved after 1850. Britain's informal financial imperialism was masked, in New Zealand before 1885 and in Australia before 1890, by the ease with which the colonists could raise capital in London and, therefore, keep imports at a level which allowed rapid growth to take place. What was, in effect, a privileged access to City funds fostered, to some degree, the illusion of economic autonomy in the same way that Britain's own defence umbrella and the remoteness of the Antipodes from the main centres of military conflict encouraged some colonists to believe that they were free of European squabbles and beyond the control of the great powers. Lending was not, of course, an arbitrary process. Although the Baring Crisis influenced British attitudes to all foreign lending, the drying up of loans to New Zealand and Australia also reflected the declining profitability of major activities in both countries.[99] In that sense, the crises described were internally generated rather than wilfully imposed from without. Nonetheless, what the crises did illustrate vividly was that development which failed to produce sufficient export income would ultimately lead to disaster and to the tightening of London's grip on colonial economic life.

The upheavals of the 1880s and 1890s certainly left a permanent mark on Australasian society. In the case of Australia, it has been argued that the crisis gave birth to a 'national bourgeoisie' capable of organising industrial growth under the shelter of protection and simultaneously lessening Australia's dependence on Britain.[100] The growth of manufacturing before 1914 was significant, as was the development of a national capital market.[101] However, Australia's ability to meet her own needs for capital after 1890 partly reflected the low level of economic activity and of investment: when, after 1910, the economy began to move towards full employment, British investment in Australia rose rapidly again. And, as we shall see, Australia borrowed heavily in London in the 1920s. It is also important to remember that the growth of import substitution under protection was a necessity if Australians were to meet financial

99. For the New Zealand case see Hawke, *The Making of New Zealand*, p. 82.

100. This is a simplified version of the thesis argued by Schwartz, *In the Dominions of Debt*, Ch. 4.

101. Ian M. Drummond, 'Government Securities on Colonial New Issue Markets: Australia and Canada, 1895–1914', *Yale Economic Essays*, I (1961).

obligations in London at a time when their credit was poor: local production reduced imports and released sterling for debt repayments. Australian industrialism, in that sense, complemented Britain's own peculiar capitalist structure. So, although the influence of domestic manufacturing increased over time, it would be difficult to argue that it resulted in any marked reorientation of policy or greatly disturbed the links between Australia's overseas interests and London finance. The crisis of the 1890s also sharpened class antagonisms in Australia and promoted the development of Labour parties, at both state and Commonwealth levels. These parties supported protection and a white Australia policy, and were suspicious of the imperial link and of Britain as 'the headquarters of the Money Power'.[102] But, once in office, Labour did little to alter the fundamentals of the Anglo-Australian economic relationship.

In New Zealand, where the population was too small to support as important a manufacturing sector as in Australia, wool and land exerted a greater sway. The traumas of the 1880s and 1890s gave a shattering blow to their social and political authority, and 'the old "Establishment" dominated by squatters, speculators, merchants, British gentlemen and their ladies' collapsed as wool declined in significance and dairy farming, dominated by small farmers, became the leading industry.[103] By the 1890s, New Zealand was ruled by a radical party with a mandate to create a welfare state, and the political dominance of the local gentry was over. But the dairy farmers were as dependent as the wool growers upon the British market, the problem of debt repayment remained as anxious and unremitting as in the past, and further heavy borrowings were necessary before 1914.[104]

In the sequel, both countries came out of depression with more efficient and diversified export sectors and both developed a greater ability to finance their own investment needs, although growth, especially in Australia, was much slower after 1890 than in the previous 30 years.[105] Depression brought home the importance of

102. Love, *Australia and the Money Power*, p. 47. On the rise of Labour after 1890 see McIntyre, *Oxford History of Australia*, IV, Chs. 3 and 4.

103. Sinclair, *History of New Zealand*, p. 166. On changes in land ownership and use see J.D. Gould, 'The Twilight of the Estates, 1891–1910', *Austral. Econ. Hist. Rev.*, X (1970).

104. On New Zealand see also Schwartz, *In the Dominions of Debt*, Ch. 5. For a more global perspective see Denoon, *Settler Capitalism*, Ch. 3.

105. Growth of GDP was estimated at 4.7 per cent per year for 1861–90 and at 2.4 per cent for 1891–1913. Rates of growth of GDP per capita were 1.2 per cent and 0.4 per cent per annum respectively. See Butlin, 'Some Perspectives on Australian Economic Development', Table 6.6, p. 284.

exports to prosperity and to financial stability as never before. It was inevitable that, by the 1890s, Australia and New Zealand should be at the forefront of demands for a preferential position in the British market.[106] From the colonial perspective, the logical consequence of extensive trade and financial commitments to Britain was that the parent country should abandon free trade.

CANADIAN UNITY AND BRITISH FINANCE

If Australia and New Zealand were economic satellites of Britain after 1850 in the manner described, this was not true in the same sense of the North American colonies, which were less successful as exporters of staples until around 1900 and where the influence of the United States was already strong at mid-century. Even in 1850, despite the growth of a banking system on the British model which eschewed American-style industrial lending, and despite British predominance in Canadian trade, only one important bank was British in origin, and the colonies held their reserves not in London but in New York.[107] What can be said is that the independence of the colonies from the USA and the creation of British North America in its modern form would have been most unlikely if the former had been unable to tap capital sources in London and if British governments had not occasionally been willing to use the leverage which London's financial predominance gave them. North America presented particularly acute problems for imperial statesmen who recognised the need for self-government, but feared its consequences in the age of free trade.

Geographically, the colonies were no more than the northerly fringes of the rapidly expanding United States,[108] and only common

106. The pressures for preferences in New Zealand are discussed in Sinclair, *History of New Zealand*, pp. 223–4.
107. As early as 1851 the Canadians had adopted the decimal system and the dollar. The connection between the USA and Canada had become so intimate by the 1870s that Canadian banks, taking advantage of legislative restrictions on their American counterparts, were setting up branches in New York and playing a significant role in the finance of Anglo-American trade. See E.P. Neufeld, ed. *Money and Banking in Canada: Historical Documents and Commentary* (Toronto, 1964), pp. 128–9 and 163–9. On the banking system as a whole see Pomfret, *The Economic Development of Canada*, pp. 168ff; Marr and Paterson, *Canada: An Economic History* pp. 249–52; Naylor, *The History of Canadian Business*, I, Ch. III; and Craig McIvor, *Canadian Monetary, Banking and Fiscal Development* (Toronto, 1958).
108. The best general histories of Canada are by Pomfret and by Marr and Paterson cited in n. 9, and by W.J. Easterbrook and H.G.J. Aitken, *Canadian Economic History*

dependence on the preferential system had given them any sense of unity. After the Napoleonic Wars, the province of Lower Canada (Ontario) had flourished as its agricultural frontier expanded and as its population increased fivefold between 1815 and 1850.[109] But much of the prosperity of the province – and of the small but cosmopolitan community centred on Montreal in the French-speaking province of Upper Canada (Quebec) – depended upon the ability to use the St. Lawrence Seaway as a conduit for trade between Britain and the midwest of America.[110] To this end, large sums were spent, both privately and publicly, upon the construction of a series of canals to improve the competitiveness of the seaway. Capital for these purposes was in short supply in the late 1830s, and the British government turned this to its political advantage in 1841 by offering a guarantee of interest on a loan for canal construction as an inducement to the provinces of Lower and Upper Canada to unite under the name of Canada. In the process, Britain hoped both to improve the colony's credit rating in London and to subordinate and assimilate the fractious French in a British-dominated union.[111] The importance of the seaway was further underlined in 1842, when the British offered a substantial preference on wheat shipped from Canadian ports.[112]

The ending of preferences after 1846 badly hurt many North American export industries, including the timber trades of the Maritime Provinces of Nova Scotia and New Brunswick, and triggered a movement in Montreal, the financial and commercial centre of the St Lawrence trading system, in favour of joining the United States. The problem was compounded by the growing power of the United States, as the frontier swept westwards and as the Union's manufac-

(Toronto, 1956). See also H.G.J. Aitken, 'Defensive Expansionism: the State and Growth in Canada', in Aitken, *The State and Economic Growth*; O.J. Firestone, *Canadian Economic Development, 1867–1953* (Income and Wealth Series, VII, 1958); and idem, 'Development of Canada's Economy, 1850–1900', in *Trends in the American Economy in the Nineteenth Century* (Studies in Income and Wealth, XXIV, Princeton, NJ, 1960). See also the discussion of Canada in the context of a wide review of Anglo-American relations in Hyam, *Britain's Imperial Century*, Ch. 6.

109. Marr and Paterson, *Canada: An Economic History*, pp. 87–95; Aitken, 'Defensive Expansionism', pp. 88ff.

110. The classic study here is Donald G. Creighton, *The Commercial Empire of the St. Lawrence* (Toronto, 1937).

111. Marr and Paterson, *Canada: An Economic History*, p. 98; Easterbrook and Aitken, *Canadian Economic History*, p. 269. On the importance of the canals in stimulating demand for British capital see H.C. Pentland, 'The Role of Capital in Canadian Economic Development before 1875', *Canadian Journal of Economics and Political Science*, XVI (1950).

112. Easterbrook and Aitken, *Canadian Economic History*, p. 352.

turing and military might grew with frightening speed, threatening to pull the small colonial outposts irresistibly into its orbit. One manifestation of American power was the rapid spread of railways south of the border, which increased the competitiveness of the east coast ports. Together with the loss of the wheat preference, this threw the future of the 'commercial empire' of the St Lawrence into doubt and threatened to leave the province of Canada with enormous unproductive debts.

At the same time, British governments were reluctantly recognising that Britain's political presence in North America was a constant provocation to the United States and that the colonies could not be defended against her in the long term.[113] In any case, public opinion in Britain was impatient of high military expenditure in North America, partly because the costs of defence appeared to cancel out the benefit of the connection, and partly because of the assumed correspondence between political freedom and military self-help. When the colonies claimed political freedom, the British authorities argued that, in return, the local communities should assume more of their own defence burden. Not surprisingly, the Canadians, while eagerly claiming the political privileges, baulked at the economic price. Wrangles over the issue of the distribution of military burdens between Britain and Canada harmed relations for years and provoked the most famous outbursts of anti-imperial and anti-colonial sentiment in mid-Victorian Britain.[114] There was also a feeling in some business circles in Britain that it would be madness to antagonise, or at the worst go to war with, Britain's best customers for the sake of a few, relatively unimportant possessions[115] and that abandoning them to their fate was a small price to pay for continued American goodwill.

A few radicals might be prepared to abandon the empire: no English ministry could take such a cavalier attitude. Keeping Canada independent held open a potentially valuable market, maintained a

---

113. At the same time as they were facing the problem in the north, the British were withdrawing from central America under US pressure. See Kenneth Bourne, *Britain and the Balance of Power in North America, 1815–1908* (1967), Ch. 6. On Britain's tacit recognition of the need to withdraw from the North American continent, see W.L. Morton, *The Critical Years: The Union of British North America, 1857–1873* (Oxford, 1964), p. 216. The most recent detailed study of US–Canadian relations from this angle is R.C. Stuart, *United States Expansionism and British North America, 1775–1871* (Chapel Hill, NC, 1988).

114. Stembridge, *Parliament, the Press and the Colonies*, passim.

115. See, for example, Richard Cobden's speech at Manchester in 1849, quoted in George Bennett, *The Concept of Empire, 1774–1947* (1953), pp. 169–70.

British presence on the American continent, slowed down the other-wise inevitable rise of the United States to world power status and limited the spread of its dangerously republican philosophy. As Russell, then Prime Minister, argued in 1849, 'the loss of any great portion of our Colonies would diminish our importance in the world, and the vultures would soon gather to despoil us of other parts of our Empire, or to offer insults to us which we could not bear'.[116]

The question before a succession of concerned British statesmen and officials was, therefore, a difficult one: how to ensure Canadian independence from the United States, and to maintain as much as possible of the British presence in North America, while supervising political and military withdrawal and tacitly recognising United States' hegemony on the American continent? The answer was to use British political and economic influence to sustain, and enhance the fortunes of, those collaborative agents in Canada who had a vested interest in the imperial link.

British support for North American independence would have been unavailing had it not met with an enthusiastic local response. Colonial governments and the business elites who supported them needed a British presence in Canada. Despite a brief flirtation with the idea of annexation to the United States when preferences came to an end, most of the politically and economically powerful groups had benefited from the old system and were keen to avoid the competition and loss of prestige which absorption by the United States might entail.[117] They preferred independence; but that was possible only with the support of British capital, whether publicly or privately subscribed. As an American historian of Canadian railway develop-ment has recently expressed it:

> The decision to opt for British rather than American dominance reflected the persistence of traditional ties and the more lucrative British market. Because of traditional sentiment and geographical separation, British capital and control was not commonly perceived as foreign dominance: similar American participation was.[118]

There were two main phases in Canadian development in which Britain's 'indirect imperialism'[119] helped to shape a distinctive North

---

116. Russell to Grey in Grey Papers, University of Durham, quoted in John B. Ingham, 'Power to the Powerless: British North America and the Pursuit of Reciproc-ity, 1846–1854', *Bulletin of Canadian Studies*, VIII (1984), p. 125.

117. Gerald J. J. Tulchinsky, *The River Barons: Montreal Businessmen and the Growth of Industry and Transportation, 1837–53* (Toronto, 1977), Ch. 13.

118. Peter Baskerville, 'Americans in Britain's Backyard: the Railway Era in Upper Canada, 1850–1880', *Bus. Hist. Rev.*, LV (1981) p. 324.

119. Ibid. p. 335.

America. The first was the attempt between the late 1840s and the early 1860s to achieve growth through closer economic ties with the United States; the second included the emergence of a united Canada from the British North America Act of 1867 and the acceptance of the reality of Confederation by the United States in the Treaty of Washington signed in 1871.

In the late 1840s both Grey, as Colonial Secretary, and Elgin, the Governor General, realised that the independence of the British North American colonies from the United States depended ultimately upon their ability to maintain economic prosperity. Reciprocity – free trade in natural products with the United States – was one way of achieving growth since it offered the chance of channelling the products of the American mid-west up the St Lawrence Seaway. The British government undertook to negotiate with the United States on the colonies' behalf, and the Reciprocity Treaty was signed in 1854.[120] Fostering colonial unity was seen as another important means of encouraging a viable economy. After 1846, Grey and Elgin tried to barter an imperial guarantee for the building of a Quebec–Halifax railway against an acceptance by the Canadians of the responsibility for the bulk of their own military expenditure. A united Canada would have good credit rating in London: both Grey and Elgin recognised that lack of capital was one of the colonies' crucial problems and that, initially, only government help could give Canadian enterprises the standing which would make them credit-worthy in the City of London.[121]

The policy foundered on intercolonial squabbles, the inability to agree on the colonies' contribution to their own defence and parliamentary cheeseparing over guarantees for railway capital. But, despite hostility to the colonies in some quarters in Britain, proposals of the kind favoured by Grey and Elgin remained on the Anglo-Canadian agenda throughout the 1850s and 1860s.[122] In the early 1850s,

120. D.G. Masters, *The Reciprocity Treaty of 1854* (Toronto, 1963); Robert Ankli, 'The 1854 Reciprocity Treaty', *Canadian Journal of Economics*, 4 (1971); Ingham, 'Power to the Powerless', passim. For the British recognition of the importance of the treaty at this crisis point in Canadian history see A.G. Doughty, ed. *The Grey–Elgin Papers, 1846–52* (Ottawa, 1937), pp. 363–413, 465–66, 471.

121. For something of the flavour of the arguments and proposals which preoccupied Grey and Elgin see Doughty, *The Grey–Elgin Papers, 1846–52*, pp. 26, 37, 252–4, 257–61, 263, 266–7, 276–7, 349, 351, 392, 419, 437, 448, 608–12, 1591, 1593. See also W.P. Morrell, *Colonial Policy in the Age of Peel and Russell* (Oxford, 1930), pp. 436–44.

122. Donald Roman, 'The Contribution of Imperial Guarantees for Colonial Railway Loans to the Consolidation of British North America, 1847–65' (unpublished D.Phil thesis, Oxford, 1978). J.A. Gibson, 'The Duke of Newcastle and British North American Affairs, 1859–64', *Canadian Hist. Rev.*, XLIV (1963); and P.B. Waite, 'A Letter from Leonard Tilley on the Intercolonial Railway, 1863', *Canadian Hist. Rev.*, XLV (1964), give insights into particular episodes.

prompted by legislation guaranteeing returns on railway investment passed by the Canadian Parliament[123] and by the world economic boom driven by gold discoveries in the United States and Australia, private capital began flowing to North America in abundance. British savings poured into the Grand Trunk and other railways built by British contractors and run by British managements; as much capital per head was invested in North America in the 1850s as in the days of the famous wheat boom of 1900–14.[124]

The great mediators between the City and the colonies at the time, and for many years after, were the banking families of Barings and Glyn, Mills, who acted as agents for the colonies in London.[125] Without their help the Grand Trunk might never have been completed, and their willingness to hold its securities, and those of colonial governments, often kept up the price of North American stocks: in 1860, for example, Barings were effectively subsidising the Grand Trunk to the extent of £1.2m. through loans and holdings of its securities.[126] Whether this was a very profitable business for the bankers is doubtful; but holding the agency of governments, even impoverished ones, and involvement in high profile projects such as the Grand Trunk, brought a degree of prestige which enhanced business in general.[127] The power of the bankers was also considerable. After protests by both Barings and Glyn, Mills, Canada passed an Act in 1851 which declared that the province would not increase its debt 'without the consent of the Agents through whom loans may have been negotiated in England, or the previous offer to pay off all debentures then outstanding'.[128] Ten years later, hints by Barings and

123. For some interesting aspects of this see Michael J. Piva, 'Continuity and Crisis: Francis Hincks and Canadian Economic Policy', *Canadian Hist. Rev.*, LXVI (1985).

124. Penelope Hartland, 'Factors in the Economic Growth of Canada', *Jour. Econ. Hist.*, XV (1955), p. 14.

125. On the origins of the British bankers' concern with Canada see M.L. Magill, 'John H. Dunn and the Bankers', in Johnson, *Historical Essays on Upper Canada*.

126. Roger Fulford, *Glyn's, 1753–1943: Six Generations in Lombard St.* (1953), p. 155; Philip Ziegler, *The Sixth Great Power: Barings, 1762–1929* (1988), p. 226; D.C.M. Platt and J. Adelman, 'London Merchant Bankers in the First Phase of Heavy Borrowing: the Grand Trunk Railway of Canada', *Jour. Imp. and Comm. Hist.*, XXVIII (1990), pp. 218–23.

127. On accepting the Agency in 1837, Glyn wrote that 'there is no salary or emolument but it is a feather': Glyn to Sir George Grey, 10 June 1837, quoted in Fulford, *Glyn's*, p. 146. On the other hand, it is arguable that, by the late 1850s, Barings and Glyn's commitment to the Grand Trunk was such that they had to support it because their reputations were linked with its survival. Platt and Adelman, 'London Merchant Bankers in the First Phase of Heavy Borrowing', p. 221.

128. Quoted in Fulford, *Glyn's*, p. 153. See also Platt and Adelman, 'London Merchant Bankers in the First Phase of Heavy Borrowing', p. 216.

Glyn's that they would jointly take possession of the Grand Trunk's property in lieu of debts galvanised the government of Canada into action to help the railway out of its financial difficulties.[129]

The strategy based on Reciprocity and the Grand Trunk began to collapse in the late 1850s, beginning with the financial crisis of 1857, after which capital and trade flows both slowed significantly. The basis of this 'American' policy was also destroyed by the Civil War, when victory by the protectionist northern states doomed the Reciprocity Treaty and aroused new fears of American expansion into the north. The Confederation of the colonies under a strong Dominion government in 1867 was, on the Canadian side, the direct outcome of their failure to tap the American market successfully.[130] With their mid-west ambitions blocked, the colonists turned to their only alternatives – unity and a concerted effort to develop the Canadian west before it was absorbed by their neighbour. Such a grandiose project required immense capital resources, mainly for railways, and Confederation was one means of attracting them. Harold Innis, the famous Canadian economic historian, once wrote: 'The constitution of Canada, as it appears on the statute book of the British Parliament, has been designed to secure capital for the improvement of navigation and transport'.[131]

In other words, Confederation like the union of Quebec and Ontario in 1840 was, among other things, a way of improving Canada's credit rating in London after the railway schemes of the 1850s had ended in disappointment. Or, as a more cynical historian has put it:

> Canadian 5 per cent bonds had fallen seriously in London to the level of 71 . . . [but] on the day the Confederation resolution reached London they rose to 75. When the full texts arrived they rose to 92, lending considerable credence to the view that the Baring Bros. were the true fathers of Confederation.[132]

---

129. Ziegler, *The Sixth Great Power*, p. 226. For a Canadian view of the role of English bankers in North America at the time see Naylor, *History of Canadian Business*, I, pp. 23–8. On the Grand Trunk itself see George Parkin de Twenebroker Glazebrook, *A History of Transportation in Canada*, I (Toronto, 1967), pp. 152ff; and Archibald William Currie, *The Grand Trunk Railway of Canada* (Toronto, 1957).

130. Masters, *The Reciprocity Treaty*, Ch. 6 and pp. 130–6.

131. Harold A. Innis, *Essays in Canadian Economic History* (Toronto, 1956), p. 395; cf. also p. 174. For similarly forthright statements see Donald G. Creighton, *British North America at Confederation* (Toronto, 1939), p. 9; and Peter J. Smith, 'The Ideological Origins of Canadian Confederation', *Canadian Journal of Politics*, 20 (1987), p. 28.

132. Naylor, 'The Rise and Fall of the Third Commercial Empire of the St. Lawrence', p. 15.

Support for a federal solution to Canada's difficulties also took on a new urgency in Britain in the mid–1860s. Colonial military expenditure had to be trimmed to meet Gladstone's need for budgetary stringency and in recognition of new threats in Europe, just when the possibility of a conflict over Canada with an angry and militarily awesome Northern United States was at its height.[133] Confederation – a strong, united but independent Canada – suited Britain's needs; after 1863, when the colonists began to take what the British considered to be a more mature attitude to their own military responsibilities, London was willing to improve its offer of financial help to British North America considerably. Without this offer the Quebec–Halifax or Intercolonial Railway, completed in 1871, would not have been built and the Maritimes would not have agreed to Confederation. Without Confederation, it would have been impossible to raise the funds to buy out the Hudson's Bay Company and to begin the conquest of the western prairies, which were so vital to the development of an independent Canadian economy. In pursuit of the objective of union, the Liberal government in Britain was not averse to applying a good deal of economic and political pressure on doubtful or hesitant elements in Canada.[134]

The main support for the new Dominion of Canada came from the wealthiest province, Ontario, and was composed of

> ambitious, dynamic, speculative and entrepreneurial business groups who aimed to make money out of the new business community or to install themselves in the strategic positions of power within it – the railway promoters, banks, manufacturers, land companies, contractors.[135]

They provided the collaborating economic elite who clung to, and depended upon, British power and British capital. The British government gave them strong support and was not afraid to bully or cajole other colonists who had their doubts about the benefit of a

133. C.P. Stacey, 'Britain's Withdrawal from North America, 1864–1871', *Canadian Hist. Rev.*, XXXVI (1955); idem, *Canada and the British Army, 1846–1971: A Study in the Practice of Responsible Government* (Toronto, 1963).

134. A.B. Erickson, 'Edward T. Cardwell: Peelite', *Transactions of the American Philosophical Society*, NS, XLIX, Pt. II (1959), pp. 35–9; D.M.L. Farr, *The Colonial Office and Canada, 1867–87* (Toronto, 1955), Ch. 3; P.B. Waite, 'Edward Cardwell and Confederation', *Canadian Hist. Rev.*, 4 (1962). For the direct part played by British investors in shifting attention to the idea of linking Canada and the Maritimes with the Pacific Coast see John Bartlett Brebner, *North Atlantic Triangle: The Interplay of Canada, the United States and Great Britain* (New Haven, Conn., 1946), pp. 174–7; Glazebrook, *A History of Transportation*, II, p. 3; Arthur R.M. Lower, *Colony to Nation: A History of Canada* (Toronto 1964), pp. 316–17; and Elaine Allen Mitchell, 'Edward Watkin and the Buying-Out of the Hudson's Bay Company', *Canadian Hist. Rev.*, 34 (1953).

135. Frank H. Underhill, *The Image of Confederation* (Toronto, 1964), pp. 24–26.

united North America. The Canadian Liberal, Edward Blake, looking back from 1876, felt that Confederation had been 'prematurely forced' on the colonies and that 'N[ew] B[runswick] was frightened into it, N[ova] S[cotia] coerced into it, the North West, B[ritish] C[olumbia] and P[rince] Edward Island bought into it'. Blake was rather disenchanted by the time he wrote this, but it is an exaggeration, not a wild untruth.[136]

Confederation would have had poor prospects without the acquiescence of the United States. The Treaty of Washington in 1871 underwrote the decision of 1867 since the United States accepted Canadian political independence in return for a tacit recognition of its own military hegemony in Northern America – implied by British military withdrawal – and improved fishing rights for American vessels in Canadian waters.[137] The latter concession deeply offended the Maritime provinces, and the Dominion government could be induced to accept it only in return for a guarantee by Britain of a considerable part of the initial expenditure on the Canadian Pacific Railway, the key both to Canadian control of the Western Prairies and to the incorporation into the union of the most westerly settlement, British Columbia.[138]

Tariffs also made a significant contribution to the process of organising and maintaining a united Canada. In the late 1850s, tariffs were justified as a way of raising revenue to pay debts and hence of maintaining the credit-worthiness of the public authorities. The British disliked the tariff immensely: Grey was particularly hostile.[139] But free trade seemed incompatible with the development of an independent Canada, and in the face of this conundrum the British

136. Blake to McKenzie, 1 July 1876, in *Dufferin-Carnarvon Correspondence, 1874–78* (Toronto, 1955), p. 397. As a leading historian of the white empire recently put the matter: 'the gentlemen who made mid-Victorian policy conveyed their intentions through the velvet glove rather than the bludgeon, and were adept at hinting that it might contain metal'. See Ged Martin, 'Launching Canadian Confederation: Means and Ends, 1836–1864', *Hist. Jour.*, 27 (1984), p. 601.

137. Morton, *The Critical Years*, pp. 250–8, links the treaty firmly with Confederation. For the wider context of Anglo-American relations see M.M. Robson, 'The Alabama Claim and the Anglo-American Reconciliation, 1865–71', *Canadian Hist. Rev.*, 42 (1961).

138. Morton, *The Critical Years*, pp. 266–7; Farr, *The Colonial Office and Canada*, pp. 85–91. On the earlier incorporation of British Columbia within the empire see B.M. Gough, '"Turbulent Frontiers" and British Expansion: Governor James Douglas, the Royal Navy, and the British Columbia Gold Rushes', *Pacific Historical Review*, XLI (1972).

139. Though, in supporting the Reciprocity Treaty idea, Grey and other British statesmen were acquiescing in a policy which allowed Canada to impose discriminatory duties on Britain and other countries. See Masters, *The Reciprocity Treaty*, pp. 56–8.

quietly abandoned their opposition, even though the tariff gave some protection to local manufacturing.[140]

Protection took on a heightened significance in the 1880s. The vague developmental ideas which lay behind Confederation broadened into the so-called 'National Policy' of Macdonald's Conservatives in 1879, when the project of western development took on its final shape. The west could not be conquered without the Canadian Pacific Railway, and a steady supply of settlers was needed to produce the wheat which would ultimately pay for the capital raised in London for prairie investments. Success on the prairies also required a high-tariff policy to raise resources for the Dominion, which underwrote a great many of the new projects, and to protect the industry in eastern Canada which would supposedly thrive on western growth.[141] Recently, some Marx-inspired historians have argued that the commercial and financial oligarchs who were the chief architects of the National Policy designed it specifically to encourage direct US industrial investment and to limit the power of Canadian manufacturing.[142] Although the importance of the bankers and merchants in Canada's political economy is not in doubt,[143] it must be remembered that the invasion of Canada by American industrial capital did not begin in earnest until after 1900 and that the tariff gave an immediate fillip to import substitution.[144] Insofar as the rise of manufacturing aided Canadian growth, it also swelled the tax revenues of the Dominion and provincial governments and eased the growing burden of debt repayments, including those due in London. Nor, given the overall importance of Canada to British trade and finance, would it

140. On tariff policy see Masters, *The Reciprocity Treaty*, pp. 64–7: the connection between thinking on the tariff issue in the 1850s and the later National Policy is stressed in Morton, *The Critical Years*, pp. 65–7, and in A.A. Den Otter, 'Alexander Galt, the 1859 Tariff and Canadian Economic Nationalism', *Canadian Hist. Rev.*, LXIII (1982).

141. The best introduction to the National Policy is still probably V.C. Fowke, 'The National Policy – Old and New', *Canadian Jour. Econ. and Pol. Sci.*, XVIII (1952); 'The National Policy and Western Development in N. America', *Jour. Econ. Hist.*, XVI (1956), and *The National Policy and the Wheat Economy* (Toronto, 1957).

142. Naylor, 'The Rise and Fall of the Third Commercial Empire of the St. Lawrence', pp. 19ff.

143. Judith Teichmann, 'Businessmen and Politics in the Process of Economic Development: Argentina and Canada', *Canadian Jour. Pol.*, 15 (1982), pp. 56–7.

144. L.R. McDonald, 'Merchants against Industry: An Idea and its Origins', *Canadian Hist. Rev.*, LVI (1975); Glen Williams, 'The National Policy Tariffs: Industrial Underdevelopment through Import Substitution', *Canadian Jour. Pol.*, 12 (1979), pp. 333–8. For another interesting comment on the Naylor thesis see Pomfret, *The Economic Development of Canada*, pp. 142–5. For the attitudes of Canadian businessmen to the penetration of American capital see Michael Bliss, *A Living Profit: Studies in the Social History of Canadian Business, 1883–1911* (Toronto, 1974), pp. 109–111.

have been wise for British governments to support the complaints of their manufacturers too strongly or to 'allow particular manufacturing interests in Britain to overrule the general interests of British capital'.[145]

Table 8.2 Net capital inflows: Canada, 1871–1915

	$m	% of GNP
1871–75	166	7.0
1876–80	93	3.3
1881–85	167	5.2
1886–90	242	6.4
1891–95	202	4.6
1896–1900	124	2.5
1901–05	317	5.3
1906–10	784	9.2
1911–15	1515	12.4

Source: W.L. Marr and D.G. Paterson, *Canada: An Economic History* (Toronto, 1980), Table 9.1, p. 267.

For a generation after Confederation the National Policy gave Canadians something to fight over rather than offering them a sense of shared achievement. While the grain frontier remained south of the Canadian border, the western frontier of the United States was a magnet for migrants and capital. Slow development in western Canada meant a high burden of public indebtedness: about £170m. worth of capital was imported between 1870 and 1895, roughly 5 per cent of national income at that time (Table 8.2). It also brought high tariffs and lower living standards, especially for those dependent on imported goods.[146] Given many financial as well as technical problems, the building of the Canadian Pacific took much longer than expected and, although the company was formed in Canada, the project might have foundered without London's support and particularly much timely help from Barings. Barings marketed a considerable amount of Canadian Pacific stock, around £10m. all told in the 1880s,

145. Williams, 'The National Policy Tariffs', p. 361.
146. Charles M. Studness, 'Economic Opportunity and the Westward Migration of Canadians during the late 19th Century', *Canadian Jour. Econ. and Pol. Sci.*, XXX (1964). For various criticisms of the National Policy, both contemporary and recent, see Melville H Watkin, 'Economic Nationalism', ibid. XXXII (1966); Ian Grant, 'Erasmus Wiman: a Continentalist Replies to Canadian Imperialism', *Canadian Hist. Rev.*, LIII (1972); and Goldwin Smith's famous *Canada and the Canada Question* (1891).

and often held parts of it for considerable periods when the London market was averse to Canadian securities.[147]

Resentment against the National Policy threatened the unity of the Dominion and fuelled an interest in free trade and in closer links with the United States in the 1880s.[148] This movement failed because of the extent of the interests tied to the National Policy, especially in the relatively highly populated manufacturing centres of Eastern Canada which benefited from protection, and because of constant fears of United States' annexationist designs. Macdonald, the leading force behind the National Policy, continually emphasised its compatibility with the British connection;[149] in 1891, he tried to revive enthusiasm for it by arguing for a preference in the British market, pulling Canada away from the United States, guaranteeing export markets and ensuring the payment of debts.[150] The National Policy was, indeed, the clearest expression of the fundamental fact that 'the empire was no longer held together by diplomatic bonds but by the financial commitments made by many influential British investors'.[151]

Macdonald's Liberal successors, who held power in the late 1890s, were more interested in free trade; but the National Policy and its aims were so entrenched in Canada by this time that the Liberals ended by offering the British preferential concessions on imports in 1897 in the hope of stimulating similar concessions on Canadian exports to Britain.[152] Besides its economic advantages, enthusiasm for the imperial cause was also a useful way in which Canadians could emphasise their distance from the United States, as support for Britain

147. D.C. Masters, 'Financing the CPR, 1880–5', *Canadian Hist. Rev.*, XXIV (1943); Ziegler, *The Sixth Great Power*, pp. 227–8; Glazebrook, *History of Transportation*, II, pp. 77, 85–9.

148. This is a major theme of Robert Craig Brown, *Canada's National Policy, 1883–1900: A Study in Canadian-American Relations* (Princeton, NJ, 1964). See also Bliss, *A Living Profit*, pp. 97–106.

149. In 1881 Macdonald claimed that, 'if our scheme is carried out, the steamer landing at Halifax will discharge its freight and emigrants upon a British railway, which will go through Quebec and through Ontario to the Far West, on British territory, under a British flag, under Canadian laws and without any chance of either the immigrant being deluded or seduced from his allegiance or proposed residence in Canada'. Quoted in Fowke, 'National Policy and Western Development in N. America', p. 476.

150. Brown, *Canada's National Policy*, Ch. 7. See also Edward Vickery, 'Exports and North American Economic Growth: "Structuralist" and "Staple" Models in Historical Perspective', *Canadian Jour. Econ.*, 7 (1974).

151. A.A. den Otter, *The Galts and the Development of Western Canada* (Edmonton, 1982), p. 43.

152. Brown, *Canada's National Policy*, Ch. 8; Norman Penlington, *Canada and Imperialism, 1896–1899* (Toronto, 1965), pp. 45–52.

in the Boer War illustrates.[153] Given the extent to which Canada's determination to avoid the American embrace put her in the hands of the London money market, it is clear that the Canadians, when they had to choose, preferred informal economic dominance from London to political control by the United States.[154] On the British side, it was rapidly recognised after 1867 that any overt interference in the Dominion's internal affairs would only breed resentment and hostility, and endanger imperial relationships.[155]

From 1895, when the grain frontier shifted across the 49th parallel, the National Policy began to pay off. The great wheat boom[156] was initially developed by Canadian savings and Canadian labour but, given the initially slow growth of exports and the rapid rise in imports as infrastructural investment increased, it could be sustained, after the turn of the century, only by large inflows of capital and labour. Migration from Britain rose sharply in the decade before the World War I;[157] between 1900 and 1914, Canada imported about

153. Penlington, *Canada and Imperialism*, pp. 218–60.

154. Penlington argues that the interest in imperial unity represented a tacit Anglo-Canadian alliance to prevent Canada being swallowed up by the United States. 'It was the condition of Canada's freedom and potential nationhood during the country's dejected and difficult childhood in the last decades of the nineteenth century'. See *Canada and Imperialism*, p. 261.

155. Farr's book, *The Colonial Office and Canada*, explores the emergence of a relationship with Britain which, in Lord Carnarvon's words, was 'political rather than colonial' (p. 309).

156. For studies of the wheat boom see John Archibald Stovel, *Canada in the World Economy* (Cambridge, Mass., 1959), pp. 104–24; A.K. Cairncross, *Home and Foreign Investment, 1870–1913* (Cambridge, 1953), Ch. III; D.C. Corbett, 'Immigration and Economic Development', *Canadian Jour. Econ. and Pol. Sci.*, XVII (1951); and G.M. Meier, 'Economic Development and the Transfer Mechanism: Canada, 1859–1913', ibid. XIX (1953); Robert E. Ankli, 'The Growth of the Canadian Economy, 1896–1920: Export-led and/or Neo-Classical Growth', *Expl. Econ. Hist.*, 17 (1980).

157. A small but significant proportion of migrants to Canada could be classed as English gentlemen. As public school numbers increased, competition in Britain for places on the land (suffering from the effects of agricultural depression) and in the professions was so great that, after 1870, around 10 per cent of the products of the 'best' schools were going abroad to seek their fortunes. Emigration to Canada appealed to the young, the athletic and the adventurous: 'in the minds of many of the emigrants, Canada was simply a remote, somewhat rugged, part of Great Britain'. It offered the prospect of landownership – land could be had for a penny an acre in the west in the early days – and other eligible gentlemanly occupations. Sport was another attraction, the coyote taking the place of the fox on the frontier. Public-school migrants kept in close touch with home, attracting investment and providing openings for new waves of gentlemanly emigration. They were concentrated enough in some places to set the social tone as in, for example, Victoria, British Columbia. These 'older established communities provided social diversion, financial security, and enough novelty to keep life interesting', and, in return, they 'provided Canada with a cultured white collar labour force . . . which was . . . vital in turning the cogs of the nation's commercial and administrative machinery'. Patrick A. Dunae, *Gentlemen Emigrants: From the British*

$2,500m. (or £500m.) of capital, 70 per cent of which came from Britain. Capital imports were equivalent to about one-half of domestic capital formation in the last few years before the war,[158] or 12 per cent of gross national product (Table 8.2). A large percentage of British capital went into railway investment: 10,000 miles were opened for traffic in 1911–15,[159] by which time Canada was showing alarming signs of the over-borrowing which had earlier afflicted Australia and New Zealand.

The economic integration of east and west after 1870 formed the basis for an independent Canadian state in the twentieth century; and it was financed to a large degree by London bankers. Looking back at three generations of economic change in Canada, one Canadian historian has claimed that

> It was not the Fathers of Confederation but Lombard Street which built the canals, the railways, financed the lumber and grain trades, the mines and the industries without which Canadian provinces would now be states in the American union.[160]

US investment, especially in industry, goes unrecognised here along with Canadian entrepreneurs' own considerable contribution to growth; but the quotation is useful in highlighting the often underrated significance of British investment not only to Canada's growth but also to its existence as an independent entity.

London's stake in the wheat boom only emphasised the extent to which Canada had become dependent on the City over the previous two generations. By 1913 Canada was paying roughly £20m. a year in interest to Britain on investments in railways and other public utilities.[161] British manufacturers had done less well. Canadian tariffs ensured debt repayment but also brought heavy competition. The British also found it increasingly difficult to meet the American

---

Public Schools to the Canadian Frontier (Vancouver, 1981). Quotations are from pp. 67 and 79.

158. Stovel, *Canada in the World Economy*, Table 9, p. 12. There are annual estimates of portfolio investment in Canada in Matthew Simon, 'British Investments in Canada, 1865–1914', *Canadian Jour. Econ.*, III (1970). The limited nature of the market for securities in Canada itself is emphasised in R.C. Michie, 'The Canadian Securities Market, 1850–1914', *Bus. Hist. Rev.*, 62 (1988).

159. Kenneth A.H. Buckley, *Capital Formation in Canada, 1896–1930* (Toronto, 1955), Table XII, p. 30. British investors dominated the Canadian market in railway and government stocks. They held 60 per cent of the shares of the CPR in 1913. Michie, 'The Canadian Securities Market', pp. 38–41.

160. Magill, 'John H. Dunn and the Bankers', p. 214.

161. This is based on the assumption of an average return of 5 per cent on British investment in Canada.

Table 8.3 Shares in Canadian foreign trade, 1851–1911 (%)

	1851[a]	1860[a,b]	1870[a]	1880	1890	1900	1911
Imports for consumption							
UK	59.3	44.4	57.1	47.8	37.5	24.2	24.3
USA	37.0	51.1	32.2	40.0	46.4	60.1	60.9
Others	3.7	4.5	10.7	12.2	16.1	15.7	14.8
Exports of foreign and domestic produce							
UK	58.8	38.1	43.3	54.6	50.5	53.9	48.2[c]
USA	35.3	57.1	44.8	37.1	41.2	36.4	37.9[c]
Others	5.9	4.8	11.9	8.3	8.3	9.7	13.9[c]

Sources: O.J. Firestone, 'Canada's Foreign Trade, 1851–1900', in *Trends in the American Economy in the Nineteenth Century*, Table 3, p. 766; M.C. Urquhart and K.A.H. Buckley, *Historical Statistics of Canada* (Cambridge, 1965), pp. 181–2.

Notes: [a] The figures for 1851, 1860 and 1870 are for the four major colonies only.
 [b] Figures for 1860 are strongly influenced by the short-lived Reciprocity Treaty with the United States.
 [c] Export of domestic produce only.

import challenge. Britain's direct investment in Canada was small compared with that of the United States, and attempts by British manufacturers to get behind the tariff were neither frequent nor very successful.[162] Britain's share of Canadian imports fell steadily, despite the preferences of 1897 and the flow of British capital into Canada, while Britain's share of Canadian exports, necessary to debt payment, rose significantly after 1870 (see Table 8.3). Even between 1911 and 1913, when British capital was flooding in, Britain's share of Canada's exports failed to improve.[163] Much of Canada's borrowings were spent on imports from the United States and became part of the burden of dollar settlements in the multilateral system described earlier.[164] Besides the natural geographical advantage possessed by the United States, the erosion of Britain's position as a manufacturing

162. Donald G. Paterson, *British Direct Investment in Canada, 1890–1914: Estimates and Determinants* (Toronto, 1976).
163. G.L. Reuber, *Britain's Export Trade with Canada* (Toronto, 1960), Table I, p. 6. The failure of British manufacturers to take maximum advantage of the flow of British capital to Canada after 1900 was noted by contemporaries with alarm. *Royal Commission on the National Resources, Trade and Legislation of Certain Portions of His Majesty's Dominions*, Minutes of Evidence, Pt. I (Cd 8458) 1917, p. 416; and ibid. *Fifth Interim Report* (Cd 8457) 1917, paras. 23–5.
164. S.B. Saul, *Studies in British Overseas Trade, 1870–1914* (Liverpool, 1960), p. 186.

exporter to Canada was also due to local protectionism and lack of competitiveness.[165] Nonetheless, in Canada as in Australia, the rise of import-substituting manufactures, insofar as they reduced imports, made it easier for the colonies to find the sterling with which to pay interest on their debts and thus strengthened the financial side of the imperial equation.

The Dominion of Canada was an artificial creation. Its chief motive force was undoubtedly local, but without substantial British support, particularly the support of British capital, it is doubtful if the enterprise could have been sustained. From the British angle, a politically independent, but economically dependent, Canada was an excellent offset to the rising power of the United States on the American continent, and brought both political and material gains. On the other hand, a united Canada was not possible without protection; it was the effects of this protection, and of declining manufacturing competitiveness, which were rapidly undermining Britain's commodity exports by 1914, while finance, commerce and services sustained her informal economic empire in Canada.

BRITAIN AND THE WHITE EMPIRE AFTER 1850

Britain's economic influence upon the white colonies was exercised via factor movements and her predominant position in world trade. It was powerful enough to sustain a range of collaborative groups whose leverage on the colonial frontier was sufficient to keep these countries within the international system dominated by Britain. There were many prominent figures in these colonies who felt that 'national pride and economic security were both jeopardized by reliance on a few export staples'; but 'when it came to the point, the rulers of the prairies and the villages would take only such measures as were compatible with the needs of export production and the demands of export producers'.[166] The 'point' usually came when countries experienced balance of payments crises or ran into other problems over borrowing in London and repaying debt: it was then that London could exact ultimate authority over their economic policies, since it was only by playing by the City's rules that the dominant economic elites could re-establish their credit-worthiness and retain their credibility locally.

165. Ibid. Ch. VII.
166. Denoon, *Settler Capitalism*, p. 223.

Dependence upon Britain and upon the world economy was certainly not incompatible with rapid growth, nor was the diversification of the economy out of primary production impossible. In terms of the production of manufactured goods per head of population, Canada, Australia and even New Zealand ranked higher than Germany in 1913.[167] Also, given strong local pressures for reducing dependence on primary output, diversification was no bar to a smooth relationship with Britain. In the Canadian case, the very process of creating a state strong enough to resist the pressures of the United States meant a National Policy within which protection and industrialisation were indispensable. In addition, the enormous annual debt payments which the future Dominions had to make gave them an added reason to succour local manufacturers since keeping down the rate of growth of imports was one way of generating the export surplus needed to pay their creditors. This is a further reason, other than slower growth and the rise of competition why, after 1880, the white colonies proved to be a disappointment to English manufacturers. Leaving aside South Africa, their 14 per cent share of British domestic exports in 1881–5 was not achieved again until 1911–13. In the same period, their share of Britain's imports rose from 9.2 per cent to 11.9 per cent.

The relentless pressure of debt repayment and dependence upon the British market also lay behind the colonies' growing interest in economic privileges within the empire and helped to define the precise character of this interest. An imperial tariff, if it meant, as Chamberlain hoped, a free-trading empire discriminating against foreigners, alarmed them deeply since it would have exposed their manufactures to British competition. Mutual preferences, however, offered them a more secure place in Britain's market and did not imperil their right to protect their manufacturers. It was the only practical kind of unity in which the white colonies were really interested and it is an eloquent expression in itself of the complex nature of their dependence upon Britain. Before 1914, of course, the British electorate rejected Chamberlain's attempt to persuade them to accept such a system of preferences, and British governments felt embarrassed when, first Canada and then Australia and New Zealand, granted them to the mother country. The range of Britain's economic interests was much wider than simply the empire: from a metropolitan perspective, if the imperatives of debt repayment and dependence upon the British for export markets were the criteria for preferences then they ought to

167. Lewis, *Growth and Fluctuations*, Table 7.1, p. 163.

have been offered to Argentina as well as to Australia or New Zealand.[168] It was only after 1918, when Britain had become more dependent on her economic connections with the empire, that a preferential system began to seem worth while to more than a minority of her own economic interest groups. Even then, the benefits could be obtained only at the expense of some valuable links with non-empire countries such as Argentina and Denmark.

The international system in the late nineteenth and early twentieth centuries was not incompatible with the diversification of white colonial economies, and in some ways encouraged it. By the same token, the cosmopolitan economic policy of Britain may have harmed the growth of her own manufacturing industry in the long run by exposing it to competition both at home and in colonial markets. Peripheral industry was not suppressed for the sake of metropolitan capitalism; instead metropolitan industry, as Chamberlain realised, was to some extent sacrificed to the interests of metropolitan finance.

168. 'Argentina and parts of China were more closely linked with Britain through trade and investment in 1913 than were Canada and the West Indies': Saul, *Studies in Overseas Trade, 1870–1914*, p. 228.

CHAPTER NINE

Calling the New World into Existence: South America, 1815–1914[1]

Britain's relations with South America in the nineteenth century are recognised by historians of all persuasions as providing the crucial regional test of theories of informal imperialism. With the minor exception of Guyana (a seventeenth-century settlement which was reinforced during the French Wars), Britain neither sought nor acquired territorial rights on the South American mainland. Consequently, the argument that Britain exercised imperialist control over the continent can be sustained only if it can be shown that the newly liberated states became card-carrying, if not flag-waving, members of her informal empire. Gallagher and Robinson's celebrated article made precisely this claim by suggesting that Britain aimed at 'indirect political hegemony' in South America in order to promote her commercial interests there.[2] However, Platt has demonstrated that British governments intervened in South America's internal affairs only when international law had been broken or when British lives and property were at risk.[3] It is possible to argue that Platt's own

---

1. 'I called the New World into existence to redress the balance of the Old'. Canning, 1826, quoted in William W. Kaufmann, *British Policy and the Independence of Latin America, 1804–1828* (New Haven, Conn., 1951), p. 220. The present chapter deals with the continental mainland and therefore refers to South America. The larger entity, Latin America, which also covers Central America, Mexico, and (in some usages) parts of the Caribbean, is referred to only where other sources cited here have used it as their unit of analysis. We are grateful to Dr Rory Miller for his helpful comments on this chapter.

2. J. Gallagher and R. Robinson, 'The Imperialism of Free Trade', *Econ. Hist. Rev.*, 2nd ser. VI (1953), p. 8.

3. D.C.M. Platt, 'British Diplomacy in Latin America Since the Emancipation', *Inter-American Economic Affairs*, 21 (1967), pp. 21–41; idem, 'The Imperialism of Free Trade: Some Reservations', *Econ. Hist. Rev.*, 2nd ser. XXI (1968), idem, *Finance, Trade, and Politics in British Foreign Policy, 1815–1914* (Oxford, 1968), Ch. 6; and the

reading of the evidence follows the workings of the official mind rather too closely; additional sources and a different perspective have revealed instances where the rules were indeed bent in order to defend Britain's economic interests.[4] Nevertheless, on the evidence presently available, Platt's case would seem to hold for most of the continent and for the greater part of the period under review.

If, then, Britain did found an informal empire in South America, it must have been based on forms of collaborative interaction which encouraged independent states to become subordinate partners of the metropolitan power. Evidence of this development might be sought in the growth of 'complementary satellite economies';[5] it might also appear in the guise of 'cultural imperialism', whereby 'the values, attitudes and institutions of the expansionist nation overcome those of the recipient one'.[6] From this perspective, Britain's sway in South America derived from a combination of overwhelming economic power and mesmerising liberal ideology. In these circumstances, direct political interference by Britain was either unnecessary or else was likely to be counter-productive in stirring nationalist feelings.

This seemingly promising line of inquiry has also run into serious opposition. Detailed research undertaken (or directed) by Platt in particular has concluded that South American states retained economic as well as political sovereignty during the period under review.[7]

---

important case study by W.M. Mathew, 'The Imperialism of Free Trade: Peru, 1820–70', *Econ. Hist. Rev.*, 2nd ser. XXI (1968), though it should be noted, in the context of the argument developed here, that Britain's tolerant view of Peru's guano monopoly was shaped partly by the need to ensure that Peru could continue to service her debts: ibid. pp. 575–7.

4. Peter Winn, 'British Informal Empire in Uruguay in the Nineteenth Century', *Past and Present*, 73 (1976), argues that informal rule was established in the second half of the century. George E. Carl, *First Among Equals: Great Britain and Venezuela, 1810–1910* (Ann Arbor, Mich., 1980), offers an interpretation which is far more critical of Platt's position than that adopted by Miriam Hood, *Gunboat Diplomacy, 1895–1905: Great Power Pressure in Venezuela* (1975: 2nd edn, 1983, appears not to have been influenced by Carl's work). See also Holger H. Herwig, *Germany's Vision of Empire in Venezuela, 1871–1914* (Princeton, NJ, 1987).

5. Gallagher and Robinson, 'Imperialism of Free Trade', p. 9.

6. Richard Graham, 'Sepoys and Imperialists: Techniques of British Power in Nineteenth-Century Brazil', *Inter-American Econ. Aff.*, 23 (1969), p. 29; and idem, 'Robinson and Gallagher in Latin America: the Meaning of Informal Imperialism', in Wm Roger Louis, ed. *Imperialism: The Gallagher and Robinson Controversy* (1976). This approach also appears in Michael Monteon, 'The British in the Atacama Desert: the Cultural Bases of Economic Imperialism', *Jour. Econ. Hist.*, 35 (1975).

7. D.C.M. Platt, 'Economic Imperialism and the Businessman: Britain and Latin America Before 1914', in Roger Owen and Bob Sutcliffe, eds. *Studies in the Theory of Imperialism* (1972); idem, ed. *Business Imperialism, 1840–1930: An Enquiry Based on British Experience in Latin America* (Oxford, 1977). This view was anticipated by H.S.

Economic relations between Britain and South America were entered into freely because both sides wanted an open door for commerce and capital. International exchange was mutually beneficial because competitive pressures prevented Britain from establishing a monopolistic and hence an exploitative grip on markets and resources. If South America's economic prospects came to rely on a narrow range of exports, it was because specialisation followed the logic of comparative advantage and not because imperialist forces imposed deviations from the 'natural' path of development. Just as British governments avoided political interference in South American affairs, so too the unofficial mind of imperialism neither envisaged nor imposed a form of 'business imperialism' on the continent. Far from moulding South American societies in a European image, the Europeans themselves often had to adapt to the shape of local institutions.

Evaluating these claims and counter-claims has been made more difficult by the fact that the debate has shown signs of fission in recent years.[8] On the one hand, the proliferation of local studies, while correcting stereotypes of the periphery associated with conventional metropolitan-based theories of imperialism, has made it harder to generalise responsibly about the continent as a whole. On the other hand, the notion of informal empire has been lifted out of its original mid-nineteenth-century setting and attached to high-flying versions of the dependency thesis. One consequence has been to introduce a number of broad and often poorly specified propositions into the discussion; another has been to tempt participants on both sides into mixing judgements about the results of dependence with explanations of the causes of imperialism, a procedure which has an immediate appeal but which is dubious in terms of both logic and the use of historical evidence.

Ferns, *Britain and Argentina in the Nineteenth Century* (Oxford, 1960), pp. 487–91. More recently, Platt has also emphasised the role of local sources of development finance: 'Domestic Finance in the Growth of Buenos Aires', in Guido di Tella and D.C.M. Platt, eds. *The Political Economy of Argentina, 1880–1946* (1986).

8. A valuable introduction to the subjects touched on in this paragraph is Christopher Abel and Colin Lewis, eds. *Latin America, Economic Imperialism and the State: The Political Economy of the External Connection from Independence to the Present* (1985), Chs. 1–3. See also Colin Lewis, 'Latin America: From Independence to Dependence', in Peter Morris, ed. *Africa, America, and Central Asia: Formal and Informal Empire in the Nineteenth Century* (Exeter, 1984), and, for a succinct survey of the economic history of the period, Bill Albert, *South America and the World Economy from Independence to 1930* (1983). For a more general but also comprehensive guide to recent research see Leslie Bethel, ed. *The Cambridge History of Latin America*, Vols. I and II (Cambridge, 1984), Vol. III (Cambridge, 1985), and Vols. IV and V (Cambridge, 1986).

These trends have underlined the need for a restatement of the causes of British imperialism which shows an awareness of new research on the history of countries in South America and which is also anchored in a particular institutional setting, rather than derived from very general assumptions pertaining to European capitalism as a whole. Specifically, we shall apply our interpretation of imperialism to the South American case by examining how Britain administered the 'rules of the game' in her dealings with the principal players in the new states during the century after 1815. We shall return, in the conclusion, to the question of whether the game itself, as well as the way it was refereed, constituted a form of external control and, if so, whether this can be said to have been imperialistic.

A CONTINENTAL PERSPECTIVE

As the French Wars altered the map of Europe, so too they moved the boundaries of Europe's overseas empires. The Spanish empire in Latin America fell apart between 1810 and 1824, some 300 years after its foundation.[9] The equally antique Portuguese empire effectively divided itself in 1807, when the Prince Regent was hastily shipped to Brazil under British protection to escape the liberating imperialism of Napoleon's armies. The subsequent diversification of Brazil's political and commercial ties, particularly her reorientation towards Britain, provoked a conservative reaction in Portugal which in turn led Brazil to declare independence in 1822.[10] If the stages of imperial decline now appear to have been both more protracted and more complex than was once thought, they have also revealed a sequence of events which prompts comparison with other colonial systems in their terminal state: the growth of a degree of 'informal emancipation' seen in the burgeoning aspirations of colonial interest groups and the loosening of economic ties with the metropole; the attempt to impose a form of 'new imperialism' characterised by tighter centralisation and increased taxation; and the dogged failure of imperial governments to recognise

9. See particularly John Lynch, *The Spanish American Revolutions, 1808–1826* (2nd edn 1987), and Michael P. Costeloe, *Response to Revolution: Imperial Spain and the Spanish American Revolutions, 1810–1840* (Cambridge, 1986). Timothy E. Anna, *Spain and the Loss of America* (1983) emphasises the decline of central authority rather than the rise of 'nationalism'.

10. Kenneth R. Maxwell, *Conflicts and Conspiracies: Brazil and Portugal, 1750–1808* (Cambridge, 1973) deals with the antecedents; A.J.R. Russell–Wood, ed. *From Colony to Nation: Essays on the Independence of Brazil* (Baltimore, Md, 1975) explores the consequences.

political realities until long after they had materialised and been given permanent illumination.[11]

The opportunities presented by these events were not lost on British policy-makers; but they were regarded as setting the scene for extending influence rather than dominion. In 1807, in the aftermath of an unauthorised and unsuccessful attempt to annex the estuary of the River Plate,[12] Castlereagh decided that the British should present themselves in future as 'auxiliaries and protectors' rather than as conquistadors.[13] This principle was endorsed by Canning, his successor at the Foreign Office, and, with a few exceptions at moments of crisis or misjudgement, it was to guide British policy towards South America throughout the nineteenth century. Military intervention presented daunting logistical problems; it was also counter-productive in rousing opposition among nationalists whose hostility to colonial rule scarcely needed further advertisement. Persuasion rather than coercion was required if the emerging new states of Latin America were to become, in Canning's well-known phrase, both free and English.[14] Thus was a role found for South America in Britain's plans for a new world order after 1815. Liberal reforms would preserve monarchy, property and order at home, check what Canning referred to as 'the evils of democracy', and defuse the time bombs of revolution.[15] Commercial expansion abroad would deliver prosperity, and prosperity would fix in place a string of friendly states which would help to maintain stability in a world caught

11. It is true that the Portuguese empire survived until the mid-twentieth century, but since it was barely animate for much of its existence it seems permissible to treat the loss of Brazil as an episode in the story of the gradual subsidence of central authority. At all events, the foregoing comments are intended to suggest comparisons which, strangely, Latin Americanists themselves do not normally pursue (perhaps because, like other scholars in different contexts, they are already burdened by the weight of their own specialisation).

12. Kaufmann, *British Policy*, pp. 23–33.

13. Quoted in Ferns, *Britain and Argentina*, p. 48.

14. Canning to Granville, 17 Dec. 1824, quoted in Kaufmann, *British Policy*, p. 178. The intention was noted by others too. In 1843, the United States' chargé d'affaires in Brazil observed that British support for the independence of the Spanish and Portuguese colonies was 'for the purpose of making these the quasi colonies of Great Britain without the expense of their maintenance as such'. Hunte to Webster, 31 March 1843, quoted in Kinley J. Brauer, 'The United States and British Imperial Expansion, 1815–60', *Diplomatic History*, 12 (1988), pp. 23–4

15. Canning to A'Court, 31 Dec. 1823, quoted in Kaufmann, *British Policy*, p. 203. Bentham was fascinated by the changes taking place in Spanish America and by the prospects of realising a utilitarian utopia there. He maintained a weighty correspondence with leaders of the new states, notably Rivadavia and Bolívar, and supplied them with constitutions designed to have universal applicability. See Mirian Williford, *Jeremy Bentham on Spanish America* (Baton Rouge, La, 1980).

between the old, 'worn out' monarchies of continental Europe and the 'youthful and stirring' nations headed by the United States.[16]

Transplanting liberal principles proved to be more complicated than was originally supposed. Britain's hopes that a clutch of viable but also pliable monarchies would arise from the debris of the Iberian empires were quickly disappointed.[17] Brazil alone preserved a monarchical system, but it rested on slavery and the slave trade, which Britain was committed to abolish. Elsewhere, British liberalism had to make its way in the new republics, where democratic and populist sentiments also flourished. If eminent members of the first generation of South American leaders, notably Bolívar and O'Higgins, were dazzled by liberal principles, their successors were more inclined to draw on a *mélange* of ideas, using ingredients from France and the United States as well as from Britain, and were ready at times to capitalise on conservative reactions to liberalism.[18] Against the promise of new 'quasi-colonies' of European settlement, stood social realities which did not fit the template of the British political system. The societies which emerged from the struggles for independence possessed neither a solid urban middle class nor a progressive aristocracy, and their open frontiers encouraged a form of extreme democracy which soon began to throw up strong men, usually on horseback, whose purpose was to bring discipline to the unruly world of the gauchos.[19] None of this was quite what Canning had envisaged. Hobbes's wilderness was not easily made into Locke's garden.

Commercial progress was also disappointing. There was undoubtedly some promise and much enthusiasm during the first years of independence. Commercial treaties with Argentina in 1825 and Brazil in 1827 boosted British interests, and by 1850 Britain was firmly established as South America's leading trading partner.[20] But the

16. Canning to Frere, 8 Jan. 1825, quoted in ibid. p. 201.

17. Kaufmann, *British Policy*, p. 38.

18. See, for example, Rivadavia's experiments in Argentina in the 1820s, discussed by Ferns, *Britain and Argentina*, pp. 111–18, and for the transition from liberalism to conservatism Simon Collier, *Ideas and Politics of Chilean Independence, 1808–1833* (Cambridge, 1967).

19. On these subjects Ferns, *Britain and Argentina*, remains as fresh and perceptive as when it was first published in 1960. See especially pp. 84–6 and Chs. 7 and 10; also idem, 'Latin America and Industrial Capitalism – The First Phase', *Sociological Review*, Monograph No.11 (1967). The rise of Argentina's first important strong man is also well covered in John Lynch, *Argentine Dictator: Juan Manuel de Rosas, 1829–1852* (Oxford, 1981).

20. On the treaty with Argentina see Ferns, 'Latin America and Industrial Capitalism', pp. 13–17. The terms imposed on Brazil (which were more favourable to Britain) are described by Alan K. Manchester, *British Preëminence in Brazil: Its Rise and Decline. A Study in European Expansion* (Chapel Hill, NC, 1933), Ch. 8. British trade is dealt with by D.C.M. Platt, *Latin America and British Trade, 1806–1914* (1972).

volume of commerce remained small, partly because Britain's conversion to free trade was still incomplete, and partly because limitations of transport (and allied services) put much of the mainland beyond the reach of external influences.[21] In the republics, moreover, economic development was also hampered by the extreme social fluidity and continuing political uncertainty which characterised the years after independence. Consequently, the period was marked less by the penetration of capitalism than by checks to its advance, including in some instances a flight into self-sufficiency.[22]

A similar sequence of optimism and disillusion was experienced by British investors. The achievement of independence in the early 1820s encouraged a speculative boom which reached its peak in 1825 with the formation of the British Churning Company, whose alleged purpose was to export Scottish milkmaids to tend Argentine cows.[23] When the market began to trade in fantasies of this order, a crash was inevitable. It duly came in 1826, and was followed by widespread default, withdrawal and protracted debt negotiations.[24] Short-lived though it was, the investment boom provided some interesting anticipations of the future. It was, first of all, an early experiment in extending the British system of lending money to the state in the expectation that it would eventually be returned.[25] As such, it has to be seen in the context of the moves towards free trade in the 1820s and the beginnings of the diversification of British capital flows abroad. The boom also underlined the importance of the link between overseas investment and nation-building. Britain's interest in promoting stable and progressive governments in South America, as elsewhere, was financial as well as political. Since there could be no sovereign debt without sovereignty, political unification was a prerequisite of loans to foreign governments, and Britain's recognition of new states was crucial to their credit-rating.[26] The resulting mutual interest in government finance created

---

21. Platt, *Latin America and British Trade*, p. 37; François Crouzet, 'Angleterre-Brésil, 1697–1850: un siècle et demi d'échanges commerciaux', *Histoire, Economie et Société*, 2 (1990).

22. Abel and Lewis, *Latin America*, pp. 96–7; See also Platt, *Latin America and British Trade*, pp. 3–34, and the case study by William Paul McGreevey, *An Economic History of Colombia, 1845–1930* (Cambridge, 1971), which shows that economic change was very limited until the 1890s.

23. Kaufmann, *British Policy*, p. 180.

24. Frank G. Dawson, *The First Latin American Debt Crisis: The City of London and the 1822–25 Loan Bubble* (New Haven, Conn., 1990); C. Marichal, *A Century of Debt Crises in Latin America: From Independence to the Great Depression, 1820–1930* (Princeton, NJ, 1989), Ch. 2.

25. Ferns, *Britain and Argentina*, pp. 133–44.

26. Ibid. pp. 121, 314–21.

bonds between the representatives of foreign creditors and the leaders of new states which foreshadowed the relationship that was to develop more fully later on.[27]

It was in the second half of the century, following the growth of the international economy, that South America became, from the British point of view, a success story. During this period, the principal states developed classic export economies, shipping cereals, beef, coffee and minerals, and importing a range of manufactures, beginning with textiles and progressing to capital goods for railways and other public utilities.[28] As a result, Britain's total trade with Latin America experienced a threefold increase in value between 1865 and 1913.[29] Looked at from another angle, Latin America received about 10 per cent of Britain's exports (and re-exports) between 1850 and 1913, and accounted for about the same proportion of Britain's retained imports during the same period.[30] These shares were larger than those of any other continent or country within the empire, apart from India.

Even more striking was Latin America's role as a recipient of British capital.[31] In the case of publicly issued capital (for which reasonable measures exist), British holdings in Latin America rose from a modest £81m. in 1865 to a massive £1,180m. in 1913. The rate of growth of investment was much faster than in the case of commodity trade; it was also more significant in proportionate terms, for in 1913 Latin America accounted for approximately 25 per cent of all British publicly issued overseas assets, a figure which put the continent in the first rank of international debtors in the non-industrialised world. Given that privately placed direct investment was also growing rapidly, especially from the 1890s, it is evident that, on financial grounds alone, Latin America merits close attention in any study of Britain's overseas interests and policy in the nineteenth century.[32]

27. Marichal, *A Century of Debt*, pp. 34–5, 40–1. On the links between Barings and Rivadavia in the 1820s see Ferns, *Britain and Argentina*, pp. 134–44.

28. On these subjects see Platt, *Latin America and British Trade*.

29. B.R. Mitchell and P. Deane, *Abstract of British Historical Statistics* (Cambridge, 1962), pp. 321–3. As we have noted in other contexts, the quantitative data need to be used cautiously and as measures of broad tendencies only. Some of the main difficulties are discussed by D.C.M. Platt, 'Problems in the Interpretation of Foreign Trade Statistics Before 1914', *Jour. Latin Am. Stud.*, 3 (1977).

30. Mitchell and Deane, *Abstract*, pp. 321–3; Platt, *Latin America and British Trade*, pp. 251, 275–6.

31. See Irving Stone, 'British Direct and Portfolio Investment in Latin America Before 1914', *Jour. Econ. Hist.*, 37 (1977); and, for greater detail, idem, *The Composition and Distribution of British Investment in Latin America, 1865–1913* (1987).

32. Although Platt has produced revised and reduced figures for British investment overseas, he has also confirmed South America's importance as a recipient of British capital. See D.C.M. Platt, *Britain's Investment Overseas on the Eve of the First World War* (1986).

This mountain of British investment stood behind South America's economic development down to World War I. Cheap manufactured goods had been available since the 1820s, but sales to South America could not expand until her exports found a market. This constraint was overcome by investment in low-cost transport and credit facilities which, in turn, was encouraged by the adoption of free trade in the 1840s. Regular steamship services (and falling freight rates) brought a generation of specialised, competitive merchants to South America;[33] the first wave of joint-stock banks and insurance companies soon followed (stimulated, too, by the Companies Acts of 1858–62); and submarine cables, the latest aids to market perfection, were laid in the 1860s and 1870s.[34] Improvements in communication spread an awareness of new opportunities far beyond business circles and encouraged a swelling number of immigrants, mostly from Spain and Italy, whose mobility and vigour played a vital part in speeding urbanisation and in colonising South America's abundant land resources.[35]

Economic growth also gave decisive impetus to the development of the state. The expansion of exports raised yields from tariffs, provided the means of servicing foreign loans, and thus created an effective revenue basis for the exercise of centralised political authority. The rise of large estates and ranches, and the spread of urban business and professional employments, both consolidated new property rights and defined the principal political constituency in the republics. From this confluence of economic and institutional trends emerged the landed and urban elites who exercised power in the second half of the century. In matters of overseas business, external policy and cultural orientation, the elites became closely associated with the representatives of foreign interests whose financial support played a crucial role in sustaining the configuration of economic and political power in South America. The liberal hour, which Canning had so eagerly anticipated, had finally come.

However, the growth of new opportunities in South America also

---

33. Robert G. Albion, 'British Shipping and Latin America, 1806–1914', *Jour. Econ. Hist.*, 11 (1951); Robert Greenhill, 'Shipping, 1850–1914', in D.C.M. Platt, ed. *Business Imperialism, 1840–1930* (Oxford, 1977); Juan E. Oribe Stemmer, 'Freight Rates in the Trade Between Europe and South America, 1840–1914', *Jour. Latin Am. Stud.*, 21 (1989).

34. The pioneering study of British banking is David Joslin, *A Century of Banking in Latin America* (1963). The starting point for more recent studies is the important work of Charles Jones. See, for example, 'Commercial Banks and Mortgage Companies', in Platt, *Business Imperialism*, and 'Insurance Companies', in ibid.

35. Nicolás Sánchez-Albornoz, 'The Population of Latin America, 1850–1930', in Bethel, *Cambridge History of Latin America*, Vol. 4, Ch. 4.

attracted foreign competition, especially from the 1880s, and there followed a 'scramble' for influence in the continent which suggests comparisons with other parts of the world, though these have yet to be given serious consideration by historians of imperialism.[36] Admittedly, overt diplomatic confrontation was confined to the Venezuela boundary dispute, which threatened to become a major crisis in 1895 and again in 1902–3, and to the passing possibility of external involvement in the War of the Pacific (1879–83), though it is interesting to note that there were widespread fears in South America, especially at times of financial crisis in the 1890s, that Britain, the major creditor, might resort to formal intervention.[37] The principal manifestations of international rivalry were less visible, but no less important, and took the form of a struggle for control of trade and finance. The United States, continuing its slow southwards advance, attempted to capture Brazil's export trade.[38] Germany made a bid for informal influence by mounting an export drive consisting of manufactures, military aid, and settlers backed by the Deutsche Ueberseeische Bank (1886), which aimed at freeing German trade from its dependence on British finance.[39] France, capitalising on long-standing connections and republican sympathies, also tried to enlarge her share of trade and investment, particularly through the agency of the Crédit Mobilier and the Banque de Paris et des Pays Bas.[40]

Britain reacted vigorously to this new foreign challenge by tightening her grip on areas which were considered to be worth holding, very much as she did in the Ottoman Empire, China and Africa. Hence, attention was concentrated increasingly on the three most important countries, Argentina, Brazil and Chile, which, on the eve of World

36. This is a curious omission, given the importance attached by historians of imperialism to the debate on informal empire earlier in the century. There is room for a book synthesising existing case studies and setting them in a wider context.

37. For the Venezuelan crisis see the references in n.4. The point of departure for studies of the war between Chile and Peru is now William F. Sater, *Chile and the War of the Pacific* (Lincoln, Nebr., 1986). On South America's fear of intervention (a subject neglected by historians of imperialism) see Joseph Smith, *Illusions of Conflict: Anglo-American Diplomacy Toward Latin America, 1865–1896* (Pittsburgh, Pa, 1979), pp. 179, 186–7, 205–9.

38. Smith, *Illusions of Conflict*, pp. 118–21, 130–4, 143–55.

39. Ian L.D. Forbes, 'German Informal Imperialism in South America Before 1914', *Econ. Hist. Rev.*, 2nd ser. XXXI (1978); Warren Schiff, 'The Influence of the German Armed Forces and War Industry on Argentina, 1880–1914', *Hisp. Am. Hist. Rev.*, 52 (1972); Jürgen Schaefer, *Deutsche Militärhilfe an Südamerika: Militär-und Rüstungsinteressen in Argentinien, Bolivien, Chile vor 1914* (Düsseldorf, 1974) similarly emphasises the link between military aid and the growth of the munitions industry in Germany.

40. Andres M. Regalsky, 'Foreign Capital, Local Interests and Railway Development in Argentina: French Investments in Railways, 1900–1914', *Jour. Latin Am. Stud.*, 21 (1989).

War I, accounted for 85 per cent of Latin America's foreign trade and 69 per cent of all publicly issued British capital placed in the continent.[41] Diplomatic support for British interests was strengthened, though selectively and discreetly, and British firms pushed further into the economies of these countries by stepping up direct investment in utilities, export production, and manufacturing, and by securing banking business which previously had been considered to lie beyond the bounds of conservative practice.[42]

Although it is impossible in the present state of knowledge to reach precise conclusions about the outcome of this contest, the broad trends are reasonably clear. On the eve of World War I, Britain still dominated the export sectors of the three leading South America countries, but her share of overseas trade had fallen from the peaks reached in the third quarter of the nineteenth century, when foreign competition was limited, and she had virtually given up some of the smaller and more difficult markets. Even in the cases of Argentina and Brazil, Britain's share of the import trade had dropped from over 50 per cent in the middle of the century to 31 per cent and 25 per cent respectively in 1912, whereas Germany, advancing from an insignificant base, supplied 17 per cent of the goods imported into each of these markets.[43] Admittedly, data pointing to relative decline have to be seen in the context of very substantial increases in total trade; but it is possible, nevertheless, to link the evidence to theories which seek to explain industrial retardation in the late-Victorian era and, by extension, to use it to support the conventional view that Britain was a waning imperial power whose hardening arteries prevented her from keeping up with younger, fitter rivals.

By concentrating on commodity trade, however, this perspective neglects a vital consideration, namely that Britain's competitors were unable to dent her supremacy in finance and commercial services. In 1914, the City and sterling still dominated short-term trade finance and the market for long-term development capital. The City's discount rates were cheaper than those available elsewhere, and the London capital market was simply too big and too well organised to allow its

41. The figures relate to 1910 and 1913 respectively. See Platt, *Latin America and British Trade*, p. 276, and Stone, 'British Direct and Portfolio Investment', Table 2, p. 695. On the trend towards concentration see Platt, *Latin America and British Trade*, pp. 116–21, 276.
42. Smith, *Illusions of Conflict*, pp. 179, 196; Charles Jones, 'The State and Business Practice in Argentina, 1862–1914', in Abel and Lewis, *Latin America*, pp. 184–98.
43. Forbes, 'German Informal Imperialism', p. 398.

smaller and less experienced competitors to make much headway.[44] The principal British banks retained their leading positions in South America in both established and developing sectors of the economy;[45] British shipping stayed well ahead of its rivals in the carriage of South America's overseas trade.[46] The United States was able to move into Mexico and Central America, but made little progress further south before World War I.[47] Trade between Germany and South America also expanded, but much of it, too, depended on British finance.[48] Germany and France made modest inroads into Britain's share of the large and rapidly expanding long-term loan business, but their advance fell far short of expectations. Too often they were pushed into less enticing countries or riskier sectors of the economy, along with members of the City fringe.[49] Although British finance and commercial services continued to support Britain's share of exports to South America, they played an increasing role in promoting the exports of rival powers, as well as exports from the continent itself.[50] This development, the product of Britain's position as a mature creditor, was both a measure of the strength of Britain's financial sector and a recognition of the need to provide debtors with the means of meeting their obligations. It underlined, once again, the crucial importance of free trade in sustaining Britain's multilateral ties and generating the invisible earnings which had become such a vital entry in the balance of payments.

We may now reduce the scale of the enquiry to consider how Britain maintained her position in the three most important countries: Argentina, Brazil and Chile. This change of focus will supplement our

44. As German businessmen, among others, acknowledged. See Forbes, 'German Informal Imperialism', p. 393.

45. Marichal, *A Century of Debt*, p. 147, and (for a helpful guide to the main foreign banks) pp. 257–68; Jones, 'Commercial Banks', pp. 26–9, 37–9, 47, 52; idem, 'The State and Business Practice', pp. 184–98. Banking also remained highly profitable: see Joslin, *A Century of Banking*, pp. 108–11.

46. Platt, *Latin America and British Trade*, pp. 120–1; Greenhill, 'Shipping', p. 120.

47. Platt, *Latin America and British Trade*, pp. 277–8; Smith, *Illusions of Conflict*, pp. 45–6, 118, 140-1, 153, 166–7, 190.

48. See Holger Herwig's critical review of R. Fiebig-von Hase, *Lateinamerika als Konfliktherd der deutsch-amerikanischen Beziehungen, 1890–1903: vom Beginn der Panameri-kapolitik bis zur Venezuelakrise von 1902/3* (Göttingen, 1986), *Hisp. Am. Hist. Rev.*, 68 (1988), p. 400.

49. Platt, *Latin America and British Trade*, p. 120, and the illustration given by Regalsky, 'Foreign Capital', p. 452. On the speculators see W.R. Reader and J. Slinn, *A House in the City: Foster and Braithwaite, 1825–1975* (1980), pp. 70–9, and Harris G. Warren, 'The Golden Fleecing: the Paraguayan Loans of 1871 and 1872', *Journal of Inter-American Economic Affairs*, 26 (1972), pp. 11–13.

50. Joslin, *A Century of Banking*, p. 107; Platt, *Latin America and British Trade*, pp. 283–4, 293.

generalisations with a measure of disaggregation and add detail to our broad historical characterisation of the continent as a whole.[51]

ARGENTINA

It is evident from the commercial data alone that Britain's position in South America as a whole depended heavily on her ability to retain her stake in Argentina. By 1913, the republic was responsible for 42 per cent (a total of £23m.) of Britain's exports and re-exports to Latin America. Argentina's share of the import trade was even more striking, and in 1913 amounted to 58 per cent (£43m.) of the total entering Britain from Latin America, a figure which placed Argentina above any of the white-settled parts of the empire.[52] In 1913, too, Argentina accounted for no less than 41 per cent (£480m.) of all publicly issued capital directed to Latin America from Britain.[53] Free trade gave Argentina's wheat and beef entry to Britain; Argentina's relatively open economy provided a market for British manufactures. Although Argentina's industrial sector was beginning to increase its share of national output, import substitution had not proceeded very far by 1914, and the market for Britain's traditional staple, cotton goods, remained strong.[54] Admittedly, Britain did not enjoy the same advantages in Argentina as she did in Canada and Australia, where kinship ties strengthened consumer loyalty. In Argentina, where the majority of immigrants came from southern Europe, competition was bound to be fiercer;[55] as Britain's share of Argentina's foreign trade began to be squeezed, especially after 1900, a number of British firms

51. If space allowed, this exercise would be carried much further, though it is worth noting that even historians who specialise on South America have not yet fully colonised the area between high-level generalisations about the continent as a whole and low level studies of particular regions or countries. The acknowledged starting point for such an exercise is Fernando Henrique Cardoso and Enzo Faletto, *Dependence and Development in Latin America* (Berkeley, Calif., 1979). See also the suggestive contributions by Carlos F. Díaz Alejandro, 'Open Economy, Closed Polity?', *Millennium*, 10 (1981), and Ian Roxborough, 'Unity and Diversity in Latin American History', *Jour. Latin Am. Stud.*, 16 (1984).

52. Mitchell and Deane, *Abstract*, pp. 321–3.

53. Stone, 'British Direct and Portfolio Investment', Table 2, p. 695.

54. E. Gallo, 'Agrarian Expansion and Industrial Development in Argentina, 1880–1930', *St. Antony's Papers*, 22 (1970), p. 50. Roger Gravil, *The Anglo-Argentine Connection, 1900–1939* (Boulder, Colo., 1985), pp. 88–9.

55. The population of Argentina more than doubled (from 1.8 million to 4 million) between 1869 and 1895, principally as a result of immigration. Reber, *British Mercantile Houses*, p. 34.

turned to safer, imperial markets.[56] Nevertheless, in 1914 Britain's position in Argentina remained substantially intact because it rested on supports which newcomers could neither match nor overturn: British finance and commercial services, and the co-operation of the wealthy and politically powerful Anglo-Argentine elite in Buenos Aires.[57]

Commercial expansion brought considerable gains to both Britain and Argentina, though the precise relationship between private profits and social benefits is not easily determined. On the British side, the developing connection with Argentina provides a prime example of the extension abroad of the financial and service interests centred on London and the Home Counties, and of their (increasingly ambiguous) alliance with provincial export industries. Argentina's willing acceptance of British finance was symbolised by the appointment of Barings as bankers to the government in 1857 and by the settlement (with interest) in the same year of the defaulted Buenos Aires loan of 1824.[58] The resumption of foreign borrowing in the 1860s encouraged British merchants in Buenos Aires to begin to specialise in finance and in commercial services other than handling goods,[59] and it also influenced the moves which led to the formation of the London and River Plate Bank in 1862.[60] The Bank's investors were drawn initially from the ranks of City merchants and bankers, and subsequently from a wider circle encompassing London's 'professions and gentlemen'.[61] Their risk was well taken: the Bank was not only the first but also the most consistently profitable of the foreign commercial banks in Argentina.[62]

A representative, if unusually successful, example of these new interests was Charles Morrison (1817–1909), a City-based financier who became one of the wealthiest Englishmen of his generation, having a fortune of nearly £11m. at the time of his death, as well as

56. Platt, *Latin America and British Trade*, p. 166. Platt's study has now to be considered in the light of Gravil, *Anglo-Argentine Connection*, who takes a more critical view of the marketing performance of British firms. On the business community see Reber, *British Mercantile Houses*, Ch. 3.

57. On the relationship between exports of capital and exports of goods, see A.G. Ford, *The Gold Standard, 1880–1914: Britain and Argentina* (Oxford, 1962), S.B. Saul, *Studies in British Overseas Trade, 1870–1914* (Liverpool, 1960), pp. 72–95, and Gravil, *Anglo-Argentine Connection*, pp. 102–3.

58. Marichal, *A Century of Debt*, p. 92; D.C.M. Platt, 'Foreign Finance in Argentina for the First Half Century of Independence', *Jour. Latin Am. Stud.*, 15 (1983), pp. 32–3.

59. Reber, *British Mercantile Houses*, pp. 33, 58, 72, 123, 140–3.

60. Joslin, *A Century of Banking*, Ch. 3.

61. Ferns, *Britain and Argentina*, pp. 335–6; also Reber, *British Mercantile Houses*, pp. 120–22, 158.

62. Joslin, *A Century of Banking*, pp. 108–11.

extensive landed property.[63] Morrison and his business associates made their money through a mixture of overseas and home-based ventures, all of which were in the fields of banking, handling and communications (and none of which came very close to manufacturing or mining). Morrison began to focus on Argentina in the 1860s, when circumstances favoured new inflows of foreign capital. He acquired the Mercantile Bank of the River Plate in 1881, invested directly in a range of public utilities in the 1890s, and by 1900 controlled nearly 10 per cent of all British investment employed in Argentina. Evidently, the investment was profitable; but it was also principled. Morrison was a liberal idealist who viewed Argentina as a great democratic republic in the making, a new United States which would realise and renew the virtues of individualism, private property, and minimal government. He never turned to British officialdom for support in Argentina, but preferred, like Canning, to place his faith in the emergence of independent but culturally subservient satellites. In helping to fashion this destiny, Morrison also began to interfere, like his contemporaries in India and Africa, in the lives of those he sought to liberate.

The ability to borrow on a massive scale and to make repayment through exports of primary products became the basis of the power and prosperity of the 400 or so wealthy landed families who formed the Argentine elite, and also of their allies in banking and commerce.[64] General Rosas had tamed the gauchos in the 1830s and 1840s, but in doing so had increased the burden of taxation and decreased his popularity; his removal in 1852 symbolised a commitment to a pacific and outward-looking economic programme which aimed to raise revenues less painfully, through export expansion, and thus to minimise the risk of political discontent.[65] Having settled the defaulted debt of 1824, Argentina's new leaders used fresh foreign loans to complete the unification of the republic in the 1860s and to 'pacify' the Indians in the following decade. Both measures were crucial to improving Argentina's credit-rating and to expanding the land available for export production.[66] Thereafter, policy continued to favour agricultural exports rather than local industries: low duties were

---

63. Charles A. Jones, 'Great Capitalists and the Direction of British Overseas Investment in the late Nineteenth Century', *Bus. Hist.*, 22 (1980).

64. David Rock, *Politics in Argentina, 1890–1930: The Rise and Fall of Radicalism* (Cambridge, 1975), pp. 2–3; A. Ferrer, *The Argentine Economy* (Berkeley, Calif., 1967), p. 98.

65. Ferns, 'Latin America', pp. 18–21.

66. Ferns, *Britain and Argentina*, Chs. 10–11; idem, *Argentina* (1969), pp. 92–6; Platt, 'Foreign Finance in Argentina', pp. 32–3.

applied to external trade, internal tariffs were reduced or eliminated, and financial guarantees were given to a number of railway projects which aimed at enlarging the export sector.[67] These developments were accompanied by a process of cultural assimilation which steadily absorbed key members of the elite. Rosas, having left Argentina with British help, enjoyed a long retirement 'very like a country gentleman' on his Hampshire estate.[68] Under his successors, Britain's civilising mission reached its highest stage: Pellegrini, who was related to John Bright, was educated at Harrow; Roca and Juárez Celmán, among others, sent their children to English public schools and built English-style mansions on the pampas; a replica of Harrods, a shrine for elite consumers, was opened in Buenos Aires in 1912.[69]

The wisdom of adhering to a cosmopolitan policy based on free trade aroused opposition in both countries, particularly in the provinces, which resented the power of the centre and jibbed at the idea that the alliance between two privileged capital cities was in the best interests of society as a whole. As some manufacturers in the British Midlands became attracted to tariff reform, so leading figures in a number of 'secondary cities' in Argentina began to argue for a policy of indigenisation.[70] These reactions were undoubtedly significant in pointing the way towards future developments, but they made little impression on the status quo before 1914. Argentina's international commercial policy continued to be formulated in Buenos Aires, where differences between Argentine and British interests involved a questioning not so much of the relationship itself as of the distribution of the benefits.[71]

The central requirement of the commercial pact between Britain and Argentina was that sovereign debts should be honoured. Exceptional circumstances demanded flexibility, but the rule itself was not to be broken. Argentina's acceptance of this principle, first signified by

67. Donna J. Guy, 'Carlos Pellegrini and the Politics of Early Argentine Industrialization, 1873–1906', *Jour. Latin Am. Stud.*, ll (1979); idem, 'Dependency, the Credit Market, and Argentine Industrialization, 1860–1940', *Bus. Hist. Rev.*, 58 (1984); Colin M. Lewis, *British Railways in Argentina, 1857–1914: A Case Study of Foreign Investment* (1983), pp. 10–12.

68. Ferns, *Britain and Argentina*, pp. 217, 286.

69. Ibid. pp. 402–3, 423. Julio Roca was President from 1880 to 1886 and from 1898 to 1904; Miguel Celmán (his brother-in-law) from 1886 to 1890; and Carlos Pellegrini from 1890 to 1892. On Harrods see Gravil, *Anglo-Argentine Connection*, pp. 94–5.

70. On the provincial towns, see James Scobie, *Secondary Cities of Argentina: The Social History of Corrientes, Salta, and Mendoza, 1850–1910* (Stanford, Calif., 1988), which complements his *Buenos Aires: From Plaza to Suburb, 1870–1910* (Oxford, 1974).

71. Rock, *Politics in Argentina*, p. 7.

repaying the defaulted loan of 1824, was next tested by the world financial crisis of 1873, which trapped a number of primary-producing countries between fixed obligations and falling revenues. President Avellaneda immediately declared that Argentina would 'willingly suffer privations and even hunger' to maintain the international reputation and credit-rating of the national government, and he lost no time in introducing an austerity programme.[72] Both the declaration and the policy were welcomed by the City, which produced a vital short-term loan (advanced by Barings in 1875–6) enabling Argentina to continue to service its debts.[73]

The crisis of the mid–1870s also provides an insight into the way in which the central government clamped down on provincial discontent, when it was seen to threaten the national interest.[74] As Argentina's exports faltered in the world recession, doubts were raised about the stability of several local banks which had advanced money on the security of mortgages and other fixed assets in the province of Santa Fe. Anxious customers in the port of Rosario began to move deposits from the Banco National and the Provincial Bank of Santa Fe to the London and River Plate Bank, which had followed a more conservative policy in the years before the slump. The provincial government tried to halt the drain by forbidding the London and River Plate Bank to issue notes, by taxing its operations (but not those of its rivals) and by seizing its gold reserves. Britain's threats to use the navy to restore the Bank's property left both national and provincial governments unmoved. What persuaded Buenos Aires to act was partly the fact that the closure of the London and River Plate Bank had brought trade in Rosario to a stand-still, thus depriving the national government of customs revenue at a vital moment, but mainly the realisation that the dispute would severely damage Argentina's standing in the City. The matter was finally settled when the Argentine government made a loan to the Santa Fe authorities in exchange for an agreement that it would return the London and River Plate Bank's gold reserves and allow it to resume operations. What British naval power had failed to do, the implied threat of the withdrawal of financial aid in London had accomplished instead.

The Argentine elite was also quick to see where its interest lay in the more severe economic blizzard which blew up with the Baring Crisis

72. Marichal, *A Century of Debt*, p. 105.
73. Ibid. pp. 105–6.
74. For the episode which follows see Joslin, *A Century of Banking*, pp. 45–50; and Ferns, *Britain and Argentina*, pp. 381–4.

in 1890.[75] During the 1880s, when the financial problems of the previous decade had been overcome, British investors poured capital into Argentine government stocks, railways and utilities on an unprecedented scale. Since returns on investments in infrastructure were invariably delayed, there was a danger that Argentina would run into a development crisis if external obligations leaped too far ahead of export earnings. In 1890, when the cost of servicing the foreign debt had risen to 60 per cent of the value of Argentina's export earnings, and with export prices falling, the alarm bells began to ring. The fact that Argentina's economic policy had become increasingly detached from the discipline of the gold standard undoubtedly made matters worse. The initial response of Juárez Celmán's government (1886–90) was to appease domestic interests by allowing the peso to depreciate and by printing inconvertible paper money. Given that Argentina's external debts were payable mainly in gold or gold-backed currencies, this course of action, if pursued, would have led to default. However, to the extent that there was a crisis of management as well as of development, a heavy responsibility also lay with the expatriate banks, which entered too willingly into the cavalier spirit of the times.[76] Barings in particular had become caught up in what the *Bankers' Magazine* aptly called 'gaucho banking', and had taken exposed positions, partly in the belief that the boom had still some way to run and partly in response to growing competition from foreign banks.[77] In November 1890, Barings suddenly found themselves holding massive quantities of Argentine government bonds which the market no longer wanted. The Baring Crisis struck at the heart of the British financial system: if the unthinkable happened and Barings were made bankrupt, large segments of the City of London, including the Bank of England, might also be pulled down. In this way, Baring's imprudence tested the strength of the whole financial edifice which had been built in London in the course of the nineteenth century.[78]

From the British perspective, the solution to the crisis fell into two

75. A full account is given by Ferns, *Britain and Argentina*, pp. 102–20. See also his *Argentina*, pp. 94–114, 119, 124, and for a different perspective, based on local sources, John E. Hodge, 'Carlos Pellegrini and the Financial Crisis of 1890', *Hisp. Am. Hist. Rev.*, 50 (1970). A valuable recent appraisal is Marichal, *A Century of Debt*, Ch.14. The fundamental economic analysis remains A.G. Ford, 'Argentina and the Baring Crisis of 1890', *Oxford Economic Papers*, 8 (1956), and, for the wider context, idem, *The Gold Standard*.

76. Driven partly by foreign rivalries. See Charles Jones, 'Commercial Banks', pp. 37–9; and idem, 'The State and Business Practice in Argentina, 1862–1914', in Abel and Lewis, *Latin America, Economic Imperialism*, pp. 185–90.

77. Quoted in Marichal, *A Century of Debt*, p. 15l.

78. For reactions in London see pp. 153–8.

connected parts: one centred on keeping Barings afloat; the other depended on persuading Argentina to co-operate in paying its debts. Barings was saved by an impressive example of self-help when the joint-stock and private banks in the City formed a fighting fund of £17m., backed by the Bank of England and, unofficially, by the Treasury, to meet its most pressing obligations. Thus were the entrenched precepts of *laissez-faire* swiftly discarded in favour of rapid official intervention: the government simply could not allow one of the most prestigious merchant banks in the City to go into liquidation. The second step was more difficult and involved delicate negotiations to safeguard the interests of creditors without provoking a nationalist reaction, and with it the threat of repudiation. Although some senior employees of British banks made an unofficial and rather vague request for intervention at a moment when alarm turned to panic in 1891, the leading figures in the City and in Whitehall held consistently to the view that a satisfactory outcome would emerge from discussion rather than from coercion. Consequently, though Lord Salisbury was prepared to nudge the Argentines from time to time, he would not prejudice negotiations over the debt by appearing to threaten the use of force.[79] Argentina was not, in any sense, Egypt.

This strategy amounted to a vote of confidence in the Argentine elite. Even before the crisis broke, Juárez Celmán's administration had shown signs of conversion to fiscal rectitude by trying to cut public expenditure. Indeed, Celmán's tentative reforms were largely responsible for generating the opposition which led to his downfall in 1890. Pellegrini, his successor, moved swiftly to reassure foreign creditors. On hearing news of Baring's imminent collapse, he declared: 'rather than suspend service on the debt I would prefer to renounce the presidency',[80] and his economic programme was designed to 'scrape up every loose peso in the Republic in order to meet government costs and hasten the day when Argentina's obligations to its foreign creditors could again be met'.[81] *The Times* nodded approvingly: 'all the wisest Argentine citizens are anxious to secure the credit of their country, and they are setting about it in the proper way'.[82] The election of Sáenz Peña, the nominee of the landed interest, to replace Pellegrini in 1892 further strengthened the confidence of foreign creditors. Sáenz Peña's victory not only eliminated an opposition candidate who stood for a far less cooperative programme, but also brought to office Juan

79. Joslin, *A Century of Banking*, pp. 103–4; Ferns, *Britain and Argentina*, pp. 464–7.
80. Quoted in Marichal, *A Century of Debt*, p. 159.
81. Hodge, 'Carlos Pellegrini', p. 509, n.35.
82. 21 Aug. 1891. Quoted in Smith, *Illusions of Conflict*, p. 188.

Romero, who was regarded by the British Minister in Buenos Aires as being 'a sure guarantee towards a sound and honest administration of the Ministry of Finance.'[83]

When negotiations over the debt began, at the close of 1890, British interests were entrusted to a committee led by Lord Rothschild, whose immediate concern was to protect the value of the bonds held by Barings and other British investors.[84] The German and French banks were aware that their own claims took second place in this British design, but they were unable to shape the negotiations to suit their own interests. In essence, Rothschild devised what today would be called a rescheduling agreement: a limited advance was made to enable Argentina to meet her short-term liabilities and to postpone the resumption of full debt service for three years, thus avoiding default; in exchange, the Argentine government entered into an implicit agreement to adopt deflationary policies to bring the balance of payments into equilibrium. Rothschild's deal undoubtedly preserved Britain's financial standing and saved Baring's position in Argentina. The alternative, allowing substantial new borrowing, would have undercut the price of Baring's bonds and would also have given opportunities to foreign banks at a moment when the City was unwilling to make new loans to Argentina. By the same token, however, the transfer of funds was not large enough to refuel the Argentine economy, and the imposition of deflationary policies provoked an anti-British reaction which led to Pellegrini's fall in 1892.

A new settlement was reached in the following year.[85] As the immediate threat of default and liquidation receded, both sides were willing to take a longer view of the debt problem. Much of the initiative for the Romero Arrangement, as it was called, came from Argentina, though it is worth noting that British interests were represented by the reconstituted and revived firm of Barings, a fact which suggests that the City was ready to resume business as usual. Under the Romero Arrangement, Argentina was allowed to settle its outstanding external debts by making reduced interest payments for five years and by suspending payments on the sinking fund for a decade. By adjusting Argentina's repayments to suit her capacity,

83. Welby to Rosebery, 14 Sept. 1892. Quoted in Ferns, *Britain and Argentina*, p. 471.

84. Marichal, *A Century of Debt*, pp. 159–60.

85. A good account is in Marichal, *A Century of Debt*, pp. 159–70. Albert Fishlow, 'Lessons from the Past: Capital Markets During the Nineteenth Century', *International Organization*, 39 (1985), pp. 410–11, correctly stresses the part played by the revival of exports in the success of the Arreglo Romero.

Britain acknowledged the difficulties of the republic's economic situation; by assigning revenues to debt payments, and by pursuing cautious domestic fiscal and monetary policies, Romero's plan was reassuringly orthodox. The fact that the plan worked, however, owed much to the coincident revival of the export economy, which boosted foreign exchange earnings and government revenues. Good management and good luck enabled Argentina to resume full interest payments in 1897, one year ahead of schedule, and to return to the gold standard in 1899 after an absence of twenty years. Thus purged, and with her credit-worthiness restored, Argentina was ready to begin borrowing heavily again during the boom years which lasted to 1913.[86]

The wider consequence of the Baring settlement was to facilitate the penetration of the Argentine economy by British firms, thus giving impetus to a process which had been under way since the 1860s, when the large joint-stock banks began a financial advance which gave British companies a substantial stake in railways and public utilities, as well as in banking and insurance.[87] The Baring Crisis brought down the two large Argentine banks, the National and the Banco de la Provincia, and left the London and River Plate Bank in a virtually unassailable position. As the economy revived, the London and River Plate took the lion's share of renewed business, and was able to return consistently impressive profits down to 1914.[88] The crisis also put an end to Argentina's attempt to build a nationally owned rail network. The need to cut expenditure and generate income during the 1890s forced the Argentine government to 'privatise' much of the railway system by selling state companies to foreign, principally British, firms.[89] A review of the railway code in 1907 (the Mitre Law), produced a new set of favourable conditions for the further expansion

86. Succinct overviews of this period can be found in Tulio Halperin, 'The Argentine Export Economy: Intimations of Mortality, 1894–1930', and David Rock, 'The Argentine Economy: Some Salient Features', both in Guido di Tella and D.C.M. Platt, eds. *The Political Economy of Argentina, 1880–1946* (1986).

87. These developments have been traced in a series of important essays by Charles Jones: 'Commercial Banks' and 'Insurance Companies', in Platt, *Business Imperialism*; 'The State and Business Practice', in Abel and Lewis, *Latin America*; and 'Great Capitalists'. See also Reber, *British Mercantile Houses*, Ch. 4, and Joslin, *A Century of Banking*, Ch. 4. British purchases of public utilities after the Baring Crisis are dealt with by Linda and Charles Jones and Robert Greenhill, 'Public Utility Companies', in Platt, *Business Imperialism*.

88. Joslin, *A Century of Banking*, Chs. 6–7; Jones, 'Commercial Banks and Mortgage Companies'.

89. This was part of a deal, approved by the City, which ended government subsidies to a number of railway lines. See Lewis, *British Railways*, pp. 86–7, 118–20; and Marichal, *A Century of Debt*, pp. 168–9.

of the private rail network, and with it of British control.[90] Argentina's tariff policy was equally friendly to foreign business interests, and was aimed principally at collecting the revenues needed to fund the administration and to service external debts. From the 1890s onwards Argentina developed a sizeable surplus on her visible trade with Britain, and this was needed to meet obligations on her invisible and capital accounts. Preserving the openness of the economy was an essential element in the smooth flow of international payments, even though it limited the extent to which tariffs could be used to protect local industries.[91]

Argentina's almost automatic orthodoxy in financial matters after 1892 symbolised the recognition by the elite that its hold on power depended on the ability of both government and private firms to continue to raise funds in London. Alternative sources in Paris, Berlin and New York were tried but found wanting.[92] Had good relations with the City broken down, the Argentine government would have been forced to finance its development programme from domestic savings, a course which was so fraught with economic problems and political risks that it was scarcely contemplated, even by the country's emerging radical and socialist parties.[93] Britain's instincts, refined by decades of experience in appraising foreign debtors, proved correct: in the end, and despite attempts at deviation, Argentina played by the approved rules of financial orthodoxy. The expansionist years which followed the Baring Crisis delivered considerable rewards. They confirmed the dominance of the Anglophile elite in Argentina, underwrote the political stability of the republic, and softened criticism of the inequalities generated by the export sector. In Britain, the boom produced steady profits on secure investments for a sizeable comple-

90. Regalsky, 'Foreign Capital', pp. 447–52. Lewis, *British Railways*, pp. 193–6, underlines the wider significance of the Law in cementing relations between British investors and the Argentine government.

91. Guy, 'Carlos Pellegrini', and idem, 'Dependency'.

92. These efforts merely underlined the supremacy of British finance. See Ferns, *Britain and Argentina*, pp. 69, 108–9; Gravil, *Anglo-Argentine Connection*, pp. 24–7; Marichal, *A Century of Debt*, p. 161. After the failure of negotiations with the United States in 1892, the US Consul in Buenos Aires reported ruefully that the British were involved in 'everything, except politics, as intimately as though it were a British colony'. Quoted in Smith, *Illusions of Conflict*, p. 190.

93. Rock, *Politics*, Chs. 3–4. Indeed the rapidity of socio-economic change in Argentina began to provoke a conservative, anti-development reaction after 1900. See David Rock, 'Intellectual Precursors of Conservative Nationalism in Argentina, 1900–1927', *Hisp. Am. Hist. Rev.*, 67 (1989). Provincial resentment at foreign control undoubtedly found expression in disputes over the way in which railways and other public utilities were operated. But discontent was contained before 1914, partly at least because of the need to retain the confidence of the City.

ment of investors. The fact that British investment in Argentina financed an increasing volume of manufactured imports from rival industrial powers was a disappointment for the Midlands and the north of England which the Home Counties were well able to tolerate.[94]

BRAZIL

Brazil and Chile were in many respects very different from Argentina, as well as from each other: Brazil was Portuguese-speaking, and it was also a monarchical, slave-holding society for the greater part of the nineteenth century; Chile, though Spanish-speaking like Argentina, looked towards the Pacific instead of the Atlantic and depended on mining rather than on agriculture for its prosperity. Nevertheless, from the point of view of the present study, the interest of these countries lies in the fact that, despite their differences, they entered and participated in the international economy on broadly similar terms, which in both cases were drawn up principally by Britain.

In many ways, Brazil was Britain's most accommodating and most successful satellite in South America during the first half of the nineteenth century.[95] The weak monarchy, which owed its presence to British support, readily bent before Britain's demands by conceding a one-sided Commercial Treaty in 1827, and a congenial alliance emerged thereafter between an oligarchy of slave-holding sugar and coffee producers and British import-export merchants. Brazil also behaved as a model debtor, surviving the financial crisis of 1825 and, uniquely, continuing to service her foreign loans. Throughout this period, the government adhered to orthodox fiscal and monetary policies, retained its credit-worthiness, and had no difficulty in raising money in the City when loans to South America resumed in the 1850s.[96] It is scarcely surprising that Brazil has been referred to, during its first phase of independence, as being a virtual British protectorate.[97]

However, it has also been claimed that British influence declined in the second half of the century, as Brazil regained tariff autonomy after

94. On the growing divorce between British investment and British exports see Gravil, *Anglo-Argentine Connection*, pp. 95–104.

95. Manchester, *British Preëminence*. For the wider context see G. Clarence Smith, *The Third Portuguese Empire, 1825–1975: A Study in Economic Imperialism* (1985).

96. Marichal, *A Century of Debt*, pp. 34–5, 48–9, 55, 80.

97. Manchester, *British Preëminence*, p. 220. The definitive account of the institutional underpinnings of Brazil's dependence is Richard Graham, *Patronage and Politics in Nineteenth-Century Brazil* (Stanford, Calif., 1990).

1844, as Britain's share of commodity trade fell thereafter, and as her diplomatic standing suffered as a result of conflict over the abolition of the slave trade and the growing presence of the United States.[98] This argument is open to question. Replacing special commercial privileges with most-favoured-nation treatment was fully in line with Britain's move towards free trade and also generated goodwill in Brazil; Britain's performance with respect to commodity trade has to be set in the context of her increasing role as a supplier of capital;[99] the dispute over abolition, though serious, did not hamper Britain's position in the long run; and the United States was unable to upset British parmountcy before 1914. In fact, as we shall try to show, the expansion of finance and commercial services after 1850 both enlarged Britain's stake in Brazil and boosted her influence there.

Britain achieved in Brazil what she failed to bring about in Africa: the conversion of a slave-holding state to one capable of sustaining new and much expanded forms of 'legitimate' commerce on terms which were still consistent with the maintenance of sovereign independence. During the 1840s, Brazil found herself on the receiving end of Palmerston's renewed efforts to put down the slave trade and open new markets, and in 1851, after considerable opposition, the emperor agreed to implement measures which brought slave imports to an end.[100] Depriving the oligarchy of one of its main economic props was scarcely a popular act among privileged circles in Rio de Janeiro. At the same time, it made the Brazilian government even more dependent upon British support and ensured that it cooperated in maintaining an open commercial regime which was attractive to foreign firms and pursued orthodox fiscal and monetary policies which won the approval of the City.[101] Signs of the emergence of a new 'alliance for progress' quickly made their appearance. Rothschilds became official bankers to the Brazilian government in 1855, complementing the position of Barings in Argentina, and the London and Brazilian Bank was founded in 1862 by merchant-financiers in the City and in Rio to channel funds into the

98. See, for example, Nathaniel H. Leff, *Underdevelopment and Development in Brazil*, II (1982), Ch. 4, which develops the main theme of Manchester's study, *British Preëminence*.

99. As Manchester himself was careful to point out in *British Preëminence*, pp. vii–viii, 336, 341.

100. His decision was strongly influenced by the need to maintain Brazil's credit-rating in London in readiness for war with Argentina and Uruguay. See Graham, *Britain and the Onset of Modernisation*, pp. 162–9. For further references see Seymour Drescher, 'Brazilian Abolition in Historical Perspective', *Hisp. Am. Hist. Rev.*, 68 (1988), and Robert Levine, 'Turning On the Lights: Brazilian Slavery Reconsidered One Hundred Years After Abolition', *Latin Am. Research Rev.*, 24 (1989).

101. Joslin, *A Century of Banking*, pp. 62–71.

'modern' sector of the economy.[102] A flow of new loans (though still on a small scale) soon followed, first to refinance government debt and then to promote railway construction.[103] The country's excellent credit record and continuing good relations with Rothschilds paid its own dividend: when the world financial crisis struck South America in 1873, Rothschilds were able to place a large issue of Brazilian bonds on the London market which enabled the government to continue to service its external debts and thereby retain its stability.[104] Not surprisingly, differences between Britain and Brazil were settled informally and in the knowledge that 'adverse publicity' would 'injuriously affect' the standing of Brazil's credit in the London money market.[105]

During the period which followed the abolition of the slave trade, Brazilian elites, outside the diminishing band of slave-owners, imbibed liberal values with undiluted enthusiasm. Brazilian ministers in London were so Anglophile that Lord Salisbury even joked of one of them that he could speak no Portuguese.[106] Rio de Janeiro, like Buenos Aires, was strongly influenced by the values and style of London and Paris, and English (replacing French) became the preferred language of commerce.[107] Brazilian entrepreneurs, such as Andre Reboucas, had no doubts about the beneficial effects of foreign capital, 'which comes principally from London, which, thanks to the wisdom of the Anglo-Saxon race, is the treasury of the whole world'.[108] Politicians, too, became standard-bearers of British liberalism, absorbing its anti-democratic slant while also deploying arguments against royal absolutism first devised in seventeenth-century England. As the celebrated abolitionist, Joaquim Nabuco, put it: 'When I enter the Chamber [of Deputies] I am entirely under the influence of English liberalism, as if I were working under the orders of Gladstone. This is really a result of my political education: I am an English liberal . . . in the Brazilian Parliament'.[109]

If Britain's relations with Brazil were cordial to the point of warmth, they were also circumscribed by the relatively slow pace of economic development. The prohibition of imports of slaves had created a growing problem of labour supply which could not be met,

---

102. Ibid. pp. 64–5, 70–2.
103. Marichal, *A Century of Debt*, pp. 80, 92, 94–7.
104. Ibid. pp. 104–6.
105. F.O. memo. by Davidson, 25 Jan. 1888, FO 13/642. Quoted in Smith, *Illusions of Conflict*, p. 18.
106. Graham, *Britain and the Onset of Modernisation*, pp. 100–2.
107. Ibid. Ch. 4. See also Jeffrey D. Needell, *A Tropical Belle Epoque: Elite Culture and Society in Turn-of-the-Century Rio de Janeiro* (Cambridge, 1988).
108. Quoted (1883) in Graham, *Britain and the Onset of Modernisation*, p. 202.
109. Quoted (n.d.) in ibid. p. 263.

while the institution of slavery persisted, by free immigrant labour. In the 1870s and 1880s labour scarcity became the crucial bottleneck to export-led growth, and the failure of the aged emperor to introduce the necessary reforms undermined support for his government, especially among the new and increasingly important coffee-producers in the São Paulo region.[110] The abolition of slavery in 1888 came too late to save either the monarch or the monarchy; by then, discontent in influential civil and military circles had acquired too much momentum. The proclamation of the first republic in 1889, and the constitution introduced in 1891, confirmed the accession to power of a modernising but also conservative oligarchy, which, broadly speaking, represented the interests of the elites of São Paulo and Rio de Janeiro and (by devolving a degree of authority) the most prominent of their counterparts in the provinces.[111]

This considerable upheaval, far from signalling the decline of British influence, offered fresh opportunities to City and service interests. Despite its long association with the Brazilian monarchy, the City did not allow sentiment to extend to the point of backing a loser. British interests detached themselves from the *ancien régime*, supported the abolition of slavery, funded the transition to free labour, and (after an initial period of customary caution) favoured the creation of the Republic as being the best means of combining economic progress with political stability.[112] On this point agreement was mutual. The new rulers were particularly anxious to secure Britain's recognition of the Republic because, as the British ambassador noted, 'it is in London that they doubtless hope to raise further loans'.[113] Subsequently, they demonstrated the extent of their 'like-mindedness' by the resolute measures they took to maintain the open

110. See particularly Stanley J. Stein, *Vassouras: A Brazilian Coffee County, 1850–1900* (Cambridge, Mass., 1957), pp. 250–76, and Warren Dean, 'The Green Wave of Coffee: Beginnings of Tropical Agricultural Research in Brazil (1885–1900)', *Hisp. Am. Hist. Rev.*, 69 (1989).

111. Eugene W. Ridings, 'Class Sector Unity in an Export Economy: The Case of Nineteenth-Century Brazil', *Hisp. Am. Hist. Rev.*, 58 (1978), and idem, 'Business, Nationality and Dependency in Nineteenth-Century Brazil', *Jour. Latin Am. Stud.*, 14 (1982). For a fascinating study of the adaptations made by one of the 'great families' over four generations see Darrell E. Levi, *The Prados of São Paulo, Brazil: An Elite Family and Social Change, 1840–1930* (1987).

112. Graham, *The Onset of Modernisation*, pp. 172–85; Smith, *Illusions of Conflict*, pp. 169–80; R.F. Colson, 'European Investment and the Brazilian Boom, 1886–92: the Roots of Speculation', *Ibero-Amerikanisches Archiv*, 9 (1983); Marshall C. Eakins, 'Business Imperialism and British Enterprise in Brazil: The St. John d'el Rey Mining Company Limited, 1830–1960', *Hisp. Am. Hist. Rev.*, 66 (1986).

113. Wyndham to Salisbury, 24 July 1890, FO 13/666. Quoted in Smith, *Illusions of Conflict*, p. 162.

economy and to hold the confidence of foreign investors.[114] They were rewarded by the rapid expansion of the export sector, driven by flows of foreign capital, and by a sharp rise in living standards among elite groups in the years down to World War I.

Britain's share of Brazil's foreign trade continued to fall during this period. As far as the import trade was concerned, the decline was gradual rather than dramatic: Britain supplied about one-third of Brazil's imports during the last years of the monarchy, and her share dropped to about one-quarter (though of a much larger total) on the eve of World War I.[115] In the case of the export trade, the fall was much more pronounced: Britain's share dropped from 23 per cent to 13 per cent between 1880 and 1900 following the growth of coffee and rubber exports, which went increasingly to the United States.[116] But, as in the case of Argentina, trends in commodity trade provide an imperfect index of Britain's presence and influence. It was in Britain's interest as a mature creditor to encourage Brazil to find markets for her exports, wherever they might be, so that she could acquire the foreign exchange needed to service her debts, as well as to buy imports (including manufactures from Britain). And, as Brazil became a mature debtor, the proportion of export receipts devoted to debt service grew, while that spent on commodity imports declined. Moreover, the financing, shipping and insuring of Brazil's overseas trade remained overwhelmingly in British hands down to 1914, irrespective of its destination.[117] Above all, Britain continued to be responsible for the major share of the vastly expanded flows of foreign capital (portfolio and direct) which accompanied the creation of the Republic and continued down to the final boom on the eve of World War I.[118]

114. The United States tried to create a 'special relationship' with Brazil by negotiating a reciprocal trade treaty in 1891, but this was unsuccessful and was annulled in 1894. See Smith, *Illusions of Conflict*, pp. 143–53, 164–9.

115. Forbes, 'German Informal Imperialism', p. 398; Platt, *Latin America and British Trade*, pp. 98–9.

116. Leff, *Underdevelopment*, II, p. 85.

117. Platt, *Latin America and British Trade*, pp. 291–3; Greenhill, 'Shipping', in Platt, *Business Imperialism*, p. 120; Joslin, *A Century of Banking*, p. 110; Graham, *The Onset of Modernisation*, pp. 88–91, 94–7, 303.

118. Leff, *Underdevelopment*, Table 43, p. 77; Platt, *Latin America and British Trade*, pp. 286–93; Marichal, *A Century of Debt*, pp. 126–7. According to Peter Uwe Schliemann, *The Strategy of British and German Direct Investors in Brazil* (Farnborough, Hants. 1981), p. 99, Britain's share of foreign investment in Brazil fell from 78 per cent of the total in the period 1860–1902 to 53 per cent in the period 1903–13. However, we know from Stone, 'British Direct and Portfolio Investment', pp. 710–20, that the 11 per cent attributed by Schliemann to Canada for the latter period was in fact raised by the City, and Albert estimates that Britain's share was 62 per cent in 1914 (*South America*, p. 21).

As in the case of Argentina, British claims and Brazilian responses are well illustrated by the tests of conduct and policy imposed by financial crises, the most important of which occurred in 1898 and 1913.[119] Brazil escaped the wash created by the Baring Crisis, despite having borrowed heavily in the late 1880s, because her credit rating was supported by buoyant coffee prices. However, a fall in coffee prices from the mid–1890s combined with a depreciation of the *milreis* (a legacy of currency inflation during the early years of the Republic) presented the government with a considerable transfer problem.[120] The official response was entirely orthodox, if also unsuccessful. A deflationary programme was drawn up in 1894, but serious political disorder prevented it from being implemented. In 1895 the government used a loan of £7.2m., originally raised in London, to defend the exchange rate, and followed this in 1896 with large tariff increases and a credit squeeze. However, when coffee prices slumped further in 1896 and 1897 so did the *milreis*. In 1898 the service charge on Brazil's external debt accounted for half the federal budget, and the Republic faced a major balance of payments crisis. At this point, having failed to solve the problem by itself, the government was forced to turn to the City for assistance.

The Funding Loan of 1898 was very similar to the loan devised for Argentina in 1891, and was also arranged by Lord Rothschild. The Brazilian government was advanced £10m. over three years to cover its debt service, and was allowed to suspend amortisation payments until 1911. With the good news came the bad: in return, Brazil was obliged to impose severe deflationary measures and to pledge the whole of her receipts from customs duties to meet debt payments. Lord Rothschild, anticipating that the resolve of the recipients might weaken, took care to point out, in a manner which was unauthorised but managed to sound authoritative, that the alternative, repudiation, would involve not only 'the complete loss of the country's credit' but

119. Special mention must be made of the important contributions of Topik and Fritsch, which have made possible a reappraisal of the history of fiscal and monetary policy during this period. See Steven Topik, 'The Evolution of the Economic Role of the Brazilian State, 1889–1930', *Jour. Latin Am. Stud.*, 11 (1979); 'State Intervention in a Liberal Regime: Brazil, 1889–1930', *Hisp. Am. Hisp. Rev.*, 60 (1980); 'The State's Contribution to the Development of Brazil's Internal Economy, 1850–1930', *Hisp. Am. Hist. Rev.*, 65 (1985); *The Political Economy of the Brazilian State, 1889–1930* (Austin, Tex., 1987); and Winston Fritsch, *External Constraints on Economic Policy in Brazil, 1889–1930* (1988).

120. See Topik, 'The Evolution of the Economic Role', pp. 330-1; Fritsch, *External Constraints*, pp. 4–11; Graham, *The Onset of Modernisation*, pp. 103–5; and the illuminating essay by Jeffrey D. Needell, 'The *Revolta Contra Vacina* of 1904: the Revolt Against "Modernisation" in *Belle Epoque* Rio de Janeiro', *Hisp. Am. Hist. Rev.*, 67 (1987).

might also 'greatly affect Brazil's sovereignty, provoking complaints that could arrive at the extreme of foreign intervention'.[121] Brazil's President, Campos Sales (1898–1902), responding to both carrot and stick, duly administered the medicine: harsh deflationary policies were applied; the radical opposition to foreign influence was broken; coffee prices fortuitously recovered; the *milreis* rose; and debt payments were resumed on time.

The most important single consequence of the crisis of 1898 was to draw both government and creditors further into the economy. Brazilian governments adopted interventionist policies in order to have more effective means of maintaining a liberal trade regime – a paradox already worked out within the British empire by the Government of India; and foreign creditors collected additional gains from Brazil's indebtedness in much the same way as they did in Argentina and (in a somewhat different form) in China. Both trends were an indication of the central and expanding role of external finance in Brazil's economy and, indirectly, in the politics of the Republic too.

The priority attached to maintaining Brazil's credit-worthiness can clearly be seen in the measures taken by Rodrigues Alves, a 'conspicuous advocate of deflationary policies', who replaced Campos Sales as President in 1902.[122] Alves masterminded Brazil's return to the gold standard by reorganising the Banco da Republica (which became the Banco do Brasil in 1905) and by setting up a complementary body, the Treasury Conversion Office, in the following year.[123] The Banco do Brasil, which was under government control, had most of the powers of a central bank and was charged particularly with managing the exchange rate; the Conversion Office, as its name implies, issued notes against equivalent gold deposits in much the same way as the Currency Boards did in Britain's colonies.[124] The aim was to give greater stability to the exchange rate by holding it between fixed gold import and export points, and to provide an automatic adjustment for movements beyond these points by linking the balance of payments to the supply of money and credit in the domestic economy, ultimately by moving gold in and out of the country. These measures, it was hoped, would boost the confidence of foreign investors, maintain inflows of foreign capital, and enable Brazil to steer clear of financial crises of the magnitude which had

121. Quoted in Topik, 'The Evolution of the Economic Role', p. 331.
122. Fritsch, *External Constraints*, p. 10.
123. Argentina set up a similar Conversion Office in 1899 to maintain the stability of the peso. Joslin, *A Century of Banking*, p. 139.
124. Brazil's reserves, like Argentina's, were also held in London.

struck in 1898. The commercial banks, encouraged to operate freely in this congenial climate, made more than hay: the leading British concerns (the London and Brazilian and the London and River Plate) attracted business from local banks, which had suffered during the crisis of 1898 and in its aftermath, and by 1913 held about one-third of all deposits in the Brazilian banking system.[125]

Other important government initiatives taken during the period 1898–1914 can also be seen to have complemented the primary aim of supporting Brazil's international credit rating. The nationalisation of a number of railway lines in 1901, far from striking a blow at expatriate control, was favoured by foreign investors because it reduced the burden on the state budget caused by the need to provide private companies with subsidies.[126] The substantial tariff increases which occurred in 1895 and 1906 were imposed principally for revenue purposes, not as concessions to local manufacturers, and were viewed by investors as being necessary for budgetary stability. Any protectionist effects were secondary; and if protection harmed some of Britain's manufactured exports, it also created opportunities for British financiers and entrepreneurs who were prepared to accept the risks of direct investment.[127] Finally, it is now clear that even the scheme devised in 1906 to stabilise coffee prices was aimed mainly at reassuring external creditors that funds would be available for debt service.[128] The initial plan favoured coffee producers, but it was condemned by Lord Rothschild, among others, as being 'an artificial expedient', and quickly withdrawn.[129] The plan eventually approved by Congress fell well short of the demands of producers, and also had to be backed by foreign loans, which the City obligingly supplied. In this way, Brazil lost control over its coffee sales, which in 1908 passed to a committee based in London (and headed by Baron Schroder). A measure of the London committee's success in determining coffee prices is that it finally provoked the United States into taking anti-trust proceedings in 1912.

Despite its exemplary fiscal and monetary policies, Brazil experienced a second major financial crisis in 1913, when swelling debt commitments, encouraged by a decade of export expansion, inter-

125. And over one-quarter in Argentina and Chile. Joslin, *A Century of Banking*, p. 110.
126. Topik, 'The Evolution of the Economic Role', pp. 335–7. Other lines were 'privatised', as in Argentina, to raise capital and to economise on running costs.
127. Graham, *The Onset of Modernisation*, pp. 110-11 and Ch. 5.
128. Fritsch, *Economic Constraints*, Ch. 2.; Topik, 'The Evolution of the Economic Role', pp. 330–4;
129. Quoted in Fritsch, *Economic Constraints*, p. 14.

sected with falling export proceeds.[130] When foreign creditors took fright in 1912, Brazil was unable to attract fresh capital from abroad, despite her good record and continuing adherence to orthodox policies. A financial mission sent by Rothschilds in 1913 eventually raised a large loan of £20m. from an international consortium. But the conditions were as severe as those imposed in 1898, and even went beyond them in demanding direct control of important instruments of Brazilian policy. These requirements were reinforced by the Foreign Office, which instructed the British Legation in Rio de Janeiro to 'press the Brazilian Government to meet outstanding British claims out of the proposed new loan and to point out that a continued failure to settle is likely seriously to impair Brazilian credit in England'.[131] The Brazilian government wriggled but could not escape, and finally accepted the terms offered. In the event, the agreement did not become operative; but it was the outbreak of war, not the decline of imperial energies, that saved Brazil from greater subjection to foreign control.

CHILE

A similar story of British dominance can be told in the case of Chile. The period after independence in 1818 was marked by a push for export growth, and by the emergence of an oligarchy which depended on international trade for its affluence and power.[132] In this process the British, the master craftsmen of nation-building, were ever at hand, supplying the principles of political economy, the international trade connections, and the loans which helped to shape the rentier mentality and aristocratic authoritarianism of Chile's almost gentlemanly elite, the appropriately named Bigwhigs. After a slow start, as elsewhere in South America, the economy entered a period of more rapid growth from the middle of the century, as a result of the shift to free trade and increased demand for Chile's principal exports, first copper and silver, and then nitrates. British merchants handled most of Chile's imports and exports, British shipping carried the trade,

130. Ibid. pp. 28–31.
131. Robertson to Grey, 9 July 1914, FO 371/1916. Quoted in Fritsch, *Economic Constraints*, pp. 218–19.
132. Thomas F. O'Brien, *The Nitrate Industry and Chile's Crucial Transition, 1870–1891* (1982), Ch. 1; Luis Ortega, 'Economic Policy and Growth in Chile from Independence to the War of the Pacific', in Abel and Lewis, *Latin America*.

British banks financed both commerce and transport, and the City dominated the expanding government loan business.[133] The noted Chilean historian and publicist, Benjamin Mackenna, observed in 1880 that

> There does not exist in the whole globe a country whose prosperity or adversity has a more direct influence as regards Chile than that which affects the welfare of the vast Empire of Great Britain, the Modern Rome.[134]

Mackenna gave particular emphasis to the role of British capital, and commented with some pride that the republic's debts were repaid with 'English punctuality'.[135] A visitor from the United States put the matter rather more tersely: 'this city', he said of Valparaiso in 1885, 'is nothing more than an English colony',[136]

The extent to which Chile's fortunes, indeed her very existence, had become bound up with the international economy was demonstrated dramatically during the 1870s, which began with a trade depression and ended in warfare.[137] Although Chile escaped the immediate consequences of the global financial crisis of 1873, export prices fell and the debt burden rose as the 1870s advanced, causing serious hardship and generating opposition to the ruling oligarchy's resolutely orthodox economic policies. By the close of the decade, the financial situation had reached a critical stage: in 1877 debt service absorbed 44 per cent of public expenditure, and in the following year Chile's reserves dropped to such a low point that the government was forced to suspend convertibility and raise import tariffs.[138] The Minister of Finance tried to reassure Britain of Chile's continuing commitment to 'the liberal principles which form the basis of our customs system', but the City feared that default was imminent and

---

133. Rothschilds became official bankers to the Chilean government, as they did in Brazil. The role of British merchants is discussed by John Mayo, *British Merchants and Chilean Development, 1851–1886* (Boulder, Colo., 1987), Chs. 1–5. See also idem, 'Before the Nitrate Era: British Commission Houses and the Chilean Economy, 1851–80', *Jour. Latin Am. Stud.*, 11 (1979), and Thomas F. O'Brien, 'The Antofagasta Company: A Case Study of Peripheral Imperialism', *Hisp. Am. Hist. Rev.*, 60 (1980), (and the debate in ibid. pp. 676–84). Valuable information can also be found in William M. Mathew, *The House of Gibbs and the Peruvian Guano Monopoly* (1981).

134. Quoted in Mayo, *British Merchants*, p. 236.

135. ibid.

136. ibid.

137. On these events, see William F. Sater, 'Chile and the World Depression of the 1870s', *Jour. Latin Am. Stud.*,5 (1979); idem, *Chile and the War*; O'Brien, *The Nitrate Industry*, Chs. 2–3; and Luis Ortega, 'Nitrates, Chilean Entrepreneurs and the Origins of the War of the Pacific', *Jour. Latin Am. Stud.*, 16 (1984).

138. Ortega, 'Economic Policy', p. 159.

refused to bail out the government by issuing a new loan.[139] After a brief interlude of fantasy, occupied by a memorable scheme for turning copper into gold, the government faced up to a hard choice: it could either implement internal reforms, which meant imposing income tax and capital gains taxes on the wealthy, or it could gamble on an external solution to its domestic problems. Predictably, perhaps, it chose the latter.

The War of the Pacific, which began in 1879, was a struggle between Chile on the one side and Bolivia and Peru on the other for control of rich nitrate and guano deposits in the provinces of Atacama and Tarapacá.[140] Although Atacama belonged to Bolivia and Tarapacá to Peru, Chile had invested heavily in both, and all three countries viewed the resources of these provinces as providing a solution to their desperate financial problems. Domestic impulses were greatly complicated by external involvement. British investors in Chile stood to gain from a Chilean victory; but British creditors in Peru, struggling to salvage something from that country's massive default in 1876, were concerned to protect their assets there. In addition, British policy had to take account of the French presence, as a creditor in Peru and as a power with wider ambitions on the Pacific coast, and of opposition from the United States to any further extension of European influence in South America. Given these complex elements of causation and momentum, the claim that the conflict was 'an English war' provoked by a conspiracy of financial interests is now seen to be far too crude.[141] What can be said is that, once the war was underway, Britain's antennae searched for a solution which protected her financial interests in both Chile and Peru. Early signs of Chile's success led in 1880 to an informal agreement whereby Chile would look after the claims of British creditors in Tarapacá in exchange for Britain's benign neutrality in the conflict. As a result, Chile also secured the active backing of bondholders in London as well as support locally from British firms which were likely to benefit from an extension of Chile's borders.[142]

---

139. Quoted in ibid. p. 164.

140. The standard account is now Sater, *Chile and the War*.

141. This contemporary claim (made especially by the United States) is evaluated in V.G. Kiernan, 'Foreign Interests and the War of the Pacific', *Hisp. Am. Hist. Rev.*, 35 (1955).

142. The Peruvian debt was a major issue in its own right which cannot be covered in the space available here. The authoritative study is by Rory Miller, 'The Making of the Grace Contract: British Bondholders and the Peruvian Government, 1885–1890', *Jour. Latin Am. Stud.* 8 (1976). See also idem, 'British Firms and the Peruvian Government, 1885–1930', in Platt, *Business Imperialism*, and 'The Grace Contract, the

British policy paid dividends. When the war ended, with Chile's victory in 1883, the nitrate provinces were delivered into Chilean hands. Thereafter, Chile's revenues grew rapidly, the position of the ruling elite was re-established, and her policy of co-operation with foreign interests was confirmed and extended. But Chile had to share her triumph by fulfilling her bargain with Britain. Consequently, the newly conquered Peruvian nitrate fields were returned to private foreign ownership, a move which placated the bond-holders even if it did not solve all their problems.[143] But, as the Chilean government realised, repudiating their claims would have seriously damaged the country's credit-rating in London.[144] Moreover, revenue considerations, and the urgent need to service the external debt, made concessions to foreign mining companies imperative. The imposition of a uniform tax on nitrate exports eliminated most of the small Chilean firms and enabled expatriate companies to dominate the industry. By 1890, Britain owned 69 per cent of the capital employed in the nitrate industry and took 80 per cent of Chile's exports.[145] Britain's financial and cultural dominance had been consolidated, French ambitions had been frustrated, and Washington's fears of the spread of London's influence had been realised.

Among those who did well out of the war was John North, a British engineer turned entrepreneur whose shrewd investment in the Tarapacá mines enabled him to build up a syndicate which in 1890 accounted for about 68 per cent of the authorised capital of all British firms engaged in the nitrate industry.[146] North's entrepreneurship was

---

Peruvian Corporation and Peruvian History', *Ibero Amerikanisches Archiv*, 9 (1983). Miller shows that the settlement finally reached in 1890 involved considerable intervention by the Foreign Office, and was made possible on the Peruvian side by the realisation that future economic development depended on restoring credit-worthiness in London.

143. Chile's Minister of Finance was well aware that the bond-holders had been influential in Europe in 'preventing the Peruvians from acquiring war materials and creating for us a beneficent atmosphere in the opinion of these peoples'. Malte to Sotomayor, 6 Feb. 1880. Quoted in O'Brien, *The Nitrate Industry*, p. 51.

144. O'Brien, *The Nitrate Industry*, pp. 52–5.

145. Joseph R. Brown, 'The Frustration of Chile's Nitrate Imperialism', *Pacific. Hist. Rev.*, 32 (1963), p. 389; Thomas F. O'Brien, 'Chilean Elites and Foreign Investors: Chilean Nitrate Policy, 1880–82', *Jour. Latin Am. Stud.*, 11 (1979); Smith, *Illusions of Conflict*, p. 192.

146. On North see Harold Blakemore, *British Nitrates and Chilean Politics, 1886–1896: Balmaceda and North* (1974), pp. 38–42; O'Brien, *The Nitrate Industry*, pp. 64–77, 113–22; Robert Greenhill, 'The Nitrate and Iodine Trades, 1880–1914', in Platt, *Business Imperialism*, pp. 236–8; and Monteon, 'The British in the Atacama Desert', pp. 127–33. The estimate of North's holding is taken from O'Brien, *The Nitrate Industry*, p. 119.

in the cavalier style appropriate to a man who bestowed upon himself the honorary title of colonel. But he mastered the intricacies of the stock exchange as well as the challenges of the frontier, cultivated the friendship of Nathan Rothschild and Randolph Churchill, and stoked the excitement which produced the mania for shares in nitrate companies in the late 1880s. Yet North, like Rhodes, was too much of a 'mushroom gentleman' to acquire significant influence in top circles in the City. His business interests intersected with those of senior members of the merchant-banking fraternity at certain points, which was significant in itself, but he was never fully accepted in 'society', despite the lavish hospitality he offered visitors to his estate in Kent in an effort to earn the spurs to match his assumed rank.

North's share-dealings made him, briefly, a controversial figure in London when the nitrate bubble burst in 1891, while allegations that he was behind the conspiracy which overthrew President Balmaceda in the same year brought him permanent notoriety in Chile. Both episodes have their importance. But the interest of the second lies less in determining North's exact role, than in demonstrating the extent to which the fortunes of the political elite, and the shape of politics itself, had become bound up with the development of the nitrate industry.[147] By the close of the 1880s, North had extended his activities into railways and banking, and was using his control of freight rates to increase his dominance of the mining industry, a strategy that was given added urgency by the collapse of nitrate prices in 1890. At this point, however, North's plans ran into President Balmaceda's attempts to increase Chile's share of the profits from nitrates and to redirect them away from Congress and towards his own supporters. These conflicts led to civil war in 1891, and to the overthrow of Balmaceda later in the same year. There is no proof that North had a direct part in the president's downfall, though it is clear that he favoured Congress, and that his sympathies were shared by British business and the navy, which 'rendered material assistance to the opposition and committed many breaches of neutrality'.[148]

147. The most detailed attempt to demonstrate North's involvement is by Osgood Hardy, 'British Nitrates and the Balmaceda Revolution', *Pacific Hist. Rev.*, 17 (1948). Blakemore, *British Nitrates*, argues that the war was essentially a matter of internal politics. O'Brien, *The Nitrate Industry*, presents an excellent synthesis of external and internal causes. See also Michael Monteon, *Chile in the Nitrate Era: The Evolution of Economic Dependence, 1880–1930* (Madison, Wis., 1982), pp. 41–7. The earlier literature is assessed by Harold Blakemore, 'The Chilean Revolution of 1891 and its Historiography', *Hisp. Am. Hist. Rev.*, 45 (1965). It is curious that obvious comparisons and contrasts with events in South Africa have yet to be explored.

148. Kennedy to Sanderson, 15 Sept. 1891, FO 16/266. Quoted in Smith, *Illusions of Conflict*, p. 196.

The establishment of parliamentary government in 1892 returned to power members of the elite who held a more tolerant view of foreign enterprise. British investment rose rapidly during the 1890s, British firms increased their involvement in nitrate mining, and British banks retained their supremacy.[149] Nevertheless, North was unable to impose himself on Chile, as, with weighty political associates, the mine-owners were able to do in the Transvaal. The rewards of victory were shared, after 1892 as after 1883. The new government frustrated North's planned railway monopoly, and the cartels he organised in the nitrate industry were not very successful. In any case, in the years following North's death in 1896, Chilean capital began to play a larger part in the industry, and the government itself became more sympathetic to the idea of rigging the market, if possible. In fact, the Chilean elite gained greatly from Britain's control of the nitrate industry, which produced 43 per cent of all government revenues between 1880 and 1920, allowed foreign borrowing to take place, and enabled debt service to be sustained without raising internal taxes.[150] But this does not mean that the economy and the elite were independent of Britain. As in the cases of Argentina and Brazil, the maintenance of affluence and authority in Chile still depended ultimately on fulfilling a set of policy requirements which met the needs of the senior partner and external creditor.

THE SPREAD OF INFORMAL INFLUENCE

South America had its place, with other continents, in Britain's grand design for a creating a developing yet stable world system after 1815. But results failed to match intentions, and the post-imperial order

149. O'Brien, *The Nitrate Industry*, p. 144; Joslin, *A Century of Banking*, pp. 110, 185. The rise to prominence of British banks and insurance companies was also bound up with the development of the nitrate industry. See Mayo, *British Merchants*, pp. 201–7. Britain's share of Chile's import trade began to slip after the turn of the century, as Germany, in particular, made her presence felt. But (as we have argued for Argentina and Brazil) this trend was related to the expansion of Britain's role as a creditor and is not to be seen as a sign of a general decline in her influence.

150. Joseph R. Brown, 'Nitrate Crises, Combinations and the Chilean Government in the Nitrate Age', *Hisp. Am. Hist. Rev.*, 43 (1963); Greenhill, 'The Nitrate and Iodine Trades'; Brown, 'The Frustration of Chile's Nitrate Imperialism', p. 396. Moreover, after a brief stay on the gold standard (1895–8), Chile reverted to inconvertible paper. This can be read as an indulgence for exporters and as a lapse from the City's ideal of the perfect debtor, but it did not alter the fact that debts still had to be serviced promptly.

was not transformed into a new empire of informal sway. South America was indeed free but she was not, in the mid-Victorian period, English. From 1850, however, the position began to change, and after 1875 the extension of finance and commercial services gave Britain a much more visible and effective presence in the republics.

The expansion of British interests was part cause and part consequence of a hitherto underestimated 'scramble' for South America which merits comparison with the rivalry of the great powers for control of Africa, the Ottoman Empire and China during the same period. As elsewhere, Britain's role was not merely passive and reactive. She was creating a position not simply defending one, and she took vigorous, if largely unofficial, action to promote her interests. The main impulses for expansion came from the centre, specifically from the rapid growth of foreign lending and the subsequent integration of the republics into recurrent cycles of development debt. Crises on the periphery were basically symptoms of this evolution, even though (as in the case of North's activities in Chile) they often assumed a semi-detached character. This is not to suggest that British policy was determined by bond-holders or mine-owners; it is rather to recognise the extent to which economic policy and political alliances in the republics had become shaped by external considerations, and above all by the need to retain the confidence of British creditors. But it is also true, in South America as in other parts of the world, that the Foreign Office departed increasingly from its non-interventionist ideals, not just in response to new foreign rivals, but in acknowledgement of the fact that Britain's economic stake in South America had reached a size which compelled attention and sometimes action too.

There was, of course, no formal partition of South America. Considerations of cost, logistics and diplomacy were always on hand to restrain the major powers at moments of crisis. Far more important, however, was the fact that official political intervention was rarely demanded by economic interests; nor was it seen by the Foreign Office to be appropriate. The Latin American republics were treated as countries of white settlement, rather like the Dominions, and were regarded as having much greater potential both for economic development and for 'responsible' government than the 'oriental' societies which caused Lord Salisbury to furrow his brow and harden his heart. Consequently, as we have seen, British strategy relied on self-policing and self-regulating mechanisms, and especially on the disciplines imposed on South American governments by their need to remain credit-worthy. This does not mean that the recipients were conditioned by ideological training to accept a subservient role. The elites of Argentina, Brazil and Chile were responsible for their own decisions and they acted in what they took to be their own interests. Cultural imperialism did not produce economic dependence. At the same time, the emergence of the remarkable degree of 'like-mindedness' among the principal creditors and debtors greatly assisted the process of understanding and conforming to the rules of the game. When the rules were broken, the penalties were severe: Peru was ostracised by the City following its bad default of 1876, and its subsequent economic development was seriously hampered by its inability to borrow abroad; elsewhere, financial crises were met by the standard penalties of retrenchment and deflation which were imposed, directly or indirectly, by external creditors.

Britain emerged from the 'scramble' with her position strengthened in a number of key areas. The fact that she reduced her presence in several of the smaller republics was less a sign of weakness or failing purpose than a recognition of the much greater potential of Argentina, Brazil and Chile. And evidence of Britain's declining share of commodity trade has to be set in the context of her expanding role as South America's chief foreign lender. Successive debt crises gave Britain more, not less, influence in the three major republics. Private investors moved further into the economy through purchases of public utilities and banks, and by investing directly in manufacturing and processing activities, while in the public sector fiscal and monetary priorities were set by borrowing requirements which were linked to the needs of open, export economies. Consequently, public expenditure, tariffs and the exchange rate, as well as the supply of money and credit to the domestic economy, were all profoundly affected by foreign influences.[151] Moreover, as we have seen, both the expansion of the public sector and the purpose of state intervention were significantly shaped by external considerations, as, beyond this, were the structure of elite politics and the ebb and flow of party rivalries.[152]

This degree of penetration, direct and indirect, must surely be seen as infringing the sovereignty of the recipients, even as it boosted their incomes. If Gallagher and Robinson overestimated the extent of Britain's informal empire in the mid-Victorian era, Platt has underes-

151. Charles Jones, '"Business Imperialism" and Argentina, 1875–1900: a Theoretical Note', *Jour. Latin Am. Stud.*, 12 (1980).

152. This is well brought out by Fritsch's discussion of the relationship between the balance of payments, the exchange rate, and interest-group politics in Brazil (*External Constraints*, Chs. 1–2).

timated its size during the Edwardian period. The argument that the republics entered the international economy freely, profited from overseas commerce, and gained from competition among the expatriate firms does not prove that the relationship between Britain and South America was simply one of interdependence based on mutual business interests. It is misleading to suppose, for example, that Argentina's growing balance of trade surplus after 1900, and the weakening position of Britain's exports, are evidence that the republic was beginning to free itself from economic dependence. When returns on investments and other invisibles are included, Britain still had a comfortable surplus on the balance of payments (current account) in 1913. Moreover, as we argued earlier, the appearance of a trade deficit with the republics was a necessary function of Britain's development as a mature creditor: without open access to the British market, South American exporters could not have earned enough sterling to pay their debts, to maintain their credit-worthiness, and hence to support the free trade–foreign investment syndrome in Britain. It is an ironic comment on this system, as it had evolved in the late nineteenth century, that, had Britain's manufactured exports become more competitive, they might have damaged London's position at the centre of the international economy by reducing the ability of borrowers, like Argentina, to pay their debts. Similarly, the fact that, in times of boom, the republics often ran economic policies which would have horrified Gladstone is not to be read as evidence of growing economic freedom. In periods of prosperity, inflationary policies were no obstacle to debt repayment; in periods of depression they were, and conformity to norms which satisfied London was both expected and usually achieved.

The argument that relations, being interdependent, were approximately equal is also hard to sustain.[153] British financiers, like Morrison, thought of Argentina as being subservient, and even Anglophile leaders, like Pellegrini, feared British intervention at times of crisis. It has yet to be suggested that South American entrepreneurs saw Britain as a satellite or that Queen Victoria's ministers were much exercised by the prospect of Argentine troops occupying the City. Interdependence is clearly consistent with wide variations in degrees of independence and dependence. Britain invested heavily in the United States in the nineteenth century but contributed only a very small percentage of the republic's total capital formation, and conse-

153. We disagree here with Ferns (*Britain and Argentina*, pp. 487–9) as well as with Platt.

quently had less influence there than in countries such as Australia, Canada and Argentina, which relied more heavily on British finance. Approximately half of Argentina's fixed capital assets (excluding land) were foreign-owned in 1913, principally by the British,[154] whereas hardly any British assets were held by Argentine investors. Argentina also depended on Britain for about 28 per cent of her foreign trade in 1913, while Britain conducted less than 5 per cent of her overseas trade with Argentina.[155]

None of this is to be read as an attempt to resurrect crude versions of the dependency thesis; as pointed out earlier, the fact of dependence ought to be separated from a consideration of its consequences for economic development and social welfare. But, if the historian's task is to explain the structures of the past, then the evolution of Argentina, Brazil and Chile since independence cannot be understood without reference to the pervasive effects of British influence in the period down to 1914. Clearly, Britain's power was not felt in South America as it was in India and Africa, but Britain's influence was exercised in much the same way as it was in Canada and Australia.[156] Argentina was shortly to be thought of as an 'honorary dominion', and that is probably as accurate a description as the imperfect terms available to historians of imperialism will allow.

154. Ferrer, *The Argentine Economy*, p. 103.
155. Platt, *Latin America and British Trade*, p. 111.
156. For some illuminating comparisons, drawn principally from the perspective of economic development problems, see Barrie Dyster, 'Argentine and Australian Development Compared', *Past and Present*, 84 (1979); D.C.M. Platt and Guido di Tella, eds. *Argentina, Australia and Canada: Studies in Comparative Development, 1870–1965* (1985); and Carl E. Solberg, *The Prairies and the Pampas: Agrarian Policy in Canada and Argentina, 1880–1930* (Stanford, Calif., 1987).

CHAPTER TEN

'Meeting her Obligations to her English Creditors': India, 1858–1914[1]

When Disraeli dubbed India a 'jewel in the Crown of England', both the example and its symbolism were well chosen, as the subsequent popularity of the phrase amply confirms.[2] In the mid-nineteenth century, even observers of the political scene who were generally indifferent to empire could scarcely overlook Britain's connections with India. The sub-continent had already acquired the special value that attaches to ancient possessions; the weight of her presence within the empire ensured that discussion of her future readily transcended the levels occupied by particular pressure groups and entered the sphere reserved for matters of national interest. From this point onwards, moreover, the history of India under the Raj showed 'the face of the future' to much of the rest of the empire as she passed from acquisition to colonial management and on to the transfer of power. Theorists of empire may bypass Tonga and may regard Uganda as being an exception to the rule, whatever it may be, of imperial growth and decay; but no serious account of British imperialism can omit India or treat her as an anomaly, and no plausible explanation of the purpose of empire-building can afford to stumble over the sub-continent.

---

1. The quotation is taken from an India Office Memorandum, 1907, cited on p. 342.
2. George Erle Buckle, *The Life of Benjamin Disraeli: Earl of Beaconsfield* (1920), V, p. 195.

INTERPRETATIONS OF THE IMPERIAL PURPOSE

Not surprisingly, the numerous historians who have appraised India's role in the empire during the nineteenth century have all agreed upon her importance, whether they have chosen to stress economic ties with the metropole, the contribution made by the Indian Army, or the political and diplomatic commitments entered into by London (and its sometimes wayward representatives on the frontier) in pursuit of strategic priorities.[3] Nevertheless, the substantial scholarly literature which has illuminated these and allied subjects has yet to resolve the central question of the determinants of the British presence in India. This is partly because much recent work on the imperial connection has been concerned with rather different issues, such as techniques of colonial management and the costs and benefits of British rule, but it is principally because the main thrust of research during the past generation has been directed towards investigating the internal history of India. The results of this sustained effort constitute a remarkable historiographical advance. But one consequence of this concentration of interest has been that wider issues concerning the nature of the British presence in India and the purpose of imperial policy have become unfashionable and consequently have lost the central place in the literature that they once enjoyed.[4]

Of the global theories of imperialism that have dealt with India, Marx's analysis is outstanding among those advanced by contemporary observers, and it remains a powerful influence today.[5] The 1850s were for Marx a decisive moment of transition, a time when the obstructive 'moneyocracy' and 'oligarchy' of City and landed interests yielded to the progressive 'millocracy' of Manchester and its allies.

3. References to this literature can be found in C.A. Bayly, 'English-Language Historiography on British Expansion in India and Indian Reactions since 1945', in P.C. Emmer and H.L. Wesseling, eds. *Reappraisals in Overseas History* (Leiden, 1979); Neil Charlesworth, *British Rule and the Indian Economy, 1800–1914* (1982); Sumit Sukar, *Modern India, 1885–1947* (New Delhi, 1983); R.J. Moore, 'India and the British Empire', in C.C. Eldridge, ed. *British Imperialism in the Nineteenth Century* (1984); and William A. Green and John P. Dewey, 'Unifying Themes in the History of British India, 1757–1857: an Historiographical Analysis', *Albion*, 17 (1985).

4. For a valuable synthesis of research on the role of the periphery see C.A. Bayly, *Indian Society and the Making of the British Empire* (Cambridge, 1988). Some of the consequences of over-specialisation are considered in Irfan Habib's review of Dharma Kumar, ed. *The Cambridge Economic History of India, II, 1757–c.1970* (Cambridge, 1983): 'Studying a Colonial Economy – Without Perceiving Colonialism', *Mod. Asian Stud.*, 19 (1985).

5. For a stimulating account of Marx's views on India see V.G. Kiernan, *Marxism and Imperialism* (1974). The debate about the relationship between early and late Marx is treated by Suriti Kumar Ghosh, 'Marx on India', *Monthly Review*, 35 (1984).

Marx viewed the Indian Mutiny of 1857, and the transfer of administrative control from the East India Company to the crown in the following year, as symbolising an important stage in the global spread of industrial capitalism. Ending the East India Company's powers of patronage would deprive aristocratic families of administrative and military places for their younger sons; opening India to the full blast of competition from modern manufactures would fuel Britain's economic development, enhance the power of the rising industrial bourgeoisie, and stimulate the process of modernisation in India herself. Until recently, Marx argued:

> the interests of the moneyocracy which had converted India into its landed estates, of the oligarchy who had conquered it by their armies, and of the millocracy who had inundated it with their fabrics, had gone hand in hand. But the more the industrial interest became dependent on the Indian market, the more it felt the necessity of creating fresh productive powers in India, after having ruined her native industry.[6]

It was now time for the Indian economy to be refashioned:

> The millocracy have discovered that the transformation of India into a reproductive country has become of vital importance to them, and to that end it is necessary above all to gift her with means of irrigation and of internal communication.[7]

Despite its vision and incisiveness, Marx's interpretation fits uncomfortably with the evidence now available, principally because it overstates the role of the forces associated with industrialisation. In reality, industrialists exerted only limited influence on policy-making in Britain, and modern manufacturing itself made slow progress in India.

The most prominent liberal theory, on the other hand, has explained nineteenth-century imperalism without fully incorporating India.[8] This oddity has arisen because attention has been focused on the concept of informal empire and on the transition to formal rule. One result of this emphasis, less remarked than perhaps it ought to be, has been to move India to the margins of the debate over the causes of British imperialism in the nineteenth century. Since India was already part of the empire, it is clearly unsuitable territory for discussing either the existence of informal influence or the shift to formal rule during the last quarter of the century. Participants in this

---

6. Karl Marx and Frederick Engels, *Collected Works*, XII (1979 edn), pp. 154–5.
7. Ibid. pp. 218–19.
8. J. Gallagher and R. Robinson, 'The Imperialism of Free Trade', *Econ. Hist. Rev.*, 2nd ser. VI (1953).

controversy tend to treat India as part of the furniture of empire, an eighteenth-century legacy whose provenance is to be explained by specialists of that period. Consequently, attention has been directed away from causation and towards questions of colonial management and its effects on India. Given that India's weighty presence within the empire is acknowledged by historians of varying persuasions, the minor part assigned to her by current theories of nineteenth-century empire-building remains a troublesome paradox. Furthermore, if the partition of Africa is to be presented as 'a gigantic footnote to the Indian empire', as one celebrated analysis claims,[9] it becomes doubly necessary to examine Britain's purpose in the sub-continent.

The view advanced here dissents from both of the foregoing interpretations. India was neither a vehicle for the industrial bourgeoisie nor a fixture that had to be defended simply because she had already been acquired by eighteenth-century enthusiasts. We shall argue instead that the longevity of Britain's presence in India provides a particularly apposite illustration of our argument about the long-run evolution of gentlemanly capitalism. The demise of the East India Company in 1858 can still be treated as a turning point in Anglo-Indian relations; but the event signified the extension abroad of the new service order following the transition from Old Corruption, rather than the triumph of the industrial bourgeoisie, as Marx supposed. The new class of officials and investors did not eject the landed and military interests which, with the East India Company, had dominated British India since the mid-eighteenth century; nor did they seek to do so. Instead, there was a progressive change in the complexion of the British presence in India which reflected the realignment of socio-economic forces that was taking place at home after 1815. As Pitt's quest for 'economical reform' eventually had its issue in Gladstonian finance, so the principles of sound money, free trade and efficient administration were slowly impressed on India. And, as peculation gave way to speculation, and speculation to serious long-term investment, so the official mind became increasingly concentrated on maintaining the credit-worthiness of the Raj and on ensuring that India's mounting external financial obligations were met. These priorities, as we shall see, were a reflection of India's growing importance in London's management of the international economy, and they provided a compelling motive for continuing to

9. R.E. Robinson and J. Gallagher, 'The Partition of Africa', in F.H. Hinsley, ed. *New Cambridge Modern History*, XI (Cambridge, 1962), p. 616.

control the sub-continent and for defending it from the various external threats that preyed on the minds of successive Viceroys.

This argument does not presume that the history of the Raj stands as a proxy for the history of India. As recent research has demonstrated, pre-British India extended long lines of continuity into the nineteenth century, entangling the new rulers and helping to shape English liberals into oriental despots.[10] But it has also shown that they were aware of the paradox and made good use of it. The managers of the Raj took readily to India partly because they were able to merge their own rent-seeking and capitalist purposes with the apparatus of 'military fiscalism' left by the Mughals,[11] and partly because their programme of 'economical reform' recognised the importance of grounding political stability in existing institutions in other parts of the world, as it did at home. Moreover, gentlemen fashioned for leadership in a society that was only just beginning to move, slowly and reluctantly, towards democracy, took readily to paternalism abroad, and they reconciled their belief in individualism with the adoption of increasingly *dirigiste* policies by arguing that firm direction was needed to prepare 'backward' societies for a more liberal order. Thus, as the British adapted to India, they also imposed on her by selecting from what they found there, and by seeking to reinforce, discard and invent traditions in the manner of those who were accustomed to applying Whig measures for Tory purposes.

PRELUDE, 1757–1857

The slow and discontinuous acquisition of India spanned nearly a century, beginning with the take-over of Bengal after the Battle of Plassey in 1757 and culminating in a clutch of acquisitions in the middle of the nineteenth century: Sind and the Punjab in 1843 and 1849; Berar and Oudh in 1853 and 1856.[12] Although the chronology of Britain's advance into India provides an approximate match with the timing of

10. See, for example, Eric Stokes, 'The First Century of British Rule in India', *Past and Present*, 58 (1973); P.J. Marshall, *Bengal: The British Bridgehead: Eastern India, 1740–1828* (Cambridge, 1987); and C.A. Bayly, *Imperial Meridian: The British Empire and the World, 1780–1830* (Cambridge, 1989).

11. On this theme see the important contributions by D.A. Washbrook, 'Law, State and Agrarian Society in Colonial India', *Mod. Asian Stud.*, 15 (1981), and Burton Stein, 'State Formation and Economy Reconsidered', *Mod. Asian Stud.*, 19 (1985).

12. To which must be added Burma. See Oliver B. Pollack, *Empires in Collision: Anglo-Burmese Relations in the Mid-Nineteenth Century* (Westport, Conn., 1979).

the Industrial Revolution, it has proved difficult, despite numerous heroic attempts, to demonstrate that the growth of empire in India was either a cause or a result of the rise of modern manufactures in England. It was not until the 1840s that products of the Industrial Revolution began to feature prominently among India's imports, and it was only in the second half of the century, after territorial annexations had been made, that this trade assumed weighty proportions.[13] If this evidence suggests that standard theories of economic imperialism are poorly aligned with the results of modern research, it has also given further impetus to the argument that the causes of expansion are to be found on the periphery rather than in the metropole.[14] The application of the 'excentric' thesis to India has the considerable merits of incorporating evidence from local studies and of drawing attention to various forms of sub-imperialism promoted by expansionists on the turbulent frontiers of empire. But, as we noted at the outset of this study, sub-imperialism does not explain imperialism, and to show that actions on the frontier were not always directed from London is not to explain why the actors were there in the first place.

A more illuminating approach, we suggest, is to view expansion into India from the mid-eighteenth century as illustrating the extension abroad of the social forces that dominated the polity at home after 1688. The emerging but still incomplete alliance between land and money in eighteenth-century England created a state that centred power on landed property and funded it by means of a fiscal system that was designed to support privilege without provoking discontent on a scale sufficient to overturn it. These aims, and the values that accompanied them, were extended to India: power was to be founded ultimately on the land, and revenue became and remained the central preoccupation of policy, the more so because India's role was to be that of a tributary province. The main problem addressed by successive generations of administrators was not how to open India to British manufactures, but how to secure the revenue base of Britain's rule. The principal oscillations in policy, which swung from defending the East India Company to abolishing it, and from introducing Benthamite reforms to entrenching India's many princes, can all be traced to this enduring fiscal imperative.

The East India Company was undoubtedly the most impressive

---

13. K.N. Chaudhuri, 'India's Foreign Trade and the Cessation of the East India Company's Trading Activities, 1828–40', *Econ. Hist. Rev.*, 2nd ser. XIX (1966).

14. Bayly, *Indian Society*, presents the view from the periphery; idem, *Imperial Meridian*, links the periphery to developments in the metropole in ways that are, we believe, consistent with the view expressed here.

overseas manifestation of the alliance between land and finance in the eighteenth century. Initially, the Company was the vehicle of City merchants rather than of large landowners, but both groups had political interests, centred on London and the court, in its fortunes, and their joint commitment was reinforced as the century advanced by the Company's growing preoccupation with raising the revenue to pay for its administrative and military overheads.[15] Moreover, during the second half of the century, the landed families who were the chief beneficiaries of patronage came to appreciate the Company's job-creating potential once it had scoured the treasuries of the nawabs and had fastened upon the remnants of Mughal administration.[16] Thereafter, as government accompanied commerce in India, so policy was increasingly influenced by the values of the magnates who controlled the English state in the eighteenth century. They exported their notions of property rights to India, looked to agriculture to generate rents, and tried to identify or create an indigenous gentry and a compliant yeomanry who would both work the land and police it.[17] By the close of the century, Company rule had come to advertise the moral virtues as well as the political imperatives of military discipline and obedience to central authority. In this respect, too, Britain's presence in India reflected the changing contour of events at home, as the experience of the American Revolution and the French Wars promoted a brand of 'new conservatism' which sought to discipline the unpropertied and the un-Godly, and readily endorsed the use of force to maintain civil order and to uphold the inequalities of the 'balanced' constitution.[18]

It is important to emphasise at this point that the Company can no longer be portrayed as being a creaking, mercantilist monopoly whose

15. H.V. Bowen, 'Investment and Empire in the Late Eighteenth Century: East India Stockholding, 1756–1791', *Econ. Hist. Rev.*, 2nd ser. XLII (1989). We are grateful to Dr Bowen for his advice on this subject.

16. P.J. Marshall, *East Indian Fortunes: The British in Bengal in the Eighteenth Century* (Oxford, 1976), Chs.1, 7, 8, 9.

17. For example: Rajat Ray and Ratna Ray, 'Zamindars and Jotedars: A Study of Rural Politics in Bengal', *Mod. Asian Stud.*, 9 (1975); Michael H. Fisher, 'Indirect Rule in the British Empire: the Foundations of the Residency System in India (1764–1858)', *Mod. Asian Stud.*, 18 (1984); Michelle B. McAlpin, 'Economic Policy and the True Believer: the Use of Ricardian Rent Theory in the Bombay Survey and Settlement System', *Jour. Econ. Hist.*, 44 (1984). Broader studies include: W.J. Barber, *British Economic Thought and India, 1600–1858* (Oxford, 1975), and Thomas R. Metcalf, *Land, Landlords and the British Raj* (Berkeley, Calif., 1979).

18. P.Langford, 'Old Whigs, Old Tories and the American Revolution', in P. Marshall and G. Williams, eds. *The British Atlantic Empire Before the American Revolution* (1980); Linda Colley, 'The Apotheosis of George III: Loyalty, Royalty and the British Nation, 1760–1820', *Past and Present*, 102 (1984).

historic role was to impede the progessive forces of British industry before finally being destroyed by them. It has now been shown that the Company was a much more innovative and efficient organisation than it has been given credit for.[19] It was undoubtedly a privileged club, but it was also a capitalist enterprise that generated as well as recycled wealth and achieved striking productivity gains in the transactions sector. In short, the Company provides an excellent example of the innovations we have identified as constituting the commercial and financial revolution of the eighteenth century. To the extent that the Company produced and integrated income streams from different countries, it can also be seen as forming a prototype for the multinational corporations that were to develop in the twentieth century. Imperfections in the Company's monopoly allowed private traders to make their way into new markets, whether by licence or by unauthorised enterprise, and the Company's inability to police all of its expanding frontiers meant that it was unable to hold back further commercial innovation, even if it wanted to. Both the Company and the private traders dealt with and sometimes borrowed from bankers and merchant princes who represented an indigenous, Indian brand of commercial capitalism. But they also enjoyed a growing competitive advantage in finance and distribution, as well as in techniques of coercion. Indian handicrafts were able to resist competition from British manufactures during the first half of the nineteenth century, whereas Indian banking and shipping were displaced from international commerce during this period.[20]

How far the Company could have extended its commercial efficiency into the nineteenth century is now a hypothetical question because its fortunes became increasingly bound up with the obligations it had assumed in administering India on behalf of the home government. The extension of empire and the financial health of the Company formed a circle that was both virtuous and vicious: territorial expansion was undertaken commonly to secure additional revenue, and thus to enable the Company to meet its financial obligations; but the costs of expansion frequently ran ahead of the

19. On the rehabilitation of the Company's commercial performance see K.N. Chaudhuri, *The Trading World of Asia and the English East India Company, 1660–1760* (Cambridge, 1978), and Ho-cheung Mui and Lorna H. Mui, *The Management of Monopoly: A Study of the East India Company's Conduct of its Tea Trade, 1784–1833* (Vancouver, 1984).

20. Frank Broeze, 'Underdevelopment and Dependency: Maritime India during the Raj', *Mod. Asian Stud.*, 18 (1984). The debate on handicrafts is summarised in Charlesworth, *British Rule*, pp. 32–6. See also Colin Simmons, '"De-industrialisation", Industrialisation and the Indian Economy, 1850–1947', *Mod. Asian Stud.*, 19 (1985).

estimates, and thus threatened to wreck rather than rescue the Company's finances. Naturally, London expected the Company's officials to create virtuous circles and avoid vicious ones, and important changes of policy towards the Company and the administration of India were invariably designed to achieve this result. When the Company's accumulating failures demonstrated its inability to achieve the near-impossible task it had been set, its powers were finally transferred to the crown in 1858.

The need to keep remittances flowing to London became a fixed priority in Britain's relations with India from the late eighteenth century onwards. Clive commandeered the revenues of Bengal for this purpose in the 1760s, and continuing fiscal imperatives go far towards explaining the territorial acquisitions made by his successors, their preoccupation with improving India's system of taxation, and official concern to develop an export surplus. During the first half of the nineteenth century, £3m.–4m. a year was required to meet official obligations (mainly pensions and equipment) and to pay dividends to the Company's shareholders in London, an additional amount (ranging from £0.5m. to £1.5m.) was needed for private remittances, and a further sum (which is not easily calculated) had to be found to settle India's invisible imports, such as freight charges, insurance and banking services.[21] The growth of India's external financial obligations at this time foreshadowed the future of countries which were drawn into Britain's orbit as overseas debtors later in the century; it also helps to account for the development of a multilateral trading system and for an emerging commitment to free trade during the first half of the nineteenth century.[22]

The revisions made to the East India Company's charter in 1813 and 1833 provide a clear illustration of the role of fiscal priorities in determining policy. The abolition in 1813 of the Company's formal monopoly of trade with India was essentially a wartime measure which was implemented principally to improve the flow of Indian commodities to Britain. The decision was not taken at the behest of a lobby representing Britain's new manufactures (though exports of cotton goods began to grow thereafter), but with one eye on placating provincial outports and the other on the ambitions of London

21. Bayly, *Indian Society*, pp. 116–17; Marshall, *Bengal*, pp. 104–5; Chaudhuri, 'India's Foreign Trade', pp. 355–60.
22. Marshall, *Bengal*, pp. 105–6, 118–19, 133; Rudrangshu Mukherjee, 'Trade and Empire in Awadh, 1765–1804', *Past and Present*, 94 (1982), pp. 89–90, 99–100; Chaudhuri, 'India's Foreign Trade', pp. 355, 358–63.

merchants whose commercial interests had outgrown the bounds set by Company control.[23] In this respect, the action taken in 1813 pointed towards the regime of freer trade that Lord Liverpool's government began to install in the 1820s, and marked a further step towards shifting the responsibility for generating an export surplus away from the Company and towards private traders.

Similar considerations underlay the decision to end the Company's remaining commercial privilege, its monopoly of trade with China, in 1833.[24] An economic depression in Britain in 1829 hit the price of India's exports, especially indigo, and brought down many of the Agency Houses, the large, private commercial firms which financed the planters. This crisis came at a time when the Company was trying to cope with a legacy of heavy military expenditure, and it raised doubts about India's ability to meet her external obligations. The need to secure the means of maintaining the flow of remittances to London provided a strong incentive for promoting exports, and led in particular to attempts to open up trade with China. The end of the Company's last monopoly was not the outcome of pressure exerted by Manchester's manufacturers but the result of efforts made by merchants based in London and India who were keen to open markets for Indian cotton goods and opium in south-east Asia and the Far East. These pressures continued after 1833, and eventually culminated in the Opium War of 1839–42.[25] Meanwhile, the Company responded to the loss of its monopoly of trade with China by expanding into Sind and the Punjab in the 1830s and 1840s in the hope of annexing new sources of revenue.

The amendments to the East India Company's charter accompanied wider experiments in what, today, would be called development policy.[26] Even the Wellesleys, whose instinct was to preserve British interests in India by installing an effective despotism backed

23. Anthony Webster, 'The Political Economy of Trade Liberalisation: the East India Company Charter Act of 1813', *Econ. Hist. Rev*, 2nd ser. XLIII (1990), and the further references given there.

24. Amales Tripathi, 'Indo-British Trade Between 1833 and 1847 and the Commercial Crisis of 1847/8', *Indian Hist. Rev.*, I (1974), pp. 306–11; Chaudhuri, 'India's Foreign Trade', pp. 345–6, 349–50, 361–2; Anthony Webster, 'British Export Interests in Bengal and Imperial Expansion into South-East Asia, 1780–1824: the Origins of the Straits Settlements', in Barbara Ingham and Colin Simmons, eds. *Development Studies and Colonial Policy* (1987), pp. 138–74; Douglas M. Peers, 'Between Mars and Mammon: the East India Company and Efforts to Reform its Army, 1796–1832', *Hist. Jour.*, 33 (1990); idem, 'War and Public Finance in Early Nineteenth-Century British India: the First Burma War', *Internat. Hist. Rev.*, 11 (1989).

25. See below, pp. 424–6.

26. This theme can be followed in W.J. Barber, *British Economic Thought and India, 1600–1858: A Study in the History of Development Economics* (Oxford, 1975).

by 'salutory terror',[27] were keen to expand trade for revenue purposes and acknowledged the desirability of making London 'the throne of commerce of the world'.[28] The next generation of rulers, represented by Bentinck and Dalhousie, envisaged the 'improvement' of India through the application of utilitarian principles which would strengthen both the institutional basis of political stability and the means of funding British rule.[29] The attack on corrupt practices, like the quest for efficiency, was part of a programme which aimed at establishing a stable but also progressive propertied order in India. Bentinck, who was Governor-General between 1828 and 1835, hoped to open India to white settlers and foreign capital, and also to 'raise a middle class of native gentlemen' who would act as agents of development.[30] In the 1840s, when optimism about the speed of India's development had been dulled by a heightened awareness of the obstacles to change, talk of 'founding British greatness on Indian happiness',[31] gave way to more pragmatic considerations. Dalhousie, the Governor-General from 1848 to 1856, continued to plan for development, but concentrated on the application of Western technology, especially to the field of communications.[32]

Two features of this development programme deserve emphasis in the context of the argument advanced here. To begin with, it is important to note that the experiments practised on India were very similar to those attempted on other parts of the world, where Britain made equally determined, if less direct, efforts to establish compliant satellites during the first half of the nineteenth century. Furthermore, policies of 'improvement' in India, as elsewhere, were projections abroad of the changes occurring in Britain following the first tentative moves towards free trade, fiscal discipline and political reform in the

27. Douglas M. Peers, 'The Duke of Wellington and British India during the Liverpool Administration, 1819–27', *Jour. Imp. and Comm. Hist.*, XVII (1988), p. 20. Wellington (then Arthur Wellesley) saw active service in India between 1796 and 1805.

28. Ricahard Wellesley, Governor-General from 1798 to 1805, quoted in Bayly, *Indian Society*, p. 83.

29. The classic study is Eric Stokes, *The Utilitarians and India* (Oxford, 1958).

30. John Rosselli, *Lord William Bentinck: The Making of a Liberal Imperialist* (Berkeley, Calif., 1974), p. 208; P.J. Marshall, 'The Whites of British India, 1780–1830: a Failed Colonial Society?', *Internat. Hist. Rev.*, 12 (1990). The career of the most famous of India's western-style entrepreneurs of the period, Dwarkanath Tagore (1794–1846), is placed in a comparative context by Rhoads Murphey, *The Outsiders: The Western Experience in India and China* (Ann Arbor, Mich., 1977), pp. 73–6. On the pursuit of Bentinck's reforms in the late 1830s see Dayal Dass, *Charles Metcalf and British Administration in India* (New Delhi, 1988).

31. Bentinck, quoted in Hyam, *Britain's Imperial Century*, p. 216.

32. Suresh Chandra Ghosh, 'The Utilitarianism of Dalhousie and the Material Improvement of India', *Mod. Asian Stud.*, 12 (1978).

aftermath of the Napoleonic Wars. India was still marked out as the patrimony of aristocrats and gentlemen, but estate management was to be conducted more responsibly than in the days of Clive and Hastings.[33] Although Company servants continued to be appointed through the patronage network, increasing numbers of them bore the imprint of Haileybury, absorbed the spirit of improvement, and stiffened it with the moral fibre of evangelical Christianity.[34] The second aspect of the reforming endeavour that needs to be stressed is its limited success. Beyond the rhetoric and the firm intentions lay a sub-continent that had been affected but not transformed by a century of British rule. The settlers' frontier proved to be abortive; the attempt to raise an indigenous 'middle class' touched a handful out of millions; and the alliance with land-holders weighed heavily on the taxable peasants who were supposed to be candidates for improvement. Above all, India's economic potential remained, if not untapped, unrealised: export growth was still restricted, difficulties remained in transferring remittances to London, and the City showed itself to be reluctant to place sizeable long-term investments in the sub-continent. In these respects, Britain's formal authority was rather more extensive than her informal influence, and the limitations of her ambitious development programme were manifest in India as they were in other parts of the world.

THE EXTENSION OF THE GENTLEMANLY ORDER

Placed in this long perspective, the Indian Mutiny in 1857 and the transfer of civil authority from the East India Company to the crown in the following year can be seen as the culmination of a long transition which complemented, not the Industrial Revolution, but the demise of Old Corruption and the adoption at home of a peculiarly British brand of conservative reform. The end of the Company's official role in governing India was the final act in a process that had seen the progressive separation of economic and

33. J. Majeed, 'James Mill's "The History of British India" and Utilitarianism as a Rhetoric of Reform', *Mod. Asian Stud.*, 24 (1990); Ram Parkash Sikka, *The Civil Service in India: Europeanisation and Indianisation under the East India Company (1765–1857)* (New Delhi, 1984); Marshall, 'The Whites of British India'.

34. The pioneering study is B.S. Cohn, 'Recruitment and Training of the British Civil Servants in India, 1600–1860', in R. Braibant, ed. *Asian Bureaucratic Systems Emergent from the British Tradition* (Durham, NC, 1966). An important example is Peter Penner, *The Patronage Bureaucracy in North India: The Robert M. Bird and James Thomason School, 1820–1870* (Delhi, 1986).

political powers in India and the growing specialisation of functions that Adam Smith and Max Weber regarded, from different standpoints, as being the hallmark of the modern world. Exactly why the Mutiny occurred is a much-debated issue that cannot be explored here; but it seems clear that the general failure of policies of development and reform provoked one kind of discontent and their modest success among particular social groups and in specific regions another, and that the two came together momentarily in 1857.[35] The resulting upheaval discredited the Company and finally forced London to take greater control of India's affairs by making the Governor-General directly accountable to the Secretary of State and parliament, not least, as we shall see, in matters of finance.[36]

The settlement which followed the transfer of power in 1858 reinforced the traditional priorities of British policy and put in place more effective means of achieving them. The creation of a new Government of India backed by an imperial guarantee upgraded the credit-rating of the state, increased the confidence of overseas investors, and greatly improved the prospects of raising foreign loans. Public finance was remodelled on Gladstonian lines and economic policy was tied to the universal principles of balanced budgets, sound money, free trade, and non-discriminatory revenue taxes.[37] One of the principal items of expenditure, the Indian Army, was brought under government control but at the same time placed on the official payroll, thus increasing the security and attractiveness of military employment. These measures gave renewed impetus to India's faltering development programme, but they also kept it on the pragmatic lines laid down by Dalhousie. British rule remained interventionist, but departures from the ideal of minimal government were justified in the case of India (as of 'backward' countries in general) by the authority of John Stuart Mill, among others, and had their rationale in the need to raise revenue as well as to keep order.[38]

After 1858, however, intervention assumed an increasingly econ-

35. The vast literature on the Mutiny can be approached through Bayly, *Indian Society*, Ch. 6 and the references given on pp. 222–3.

36. A summary of the constitutional changes is given in R.J. Moore, *Liberalism and Indian Politics, 1872–1922* (1966), pp. 6–8.

37. The main changes were made in 1859–60 by James Wilson, the first Indian Finance Member of the Council of India (and also the founder of *The Economist*). See Sabyasachi Bhattacharyya's valuable (and rather neglected) study, *Financial Foundations of the British Raj* (Simla, 1971), pp. xlviii–li, and 3–4; and, more generally, Raymond W. Goldsmith, *The Financial Development of India, 1860–1977* (New Haven, Conn., 1983). For the policy in action see, for example, Edward C. Moulton, *Lord Northbrook's Indian Administration, 1872–1876* (Bombay, 1968), Ch. 2.

38. Bhattacharyya, *Financial Foundations*, p. lxxv.

omic character: the search for revenue led the government to promote mining and manufacturing activities as well as public utilities, especially railways and irrigation. Military intervention, on the other hand, lost its place as an established means of enlarging the treasury. It was a tempting strategy, but it had also proved to be a costly one, and after the Mutiny no government was prepared to risk actions that might stir the deep waters of Indian society. On the contrary, the Mutiny drew the Government of India into a closer partnership with land-holders and princes.[39] The result, a conservative 'alliance for progress', aimed at winning political support by picking a route to economic development that was consistent with social stability. In this respect, policy in India can be compared to that adopted towards other 'oriental societies', as Lord Salisbury called them, during the second half of the nineteenth century, when the idea of the brotherhood of man gave way to the notion of a hierarchy of racial types, each arranged into appropriate social classes, whose spiritual and material improvement were to be entrusted to the paternal direction of gentlemanly rulers.

From the 1850s, India became a notable outpost of the new service and financial order which had come to prominence in Britain following the demise of Old Corruption and the growth of sterling's role as a world currency.[40] The main instruments of British policy in India, the army and the civil service, employed only a small number of white officials. But their hands were on the levers of power: they controlled the means of coercion, they collected and allocated India's vast revenues, and their values helped to shape policy and its execution. From the 1850s, military and civil appointments in India became a large, vested interest of the educated upper middle class. In 1913–14, for example, the Government of India devoted no less than £53m. (65 per cent of the total budget of £82m.) to the army and the

39. There is now a huge literature exploring the regional variations of the post-Mutiny settlement. See, for example, Thomas Metcalf, *Land, Landlords and the British Raj* (Berkeley, Calif., 1979). The Punjab is a particularly good example in the present context because it remained conspicuously loyal in 1857 and was rewarded thereafter. The Punjab also became the most important source of military recruitment for the Raj, and accounted for three-fifths of the Indian Army in 1914. See I. Talbot, *Punjab and the Raj, 1849–1947* (New Delhi, 1988). The 'princely states', however, have been unduly neglected. See S.R.Ashton, *British Policy Towards the Indian States* (1982), and John Hurd, 'The Economic Consequences of Indirect Rule in India', *Indian Econ. and Soc. Hist. Rev.*, 12 (1975).

40. On the London headquarters see Arnold Kaminsky, *The India Office, 1880–1910* (Westport, Conn., 1986). The Permanent Under-Secretary from 1883 to 1909, Sir Arthur Godley (later Lord Kilbracken), was educated at Rugby and Balliol College, Oxford, and had previously served as Gladstone's Private Secretary.

civil administration.[41] Imperial service enabled the mainly southern, professional and public-school culture to reproduce itself abroad and also, as we shall see, to create facsimiles among elites in the new colonies established in Asia and Africa.

Despite outspoken criticism from Manchester radicals, who deplored the 'waste' of Indian revenues on military expenditure,[42] the Indian Army remained vital to Britain's presence in Asia, both for reasons of internal security and for policing the vast region stretching from the Eastern Mediterranean to China. Without the Indian Army, and the Indian revenues that sustained it, Britain would not have been able to maintain her position east of Suez, and her status as a great power would have been seriously impaired.[43] From the 1850s onwards, the officer class was drawn mainly from the sons of professional families clustered in and around London and from the provincial gentry, though room was also found for recruits from the 'Celtic Fringe'.[44] In 1853, Cobden observed that 'our system of military rule in India has been widely profitable to the middle and upper classes in Scotland, who have more than their numerical share of its patronage', a fact that, in his view, partly explained their lack of interest in the Peace Society.[45] Colonial service helped to incorporate the articulate products of Scottish and Irish universities into a predominantly English-run enterprise and gave them a stake in defending national, that is to say British, interests. The social fusion, via public schools, of segments of the gentry and the middle class produced a formidable British hybrid: the Christian gentleman who combined measured refinement with licensed muscularity.

Parallel developments affected the Indian civil service after the East India Company's patronage machine was dismantled in the 1850s. Following an uncertain start, the introduction of an examination-based, meritocratic system forged close links between public schools, universities and colonial service, and created new employment oppor-

41. *Statistical Abstract of British India, 1911–12 to 1921–22* (1923), p. 126. The most thorough analysis of government expenditure during the period under review is A.K. Banerji, *Aspects of Indo-British Economic Relations, 1858–1898* (Bombay, 1982).

42. R.J. Moore, 'Imperialism and Free Trade Policy in India, 1853–4', *Econ. Hist. Rev.*, 2nd ser. XVII (1964), p. 139. For official salaries see Banerji, *Aspects*, p. 145.

43. On the connection between finance and defence see B.R. Tomlinson, 'India and the British Empire, 1880–1935', *Indian Econ. and Soc. Hist. Rev.*, 12 (1975).

44. P.E. Razzell, 'Social Origins of Officers in the Indian and British Home Army, 1758–1962', *Brit. Jour. Soc.*, 14 (1963). The aristocracy found employment in the Home Army more congenial.

45. Cobden to McLaren, 15 Sept. 1853. Quoted in J. Morley, *The Life of Richard Cobden*, II (1881), p. 144.

tunities, especially for professional families in south-east England.[46] Three-quarters of the recruits who entered the Indian Civil Service through the examination system between 1860 and 1874 were drawn from this class and a further 10 per cent came from the aristocracy and the landed gentry.[47] The competitive apparatus was not designed to open the corridors of power to ordinary citizens, and it created only limited opportunities for aspirants who saw in colonial service a means of attaining gentlemanly status.[48] The aim, as stated by Gladstone in 1854, was to 'strengthen and multiply the ties between the higher classes and the possession of administrative power'.[49] Emphasis was placed on the continuing vitality of the notion that gentlemen were uniquely qualified to become ideal administrators because of 'their capacity to govern others and control themselves, their aptitude for combining freedom with order, their love of healthy sports and exercise'.[50] The reformed civil service was more an act of management than an abrogation of privilege.[51] It was a response by the political elite to criticism of the patronage system, and it anticipated the expansion of demand for employment from the newly enfranchised middle classes. In the manner of British reforms, it looked more radical than it was. The army officer in India thus had his counterpart in the civil servant: both shared a common set of values and carried a blueprint, joining universal principles with worldly pragmatism, of how society – any society – ought to be governed.

A renewed effort was also made after the Mutiny to regroup India's large land-holders behind the Raj and to reinforce their position in the

46. B.B. Misra, *The Bureaucracy in India: An Historical Analysis up to 1947* (Delhi, 1977); J.M. Compton, 'Open Competition and the Indian Civil Service, 1854–76', *Eng. Hist. Rev.*, LXXXIII (1968), pp. 265–84; C.J. Dewey, 'The Making of an English Ruling Caste: The Indian Civil Service in the Era of Competitive Examination', *Eng. Hist. Rev.*, LXXXVIII (1973); R.J. Moore, *Sir Charles Wood's Indian Policy, 1853–66* (Manchester, 1966), Ch. 6. See also Philip Mason, *The Men Who Ruled India* (1985).

47. Bradford Spangenberg, *British Bureaucracy in India: Status, Policy and the I.C.S. in the Late Nineteenth Century* (New Delhi, 1976), pp. 19–20. (On the question of the wider interpetation of the data, we may note in passing that Spangenberg's undoubtedly healthy revisionism appears not to have converted specialists. Broadly similar criticisms of the stereotype of selfless, Platonic guardians have been made with more restraint by Misra, *The Bureaucracy*, Ch. 3 and pp. 200–10, whose assessment is consistent with the argument advanced here.)

48. Ibid. pp. 256–7.

49. Quoted in Compton, 'Open Competition', p. 266.

50. Quoted from a Parliamentary Paper of 1854 by Compton, 'Open Competition', p. 269.

51. J.M. Bourne, *Patronage and Society in Nineteenth-Century England* (1986), pp. 45–6, 127, 181.

great chain of command which joined London to the sub-continent's far-flung provinces. This was achieved by endorsing their privileges and incorporating them as junior partners into the imperial enterprise.[52] As the cult of royalty was elaborated at home, so the panoply of nobility was revived in India. The two came together in 1877, when the Queen was proclaimed empress of India and a huge 'royal assemblage' was staged in Delhi to pay homage to the monarch and to impress her subjects.[53] Lytton, the Governor-General and prospective Viceroy, had no doubt about the material value of this political ritual: 'the cost of the Assemblage', he calculated, 'will really be very moderate, and the effect of it may save millions'.[54] The new generation of mighty but loyal subjects was also educated for its imperial role. Those who were to exercise authority under British supervision were to be 'brought up as a gentleman should be' by establishing 'an Eton in India'.[55] In fact, several Etons were founded in India during the last quarter of the century with the aim of inculcating 'a healthy tone and manly habits' among future leaders.[56] In India, as elsewhere in the empire, team games became a means of moral instruction and not merely of physical exercise. The belief that sport was an allegory of life, and that life, like the body politic, was a matter of balancing individual rights and public duties through a mixture of effort and discipline was successfully conveyed to the children of India's elite, who learned the 'rules of the game' through the patient art of cricket.[57]

It is not surprising to find that the aims of the official 'caste' in India closely resembled those of the political elite at home, given the strong element of homogeneity in the recruitment and training of both. The central dilemma of policy remained unchanged after 1858, as before: how to produce sufficient revenue to meet India's financial obligations and defence commitments without provoking internal discontent on a

52. See n.39 above.

53. Alan Trevithick, 'Some Structural and Sequential Aspects of the British Imperial Assemblages at Delhi, 1877–1911', *Mod. Asian Stud.*, 24 (1990). The important general study is Bernard Cohn, 'Representing Authority in Victorian India', in Eric Hobsbawm and Terence Ranger, eds. *The Invention of Tradition* (Cambridge, 1983).

54. Lytton to Morley, 29 Oct. 1876, quoted in Trevithick, 'Structural and Sequential Aspects', p. 563.

55. J.A. Mangan, *The Games Ethic and Imperialism* (1986), p. 125.

56. Ibid. p. 133. The Etons were complemented by Oxfords, whose origins have been studied by Robert Frykenberg, 'Modern Education in South India, 1784–1854: its Roots and Role as a Vehicle for Integration Under Company Raj', *Am. Hist. Rev.*, 91 (1986).

57. Donald Linster-Mackay, 'The Nineteenth-Century English Preparatory School: Cradle and Creche of Empire?', in J.A. Mangan, ed. *Benefits Bestowed? Education and British Imperialism* (Manchester, 1986). In England, it was also possible to explain the Holy Trinity in terms of three stumps and one wicket (ibid. p. 69).

scale that would raise the costs of maintaining order and unnerve foreign investors. After the Mutiny, however, the problem could no longer be attacked by tribute-gathering military expeditions; and the land tax could not be increased without raising the spectre of social protest and civil disorder. One solution was to raise agricultural productivity, but this was a gradual as well as a formidable task. A more promising alternative was to promote the export sector by a series of official 'pump-priming' development initiatives (which had the advantage of keeping the political and social consequences of economic policy in view), and to increase the proportion of revenue derived, directly or indirectly, from foreign trade.[58]

Judged by indices of volume and value, the export drive produced impressive results. India's overseas trade grew rapidly in the second half of the nineteenth century as she became fully incorporated into the international economy. Export values increased nearly five times between 1870 and 1914, as jute, cotton, indigo and tea flowed to Europe and rice and opium to the Far East.[59] In exchange, India absorbed increasing quantities of manufactured goods, especially from Britain. Her share of Britain's exports jumped from about 8 per cent in the early 1870s to about 13 per cent in the early 1880s, a figure that was almost maintained (though not exceeded) down to 1914.[60] This was a sizeable proportion, given Britain's numerous world-wide trading connections, and it made India her most important market in the empire.[61] It also made Britain India's principal trading partner: she supplied about 85 per cent of India's imports in the 1890s, and the proportion, though falling, was still over 60 per cent on the eve of World War I.[62] About two-thirds of Britain's exports to India in 1880–84 consisted of cotton goods, and the figure was still around three-fifths in 1913. Moroever, the volume and value of cotton goods exported to India grew much faster than to other markets in the second half of the century. In terms of value alone, India's share of Britain's exports of cottons rose from 18 per cent in 1850 to a peak of 27 per cent in 1896, and was still around 20 per cent in 1913.[63]

58. On the oscillations of policy between the twin objectives of development and stability see D.A. Low, *Lion Rampant: Essays in the Study of British Imperialism* (1973), Ch. 2, and Barber, *British Economic Thought*.

59. Charlesworth, *British Rule*, pp. 48–9.

60. Mitchell and Deane, *Abstract of Historical Statistics*, pp. 324–6.

61. Tomlinson, 'India and the British Empire', p. 339.

62. Calculated from K.N. Chaudhuri, 'Foreign Trade and the Balance of Payments (1757–1947)', in Kumar, *Cambridge Economic History*, II, pp. 832–7.

63. D. Farnie, *The English Cotton Industry and the World Market, 1815–1896* (Oxford, 1979), Table 5, p. 91, Table 6, p. 98, Table 7, p. 118, and the authoritative discussion in Ch. 3.

How far this impressive record is to be attributed to official policy and how far to wider developments stimulating the international economy is a matter that needs dissecting, though it is not an operation that needs to be performed here. Evidently, some weight has to be attached to the rise of consumer demand in Europe, to railway construction in India from the 1850s, and to the opening of the Suez Canal in 1869.[64] It is equally clear that Britain's export industries gained greatly from the extension of British sovereignty over India and in particular from the transfer from Company to crown rule in 1858. As Dilke observed in 1869:

> Were we to leave Australia or the Cape, we should continue to be the chief customers of these countries: were we to leave India or Ceylon, they would have no customers at all; for, falling into anarchy, they would cease at once to export their goods to us and to consume our manufactures.[65]

Given that 'anarchy' could mean no more than India's refusal to cooperate with the international commercial order which Britain policed on behalf of the 'civilised' world (as the fate of Egypt subsequently made clear), Dilke's assessment was probably correct. The full value of British rule, the return on political investments first made in the eighteenth century, was not realised until the second half of the nineteenth century, when India became a vital market for Lancashire's cotton goods and when other specialised interests, such as jute manufacturers in Dundee and steel producers in Sheffield, also greatly increased their stake in the sub-continent.

Manchester's role is particularly relevant here because it provides a crucial test of the extent to which industrial lobbies were able to influence imperial policy. Increasing reliance upon the Indian market undoubtedly gave Manchester a keen interest in the development of the sub-continent, even though the link between commerce and empire-building remained a constant embarrassment to the Gladstonian wing of the Liberal Party.[66] At times of crisis, when raw cotton was in short supply or when export markets sagged, Manchester banged the drum for development and campaigned vigorously for

64. John Hurd, 'Railways and the Expansion of Markets in India, 1861–1921', *Expl. Econ. Hist.*, 12 (1975); J. Forbes Munro, 'Suez and the Shipowner: the Response of the Mackinnnon Shipping Group to the Opening of the Suez Canal, 1869–84', in Lewis R. Fischer and Helge W. Nordwick, eds. *Shipping and Trade, 1750–1950: Essays in International Maritime Economic History* (Pontefract, 1990).

65. C.W. Dilke, *Greater Britain*, I (1868), pp. 394–5.

66. W.E. Gladstone, 'Aggression on Egypt and Freedom in the East', *Nineteenth Century*, II (1877), p. 153.

increased spending on public works, for a guaranteed return on capital invested in Indian railways, and for low and non-discriminatory tariffs.[67] Given the importance of the Indian market, it is not surprising that Manchester's antennae were particularly sensitive to tariff issues. In 1859, for example, when the Government of India doubled the import duties paid on cotton goods as a means of meeting the heavy costs of the Mutiny, Lancashire protested vigorously and the tariff was reduced in 1862.[68] In 1874, Manchester was faced with a further threat to its prosperity, when a downturn in international trade coincided with the growth of competition from import-substituting manufactures in India. The Lancashire lobby pressed for the removal of duties on imported cottons, and in 1882, after a period of sustained agitation, the Government of India obliged.[69] When budgetary difficulties forced the government to reintroduce import duties in 1894, cotton goods and yarn were at first exempted. When they were included, later in the same year, strong representations from Manchester ensured that the duty was held at a low level (and was reduced in 1896), and that a 'countervailing' excise was imposed on Indian cotton manufactures.[70]

The activities of the textile lobby deserve emphasis because they provide a clear indication of the ways in which a major manufacturing interest could influence imperial policy at moments when it felt particularly threatened. Nevertheless, it would be mistaken to conclude from this evidence that the 'millocracy' had won a dominant role in the formulation of economic policy, even in the mid-Victorian era, when its influence was probably at its height, and even in India, where its stake was greater than in any other part of the empire. An assessment of the benefits derived by British exporters from the

67. See D. Thorner, *Investment in Empire: British Railway and Steam Shipping Enterprise in India, 1825–1849*, (Philadelphia, Pa, 1950), Ch. 1; Moore, 'Imperialism and "Free Trade" Policy', pp. 135–45; idem, *Sir Charles Wood*, Ch. 6; A.W. Silver, *Manchester Men and Indian Cotton, 1847–72* (Manchester, 1966); Peter Harnetty, *Imperialism and Free Trade: Lancashire and India in the Mid-Nineteenth Century* (Manchester, 1972); and Dwijendra Tripathi's assessment of the cotton supply problem during the American Civil War: 'Opportunism of Free Trade: Lancashire Cotton Famine and Indian Cotton Cultivation', in Sabyasachi Bhattacharya, ed. *Essays in Modern Indian Economic History* (New Delhi, 1987). See also Ian Inkster, 'The "Manchester School" in Yorkshire: Economic Relations Between India and Sheffield in the Mid-Nineteenth Century', *Indian Econ. and Soc. Hist. Rev.*, 23 (1986).

68. Peter Harnetty, 'The Imperialism of Free Trade: Lancashire and the Indian Cotton Duties, 1859–1862', *Econ. Hist. Rev.*, 2nd ser. XVIII (1965).

69. Harnetty, *Imperialism and Free Trade*, Ch. 2.; Ira Klein, 'English Free Traders and Indian Tariffs, 1874–96', *Mod. Asian Stud.*, 5 (1971).

70. Peter Harnetty, 'The Indian Cotton Duties Controversy, 1894–1896', *Eng. Hist. Rev.*, LXXVII (1962); Klein, 'English Free Traders'.

possession of India needs to be related to the aims and ambitions of India's rulers, both in Britain and in the sub-continent. Seen from this perspective, the Lancashire lobby appears to have been far less powerful than Marx supposed; its successes were achieved largely because its aims were congruent with those of India's rulers.

Manchester did indeed press for 'public works', but these were already part of the Government of India's development plans, and had been since at least the 1820s. Governments did not need to be persuaded of the importance of railways in 'opening up' the country because they were an integral feature of the Victorian conception of civilisation and improvement. If the main lines were built to assist economic development, they were also designed to serve the wider administrative and military needs of government, including increasing India's revenue potential.[71] Temporary inducements were offered to help prime the pump, but they were quickly discarded when fiscal problems arose. The Government of India refused to provide financial guarantees for the construction of new railway lines during the period of financial stringency which followed the Indian Mutiny, despite the fact that pressure from Manchester was then at its height, because balancing the budget was a higher priority.[72] In fact, Manchester had virtually no success in directing economic policy along paths that were not already marked out. It was unable to achieve significant representation on the Council of India (the body set up in 1858 to advise the Secretary of State), and its attempts to shape policy towards land, settlement and administration failed, as – predictably – did its effort to secure reductions in the 'large salaries' paid to India's rulers.[73] When accumulated frustration led Manchester to campaign for the removal of the Secretary of State, Sir Charles Wood, in 1862–3, the manufacturing interest was put firmly in its place. Palmerston shared Wood's opinion of 'parvenu capitalists', and he fully endorsed Wood's view that 'India was governed for India and . . . not for the Manchester people'.[74]

71. W.J. MacPherson, 'Investment in Indian Railways, 1845–75', *Econ. Hist. Rev.*, 2nd ser. VIII (1955), p. 179; R.O. Christensen, 'The State and Indian Railway Performance, 1870–1920. Part II: The Government, Rating Policy and Capital Funding', *Jour. Transport Hist.*, 3 (1982).
72. MacPherson, 'Investment', p. 186; Harnetty, *Imperialism and Free Trade*, p. 81; C.J. Dewey, 'The End of the Imperialism of Free Trade: the Eclipse of the Lancashire Lobby and the Concession of Fiscal Autonomy to India', in C.J. Dewey and A.G. Hopkins, eds. *The Imperial Impact: Essays in the Economic History of India and Africa* (1979), pp. 58–9.
73. Silver, *Manchester Men*, pp. 109–11, 152, 249–54; Arthur Redford, *Manchester Merchants and Foreign Trade, II, 1850–1939* (Manchester, 1956), p. 29.
74. Silver, *Manchester Men*, pp. 144, 222 and Ch. 7; Moore, *Sir Charles Wood*, is important for policy as a whole during this period.

Even in the area of tariff policy, Manchester's success was heavily qualified. When the Government of India increased tariffs, it was not because it disagreed with Manchester over the principle of free trade, but because it was driven by fiscal need. This was the case in both 1859 and 1894. In cutting the rate from 10 per cent to 5 per cent, the concession made in 1862 merely returned traders to the position they had been in before the emergency brought about by the Mutiny. The outcome of the negotiations of 1894–6 cannot be counted as a victory for Manchester either, and was not seen in this light by contemporaries, because it established the principle that, in times of need, the Government of India could and would impose a tariff on imports from Britain.[75] Manchester 'reluctantly acquiesced' in the final deal, tried to have it revised, and was defeated in 1903.[76] When tariffs were reduced, it was largely because minimal rates were regarded as being the natural goal of commercial policy, and not because a reluctant government was bent to the will of the industrial lobby.[77] This reasoning undoubtedly applied to the cuts made in 1882, which were allowed only because the government's budgetary position had improved.

A full analysis, which cannot be pursued here, should also place these episodes in the wider context of the evolution of Anglo–Indian relations in the late nineteenth century.[78] In reducing India's tariffs in 1882, for instance, the British government was seeking both to increase the grip of the metropole at a time when the Indian administration appeared to be strengthening its autonomy and to capture the important Lancashire vote at a moment of extreme political fluidity. Similarly, by reimposing duties on imported cotton goods in 1894 and frustrating Manchester's attempts to curtail local competitors, the Government of India was showing an awareness of the need to blunt the edge of nationalist opposition by extending its appeal to progressive elements in India.[79] Even Manchester's least

75. Tomlinson, 'India and the British Empire', p. 345.

76. Redford, *Manchester Merchants*, p. 43.

77. Tomlinson, 'India and the British Empire', pp. 342–5; Klein, 'English Free Traders', pp. 251–71; Dewey, 'The End of the Imperialism of Free Trade'.

78. Dewey, 'The End of the Imperialism of Free Trade', pp. 35–44, 50–2, 55–65. Dewey's study, referred to in full in n.72, provides an excellent account of this context and one, moreover, that has important implications for the study of British imperialism beyond the realm of Anglo–Indian relations.

79. On official awareness of the need to placate nationalist feeling see Marc Jason Gilbert, 'Lord Lansdowne and the Indian Factory Act of 1891: a Study in Indian Economic Nationalism and Proconsular Power', *Journal of Developing Areas*, 16 (1982); Ira Klein, 'Politics and Public Opinion in Lytton's Tariff Policy', *Jour. Indian Hist.*, 45 (1967); and Howard Brasted, 'Indian Nationalist Development and the Influence of Irish Home Rule, 1870–1886', *Mod. Asian Stud.*, 14 (1980). On the growth of competition from Bombay see Farnie, *English Cotton Industry*, pp. 111–12.

qualified successes have to be viewed as part of a process whereby liberal, free-trading interests were given a stake in empire and consequently had their opposition to imperialist expansion compromised. Concessions over tariffs helped to mute potentially serious criticisms of the burdens placed on the Indian budget by the army and the bureaucracy, and persuaded anti-imperialists to acquiesce in the wider aims of the Raj. Gladstone's anguish, as he saw his cosmopolitan principles transformed into imperialist actions, was only the most public example of a process that infected an increasingly vocal segment of the Liberal Party and eventually spread far beyond it.

It is important to recognise, too, that neither Manchester nor industry as a whole ought to be used as a proxy for British business in India. Other sizeable commercial interests, notably in finance and shipping, were also growing rapidly in the second half of the century.[80] After 1858, India attracted an increasing flow of investment from London, and accounted for approximately £286m. of the capital raised on the London stock market between 1865 and 1914.[81] This figure was about 18 per cent of the total placed in the empire, and made India second only to Canada as a recipient of British investment. India's share was even higher at the beginning of the period, when the railway boom was at its peak, but underwent a decline towards the close of the century as other regions (such as Australia) came to the fore, though the total invested annually continued to increase. In addition, substantial sums entered India as direct investments, typically in commerce, services and plantations, though in this case the total can scarcely be guessed at.[82] Thus, as the patronage system served by the East India Company withered away, there arose a new, larger vested interest which relied on rentier incomes from safe overseas investments. Manchester may have pushed hard to secure financial guarantees for railway construction, but the principal beneficiaries were middle-class investors in London and the Home Counties.[83] This constituency of southern investors, and its insti-

80. For an introduction to the history of expatriate business in India from the mid-nineteenth century see B.R. Tomlinson, 'British Business in India, 1860–1970', in R.P.T. Davenport-Hines and Geoffrey Jones, eds. *British Business in Asia Since 1860* (Cambridge, 1989).

81. Lance Davis and Robert A. Huttenback, *Mammon and the Pursuit of Empire: The Political Economy of British Imperialism, 1860–1912* (Cambridge, 1986), Table 2.1 (intermediate estimate), pp. 40–1, and 43–53; D.C.M. Platt, *Britain's Investment Overseas on the Eve of the First World War* (1986), pp. 88–9.

82. Platt, *Britain's Investment*, pp. 54–7; Tomlinson, 'British Business', pp. 114–16.

83. MacPherson, 'Investment in Indian Railways', pp. 181–4. MacPherson's evidence on India fits neatly with the broader conclusions reached by Davis and Huttenback, *Mammon*, Ch. 7.

tutional representatives in banking and shipping, fell in readily behind the flag of empire and gave full support to policies of free trade and sound money. If British rule in India was helpful to British industry, it was vital to British investment.

The growth of British trade and investment in the second half of the century was bound up with important institutional changes in banking and finance, though these have only recently begun to receive the historical attention they deserve.[84] India's external commerce had long suffered from inadequate credit facilities, and this problem had impaired the smooth functioning of multilateral trade and especially the transfer of funds to London. A solution to these difficulties was a central part of the settlement which followed the end of Company rule. The new administration developed an efficient system of making remittances by using Council Bills, which were sold in India for rupees and redeemed in London for sterling, redefined the role of the four semi-official Presidency Banks to bring them into line with sound banking principles, and pressed on with measures to standardise India's currencies.[85] It also created a climate of confidence which encouraged the spread of private commercial banks. Out of the banking boom that followed in the 1860s and 1870s emerged the National Bank of India, which was founded in Calcutta in 1863.[86] The National Bank began as a rupee-based bank and with a complement of Indian and expatriate directors. But it soon moved its headquarters to London (in 1866), denominated its reserves in sterling and steadily anglicised its personnel and ethos. Besides financing overseas trade, the National Bank invested in the production of tea, coffee, cotton and indigo, and, significantly, in Indian cotton mills.

84. Tomlinson, 'British Business', pp. 93–4.
85. B.R. Tomlinson, 'Exchange Depreciation and Economic Development: India and the Silver Standard, 1872–1893', in Clive Dewey, ed. *Arrested Development in India: The Historical Dimension* (Manohar, 1988), pp. 223–38 (on the use of Council Bills); Amiya Kumar Bagchi, 'Anglo-Indian Banking in British India: From the Paper Pound to the Gold Standard', *Jour. Imp. and Comm. Hist.*, XIII (1985). On the early history of banking see Amiya K. Bagchi, *The Evolution of the State Bank of India: The Roots, 1806–1876*, I, *The Early Years, 1806–1860*, and II, *Diversity and Regrouping, 1860–1876* (Bombay, 1987). On currencies see S. Ambirajan, *Political Economy and Monetary Management: India, 1766–1914* (New Delhi, 1984), pp. 76–85 and Ch. 6; and John S. Deyell and R.E. Frykenberg, 'Sovereignty and the "Sikha" under Company Raj: Minting Prerogative and Imperial Legitimacy in India', *Indian Econ. and Soc. Hist. Rev.*, 19 (1982).
86. Geoffrey Tyson, *100 Years of Banking in Asia and Africa* (1963). Frank H.H. King, *A Concise Economic History of Modern China* (New York, 1968), Ch. 3, traces the links between banks operating in India and China. Unfortunately, there is no equivalent study for India of King's monumental history of the Hongkong and Shanghai Bank (which we have used extensively in Chapter 13).

By 1900 the Bank had 19 principal offices spanning Ceylon, Burma and East Africa, as well as India. By then, too, the Bank had become part of the City hierarchy and had developed ties with Whitehall and the Indian Civil Service which led to seats on the Board of Directors for a number of retired officials.

The transition from Company to crown control also provided a boost to shipping services, which were needed for government business as well as for private trade. When Sir William Mackinnon's shipping group secured the official mail contracts for India in the early 1860s, the government provided him with a maritime subsidy that paralleled the inducements offered on land to investors in the railway system, except that it lasted a good deal longer.[87] Consequently, Mackinnon was well placed to take advantage of the growth of trade that followed the opening of the Suez Canal in 1869, and his firm, Mackinnon Mackenzie, also spread into various land-based enterprises, including jute and cotton mills. Mackinnon's official connection gave him ready access to policy-making circles in India, and he established a particularly close relationship with the Governor of Bombay, Bartle Frere, a like-minded imperialist who was equally keen to capitalise on the link between profit and patriotism.[88] In the 1870s, Mackinnon shifted his head office from Clydeside to London, where he cultivated connections in Whitehall and acquired directorships in the City, including a seat on the board of the National Bank of India.

When Mackinnon died in 1893, his empire was inherited by James Mackay (later Lord Inchcape), who showed himself to be equally skilled in using political contacts to oil the machinery of commerce.[89] In the 1890s, Mackay became President of the Bombay Chamber of Commerce and a member of India's Legislative Council, and he established a privileged relationship with Lansdowne, who was Viceroy from 1888 to 1894. After the turn of the century, Mackay, like his predecessor, acquired directorships of leading banks in London, and he also became a tireless and ubiquitous member of numerous Whitehall committees. He received a knighthood for his work on Indian currency reform, and a peerage in 1911 as compensa-

87. J. Forbes Munro, 'Shipping Subsidies and Railway Guarantees: William Mackinnon, Eastern Africa and the Indian Ocean, 1860–93', *Jour. African Hist.*, 28 (1987); idem, 'Scottish Overseas Enterpise and the Lure of London: the Mackinnon Group, 1847–1893', *Scottish Econ. and Soc. Hist.*, 8 (1988); and Stephanie Jones, *Two Centuries of Overseas Trading: The Origins and Growth of the Inchape Group* (1986).

88. See pp. 387–90.

89. Stephanie Jones, *Trade and Shipping: Lord Inchcape, 1852–1932* (Manchester, 1989).

tion for failing to become Viceroy two years earlier. He was Morley's choice but he received Asquith's veto. Intimate though the connections between acceptable commerce and high politics had become, there were still lines to be drawn, and Asquith did not intend to appoint a businessman to the viceroyalty, even one who had once been a prominent member of the Bombay Hunt.

The twin imperatives of holding the Raj together and keeping faith with external creditors exercised a pervasive, almost determining, effect on British policy in India. Between 1858 and 1898 India's remittances to external creditors averaged nearly half the value of her exports: about 30 per cent of the total represented payments for private services, including interest on investments and repatriated profits, and the remaining 20 per cent was accounted for by official obligations, the 'Home Charges', which consisted of pension and leave payments, bills for military equipment and stores, and interest on the public debt.[90] Successive Viceroys frightened themselves with the recurring nightmare that India might default on her external obligations. The fear was graphically expressed by Lord Mayo in 1869:

> We hold India by a thread. At any moment a serious danger might arise. We owe now £180 millions, more than 85 per cent of which is held in England. Add £100 millions to this and an Indian disaster would entail consequences equal to the extinction of half the National Debt. The loss of India or a portion of it would be nothing as compared to the ruin which would occur at home.[91]

Although the budgetary position improved in the 1880s, by the 1890s external obligations were rising faster than income from customs duties and the land tax, and could no longer be covered by the export surplus. As a result, India was able to balance her payments only by further borrowing.[92] Failure to service these obligations would have been disastrous for British rule in India and would have had far-reaching repercussions on the international economy and on Britain too, as Mayo clearly saw.

90. The fullest account of the 'Home Charges' and of the associated 'Drain' from India is in Banerji, *Aspects*, Chs. 4 and 8 and Appendix II. See also K.N. Chaudhuri, 'India's International Economy in the Nineteenth Century: an Historical Survey', *Mod. Asian Stud.*, 2 (1968), B.R. Tomlinson, *The Political Economy of the Raj, 1914–1947* (Cambridge, 1979), Ch. 11 and Table 1.1, p. 18, and James Foreman-Peck, 'Foreign Investment and Imperial Exploitation: Balance of Payments Reconstruction for Nineteenth-Century Britain and India', *Econ. Hist.Rev.*, 2nd ser. XLII (1989).

91. Mayo to Argyll, 17 May 1869, quoted in S. Gopal, *British Policy in India, 1858–1905* (Cambridge, 1965), pp. 91–2.

92. Banerji, *Aspects*, Table 34, pp. 168–9, Table 38, p. 220, and Tables 40a and 40b, pp. 236–7; Dietmar Rothermund, *An Economic History of India* (1989), p. 43.

To prevent Mayo's nightmare from becoming a reality, India had to generate a sizeable export surplus and keep a firm grip on expenditure. Export earnings could not be boosted by bilateral exchange because India ran a growing trading deficit with Britain from the 1870s. The great merit of free trade, the quality which made it a much-prized orthodoxy, was that it allowed India to settle her trade deficit with Britain by using profits from exports shipped to countries elsewhere in Asia and in continental Europe. Moreover, this surplus was vital to the maintenance of the pattern of multilateral settlements which enabled Britain, in turn, to settle more than two-fifths of her own trading deficits, principally with Europe and North America.[93] The essence of this relationship was fully appreciated by contemporaries, as a memorandum from the India Office made clear in 1907:

> The aggregate exports from India to Asiatic and African ports, including the Crown Colonies of Ceylon, the Straits Settlements, and Mauritius, exceed in value her export trade with the continent of Europe. The balance of trade in both cases is largely in India's favour, and represents the sources from which she satisfies the heavy balance against her on her trading, debt, and administrative accounts with the United Kingdom.[94]

The India Office also noted that India had 'a large net balance in its favour on its trade with America as a whole, which no doubt finds its way to the United Kingdom in adjustment of international trade'.[95] The memorandum concluded that 'as a debtor country India requires the freest possible market for its exports, and as a poor country it requires cheap imports', and that 'any diminution of India's trade with those foreign countries that are the largest buyers of her exports would at once lessen her power of buying English produce and meeting her obligations to her English creditors'.[96]

The priority attached to upholding the multilateral payments system by means of free trade greatly reduced the scope for concessions to British industry. The India Office foresaw that, if British manufacturers were given preferential treatment in India, it 'would be likely to give rise to demands for other changes in the fiscal system

---

93. S.B. Saul, *Studies in British Overseas Trade, 1870–1914* (Liverpool, 1960), Chs. 3–4, and the discussion in Banerji, *Aspects*, pp. 18–23. India's multilateral settlements are considered further in A.J.H. Latham, 'Merchandise Trade Imbalances and Uneven Economic Development in India and China', *Jour. Eur. Econ. Hist.*, 7 (1978), pp. 37–40.

94. India Office, 'Memorandum on Preferential Tariffs in their Application to India', in *Papers Laid Before the Colonial Conference, 1907*, Cd 3524 (1907), p. 1,155. We are indebted to Dr B.R. Tomlinson for providing this reference.

95. Ibid. p. 1,155.

96. Ibid. p. 456.

of the country which would be very difficult to refuse', and in particular would encourage agitation in support of India's own import-substituting industries.[97] Consequently, successive Viceroys were unresponsive to Manchester's pleas for action to control India's burgeoning textile industry. When the Lancashire lobby attempted to eliminate the competitive advantage of its Bombay rivals by imposing factory legislation on India in 1891, the Viceroy devised an alternative that offered some safeguards to Indian workers but none to Manchester, and was accordingly received favourably by nationalist opinion.[98] Indeed, since local manufactures economised on imports, helped to balance the budget and hence maintained the confidence of overseas investors, the Government of India had good reason for encouraging them. As Lord Northbrook observed in 1874: 'I am very happy also on the progress of Indian manufactures ultimately. Whisper it not in Manchester'.[99] In the 1880s, Lord Ripon's policy of favouring local manufacturers for government purchases stimulated a wide range of industries and culminated in the development of a state-operated iron and steel plant.[100] Curzon's efforts to promote manufacturing in India after the turn of the century aroused renewed alarm in Lancashire. But the textile lobby's representations were again ineffective because the Viceroy's policy, though interventionist, was not protectionist and did not endanger budgetary stability.[101]

The need to keep a tight grip on expenditure had an influence that extended beyond the realm of economic policy and into administration and defence. As noted earlier, considerations of cost encouraged the adoption of cheap methods of internal control based on indirect rule and the mystique of racial supremacy.[102] After the Mutiny, fiscal imperatives also hastened moves towards political decentralisation which aimed at defusing opposition and generating fresh sources of revenue in the provinces.[103] In the manner of colonial

97. Ibid. pp. 456–7.
98. Gilbert, 'Lord Lansdowne', pp. 357–72.
99. Northbrook to Clerk, 27 Feb. 1874, quoted in Gopal, *British Policy*, p. 109.
100. Sunil K. Sen, 'Economic Measures of Lord Ripon's Government, 1880–84', in Bhattacharya, *Essays in Modern Indian Economic History*, pp. 217–23.
101. Clive Dewey, 'The Government of India's "New Industrial Policy", 1900–1925: Formation and Failure', in K.N. Chaudhuri and C.J. Dewey, eds. *Economy and Society: Essays in Indian Economic and Social History* (Delhi, 1979), pp. 231, 238.
102. See, for example, Michael H. Fisher, 'Indirect Rule in the British Empire: the Foundations of the Residency System in India (1764–1858)', *Mod. Asian Stud.*, 18 (1984); Robert Frykenberg, 'Elite Groups in a South Indian District, 1788–1858', *Indo-British Review*, 10 (1983); Frances M. Mannsakar, 'East and West: Anglo-Indian Racial Attitudes as Reflected in Popular Fiction, 1890–1914', *Victorian Studies*, 24 (1980).
103. Tomlinson, 'India and the British Empire', pp. 347–9.

solutions, this strategy created new problems by lending impetus to the formation of the Indian National Congress in 1885, and it prompted further constitutional concessions (the Morley-Minto reforms) after the turn of the century.[104] In essence, Britain's aim was to group conservative elements (Muslim and Hindu) behind the Raj and to head off militant nationalists by promoting a 'loyal opposition' in the hope of incorporating it.[105] Unrest, it was widely believed, was bad for investment. The need to hold defence expenditure down left its mark on India's external relations too. The cost of stabilising frontiers with Persia, Afghanistan and Tibet, for example, acted as a check on military action and eventually pushed Britain into an agreement with Russia in 1907, against the wishes of an influential group which favoured a more bellicose stance.[106]

The Government of India's internal fiscal and monetary reforms were complemented by a policy that aimed at stabilising the external value of the silver rupee to ensure the smooth payment of international obligations and to maintain the confidence of foreign investors. The process of internal reform was completed in the late 1850s and in the 1860s, as part of the administrative settlement that followed the abolition of Company rule. But serious problems arose on the external account from the 1870s, when falling world prices for silver led to the progressive depreciation of the rupee against sterling.[107] The Government of India found itself in difficulties because it raised its revenues in rupees and had to make payments in London in sterling. Initially, the budgetary consequences of this adverse trend were offset to some extent by the fact that the depreciation of the rupee raised the price of imports, encouraged import-substitution, and boosted India's exports.[108] From the mid–1880s, however, taxes

104. A. Seal, *The Emergence of Indian Nationalism* (Cambridge, 1968); Gordon Johnson, *Provincial Politics and Indian Nationalism: Bombay and the I.N.C., 1880–1915* (Cambridge, 1973); Stanley Wolpert, *Morley and India, 1906–1910* (Berkeley, Calif., 1967); and Pardaman Singh, *Lord Minto and Indian Nationalism, 1905–1910* (Allahabad, 1976).

105. This is well brought out by Singh, *Lord Minto*.

106. Ira Klein, 'The Anglo-Russian Convention and the Problems of Central Asia, 1907–1914', *Jour. Brit. Stud.*, 11 (1971); Sheh Mahajan, 'The Problems of the Defence of India and the Formation of the Anglo-Russian Entente, 1900–1907', *Jour. Indian Hist.*, 58 (1980).

107. Ambirajan, *Political Economy*, Ch. 7; Banerji, *Aspects*, Ch. 10. See also Arnold Kaminski, '"Lombard Street" and India: Currency Problems in the Late Nineteenth Century', *Indian Econ. and Soc. Hist. Rev.*, 17 (1980).

108. Banerji, *Aspects*, Ch. 10; Chaudhuri, 'India's International Economy', pp. 47–50. To the extent that the decline in the value of the rupee represented an adjustment to a chronic balance of payments deficit, as well as to a fall in the price of silver, it would have reinforced the trend towards higher import prices and given further encouragement to import-substitution.

had to be increased to secure the additional rupees needed to meet external obligations, and there were worrying signs that taxpayers were beginning to feed their discontent into the embryonic nationalist movement. Investors were also losing confidence in the rupee, and the expatriates who ran the Indian Civil Service and the Indian Army were becoming anxious about their declining ability to purchase sterling assets. By the 1890s, the effective devaluation of the rupee had reached a point where action had to be taken to protect the value of external payments, and the problem was eventually resolved, after a formidably complicated and protracted debate, by moving the rupee to a gold–exchange standard from 1898.

The interest of this outcome, in the present context, lies in the evidence it provides about the motives of contending parties to the debate and about their influence on policy. Sterling's growing strength against the rupee presented British industrialists, headed by Manchester, with an increasingly difficult market. Manchester wanted a solution that would help to restore its position in the Indian market and also undercut the competitive advantage of Bombay cottons in the Far East. After some uncertainty, the Manchester interest put its weight behind a bimetallist solution as being the one best calculated to achieve this result and also to prevent the Government of India from raising import duties.[109] This proposal, though propelled with considerable force, left scarcely a mark on the defenders of monetary orthodoxy: not only was bimetallism rejected, but also duties were imposed on imported cotton goods in 1894, as we have seen.[110] The Government of India favoured the introduction of a gold standard, which it considered to be the most effective way of overcoming the problem of remitting the Home Charges and of protecting the salaries of its officials.[111] The alternative was to compensate for the decline of the rupee by further tax increases, but senior officials in India opposed this course of action because they feared its political consequences.[112] Their arguments carried considerable weight in Whitehall and the City, where monetary orthodoxy held sway and where there was a strong vested interest in safeguarding the value of funds transferred from India to Britain.[113]

109. Redford, *Manchester Merchants*, pp. 34–42.
110. Ambirajan, *Political Economy*, pp. 119–20, 130–2, 144–5. Powerful interests involved in India's export trade (notably the British-dominated tea industry) wished to retain the silver standard, but they, too, were disappointed. See Tomlinson, *Political Economy*, p. 17.
111. Ambirajan, *Political Economy*, pp. 100, 178.
112. Ibid. pp. 100, 108, 128–9, 137, 142, 178.
113. This is not to suggest that there was a unanimous view in the City of how this could be achieved. For a summary of the discussion see pp. 151–3.

In the event, a gold-exchange standard was established in preference to a gold standard, partly because it was cheaper and partly because Whitehall was concerned that the adoption of a full gold standard would increase the independence of the authorities in India.[114] Manchester's defeat brought only incidental compensation: raising the exchange rate of the rupee against silver reduced the currency advantage of Bombay's textile exports, but the adjustment was insufficient to halt the advance of competition from Indian manufactures.[115] The Government of India secured its principal objectives, though it was not immediately reconciled to a gold-exchange system without a local, gold-based currency. The City's gains were considerable and unqualified: the new arrangements drew India more firmly into the orbit of London finance and did so at minimum cost and risk; and the removal of uncertainty over remittances encouraged a flow of new investment into the sub-continent.[116] The result was a triumph for the Gold Standard Defence Association, an alliance of City bankers and Whitehall officials whose purpose was to block deviations from orthodoxy of the kind proposed by Manchester and its allies.[117]

On the eve of World War I, India was still the largest market for Britain's exports in the empire, and was particularly important for the older staple manufactures, such as textiles and metal products.[118] Yet India, like many other parts of the empire, disappointed the expectations of a generation of British industrialists in the period before 1914. As we have seen, India's share of Britain's exports reached a peak early in the 1880s, while Britain's share of India's imports fell steadily during the second half of the nineteenth century.[119] To some extent, of course, the expectations of manufacturers were, as ever, exaggerated, not least because India remained resolutely poor and the new frontiers opened by the railway either lacked potential or were slow to realise it. Nevertheless, it is hard to avoid the conclusion that free trade provided ambiguous benefits for British

114. Ambirajan, *Political Economy*, pp. 152–7, 164–9, 182. On the difficulties of establishing a full gold standard see ibid., Ch. 6 and p. 123, and Banerji, *Aspects*, p. 225.

115. Farnie, *English Cotton Industry*, pp. 111–13.

116. Ambirajan, *Political Economy*, pp. 100, 167–71, 176; Banerji, *Aspects*, pp. 115–18; Chaudhuri, 'India's International Ecnomy', pp. 47–50; and the data in Davis and Huttenback, *Mammon*, pp. 41, 44–5.

117. E.H.H. Green, 'Rentiers versus Producers? The Political Economy of the Bimetallic Controversy', *Eng. Hist. Rev.*, LIII (1988).

118. Tomlinson, *Political Economy*, pp. 2–3.

119. Calculated from Chaudhuri, 'Foreign Trade', pp. 832–7. See also Tomlinson, 'India and the British Empire', p. 339.

industry in India, as indeed elsewhere. The open door offered a market for British goods, but it allowed entry to foreign rivals, too, and it did nothing to halt the development of indigenous competitors.[120] Moreover, India's need to generate an export surplus to fund her remittances to London gave the Government of India an incentive to restrain imports, where possible, and to promote import-substituting activities. But Manchester was tied into free trade as she was tied into the empire: had Britain adopted protectionism, India would have followed suit, and Manchester would have suffered more from the change than from continuing to endure the rigours of free trade.[121] Similarly, although Manchester found few favours within the empire, her prospects were still better there than in countries that were neutral but uncongenial, or unfriendly and therefore forbidding.

FINANCIAL IMPERATIVES AND BRITISH RULE

Despite the insights that he offered into events in India, Marx was mistaken in supposing that the demise of the East India Company symbolised the rise of the 'millocracy'. British policy towards India cannot be understood on the assumption that the industrial bourgeoisie finally grasped the levers of power in 1858. But this does not imply that 'economic' explanations of empire-building ought to make way for 'political' alternatives, still less that this polarity provides a satisfactory framework of analysis. Nor does it mean that the causes of Britain's presence in India can be left to historians of the eighteenth century, while historians of the nineteenth century concentrate on techniques of control and the consequences of imperial rule.

It is more plausible to interpret India's enlarged role within the imperial system between 1858 and 1914 as representing the extension abroad of the financial and service interests that had achieved prominence at home following the demise of Old Corruption and protectionism. These interests had already begun to shape India's international trade and the character of the Raj before 1858. The

120. Belgian iron and steel products and German textiles provided increasing competition after about 1900; whatever the fate of Indian handicraft workers earlier in the century, the new textile industry in Bombay made considerable headway under British rule from the 1880s onwards. See M.D. Morris, *The Emergence of an Industrial Labour Force in India: A Study of the Bombay Cotton Mills, 1854–1947* (Berkeley, Calif., 1965); and Makrand Mehta, *The Ahmedabad Cotton Textile Industry: Genesis and Growth* (Ahmedabad, 1982).

121. As contemporaries were well aware: Redford, *Manchester Merchants*, p. 46.

transition to crown rule after that date marked the assumption of authority by the new gentlemanly meritocracy and its 'like-minded' associates in finance and commercial services, the quantitative expansion of the economic influences they represented, and the installation of the Gladstonian orthodoxies of free trade, sound money and balanced budgets. In India, as in other parts of the empire which had to make large remittances to London, financial priorities overrode the claims of British industry. Moreover, since the multilateral trade regime was crucial to settling Britain's balance of payments, the gains accruing to finance and commercial services from free trade could also be presented as being of national rather than merely of sectional importance. British governments were concerned to keep industry content, especially at times of crisis, but in the last resort it was more important that India's debts were settled than that British goods were bought.

British industry, especially textiles, also gained from Britain's control of India and from the transfer from Company to crown rule in 1858. But Manchester's power was limited, even in India, the case which ought to provide an impressive illustration of the ability of manufacturers to shape imperial policy. The influence of the industrial lobby reached its height in the middle of the century rather than later on, when the new service interests had taken a firm grip on the formulation of policy and on the shape of India's international economic relations. Even so, manufacturers gained most where their aims were congruent with those of the civil and commercial service elite, whose main concern was to ensure that there were no impediments to the flow of India's multilateral trade and remittances. As the manufacturing interest became tied into the empire, so it lost its anti-imperialist stance; as it was offered a large new market, so too it lapsed into a conservative reliance on old staples. And, just as India became firmly incorporated into Britain's burgeoning service economy, so Manchester's fortunes came to depend increasingly on the southern-based diaspora whose leaders in London and far-flung representatives east of Suez were at once strong advocates and principal beneficiaries of the Raj.[122]

India, then, is no exception to the rules of imperial expansion: it offers, as it ought to do, a prime example of the gentlemanly forces which promoted expansion in the eighteenth century and, in their stronger, reconstructed form, shaped the Raj in the nineteenth and

---

122. The commitment of the educated classes to the imperial cause was emphasised by H.N. Brailsford, *The War of Steel and Gold* (1915), pp. 86–8.

twentieth centuries. Moreover, the chronology of expansion in India fits the pattern of causation identified in this study in reflecting not only the shift from Old Corruption and protectionism to the new meritocracy and free trade, but also in demonstrating the limits to the realisation of imperialist intentions before the mid-nineteenth century and the greater extent to which they were implemented thereafter. In offering this long perspective, India also provides a unique illustration, outside the white empire, of British imperialism untrammelled by foreign rivals. The British worried permanently about unstable frontiers, but inside India their policies were shaped without reference to the interests of foreign powers. The Indian example, we suggest, reveals the priorities of policy particularly clearly, and in doing so erects a signpost to other cases of imperialism where Britain's motives were complicated and often clouded by the presence of foreign rivals. Of course, motives identified in India cannot be transported to explain other episodes; but, where similarities already exist, it is instructive to bear the Indian case in mind, given the tendency of current intepretations, especially of the partition of Africa and the scramble for China, to assume that Britain was a defensive if not a declining power and to treat her actions as being reactions to initiatives taken by more athletic rivals.

This analysis suggests that India ought to be reincorporated into the study of empire-bulding in the nineteenth century rather than treated as a special case or as an imperfectly explained legacy of the eighteenth century. If this argument has merit, then India's significance for theories of imperial expansion extends far beyond her own frontiers: the multilateral trading ties and financial flows that Britain established with the sub-continent foreshadowed bonds of incorporation that were forged with other parts of the underdeveloped world and with the colonies of white settlement during the second half of the nineteenth century; the defence of vital interests in India, once they are defined, helps to explain how Britain's imperial design came to be tacked on to parts of the Middle East, south-east Asia and China. These ramifications cannot be explored here, but the comparison with the many other countries that experienced the 'debt crisis' of the late nineteenth century needs to be firmly identified, if only to suggest a route for future research. In Australia, New Zealand and Argentina, which were on a gold standard, devaluation was ruled out at times of crisis and deflationary policies were imposed. In Egypt and the Ottoman Empire, as we shall see, the bailiffs were sent in to deal with default. In India the bailiffs were already present, and 'sound' management combined with the unplanned depreciation of the silver rupee enabled the government to escape the most extreme consequences of indebtedness – economic chaos and political upheaval. The case of China, which was also on a silver standard, is particularly interesting in this connection. The depreciation of China's silver currency appears not to have stimulated exports to any noticeable extent, but it does seem to have aroused concern among external creditors about the security of their investments, and it may have encouraged them to try to take a firmer grip on the management of China's finances.

At this point speculation runs ahead of research: but it should at least be clear from the foregoing comments that gentlemanly interests were very much to the fore in India, and that, in forging India's links with the international economy, they created, and often foreshadowed, relations of the kind that Britain established elsewhere in the world after 1850. By perceiving these connections, we can improve our appreciation of the value of the jewel in the crown and the reasons for keeping it polished and protected.

CHAPTER ELEVEN

'The Imperious and Irresistible Necessity': Britain and the Partition of Africa[1]

Nowhere does the weight of historiography press so insistently upon the study of imperialism as in the case of the partition of Africa. So much has been written on this theme on behalf of so many competing theories that few interpretations, even of points of detail, can resist the absorptive power of the existing literature.[2] Given that the quality of this research is as impressive as its weight, it might be thought that the subject now requires fine-tuning rather than thorough reappraisal. However, the growth of knowledge has had the perplexing result of making it easier to say what is wrong with current interpretations than what is right. Historians who wish to move beyond this point appear to face a choice between retreating to the high ground of deductive certainty and taking shelter in the empirical undergrowth. Yet, as we shall try to show, the anomalies in the literature can be resolved once the assumptions underlying existing interpretations are removed.

Marxist and Marxisant interpretations have performed particularly badly, despite some excellent research on specific subjects, largely because of their failure to relate partition to the realities of capitalist development in the late nineteenth century. Because the trail taken by the agents of advanced industrial capitalism bypassed much of Africa, the hounds seem to have lost the scent. Aside from tentative attempts

1. The quotation is from the Earl of Cromer (Evelyn Baring), *Ancient and Modern Imperialism* (1910), pp. 19–20. This study, which draws on Baring's long experience in Egypt, deploys many of the ideas which today are associated with modern studies of the 'official mind' of imperialism.

2. The fullest and most recent survey is R.A. Oliver and G.N. Sanderson, eds. *The Cambridge History of Africa*, Vol.6, *1870–1905* (Cambridge, 1985). See in particular the important contributions by Sanderson, Hargreaves, Marks, and Lonsdale, and the extensive bibliographical essay.

to treat partition as being an expression of feeble capitalist influences and atavistic social forces (a view that brings Marx uncomfortably close to Schumpeter),[3] most work in the Marxist tradition has fallen back upon very broad generalisations associating capitalism with imperialism. There is at present no study of partition from a Marxist perspective which combines a recognition of the analytical weaknesses of parts of the theory of capitalist imperialism with a detailed knowledge of the empirical literature.

Liberal interpretations, by contrast, have flourished on the diversity revealed by recent research, both on Africa and on policy-making in Europe. This evidence has been used to underline the inadequacies of standard Marxist accounts and to construct various alternatives, the most coherent, and certainly the most celebrated, being that advanced by Robinson and Gallagher.[4] However, this interpretation has now become a casualty of the work it has inspired. It commands unanimous respect among specialists but only their qualified support. To claim that imperialism was the result of crises on the periphery is to report the symptoms, not to diagnose the cause; to attribute British intervention to the actions of European rivals is to assign to others impulses which might properly be looked for at home. Indeed, were it not for the fact that metropolitan-based explanations of imperialism have been discredited by the poor performance of Marxist theories, it is unlikely that interpretations of British policy would have come to rest quite so heavily on decisions taken by other countries. However, Robinson and Gallagher's critics have in turn become victims of their own success, for they have provided explanations for every episode and often for every event, with the result that the repertoire of possibilities has become so extensive that it is almost impossible to comprehend the subject as a whole.

Disarray may well be a faithful representation of historical reality; and it also accords with a view of history which denies that there is a whole to be grasped. Nevertheless, an awareness of diversity is consistent with an explanation of partition which seeks to reconstruct the context within which numerous individual actions took place; and in our view, it is also compatible with the historian's obligation to try to advance beyond accounts which rely on 'the interplay of the

---

3. See, for example, the interesting essay by Catherine Coquery-Vidrovitch, 'De l'impérialisme britannique à l'impérialisme contemporain: l'atavar colonial', in Jean Bouvier and René Girault, eds. *L'impérialisme français d'avant 1914* (Paris, 1976).

4. Ronald Robinson and John Gallagher with Alice Denny, *Africa and the Victorians: The Official Mind of Imperialism* (1961; 2nd edn 1981).

contingent and the unforeseen',[5] or make a virtue of surrendering in the face of the infinite complexity of events. The problem, as defined here, is to explain how Britain's changing interest in Africa influenced her presence there in the second half of the nineteenth century with the result that she moved from being a power on the coast to being a power in the land and, more than this, the most important of the continent's colonial powers. Our suggested solution will be presented in two parts. We shall begin by showing how Africa as a whole was touched by Britain's plan for harmonious world development in the nineteenth century, and how this programme was recharged and also reshaped by the extension of finance and services to Africa after 1850. The regional implications of this new impetus will then be considered by looking at Egypt, southern Africa and tropical Africa. These examples are not comprehensive, but they cover Britain's principal areas of interest, before and after partition, and thus provide a crucial test of any general interpretation of the scramble for power in Africa.

BRITAIN'S FIRST DEVELOPMENT PLAN FOR AFRICA

The decision taken in 1807 to outlaw the slave trade initiated a new era in Britain's long-standing relations with Africa.[6] Thereafter, there began a campaign to 'regenerate' the continent by promoting the 'civilising' values of commerce and Christianity.[7] This endeavour, as we have seen, touched every continent, if not quite every country. The utilitarians cut their teeth, and more besides, on India's ancient institutions; a new generation of commercial crusaders laid seige to the Sublime Porte, and Christian missionaries knocked presumptuously at China's ancient doors. But Africa, the Dark Continent, had a special appeal; for there, in the aftermath of the Atlantic slave trade, it seemed that economic backwardness and moral degeneration had reached the lowest possible levels, and it was there, consequently,

5. Fisher's widely quoted phrase has come to stand for a form of liberal individualism in historical writing and in opposition to the 'scientific' history written by Toynbee and others. See H.A.L. Fisher, *A History of Europe* (1936), p. v.

6. The substantial revisionist literature on this subject can be followed through Barbara L. Solow and Stanley L. Engerman, eds. *British Capitalism and Caribbean Slavery* (Cambridge, 1987); and David Eltis, *Economic Growth and the Ending of the Transatlantic Slave Trade* (Oxford, 1987).

7. J. Gallagher, 'Fowell Buxton and the New African Policy, 1838–1842', *Cambridge Hist. Jour.*, 10 (1950) is the starting point for what is now a substantial literature on this theme.

that the ultimate test of the supremacy of Western culture and skills was to be found.[8] The comprehensiveness of the new programme, and its confident belief that a combination of approved values and appropriate technology would both transform the world and cause it to be grateful, had no rival until the United States (unmindful of the precedent) promulgated a similar set of doctrines after 1945

The most obvious effects of this endeavour were to be seen at points on the African coast that were designated as centres of diffusion. In southern Africa, it was expected that white settlers would play the role of 'like-minded' agents of metropolitan policy.[9] Here, strategy and commerce were closely entwined, both as means and ends, from the outset. A dependable colonial community was the best long-term defence of the route to India; a prosperous and progressive colony would remain dependable and would also promote trade, spread enlightened values, and ultimately become self-support-ing. Spurred by this prospect, Britain reinforced the Cape after the French Wars by assisting emigration in 1819, and then attempted to 'Anglicise' the colony in the 1820s by crossing the social values of the English gentleman with the business ethic of the middle class.[10] Measures were taken against the slave trade and (after 1833) against the institution of slavery, and experiments with 'legitimate' commerce produced exports of wine, wool, grain and sugar.[11]

In other parts of Africa, where there were no white settlers, the universal ideals of the early and mid-Victorian periods had to be implanted into indigenous societies which themselves had very different characteristics. In west Africa, a new generation of educated, Christian Africans, who were intended to be the progenitors of a compliant middle class, arose in the main ports, and legitimate commodities, notably palm oil, began to flow from the hinterland in exchange for British cotton goods.[12] In north and east Africa, Britain had to negotiate her way in a more alien milieu. As there was no

8. For this aspect of European perceptions of Africa see A.G. Hopkins, 'Of Africa and Golden Joys', *Genève-Afrique*, 23 (1985).

9. Stanley Trapido, 'From Paternalism to Liberalism: the Cape Colony, 1800–1834', *Internat. Hist. Rev.*, 12 (1990).

10. James Sturgis, 'Anglicanisation at the Cape of Good Hope in the Early Nineteenth Century', *Jour. Imp. and Comm. Hist.*, XI (1982).

11. Robert Ross, 'The Relative Importance of Exports and the Internal Market for the Agriculture of the Cape Colony, 1770–1855', in G. Liesegang, H. Pasch and A. Jones, eds. *Figuring African Trade* (Berlin, 1986). The local currency, the Rixdollar, was tied to sterling from 1827. The 'rising gentry' also used coerced labour, as Clifton Crais has shown: 'Gentry and Labour in Three Eastern Cape Districts, 1820–1865', *South Afr. Hist. Jour.*, 18 (1986).

12. A.G. Hopkins, *An Economic History of West Africa* (1973; 1988), Ch. 4.

realistic prospect of making use of either white settlers or black Christians, working relationships were established with Muslim centralisers in Egypt and Zanzibar. In these cases, necessity imposed the virtue of tolerance, subject only to Palmerston's basic requirement that the state concerned should be 'well-kept' and 'always accessible'.[13] A combination of commercial self-interest and menace fostered the expansion of trade in raw cotton and manufactures with Egypt from the 1820s.[14] With greater effort, it also began to check the east African slave trade and encouraged a modest growth in exports of ivory, cloves and sugar.[15] In these diverse ways, new impulses from Britain touched the edges of the continent and sowed the seeds of the 'green revolution' which was eventually to produce the export-crop economies of colonial Africa.

Nevertheless, during the first half of the nineteenth century reform and development made disappointingly slow progress in Africa, as indeed elsewhere. The belief that unfree labour was incompatible with modern capitalism, though morally appealing, proved to be mistaken. The external slave trade, far from withering away, continued to flourish while it remained profitable, and the institution of slavery was strengthened as slave labour was redirected within the continent to produce new, 'legitimate' exports.[16] Consequently, the transition to legal forms of trade turned out to be far more protracted than the abolitionists had anticipated, and far more costly than successive British governments, committed to a 'leaner, fitter' public sector after 1815, had bargained for. The export of Christian values, never a serious prospect in north Africa, made disappointingly slow progress south of the Sahara. Efforts to convert Boer farmers to liberalism hastened their migration from British influence from the 1830s and generated conflicts over access to land and supplies of labour.[17]

13. Quoted in M.E. Chamberlain, *The Scramble for Africa* (1974), p. 36.
14. E.R.J. Owen, *Cotton and the Egyptian Economy, 1820–1914* (Oxford, 1969).
15. E.A. Alpers, *Ivory and Slaves in East Central Africa* (1975); Abdul Sheriff, *Slaves, Spices and Ivory in Zanzibar: Integration of an East African Commercial Empire in the World Economy, 1770–1873* (1987).
16. See, for example, Paul O. Lovejoy, 'The Characteristics of Plantations in the Sokoto Caliphate (Islamic West Africa)', *Am. Hist. Rev.*, 84 (1979); Frederick Cooper, *Plantation Slavery on the East Coast of Africa* (New Haven, Conn., 1977), and Robert Ross, *Cape of Torments* (1983).
17. The causes of 'turbulence' on the frontier during this period have been the subject of important recent research. See, for example, J.B. Peires, *The House of Phalo* (Johannesburg, 1981), and Timothy Keegan, 'Dispossession and Accumulation in the South African Interior: the Boers and Tlhaping of Bethulie, 1833–61', *Jour. African Hist.*, XXVIII (1987). The phrase itself derives from John S. Galbraith's pioneering essay, 'The "Turbulent Frontier" as a Factor in British Expansion', *Comparative Studies in Society and History*, 11 (1960).

Attempts to create model settlements in the tropics were overwhelmed by the environment they were supposed to transform.[18] As it became clear that progress required more than a short course in applied ethics, Britain's official presence became more visible: naval squadrons were strengthened; diplomatic commitments were increased by establishing consulates in ports along the coast; and political acquisitions were made at strategic points, such as Aden (1839) and Natal (1842). But coastal bases 'opened up' very little of the interior, and the increase in legitimate trade was to levels that were still trivial.[19] There was no lucky strike and no 'quick fix' before 1850. As disillusion set in, the planners began to blame the recipients rather than the plan. Some felt that the continent should be abandoned to its fate; others that it required firmer direction.[20]

This situation changed during the second half of the century in ways that are important for understanding partition. The demise of the external slave trade was complemented by a new impulse: the extension to Africa of Britain's burgeoning financial and service sector. Investment in a few promising parts of the continent, principally Egypt and South Africa, grew rapidly, and soon drew in modern banking facilities as well. The beginning of regular steamship services in the 1850s increased the capacity and cut the cost of ocean transport; and the appearance, particularly from the 1880s, of 'megamerchants' and investment groups introduced forms of commercial organisation which were designed to be more successful than their predecessors in penetrating the interior.[21] In the British case, the 'large firm' emerged in the transactions sector much earlier than it did in manufacturing. The impetus for this development, as we have seen in other parts of the world, came from Britain's unique role and continuing dynamism in international commerce. Steamship, mining and trading companies all had to become larger in the late nineteenth century if they were to be successful, especially on the frontiers of empire. Small firms lacked the resources to buy and run steamships,

18. Most famously in the case of the Niger expedition. See C.C. Ifemesia, 'The "Civilising Mission" of 1841', *Jour. Hist. Soc. Nigeria*, 2 (1962).

19. The disillusion of the time is well captured by John S. Galbraith, *Reluctant Empire: British Policy on the South African Frontier, 1834–54* (1963). Problems of quantifying African trade during this period are discussed in Liesegang, Pasch, and Jones, *Figuring African Trade*.

20. A very similar sequence characterised the development drive which followed World War II.

21. A.G. Hopkins, 'Imperial Business in Africa, Part II: Interpretations', *Jour. African Hist.*, 18 (1976); S.D. Chapman, 'British-Based Investment Groups Before 1914', *Econ. Hist. Rev.*, 2nd ser. XXXVIII (1985), and the discussion in ibid. XL (1987).

to finance and manage complex mining operations, and to act as quasi-bankers, advancing credit, often over long periods, to indigenous traders and producers. Moreover, large firms operating in frontier conditions readily acquired political connections and often official functions too, both of which were helpful in reducing risk and suppressing competitors. Steamship companies secured subsidies in return for services to imperial communications; large commercial firms were sometimes awarded royal charters for acting as proxies for officialdom, and particularly for meeting protection costs which the Treasury was unwilling to bear.

The men who created these firms were adventurers as well as entrepreneurs. They were rarely gentlemen by birth, and their willingness to cut corners on the frontiers of empire was often frowned on in London. But, being on the make, they were also gentlemen in the making. As such, they took readily to the imperial mission and helped to rejuvenate it in the second half of the nineteenth century. Imperialism, however, was much more than a cover for new business interests: it gave private ambitions a wider purpose and enhanced their standing. The most successful of the entrepreneurs who descended on Africa carried the gentlemanly code with them. They saw themselves as being Christian knights engaged in a civilising mission and performing a patriotic duty, which in turn expressed their loyalty to the crown – and hence their acceptance of the social order it represented.[22] At the highest levels, business success and social advancement required connections in London, principally within the City and parliament. Thus, Goldie made use of first a Baron (Aberdare) and then an Earl (Scarborough) as chairmen of the Royal Niger Company, and Mackinnon mobilised the Duke of Sutherland to promote the Imperial British East Africa Company. As might be expected, Rhodes went a step further: he acquired a brace of Dukes (Abercorn and Fyfe), and cultivated good relations with Lord Rothschild. Currie, the shipping magnate whose steamers dominated the routes to South Africa, enjoyed Gladstone's friendship and also took a direct path to influence by becoming a Liberal MP in 1880.[23] In return came a good deal of local authority in Africa, a

22. Rhodes's mixture of hard-headedness and fantasy is well known, but see, too, D.J.M. Muffett, *Empire Builder Extraordinary: Sir George Goldie and His Philosophy of Government and Empire* (Douglas, I.o.M., 1978).

23. Alfred Jones, whose companies controlled British shipping to West Africa was less interested in high society. But he recognised the need to represent his interests in London and he was prepared (exceptionally) to cut his profit to secure a knighthood. See P.N. Davies, *Sir Alfred Jones: Shipping Entrepreneur Par Excellence* (1978), pp. 69–70.

sprinkling of knighthoods, and some recycling of wealth into estates, usually in the south of England.[24]

If Africa's colonial entrepreneurs were proto-gentlemen, their associates, the explorers and the representatives of the Church Missionary Society, tended to be drawn from established gentry families and from the professional classes of southern England.[25] They, too, helped to revitalise the development drive in the second half of the century. A society that had given up protection for free trade took readily to the need to open new frontiers and gave explorers considerable status; one that had committed itself to creating 'like-mindedness' (where it could not readily be found) was also likely to inspire missionary activity. Not surprisingly, reports from both sources were cast in the image of metropolitan society, and were accompanied by renewed optimism about Africa's potential and Britain's ability to push the frontiers of economic growth inland, especially by means of the railway and the telegraph – 'the keys to the continent', as Rhodes called them.[26] Societies which showed signs of gentility were marked out as being ready for development by settlement or assimilation; those which did not were deemed to require developing by others. This more assertive attitude was endorsed by the Church Missionary Society, whose vision of spiritual egalitarianism retreated before the advance of militant evangelical influences in the late nineteenth century, and by the new academic disciplines of anthropology and phrenology, which lent scientific credence to the congenial view that the service class of the Home Counties was destined to dominate the world.[27] These ideas, and others linking racism to patriotism, were translated by the new popular press in a manner which encouraged statesmen to give increasing consideration to the use imperial issues might serve in an era of semi-democratic politics.

This argument is not to be read as disparaging the part played by manufacturers, who undoubtedly showed a keen awareness of the

24. A neat and little known example is provided by Frederick Stow, one of the founders of De Beers, who retired to Sussex and became a landed gentleman and supporter of the local hunt, though he also maintained his interest in the 'white man's cause' in South Africa. See Rob Turrell, 'Sir Frederick Philipson Stow: the Unknown Diamond Magnate', *Bus. Hist.*, 28 (1986).

25. On this subject see the important article by Roy C. Bridges, 'The Historical Role of British Explorers in East Africa', *Terrae Incognitae*, 14 (1982).

26. Lois A.C. Raphael, *The Cape to Cairo Dream: A Study in British Imperialism* (New York, 1936), pp. 69–70.

27. On the changing mood of the missions see Andrew Porter, 'Cambridge, Keswick and Late Nineteenth-Century Attitudes to Africa', *Jour. Imp. and Comm. Hist.* V (1976); and idem, 'Evangelical Enthusiasm, Missionary Motivation and West Africa in the Late Nineteenth Century: the Career of G.W. Brooke', ibid. 6 (1977).

need to open markets for old staple exports outside Europe and the United States, particularly in the last quarter of the century.[28] But to an extent which has been underestimated, the manufacturing interest rode on the back of the new expansionist wave rather than created it. By the late nineteenth century the manufacture of cotton goods, the principal export to Africa, had ceased to be characterised by striking productivity gains, and further growth had come to depend increasingly on improvements in the transactions sector, especially transport and finance. Expansion also required political influence, in Africa and in London, and here too manufacturers relied to a considerable degree on the representations and actions of financial and commercial houses, while also, of course, making use of their own trade organisations and members of parliament

The combination of capital and commercial innovation undoubtedly made inroads into Africa during the second half of the nineteenth century, though the poor quality of the data does not allow the results to be traced with any degree of precision.[29] Some approximate orders of magnitude are provided by Austen's calculations, which show that Africa's share of British exports (excluding trade with Egypt) rose from less than 3 per cent in the middle of the century to 4.3 per cent in 1890 and to 8.3 per cent in 1906.[30] The proportions were indeed small, and the striking gains came after partition rather than before. But these are not reasons for dismissing the importance of Britain's trade with Africa on the eve of partition. The fact that the proportion was rising shows that Africa was a growth area for Britain's exports, and such areas were in short supply in the late nineteenth century. Moreover, since Britain's total exports were expanding globally, the increasing share taken by Africa represents a considerable gain in absolute terms. However, the real significance of the data lies in their regional basis. In the 1880s three-quarters of Britain's direct trade with Africa (imports and exports amounting to about £30m. a year) was conducted with Cape Colony, Natal and Egypt.[31] This figure (£22.5m.) was larger than Britain's trade with the whole of China

28. W.G. Hynes, *The Economics of Empire: Britain, Africa, and the New Imperialism, 1870–95* (1979). The authoritative account of Manchester's difficulties at this time is D.A. Farnie, *The English Cotton Industry and the World Market, 1815–1896* (Oxford, 1976), Ch. 5.

29. See Leisegang, Pasch and Jones, *Figuring African Trade*.

30. Ralph A. Austen, *African Economic History: Internal Development and External Dependency* (1987), pp. 277–80.

31. Colin Newbury, 'On the Margins of Empire: the Trade of Western Africa, 1875–1890', in Stig Forster, Wolfgang Mommsen and Ronald Robinson, eds. *Bismarck, Europe and Africa* (Oxford, 1988), pp. 41, 49.

(including Hong Kong) during this period and slightly more than half the value of her trade with Latin America. When it is remembered that these were also the areas of Africa that attracted British investment after 1850, the significance of a regional approach to partition becomes apparent. This was certainly the perspective adopted by contemporary business opinion in London, which had no doubt that South Africa and Egypt were the parts of the continent that really mattered.[32]

The pace of commercial expansion during the second half of the century had profound effects on the African side of the frontier, though these are still imperfectly understood. However, research now available suggests that the various 'crises on the periphery' which have attracted the attention of historians of partition derived from structural changes to societies which were adapting to the demands of the new international economic order, and that these adjustment problems were greatly magnified by the renewed development push after 1850. The evidence also indicates that African polities produced a cluster of hybrid and often assertive responses to external forces and were not simply 'undermined' by them to the extent that 'law and order' had to be reimposed. Slave-raiders in west Africa achieved some success in adjusting to the palm oil trade and to competition from new small producers; hunters in east Africa momentarily held back the clock of history by making windfall gains during the ivory boom. Ismail in Egypt and Kruger in the Transvaal actively sought to use external influences to reinforce their independence. The problem was not that societies in Africa were unresponsive, but that Britain's presence was marked by increasing demands and diminishing tolerance in the second half of the century. From that point onwards the machinery of adjustment became vulnerable to short-term fluctuations in international trade, transmitted mainly by falling export prices and credit restrictions, and to random influences on the domestic economy, such as the size of the harvest and the incidence of disease. When these struck, as they did in different parts of Africa during the last quarter of the century, local crises were easily precipitated. In these circumstances, it was virtually impossible for African states to pass Palmerston's test: those which ran into difficulties failed because they were no longer 'well-kept', while those which turned Cobden's international principles to national advantage failed because they had ceased to be 'always accessible'.

This assessment suggests the need to question the conventional

---

32. Newbury, 'On the Margins', p. 50.

view that Britain's policy towards frontier disputes was essentially restrained and reactive. This characterisation undoubtedly represents the ideal of a low-cost, harmonious international order which inspired in the official mind a degree of coherence and a sense of purpose that it might otherwise have lacked. But in the real world the rules had long been bent where they had not been broken, despite Britain's aversion to territorial acquisition and desire for economy in public expenditure. To cite just a few examples from different parts of Africa: Britain had established a colony in Lagos in 1861 and had fought wars with Asante in 1863 and 1874; she had invaded Ethiopia in 1867–8 and had appointed a Consul-General at Zanzibar in 1873; she had annexed Griqualand West in 1871, the Transvaal in 1877, and Walvis Bay in 1878; and she had fought one war with the Zulu in 1879, and another with the Boers in 1880–81. These events certainly looked (and felt) aggressive from an African point of view. Although their precise causes are open to discussion and need to be attuned to particular circumstances, the fact that they occurred at all can be understood only in the context of the quickening beat of impulses transmitted from the metropole, which placed Britain in a position where circumstances 'forcing' her to take action on the frontiers of empire were much more likely to arise.

For the same reasons, it is also necessary to pause before assigning the responsibility for Britain's actions to foreign rivals. This exercise is partly flawed by its circularity: British historians tend to blame the French; but French historians tend to accuse Germany or Belgium; and German and Belgian historians are inclined to attribute responsibility to Britain and France.[33] This line of argument also suffers from empirical difficulties. It has to be remembered that Africa's most important commercial, financial and diplomatic ties in the period down to partition were with Britain, not France (still less with Germany, Belgium or Portugal). The entry of foreign rivals was undoubtedly a complication for British policy. But France and Germany had more influence in tropical Africa, at the margins of Britain's interests, than in Egypt and South Africa, which were central to her position in the continent. Britain had her own reasons for safeguarding her position in Africa. Appearances did not deceive; the tail did not wag the dog.

The general direction of the argument should now be clear. The

---

33. An illuminating (and probably chastening) historiographical study of the application of national traditions to international history could be written on this subject.

next step is to consider its application to different parts of the continent. Schematically, Britain's presence in Africa can be considered along two axes: one, running from north to south, charts the extension abroad of the new financial and service sector; the other, drawn more tentatively from west to east across the tropics, represents less substantial speculative and manufacturing interests. This division, we suggest, reflects the realities of British capitalism because it gives appropriate weight to the influence exerted by the gentlemanly complex in London and the Home Counties. It also accords with the realities perceived by British diplomats. Since the continent was not united, even in the loose sense that applied to the Ottoman Empire and China, there could be no 'one Africa' policy. Officials had divided Africa in their minds long before they had begun to partition it in reality. As we shall now see, Britain fastened upon the most promising parts of the continent, where her economic and political purposes were more or less congruent, and did not let go.

THE OCCUPATION OF EGYPT

The first, decisive advance inland on the route which Rhodes was later to envisage joining the Cape to Cairo took place in 1882, when British troops occupied Egypt.[34] This event sparked a lively debate among contemporaries, and it has made a distinctive contribution to theories of imperialism from that time to the present day. As far as modern scholarship is concerned, the Egyptian case is best known for the central role assigned to it by Robinson and Gallagher in *Africa and the Victorians*.[35] In their view, the occupation of Egypt was the product of a crisis on the periphery prompted by a proto-nationalist revolt. Britain was reluctant to intervene, but did so because the breakdown of law and order posed a threat to her strategic interest in the Suez Canal, which guarded the route to India. This decision had far-reaching consequences: it destroyed the informal understandings which had governed the major powers in their dealings with Africa, drove the French to seek compensation in west Africa, and pushed

34. The interpretation which follows is based on A.G.Hopkins, 'The Victorians and Africa: a Reconsideration of the Occupation of Egypt, 1882', *Jour. African Hist.*, 27 (1986), and the references given there. The account presented here makes use of some additional sources, and has also benefited from advice generously offered by Profs. G.N. Sanderson and Juan Cole.

35. Set out in Chapter 4 and followed in subsequent chapters.

the British up the Nile and into east Africa in pursuit of strategic security. Southern Africa was too remote to become the final domino in this particular 'great game', but British policy towards the Boer republics nevertheless exemplifies the paramountcy of 'excentric' and strategic considerations in understanding the essentially defensive imperialism of the late Victorians.

Robinson and Gallagher's view of events is indeed very close to the official interpretation put forward at the time.[36] The question, however, is whether the authorised version also provides an acceptable explanation of the problem under review, and the evidence now available suggests that it does not. As we shall see, the official account was formulated with at least one eye on the need to ensure that the controversial decisions taken by Britain presented her in a favourable light; the other was uninterested in recording causes of actions which lay beyond the immediate reasons given for them by the participants themselves. A more plausible interpretation, we suggest, is one that sees the crisis of 1882 as a moment of conjuncture arising out of the long-term interaction between the expansion of British interests and the aspirations of Egypt's rulers.

Britain's commercial ties with Egypt grew rapidly after 1815. Manchester's quest for new markets coincided with the modernising policies of Egypt's ruler, Mohammed Ali, and led to the development of a sizeable export sector based on the exchange of cotton goods for raw cotton.[37] However, this emerging complementarity could not disguise the fact that Mohammed Ali was a centralising autocrat who favoured state monopolies and protectionism, and had expansionist ambitions of his own, whereas Britain was treading a path towards free trade and minimal government, and needed to create obedient and pacific satellites. The spread of cash crops had already begun to have destabilising consequences within Egypt in the 1820s, and these led, indirectly, to expansionist ventures in the 1830s.[38] After 1838, when Britain imposed free trade on the Ottoman Empire (of which Egypt was formally a part), Mohammed Ali's chances of achieving economic independence disappeared. State monopolies were destroyed, military expansion was checked, and Egypt's rulers were forced to rely increasingly on internal taxation and foreign borrowing.

The assimilation of Egypt into Britain's free-trading regime generated a substantial increase in foreign trade and investment from the

36. See, for example, Cromer, *Ancient and Modern Imperialism*.
37. E.R.J. Owen, *Cotton and the Egyptian Economy, 1820–1814* (Oxford, 1969).
38. See, for example, Fred H. Lawson, 'Economic and Social Foundations of Egyptian Expansionism: the Invasion of Syria in 1831', *Internat. Hist. Rev.*, 10 (1988).

1840s onwards. One manifestation of the growth of European influences was the rapid expansion of the principal port, Alexandria, which became a colonial enclave long before Egypt became, effectively, a colony.[39] The French presence was sizeable and pervasive; but Britain was the most important foreign trading partner, and in 1880 took 80 per cent of Egypt's exports and supplied 44 per cent of her imports.[40] Commercial expansion was accompanied by railway and harbour construction and by the installation of industrial machinery, all of which gave employment to British manufacturers and personnel. Export growth was funded largely by private capital flows, which came chiefly from British sources. State bonds began to be marketed externally from 1862, principally to finance the construction of the Suez Canal and to underwrite the military budget. British investors held more than half the public debt in 1873, shortly before a rash of short-term loans temporarily raised the proportion held by the French. Even so, the funded debt remained largely in British hands. Moreover, Britain's financial stake in Egypt increased following Disraeli's purchase of the Egyptian government's shares in the Suez Canal in 1875 and the consolidation of the public debt in 1880, which led many French investors to sell their unified bonds in London.

Britain was therefore the principal creditor when Egypt subsided into bankruptcy in 1876.[41] However, it does not follow, as a matter of logic or necessity, that financial considerations played a determining part in subsequent events leading to the occupation of Egypt in 1882. This possibility, like others, must stand or fall by empirical tests. In fact, British governments were reluctant to give guarantees to private investors because they rightly feared the consequences of signing blank cheques for City speculators.[42] At the same time, governments also acknowledged a general obligation to support Britain's interests, including her economic interests, abroad. A case for intervention could be made, for example, where British lives or

39. Michael J. Reimer, 'Colonial Bridgehead: Social and Spatial Change in Alexandria, 1850–1882', *Int. Jour. Middle East Stud.*, 20 (1988).

40. Hopkins, 'The Victorians and Africa', p. 379.

41. On default see Roger Owen, *The Middle East in the World Economy, 1800–1914* (1981), pp. 122–8; and D.S. Landes, *Bankers and Pashas: International Finance and Economic Imperialism in Egypt* (1958), Chs. 1–2.

42. This point has been firmly established by D.C.M. Platt, *Finance, Trade and Politics in British Foreign Policy, 1815–1914* (Oxford, 1968), pp. 154–80. In the case of Egypt, investors overestimated both the number of years of uninterrupted debt service available to them and the extent of the losses that would follow from default. See Gershon Feder and Richard Just, 'Debt Crisis in an Increasingly Pessimistic International Market: the Case of Egyptian Credit, 1862–1876', *Econ. Jour.*, 94 (1984).

property were endangered by the break-down of law and order. As far as Egypt was concerned, the British government had a formal commitment to ensure that the loans made to the Ottoman Empire in the 1850s would be repaid, and recognised, too, that default would have sizeable consequences for financial and manufacturing interests in Britain. The Egyptian case was one among an increasing number of others in the late nineteenth century which left open the possibility of intervention providing that the reasons were weighty and respectable, either in reality or in presentation.

It now seems clear that Britain adopted a much more assertive policy towards Egypt than Robinson and Gallagher allowed.[43] In resolving to make Egypt pay her debts, Disraeli's Conservative government (1874–80) soon blurred the line between official neutrality and unoffficial assistance. The banker, Goschen, was given semi-official support in negotiating the agreement which led to the establishment of Dual (Anglo-French) Control over Egyptian finances in 1876. Harsh measures were imposed to balance the budget and to enable debt service to be resumed; when these provoked opposition in Egypt in 1879, the government came very close to taking military action. In the event, the Khedive was deposed, the system of dual control was tightened, and the Law of Liquidation was passed in 1880. This measure consolidated the public debt and rescheduled repayments: it also bound the European signatories to see that it was carried out.

The advent of the Liberal government in 1880 altered the tone but not the direction of policy. Gladstone was vaguely in favour of the 'nationalists' in Egypt; but, unlike his fellow Liberal, John Bright, he was not against intervention at any price.[44] In this particular case Gladstone himself had good reason to calculate the cost because no less than 37 per cent of his total portfolio was invested in Egyptian stock in 1882.[45] This is not to say that Gladstone was motivated by crude self-interest; but it does suggest that he was likely to see the creditors' point of view with some clarity if it could be presented as an issue of principle, and especially one that was in the wider public interest. Gladstone was also out-manoeuvred by the hawks in his

43. Hopkins, 'The Victorians and Africa', pp. 379–83.
44. Intellectual permissiveness had already been justified, as Joseph H. Udelson's neglected study has shown: 'Britain, Russophobia and the Egyptian Question of 1882: a Study in the Philosophy of History and Linguistics', (Ph.D. thesis Vanderbilt University, 1975), pp. 326, 330, 482–4, 659 and Ch. 4.
45. H.C.G. Matthew, ed. *The Gladstone Diaries*, Vols. X and XI, *January 1881-December 1886* (Oxford, 1990), pp. lxxii. Gladstone wisely sold some of his stock in 1884, when prices had recovered.

government, headed by Hartington and Dilke, who were keen to shift the Liberals towards a strong foreign policy as a means of showing that the party could be as patriotic as the Conservatives in defending Britain's interests abroad.[46] This group began to devise ways of imposing an aggressive policy in opposition to Gladstone's internationalism, and sought specifically to replace Dual Control by British supremacy. In this aim the militants were well supported by the 'men on the spot', particularly Colvin, the British Controller-General, and Malet, the British Consul, who sent increasingly lurid reports purporting to show that Egypt would soon be governed by an authoritarian military clique dedicated to the elimination of European influences unless Britain took decisive action.

In addition, the City's involvement reached to the highest levels, and included a weighty contribution by Rothschilds, who had given substantial financial support in 1879, when Egypt's external debt was being reorganised in preparation for the Law of Liquidation.[47] Lord Rothschild himself was active in representing the interests of British investors, and so, too, was the Corporation of Foreign Bondholders, which mobilised *The Times*, the financial press, and the considerable number of members of parliament (besides Gladstone) who had a financial stake in the Egyptian economy.[48] There is little doubt that the government's purchase of shares in the Suez Canal, combined with increasing evidence of semi-official support for the various steps taken to improve the efficiency of Egypt's finances after 1875, had greatly encouraged British investors by providing an implied guarantee which, in appropriate circumstances and on a favourable interpretation, could be said to be a matter of principle.[49]

The budgetary rigours imposed by Britain and France eventually provoked a reaction in Egypt. In September 1881 Urabi, the nationalist leader, led a protest against the rapid spread of European influence, and shortly afterwards joined with the newly revived Chamber of Notables to challenge European financial control. The

---

46. M.E. Chamberlain, 'Sir Charles Dilke and the British Intervention in Egypt in 1882: Decision-Making in a Nineteenth-Century Cabinet', *Brit. Jour. Internat. Stud.*, 11 (1976).

47. B.R. Johns, 'Business Investment and Imperialism: the Relationship Between Economic Interest and the Growth of British Intervention in Egypt, 1838–82' (Ph.D. thesis, Exeter University, 1981), pp. 75–92, 107, 215, 281–2.

48. W.S. Blunt, *A Secret History of the British Occupation of Egypt* (1907: 1969), pp. 240, 294–5; Paul F. Meszaros, 'The Corporation of Foreign Bondholders and British Diplomacy in Egypt, 1876–1882', (Ph.D. thesis, Loyola University, 1973), Ch. 5; Johns, 'Business Investment', pp. 329, 376–7.

49. Johns, 'Business Investment', pp. 250–54.

Chamber accepted Egypt's obligations to its external creditors, but wanted to manage parts of the budget that were not assigned to the foreign debt. The Controllers-General interpreted this demand as being the prelude to wider claims, and immediately raised the alarm. When this happened, Dilke and his associates felt ready to act. The Joint Note issued by Britain and France in January 1882 was deliberately provocative; Granville, the moderate Foreign Secretary, was won over in March by the fear that Britain's financial interests would be damaged by the determined stance taken by the nationalists; in June Hartington threatened to split the Liberal government by resigning unless a forward policy was adopted.[50] At this point Gladstone himself agreed to sanction some form of intervention, having been persuaded that action was justified by growing 'disorder' in Egypt. An Anglo-French naval presence was planned to intimidate the nationalists. In the event, the force became a British one and it had the predictable result of strengthening Egyptian unity and increasing tension in Cairo and Alexandria. When riots broke out in Alexandria, Admiral Seymour was let off the leash: the port was bombarded, and the occupation of Egypt began. Dilke was delighted with the outcome; Malet, writing to congratulate the Foreign Secretary, observed that the action had given the Liberals 'a new lease of popularity and power'.[51]

Not surprisingly, the official version told a very different story. The Foreign Office removed a passage from the draft of the public statement admitting that intervention had been brought about by Egypt's attempts to exercise control over the budget, and instead provided a set of explanations which were calculated to impress international opinion and to soothe the sensitivities of Liberal supporters.[52] According to the authorised view, Britain was reluctant to take action but was compelled to do so by the breakdown of law and order, which put British lives and property in danger and posed a threat to the Suez Canal. Even so, Britain found herself embroiled in Egypt largely as a result of the assertiveness of the French. Milner, whose experience of Egypt formed a prelude to the acts of colonial brinkmanship he was to perform in southern Africa, helped to propagate the myth, subsequently repeated by many others, that it was the French who, 'after dragging us into the Egyptian imbroglio

50. Blunt, *A Secret History*, pp. 221–2.
51. Quoted in John S. Galbraith and Afaf Lufti al-Sayyid-Marsot, 'The British Occupation of Egypt: Another View', *Int. Jour. Middle East Stud.*, 9 (1978), p. 478.
52. Chamberlain, 'Sir Charles Dilke', pp. 238–9.

in 1882, shirked at the last moment and left us to settle the whole matter alone'.[53]

Not one of these explanations can carry the weight attached to it.[54] Despite the pressures on the Egyptian polity, it is now apparent that Egypt was not descending into anarchy on the eve of the British occupation. Law and order were maintained until the riots in Alexandria in June 1882. Furthermore, the riots were a response to the intrusion of Europe, not a cause of it, and they were far less serious than the official version of events held them to be. Their real significance was psychological and political: they catalysed the anxieties of European residents and foreign investors, and caused them to reach for the alarm cord.[55] These anxieties had grown, not because Egypt was in a state of chaos, but because the British decided that they could not trust Urabi and the nationalists. The disorder they feared was financial; and fiscal anarchy was a moral issue, not just an economic one. Resolving the confusions of Egyptian finances became, for Gladstone, a 'holy subject' – and thus a matter of principle.[56]

The Suez Canal was not at risk in 1882; nor was it thought to be the cause of intervention by Gladstone or his Foreign Secretary, Granville, or by the Admiralty (which in any case based its strategy on the Cape route until the 1890s), or by the mercantile shipping lobby.[57] The Canal did not become an issue in the public mind until two weeks before the bombardment of Alexandria, and it was only after this event that the possibility of retaliatory action in the region of Suez arose. As for the French, it is now evident that they were indeed worried about safeguarding their interests between 1875 and 1880, when their investments were in a highly exposed position. After 1880, however, French policy towards Egypt was marked by restraint. The Law of Liquidation took care of the worries of French investors. Some sold their holdings and departed. Those who remained were quite happy to have their protection provided by the world's largest security organisation – Great Britain. Moreover, after 1881 France was preoccupied by the invasion of Tunisia. The French did not lead Britain into the 'Egyptian imbroglio'. Their fleet was

---

53. Alfred Milner, *England in Egypt* (5th edn, 1894), p. 416.

54. See the evidence cited in Hopkins, 'The Victorians and Africa', pp. 373–9.

55. See Juan R.I. Cole, 'Of Crowds and Empires: Afro-Asian Riots and European Expansion, 1857–1882', *Comp. Stud. in Soc. and Hist.*, 31 (1989).

56. Matthew, *The Gladstone Diaries*, p. lxxvi.

57. Ibid. p. lxx; Udelson, 'Britain, Russophobia', p. 579. Lord Randolph Churchill's opinion, expressed in 1884, was that 'the Suez Canal was at no time in the smallest danger'. Quoted in Chamberlain, *Scramble for Africa*, p. 114.

withdrawn from Alexandria precisely because France did not want to be dragged into Egypt by Britain.

If, in its final stages, the crisis on the Egyptian periphery displayed clear signs of stage-management, its deeper origins lay in the expansion of European trade and investment after 1838, and especially in the growth of public-sector borrowing from the 1860s. British policy was assertive not because policy-makers were in the pockets of the bond-holders, but because they recognised the need to defend Britain's substantial economic interests in Egypt, and because they thought that these could be secured by a quick and inexpensive strike that would also produce political benefits at home. The outcome was what Milner called a 'veiled protectorate', which enabled Britain to retain control over the budget in much the same way as the Ottoman Public Debt Administration (with rather less power) managed the finances of the Sublime Porte. The other major consequence of the occupation of Egypt was to draw Britain into the Sudan. This further extension of British influence cannot be explored here.[58] But it is worth noting that Britain's involvement in the Sudan stemmed much more from Egypt's indebtedness than it did from a concern with the need to protect the Suez route to India. The collapse of Ismail's regime in 1879 weakened Egypt's hold over the Sudan and opened an opportunity for a coalition of slave-traders and taxpayers to unite against the reforms which Britain had tried to impose through Cairo's authority. It is understandable that the Mahdists opposed foreign influence and aimed at creating an independent Muslim state with its own fiscal system; it is not surprising either that the British decided that they could not allow 'disorder' to persist in the Sudan when it endangered the settlement they had just imposed on Egypt.

CRISIS AND WAR IN SOUTH AFRICA

As Egypt was being occupied, so Britain was beginning to grapple with problems at the other end of the continent that were to lead, somewhat later and by an even more complex route, to the acquisition

---

58. See G.N. Sanderson, *England, Europe, and the Upper Nile, 1882–1899* (Edinburgh, 1965); Robert O. Collins, *King Leopold, England and the Upper Nile, 1899–1909* (New Haven, Conn., 1968); idem, *Land Beyond the Rivers: The Southern Sudan, 1898–1918* (New Haven, Conn., 1971). An illuminating example of recent research is Yitzhak Nakesh, 'Fiscal and Monetary Systems in the Mahdist Sudan, 1881–1898', *Int. Jour. Middle East Stud.*, 20 (1988).

of the greater part of southern Africa. The impulses which carried Britain northwards into central Africa, culminating in the Boer War and the eventual Union of South Africa under British rule in 1910, also inspired among contemporaries a debate over the causes of imperialism which continues to stimulate scholars today.[59] At one extreme is the interpretation, formulated by Hobson, that events in southern Africa were driven by a conspiracy of financiers who hijacked the apparatus of state power in the interests of private profit; at the other extreme is the view that agents of the state on the periphery of empire harnessed both Whitehall and the mine-owners for their own (greater or lesser) ends. In between stand many floating voters who see the complexity of events rather more clearly than their underlying purpose. The principal problem, as in the case of Egypt, is to trace the ties that bound economics, strategy and private ambition, without also collapsing the argument into poorly specified generalities about the defence of British supremacy.

The extension of free trade from the 1840s and the advent of banking and steamship services during the 1860s gave fresh impetus to the Cape's agricultural exports (notably wool) and offered a small but growing market for British manufacturers.[60] By promising to underpin the prosperity of the settler community, these developments also held out the hope of securing Britain's strategic interest in the route to the Far East. This concern was enhanced as Britain's financial and commercial stake expanded, particularly in India, during the second half of the nineteenth century, and the Cape route retained its high priority, even after the opening of the Suez Canal in 1869.[61] Nevertheless, the vision of self-supporting communities of loyal settlers failed to materialise. Degrees of self-government were indeed

59. We are indebted to Dr Iain Smith of the University of Warwick for his generosity in allowing us to read sections of his forthcoming study of the Anglo-Boer War and for his comments on the numerous baffling intricacies of this subject. See also his overview: 'The Origins of the South African War (1899–1902): a Reappraisal', *South African Historical Journal*, 22 (1990). See, too, Shula Marks, 'Scrambling for South Africa', *Jour. African Hist.*, 23 (1982), and idem, in Oliver and Sanderson, *The Cambridge History of Africa*, Vol.6, Chs.7–8.

60. The spread of 'legitimate' commerce in southern Africa is dealt with by Malyn Newitt, 'Economic Penetration and the Scramble for Southern Africa', in Peter Morris, ed. *Africa, America and Central Asia: Formal and Informal Empire in the Nineteenth Century* (Exeter, 1984). See also A.G. Hopkins, 'Imperial Business in Africa, Part II: Interpretations', *Jour. African Hist.*, 18 (1976); and on specific themes Andrew Porter, *Victorian Shipping. Business and Imperial Policy: Donald Currie, the Castle Line and Southern Africa* (Woodbridge, 1986), and V.E. Solomon, 'Money and Banking', in F.L. Coleman, ed. *Economic History of South Africa* (Pretoria, 1983), pp. 141–2.

61. D.A. Farnie, *East and West of Suez: The Suez Canal in History, 1854–1856* (Oxford, 1969), pp. 293–4, 334, 455.

conferred, but the trekkers in the Transvaal and the Orange Free State were given independence (in 1852 and 1854) because they could not be Anglicised and because they were thought to be unimportant; and the Cape's qualifications for 'responsible government' were hurried on in 1872 so that it could play its part in sustaining Britain's interests without also remaining a burden on the defence budget.[62]

Recent research on southern Africa has revealed in considerable detail the processes by which the expansion of agriculture and pastoralism in the second half of the nineteenth century increased competition for land and labour and generated economic disputes which rapidly assumed a political form.[63] It has also shown how exposure to free trade hit agricultural exports from the 1870s and stepped up pressure from farmers to cut labour costs, and how this turn of events became caught up with the natural disasters of drought and rinderpest which struck much of southern Africa after 1869.[64] In the Western Cape, wine producers and wheat farmers facing the cold winds of free trade and indebtedness were also confronted with the unbending orthodoxy of imperial finance in the shape of the Standard Bank. These developments cut into the support which the colonial government had built up during more prosperous times, generated demands for protection and for 'country' banks, and helped to stimulate Afrikaner nationalism.[65] A broadly similar picture has emerged from research on Natal, where depressed exports, difficulties over labour supply and rural indebtedness also promoted political disaffection.[66] It is now apparent that turbulence on the southern

62. The antecedents are dealt with by Basil A. Le Cordeur, *The Politics of Eastern Cape Separatism, 1820–1854* (Cape Town, 1981).

63. Only a selection of recent important work can be cited here: William Beinart, *The Political Economy of Pondoland, 1860–1930* (Cambridge, 1982); Philip Bonner, *Kings, Commoners and Concessionaires: The Evolution and Dissolution of the Nineteenth-Century Swazi State* (Cambridge, 1983); Colin Bundy, *The Rise and Fall of a South African Peasantry* (1979); Peter Delius, *The Land Belongs to Us: The Pedi Polity, the Boers and the British in the Nineteenth-Century Transvaal* (1984).

64. C. Van Onselen, 'Reactions to Rinderpest in Southern Africa, 1896–7', *Jour. African Hist.*, 13 (1972); Charles Ballard, 'The Repercussions of Rinderpest: Cattle, Plague and Peasant Decline in Colonial Natal', *Int. Jour. African Hist. Stud.*, 19 (1986).

65. These developments are discussed in important contributions by Hermann Giliomee, 'The Beginnings of Afrikaner Nationalism, 1870–1915', *South Afr. Hist. Jour.*, 19 (1986), and idem, 'Western Cape Farmers and the Beginnings of Afrikaner Nationalism, 1870–1915', *Jour. Southern African Stud.*, 14 (1987). See also Arthur Webb, 'Early Capitalism in the Cape: the Eastern Province Bank, 1839–73', in Stuart Jones, ed. *Banking and Business in South Africa* (New York, 1988).

66. Peter Richardson, 'The Natal Sugar Industry, 1849–1905: an Interpretative Essay', *Jour. African Hist.*, 23 (1982), pp. 522–6; Ritchie Ovendale, 'Profit or Patriotism: Natal, The Transvaal and the Coming of the Second Anglo-Boer War', *Jour. Imp. and Comm. Hist.*, VIII (1980).

African frontier after 1850 resulted not only from attempts to escape the forces of modernisation but also from the consequences of their ambiguous embrace.

The issues facing British policy from the 1870s extended beyond the control of uncertain frontiers and centred increasingly on securing the economic base of the colony itself. The discovery of diamonds in 1867 and the exploitation of the rich reserves at Kimberley from 1870 appeared to be the 'lucky strike' that policy-makers had long been waiting for. By annexing Griqualand West in 1871, Britain gained control of the principal mines and with them a means of funding responsible government at the Cape, and the imperial government seized the opportunity to uncouple the colony from its reliance on the Treasury and to link it instead with the London money market.[67] However, the lucky strike did not produce an instant solution to the problem of marrying economic resources to political authority. The diamond mines quickly generated a substantial demand for labour which was met initially from settler farming areas, thus adding to the difficulties which agriculture was already experiencing.

It was the attempt to deal with this question that underlay Carnarvon's drive for a South African Confederation after he became Colonial Secretary in 1874.[68] Carnarvon's design was to turn central Africa and Mozambique into labour reserves for the mines and farms of the south. This strategy was linked to a revival of the anti-slavery campaign in East Africa and to the spread of steamship and banking services northwards along the south-east coast of Africa; it culminated

67. Andrew Porter, 'Britain, the Cape Colony, and Natal, 1870–1914: Capital, Shipping and the Colonial Connexion', *Econ. Hist. Rev.*, 2nd ser. XXXIV (1981).

68. The historical significance of Carnarvon's plan has been emphasised by Norman Etherington, 'Labour Supply and the Genesis of South African Confederation in the 1870s', *Jour. African Hist.*, 20 (1979). See also R.L. Cope's important contributions: 'Strategic and Socio-Economic Explanations for Carnarvon's South African Confederation Policy: the Historiography and the Evidence', *History in Africa*, 13 (1986), and 'The Sources of Lord Carnavon's South African Confederation Policy', *Int. Jour. African Hist. Stud.*, 20 (1987). An additional dimension is revealed by John Wright and Andrew Manson, *The Hlubi Chiefdom in Zululand-Natal* (Ladysmith, 1983).

Henry Herbert (1831–90), the 4th Earl of Carnarvon, was educated at Eton and Oxford and held posts in every Conservative government between 1858 and 1886, including the office of Colonial Secretary in 1886–87. Carnarvon was a Tory grandee dedicated to maintaining his estates (amounting to nearly 36,000 acres), to securing the future of his dynasty, and to the survival of the great landowners in an era of free trade and increasingly democratic politics. As an aristocrat and a gentleman, he believed that the 'duties of property' were linked to the 'right to rule'. The agricultural depression caused him to channel funds into securities and land in the colonies from the late 1870s. His son, the 5th earl, married a daughter of Alfred de Rothschild in 1895, principally 'to induce solvency'. See A. Adonis, 'The Survival of the Great Estates: Henry, 4th Earl of Carnarvon and his Dispositions in the 1880s', *Historical Research*, 64 (1991).

in the annexation of the Transvaal in 1877.[69] Carnarvon's plan failed
because of the hostile reactions it provoked in South Africa, and
because diamonds were unable to generate the resources needed to
carry Confederation through, with the result that independence had
to be restored to the Transvaal in 1881.[70] But the plan deserves
emphasis for the way it foreshadowed the future in recognising the
centrality of the labour question and in seeking to solve the Cape's
economic problems by mounting a 'big push' inland. It was a
conscious expansionist scheme directed from the metropole, albeit
with support from business interests in South Africa, and not merely
an aberrant reaction to chance events occurring spontaneously on the
periphery.

The problems raised by the shift from agricultural to mineral
exports became both more complex and more intractable after the
discovery of gold on the Rand in 1886.[71] The ensuing gold rush
greatly hastened the pace of economic change by attracting foreign
capital, manufactures and settlers, and by drawing more labour away
from the hard-pressed farming communities whose prosperity and
loyalty were supposed to uphold Britain's interests in southern Africa.
By the close of the 1890s the Rand had become the largest single
producer of gold, being responsible for over one-quarter of world
output; by 1906–10 gold accounted for about two-thirds of the value
of South Africa's exports.[72] In 1899, on the eve of the Boer War,
investment in the gold-mines stood at about £74m.: recent research
has drawn attention to the sizeable stake held by French and German
investors, but it has also underlined the continued paramountcy of
Britain, which was responsible for 60–80 per cent of the total.[73]
Similarly, though Britain's share of South Africa's external trade

69. Norman Etherington, 'Frederick Elton and the South African Factor in the
Making of Britain's East African Empire', *Jour. Imp. and Comm. Hist.*, IX (1980).

70. Exactly how much independence was restored was to become a matter of
dispute: Britain subsequently claimed that the Transvaal was independent in internal
but not external affairs. See D.M. Schreuder, *Gladstone and Kruger: Liberal Government
and Colonial Home Rule, 1880–85* (1969).

71. The best single guide to this vast subject is Peter Richardson and Jean Jacques
Van–Helten, 'The Gold Mining Industry in the Transvaal, 1886–99', in Peter Warwick,
ed. *The South African War: The Anglo-Boer War, 1899–1902* (1980).

72. Jean Jacques Van–Helten, 'Empire and High Finance: South Africa and the
International Gold Standard, 1890–1914', *Jour. African Hist.*, 23 (1983), p. 536; Peter
Richardson and Jean Jacques Van–Helten, 'The Development of the South African
Gold Mining Industry, 1895–1918', *Econ. Hist. Rev.*, 2nd ser. XXXVII (1984), p. 19.

73. R.V. Kubicek, *Economic Imperialism in Theory and Practice: The Case of South
African Gold Mining Finance, 1886–1914* (Durham, NC, 1979); Van–Helten, 'Empire
and High Finance', p. 539; Richardson and Van–Helten, 'Development of the South
African Gold Mining Industry', pp. 21–2.

declined under the pressure of foreign competition, in 1900 she still supplied two-thirds of the rapidly expanding import trade, which, with a value of £15m., made South Africa her largest single market in the continent.[74]

The discovery of gold made it clear that prosperity and authority in South Africa would in future rest on minerals rather than agriculture. However, since the richest gold deposits were located in the Transvaal, the Boer Republic which Britain had recently fought, annexed and relinquished for the second time in the century, a sizeable political obstacle stood between Britain and the realisation of this new potential. The discovery of gold gave the Republic the resources to underwrite its political independence, and the Boer leaders, headed by Kruger, took the opportunity to embark on a programme of modernisation and expansion.[75] The prospect of being able to finance a railway link to Lourenço Marques promised to give the Transvaal an independent route to the sea; while the new-found prosperity of the Republic strengthened ties with the Orange Free State and encouraged the depressed farming areas of the Cape and Natal to look northwards for their future, thus threatening to deprive Cape Town of a large part of its hinterland.[76] Had Britain's interests in southern Africa been purely strategic, she might have been able to tolerate these developments. But her commitments, like her ambitions, had spread far beyond the narrow confines of a naval base. The Transvaal could no longer be ignored: the question now was how to bring it into line with British interests.

In the absence of a sturdy Anglophile yeomanry, and in the face of a new mining frontier populated by entrepreneurs whose activities were some way removed from gentlemanly norms and conduct, British policy took a further turn away from cultural idealism and towards political realism. Two main strategies were adopted from the

74. Jean Jacques Van-Helten, 'German Capital, the Netherlands Railway Company and the Political Economy of the Transvaal, 1886–1900', *Jour. African Hist.*, 29 (1978), p. 376.
75. For a summary of the revisionist view of Kruger, which now views him as trying to combine the defence of traditional rural Akrikaner interests with a programme of state development, see Richardson and Van-Helten, 'The Gold Mining Industry', pp. 30–35; and, for a detailed illustration, Van-Helten, 'German Capital'.
76. Ovendale, 'Profit or Patriotism'. The position of the Orange Free State has been rescued from unjust neglect by Timothy Keegan, who has shown that the republic was balanced between an urban, commercial and professional English-speaking community and rural Afrikaner communities led by magnates who stood to gain from rising demand for food in the Transvaal: 'The Political Economy of the Orange Free State, 1880–1920', Institute of Commonwealth Studies, London, S. African History Seminar, 1977.

1880s: one made use of British finance to re-establish Britain's influence within the Transvaal: the other involved licensing colonial agents, above all Rhodes, to curb the Republic's expansionist tendencies outside its frontiers.

Although British governments could not direct British finance, they could reasonably hope that the Transvaal's dependence upon the London money market would cause Kruger, as it had caused others, to think twice before embarking on policies that were inimical to British interests. This hope was not left entirely to chance. In 1892, for example, official encouragement was given to Rothschilds when they sought City support in raising a loan (of £2.5m.) for the Transvaal, and the terms of the loan gave Britain a degree of leverage over the Republic.[77] But Kruger countered Britain's financial influence by attracting German capital, which assisted the formation of the National Bank of the South African Republic in 1894, despite Britain's opposition.[78] Moreover, Kruger's programme of nation-building operated against the large and predominantly British mining interest on the Rand by raising freight rates and the cost of dynamite, by impeding moves to increase the supply (and hence reduce the price) of labour, and by threatening to apply a tourniquet to Britain's plan for creating a free-trade area throughout southern Africa.[79] While it is hard to assign precise weights to the various difficulties confronting the mining industry, it seems clear that they grew more rather than less important, and that they became particularly contentious in 1895, when there was a slump in the gold market.[80]

77. Robert Vicat Turrell, '"Finance . . . The Governor of the Imperial Engine:" Hobson and the Case of the Rothschilds and Rhodes', *Jour. Southern African Stud.*, 13 (1987); Kenneth Wilburn, 'The Nature of the Rothschild Loan', *South African Journal of Economic History*, 3 (1988).

78. Van-Helten, 'German Capital'.

79. Richardson and Van-Helten, 'The Development of the South African Gold Mining Industry', pp. 27–35; A.N. Porter, *The Origins of the South African War: Joseph Chamberlain and the Diplomacy of Imperialism, 1895–1899* (Manchester, 1980), pp. 53–6.

80. We are aware that Patrick Harries has argued that the problem of labour supply has been exaggerated: 'Capital, State and Labour on the Nineteenth-Century Witwatersrand: a Reassessment', *South Afr. Hist. Jour.*, 18 (1986). Accordingly, we have not singled out this question for special emphasis; but there seems little doubt that it remained a continuing sore. See Norman Levy, *The Foundations of the South African Cheap Labour System* (1982), p. 133. We are grateful to Prof. W. Worger for his advice on this point. On the other hand, the problem of gold supplies, which we have not stressed, may well need to be entered in the list of issues at stake. We have followed the standard source – Van-Helten, 'Empire and High Finance' – but Dr Russell Ally has recently argued that this was an important matter because London needed to be confident that regular supplies of gold would continue to be shipped. We are grateful to Dr Ally for alerting us to his research on this subject, which will be greatly advanced by the publication of his Ph.D. thesis.

In devising a more assertive policy towards Boer expansionism, Britain was caught in the familiar dilemma of trying to reconcile ambition and parsimony. The solution, which had its counterparts elsewhere in Africa, was to appoint an inexpensive instrument of policy by granting a royal charter to Cecil Rhodes's British South Africa Company in 1889.[81] In securing this privilege, Rhodes was greatly assisted by Sir Hercules Robinson, the Governor of the Cape, who had sizeable investments in Rhodes's companies and who was economical with the truth in presenting the Company's credentials.[82] Rhodes had made his fortune from diamonds in Kimberley, where his success in a series of heavyweight contests with local rivals had been greatly helped by the London branch of Rothschilds, and particularly by the consolidation of De Beers in the early 1880s.[83] Subsequently, however, Rhodes was slow to recognise the potential of the Rand and failed to lay hands on the most promising gold-fields. Commercial disappointment led him to search for a second Rand further north, and it was at this point that his potential as an agent of imperial policy manifested itself. Rhodes had already played a part in the negotiations which led to the acquisition of Bechuanaland, to the west of the Transvaal, in 1884–5. His subsequent manoeuvres, especially his cavalier use of military and political means to boost his company's sagging fortunes, brought Mashonaland and Matabeleland (to the north) under British control between 1888 and 1893.[84] As it happened, none of these vast acquisitions yielded a second Rand, and in 1894 Rhodes fixed his gaze firmly on the Transvaal, where gold-production was beginning to shift from out-crop to deep–level operations.[85] Rhodes's own company, Consoli-

81. John S. Galbraith, 'Origins of the British South Africa Company', in John E. Flint and Glyndwr Williams, eds. *Crown and Charter: The Early Years of the British South Africa Company* (Berkeley, Calif., 1974). The most recent biography is Robert I. Rotberg, *The Founder: Cecil Rhodes and the Pursuit of Power* (Oxford, 1988).

82. Kenneth O. Hall, *Imperial Proconsul: Sir Hercules Robinson and South Africa, 1881–1889* (Kingston, Ontario, 1980).

83. C.W. Newbury, 'Out of the Pit: the Capital Accumulation of Cecil Rhodes', *Jour. Imp. and Comm. Hist.*, X (1981); idem, 'Technology, Capital, and Consolidation: the Performance of De Beers Mining Company Limited, 1880–1889', *Bus. Hist. Rev.*, 61 (1987); and R.V. Turrell, 'Rhodes, De Beers and Monopoly', *Jour. Imp. and Comm. Hist.*, 10 (1982).

84. The precise relationship between Rhodes's business fortunes and his political activities during this period has still to be determined. See I.R. Phimister, 'Rhodes, Rhodesia and the Rand', *Jour. Southern African Stud.*, 1 (1974), and idem, *An Economic and Social History of Zimbabwe, 1890–1948* (1988), pp. 4–19; but also Jeffrey Butler, 'Cecil Rhodes', *Int. Jour. African Hist. Stud.*, 10 (1977), pp. 265–9. We are grateful to Prof. Phimister for his advice on this phase of Rhodes's career.

85. Richardson and Van-Helten, 'The Development of the South African Gold Mining Industry', pp. 28–9; Phimister, 'Rhodes', p. 80.

dated Goldfields, in association with Wernher Beit, the largest of the mining firms, was this time well placed to take advantage of the industry's need for finance and of the process of amalgamation which accompanied it by drawing on his valuable City connections and his particular association with Rothschilds.[86] He was now in a good position to contemplate the industry's growing differences with Kruger and to consider a solution that would also further his wider political ambitions.

It was in these circumstances that Jameson, Rhodes's lieutenant, mounted his ill-judged coup against the Transvaal in 1895. The Jameson Raid was a wild attempt, launched by 'men on the spot', to solve disputes arising on the 'turbulent frontier' of empire; but its significance extended far beyond the actions of local buccaneers. Rhodes undoubtedly used his royal charter and his position as Prime Minister of the Cape for his own complex purposes, which included dreams of re-annexing the United States as well as plans for painting the map red in Africa and adding hugely to his own business empire there.[87] Yet to confine the explanation of this episode to Jameson or even to Rhodes is to adopt an excessively narrow view of causation. Sections of the mining interest were heavily implicated too.[88] Firms such as Wernher Beit, which had made long-term investments in both deep and outcrop mining, saw a chance to install a regime that would settle their immediate grievances, deal with the problem of labour supply, and provide a political framework favourable to international investment. Successive British governments also played a considerable part in bringing about an event which they had not

86. Chapman's attempt to minimise the role of Rothschilds and of London generally is hard to sustain against the evidence advanced by Turrell and Van-Helten. Rothschilds feared the economic consequences of Rhodes's political ambitions, but they remained heavily committed to his business ventures. See S. Chapman, 'Rhodes and the City of London: another View of Imperialism', *Hist. Jour.*, 28 (1985); R.V. Turrell and Jean Jaques Van-Helten, 'The Rothschilds, the Exploration Company, and Mining Finance', *Bus. Hist.*, 28 (1986); Turrell, '"Finance, the Governor of the Imperial Engine"', pp. 427–31, and Van-Helten, 'Empire and High Finance', pp. 539, 541–2. On the complexities of the process of amalgamation see Richardson and Van-Helten ('The Development of the South African Gold Mining Industry'), who also point out that the industry remained dependent on foreign finance until *after* the Boer War (pp. 334–6).

87. On Rhodes's political exploits see Paul Maylem, *Rhodes, the Tswana and the British: Colonialism, Collaboration and Conflict in the Bechuanaland Protectorate, 1885–1902* (1980), and A. Keppel-Jones, *Rhodes and Rhodesia: The White Conquest of Zimbabwe, 1884–1902* (Kingston, Ontario, 1984).

88. The best account of this question is Richard Mendelsohn, 'Blainey and the Jameson Raid: the Debate Renewed', *Jour. Southern African Stud.*, 6 (1980). Mendelsohn's conclusion is endorsed by Richardson and Van-Helten, 'The Development of the South African Gold Mining Industry', p. 326.

377

planned. In granting a royal charter to the British South Africa Company, the imperial government took a conscious risk: the hope was that the aristocrats on the board of directors, combined with Lord Rothschild's influence, would make Rhodes an obedient agent of empire, and a chance was taken on the consequences that might follow if Rhodes slipped the leash when his territorial instincts were aroused. Moreover, it is now clear that the British government, under Salisbury's direction, was tightening the screws on Kruger in 1894–5, and was coming round to the view, always ominous for the prey of empire, that the Transvaal was an anomaly which, in a properly ordered world, ought to be governed by Englishmen.[89] Chamberlain, the Colonial Secretary, may not have connived in the Raid, but he gave 'indirect private encouragement to the plotters',[90] who, since they had already been used to encircle the Transvaal, might reasonably have concluded that they were now being encouraged to go over the top.

The chain of causation thus stretches back to the metropole. British governments were not the tools of mining magnates, nor were British financiers keen to fund Rhodes's political ambitions. But their hands were in the pot. As the wealth of the Transvaal drew in British capital and trade, so Kruger's policies made it increasingly unlikely that indirect means would suffice to winch the Republic back into Britain's sphere of influence. The conditions developing in the mid-1890s were such as to encourage men of Jameson's stamp to put up schemes of the kind he in fact concocted. The temptation of a quick and cheap solution to the Transvaal 'problem' was not easily turned down, and the notion that a change of government would also be popular within the republic gave a quasi–liberal tinge to the venture. The conspirators themselves were only a small group, but there were others, in higher places, who were looking elsewhere when the Raid took place.

The failure of the Jameson Raid diminished Rhodes as a political force, and ultimately widened the gulf between Britain and the Transvaal. In the short run, however, it led to renewed efforts to control the republic by more peaceful means under the supervision of London. The Colonial Office continued to make use of the 'good offices' of the City, especially Rothschilds, and tried in particular to limit the Transvaal government's access to foreign capital.[91] In 1898, when Milner, the British High Commissioner, learned of the Trans-

89. This point is firmly established by Porter, *The Origins of the South African War*, pp. 53–7, 73.
90. Ibid. p. 80; see also pp. 69, 79–85.
91. Turrell, '"Finance . . . The Governor of the Imperial Engine"'.

vaal's plans for raising money in Europe, he asked the Colonial Office, 'through the international influence of big financial houses in London, to make difficulties for the Transvaal government in borrowing money'. The Colonial Office, having consulted Lord Rothschild, replied that 'any loan could be stopped and would be in London and possibly in Paris, but we cannot influence the market in Holland or Germany'.[92] In the event, £2m. was raised, largely in Germany, where the City's writ did not run, and the Transvaal was able to stiffen its defences and its foreign policy. There was a possibility, too, that the mine-owners might strike a deal with the Transvaal which, in settling their complaints, would also enhance British influence. Kruger's response to this prospect was to set up an Industrial Commission in 1897; but his attempt to win over the mine-workers by criticising their employers, his incomplete implementation of the Commission's recommendations in 1898–9, and the Randlord's insistence on linking the industry's problems to wider political issues ensured that no reconciliation took place.[93] The final means of exercising indirect influence depended on the Trojan Horse containing the *uitlanders (foreigners)*. Chamberlain and Milner quickly developed a commitment to these predominantly British settlers in the Transvaal, and pressed for an end to the economic and political discrimination which they suffered.[94] Their hope was that an enlarged electorate would provide a constituency for more liberal Boer political figures and would swing the Republic back into Britain's orbit. But Kruger could not extend the franchise without risking political defeat, and his re-election in 1898 damaged Britain's plans for applying this essentially Gladstonian formula of voluntary and low-cost political reform.

The failure to control the Transvaal by informal means opened the door to the advocates of force. Foremost among these was Milner, whose short fuse was readily set alight, and whose impatience was quickly communicated to others. But this does not mean, as some scholars have argued, that the Boer War was caused primarily by Milner and his policies.[95] Although Milner helped to stir the pot, he did not supply the ingredients. More important agents were the imperial government and, indirectly, the mine-owners. Neither

92. Quoted in Van-Helten, 'German Capital', p. 384.
93. Smith, 'Origins of the South African War'.
94. Diana Cammack, 'the Politics of Discontent: the Grievances of the Uitlander Refugees, 1899–1902', *Jour. Southern African Stud.*, 8 (1982); Porter, *The Origins of the South African War*, pp. 104–5.
95. For example, Thomas Pakenham, *The Boer War* (1979).

wanted war; both exerted the pressures that brought it about. The imperial government knowingly adopted a high-risk policy.[96] Salisbury and his Cabinet were not driven off course by the men on the spot. Although they did not want a costly war, they accepted the possibility of hostilities, they continued to apply pressure to Kruger, and they became more insistent after 1898, when the Anglo-German agreement removed the Transvaal's best chance of securing external support.[97] Britain's determined stance owed little to strategic considerations: by the 1890s her interests and ambitions in South Africa had far outgrown the requirements of a naval base, as Lord Selborne's memorandum, written from the Colonial Office in 1896, makes quite plain.[98] In any case, it was not necessary to go to war with the Transvaal in order to protect Simonstown, which was 800 miles to the south and not under any threat.[99] As for the randlords, they had been tempted by the prospect of a quick, cheap coup in 1895, but they also had good reason to stop short of war in 1899 because a major conflict would have interrupted output and damaged investment. Nevertheless, the mine-owners played their part in a dangerous game. They pressed their grievances against Kruger's government in 1899, generalised them to include political questions, and associated themselves with Milner to an extent that compromised the search for a peaceful settlement.

A full appreciation of the motives behind Britain's determination to go to war in 1899 requires a longer perspective than that provided by the events of the previous few years. What Carnarvon strove for in the 1870s, Salisbury, Chamberlain and Milner achieved, if at a high cost, twenty years later. Carnarvon himself had played a significant part in steering through parliament the British North America Act, which brought the Dominion of Canada into being. The Act of 1867 was the culmination of a highly successful strategy which aimed at keeping Canada within Britain's economic orbit for much longer than

96. Porter, *The Origins of the South African War*, pp. 17, 253. Porter also argues, against the 'peripheral' view of empire building, that politicians were becoming increasingly responsive to public opinion in the metropole (pp. 246–7).

97. Ibid. pp. 159–60. It was at this point, too, that German mining interests on the Rand shifted their support from Kruger and moved behind the idea of a British-dominated South Africa. See Van-Helten, 'German Capital', pp. 386–8. When the 'small war' became a big one, Britain had to turn to the New York money market for assistance. See Kathleen Burk, 'Finance, Foreign Policy and the Anglo-American Bank: the House of Morgan, 1900–31', *Historical Research*, 61 (1988), pp. 199–201.

98. Selborne's Memorandum, dated 30 March 1896, is quoted at length in Robinson and Gallagher, *Africa and the Victorians*, pp. 434–7.

99. Cope, 'Strategic and Socio-Economic Explanations', is decisive on this question.

would otherwise have been possible, given the rising influence of the United States.[100] Carnarvon tried to apply the same formula to South Africa, and for the same reasons, namely that unity was thought to be a prerequisite of local prosperity, sound credit and political stability under British authority, and would add to the strength of the empire.

Selborne's influential memorandum of 1896 was based on the same assumptions. What had changed since Carnarvon's time was that the power and potential of the Transvaal had greatly expanded, and the prospect of a Canadian solution to Britain's problems in South Africa was now threatened by the emergence of a rival possibility: the creation of a 'United States of South Africa' under Afrikaner control.[101] This prospect not only stirred up uneasy memories of colonial revolt but also aroused anxieties about a weakening of Britain's economic and political influence in the world. Union under the imperial flag was intended to forestall such a calamity by bringing the aspirations of the Afrikaners under control in much the same way as the problem of the French settlers in Canada had been dealt with; that is, by winning their loyalty through the creation of prosperity and by giving them the opportunity to cooperate, politically as well as economically, in the imperial adventure. These wider considerations enabled British politicians to generalise the issues in dispute and to present them in terms of the national interest. In September 1899 Chamberlain could claim that 'What is now at stake is the position of Great Britain in South Africa – and with it the estimate formed of our power and influence in Colonies throughout the world'.[102] Comforted by their own propaganda, policy-makers discounted the opposition; at this point the drums began to roll.

SELECTIVE ACQUISITIONS: TROPICAL AFRICA

Compared to the weight of Britain's interests in Egypt and southern Africa, tropical Africa was scarcely able to turn the scales. Despite its vast size, this region accounted for only a minute share of Britain's

100. See pp. 261–6. The application of these ideas to South Africa is well brought out by J.S. Marais, *The Fall of Kruger's Republic* (1961).

101. Selborne's Memorandum (see n. 98) is evidence of this concern, which is also apparent in Chamberlain's Cabinet Memorandum of 6 Sept. 1899, quoted in J.A.S. Grenville, *Lord Salisbury and Foreign Policy: The Close of the Nineteenth Century* (1964), pp. 257–8.

102. Colonial Office Memorandum, 7 Sept. 1899, quoted in Ovendale, 'Profit or Patriotism', p. 226.

overseas trade and had very limited strategic significance. Nevertheless, Britain secured two large slices of west Africa, Nigeria and the Gold Coast, and a substantial chunk of east Africa, based on Kenya and stretching inland to include Uganda. If the partition of tropical Africa has long posed a problem for theorists of imperialism committed to the quest for 'surplus capital', it has also raised difficulties for those who have turned to alternative geopolitical explanations of empire-building. These dilemmas can be resolved, we suggest, once it is recognised that Britain was prepared to promote her interests in tropical Africa, but was constrained (as in the Middle East and China) by the extent to which private enterprise was willing to fund the maintenance or extension of British claims. Since the City took a generally unfavourable view of tropical Africa, advocates of a forward policy faced an uphill struggle, and large parts of the region were taken over by foreign rivals who had been denied more attractive opportunities elsewhere. In general, Britain enlarged her sphere of influence in areas where the value of existing trade indicated that expansion would be self-supporting, or where anticipated returns, combined with arguments about the national interest, enabled committed pressure groups to squeeze a limited measure of support from the 'Gladstonian garrison' in the Treasury.

Early expectations that the 'Bible and plough' would transform the societies and economies of west Africa were disappointed. 'Legitimate' commerce expanded after 1807, but the rate of growth was modest and was hampered in particular by the persistence of the overseas slave trade.[103] Moreover, Britain's political and cultural influence was confined to a handful of entrepôts, which provided indirect and very limited control over affairs in the interior.[104] After 1850, however, the pace of change quickened, and the value of west Africa's external trade doubled between 1865 and 1885 as a result of the elimination of the overseas slave trade, the advent of regular steamship services, and buoyant prices for 'legitimate' exports.[105] These developments were also accompanied by an increase in the volume of commercial capital tied up in goods and advances to local merchants. From the City's perspective, however, the region still

103. David Eltis and Lawrence Jennings, 'Trade Between Western Africa and the Atlantic World in the Pre-Colonial Era', *Am. Hist. Rev.* 93 (1988).
104. Martin Lynn, 'The "Imperialism of Free Trade" in West Africa, c.1800–c.1870', *Jour. Imp. and Comm. Hist.*, 15 (1986).
105. Newbury 'On the Margins of Empire', pp. 41–2; Martin Lynn, 'From Sail to Steam: the Impact of the Steamship Services on the British Palm Oil Trade with West Africa, 1850–1890', *Jour. African Hist.*, 30 (1989).

deserved its zero credit-rating: African states were in no position to attract foreign capital, even if they wanted to; and private investment inland awaited firm evidence, which never materialised, of the existence of a tropical Klondike.

During the last quarter of the century, commercial expansion was checked by falling export prices and reduced rates of growth.[106] Although import prices fell too, the indications are that the (net barter) terms of trade moved against primary producers.[107] These trends, transmitted from the metropolitan centres of demand, squeezed profit margins on the periphery and sharpened commercial conflict between merchants and producers. The declining performance of the export sector needs also to be seen in a longer perspective of structural change which affected both production and distribution. The shift to 'legitimate' commerce encouraged the rise of small export producers, caused large producers to intensify the use of slave labour, and had far-reaching social and political repercussions within west Africa which have still to be fully explored.[108] However, it seems clear that the fall in export prices reduced the chances of an orderly commercial transition and provided material for the claim, made by Europeans on the coast, that Africans were incapable of 'running their own affairs'. The growing volume of trade after 1850 had important consequences for the distributive system because it increased the credit requirements of the export sector and generated a demand for improved harbours and expanded on-shore facilities, including railways, to reduce the cost and hence restore the profitability of west African trade.[109] Credit became an especially critical issue because of the existence of non-convertible currencies, such as cowries, which were rapidly depreciating in value, and because of the lack of acceptable forms of security, such as transferrable land.[110] The peri-

106. The analysis here broadly follows A.G. Hopkins, *An Economic History of West Africa* (1973: 1988), Ch. 4, and the work of Hargreaves and Newbury cited in n. 111.

107. Newbury, 'On the Margins of Empire', offers a valuable assessment of the relationship between commercial fluctuations and political action.

108. Hopkins, *Economic History of West Africa*, Ch. 4. The most important recent work is that undertaken by Robin Law, of the University of Stirling, 'The Historiography of the Commercial Transition in Nineteenth-Century West Africa', in Toyin Falola, ed. *African Historiography: Essays in Honour of Ade Ajayi* (1991).

109. C.W. Newbury, 'Credit in Early Nineteenth-Century West African Trade', *Jour. African Hist.*, 13 (1972); idem, 'On the Margins of Empire', p. 39.

110. Jan S. Hogendorn and Marion Johnson, *The Shell Money of the Slave Trade* (Cambridge, 1986) is the definitive account. For one detailed study of the decline of cowrie currency see A.G. Hopkins, 'The Currency Revolution in South-West Nigeria in the Late Nineteenth Century', *Jour. Hist. Soc. Nigeria,* 3 (1966). On the attempt to introduce British ideas of rights in land see A.G. Hopkins, 'Property Rights and Empire Building: Britain's Annexation of Lagos, 1861', *Jour. Econ. Hist.*, 40 (1980).

odic dips in export performance in the last quarter of the century caused acute problems for European wholesalers who, in the absence of modern banks, were also the principal suppliers of commercial credit on the west coast.

Deteriorating conditions of trade intersected with international rivalries, sharpening tensions among the major powers and in turn being aggravated by them.[111] The French began to advance inland from Senegal in 1879 and stepped up their efforts to control the lower Niger in the early 1880s; the Germans laid claim to Togo and Cameroun in the mid–1880s.[112] These moves aroused both cupidity and anxiety among Britain's representatives in west Africa: the optimists began to propagate the idea that the interior was an area of vast and easily realised potential; the pessimists expressed fears that it would soon be absorbed into protectionist regimes which would discriminate against British trade and cut into the revenues supporting Britain's outposts on the coast.

As the evidence began to indicate that the grand experiment in 'legitimate' commerce was faltering and might even founder, merchants and officials on the west coast started to agitate for a more overt defence of Britain's position to fend off the encroachments of foreign rivals and to promote a new development drive which would carry the commercial revolution inland.[113] Successive British governments responded to these pressures in two ways: by trying to preserve a large free-trade zone in west Africa, and by annexing regions that were particularly important for British commerce.

The threat to free trade had to be taken seriously because Britain was west Africa's principal foreign trading partner and consequently had interests throughout the region. Moreover, as we have seen in

---

111. Historians of West Africa are heavily indebted to the authoritative work of Hargreaves and Newbury on this subject, though only a selection of their important contributions can be referred to here. See, in particular: J.D. Hargreaves's trilogy, *Prelude to the Partition of West Africa* (1973), *West Africa Partitioned: The Loaded Pause, 1885–1889* and *West Africa Partitioned; The Elephants and the Grass* (1985); and C.W. Newbury, *The Western Slave Coast and its Rulers* (Oxford, 1966), 'The Tariff Factor in Anglo-French West African Partition', in Prosser Gifford and William Roger Lewis, eds. *France and Britain in Africa* (New Haven, Conn., 1971), and 'Trade and Authority in West Africa from 1850–1880', in Lewis Gann and P. Duignan, eds. *Colonialism in Africa*, Vol. I (Cambridge, 1969).

112. It is now clear that the French decision to advance inland from Senegal was taken before Britain's occupation of Egypt in 1882 and therefore cannot have been caused by it. See C.W. Newbury and A.S. Kanya-Forstner, 'French Policy and the Origins of the Scramble for West Africa', *Jour. African Hist.*, 10 (1969).

113. William G. Hynes, *The Economics of Empire: Britain, Africa and the New Imperialism, 1870–95* (1979); B.M. Ratcliffe, 'Commerce and Empire: Manchester Merchants and West Africa, 1873–95', *Jour. Imp. and Comm. Hist.*, 6 (1979).

other parts of the world, Britain had a general interest in maintaining the open door because she had a powerful stake in preserving the pattern of multilateral settlements that underpinned her own position as the world's largest international trader and supplier of capital. In west Africa, as with the Congo, Portuguese Africa and south-west Africa, the Foreign Office was concerned less with sovereignty than with access: if foreign rivals could be persuaded not to discriminate against British goods and capital, then Britain's interests could be upheld without the burdens of territorial responsibility.[114] In pursuit of this goal, the Foreign Office embarked on a campaign of perpetual negotiation to secure agreements on tariffs and, by association, on boundaries too.[115] This strategy was hampered because the resources available for diplomacy were limited. No counterpart to the Hong-kong and Shanghai Bank stood alongside the Foreign Office in tropical Africa because, in contrast to China, indigenous states in the west and east of the continent were unable to fund sizeable foreign loans. Nevertheless, Britain's negotiators achieved impressive results: a series of agreements, beginning in 1882 and culminating in the Anglo-French settlement of 1898, went a long way towards preserving an open door to west Africa, principally by limiting the extension of the discriminatory system in force in Senegal.

In the areas that were to become the colonies of Nigeria and the Gold Coast, the balance of costs and returns appeared to justify a more vigorous policy. On the lower Niger there were indications that mercantile enterprise could become self-supporting. Goldie's United African Company, formed in 1879, had engaged the French firms in economic warfare and had emerged victorious in 1885.[116] With its London base and its complement of aristocrats and reputable financiers, the National African Company, as it had (significantly)

114. For examples of the ways in which capital and trade crossed colonial boundaries see: W.G. Clarence Smith, ed. 'Business Empires in Equatorial Africa', *African Econ. Hist.*, 12 (1983); Ronald Dreyer, 'Whitehall, Cape Town, Berlin and the Economic Partition of South-West Africa: the Establishment of British Economic Control, 1885–94', *Jour. Imp. and Comm. Hist.*, XV (1987); Richard A. Voeltz, 'The European Economic and Political Penetration of South-West Africa, 1884–1892', *Int. Jour. African Hist. Stud.*, 17 (1984); S.E. Katzenellenbogen, 'British Businessmen and German Africa, 1885–1919', in B.M. Ratcliffe, ed. *Great Britain and her World* (Manchester, 1975), pp. 258–9; and A.G. Hopkins, 'Big Business in African Studies', *Jour. African Hist.*, 28 (1987), pp. 130–1.

115. The progress of this campaign can be followed through the work of Hargreaves and Newbury cited in n. 111 above.

116. C.W. Newbury, 'The Development of French Policy on the Lower and Upper Niger, 1880–98', *Jour. Mod. Hist.*, 31 (1959), pp. 16–26.

become in 1882, was an acceptable candidate for an official charter.[117] It duly became the Royal Niger Company in 1886, and was granted extensive commercial rights in exchange for repelling further French incursions.[118] In Lagos, Governor Carter was allowed to mount an expedition into Yorubaland in 1892, following considerable mercantile pressure and after agreement had been reached to pay for the campaign by raising import duties.[119] When Joseph Chamberlain became Colonial Secretary in 1895, a firmer line was taken towards reserving the remaining areas of British interest. Britain's new frontiersmen, coordinated by what Lugard called the 'Birmingham Screw Policy', subdued the Asante in the central region of the Gold Coast and took hold of northern Nigeria, thus pushing the French into the 'lighter soils' of the desert edge.[120] Beyond this point, however, Chamberlain's plans for cultivating his 'undeveloped estates' had only limited success. The advocates of subsidised development in the tropics were no match for the defenders of fiscal orthodoxy in the Treasury.[121] Chamberlain's defeat on this question, as on the larger issue of tariff reform, confirmed the supremacy of the principles of free trade and sound money and made clear to assailants the high price that would be exacted for attacking them.

British policy towards east Africa was broadly similar to that applied to the west coast, though in the eastern part of the continent the development of 'legitimate' commerce occurred later and was on a much smaller scale. The aspirations, however, were much the same: the Foreign Office identified a promising entrepôt and agent in Zanzibar and its sultan, imposed an anti-slave-trade treaty in 1845, and stood back to observe the anticipated expansion of 'legitimate' commerce. Both the principal exports, ivory and cloves, responded to the growth of external demand, but neither was capable of serving as the basis of long-term export development. Ivory depended upon

117. The Chairman, Lord Aberdare, was a prominent Liberal politician and a close friend of Gladstone and Lord Granville, the Foreign Secretary. Charles Mills of the leading merchant bank, Glyn, Mills & Currie, was also on the board. See J.E. Flint, *Sir George Goldie and the Making of Nigeria* (1960), pp. 45–6.

118. Flint, *Sir George Goldie*, Ch. 4.

119. A.G. Hopkins, 'Economic Imperialism in West Africa: Lagos, 1880–1892', *Econ. Hist. Rev.*, 2nd ser. XXI (1968).

120. Hargreaves, *West Africa Partitioned: The Elephants and the Grass*, pp. 201–8, 208–24, 224–35.

121. R.E. Dumett, 'Joseph Chamberlain, Imperial Finance and Railway Policy in British West Africa in the Late Nineteenth Century', *Eng. Hist. Rev.*, XC (1975). See also the perceptive comment by Hargreaves, who points out that Lord Salisbury had a larger as well as a sounder view of which parts of the world were of economic value: *West Africa Partitioned: The Elephants and the Grass*, pp. 230–31.

essentially finite resources, which began to decline from the mid-1870s, while the production of cloves was confined to coastal estates which continued to employ slave labour.[122] As in the case of the west coast, abolitionist measures initially weakened or diverted the slave trade without destroying it, and caused serious discontent among slave-holders and traders.[123] One result was a political crisis in Zanzibar which drew in British intervention in 1859–61 but left the problem of reconstructing the export economy unresolved. With the completion of the Suez Canal in 1869 and the advent of the steamship, the pressure for change began to quicken. The prospect of 'opening up' the east coast attracted entrepreneurs who saw the potential of improved communication with Europe and of closer integration with the Indian Ocean economy. It also helped to revitalise the abolitionist movement by stimulating both the navy and the missions, and it merged with the activities of explorers to contribute to the 'Afromania' which infected influential segments of public opinion during the period of the scramble.[124]

This renewed effort to pull east Africa into line with British policy was signalled by the appointment of Sir John Kirk as Consul-General at Zanzibar in 1873. It has long been known that Kirk made a determined effort to use the Sultanate as an instrument of British policy by securing a new treaty abolishing the slave trade and by backing it with naval and military force.[125] What has only recently been revealed, however, is the extent to which the growing assertive-

122. These subjects have been well covered by Abdul Sheriff, *Slaves, Spices and Ivory in Zanzibar: Integration of an East African Commercial Empire into the World Economy, 1770–1873* (1987), and F.Cooper, *Plantation Slavery on the East Coast of Africa* (New Haven, Conn., 1977).

123. Unfortunately, the ramifications of these changes in the East African interior have yet to be studied in the detail needed to sustain a plausible generalisation on this subject. Interesting case studies include: Charles H. Ambler, *Kenyan Communities in the Age of Imperialism: The Central Region in the Late Nineteenth Century* (New Haven, Conn., 1987); Ronald R. Atkinson, 'A History of the Western Acholi of Uganda, c.1675–1900' (Ph.D. thesis Northwestern University, 1978); and Thomas J. Herlehy, 'An Economic History of the Kenya Coast: The Mijkenda Coconut Palm Economy, 1800–1980' (Ph.D. thesis, Boston University, 1985). There are many suggestive comments in John Lonsdale's important contribution, 'The European Scramble and Conquest in African History', in Oliver and Sanderson, *The Cambridge History of Africa*, Vol. 6, which deserve further research. On the slave trade see W.G. Clarence Smith, ed. 'The Economies of the Indian Ocean Slave Trade', *Slavery and Abolition*, 9 (1988).

124. R.J. Gavin, 'The Bartle Frere Mission to Zanzibar, 1873', *Hist. Jour.*, 5 (1962); Raymond Howell, *The Royal Navy and the Slave Trade* (1987); R.M. Githige, 'The Issue of Slavery: Relations Between the C.M.S. and the State on the East African Coast Prior to 1895', *Journal of Religion in Africa*, 16 (1986); Bridges, 'The Historical Role of British Explorers'.

125. R. Coupland, *The Exploitation of East Africa, 1856–1890* (1939), Ch. 12.

ness of official policy was both matched and influenced by the attitude of private interests.

One important source of support for an expansionist policy came from southern Africa, where the mining firms were quick to see a possible connection between ending the east African slave trade and developing a flow of cheap labour for the mines.[126] In the 1870s, Frederick Elton, a former Indian Army officer who was involved in diamond-mining with one of Rhodes's brothers, made himself a powerful advocate of the need to advance 'commerce and civilisation' in east Africa. Elton was used as an unofficial consultant to the Foreign Office on central and east African affairs, became Britain's Consul in Mozambique in 1875, and lent strong support to Carnarvon's drive for a south African confederation in the late 1870s.

A second connection was with British shipping and mercantile interests in India, and particularly with William Mackinnon, who founded the British and India Steam Navigation Company in 1862 and had substantial commercial interests in the firm of Smith, Mackenzie.[127] Mackinnon recognised the implications of the opening of the Suez Canal and moved swiftly to secure prime positions in east Africa, linking Aden and Zanzibar by steamer in 1872 and extending his trading activities to Zanzibar shortly afterwards. Mackinnon had close ties with Elton and also with the governor of the Cape, Sir Bartle Frere, both of whom supported his schemes for controlling the shipping lanes of the east coast, and he was intimately associated, too, with the Church of Scotland mission in Livingstonia. Mackinnon, however, was much more than a sub-imperialist on the margins of empire. His close associates in Britain included James Hutton, the wealthy and politically active Manchester businessman who had a particular interest in tropical Africa, and the Duke of Sutherland, an enthusiast who was prepared to cover the world with railway lines, and sometimes to finance them. Moreover, in the mid–1870s Mack-

---

126. Etherington, 'Frederick Elton'.

127. Our understanding of Britain's imperial interests in East Africa during this period is being transformed by J. Forbes Munro's research on Sir William Mackinnon. See 'Shipping Subsidies and Railway Guarantees: William Mackinnon, Eastern Africa and the Indian Ocean, 1860–93', *Jour. African Hist.*, 28 (1987); and 'Suez and the Shipowner: the Response of the Mackinnon Shipping Group to the Opening of the Suez Canal, 1869–84', in Lewis R. Fischer and Helge W. Nordvick, eds. *Shipping and Trade, 1750–1950: Essays in International Maritime Economic History* (Pontefract, 1990). Mackinnon also had close connections with the National Bank of India, which established a branch in Zanzibar in 1892. See Geoffrey Tyson, *100 Years of Banking in Asia and Africa* (1963), pp. 111–13. His business interests in Smith, Mackenzie are dealt with by Stephanie Jones, *Two Centuries of Overseas Trading: The Origin and Growth of the Inchcape Company* (1986), Ch. 4.

innon himself moved his headquarters from Glasgow to London because he wanted to have better access to the City's commercial services and to the higher circles of political influence.[128] Mackinnon provides a good example of a particular type of business imperialist who was emerging in the second half of the nineteenth century as a result of the extension abroad of the new service sector: he supported free trade but also relied on imperial contracts and subsidies; he stood for private enterprise but also bent the arm of government when he could; he pursued profit but also invested in philanthropy and placed them both under the banner of an onward-marching Christianity.

It is now evident that there was a vocal and growing lobby of private and official interests pushing an expansionist policy in east Africa from the 1870s onwards.[129] In 1877 Mackinnon declared himself ready to take on the administration of the whole region from the coast to Lake Victoria; in 1884 Harry Johnston, a young proconsul in the making, wrote lyrical, almost chimerical, reports on the region, extolling its market potential, its unfathomed resources, and its suitability for European settlement; more important still, by 1884 the Foreign Office was making quantitative assessments of east Africa's commercial potential, and had also persuaded itself that the indigenous population would welcome the establishment of good government – a sure sign that the Titans of officialdom were preparing to accept yet another burden. But, if interest in east Africa was more economic than strategic, it was also largely speculative.[130] Britain's commercial stake there was minuscule, even compared to west Africa, and there was little financial interest beyond that involved in foreign trade. Advocates of expansion spoke of a new India and a new Australia, but the City's scepticism and the Treasury's opposition combined to prevent this Atlantis from materialising.

128. J. Forbes Munro, 'Scottish Overseas Enterprise and the Lure of London: the Mackinnon Group, 1847–1893', *Scottish Econ. and Soc. Hist.*, 8 (1988).

129. This point has been established by M.E. Chamberlain in an important and still unjustly neglected article: 'Clement Hill's Memoranda and the British Interest in East Africa', *Eng. Hist. Rev.*, LXXXVII (1972). See also Hynes, *The Economics of Empire*, pp. 77–83, 127–9. In the mid–1880s the lobby was able to call upon Lord Aberdare (see n. 117), Chamberlain, Dilke, Kimberley (the Secretary of State for India), and a clutch of Lancashire MPs; it also had the sympathy of Lord Rothschild.

130. The idea (associated with Robinson and Gallagher, *Africa and the Victorians*) that Britain's concern in East Africa was largely strategic not only neglects the economic considerations summarised here, but also is hard to reconcile with the fact that Britain was unperturbed by the French acquisition of Madagascar in 1883–5, and that the Admiralty had no interest in making use of Mombasa at this time. There were plenty of bases: the real test was controlling the high seas. See Chamberlain, *The Scramble*, pp. 63–4.

As in the case of west Africa, the aims of the commercial lobby were helped along by the actions of foreign rivals. In 1885, when Germany declared protectorates over a region which included some of the principal trade routes to Zanzibar, the opponents of British expansion could no longer rely on traditional arguments for non-intervention.[131] In the following year, an agreement was reached with Germany which divided the hinterland of Zanzibar between the two powers (largely at the sultan's expense), preserved the principle of free trade in both spheres, and allocated the northern section (later to become Kenya) to Britain. Mackinnon and his associates did not gain all they wanted, but they did secure the area which was thought to have the greatest potential.[132] In a further agreement, reached in 1890, Germany effectively recognised Britain's paramount position in east Africa in exchange for Heligoland, an island in the North Sea which, in the eyes of the Foreign Office, was even less valuable than tropical Africa.[133]

The administration of this huge territory was assigned to a new chartered company, the Imperial British East Africa Company, which was formed by Mackinnon in 1888.[134] Mackinnon's company extended its domain inland in the hope of annexing the fabled (and indeed mythical) wealth of the interior, headed off German expansion, and laid claim to Uganda; but it failed to draw in either capital or settlers, and by 1890 was virtually bankrupt. When Mackinnon appealed for a financial guarantee to build a railway from Mombasa to Lake Victoria, parliament turned the proposal down, and in 1892 the company threatened to withdraw from Uganda unless it received a subsidy to cover its administrative overheads. This was a threat that Gladstone in particular welcomed, but the Prime Minister was again out-manoeuvred, as he had been in the case of Egypt, by the forward party in the Cabinet, this time led by the Foreign Secretary, Rosebery, who dusted off and deployed much the same arguments as Hartington and his associates had used in 1882.[135] In this case, 'anarchy' in the

131. As H.P. Merritt has shown, the British were not alone in being dazzled by the commercial potential of East Africa: 'Bismarck and the German Interest in East Africa', *Hist. Jour.*, 21 (1978).

132. Chamberlain, 'Clement Hill', pp. 545–6.

133. William Roger Louis, 'The Anglo-German Hinterland Settlement of 1890 and Uganda', *Uganda Jour.*, 27 (1963).

134. J.S. Galbraith, *Mackinnon and East Africa, 1878–95* (Cambridge, 1972) remains the most detailed account, though it must now be read in the light of Munro, 'Shipping Subsidies'.

135. However, contrary to an often-repeated statement, he did not threaten to resign: Gordon Martel, *Imperial Diplomacy: Rosebery and the Failure of Foreign Policy* (1986), pp. 80–6.

interior was linked not only (and improbably) to the claim that Uganda was strategically important to Egypt, but also to the alleged revival of the slave trade and the danger to Christian missions in the region. The press responded, public opinion was aroused, and the government appointed a commissioner to recommend a solution.[136] The Commissioner, Sir Gerald Portal, was Consul-General in Zanzibar and was therefore familiar with the issues. He had two other qualities: he was an ambitious imperialist who saw himself running a 'vast equatorial empire' and he was Rosebery's nominee.[137] The result, in the words of another well-placed imperialist, was 'a foregone conclusion'.[138] Uganda became a British protectorate in 1894, and Mackinnon's much-prized and hugely expensive railway followed soon afterwards, with some assistance from Joseph Chamberlain. Mackinnon's ambition had given Britain a stake in Uganda; Rosebery's ensured that it was firmly planted. It was left to others to try to create a viable unit out of what some contemporaries had already characterised as being a white elephant.[139]

FROM PARTITION TO PARAMOUNTCY

From the perspective of this study, there is an argument to be made for reducing the attention customarily paid to the partition of Africa because the importance of the continent, as measured by trade and financial flows, did not give it a high ranking among Britain's international trading partners or even among regions that felt the force of her imperialist ambitions. Moreover, Africa was not a single state with one central government but a continent with numerous very different states, and this presents a problem of categorisation that is either not found or is far less prominent than in the other cases we have considered. This degree of diversity suggests that it might be illuminating to repartition the literature on the scramble, so that Egypt is considered with the Ottoman Empire, southern Africa with regions of white settlement (including Latin America), west Africa with other tropical export economies, and east Africa with the

136. Anthony Low, 'British Public Opinion and the Uganda Question: October–December, 1892', *Uganda Jour.*, 18 (1954); Gordon Martel, 'Cabinet Politics and African Partition: the Uganda Debate Reconsidered', *Jour. Imp. and Comm. Hist.*, XIII (1984).
137. Martel, *Imperial Diplomacy*, p. 87.
138. Harry Johnston, *The Uganda Protectorate* (1904), p. 234.
139. Cartoon in *Punch*, 22 Oct. 1892.

expanding Indian Ocean complex. However, given that partition has been treated for so long as a subject with continental boundaries and is so firmly entrenched in the literature as the classic case of late-nineteenth-century imperialism, there are compelling historiographical reasons why we have situated our own interpretation in the context of the existing literature, and have tried to provide an adequate, if compressed, account of the voluminous research which the subject has generated.

By 1900, when the dust of partition had settled, it could be seen that Britain had secured the most valuable parts of Africa and had also preserved access to large parts of the continent that were not under her direct control. This outcome is not immediately apparent from the map of Africa, which shows that large areas were allocated to other colonial powers; but size is a poor measure of value, and there is no doubt that the continent's trade and finance were concentrated overwhelmingly on British territories, and remained so during the colonial era.[140] Moreover, Britain achieved considerable success in preserving access to regions which fell under foreign control: Belgium, Portugal, Germany and even France were all bound, albeit in different ways, to preserve elements of the open door in their African colonies. Agreements to maintain free trade, though qualified in a number of respects, fitted the needs of Britain's system of multilateral payments and enabled her finance to flow readily over foreign boundaries.[141] This point deserves emphasis because it is commonly underestimated in studies of partition, which are concerned, understandably but also incompletely, with the formal division of territory.

Britain's success is not readily explained by the existing historiography, despite its richness and refinement, because it remains tied too closely to the arguments mobilised by contemporary observers – often for a moral or political purpose.[142] Current interpretations either fasten a misleading stereotype of capitalist development on to Africa or assign too much weight to other parties, whether foreign rivals or proto-nationalists. Just as there are well-known difficulties in finding

140. See Volume II, p. 203.
141. This theme is explored in the references given in n. 114. The case of South West Africa, where German rule was dependent on British capital, is particularly telling – and has been well told: Dreyer, 'Whitehall, Cape Town'; Richard A. Voeltz, *German Colonialism and the South-West Africa Company, 1894–1914* (Athens, Ohio, 1988).
142. For the origins of the most influential radical and liberal interpretations of partition see Hopkins, 'The Victorians and Africa', pp. 364–70; and for an assessment of the applicability of Hobson's views see P.J. Cain, 'Hobson Lives? Finance and British Imperialism, 1870–1914', in Simon Groenveld and Michael Wintle, eds. *State and Trade: Government and Economy in Britain and the Netherlands since the Middles Ages,* (Zutphen, 1992).

'surplus' capital and conspiracies of bond-holders, so there are equally serious problems with the currently influential view that Britain was an ageing, defensive power struggling to fend off new challenges to her dominance. France and Germany complicated Britain's pursuit of her interests, but were not the main cause of her actions, and their chief influence was felt in tropical Africa, at the margins of Britain's principal areas of involvement. Strategic arguments have also been greatly overestimated. They were used mainly as a legitimation for action in Egypt and east Africa, were largely irrelevant in south Africa, and were non-existent on the west coast. As for proto-nationalism, while it is undeniable that there were numerous crises on the African frontier during the period of partition, an examination of their origins indicates that their prime cause lay in Europe rather than on the periphery.

This does not mean that we are obliged to fall back on the argument that partition was 'a remarkable freak' in the annals of imperialism.[143] The central fact which needs to be explained is that Britain began and ended partition as the dominant foreign power in Africa. To assume that she was ageing, declining and retreating is unhelpful; to invoke the flexible laws of chance is to abandon the possibility of providing a systematic account of a momentous historical event. The interpretation advanced here suggests that Britain had independent reasons for taking action to increase her grip on Africa. The impulses motivating policy can be traced to the metropole, and particularly to the expansion after 1850 of the gentlemanly occupations and values we have identified. Indeed, Britain's actions in partitioning Africa followed the contours of this development: the main weight of her interests lay in Egypt and southern Africa, where City and service interests were most prominently represented, and it was there that Britain showed the greatest vigour in promoting her claims.

The occupation of Egypt was closely linked to restoring the health of public finance. The course of treatment was connected, in turn, to the internal politics of the Liberal Party, through which it was generalised as an issue of principle and elevated to the status of a national interest. The occupation of southern Africa was also a result of Britain's growing stake in the region, where her investments had risen substantially following the discovery of minerals. But the Anglo-Boer War was not fought at the behest of the mine-owners

---

143. R.E. Robinson and J. Gallagher, 'The Partition of Africa', in *New Cambridge Modern History*, Vol. XI (Cambridge, 1962), pp. 593–4.

any more than it was fought to secure a naval base or to realise the dreams of an ambitious proconsul. The decision was made because Britain was an expanding power which sought to create in Africa a dynamic economic and political satellite of the kind already in evidence in Australia, Canada, New Zealand and, it should be added, Argentina. Kruger's plans for achieving greater political independence cut across the trajectory of British policy by threatening to confine Britain's influence to the Cape and by perpetuating uncertainties about the long-term future of the mining industry. Whether war was necessary to achieve Britain's purpose, or was even desired by those who were responsible for bringing it about, are questions that this study can put to one side. But it is hard to imagine that Britain would have involved herself to the point where war became inevitable had the Transvaal been devoid of resources; and it is worth observing that Lord Salisbury was quite content to leave the French to federate vast areas of desert and savanna in west Africa.

In tropical Africa the shortage of investment limited Britain's presence and handicapped her diplomacy, in much the same way as it did in Persia. In the absence of a powerful City interest, the Foreign Office had to rely on chartered companies, which in turn required subsidies (in the shape of commercial rights and guarantees) in exchange for political services. Organisations such as the Royal Niger Company and the Imperial British East Africa Company represented gentlemanly capitalist interests in a dilute form. In these circumstances, they acted in association with or alongside other mercantile and shipping interests, and with the missions, to a greater extent than was usual elsewhere. In west Africa, mercantile pressure groups also joined with British Chambers of Commerce representing manufacturers who were keen to preserve markets for their goods. But this example is an exception that proves the rule: policy in Britain's principal spheres of interest throughout the world was not made by the manufacturing lobby and was influenced by it only to a limited extent. Even in west Africa, manufacturing interests made headway only because their demands were consistent with free trade and, in general, with principles of sound finance.[144] This loose coalition of pressure groups nevertheless managed to secure a substantial part of its demands, principally because the financial and diplomatic cost of acceding to them was very limited. The commercially attractive parts of west Africa were retained, and the most promising parts of east

144. Typically by raising customs duties to pay for military operations and the costs of administration.

Africa were marked out for future use. Even when only half exerting herself, Britain was still able to outdistance her new foreign competitors.

In retrospect, we can now see that the problem was not that Britain's informal empire had broken down but that it had never come into being except, for an illusory moment, in Egypt. Elsewhere, political alliances were transitory where they were not abortive: sultans and chiefs were too often weak reeds; the Boers were too strong to be bent. The difficulty was rather that the rapidity of economic change affecting Africa after 1850 outpaced the rate of institutional adjustment needed to support it. The old staple industries may have begun to seek refuge in tropical markets, but the dynamic and highly competitive sector of the economy in London and the south-east was pushing back new frontiers at an unsettling speed. Viewed from this perspective, Britain was an advancing not a retreating power. It was not the arteries that hardened but the pulse that quickened. None of this meant that Britain was bent on annexation, but it did mean that attempts to exert influence and to ensure that small states were 'well kept' and 'always accessible' were more likely to create conditions which placed annexation on the agenda. Men like Colvin, Rhodes, Goldie and Mackinnon undoubtedly made sure that it stayed there. Nevertheless, the crucial decisions were taken in London. Salisbury, Hartington, Rosebery and Chamberlain knew what they were doing even if they did not always entirely approve of their own actions or control all of the consequences. Accidents did indeed occur during the partition of Africa, but they can be understood only in the context of an event that was not, in itself, accidental.

The causes of actions must not be inferred from their consequences; at the same time, it is surely not fanciful to see, in the colonial settlement, the resolution of the problems which had led to partition. In Egypt, Baring's tax-gathering efficiency and rigorous control of expenditure balanced the budget and encouraged renewed flows of foreign capital from the 1890s onwards.[145] In South Africa, the period of post-war reconstruction witnessed the abolition of the most contentious of the Transvaal's monopolies, the implementation of measures to improve the supply of labour to the mines, and the accommodation of mining and political interests.[146] Carnarvon's

145. Bent Hanson, 'Interest Rates and Foreign Capital in Egypt under British Occupation', *Jour. Econ. Hist*, 43 (1983).
146. Diana Cammack, 'The Johannesburg Republic: the Reshaping of a Rand Society, 1900–01', *South Afr. Hist. Jour.*, 18 (1986); Alan Jeeves, *Migrant Labour in*

long-sought confederation was achieved by an act of reconciliation that was dazzling and economical, even if it was not magnanimous: the Transvaal was granted self-government in 1906, and the management of the Union of South Africa was entrusted to a predominantly Afrikaner leadership in 1910.[147] In west Africa, the creation of new colonial states and the revival of international trade after 1900 provided the tax basis for raising foreign loans and accelerated the process of export-led growth. In east Africa, house-breaking also gave way to house-keeping, though in this case the City's judgement proved to be correct: there was some potential and more big game, but also white elephants to be preserved.

South Africa's Mining Economy: The Struggle for the Gold Mines' Labour Supply, 1890–1920 (Kingston, Montreal, 1985). The precise nature of this accommodation is currently under discussion, and no doubt will remain so: see Donald Denoon, 'Capital and Capitalists in the Transvaal in the 1890s and 1900s', *Hist. Jour.*, 23 (1980). A valuable guide to this period is Deryck Schreuder, 'Colonial Nationalism and "Tribal Nationalism": Making the White South African State, 1899–1910', in John Eddy and Deryck Schreuder, eds. *The Rise of Colonial Nationalism* (Sydney, 1988).

147. Ronald Hyam and Ged Martin, *Reappraisals in British Imperial History* (1975), Chs. 8–9.

CHAPTER TWELVE

'We Offer Ourselves as Supporters': The Ottoman Empire and Persia, 1838–1914[1]

The Ottoman Empire and Persia can be placed, with China, in a distinct category of regions that presented peculiar obstacles to European expansion in the underdeveloped world. The failure of societies in these three empires to produce modernising elites which were both powerful and cooperative limited their development as independent polities along Western lines. At the same time, the presence of large, antique, yet still death-defying political structures meant that indigenous authorities could not be taken over without promoting internal disorder, incurring massive expense and risking international conflict. The conundrum posed by the attempt to secure European interests without disrupting the Middle East became known in diplomatic circles as the Eastern Question. Policy-makers in Constantinople and Tehran grappled with a more desperate dilemma – the Western Question – of how to respond to intrusive European designs without losing their autonomy.[2]

Most of the historical literature on Britain's position in the Middle East has been harnessed to two opposed interpretations.[3] One empha-

1. 'The Porte, it is abundantly proved, is not strong enough to stand alone. It must be held up. We offer ourselves as supporters on the East, Austria on the West.' Lord Salisbury, 1878, quoted in C.J. Lowe, *The Reluctant Imperialists* (1969), Vol. I, p. 19.

2. For one variation on this theme see A.J. Toynbee, *The Western Question in Greece and Turkey*, (Boston, Mass., 1922). The indigenous point of view is put by L. Carl Brown, *International Politics and the Middle East* (Princeton, NJ, 1984), and M.E. Yapp, *The Making of the Modern Near East, 1792–1923* (1987).

3. A crisp summary is provided by D.C.M. Platt, *Finance, Trade and Politics in British Foreign Policy, 1815–1914* (1968), pp. 181–5. Helpful guides to the broader historiography of the region are John R. Broadus, 'Soviet Historical Literature on the Last Years of the Ottoman Empire', *Midd. East. Stud.*, 18 (1982); Rifaat Ali Abou-el Haj, 'The Social Uses of the Past: recent Arab Historiography of Ottoman Rule', *Int. Jour. Middle East Stud.*, 14 (1982); and William J. Olson, *Britain's Elusive Empire in the Middle East, 1900–1921; An Annotated Bibliography* (1982).

sises the dominance of economic motives, both in Britain's presence in the region and in the formulation of policy in London; the other stresses the paramountcy of strategic considerations. The concern of the present study lies less with trying to reinforce one or other of these standpoints than with unravelling the ties between them. The danger of this approach is that it can readily become either over-complex and excessively narrow, or all-embracing and excessively vague. The account that follows has the specific aim of showing how the rise and retreat of British finance affected the instruments available to policy-makers and influenced both the purpose and the result of Britain's endeavours in the region.

During the first half of the period under review, economics and strategy found harmonious expression in Britain's spacious vision of a free-trading and progressive international order. Palmerston's grand design was intended to regenerate the fallen nations of the world and to uplift those which had never risen.[4] It was believed that Sultan and Shah alike would become converts to the new ideology of progress, would adopt liberal reforms and would thereby become congenial commercial clients and reliable political allies. During the last quarter of the century this optimistic view, already weathered by exposure to reality, was replaced by a colder set of calculations and accompanied by a less flattering image, especially of the Turks, whose capacity for moral improvement was downgraded after the publicity given to the Bulgarian 'atrocities'.[5] Thereafter, British policy aimed at sedation rather than conversion, and expansive plans for co-operation gave way to the calculated and admirably economical 'language of menace'.[6] As the City turned to more attractive areas of investment, so the Foreign Office was drawn further into the Middle East, meddling in local politics and trying to tempt reluctant businessmen into unpromising commercial opportunities in order to shore up Britain's strategic interests.

The growing divergence between economic and political commit-

---

4. See Alan Cunningham's illuminating article, 'The Sick Man and the British Physician', *Midd. East. Stud.*, 17 (1981), and the wider commentary in Ronald Hyam, *Britain's Imperial Century, 1815–1914* (1976), Ch. 2.

5. The use made of the Bulgarian issue in British politics is dealt with by Marvin Swartz, *The Politics of British Foreign Policy in the Era of Disraeli and Gladstone* (1985), Ch. 2.

6. The phrase was coined by Lord Dufferin, a noted practitioner, in 1881. Quoted in H.S.W. Corrigan, 'British, French and German Interests in Asiatic Turkey, 1881–1913' (unpublished Ph.D. thesis, University of London, 1954), p. 8. Corrigan's thesis deserves credit for anticipating many of the conclusions of research published subsequently.

ments is an interesting indication of shifting priorities among segments of Britain's gentlemanly elite. But it is not to be treated, crudely, as demonstrating the ultimate primacy of 'strategic' over 'economic' motives. As we shall see, economic interests continued to be well represented through the Ottoman Public Debt Administration and through specific, if limited, commitments to particular regions and sectors in both the Ottoman Empire and Persia. Moreover, to the extent that successive British governments tried to prop up both states in order to safeguard the routes to India, it was because there Britain's economic stake *was* crucial to her status as a great power. The problem was that businessmen were not prepared to defend India by making essentially political investments in the Middle East. That burden was to be borne by governments, and governments were still constrained by cost, even though the tradition of non-intervention was steadily weakening. Informal ties between the City and government, though close, did not enable ministers of state to direct flows of funds overseas. Seen in this context, the Middle East offers a good example, not of the weakness, but of the strength and independence of the City. Bankers and traders paid the region the attention they thought its economic potential deserved; the Foreign Office gave it as much political commitment as the Treasury and the Government of India were willing to finance.

THE OTTOMAN EMPIRE: FROM FREE TRADE TO FOREIGN MANAGEMENT

Britain's long-standing connections with the Middle East were greatly strengthened by success in the French Wars, which encouraged the belief that the region would readily fall into her orbit when conditions of peaceful competition returned.[7] The abolition of the Levant Company's monopoly in 1825 symbolised the transition from an era of restriction and patronage: thereafter, the number of British merchants and political representatives in the Middle East increased and the size of the Ottoman market for British manufactures expanded.[8] But the

7. The economic history of the period is covered by Roger Owen, *The Middle East in the World Economy, 1800–1914* (1981), Charles Issawi, *An Economic History of the Middle East and North Africa* (Chicago, 1982); idem, ed. *The Economic History of the Middle East, 1800–1914* (Chicago, 1966), *The Economic History of Iran, 1800–1914* (Chicago, 1971) and *The Economic History of Turkey, 1800–1914* (Chicago, 1980).

8. A.G. Wood, *A History of the Levant Company* (Oxford, 1935), pp. 198–202; D.C.M. Platt, *The Cinderella Service: British Consuls since 1825* (1971), pp. 125–131.

subsequent growth of trade, though welcome, was insufficient to offset serious problems posed by the rise of competition and protection in major outlets in Europe. It was against this background that Palmerston began his assertive quest for new markets in the late 1830s and early 1840s.[9] In the case of the Ottoman Empire, the breakthrough came in 1838, when a free-trade treaty was concluded in exchange for backing the Porte against its powerful satellite, Egypt.[10] The treaty was a typical example of its kind: tariffs were subjected to external control, state monopolies were eliminated, the capitulatory privileges of European minorities were confirmed, and Britain was guaranteed treatment as a most-favoured-nation. With the commercial treaty came a package of broader measures designed to promote institutional reforms and to support modernising elements within the Ottoman state.[11]

The Anglo-Turkish convention brought immediate and gratifying results. Ottoman foreign trade grew rapidly between 1840 and the outbreak of the Crimean War in 1854.[12] Britain's share of the total rose impressively, and Lancashire's cotton goods began to find a market worthy of their needs.[13] Moreover, Britain earned consistent surpluses on her visible trade with the Ottoman Empire and these contributed to her emerging pattern of multilateral settlements.[14] Nevertheless, the early optimism about the development potential of the Middle East was never fulfilled. Within the Ottoman Empire the reform movement made limited progress, and the most influential reformers turned out to be loyalists who wished to strengthen the empire against European incursions and to restrain the emergence of a comprador class which might become a compliant agent of foreign

9. P.J. Cain and A.G. Hopkins, 'The Political Economy of British Expansion Overseas, 1750–1914', *Econ, Hist. Rev.*, 2nd ser. XXXIII (1980), pp. 479–81.

10. The text is printed in Issawi, *The Economic History of the Middle East, 1800–1914*, pp. 38–40. See also Orhan Kurmus, 'The 1838 Treaty of Commerce Re-examined', in Jean-Louis Bacqué-Grammont and Paul Dumont, eds. *Economies et sociétés dans l'Empire Ottoman* (Paris, 1983).

11. Carter V. Findley, *Bureaucratic Reform in the Ottoman Empire: The Sublime Porte, 1789–1922* (Princeton, NJ, 1980); S. Shaw, 'The Nineteenth-Century Ottoman Tax Reforms and Revenue System', *Int. Jour. Middle East Stud.*, 7 (1975); Ehud R.Toledano, *The Ottoman Slave Trade and its Suppression, 1840–1890* (Princeton, NJ, 1983); Roderic H. Davison, *Reform in the Ottoman Empire, 1856–1876* (New York, 1973), Ch. 1

12. Sevket Pamuk, *The Ottoman Empire and European Capitalism, 1820–1913* (Cambridge, 1987), Ch. 2. Pamuk's important study provides the most rigorous analysis yet made of the Ottoman foreign trade data.

13. Halil Inalcik, 'When and How British Cotton Goods Invaded the Levant Markets', in Huri Islamoglu-Inan, ed. *The Ottoman Empire and the World Economy* (Cambridge, 1987).

14. Pamuk, *Ottoman Empire*, p. 33.

interests.[15] The Ottoman territories had difficulty generating exports to pay for additional imports, and the rate of growth of foreign trade began to slow from the 1850s once the early, easy gains from free trade had been realised.[16] As the mid-Victorian boom gathered pace, and as supplies from Russia and the United States were resumed following the Crimean War and the American Civil War, British exporters began to identify markets outside the Middle East as sources of future growth.[17]

Free trade also provided greater opportunities for British finance. In destroying state monopolies and in holding down tariff levels, the Anglo-Turkish Commercial Convention curtailed government revenues; in promoting reform it also imposed new burdens on the budget. The resulting fiscal balancing act had already become precarious when it was finally upset by the Crimean War, which drove the Ottoman government to seek external financial aid, thus anticipating a path followed by China after 1895. The fact that Britain and France decided to support the Ottomans against Russia is indicative of the importance they attached to the economic and political stake they had acquired in the Empire. Both governments encouraged subscriptions to the first Ottoman loan in 1854 and guaranteed the next one (floated by Rothschilds) in the following year.[18] This was the prelude to an extensive loan business which developed during the next 20 years to meet Ottoman needs for post-war reconstruction, 'modernisation' and – finally – current expenditure.[19] Foreign loans called into being novel agencies which specialised in attracting capital from a widening circle of investors around London (and Paris) to frontiers of risk beyond Europe.[20] The leading expatriate financial institution in the Empire, the Imperial Ottoman Bank, began its life in London as the Ottoman Bank in 1856 and received a state charter in 1863, when it became a joint Anglo-French concern.[21] The Bank was given special

15. Davison, *Reform,* pp. 49–51; Pamuk, *Ottoman Empire,* pp. 132–3.

16. Given the size and diversity of the Ottoman Empire, this is inevitably a generalisation which needs qualification. See, for example, Haim Gerber, 'Modernization in Nineteenth-Century Palestine: the Role of Foreign Trade', *Midd. East. Stud.,* 18 (1983).

17. Exports of Manchester cottons peaked in 1880. See Arthur Redford, *Manchester Merchants and Foreign Trade,* Vol. II (Manchester, 1956), p. 80.

18. O. Anderson, 'Great Britain and the Beginnings of the Ottoman Public Debt, 1854–5, *Hist. Jour.,* 7 (1964), pp. 47–8; Owen, *The Middle East,* pp. 100–1.

19. Pamuk, *The Ottoman Empire,* pp. 57–60, 176–81.

20. Leland H. Jenks, *The Migration of British Capital to 1875* (1927), Chs. 8–9; David Landes, *Bankers and Pashas* (1958), pp. 62–7; A.S.J. Baster, *The Imperial Banks* (1927).

21. A.S.J. Baster, 'The Origins of British Banking Expansion in the Near East', *Econ. Hist. Rev.,* 2nd ser. V (1934). We are grateful to Prof. Christopher Clay, who is

privileges, including a monopoly of issues of paper currency, which helped it to become the chief financial agent of the Empire; it was also the most visible manifestation of the extension abroad of the new financial instruments developed in Britain in the second half of the nineteenth century.

Initially, export proceeds were sufficiently buoyant to meet interest payments, and the level of capital flowing into Constantinople rose rapidly. By 1875 the public debt amounted to about £250m., and there was also a large, short-term floating debt.[22] However, little more than half the total nominally borrowed between 1854 and 1874 actually reached the Ottoman government, and a sizeable part of this sum was immediately recycled to repay existing loans. Much of the rest was channelled into military expenditures; some found its way into private pockets. It is over-simple to conclude that foreign loans were 'squandered' because it is now recognised that they helped to lay the foundation of a form of bureaucratic centralism that was to survive the demise of the Ottoman Empire.[23] But it is certainly true that they failed to produce the progressive, liberal reforms which commended themselves to European interests, and they may even have helped to avert them. By 1875 over half the Ottoman budget was assigned to servicing external obligations, and new loans were being raised to pay the interest on earlier debts. As the Empire's credit-worthiness dropped, interest rates rose; even so, it became harder to attract fresh capital. In 1875 the Ottoman government had to suspend payment on half its foreign debt, following a fall in export prices prompted by the financial crisis in the United States in 1873 and compounded by a series of poor harvests in Anatolia, which reduced government revenues after 1872. Default followed in 1876, and a formal declaration of bankruptcy was made three years later. The Ottoman Empire thus joined a clutch of countries, including its dissident province, Egypt, which had been pumped up by European

---

writing a history of the Imperial Ottoman Bank, for advice on his subject. At present, a number of topics still have to be clarified, among them the timing of the Ottoman Empire's shift to an effective gold standard. It would seem that Pamuk *(The Ottoman Empire,* p. 13) minimises the extent to which the Empire remained on a bimetallic standard. Evidently, the Empire's ambivalence cannot have increased the City's confidence,

22. Jenks, *Migration,* pp. 294–300; Owen, *The Middle East,* pp. 101–5; Pamuk, *The Ottoman Empire,* Ch. 4.

23. Findlay, *Bureaucratic Reform.* The revisionist view of the Ottoman reform programme is well summarised by Yapp, *Making of the Modern Near East,* pp. 97–145. For a detailed study of reform in one area see David Kushner, 'The Ottoman Governors of Palestine', *Midd. East. Stud.,* 23 (1987).

capital from the middle of the century only to fall victim to the first major debt crisis of the 'developing world' in the 1870s.

The year 1875 marks, as well as any single date can, the end of mid-Victorian optimism about the development prospects of the Ottoman Empire. Britain remained the Empire's leading foreign commercial partner, but her share of Ottoman exports reached a peak of 29 per cent as early as 1850–2 and dropped gradually to 18 per cent in 1909–11; her slice of the import trade (which was concentrated heavily on textiles) fell from a high point of 45 per cent in 1880–2 to 24 per cent in 1909–11.[24] These proportions need to be considered against the slow growth of Ottoman foreign trade as a whole between 1873 and 1898, the decline in the external terms of trade (which made it harder for Ottoman exporters to buy imported goods), and the depressingly small scale of the market, which was unable to absorb more than 1 or 2 per cent of Britain's annual exports, despite half a century of firm persuasion. Trade with the Ottoman Empire was certainly not to be given up lightly, but there was scarcely a case for defending it heavily either. The costs of intervention were an ever-present and sensitive consideration at a time when public expenditure had become linked to democratic politics in Britain. Even when anti-Russian feeling reached a peak of stridency, as it did in 1877, Salisbury's judgement was that 'it no where rises nearly to Income-tax point', and he steered his course accordingly.[25]

Britain's financial interests underwent a more immediate reversal. The City was already becoming wary of Ottoman investments in the early 1870s, and after the default of 1876 it became very difficult to tempt British capital into the region. Indeed, the longer-term trend was towards disinvestment, as British investors withdrew from the Ottoman Empire, often selling their holdings to French and German companies, and placed their money in more profitable and less risky openings elsewhere. After the 1880s, Britain ceased to be the leading source of new foreign finance in the Ottoman Empire. By 1913 her share of the Ottoman public debt had fallen to 13 per cent and her share of direct foreign investment to 15 per cent.[26] Britain's place was taken principally by her long-standing competitor, France, which held 53 per cent of the debt in 1914, and Germany, which held 21 per cent. France was also the dominant force behind the Imperial Otto-

---

24. Pamuk, *The Ottoman Empire*, Table 2.4, p. 32; idem, 'The Ottoman Empire in the "Great Depression" of 1873–1896', *Jour. Econ. Hist.*, 44 (1984), pp. 107–18.

25. Quoted in Swartz, *The Politics of British Foreign Policy*, p. 67.

26. Owen, *The Middle East*, p. 198; Issawi, *Economic History of the Middle East*, p. 69; Pamuk, *Ottoman Empire*, pp. 72–3, 76.

man Bank, which worked closely with the French government in expanding its activities from the 1890s, while Germany made increasingly effective use of its own financial agent in the Middle East, the Deutsche Bank.[27]

The events of 1875–6 led to a reappraisal of British policy towards the Ottoman Empire. It was now clear that the Empire was not going to become a progressive and self-supporting satellite bound to Britain by 'natural' ties of finance and commerce. The standing of the Empire, already damaged in British eyes by the harassment of Christian minorities, fell with its credit-rating to the point where the introduction of liberal government and institutional reforms was no longer considered to be a realistic expectation. There was even a feeling, in the 1870s, that the Empire ought to be allowed to disintegrate.[28] Ottoman bankruptcy and fear of Russian influence dictated otherwise, but disillusion with the Empire was accompanied by a stiffer and less tolerant attitude, summarised in Salisbury's view that British interests were best served by 'order and good government',[29] a formula that stood for political stability and sound finance. British governments continued to proclaim their support for the unity of the Ottoman Empire down to 1914, but they managed to combine this principle with the acquisition of semi-detached and 'unstable' segments, notably Cyprus (in 1878) and Egypt (in 1882).[30]

The City was also keen to see the unity of the Ottoman Empire upheld in order to safeguard British investments there, though it, too, was sufficiently ambidextrous to back the take-over of both Cyprus and Egypt.[31] However, as Britain's capital stake in the Empire diminished after the turn of the century, the City became more willing to consider partition as being a practical means of safeguarding specific regional commitments. As the City's interest in Constantinople diminished, so too did the influence of the British government. After efforts to tempt British capital back into the Empire to strengthen the front against Russian expansionism had failed, the

27. The definitive work on French investment is Jacques Thobie, *Intérêts et impérialisme français dans l'Empire Ottoman, 1895–1914* (Paris, 1977).

28. Swartz, *The Politics of British Foreign Policy*, pp. 28–30.

29. Quoted in Corrigan, 'British, French and German Interests', p. 4.

30. As Keith Wilson has shown, British policy did not desert Constantinople for Cairo: 'Constantinople or Cairo: Lord Salisbury and the Partition of the Ottoman Empire, 1886–1897', in Keith M. Wilson, ed. *Imperialism and Nationalism in the Middle East* (1983).

31. Swartz, *Politics of British Foreign Policy*, p. 99; A.G. Hopkins, 'The Victorians and Africa: a Reconsideration of the Occupation of Egypt, 1882', *Jour. African Hist.*, 27 (1986), pp. 379–85.

Foreign Office gave up the northern line of defence and pitched its tent in the south, where the main boundaries of commerce and investment had come to be drawn.

The City's involvement in the Ottoman Empire was therefore limited after 1875. But this does not mean that Britain's existing financial interests were abandoned. Once default had occurred, the overriding concern of British investors was to secure repayment of the Empire's outstanding obligations on the best possible terms. The Ottomans wavered, but they realised that a settlement was imperative if they were to resume borrowing, and their remaining hesitations were removed by a demonstration mounted by British warships in the Straits in 1879.[32] After lengthy negotiations, the Porte and its foreign creditors came to an agreement in 1881.[33] The outstanding debt was slightly reduced, consolidated and rescheduled; in exchange, the Ottoman government agreed to make the external debt the first charge on its revenues, to hand over the administration of a sizeable proportion of these revenues, and to cede control over tariff rates on imports and exports. The management of these concessions was entrusted to a new organisation, the Ottoman Public Debt Administration, which was established in the same year. This was a hybrid body: it was international, though in practice the two principal creditor countries, Britain and France, wielded the greatest influence; and it was private, though it also maintained very close links with official circles in Britain and France.

For the next 30 years, the Public Debt Administration was the most powerful economic agency in the Empire. In 1914 it had about 700 offices and 9,000 employees.[34] It virtually controlled central government finance, exerted great influence over railway concessions and other developmental projects (such as the silk industry), and received diplomatic support from the major powers and assistance from the principal foreign banks.[35] The Public Debt Administration proved to be an effective debt collecting agency: creditors were repaid in accordance with the terms agreed in 1881, and by the turn of the century the Ottoman government's credit-rating had improved to the

32. Donald C. Blaisdell, *European Control in the Ottoman Empire* (New York, 1929), Ch. 5.

33. On the settlement of 1881 see Blaisdell, *European Control*, Chs. 5–7; Owen, *The Middle East*, pp. 191–200; and Pamuk, *Ottoman Empire,* pp. 61–2.

34. Issawi, *Economic History of the Middle East*, p. 190.

35. Donald Quataert, 'The Silk Industry of Bursa, 1880–1914', in Islamoglu-Inan, *The Ottoman Empire*; Osman Okyar, 'A New Look at the Problem of Economic Growth in the Ottoman Empire (1800–1914)', *Jour. Econ. Hist.*, 16 (1987), pp. 40–1, 46; Pamuk, *Ottoman Empire*, pp. 16–17, 63–4.

point where it was able to float new loans. Indeed, the credit of the Empire came to rest largely on the prestige of the Public Debt Administration, which generated confidence among foreign investors and acted as a conduit for external finance.[36]

The City, however, remained sceptical, despite the persistence of several well-placed advocates. One, Edgar Vincent, was the British representative on the Council of the Ottoman Public Debt Administration in 1882–3 and Governor of the Imperial Ottoman Bank from 1889 to 1897.[37] Another, Vincent Caillard, replaced him on the Public Debt Council in 1883 and became its President (alternating with the French representative) until his retirement in 1898.[38] Vincent and Caillard are interesting examples of the new generation of financier-promoters thrown up by the growth of the City-service complex and its extension overseas after 1850. Both men came from families of substance in the south of England, were educated (together) at Eton, and found their way to the fringes of empire initially through careers in the army. They were not only officers and gentlemen, but also soldiers of fortune who became bankers of fortunes. Vincent served with the Coldstream Guards; Caillard won his spurs in the Egyptian campaign of 1882. When they entered financial administration, they combined, in a way that admirably captured the spirit of the period, a sharp eye for private profit with a more spacious view of Britain's imperial role, and they were tireless advocates of both causes. Their success owed much to their social connections. Vincent was a protégé of the Gladstone family and of George Goschen, the banker and prominent Liberal; Caillard drew upon distant family ties with Disraeli and close links with Dilke, the Liberal-imperialist. Both men had influence, but their speculative ventures led them into grey areas of international finance which did not inspire confidence in the highest

36. Okyar, 'A New Look', p. 40; Blaisdell, *European Control*, pp. 152–3.

37. R.P.T. Davenport-Hines and Jean Jacques Van-Helten, 'Edgar Vincent, Viscount D'Abernon, and the Eastern Investment Company in London, Constantinople and Johannesburg', *Bus. Hist.*, 28 (1986). Vincent (1857–1941) was also Financial Adviser to the Egyptian government, 1883–9. After he left the Imperial Ottoman Bank, he was recruited by the financier, Sir Ernest Cassel (see n.44), entered parliament as Conservative MP for Exeter, and became a director of the armaments firm, Vickers. He was elevated to the peerage in 1926 and took his title from his home in Stoke D'Abernon, Surrey.

38. R.P.T. Davenport-Hines, 'The Ottoman Empire in Decline: the Business Imperialism of Sir Edgar Vincent', Institute of Commonwealth Studies, London, 1984. We are grateful to Dr Davenport-Hines for permission to cite his unpublished seminar paper. Caillard (1856–1930) also acquired a clutch of directorships after retiring from the Ottoman Public Debt Administration, and became President of the Federation of British Industries in 1919. He was given a knighthood in 1896 but failed, despite persistent efforts, to secure a peerage.

banking circles.[39] In this matter the City's judgement was sound: Vincent steered the Imperial Ottoman Bank towards the rocks by making risky investments in South African gold-mines and had to resign in 1897; Caillard's constant intrigues and occasional misjudgements ensured that the leading merchant banks kept him at arm's length. The new clutch of Ottoman loans floated after the turn of the century attracted mainly French and German investors, and it brought them more headaches than profits.

As development prospects faded, British policy focused increasingly on the task of maintaining the stability of the Empire. This aim met the priorities of the Ottoman Public Debt Administration, which needed to control central revenues, and also of imperial strategy, which was preoccupied by the fear that foreign rivals would threaten India from bases in the Middle East. In countering this possibility, however, Britain was handicapped by her waning economic influence, as well as by her presence in Egypt and her moral support for Christian minorities within the Ottoman Empire, neither of which gave her a head start in the contest to gain leverage in Constantinople. Given these constraints, the Foreign Office fell back upon energetic diplomacy to bolster Britain's commercial presence and to create favourable alliances among rival powers and potential supporters in the region.[40]

A notable feature of this policy was the decision to step up official support for British investment in the hope that injections of capital would bolster Britain's political influence.[41] As the Foreign Secretary, Grey, observed in 1908: 'We shall make no progress till British capital of a high class takes an energetic interest in Turkey'.[42] Without formal guarantees, however, the City remained wary. Indeed, the rise of foreign competitors increased the uncertainty that already surrounded the political future of the Ottoman Empire and reinforced the cautious attitude of British investors. The closest the government came to success in the financial field was when the British-owned National

39. Davenport-Hines and Van-Helten, 'Edgar Vincent', p. 44; Davenport-Hines, 'The Ottoman Empire in Decline', pp. 5–7, 9; Corrigan, 'British, French and German Interests', pp. 59–61.

40. No attempt will be made here to provide a general survey of great-power rivalries during the final years of the Ottoman Empire. The best introduction to the voluminous literature on this subject is Marian Kent, ed. *The Great Powers and the End of the Ottoman Empire* (1984).

41. Corrigan, 'British, French and German Interests', pp. 148, 151–3, 174–5; David McLean, 'Finance and "Informal Empire" Before the First World War', *Econ. Hist. Rev.*, 2nd ser. XXIX (1976).

42. Quoted in McLean, 'Finance and "Informal Empire"', p. 294.

Bank of Turkey was formed in 1909.[43] This was a private venture headed by Sir Ernest Cassel, another financier who was willing to engage in risky overseas loans in the hope of eventually gaining access to a higher grade of business.[44] On this occasion Cassel received support from Lord Revelstoke of Barings and encouragement from the Foreign Office. Grey had high hopes that the National Bank would spearhead a revival of British influence and counter the advance of Germany. The Foreign Office played an active part in channelling business towards the Bank and in warning off potential competitors. Nevertheless, the Bank was unsuccessful and ceased operations in 1913. This was partly because official support shackled as well as sheltered enterprise by subordinating commercial decisions to political priorities. But the main reason for the Bank's failure was its inability to win the confidence of British investors.[45] British governments could influence the City but not control it, and were rarely able to mobilise the market in support of the 'national interest'. In France and Germany, law and custom gave governments greater power to direct private funds for political purposes; in Britain the City remained, in this sense, above politics.[46]

A more successful departure from mid-nineteenth-century principles of non-intervention followed the search for oil in Mesopotamia after the turn of the century.[47] This episode does not provide an

---

43. Marian Kent, 'Agent of Empire? The National Bank of Turkey and British Foreign Policy', *Hist. Jour.*, 18 (1975); McLean, 'Finance and "Informal Empire"', pp. 294–7.

44. Pat Thane, 'Financiers and the British State: The Case of Sir Ernest Cassel', *Bus. Hist.*, 28 (1986). See also Anthony Allfrey, *Edward VII and His Jewish Court* (1991). Cassell (1852–1921) was active in the Balkans, Egypt and China, as well as the Ottoman Empire. His friendship with the Prince of Wales turned out to be a profitable one: when the Prince succeeded to the throne as Edward VII, Cassel managed his portfolio and benefited in return from access to privileged information. He became known, predictably, as 'Windsor Cassel'. The family's royal connection was continued by his granddaughter, Edwina, who married Earl Louis Mountbatten, a great-grandson of Queen Victoria.

45. McLean, 'Finance and "Informal Empire"', pp. 294–7.

46. Corrigan, 'British, French and German Interests', pp. 66, 74–5; Swartz, *Politics of British Foreign Policy*, p. 88; Thobie, *Intérêts et impérialisme*, p. 719, and (for a case study) idem, 'L'emprunt Ottoman 4%, 1901–1905: le triptyque finance-industrie-diplomatique', *Relations Internationales*, 1 (1974).

47. Marian Jack, 'The Purchase of the British Government's Share in the British Petroleum Company, 1912–1914', *Past and Present*, 39 (1968); Marian Kent, *Oil and Empire: British Policy and Mesopotamian Oil, 1900–1920* (1976); Helmut Mejcher, 'Oil and British Policy Towards Mesopotamia, 1914–18', *Midd. East Stud.*, 8 (1972), pp. 377–91; idem, 'Imperial Quest for Oil, 1910–1928* (1976); G. Gareth Jones, 'The British Government and the Oil Companies, 1912–1924: the Search for an Oil Policy', *Hist. Jour.*, 20 (1977). See also Geoffrey Jones, *The State and the Emergence of the British Oil Industry* (1981).

example of capitalist investment on a scale that was generally lacking in the Ottoman Empire. On the contrary, the government intervened in 1908 to prop up a faltering concessionary company owned by a British subject, William D'Arcy. But it does demonstrate how economic resources were entwined with strategic priorities, and the extent to which the Foreign Office had accepted the need to reinforce private firms in areas of political sensitivity. Encouraged by the Admiralty, and with an eye on checking the advance of oil syndicates backed by the Deutsche Bank, the government supported the creation of the Anglo-Persian Oil Company in 1909 and acquired a controlling interest in it in 1914. Anglo-Persian was encouraged to buy out rival firms competing for oil concessions in Mesopotamia (including, ironically, one supported by the Foreign Office's other instrument, the National Bank of Turkey), and in 1912 it sponsored the Turkish Petroleum Company, which brought British and German oil interests in the region together but ensured that the Deutsche Bank group held only a minority share. Government intervention succeeded in this case because it fitted with the judgement of the market (especially after the discovery of large oil deposits in Persia in 1908), and because it involved material official participation rather than the less substantial offer of diplomatic and moral support.

Since Britain's own resources were insufficient to guarantee the friendly neutrality of the Ottoman Empire, she also defended her interests by striking bargains with rival powers. Until the close of the nineteenth century, competition with France was constrained by a common interest in the Ottoman Public Debt Administration and by Britain's concern to retain French goodwill in dealing with the Russians. From the 1890s, however, the resumption of foreign borrowing by the Ottoman Empire and the rise of German interest in the Balkans and Turkey set off a scramble for economic concessions and political influence which had parallels in other 'unclaimed' parts of the world, notably Africa and China.[48]

The chief focus of British anxiety was Germany's plan, devised between 1899 and 1903, for building a railway line between Berlin

---

48. The differing perspectives of the European powers are well covered in Kent, *The Great Powers*. But it is worth underlining the fact that recent research suggests that it is over-simple to assign Britain's problems in the Middle East to German expansion, which did not match up to the alarmist expectations of contemporary observers. See Ulrich Trumpener, *Germany and the Ottoman Empire, 1914–18* (Princeton, NJ, 1968); H.S.W. Corrigan, 'German–Turkish Relations and the Outbreak of War in 1914: a Reassessment', *Past and Present*, 36 (1967), pp. 144–52; and Gregor Schöllgen, *Imperialismus und Gleichgewicht: Deutschland, England und die orientalische Frage, 1871–1914* (Munich, 1984).

and Baghdad.[49] This ambitious scheme sounded alarms in London and Delhi because it threatened to pierce India's outer defences, and it quickly became a symbol of the global challenge which German expansion was thought to present. It therefore had to be resisted. One possibility, which arose in 1903, was to participate in the project, but this idea foundered on a mixture of anti-German feeling and dissatisfaction with terms of the proposed deal.[50] Another plan was to neutralise the German advance by combining with the French to promote alternative railway and development projects. This tactic received some impetus from the Anglo-French entente of 1904, but little was achieved in practice because official agreement was not backed by active support from either the Imperial Ottoman Bank or the City.[51] However, in 1906 Britain managed to persuade Constantinople to recognise her exclusive rights to build railways in parts of Anatolia, and the Foreign Office later gave strong backing to a British railway project in the western part of the province when it was challenged by a rival Italian concession.[52] In the event, the slow progress made by the Baghdad railway lowered anxiety levels in the Foreign Office, and Germany's growing preoccupation with European security strengthened the hand of British diplomacy in the Middle East. The outcome, the Anglo-German convention of 1914, was a satisfactory compromise which confirmed Britain's position in Mesopotamia and the Persian Gulf.[53]

An opportunity for creating an entirely new political alliance arose in 1908, when the Young Turks seized control in Constantinople and deposed the Sultan in the following year.[54] At first, the British were

49. The substantial literature on this subject is summarised in Kent, *The Great Powers*, which also provides a bibliography.

50. Richard M. Francis, 'The British Withdrawal from the Baghdad Railway Project in April 1903', *Hist. Jour.*, 16 (1973).

51. Keith A. Hamilton, 'An Attempt to Form an Anglo-French Industrial Entente', *Midd. East. Stud.*, 11 (1975).

52. David McLean, 'British Finance and Foreign Policy in Turkey: the Smyrna-Aidin Railway Settlement, 1913–1914', *Hist. Jour.*, 19 (1976).

53. The Agreement ensured that the Baghdad railway would not extend to the Gulf except under British auspices. This concession reflected the difficulties which the Germans had experienced in raising money for the project and their desire to conciliate Britain in the hope of keeping her out of the impending war with France. (For further details see the references cited in n.48). Apart from increasing their share of the Ottoman public debt, which turned out to be a bad investment, the French, too, were less of a threat to Britain's economic stake in the Middle East than is indicated by scholars who emphasise her weakness in the face of foreign competition. See, for example, William I. Shorrock, *French Imperialism in the Middle East: The Failure of Policy in Syria and Lebanon,1900–1914* (Madison, Wis., 1976).

54. Yapp, *The Making of the Modern Near East,* pp. 189–95, provides an excellent overview. See also Feroz Ahmad, 'Great Britain's Relations with the Young Turks,

inclined to interpret the revolution as representing the resurgence of liberal constitutionalism and supposed that the new rulers would naturally turn to them for guidance. This expectation was encouraged by the promptness with which the provisional government expressed its willingness to co-operate with the Ottoman Public Debt Administration[55] and helped to provide official impetus for the formation of the National Bank of Turkey. However, once it became clear that the new goverment was bent on building an independent and centralised state with German rather than British assistance, the view from London changed. The Young Turks were then portrayed as a conspiracy of Freemasons and Jews with Jacobin intentions. Not surprisingly, this bizarre interpretation hardened attitudes on both sides. Far from promoting congenial allies for Britain, the advent of the Young Turks heightened tensions within the Ottoman Empire, encouraged regional defections, and brought the European powers closer to partition.

PERSIA: FINANCIAL DIPLOMACY – WITH LIMITED FINANCE

By 1914 the main weight of Britain's trade and finance had gravitated to the southern provinces of the Empire (apart from specific interests in Anatolia), and particularly to Mesopotamia, where they formed a bridge to her interests in Persia.[56] There, too, British governments had to come to terms with the City's reluctance to invest in unpromising areas, and were forced to adopt interventionist policies to ensure that imperial commitments were met.[57]

1908–14', *Midd. East. Stud.* 2 (1966), and, for an interesting attempt to trace the roots of the movement, Carter V. Findley, 'Economic Bases of Revolution and Repression in the Late Ottoman Empire', *Comp. Stud. in Soc. and Hist.*, 28 (1986).

55. Blaisdell, *European Financial Control*, pp. 178–9.

56. R. Khalidi, *British Policy Towards Syria and Palestine, 1906–14* (1980); Stuart A. Cohen, *British Policy in Mesopotamia, 1903–1914* (Oxford, 1976); Owen, *The Middle East*, pp. 275–6.

57. The analysis which follows owes a good deal to David McLean's authoritative study, *Britain and her Buffer State: The Collapse of the Persian Empire, 1906–1914* (1979). We hope that our indebtedness to his work is consistent with the additional emphasis we have tried to supply. McLean was concerned to demonstrate that British governments adopted increasingly interventionist policies; we have tried to trace the relationship between this trend and the attitude of the City of London towards investing in the Middle East.

At the start of the nineteenth century Britain had a long-established commercial presence in the Persian Gulf, represented by the East India Company, and had also formulated plans to use Persia as a buffer in the defence of Wellesley's acquisitions in India.[58] With the end of the French Wars, Persia received the standard prescription of liberalism and coercion which Britain administered to weaker states, such as the Ottoman Empire and China, in pursuit of her economic and strategic goals. Piracy and slaving were suppressed in the Gulf, a free-trade treaty was signed in 1841, after a show of force, and a short war in 1856–7 curtailed Persia's imperial ambitions when they threatened India's land defences.[59] Thereafter the frontiers of progress were to be moved forward by private enterprise. Coastal trade was developed from the 1860s through the agency of the British and Indian Steam Navigation Company, submarine cables were laid, and the opening of the Suez Canal in 1869 held out much promise.[60] The performance, however, proved to be disappointing. A very modest market for Manchester cottons was created, but Persia's export trade lacked the dynamism to raise import-purchasing power substantially.[61] Beyond the ports, the interior remained land-locked and unrewarding, and internal reforms made even less progress than in the Ottoman Empire.[62] The two principal concessions secured by British subjects both failed: de Reuter's comprehensive rights, obtained in 1872 (mainly for railway development), ran into opposition both within Persia and from Britain and Russia; Talbot's tobacco concession, granted in 1890, aroused such popular resentment

58. There is a vast literature dealing with strategies for defending India in the nineteenth century. Recent studies with good bibliographies include: D. Gillard, *The Struggle for Asia, 1828–1914* (1977); M.E. Yapp, *Strategies of British India* (Oxford, 1980); Edward Ingram, *Commitment to Empire; Prophecies of the Great Game in Asia, 1797–1800* (Oxford, 1981); and idem, *In Defence of British India: Great Britain and the Middle East, 1775–1842* (1985).

59. J.B. Kelly, *Britain and the Persian Gulf, 1795–1880* (Oxford, 1968); Gillard, *Struggle for Asia*, pp. 20–3; Mikhail Volodarsky, 'Persia and the Great Powers, 1856–1869', *Midd. East. Stud.*, 19 (1983); idem, 'Persia's Foreign Policy between the Two Herat Crises, 1831–56', *Midd. East. Stud.*, 21 (1981); Barbara English, *John Company's Last War* (1971).

60. Stephanie Jones, *Two Centuries of Overseas Trading; The Origins and Growth of the Inchcape Group* (1986), pp. 21–3 and Ch. 3.

61. For an example of one development see Ahmad Seyf, 'Commercialisation of Agriculture: Production and Trade of Opium in Persia, 1850–1906', *Int. Jour. Middle East Stud.*, 16 (1984).

62. McLean, *Britain and her Buffer State*, pp. 19–23; Yapp, *The Making of the Modern Near East*, pp. 162–72. See also Shaul Bakhash, *Iran: Monarchy, Bureaucracy and Reform under the Qajars, 1858–1896* (1978), and Guity Nashat, *The Origins of Modern Reform in Iran* (Champaign-Urbana, ILL., 1982).

in Persia that it had to be cancelled in the following year.[63] By the close of the century it was apparent that Persia offered neither rich pickings nor the conditions to support a sustained development drive.

The City did not like what it saw in Persia. The economy was hampered by a feeble export sector, a primitive transport system, and an unstable, silver-based currency, and Persian society showed little sign of producing a congenial comprador class.[64] The Shah's government was neither stable nor progressive and looked as if it might be submerged by dissidents from within or by Russian expansionism. Moreover, the history of the concessions granted to de Reuter and Talbot showed the face of Persian hostility to foreign influences and caused a loss of confidence in the City which was reflected in Persia's declining credit rating.[65] In these circumstances, it is not surprising that the City remained uninterested in Persia throughout this period, apart from a brief speculative flutter in 1909–11. Only two foreign loans were floated in London for the Persian government: one, a modest issue of £500,000 offered in 1892, met with a poor response; the other, a more substantial loan of £1.5m. launched in 1911, was well received largely because it had official backing. The flow of private capital was also very limited, and the leading British companies, the Imperial Bank of Persia and the Anglo-Persian Oil Company, both benefited from government support.[66] Yet, without pump-priming investment, the economy would remain backward and there was no prospect of creating a strong buffer state, and without government borrowing there was no easy way of ensuring the political dependence of the Shah. Consequently, British policy towards Persia in the late nineteenth century wavered between promoting a robust state, a strategy that required finance, and leaving the country to its own devices in the hope that its neutrality could be preserved by agile diplomacy.[67]

The cheap option depended upon the goodwill of other powers, and by the close of the nineteenth century it was clear that this was in short supply. After recovering from the Crimean War, Russia

63. Geoffrey Jones, *Banking and Empire in Iran: The History of the British Bank of the Middle East*, Vol. 1 (1986), pp. 3–25, 48–52; N. Keddie, *Religion and Rebellion in Iran: The Tobacco Protest, 1891–1892* (1966).

64. On the currency question see P. W. Avery and J. B. Simmons, 'Persia on a Cross of Silver, 1880–1890', *Midd. East. Stud.*, 10 (1974). Persia's currency (the Kran) lost more than half its value against sterling between 1850 and 1890.

65. Jones, *Banking and Empire*, pp. 49–51.

66. Issawi, *Economic History*, pp. 70–1; McLean, *Britain and her Buffer State*, pp. 61–3, 143–4.

67. McLean, *Britain and her Buffer State*, pp. 29–30.

resumed her southern expansion. By the 1880s she dominated Persia's external trade (a position she retained until 1914), and had extended her railway network into central Asia and her political control south of the Caspian Sea.[68] Moreover, from the 1890s Russian capital was directed to the Persian government in a series of loans (totalling £7.5m. by 1905), which gave her considerable leverage in Tehran.[69] These developments were greeted with alarm in Britain, where it was thought that Russia's advance might stimulate disaffection in India and also pose a direct military threat in the Middle East itself.[70] As these fears multiplied, Britain responded by adopting a more interventionist approach to Anglo-Persian economic and political relations.

Early indications of this response can be found in the 1880s, when Salisbury began to stiffen British policy towards the defence of Persia. A modest start was made by subsidising steamship services on the Tigris and Karun rivers at the head of the Gulf from the 1880s.[71] A more significant development was the attempt to encourage British investment in Persia. This aim found concrete expression in the shape of the Imperial Bank of Persia, which was formed in 1889 with the backing of two highly reputable City houses, J. H. Schroder and David Sassoon & Co.[72] The Imperial Bank provides a good example of the composition and operation of Britain's burgeoning financial and service diaspora in the second half of the nineteenth century. J. H. Schroder was a well-known merchant bank run by a family which had found refuge in London during the French Wars at the beginning of the century. The Sassoons had made their fortune by accompanying the moving frontier of British influence in the Middle East, India and China before locating their headquarters in London in 1858 and establishing their reputation in the City thereafter. The family's acceptance into high society was marked by a knighthood for Albert Sassoon, the head of the firm, in 1872. The first chairman of the Bank was William Keswick, the former head of Jardine, Matheson & Co. and of the Hongkong and Shanghai Bank. The other banker on the

68. Ibid. pp. 14–19.

69. Jones, *Banking and Empire,* p. 87.

70. M.A. Yapp, 'British Perceptions of the Russian Threat to India', *Modern Asian Studies,* 21 (1987).

71. McLean, *Britain and her Buffer State,* p. 7.

72. Jones, *Banking and Empire,* pp. 20–31. For the Bank's colonial connections see also D. McLean, 'International Banking and its Political Implications: the Hongkong and Shanghai Banking Corporation and the Imperial Bank of Persia, 1889–1914', in Frank H.H. King, ed. *Eastern Banking: Essays in the History of the Hongkong and Shanghai Banking Corporation* (1983).

board of directors was Geoffrey Glyn of Glyn, Mills, Currie & Co., the leading private bank in London specialising in overseas railway and banking ventures. As in the case of the Hongkong and Shanghai Bank, cosmopolitan origins gave way to a more homogeneous pattern of recruitment as the Bank became established. The English public school and its ethos soon infused the institution and its staff: hunting, shooting and racing were among the gentlemanly sports fostered in Persia, and by 1896 the Tehran branch was able to field its own cricket team.[73]

The Imperial Bank was a private undertaking but it received the valuable endorsement of a royal charter as well as the support of the British Minister in Persia, and it was given subventions to open branches in politically sensitive areas.[74] The Bank's political ties were readily established. Its royal charter, for example, was granted after the Foreign Office had exerted pressure on the Treasury, and the lever was pulled by Sir Henry Drummond Wolff, a career diplomat with strong connections in the City and Westminster, who was sent to the Middle East in 1888 to strengthen Britain's presence there. The Bank's board of directors soon began to include prominent retired officials from Whitehall and the Indian Civil Service – a pattern of recruitment that continued in the twentieth century and characterised all of the 'colonial' banks. For its part, the Foreign Office hoped to use the Imperial Bank as a conduit for British capital, and attached particular importance to the Shah's need for foreign investment in the 1890s. As the British Minister in Tehran observed of Persia in 1903: 'The more we get her into our debt, the greater will be our hold and our political influence over her government'.[75]

The purpose was clear, but the means remained elusive. The Baring Crisis and the Australian banking collapse in the 1890s added to the City's reluctance to respond to patriotic appeals to invest in Persia without formal guarantees, which successive governments were reluctant to offer.[76] The Imperial Bank itself struggled through the 1890s with some difficulty and little profit.[77] Safe overseas investments lay outside the Middle East, and speculators preferred to take their chance with South African or Australian gold-mining shares, where there was some prospect of a tangible return. In this situation the British government was forced to depart still further from its ideal of

73. Jones, *Banking and Empire*, pp. 110, 143, 153.
74. Ibid. pp. 90–2.
75. Quoted in McLean, 'Finance and "Informal Empire"', p. 297.
76. Jones, *Banking and Empire*, pp. 17–20; McLean, 'International Banking', p. 12.
77. Jones, *Banking and Empire*, pp. 49, 53–4, 66.

non-intervention. At the Foreign Office, Lansdowne developed a more active policy after 1900, authorising two small direct loans to the Persian government in 1903 and 1904, providing subsidies for private firms and giving official backing (including assistance from secret service funds) to the Persian Transport Company, which was established in 1902 to promote road building.[78] This pattern of interference was continued by his successor, Grey, who was also an advocate of sterling diplomacy: 'the broad principle upon which we must necessarily proceed', he emphasised in 1906, 'is to obtain leverage over the Persian government by assisting them in a financial sense'.[79]

The constitutional revolution of 1906 appeared to offer a chance for Britain to apply Grey's maxim. As in the case of the Young Turks, however, the British mistook incipient nationalism and dissident provincialism for Western-style liberalism, and greatly overestimated their chances of forging new political alliances within Persia.[80] Moreover, the revolution generated a great deal of internal instability and it was not until 1909 that victory over the Shah was assured. By that time, however, British policy was increasingly constrained by a desire to placate Russia, and this meant tempering support for reform. The need to reach a settlement with Russia stemmed from the British government's recognition that the costs of halting Russian expansion in Persia were unacceptably high, and that it had also become necessary to concentrate on the threat posed by Germany. Under the terms of the Anglo-Russian Convention of 1907, the two powers agreed to respect Persia's territorial integrity, but they also divided the country into spheres of influence: one in the north assigned to Russia, another in the south-east allotted to Britain, and a third, neutral zone between them.[81] Like the Anglo-Japanese alliance of

78. McLean, *Britain and her Buffer State,* pp. 59, 68–9, 133–4. Also L.P. Morris, 'British Secret Service Activity in Khorassan, 1887–1908', *Hist. Jour.,* 27 (1984).

79. McLean, *Britain and Her Buffer State,* p. 143.

80. The constitutional movement is summarised by Yapp, *The Making of the Modern Near East,* pp. 247–60. The most interesting recent work has focused on the socio-economic causes of the revolution. See, for example, Gad Gilbar, 'The Big Merchants (tujjar) and the Persian Constitutional Revolution of 1906', *Asian and African Studies,* 2 (1976); idem, 'The Opening up of Qajar Iran: some Economic and Social Aspects', *Bulletin of the School of Oriental and African Studies,* 49 (1986); and Mohammed Reza Afshari, 'The Pīshivarān and Merchants in Precapitalist Iranian Society: an Essay on the Background and Causes of the Constitutional Revolution', *Int. Jour. Middle East Stud.,* 15 (1983). British policy is dealt with by Ira Klein, 'British Intervention in the Persian Revolution, 1905–1909', *Hist. Jour.,* 15 (1972).

81. Ira Klein, 'The Anglo-Russian Convention and the Problems of Central Asia, 1907–1914', *Jour. Brit. Stud.,* 11 (1971), pp. 126–4; and, on this subject generally, Firuz Kazemadeh, *Russia and Britain in Persia, 1864–1914: A Study in Imperialism* (New Haven, Conn., 1968).

1902, the Anglo-Russian convention was essentially a way of reducing defence costs in the face of a challenge by a third power, in this case Germany. In 1911 Britain deserted the constitutional movement and endorsed Russia's successful demands for the dismissal of the Persian government's new American financial adviser, Morgan Schuster, and for the suppression of the Persian assembly, the Majlis.[82] The buffer state was to be preserved, but by policies that favoured stability rather than reform.

After 1907, therefore, sterling diplomacy was hampered by the need to work with the Russians as well as by the continuing caution of the City. Two joint Anglo-Russian loans were approved in 1908 and 1909 in an attempt to restore political stability to Persia, though Britain hoped that they would increase her influence with anti-Russian elements within the country as well.[83] But the Foreign Office also had to intervene in 1910 to prevent the City from lending to the Shah on one of the very rare occasions when it was prepared to do so, because a loan without political strings would have jeopardised Grey's Anglo-Russian policy.[84] In 1911, when a new Persian loan of £1.25m. was placed successfully in the City, it was issued via the Foreign Office's preferred vehicle, the Imperial Bank, and with official support, as well as with the agreement of the Russians.[85] By 1914 the British government had moved very far from its ideal of non-intervention in financial affairs. In doing so, it had also lent a helping hand to the Imperial Bank, whose fortunes improved as a result of official and semi-official support for Persian loans after the turn of the century.[86]

The success of this policy could be seen in the hold which Britain took on the south-eastern sphere of influence allocated to her by the Anglo-Russian Convention, and on the coastal area of the neutral zone, where British troops were stationed after 1911. Britain's presence here was firmly based on her dominance of coastal commerce and shipping, and on her control of the customs revenues of the Gulf ports, which served as security for foreign loans.[87] Inland, important initiatives were taken to promote oil-mining and railway construction, both of which were capital intensive and vulnerable to political uncertainty. As noted earlier, the British government rescued

82. McLean, *Britain and her Buffer State*, pp. 83, 103–5; Robert A. McDaniel, *The Schuster Mission and the Persian Constitutional Revolution* (Minneapolis, Minn., 1974).

83. McLean, *Britain and her Buffer State*, pp. 89–91.

84. Ibid. pp. 93–100; Jones, *Banking and Empire*, pp. 120–1.

85. Jones, *Banking and Empire*, pp. 120–4.

86. Ibid. pp. 110, 116, 122–3.

87. McLean, 'International Banking', pp. 7–8; Marian Kent, 'Great Britain and the End of the Ottoman Empire', in Kent, *The Great Powers*, pp. 179–80.

D'Arcy's failing oil concession in 1908, following representations from the Admiralty.[88] This move was the prelude to the formation of the Anglo-Persian Oil Company in 1909 and to government control of the new firm in 1914. The contrast between the *laissez-faire* attitude adopted towards de Reuter and the assistance granted to D'Arcy provides an apt measure of the change in government policy towards private enterprise in Persia between the 1870s and the 1900s. Railway-building was long prevented by 'sterilising agreements' between Russia and Persia. But these expired in 1910 and an opportunity then arose to promote Britain's strategic and commercial interests in the south. In the following year, the Foreign Office helped to put together the Persian Railways Syndicate, a consortium consisting of British oil interests in Persia, the Imperial Bank, the Persian Transport Company, Indian shipping interests, and investment trusts in London.[89] The Syndicate was given preferential treatment by the Foreign Office, though in the event no construction took place before World War I.

By 1914 it was evident that India's line of defence had shifted from Constantinople to the Gulf, where political priorities were more compatible with Britain's commercial and financial interests. But, if the geography had changed, Britain's grip had not loosened: her influence gave her a virtual protectorate along the Gulf coastline eastwards to India, and stretched westwards to Aden and on to Egypt.

MANAGEMENT WITHOUT DEVELOPMENT

This assessment of the literature on British imperialism in the Middle East suggests revisions to the two leading interpretations referred to at the outset of the chapter. Historians who look for economic motives find themselves in difficulty when they reach the Middle East because the evidence now available fits awkwardly with the idea that British manufactures and finance swept all before them in either the Ottoman Empire or Persia. This problem has been seized upon by proponents of diplomatic or strategic interpretations of imperialism

88. See pp. 408–9.
89. Jones, *Banking and Empire*, pp. 129–31; McLean, *Britain and her Buffer State*, p. 119. For a case study of the diplomacy of railway-building see D.W. Spring, 'The Trans-Persian Railway Project and Anglo-Russian Relations, 1909–14', *Slavonic and East European Review*, 54 (1976).

who have treated the efforts of successive British governments to mobilise business interests as vindicating the belief that politics dominated economics. The only point at which the two interpretations appear to touch is in agreeing that Britain was forced to retreat in the face of the gathering power of new foreign rivals. This perception can be incorporated into the notion that industrial capitalism entered a stage of crisis in the late nineteenth century; it can be attached with equal facility to the argument that, at a time when the metropolitan economy was beginning to suffer from hardening arteries, Britain remained ambulant in the international arena only because the athletes of the Foreign Office were capable of running simultaneously in all directions.

The argument presented here has taken a rather different course. We have tried to show that the Middle East fits with our other examples of Britain's ambitious policy of global development in the nineteenth century, and that it demonstrates, too, the extent to which the realisation of this vision depended on the extension abroad of the new financial and service sector after 1850. Throughout the period under review, governments of different complexions called upon financial instruments, rather than manufacturing interests, to act as agents of economic development and political strategy. The Public Debt Administration served in this capacity in the Ottoman Empire; the Imperial Bank did its duty in Persia. Indeed, the links forged between 'colonial' banks, such as the Imperial Bank of Persia and the Hongkong and Shanghai Bank, and the ties established between these groups and the metropolitan government, suggest that a new form of financial corporatism was emerging to service the international economy long before the large firm became characteristic of industry in Britain itself.

Nevertheless, Britain's great experiment met with limited success in the Middle East, and British policy was left without the economic underpinning it needed. The central cause of this failure was the City's judgement that the Middle East was an area of high risks and generally low returns which could not compete with alternatives that were opening up elsewhere, especially in the Dominions and South Africa, during the second half of the century. The turning point here was the Ottoman default of 1875–6, which was regarded in the City as being particularly reprehensible both because of its size and because it was thought to be the product of bad management rather than of bad luck. Thereafter, the Empire was moved steadily to the periphery of Britain's international economic relations, just as representatives there of the new financial and service class, such as Vincent and

Caillard, remained on the fringe of inner City circles. The City itself was close to politicians but above politics: it could not be directed into investments that did not satisfy the judgement of the market. If the Ottoman Empire was in default, Persia was too poor to attract serious interest from the City. Consequently, British governments had to adjust their traditional attitudes towards intervention and had to supply subsidies, in one form or another, to draw investors into the region. The Imperial Bank and the activities associated with its operations in Persia provide good examples of the implementation of this policy. Although this tactic achieved a considerable measure of success, as we have seen, Britain's informal influence remained partial rather than complete, and in these circumstances diplomatic agreements were made to control rival powers, notably Russia.

Seen in this light, the Middle East offers an illustration both of the strength of the City and of the importance of strategy in imperial policy; and the two together provide little support for the view that Britain's power, however defined, was on the wane before 1914. But the City's caution is not to be taken as an indication of the weakness of British finance in the face of foreign competition. On the contrary, the small scale of Britain's investments in the Middle East was a sign of the City's strength in having a range of more promising investment opportunities available elsewhere, and in being able to resist political demands. Moreover, where they were present, the City's dispositions were shrewdly placed. The Public Debt Administration served British creditors well and also upheld Britain's wider interest in maintaining the unity of the Ottoman Empire. The Imperial Bank and related ventures in Persia benefited from official support, while other investments were made in the Gulf ports, where the returns were attractive, or secured by customs revenues.

These financial decisions undoubtedly set limits to the power behind British diplomacy in the Middle East. Even so, it is hard to reconcile the evidence with the assumption, influential though it is, that Britain was engaged in a series of rearguard actions in a long retreat from dominance. Palmerston's energetic policy was intended to open the way to informal influence; but, as we have seen, it is misleading to suppose that the result was an informal empire under British sway. It was not until the late Victorian era, when informal empire is conventionally said to have been in decline, that Britain was able to extend her grip on the Ottoman Empire and Persia. This happened, as we have shown in other cases, at the time when Britain's share of commodity trade was beginning to decline, and it is this trend which has attracted scholarly attention. A more important and somewhat less emphasised development, however, was the growing external indebtedness of first the Ottoman Empire and then Persia, which increased the leverage at Britain's disposal. As Lord Derby observed in 1879, three years after the Ottoman default: 'the daily surveillance of which Turkey is the object in her domestic affairs has reduced her sovereign authority to practically zero'.[90] Moreover, the City's caution did not, in the event, frustrate Britain's aims. It is certainly true that French, German and Russian banks increased their investments in the Ottoman Empire and the Middle East from the 1890s. But it has also to be emphasised that these investments were made at least partly because Britain's competitors did not have access to comparable opportunities in other parts of the world, that they were not particularly profitable, and that in 1914 the investors lost their money. At that point, Britain had been neither ousted from the region nor defeated in her purpose of defending India, despite the considerable effort and expenditure made by her rivals.

World War I destroyed the Ottoman Empire, but it also brought down Germany, diverted Russia and enabled Britain and France to influence the division of territory in ways that served their interests. Britain remained the dominant power in the new states that emerged from the southern provinces of the empire as well as in Persia, and she also controlled the region's important oil resources. After World War II, when Whitehall designed a new era of colonial rule, Britain aimed to reposition the empire in the Middle East and Africa. The end came in the 1950s; but its origins should not be traced so far into the past that evidence of successful expansion before 1914 is either minimised or translated, mistakenly, into the language of decline.

90. Quoted in Blaisdell, *European Financial Control*, p. 26.

CHAPTER THIRTEEN
'Maintaining the Credit-Worthiness of the Chinese Government': China, 1839–1911[1]

Hobson was not alone among contemporaries in regarding the contest for influence in China at the close of the nineteenth century as being the prelude to an economic division or even a territorial partition which would alter the course of world history.[2] In the event, China defied the odds: her vast economy was insufficiently penetrated to be either developed or undermined by Western forces; formally at least, she managed to retain her political independence, despite the manifest frailty of successive Ch'ing governments and the ultimate collapse of the Manchu dynasty in 1911. This outcome contrasts with the experience of the South American republics, which were drawn into the West's economic and cultural orbit, and of Africa, where indigenous states lost their independence and became colonies of the European powers. However, this does not mean that China escaped from imperialist impulses. The public sector, especially finance, fell under external control and this, in turn, curtailed the political independence of the central government. The Chinese case is therefore closer to that of the Ottoman Empire than it is to South America or Africa, and it raises the question of whether imperialist designs on these centralised but also sprawling polities sprang from different impulses or whether broadly similar intentions were frustrated by a series of drawn games of diplomatic chess or by forces within

1. The quotation is taken from a review of general policy made by the Hongkong and Shanghai Bank at the close of the nineteenth century. See Frank H.H. King, *The History of the Hongkong and Shanghai Bank*, I (Cambridge, 1987), p. 18.
2. P.J. Cain, 'International Trade and Economic Development in the Work of J.A. Hobson Before 1914', *History of Political Economy*, 11 (1979); Ronald Hyam, *Britain's Imperial Century, 1815–1914* (1976), pp. 360–1.

indigenous society which remain, despite the advances of modern research, in part inscrutable.

In the case of China, most answers to this question emphasise the underlying continuity of Britain's economic and political aims in the Far East during the nineteenth century and focus instead on changes in the means required to uphold them.[3] Thus, current assessments give considerable prominence to the process by which Britain shifted from a low-profile, free-trading policy to a more interventionist stance following the Sino-Japanese War of 1894–5, and attribute the change primarily to the new, assertive policies of other powers. There is less agreement about the character of the interests that were defended by this move: some interpretations point towards economic motives, but do so in ways which, though avoiding notions of capitalist conspiracies, often lack specificity; others note the relatively minor role played by China in Britain's international commerce, and give primacy to the activities of the Foreign Office in mobilising economic forces for predominantly geo-political purposes.

It is impossible to provide a comprehensive assessment of the relevant literature in the space available here, not least because a full account would need to determine the role of the complex changes taking place within China itself in the nineteenth century, and this is a vast undertaking which has yet to be attempted by historians of European imperialism.[4] However, research on the foreign, 'barbarian' presence has also advanced greatly in recent years, notably through contributions to business history, and it is now possible to offer a view of events which builds on but also adapts the positions established so far.[5] We shall try to show that Britain's interest in China, far from being static, underwent an important shift of emphasis from

3. Important discussions of these issues can be found in D.C.M. Platt, *Finance, Trade and Politics in British Foreign Policy, 1815–1914* (Oxford, 1968), Ch. 5; D.K. Fieldhouse, *Economics and Empire, 1880–1914*, Ch. 12; and in the work of David McLean cited below and summarised in 'Finance and Informal Empire Before the First World War', *Econ. Hist. Rev.*, 2nd ser. 29 (1976), pp. 300–04.

4. Though much progress has been made by historians of China. The best starting point is John K. Fairbank, ed. *The Cambridge History of China*, Vols X and XI (Cambridge, 1978 and 1980). On the other hand, as Marie-Claire Bergère has observed, these advances have tended to widen the gulf between specialists on Chinese history and analysts of international relations: 'The Issue of Imperialism and the 1911 Revolution', in Eto Shinkichi and Harold Z. Schiffrin, eds. *The 1911 Revolution in China: Interpretative Essays* (Tokyo, 1984).

5. We are especially indebted to the work of King, *History of the Hongkong and Shanghai Banking Corporation*, Vols. I and II (Cambridge, 1987 and 1988), and Roberta A. Dayer, *Finance and Empire: Sir Charles Addis, 1861–1945* (1989). Important research on the history of expatriate and local financial institutions between 1895 and 1911 is currently being undertaken by Takeshi Hamashita of the University of Tokyo.

an initial concern with markets for exports from India and Britain to a preoccupation with opportunities for finance. This trend was under way well before the Sino-Japanese War, and was an expression of developments within the international economy brought about by innovations stemming largely from British enterprise, and was not simply a response to external stimuli administered by foreign powers. The outcome was an effective if sometimes awkward collaboration between political and economic agents, principally the Foreign Office and the Hongkong and Shanghai Bank. This alliance drew the template for British policy towards China from the 1890s onwards, and was successful in its twin aims of upholding China's territorial integrity while also advancing Britain's economic, and especially financial, interests during a period of intense international rivalry in the Far East.

EXPERIMENTS WITH INFORMAL INFLUENCE, 1839–94

The peculiar mixture of compulsion and liberalism prescribed by the early Victorians as a remedy for universal ills was first applied to China in the 1830s.[6] The end of the East India Company's monopoly of the China trade in 1833 created further opportunities for private traders who were keen to expand sales of Indian cottons and opium.[7] Among them were William Jardine and James Matheson, who moved into the China trade in the late 1820s as 'free merchants' and formed what was to become one of the most famous expatriate firms operating in China, Jardine, Matheson & Co., in 1832.[8] At the same time, growing concern about providing outlets for British manufac-

6. Michael Greenberg, *British Trade and the Opening of China, 1800–1842* (Cambridge, 1951); John K. Fairbank, *Trade and Diplomacy on the China Coast: The Opening of the Treaty Ports, 1842–1854* (Cambridge, Mass., 1964); Gerald Graham, *The China Station: War and Diplomacy, 1830–1860* (Oxford, 1978).

7. P. Harnetty, *Imperialism and Free Trade: Lancashire and India in the Mid-Ninteteenth Century* (1972), Ch. 3; A. Tripathi, 'Indo-British Trade Between 1833 and 1847 and the Commercial Crisis of 1847/8', *Indian Hist. Rev.*, 1 (1974); W.E. Cheong, 'The Crisis of the East India Houses, 1830–1834', *Revue internationale de l'histoire de la banque*, 9 (1974).

8. Maggie Keswick, ed. *The Thistle and the Jade: A Celebration of 150 Years of Jardine, Matheson & Co.* (1982). It is interesting to note that the firm's headquarters were in London, where it had close City connections. Alexander Matheson, the head of the affiliated London firm of Matheson & Co., became a director of the Bank of England in 1847.

tures, which were experiencing serious difficulties in the late 1830s, generated wider interest in the potential of the fabled China market. Underlying these developments, however, was the problem that India was unable to meet her external obligations, including the Home Charges, by exporting directly to Britain, and counted on exports to China (principally opium) to balance her payments.[9] China's refusal to extend ports of entry beyond the narrow gate at Canton, combined with Commissioner Lin's ban on opium imports in 1839, therefore presented a serious threat to an emerging system of multilateral settlements and took the problem far beyond the grievances of China hands, old and new.

These issues provided the impetus behind the forceful policies which led to wars with China in 1839–42 and in 1858–60.[10] The first war ended with the Treaty of Nanking, which ceded Hong Kong, conferred rights of extraterritoriality on British citizens, opened five ports (including Shanghai) to free trade, and fixed tariffs at uniform and modest levels. These provisions were reinforced in 1854 by the creation of the Imperial Maritime Customs Administration, which placed China's tariffs under the direction of a British Inspector-General, who, according to one observer, 'came to enjoy more influence with the Foreign Office than did the British Minister in Peking'.[11] The Treaty of Tientsin, which ended the second war, opened more ports to international commerce, allowed foreign shipping to enter the Yangtse, legalised the opium trade, and levied indemnities on China which were to be paid from customs duties.

These impositions were intended to be a low-cost and ultimately self-financing means of unlocking the potential of the vast China market. Britain had no territorial designs on China: on the contrary, in exchange for concessions centred on the Treaty Ports, Britain acquired a commitment to support the government in Peking, which was thought to be the best guarantee of domestic stability and orderly commerce.[12] The Treaty Ports were to become bridgeheads to the interior, releasing the export potential of the hinterland and acting as

9. Tripathi, 'Indo-British Trade', pp. 308–11.

10. P.W. Fay, *The Opium War, 1840–1842* (Chapel Hill, N.C., 1975); Douglas Hurd, *The Arrow War: An Anglo-Chinese Confusion, 1856–1860* (1968); Britten Dean, *China and Great Britain: The Diplomacy of Commercial Relations, 1860–1864* (Cambridge, Mass., 1974).

11. Quoted in Dayer, *Finance and Empire*, p. 8. On Sir Robert Hart, the long-serving Inspector General, see Stanley F. Wright, *Hart and the Chinese Customs* (Belfast, 1950).

12. Fairbank, *Trade and Diplomacy*, pp. 464–8; Dean, *China and Great Britain*, pp. 129–32, 141–4.

funnels for a return trade in goods from Britain and India. Despite their apparent promise, these plans disappointed successive generations of China-watchers.[13] Britain undoubtedly came to dominate China's overseas trade, but the trade itself remained small and expectations of expansion had constantly to be revised.[14] Between 1840 and 1870 China supplied about 5 per cent of Britain's imports, but took less than 3 per cent of her exports. India's exports of opium increased, but the feverish calculations about clothing and equipping several hundred million Chinese turned out, not for the last time, to be fantasies. By 1896, after half a century of endeavour, China and Hong Kong between them accounted for only about 8 per cent of Britain's main export, cotton goods.[15] China's own export sector remained dependent on tea and silk, which, as we shall see, began to experience difficulties towards the close of the century. Foreign investment was also on a small scale and was confined mainly to the Treaty Ports. At the time when the Ottoman Empire was on the edge of bankruptcy, China had scarcely contracted her first foreign public loan.[16] Instead of acting as bridgeheads, the Treaty Ports became enclaves which strengthened Chinese merchants, notably the compradors, and incorporated the representatives of the West into a vibrant indigenous system of distribution.[17]

13. Rhoads Murphey, 'The Treaty Ports and China's Modernization', in Mark Elvin and G. William Skinner, eds. *The Chinese City Between Two Worlds* (Stanford, Calif., 1974); Shannon R. Brown, 'The Partially Opened Door: Limitations on Economic Change in China in the 1860s', *Mod. Asian Stud.*, 12 (1979); Thomas G. Rawski, 'Chinese Dominance of Treaty Port Commerce and its Implications, 1860–1875', *Explorations in Econ. Hist.*, 7 (1970); Robert Y. Eng, 'Chinese Entrepreneurs, the Government and the Foreign Sector: the Canton and Shanghai Silk-Reeling Enterprises, 1861–1922', *Mod. Asian Stud.*, 18 (1984).

14. Britten Dean, 'British Informal Empire: the Case of China', *Journal of Commonwealth and Comparative Politics*, 14 (1976), pp. 70–1.

15. Dean, 'British Informal Empire', p. 72; D.A. Farnie, *The English Cotton Industry and the World Market, 1815–1896* (Oxford, 1979), p. 91. Here, and throughout this chapter, we have confined our general comments on overseas trade (and investment) to broad indications of the principal trends. These are sufficient for our main purpose, though less accurate than we would like them to be. At present, however, the data contain too many uncertainties to allow a more precise analysis to be made without an extended justification, which is precluded by limitations of space. We are particularly indebted to the work of Hsiao Liang-lin, *China's Foreign Trade Statistics, 1864–1949* (Cambridge, Mass., 1974), to Hou Chi-ming, *Foreign Investment and Economic Development in China, 1840–1937* (Cambridge, Mass., 1965), and to Dr John Latham for his advice on this subject.

16. David J.S. King, 'China's First Public Loan: the Hongkong Bank and the Chinese Imperial "Foochow" Loan of 1874', in Frank H.H. King, ed. *Eastern Banking: Essays in the History of the Hongkong and Shanghai Banking Corporation* (1983). See also Shannon R. Brown, 'The Transfer of Technology to China in the Nineteenth Century: the Role of Foreign Direct Investment', *Jour. Econ. Hist.*, 39 (1979).

17. Hao Yen-p'ing, *The Comprador in Nineteenth-Century China: Bridge Between East*

The reasons for the failure of this experiment in development derive from a mixture of economic constraints and public policy choices which lies beyond the scope of this study.[18] At the time, when the outcome was unclear, British merchants continued to hope that the China market could be prised open by a combination of railways and active diplomacy, and to fear that this strategy would first be applied by foreign competitors. British governments, however, began to take a more cautious view of China's development prospects from the 1860s.[19] The Foreign Office was not prepared to see Britain's position eroded, but it was also unwilling to adopt policies which, besides being costly, might weaken the authority of Peking and stimulate the territorial ambitions of rival powers.[20] As always, opportunities had to be weighed against costs and against alternatives which, fortuitously, arose elsewhere in the middle of the century following the revival of international trade and the expansion, in particular, of the Indian market.[21]

The manifest limitations of the development drive ought not to obscure the fact that significant changes took place among the firms representing Britain's economic interests in China during the second half of the century, principally as a result of the extension of new financial and commercial services to the Far East.[22] The foundation of the Hongkong and Shanghai Bank in 1865 greatly improved credit facilities; and the advent of regular steamship services in the 1870s, coupled with the extension of the telegraph (which reached Shanghai

---

and West (Cambridge, Mass., 1970); idem, *The Commercial Revolution in Nineteenth-Century China: The Rise of Sino-Western Mercantile Capitalism* (Berkeley, Calif., 1986); Dean, 'British Informal Empire', p. 70.

18. For a lively introduction to some of the main issues see Philip C. Huang, ed. *The Development of Underdevelopment in China* (New York, 1980).

19. Mercantile and official views during this period are discussed by Nathan A. Pelcovits, *Old China Hands and the Foreign Office* (New York, 1948). This study is of lasting value, but the subject itself now needs to be reassessed in the light of the research produced since the early 1950s.

20. Marvin Swartz, *The Politics of British Foreign Policy in the Era of Disraeli and Gladstone* (1985), p. 14; Dean, 'British Informal Empire', p. 74.

21. Farnie, *English Cotton Industry*, pp. 96–106.

22. A valuable synthesis is Jürgen Osterhammel, 'British Business in China, 1860s–1950s', in R.P.T. Davenport-Hines and Geoffrey Jones, eds. *British Business in Asia since 1860* (Cambridge, 1989), pp. 190–200. See also Hao, *The Commercial Revolution*, Ch. 7; Motono Eiichi, 'The "Traffic Revolution": Remaking the Export Sales System in China, 1866–1875', *Modern China*, 12 (1986); Liu Kwang-ching, 'British-Chinese Steamship Rivalry in China, 1873–85', in C.D. Cowan, ed. *The Economic Development of China and Japan: Studies in Economic History and Political Economy* (1964); and Daniel Headrick, *Tentacles of Progress: Technology Transfer in the Age of Imperialism, 1850–1940* (Oxford, 1988), pp. 37–41.

in 1871), reduced the time taken by commercial transactions and lowered their cost. These innovations attracted new traders (such as Butterfield & Swire) to the Treaty Ports and heightened business rivalries at a time when Western firms were unable to penetrate the interior.[23] Moreover, the main lines of trade became much less profitable in the 1870s and 1880s.[24] China's import-purchasing power was affected by a decline in the profitability of tea and silk exports during the last quarter of the century, largely as a result of competition from India and Japan. Although exports received some stimulus from the fall in the value of silver from the 1870s, this was offset by adverse movements in the barter and income terms of trade. The return business in British manufactured goods also began to suffer from competition: after 1883, for example, cotton yarn from India replaced British yarn in the China market.[25] The years preceding the Sino-Japanese war were particularly poor. At the close of 1886 the British Consul in Shanghai reported that the year had ended in 'a state of depression never before witnessed in the China trade'.[26] Matters did not improve: Russell & Co., the most prestigious of the United States' firms trading in China, collapsed in 1891;[27] the Hongkong and Shanghai Bank's chief comprador became bankrupt in the following year; and the Australian banking crisis shook business confidence in 1893.[28] According to Jardine, Matheson's agent, trade in the Far East had been 'disastrous for some time'.[29]

23. On John Swire, see Sheila Marriner and Francis Hyde, *The Senior: John Samuel Swire, 1825–1898: Management in Far Eastern Shipping Trades* (Liverpool, 1967); and Shinya Sugiyama, 'A British Trading Firm in the Far East: John Swire & Sons, 1867–1914', in Shin'ichi Yonekawa and Hideki Yoshihara, eds. *Business History of General Trading Companies* (Tokyo,1987). Swires joined the growing number of provincial overseas trading firms which moved their headquarters to London in the 1870s.

24. Hao, *The Commercial Revolution*, Ch. 11; Cheng, Yu-kwei, *Foreign Trade and Industrial Development of China* (Washington, D.C., 1956), pp. 258–9; Liu Kwang-ching, *Anglo-American Steamship Rivalry in China,1862–1874* (Cambridge, Mass., 1962), pp. 117–18, 138–9, 150; Hou Chi-ming, *Foreign Investment and Economic Development in China, 1840–1937* (Cambridge, Mass., 1965), pp. 194–210, 231–2; Albert Feuerwerker, 'Economic Trends in the Late Ch'ing Empire, 1870–1911', in Fairbank, ed. *Cambridge History*, XI, Pt. 2, pp. 45–7; King, *History of the Hongkong and Shanghai Bank*, I, pp. 283–4, 426; Jerome Ch'en, *State Economic Policies of the Ch'ing Government, 1840–1895* (1980), pp. 116–20.

25. Farnie, *English Cotton Industry*, pp. 110–11.

26. Quoted in Hao, *The Commercial Revolution*, p. 324.

27. It is interesting to note that the firm was also a distant casualty of the Baring Crisis. See Hao, *The Commercial Revolution*, p. 324.

28. King, *History of the Hongkong and Shanghai Bank*, I, pp. 404–6, 433, 438–42.

29. Edward le Fevour, *Western Enterprise in Late Ch'ing China: A Selective Survey of Jardine, Matheson and Company's Operations, 1842–1895* (Cambridge, Mass., 1968), pp. 152–3.

The leading import and export firms reacted to these trends by moving out of the old staple trades and by becoming managing agencies concerned increasingly with services, notably shipping, insurance and banking, and with an array of activities connected to property and utilities in the Treaty Ports.[30] Jardine, Matheson & Co. provides a good example of this shift of interest. Reacting to competition from newcomers to the China trade, and judging that Chinese merchants would continue to handle imports and exports outside the Treaty Ports, Jardines gave up the opium trade in the 1870s and turned to shipping, banking and allied services.[31] They also started to forge alliances with progressive elements in the Chinese bureaucracy, made several small loans for political purposes in the 1870s, and showed their willingness to co-operate with the modernising programme advocated by the 'self-strengthening' movement by entering into joint ventures with Chinese entrepreneurs.[32]

These changes in the organisation and performance of the export sector had important consequences for the Hongkong and Shanghai Bank, which had become the leading expatriate bank in the Far East by the close of the nineteenth century.[33] The Bank was founded by a cosmopolitan group of local merchants primarily to finance China's overseas trade but also in the expectation that the development of the Chinese economy was imminent, and that new business, including public loans, would then materialise.[34] From the 1870s, however, the Bank found itself grappling with unexpected problems as the profitability of trade declined and as the fall in the value of silver created difficulties in meeting sterling obligations. Moreover, from the 1880s the bank began to face competition, first from the Yokohama Specie

---

30. Osterhammel, 'British Business in China', pp. 192–3. This completed an adjustment that was already under way: as early as 1851, one of the partners in Rathbone, Worthington & Co. observed that, in future: 'profits will be made as much in the management of the funds and exchanges as in any other way.' Quoted in S.G. Checkland, 'An English Merchant House in China after 1842', *Bull. Bus. Hist. Soc.*, 27 (1953), pp. 162–3. See also ibid. pp. 168, 170, 181.

31. Le Fevour, *Western Enterprise*, pp. 28–9, 48–9; Liu, *Anglo-American Steamship Rivalry*, pp. 138–9, 150; Hao, *The Commercial Revolution*, p. 173.

32. Le Fevour, *Western Enterprise*, pp. 52–3, 57–62, 125. Economic aspects of the 'self-strengthening' movement are covered by Wellington K.K. Chan, *Merchants, Mandarins and Modern Enterprise in Late Ch'ing China* (Cambridge, Mass., 1977).

33. King, *History of the Hongkong and Shanghai Bank*, I, Ch. 1.

34. Ibid. pp. 43–5, 86, 157–62, 353–5, 500–1, 523–4, 535. The career of the Bank's founder, (Sir) Thomas Sutherland, spanned banking, shipping (chairman of P&O in 1884) and politics (MP for Greenock, 1884–1900) in a way that was characteristic of imperial entrepreneurs from the second half of the nineteenth century onwards, and suggests comparison with figures such as Currie, Mackinnon and Inchcape.

Bank (1880) and then from the Deutsche-Asiatische Bank (1889).[35] The Bank had to manage its exchange dealings with great skill, and it also had to grow if it was to remain profitable and credit-worthy.

In these circumstances, the Bank was anxious to extend its business beyond its traditional concern with international trade and, if possible, into government loans.[36] The Bank had privileged access to official sources from the outset, since it acted as banker to the colonial government in Hong Kong and also to the Imperial Maritime Customs Administration, which controlled the principal security for public borrowing.[37] Only 'imperial' loans (those raised by the central government in Peking) could draw on this security which, in turn, was essential to winning the support of the London money market.[38] Not surprisingly, the Bank was keen to see the unity of China maintained, and it joined the Foreign Office in supporting the central government. However, the Ch'ing dynasty was reluctant to raise money from abroad, and did so only as a result of crises in foreign affairs, first with Japan over Formosa in 1874 and then following the Sino-French War of 1883–5. These events provided the Bank with the opportunity it had been waiting for: it issued China's first foreign loan in 1874, and followed this with further loans later in the decade and during the 1880s.[39] The first loan enabled the Bank to avoid making a loss in 1874–5; the others underpinned its profitability during a period of continuing trading difficulty.[40]

The growth of the Bank's foreign loan business also strengthened its ties with London. The Bank had the backing of the London and County Bank at the time of its foundation, and thereafter it took care to maintain close links, through its London office, with bankers of 'very high standing' in the City.[41] Its managers and shareholders became predominantly British, and its reserves were invested in British (and Indian) government securities.[42] Although the Bank lost some of its cosmopolitan origins, it remained international in its aspirations; it was never intended to serve or even to favour British industry.[43] By the 1890s, the Bank was considered to be part of the

35. Ibid. pp. 261–3, 283–4, 422, 451, 426, 440.
36. Ibid. pp. 266, 284, 298, 308–11.
37. Ibid. pp. 546–7.
38. Ibid. pp. 19, 98–100, 270, 303–4, 538–41, 546–7.
39. King, 'China's First Public Loan'.
40. Ibid. p. 261; King, *History of the Hongkong and Shanghai Bank*, I, pp. 266, 283, 308–11.
41. King, *History of the Hongkong and Shanghai Bank*, I, p. 100.
42. Ibid. pp. 98–100, 143–4, 270, 276, 311, 343.
43. Ibid. pp. 558–62.

City community. At the Bank of England's request, it subscribed to the fund raised to help out Barings in 1890, when the General Manager, Thomas Jackson, received a knighthood for 'services to British commerce in the East'.[44]

During the last quarter of the century, the changing structure of trade and growing difficulties among the expatriate firms led to renewed demands for China to be opened to foreign enterprise. This pressure reinforced and expressed a wider concern in Britain with the effects of commercial depression and foreign competition, and in turn led the Foreign Office to reconsider the extent to which it was willing to act in support of business interests in China, as indeed elsewhere. This drift in official thinking can be discerned from two episodes which arose in the mid-1880s: the first drew attention to the political implications of new lending to China; the second tested Britain's reaction to the rise of foreign competition.

In 1884, when China was technically in default on a portion of her loan repayments, the Hongkong and Shanghai Bank asked Sir Harry Parkes, the British Minister in Peking, to intervene with the Chinese authorities.[45] Parkes, who had subscribed heavily to the Bank's loans to China, duly obliged and payment was resumed. His action prompted considerable discussion in Whitehall. As always, the Treasury was alarmed at the prospect of a back-door guarantee and the Foreign Office was equally worried about unauthorised intervention. However, Sir Julian Pauncefote, then an Assistant Under-Secretary at the Foreign Office and also a substantial shareholder in the Hongkong and Shanghai Bank, argued that 'diplomatic intervention in China is a necessity in many cases where it would not be resorted to elsewhere', and pointed out that formal communications concerning the loan had to be conducted through the Legation because this was the only channel which the Ch'ing government recognised.[46] Although no official departure from existing policy was sanctioned, the episode showed that the Foreign Office was edging towards more active backing for British interests in China. Parkes's action helped to maintain the confidence of British investors, and in doing so blurred the line between loans which were guaranteed and those which were not.

Two years later, reports that a powerful German syndicate was

44. Ibid. pp. 422–3, 565.
45. Ibid. pp. 546–7. See also Platt, *Finance, Trade*, pp. 269–70.
46. King, *History of the Hongkong and Shanghai Bank*, I, p. 547; King, 'China's First Public Loan', p. 247. Pauncefote (1828–1902) was appointed Ambassador to the United States in 1893 and became a peer in 1899.

about to descend on China led to fears that British finance and manufactures would be pushed aside, and prompted a flurry of representations from Chambers of Commerce, the China lobby in the House of Commons, and influential private sources.[47] Once again, the official response was guarded; but the alarm was real and it produced a 'series of "unofficial" measures designed to support both the financial and the commercial interests of British firms in China and of British industry'.[48] This concern died away when the German venture faded in 1886, but the event offered a preview of the more serious rivalries which were to arise in the 1890s.

None of this is to suggest that big business was pushing for the partition of China; on the contrary, the large firms remained keen to cooperate with modernising elements within the bureaucracy and continued to hope that China would eventually develop along Japanese lines.[49] At the same time, the evidence now available indicates that the evolution of commerce since the mid-century had put British companies in a position where they had both the capacity and the need to develop more profitable business, that loans to Peking were seen as being a particularly attractive option, and that the Foreign Office, under both Liberal and Conservative governments, was willing to take a more assertive line on behalf of British business at times when it appeared to be under threat. The idea that British interests on the China coast remained quiescent until disturbed by the sudden outbreak of the Sino-Japanese War therefore misses a developing theme in British imperialism in the late nineteenth century, and in doing so it also presumes that policy was more reactive than was the case. As we shall now see, Britain's attitude towards China after 1894–5 was very much an extension of trends which had already begun to make their presence felt.

THE SCRAMBLE FOR CHINA, 1894–1911

If the outbreak of the Sino-Japanese War in 1894 pushed British policy further along a path it was beginning to take, it nevertheless did so at

47. David McLean, 'Commerce, Finance and British Diplomatic Support in China, 1885–86', *Econ. Hist. Rev.*, 2nd ser. XXVI (1973).

48. Ibid. p. 469.

49. King, *History of the Hongkong and Shanghai Bank*, I, p. 508; Le Fevour, *Western Enterprise*, pp. 67–9, 132–3. On the growth of manufacturing see Stephen C. Thomas, *Foreign Intervention and China's Industrial Development* (Boulder, Colo., 1984).

a pace which caused the Foreign Office to shed a number of long-standing assumptions about the future of the Far East. The hope that China would experience a measured evolution, combining economic progress with political stability and led by Britain, suddenly began to look unrealistic. In its place was thrust the prospect that Britain, the sitting tenant, might be dislodged by upstarts who had no respect for her claims. China was one of Britain's minor trading partners, but the surplus generated by existing commerce made a useful contribution to the balance of payments,[50] and the potential, especially for finance and services, was irresistible. If the China market was finally going to be opened, Britain intended to cross the threshold as fast as other entrants. The principles of free trade and the open door were bent and at points abandoned in the rush; but the Foreign Office held firmly to the policy of supporting central authority in Peking both to safeguard the security for China's foreign loans and to prevent other powers from establishing exclusive rights that would damage Britain's cosmopolitan trading relationships.[51] In doing so, Whitehall became closely involved with British commercial interests, and particularly with the Hongkong and Shanghai Bank, which regarded the preservation of China's unity as being crucial to securing new business as well as to avoiding default on existing loans.[52]

The defeat of Ch'ing forces at the hands of Japan in 1895 signalled the start of a scramble for influence and territory in China. The immediate and also the most important result of the war was to compel the government to borrow from foreign sources on a far larger scale than before. As Charles Addis (then an aspiring sub-manager with the Hongkong and Shanghai Bank) was quick to realise, Japan's victory was an opportunity rather than a set-back for British policy. China now needed Britain's protection more than ever; the indemnity imposed by Japan would have to be financed in London; and Britain would then be in a position to influence the 'development of the material resources of China'.[53] This judgement may have underestimated the obstacles to opening up the hinterland, but it was also prescient: in the 21 years between 1874 and 1895 the Bank (the principal intermediary) raised about £12m. for the Chinese

50. S.B. Saul, *Studies in British Overseas Trade, 1870–1914* (Liverpool, 1960), p. 58.

51. For a detailed study of these issues see L.K. Young, *British Policy in China, 1895–1902* (Oxford, 1970).

52. King, *History of the Hongkong and Shanghai Bank*, II, pp. 250–1, 264, 315, 506–7; Dayer, *Finance and Empire*, pp. 35–6. On the shared aims of bankers and diplomats generally see Clarence B. Davis, 'Financing Imperialism: British and American Bankers as Vectors of Imperial Expansion in China, 1908–1920', *Bus. Hist. Rev.*, 56 (1982).

53. Quoted in Dayer, *Finance and Empire*, p. 37.

government; in the four years between 1896 and 1900 it provided no less than £32m.[54] British loans to the Chinese government continued to grow after the turn of the century, albeit at a slower rate, and almost doubled in value between 1902 and 1914.[55] Addis might also have predicted that the indemnity would benefit British business with the victors as well as with the vanquished: it enabled Japan to move to the gold standard in 1897, improved her credit-rating, and thus helped her to attract substantial inflows of foreign capital, most of which came from London.[56]

The growing and increasingly overt convergence of politics and finance became apparent during negotiations over the three post-war loans that funded China's indemnity payments. In 1895, when the first loan was being discussed, the Foreign Office tried to create an international consortium that would hold China together and contain the ambitions of rival powers. The Hongkong and Shanghai Bank asked for official support, but the Foreign Office thought that formal action would simply provoke retaliation, and responded by calling on 'the assistance of the Rothschilds in preventing anything being done to prejudice British interests'.[57] The result was a cooperative agreement between the Hongkong and Shanghai Bank and the Deutsche-Asiatische Bank in conjunction with Rothschilds in London; but by the time this arrangement had been reached the loan had been won by a Russian syndicate, which had government backing (and French support). When the second loan was raised in the following year, the Anglo-German group was in place and ready to act. On this occasion the Bank of England agreed to inscribe the bonds, following pressure from the British government.[58] Addis, who was surely in a position to know, was satisfied that for practical purposes the Bank of England had provided 'one of the best guarantees'.[59] The group's bid was accepted, the flotation was successful, and the Hongkong and Shang-

54. King, *History of the Hongkong and Shanghai Bank*, II, pp. 242, 264, 312.

55. Hou, *Foreign Investment*, pp. 13–14; C.F. Remer, *Foreign Investment in China* (New York, 1933), pp. 19, 138. The data on foreign investment in China need to be treated with caution until the pioneering work of Remer and Hou has been updated.

56. R.P. Sinha, 'Unresolved Issues in Japan's Economic Development', *Scottish Journal of Political Economy*, 23 (1969), pp. 132–4; R.P.T. Davenport-Hines and Geoffrey Jones, 'British Business in Japan Since 1860', in idem, *British Business*, pp. 224–5. See also King, *History of the Hongkong and Shanghai Bank*, II, pp. 94–101.

57. F.O. Memo. by Sanderson, 20 May 1895, quoted in King, *History of the Hongkong and Shanghai Bank*, II, p. 269. On the episode as a whole, see ibid. pp. 264–75, and D. McLean, 'The Foreign Office and the First Chinese Indemnity Loan, 1895', *Hist. Jour.*, 16 (1973).

58. King, *History of the Hongkong and Shanghai Bank*, II, pp. 275–83.

59. Quoted in Dayer, *Finance and Empire*, p. 38.

hai Bank's profits jumped. The third loan, which was offered in 1898, was also given official backing, despite opposition from the Treasury, and it too was handled by the British-led consortium. As Curzon explained, in a statement that conveyed his sense of British superiority with undiplomatic frankness: 'the Government decided not merely that they were better qualified to lend the money than any others, but that in the interests of commercial expansion, which we also had in view, and in the interests of sound finance, the assistance was what might very properly be given'.[60] No doubt with the same interests in mind, the Foreign Office used the occasion to establish Britain's claim to a sphere of influence in the Yangtse Valley, the region with the greatest development potential, and to reinforce her control of the Imperial Maritime Customs Administration.[61]

International competition over shares in China's indemnity loans was complemented by a battle for railway and mining concessions which reached its height between 1895 and 1900. The scramble for concessions stemmed partly from the hope of finding new, profitable business, but also from the need to generate extra revenues to secure China's foreign loans, since the income from the Imperial Maritime Customs was fully pledged by the turn of the century.[62] Britain was well represented in the vast allocations which were made during this period, acquiring large holdings in the Yangtse Valley and securing concessions elsewhere to prevent rival powers from carving China into exclusive zones.[63] As in other parts of the world, the opening of the frontier was accompanied by the formation of new investment groups and syndicates.[64] The leading companies were not simply vehicles for expatriate firms on the China coast, but were backed by London finance and included prominent City bankers among their directors. The British and Chinese Corporation, founded in 1898, brought together Jardine, Matheson and the Hongkong and Shanghai Bank, and was connected to Rothschilds, Barings and other City banks. The Peking Syndicate (1897) and the Yangtse Valley Company (1901) were similarly constituted, and the former also included South African mining interests. These firms were essentially financial instru-

60. Quoted in King, *History of the Hongkong and Shanghai Bank*, II, p. 286.

61. Young, *British Policy*, pp. 91–2; King, *History of the Hongkong and Shanghai Bank*, II, pp. 280–81.

62. King, *History of the Hongkong and Shanghai Bank*, II, pp. 350–1; Dayer, *Finance and Empire*, p. 39.

63. E.W. Edwards, *British Diplomacy and Finance in China, 1895–1914* (Oxford, 1987), pp. 4–6 and Ch. 2; Young, *British Policy*, pp. 77–85.

64. On the details which follow see King, *History of the Hongkong and Shanghai Bank*, II, pp. 295–303; Osterhammel, 'British Business', pp. 193, 197–200.

ments rather than representatives of 'finance capital' in the sense of linking banks with industry.[65] Within the limits of prudence dictated by financial cost and diplomatic risk, the Foreign Office gave vigorous support to private enterprise in securing concessions and in diverting competitors to the fringes of the Chinese empire away from the main focus of British interests.[66]

Yet the estate remained undeveloped. Concessions were more easily won than exploited, and the attempt to move inland fuelled a reaction to foreign intrusion which culminated in the Boxer Rising in 1900.[67] Following the suppression of the Boxers, Britain consolidated her position in China by revising her treaty arrangements with the Ch'ing government. Under the terms of the Mackay Treaty (1902), China abolished certain duties on internal trade and in exchange was allowed to raise the tariff on imports.[68] Manchester opposed the increase but could make no headway against the Foreign Office and the Hongkong and Shanghai Bank, which recognised that Peking had to be provided with the means of servicing China's enlarged foreign debt. In fact, The Mackay Treaty was based upon a memorandum drawn up by Addis, now manager of the Hongkong and Shanghai Bank, and it also bound China to adopt a uniform currency, a national bank, and, when conditions allowed, a gold standard.[69]

After 1900, however, the City of London marked down the attractions of investing in China, partly because of the political risks and partly because of anxieties about the soundness of the security, which in turn reflected the increasing size of the public debt and the disappointing performance of the export economy.[70] The indemnities imposed by the foreign powers after the Boxer Rising were profitable

65. As such, they illustrate the financial and managerial innovations described by Mira Wilkins, 'The Free-Standing Company, 1870–1914: an Important Type of British Foreign Direct Investment', *Econ. Hist. Rev.*, 2nd ser. XLI (1988).

66. Platt, *Finance, Trade*, pp. 283–307; Ian H. Nish, *The Anglo-Japanese Alliance: The Diplomacy of Two Island Empires, 1894–1907* (1966), pp. 93, 233, 252, 276; and, for an example of the use of concessions to counter the expansion of other powers, A.L. Rosenbaum, 'The Manchurian Bridgehead: Anglo-Russian Rivalry and the Imperial Railways of North China, 1897–1902', *Mod. Asian Stud.*, 10 (1976).

67. For an introduction to recent research on the Boxer Rising (referred to in some studies as the Boxer Rebellion) see the special issue of *Chinese Studies in History*, 20 (1987). The geographical and social diversity of the movement is brought out well by Joseph W. Esherick, *The Origins of the Boxer Uprising* (Berkeley, Calif., 1987).

68. The Mackay Treaty also created several new Treaty Ports. The fullest account remains Pelcovits, *Old China Hands*, pp. 278–82.

69. King, *History of the Hongkong and Shanghai Bank*, II, p. 202.

70. Edwards, *British Diplomacy*, pp. 52, 63, 68, 70, 78, 83, 125; King, *History of the Hongkong and Shanghai Bank*, II, pp. 333, 351–3; Feuerwerker, 'Economic Trends', pp. 65–7.

fines which forced China into renewed borrowing, but they also reduced her ability to finance productive projects and made British investors wary of putting their money into risky, long-term development loans in China.[71] The Foreign Office complained endlessly about the lack of British enterprise, but it could neither alter the judgement of the market nor lead the City where it did not want to go. Exceptions to this rule arose only when the government provided sufficient support to reduce the risk or when the banks decided to treat particular loans as 'loss leaders' which would subsequently promote profitable business. Britain's rivals, on the other hand, generally had fewer investment opportunities and greater powers of direction over their money markets.[72] Consequently, there was growing apprehension that Britain would lose ground in the contest to win influence in Peking and to develop the mainland.

Britain's response to this challenge showed just how interdependent politics and finance had become. After 1900, intervention on behalf of British business in China became a regular feature of diplomatic activity. In 1903, for example, the Foreign Office helped to put together a syndicate to construct a railway along the Yangtse Valley, and provided official backing when it raised money in the City;[73] and in the next year government encouragement was given to a loan for building the Shanghai–Nanking line.[74] Following the Boxer Rising, Britain also had to take account of the emergence of 'Young China'.[75] As with the Young Turks and the constitutionalists in Persia, the Foreign Office hoped that the reform movement was a sign that the long-awaited conversion to Western liberalism was at hand. Having loaned money to secure concessions after 1895, Britain was prepared to lend more money after the turn of the century to enable China to recover her rights, providing that the terms were

71. King, *History of the Hongkong and Shanghai Bank*, II, p. 333.
72. Edwards, *British Diplomacy*, pp. 64–6, 85, 88, 130, 196–7; and, for the case of France, D. Gagnier, 'French Loans to China, 1895–1914: the Alliance of International Finance and Diplomacy', *Australian Journal of Politics and History*, 18 (1972).
73. D. McLean, 'Chinese Railways and the Townley Agreement of 1903', *Mod. Asian Stud.*, 7 (1973); King, *History of the Hongkong and Shanghai Bank*, II, pp. 331–7.
74. Edwards, *British Diplomacy*, Ch. 2, and pp. 64, 70. On the history of China's railways see Ralph W. Huenmann, *The Dragon and the Iron Horse: The Economics of Railroads in China, 1876–1937* (Cambridge, Mass., 1984).
75. On this subject see Chuzo Ichiko, 'Political and Institutional Reform, 1901–1911', in Fairbank, *Cambridge History*, XI; Lee En-han, *China's Quest for Railway Autonomy, 1904–1911* (Singapore, 1977); and, for case studies of the relationship between the economics and the politics of reform, Yen Chin-hwang, 'Chang Yu-Nan and the Chaochow Railway (1904–1908)', *Mod. Asian Stud.*, 18 (1984); and D. Atwell, *British Mandarins and Chinese Reformers: The British Administration of Weihaiwei, 1898–1930* (Oxford, 1986).

suitable and that the results did not weaken central authority. In a complex deal in 1905, for instance, the Colonial Office arranged for the Hongkong and Shanghai Bank to lend £1.1m. to enable China to buy out American interests in the Canton–Hankow line, and then advanced a further £3m. to redeem the railway in return for the right to build a direct link between Hankow and Hong Kong.[76]

Financial considerations also entered into various schemes which the Foreign Office devised to conciliate other powers. An obvious case was the alliance formed with the Japanese in 1902, which helped the Treasury to control naval expenditure at a critical time by making Japan Britain's watchdog in the Far East.[77] In return for guaranteeing China's territorial integrity, Japan was let off the leash in Korea, which lay beyond the bounds of British interests. With regard to the mainland itself, the chief aim of the Foreign Office was to shepherd other powers into agreements which would uphold the principles of 'responsible lending' and prevent financial competition from degenerating into territorial acquisition. This task required the cooperation of the City, but because the government could not direct the merchant banks there was often a need to draw on foreign sources to supplement British capital. This problem played a part in the decisions first to share China's post-war indemnity loans with Germany, and then to cooperate with France, in harmony with the new entente, in financing Chinese railways after 1904.[78] An allied consideration was that, since rival powers had free access to the London capital market, they did not have to be penned in by the Foreign Office. Concern that Russia and Japan, which had weak capital markets and strong government support, might use the City of London to compromise British policy ensured that their claims for shares of China's loan business were listened to more carefully than would otherwise have been the case.[79]

These developments drew the Foreign Office and the Hongkong and Shanghai Bank into an even closer partnership, despite increasing criticism – the more embarrassing because it was justified – that this involved a departure from the principle of impartiality which govern-

76. Dayer, *Finance and Diplomacy*, pp. 57–8. As far as private risk-capital was concerned, however, the City took a guarded view of China outside the treaty ports, and this limited the extent of Britain's co-operation with the self-strengthening movement. The progress of the movement after 1900 is well covered by Chan, *Merchants, Mandarins*.

77. The standard work is Nish, *Anglo-Japanese Alliance*.

78. King, *History of the Hongkong and Shanghai Bank*, II, pp. 272–5, 353; Edwards, *British Diplomacy*, pp. 64–6, 76, 85, 88.

79. King, *History of the Hongkong and Shanghai Bank*, II, pp. 484–5.

ment departments were supposed to apply in their dealings with private firms. This special relationship was the product of converging interests and was sealed by a process of osmosis which absorbed the Bank into gentlemanly culture.[80] The Bank never lost its Hong Kong base, which was the source of its strength in the Far East, but it was also steadily permeated by metropolitan values. From the 1880s, the Bank's main recruiting and training centre was located in London, and by the turn of the century it had become an institution for changing 'young gentlemen into bank clerks'.[81] Not surprisingly, the young gentlemen were drawn primarily from landed and professional families, and hardly at all from backgrounds in manufacturing. As in other parts of the empire, there was a strong admixture of promising young Scots who had been caught in the glutinously effective 'porridge trap.'[82] On both sides of the border, the Bank relied heavily on public schools to supply suitable new entrants, and it cultivated a sporting ethos which placed great emphasis on team games such as rugby and cricket. In these ways, the Bank nurtured a sense of solidarity which generated institutional loyalty among its employees, helped to define their sense of social identity, and justified the supremacy of the white man in his dealings with alien cultures. There were infrequent attempts to modify the rites of apprenticeship by attracting graduates and by encouraging Bank staff to learn Chinese, but they left little impression. Since the existing system produced satisfactory results, there seemed little reason to change the method: exchange bankers, it was said, 'were born not made'.[83]

The qualities prized by the Bank were personified by Charles Addis, the son of a Scots minister, who joined the Bank as a young clerk in 1880 and became London Manager in 1905.[84] On his return from the East, Addis was steadily absorbed into London banking and social circles, where his benefactors included Lord Revelstoke, the head of Barings. After 1905, Addis spent an increasing amount of time acting as a financial diplomat, travelling between London, Paris

80. What follows is based on King, *History of the Hongkong and Shanghai Bank*, I, Ch. 15, and II, Ch. 3; and Christopher Cook, 'The Hongkong and Shanghai Banking Corporation on Lombard Street', in King, ed. *Essays*.

81. Quoted in King, *History of the Hongkong and Shanghai Bank*, II, p. 173.

82. According to banking lore, the agents of banks operating in the Far East would dig large pits on desolate moors in Scotland, place bowls of porridge in them and thus trap unwary native youths who were searching for food. The captives were then sent down to London to be trained as bankers. See King, *History of the Hongkong and Shanghai Bank*, II, p. 173.

83. Ibid. p. 187.

84. See Dayer's excellent biography, *Finance and Empire*, and idem, 'The Young Charles Addis: Poet or Banker?', in King, ed. *Essays*.

and Berlin on behalf of the Bank and keeping in close touch with the Foreign Office.[85] He received a knighthood in 1913, and he finished his career as a director of the Bank of England and as an adviser to the Treasury and the Cabinet on financial and Far Eastern affairs before retiring to his home in Surrey. Addis was a consistent supporter of free trade, the gold standard and stable exchange rates. His vision of international development allocated non-governmental organisations, principally banks, a leading role in financing modernisation, and he regarded the British empire as being the best means yet invented of realising these cosmopolitan aspirations. His was a world in which, ideally, capital knew no national frontiers; he had no time for protectionist sentiments or for the special pleading of industrial interests whose competitive power was in decline. His approach to China was that of the modern missionary whose faith was drawn from the universal principles found in Calvinism and economics. Addis hoped that China would remain strong and independent but also that it would be converted to progress through a programme of 'responsible lending', which Britain was uniquely qualified, and therefore morally obliged, to undertake.[86]

Cooperation between the Foreign Office and the Hongkong and Shanghai Bank reached a new peak of intensity during the critical period between the fall of the Manchu dynasty in 1911 and the appointment of Yuan Shi-k'ai as President of the Republic of China in 1912. The underlying causes of the revolution of 1911 lie beyond the scope of this chapter, and in any case are still much debated among specialists.[87] But it is clear that foreign incursions since 1895 had generated growing disaffection in the provinces, which resented the increased burden of taxation imposed by the central government to meet China's external financial obligations, and that their hostility merged with mercantile and popular opposition to railway and mining concessions and to the attempts to exploit them after the turn of the century. The Ch'ing government fell between its dislike of the barbarians (manifested in its support for the Boxers), and its belated

85. King, *History of the Hongkong and Shanghai Bank*, II, pp. 412–14.
86. Ibid. pp. 517–19.
87. See, for example, Shinkichi and Shiffrin, *The 1911 Revolution*; E. Zurcher, 'Western Expansion and Chinese Reaction – A Theme Reconsidered', in H.L. Wesseling, ed. *Expansion and Reaction: Essays on European Expansion and Reactions in Asia and Africa* (Leiden, 1978); Mark Elvin, 'The Revolution of 1911 in Shanghai', *Papers on Far Eastern History*, 29 (1984); Richu Ding, 'Shanghai Capitalists Before the 1911 Revolution', *Chinese Studies in History*, 18 (1985); and compare the views of Feuerwerker, pp. 65–9 with those of Bastide-Brugière, pp. 592–9, in Fairbank, *Cambridge History*, XI.

recognition of the need for economic reform, which could be undertaken only with foreign assistance, given the reluctance of Chinese investors to back government-managed projects. For their part, the foreign powers, especially Britain, wanted to maintain the central government and one China, but the flow of loans which they supplied contributed to the downfall of both.

The immediate cause of the revolution was the outbreak of discontent which greeted the announcement of the Hukuang railway loan. The Foreign Office and the Hongkong and Shanghai Bank had been trying to tie the major powers into a general consortium to finance railway construction since 1909, and terms were finally agreed with the Ch'ing government in 1911.[88] The conditions of the Hukuang loan were not unusual, but they were agreed at a point when foreign indebtedness had become a highly sensitive political issue. Critics of the regime were also aware that the consortium was considering a further large loan to reform the Chinese currency and to assist China's long-debated transfer to the gold standard, a move that was intended partly to improve her credit-rating. As one revolutionary leader put it: 'China's present situation is that if it is not conquered by partition it will be lost by invisible financial control by foreign powers'.[89] From Britain's point of view, the events of 1911 overturned the regime supported by the foreign powers, raised the possibility of default on existing loans, and opened up the prospect of a renewed scramble for China.

Britain played a leading part in averting this outcome. In 1912, the Foreign Office and the Hongkong and Shanghai Bank led the way in forming an International Commission of Bankers to manage customs revenue, and hence to secure loan repayments, in enlarging the international consortium to include Russia and Japan (in the hope of controlling them), and in backing the provisional government under Yuan, a former Ch'ing general who had agreed to cooperate in maintaining the open door and in meeting China's external financial obligations.[90] In the following year, the consortium issued a Reorgan-

88. Different judgements on the terms of the loan are given by Dayer, *Finance and Empire*, pp. 63–4, and King, *History of the Hongkong and Shanghai Bank*, II, Ch. 7. We have followed King's fuller statement. The international politics of the loan are dealt with by K.C. Chan, 'British Policy in the Reorganisation Loan to China, 1912–13', *Mod. Asian Stud.*, 5 (1971), and Anthony B. Chan, 'British Policy in the Reorganisation Loan to China, 1912–13', *Mod. Asian Stud.*, 6 (1977). There is also a disagreement between these two writers, but the difference is unimportant from the standpoint of the present study.

89. Quoted in Dayer, *Finance and Empire*, p. 64.

90. Liu Ming-te, 'Yuan Shih-k'ai and the 1911 Revolution', *Bull. Inst. of Mod. Hist.*, 11 (1982); and, for a biography, Jerome Ch'en, *Yuan Shih-k'ai, 1859–1916: Brutus Assumes the Purple* (Stanford, Calif., 2nd edn 1972).

isation Loan of £25m., which helped Yuan to gather support, become President of the Republic, and purge the democratic wing of the reform movement. The new loan was secured on specified revenues (principally the salt tax), which were to be administered by an official appointed by the international consortium. China's credit-rating was maintained, and the issue was a success. Investors looked forward to a new era of development; borrowers looked back on a long process by which external indebtedness, contracted by successive governments, had compromised China's independence.

It was during this period that the Hongkong and Shanghai Bank's virtual monopoly of official loans to China and of unofficial influence in Whitehall came under heavy attack from British manufacturers and their sympathisers. Pauling & Co., the large railway contractors, had already made an attempt in 1908 to ensure that loans to China were tied to the purchase of British manufactures.[91] Their campaign had the support of the British Minister in Peking, Sir John Jordan, and it gained impetus from anti-German feelings expressed in *The Times* and elsewhere. The Bank defended its cosmopolitan policy on conventional free trade grounds, and its position was endorsed by the Foreign Office. As a result, Pauling's plea was turned down. In 1912, with the prospect of new and lucrative loans to China, the Bank faced direct competition from a British financier, Charles Crisp, who was prepared to offer a loan to the provisional government.[92] Although Crisp was not in the top rank of City bankers, his challenge, like Pauling's, attracted attention because it merged with growing anxiety about foreign competition in manufactured goods and with the feeling that the Bank's cosmopolitan approach to lending was damaging British exports. Since Crisp could fairly claim to be acting in the spirit of free trade and private enterprise, his bid was an embarrassment to the British government. Nevertheless, the Foreign Office leant on him heavily to try to stop the issue, and made its displeasure known when it went forward, with the result that only 40 per cent of the £5m. offered in London was subscribed by the public.[93] The official view was that Crisp's loan would enable China to evade the controls needed for 'responsible lending', a phrase which applied not only to the security of the loan but to the reliability of the lenders. This was a dubious argument in terms of free-trade orthodoxy, but it

91. Edwards, *British Diplomacy*, pp. 96, 120–1, 126, 131–5, 180.
92. King, *History of the Hongkong and Shanghai Bank*, II, pp. 490–8; Dayer, *Finance and Empire*, pp. 66–7.
93. Hou, *Foreign Investment*, p. 48; Platt, *Finance, Trade*, pp. 300–1.

demonstrated the extent to which the success of British policy towards China had come to rely on particular financial interests.

The Bank had to pay for its victory by agreeing to enlarge Britain's representation on the consortium, and thus reduce its share of loans to the Chinese government.[94] However, given that China needed some £60m. in new loans, this amendment did not have a serious effect on the Bank's position or prospects. Moreover, the newcomers to the consortium were all established City associates of the Bank, the most prominent being Barings. The loan business was opened up just enough to allow the Foreign Office to give exclusive support to the British group in the Consortium, but it was also kept in the family. Jordan continued to call for 'the organisation of British manufacturing and financial interests into one or two powerful syndicates equipped in such a way as to enable them to compete with the Associations which are being formed by our rivals'.[95] But, as the Foreign Office noted in 1914: 'It is extremely difficult to collect British firms to undertake business in China, especially mining. We are not really in touch with those sort of people'.[96] In fact, 'those sort of people' were divided among themselves as well as separated from the City. Railway interests may have been willing to ride on anti-German sentiment, but Manchester refrained from attacking either Germany or the Hongkong and Shanghai Bank's monopoly because over half of its exports to China were distributed by German firms, which were financed very largely by the City and the Bank.[97] If the future of British manufactures in China depended on the emergence of finance capitalism, then the outlook was indeed gloomy. But most of Britain's exports to China probably still gained more than they lost from free trade in 1914, even though the price was dependence on the City's financial and commercial services and exposure to foreign competition.

THE NEW FINANCIAL EMPIRE

Reflecting on Britain's relations with China, Charles Addis observed in 1905 that 'an imperial policy is essentially a commercial policy and

---

94. King, *History of the Hongkong and Shanghai Bank*, II, pp. 453, 496.
95. Quoted in Edwards, *British Diplomacy*, p. 191.
96. Ibid. p. 193.
97. See King, *History of the Hongkong and Shanghai Bank*, II, Ch. 9 and especially pp. 523, 527, 531–2, 544–5, 605, 615. The Deutsche Asiatische Bank was established to finance German exports, but it remained dependent on the London money market because it was unable to discount bills of exchange at competitive rates.

to resent the intrusion of politics into business is to do injury to both'.[98] This assessment accords not only with other contemporary opinion, whether favourable or hostile to imperialism, but also with the evidence now available on Britain's involvement with China in the period between the Opium Wars and the fall of the Manchu dynasty. The commercial policy that Addis referred to was based essentially on a continuing belief in the merits of free trade. If, in 1839, policy was influenced by the needs of manufacturing interests, by 1911 it was quite clearly shaped by considerations of finance. Moreover, even at the outset of the period, the pressure to open China was driven by a concern to ensure that India had the means of meeting her financial obligations to Britain, and to this end markets were sought for Indian as well as for British exports. Of course, British industry remained an important element in policy-making, and the potential of the China market was a permanent feature of the calculations of the Foreign Office as well as of Manchester and Birmingham. But the China market remained more of a myth than a reality. Although the value of Britain's trade with China rose after the turn of the century, her share of the total fell sharply as rival powers made inroads into the larger market created by the revival of international commerce and the partial opening of the interior, and her manufactured exports suffered badly from Japanese competition.[99]

The dynamic force, in China as elsewhere, was the growth of investment, a process both symbolised and realised by the success of the Hongkong and Shanghai Bank. As Britain lost her place in commodity trade, so she strengthened it in the field of finance. This is not to say that capital flowed readily to China: the City was generally wary of investing in the Far East, apart from Japan, and China remained, in global terms, one of Britain's minor debtors. On the other hand, China had never defaulted on a major loan. Peking's credit remained good, and secure loans authorised by the central government or anchored in the Treaty Ports, were usually taken up. It was there, in centres of political authority and international trade, that British influence was most pronounced. By 1914, Britain's holdings of Chinese government stock had grown both absolutely

98. Quoted in Dayer, *Finance and Empire*, p. 58.
99. Calculated from *Statistical Abstract for the United Kingdom, 1899–1913* (1914), and Hsiao, *China's Foreign Trade Statistics*. See also Oriental Economist, *The Foreign Trade of Japan: A Statistical Survey* (Tokyo, 1935); Cheng, *Foreign Trade*; and Hou, *Foreign Investment*. There was a decline, too, in the share of China's overseas trade handled by the 'imperial unit' of Britain, India and Hong Kong.

and relative to other foreign powers.[100] The volume of private investment flowing from Britain had risen too, as had her share of the total, most of which found safe havens in shipping, property and utilities in the major ports. This investment helped British-registered shipping to retain its lead in the carrying trade between China and other countries and to hold its share of the enlarged inter-port carrying trade. In China, as in other parts of the world, invisible earnings had come to depend increasingly on moving goods other than those produced in or required by Britain.[101]

Strategic motives played little or no part in Foreign Office thinking because China was not on the route to anywhere of importance to Britain. The wider purposes of diplomacy could undoubtedly be seen in the slow-moving and endless bargaining which aimed at deflecting or accommodating rival powers by giving them slices of other people's property, but this was neither a unique nor a pre-eminent feature of British imperialism in the Far East. In addition, there were a number of crises at various points on the periphery where Britain and China met, but the most important of these, the Boxer Rising, followed rather than caused foreign intervention, and indeed prompted the major powers to adopt a more cautious stance in their dealings with Peking. Finally, while it can be acknowledged that other states, especially Japan but also Germany, France and Russia, had considerable influence on British policy, this does not mean that changes in Britain's presence in China were simply, or even largely, responses to external stimuli. The view that policy towards China was essentially reactive needs to take account of the fact that Britain was an expanding power which gained either territory or influence in other parts of Asia too in the late nineteenth century, most obviously in Burma and Malaya, but also in Thailand, North Borneo and Japan.

The scramble for China can therefore be placed in the global context shaped by the extension of Britain's finance and services during the second half of the nineteenth century. There were many reasons why China did not suffer the same fate as Africa, but prominent among them was the fact that the continuing authority of Peking was needed to guarantee foreign loans and to underwrite the Treaty Port system, whereas in Africa viable states and central authorities had to be created before foreign lending could begin. A

100. Remer, *Foreign Investment*, pp. 19, 138; Cheng, *Foreign Trade*, pp. 88–92; Hou *Foreign Investment*, pp. 16–17. Shipping data calculated from Hsiao, *China's Foreign Trade*.

101. And, as Osterhammel notes, British trade 'in China was vastly more important than British trade with China': 'British Business', p. 215.

closer comparison can be drawn between China and the Ottoman Empire: each had a recognised central authority and far-flung, poorly integrated domains; and Britain's chief interest, in both cases, lay in public-sector loans, which in turn gave her a strong commitment to the maintenance of political stability. In both cases, too, informal influence was exerted through government borrowing rather than through trade, and tended to grow rather than diminish as the period advanced. The principal difference was not of structure but of timing. The default of 1875 removed the Ottomans from the City's list of creditable borrowers and shifted its considerable influence towards debt collection, whereas China beckoned at the close of the century as a land of promise which required sizeable foreign loans for the first time and offered adequate security (much of it under British control) for repayment. The revolution of 1911, itself caused partly by foreign indebtedness, placed Peking even more firmly under the discipline of external creditors headed by Great Britain. It is true, as we have noted, that Britain had a greater strategic interest in the Middle East, which was on the route to India, than she had in China, but this was not, as is sometimes claimed, the determining influence on policy: preserving the open door and maintaining debt service were sufficiently weighty reasons in themselves for upholding the authority of both Constantinople and Peking.

At the same time, the City's reluctance to invest beyond well-defined limits played its part in China, as in the Ottoman Empire, in drawing the boundaries of British influence and in pushing the Foreign Office towards agreements with other powers. Valuable though it was, the Yangtse Valley was scarcely the Rand of the East, and its potential could be realised only at huge expense and considerable political risk. Consequently, Britain was unable to open a vast new market for her manufactures, but she did succeed in holding China together and in expanding opportunities for finance and commercial services there. In moving towards this goal, the Foreign Office and the Hongkong and Shanghai Bank cooperated so closely that it is misleading as well as unnecessary to speak of one dominating the other, not least because they were manned by 'the same sort of people'.

PART FOUR
Rediviing the World

CHAPTER FOURTEEN

Britain, Germany and 'Imperialist' War, 1900–14

In 1913 Britain was the only nation whose economic interests were global[1] and the only one whose status as a great power rested upon world-wide commitments. She had neither the sheer size of population and territory which gave a country like Russia great power, despite her relative economic backwardness, nor the enormous internal market and wealth of natural resources which fuelled the growth of the United States. It was a recognition of the strength and the vulnerability resulting from this world-wide system which dictated the general lines of British foreign policy.[2]

THE ECONOMICS OF FOREIGN POLICY

In the first place, Britain was determined to prevent the domination of the European continent by any one power or a close combination

1. Between 1909 and 1911, 65 per cent of Britain's exports went outside Europe, and in 1910 55 per cent of her imports came from extra-European sources. The corresponding export figure for Germany, Britain's greatest trade rival, was 25 per cent. Paul Bairoch, 'Geographical Structure and Trade Balance of European Foreign Trade from 1800 to 1970', *Jour. Eur. Econ. Hist.*, III (1974), Tables 5 and 6, p. 573.
2. On British foreign policy generally see Paul Kennedy, *The Realities behind Diplomacy: Background Influences on British External Policy, 1865–1980* (1981), Pt. I; Bernard Porter, *Britain, Europe and the World, 1850–1982: Delusions of Grandeur* (1983); Kenneth Bourne, *The Foreign Policy of Victorian England, 1830–1902* (Oxford, 1970); C.J. Lowe, *The Reluctant Imperialists: British Foreign Policy, 1878–1902*, 2 Vols., (1967); C.J. Lowe and M.L. Dockrill, *The Mirage of Power: British Foreign Policy, 1902–22*, 3 Vols., (1972); M.E. Chamberlain, *'Pax Britannica'? British Foreign Policy, 1789–1914* (1988). Marvin Swartz, *The Politics of British Foreign Policy in the Era of Disraeli and Gladstone* (1985) has also proved useful in relating foreign policy to domestic politics. There is a good short summary of the main principles of nineteenth-century foreign policy in Alun Davis, 'England and Europe', in J.S. Bromley and E.H. Kossman, eds. *Britain and the Netherlands in Europe and Asia* (The Hague, 1968).

of powers. Checkmating her European rivals was of prime importance because, as a memorandum from the General Staff put it in 1911,

> Such domination or control would place at the disposal of the Power or Powers concerned a preponderance of naval and military force which would menace the importance of the United Kingdom and the integrity of the British Empire.[3]

In other words, much of the concern about Europe reflected worries about the fate of Britain's vast extra-European network upon which her economic strength – and therefore her world political status – depended. Britain's second great diplomatic concern was a close corollary of the first: the maintenance of the freest possible intercourse for trade and commerce throughout the world. Both of these aims could be achieved only through naval strength, which ensured her independence of Europe and gave her the leading position in the extra European world through control of a string of coaling stations and strategic outposts across the seas.

Besides the attainment of these diplomatic objectives, Britain had a more fundamental need, that of world peace. The whole intricate web of financial and commercial interests of which London was the centre depended upon adhering to an economic orthodoxy which would be severely tested and could even be overthrown by a protracted war or a sustained high level of defence expenditure.[4] The dangers of war were clear enough even during the brief Crimean conflict of the mid–1850s. Gladstone, one of the fathers of fiscal orthodoxy, was forced, as Chancellor of the Exchequer at the time, to borrow extensively and increase the national debt. Heavy war expenditure also led to a drain of gold and made the commercial community anxious about maintaining the convertibility of sterling, and about the high Bank Rate and the increased income tax which were necessary to stem the flow and pay for the troops. The Crimean War disturbed the status quo at a yet more fundamental level in that the disappointments of the campaign threatened to expose the amateurism of gentlemanly government and led to demands for changes which, had the war lasted longer, could have sparked off a social revolution.[5]

3. Memorandum from the General Staff, 13 August 1911. PRO Cab. 38/19/47, reprinted in Lowe and Dockrill, *The Mirage of Power*, Vol. III, p. 445.
4. Paul M. Kennedy, 'Strategy versus Finance in Twentieth Century Great Britain', *Internat. Hist. Rev.*, III (1981), pp. 45–52. This essay has been reprinted in *Strategy and Diplomacy, 1870–1945: Eight Studies* (1983). See also idem, *The Rise of the Anglo-German Antagonism, 1860–1914* (1980), pp. 295, 302–5.
5. Olive Anderson, *A Liberal State at War: English Politics and Economics in the Crimean War* (1967), Chs. 3, 4, 6, 7, and 8.

Britons had a long-standing aversion to large armies, and any attempt to produce a force which could rival that of the European powers would have involved conscription and an invasion of liberty that few politicians were willing to contemplate. Equally important in deterring militarism was the cost. A large standing army could have been created only by pushing taxation to levels that would have intensified social conflict and threatened Britain's role as an international financial market. So Britain had to rely upon the Indian Army to give her the status of a great land power; and the orbit of operations of that army was strictly limited for both political and economic reasons. What this meant in practice was that Britain's influence upon the balance of power in Europe was never as great as she often pretended. Even in Palmerston's time Britain lacked the power to enforce her will in Europe, and her bluff could be called, as was Palmerston's, by Bismarck over the Schleswig-Holstein crisis in 1863.[6] Britain's power lay outside Europe and rested upon her navy. Maintaining a large navy was the cheapest and most effective way of protecting her interests and was heartily supported not only by the political establishment but even by the City, which took it for granted that naval predominance was crucial to world peace, a form of insurance premium taken out on the wealth owned or controlled by Britain.[7]

The relationship between naval predominance, the security of Britain and her empire, and confidence in Britain as the world's banker and commercial intermediary, was very well understood before 1914. As one aristocratic member of the government expressed it during the Boer War: 'Its Credit and its Navy seem to me to be the two main pillars on which the strength of this country rests and each is essential to the other'.[8] Reconciling foreigners to this naval predominance was also thought to be a good reason for standing by free trade. As a senior member of the Foreign Office pointed out in 1907, the openness of the British market and Britain's opposition to discrimination in trade were ways of demonstrating that her control of the seas and her extensive empire were used for the benefit of others as well as herself.[9] The more Britain's international economic

---

6. Porter, *Britain, Europe and the World*, pp. 26–7.

7. Kennedy, *The Rise of the Anglo-German Antagonism, 1860–1914*, p. 305; Peter Stansky, *Ambitions and Strategies: The Struggle for Leadership of the Liberal Party in the 1890s* (Oxford, 1964), pp. 19–35, esp. pp. 24, 34.

8. See the Cabinet Memo. of 16 Nov. 1901, written by Selborne, in Lowe, *The Reluctant Imperialists*, I, p. 5.

9. Eyre Crowe's memorandum on 'The Present State of British Relations with France and Germany', 1 Jan. 1907, printed in G.P. Gooch and H. Temperley, eds.

empire expanded and the greater the cost of defending it, the more the desire to settle conflicts with other powers by discussion and rational concession became part of the furniture of the minds of the political elite.[10]

Before 1880, the need to reconcile cheap government with naval supremacy did not prove too difficult and, given the lack of competition from the other great powers, Britain managed to rule the waves and penny-pinch simultaneously.[11] Competition began to hot up and Britain's defence commitments to expand alarmingly as the formal empire grew, just as her industrial growth prospects were becoming a matter of concern and as social welfare expenditure began to rise to meet the needs of voters enfranchised in 1867 and 1884.[12] By 1900, the expansion of Britain's overseas commitments was pushing up public expenditure to the point where the alarm bells were beginning to ring. The Boer War cost 14 per cent of the national income of 1902: £160m. was added to the national debt and Bank Rate had to be raised to 6 per cent (from an average of 2 or 3 per cent in the 1890s) in order to prevent a drain.[13] The war and the subsequent naval race with Germany also provoked a more general crisis in public expenditure, opening the door both to Chamberlain's protectionist and imperial ideas and to Lloyd George's radical budgeting of 1909–14.

Moreover, the South African conflict appeared to prove that Britain had no ally of any importance, while the number of contenders for great-power status was increasing rapidly; and it was recognised that the time had arrived when, in the interests of keeping down defence expenditure and policing her empire and her economic interests

---

British Documents on the Origins of the War, Vol. III (1928), App. A. The sections on free trade are reprinted in W.H.B. Court, *British Economic History, 1870–1914: Commentary and Documents* (Cambridge, 1965), pp. 469–70. See also Gerald S. Graham, *Tides of Empire: Discursions on the Expansion of Britain Overseas* (1972), p. 82.

10. P.M. Kennedy, 'Tradition of Appeasement in British Foreign Policy, 1865–1939', *Brit. Jour. Internat. Stud.*, II (1976); W.D. Gruner, 'The British Political, Social and Economic System and the Decision for Peace or War: Reflections on Anglo-German Relations, 1800–1939', ibid. VI (1980).

11. C.J. Bartlett, ed. *Britain Pre-eminent: Studies in British World Influence in the Nineteenth Century* (1969), p. 173; Graham, *Tides of Empire*, p. 80. A recent survey of British naval history which places it within the context of a changing economy is P.M. Kennedy, *The Rise and Fall of British Naval Mastery* (1976). See also Bernard Semmel, *Liberalism and Naval Strategy: Ideology, Interest and Sea Power During the Pax Britannica* (1986).

12. Harold Sprout and Margaret Sprout, 'The Dilemma of Rising Demands and Insufficient Resources', *World Politics*, XX (1968).

13. Clive Trebilcock, 'War and the Failure of Industrial Mobilization 1899–1914', in J.M. Winter, ed. *War and Economic Development: Essays in Memory of David Joslin* (Cambridge, 1975), pp. 141, 143.

overseas, she ought to decide who were her friends and who were her enemies. The Hay-Pauncefote Treaty of 1901 with the USA and the Anglo-Japanese alliance of the following year delimited Britain's naval responsibilities in the Caribbean and Pacific respectively, helping both to head off potential conflicts and to narrow the area wherein the British had to find men and money to defend essential interests.[14] It was at this time, too, that hostility to, and fear of, Germany started to crystallise in Britain, as the former began to appear as a threat to Britain's standing in the world greater than any since that posed by France a century earlier. The conflict was analysed closely by contemporary Marxists and incorporated into their evolving critique of imperialism, a critique which perhaps deserves more attention than it has received from imperial historians during the last 30 years.[15]

MARXIST THEORY AND WORLD WAR I

Marxists viewed the last part of the nineteenth century as the end of what Lenin termed the 'free capitalist' stage of development, when the small, self-financed firm was the characteristic unit. By the end of the century the world had been 'divided up' economically, politically and strategically on the basis of this free capitalist development. Britain, as the leading economic power, had been the chief beneficiary of the division. By 1900, the free capitalist phase was giving way to a more advanced stage: 'finance' or 'monopoly' capitalism. A succession of economic crises after 1870 had produced not only an oligopolistic economic structure in the most advanced nations but also a fusion between large-scale industry and banking capital. Changes in the structure of enterprise were accompanied by shifts in the geographic

---

14. G. W. Monger, *The End of Isolation: British Foreign Policy, 1900–1907* (1963), Chs. I and 3; Zara S. Steiner, *Britain and the Origins of the First World War* (1977), Ch. 2. For a recent analysis of the connection between crises over government expenditure and Britain's foreign policy stance see Aaron L. Friedberg, *The Weary Titan: Britain and the Experience of Relative Decline, 1895–1905* (Princetown, NJ, 1988).

15. The main texts are Rudolf Hilferding, *Finance Capital: A Study of the Latest Phase of Capitalist Development* (ed. T. Bottomore, 1981); N. Bukharin, *Imperialism and World Economy* (1972 edn) and V.I. Lenin, 'Imperialism, the Highest Stage of Capitalism' (1916), in *Collected Works*, XXXII (Moscow, 1964). Commentaries sympathetic to the approach taken here can be found in Eric Stokes, 'Late Nineteenth-Century Colonial Expansion and the Attack on the Theory of Economic Imperialism: a Case of Mistaken Identity?', *Hist. Jour.*, XII (1969), to which we owe a considerable debt. See also the important contribution by Norman Etherington, *Theories of Imperialism: War, Conquest and Capital* (1984).

epicentre of capitalism: Germany and the United States superseded Britain as the front-runners in development. Whereas the growth of the United States was still largely within her own frontiers, Germany's expansion required rapid extension of her trade, commerce and capital into the world at large and, therefore, into areas largely controlled by Britain and other countries, like France, who were in relative economic decline. To assert herself as a world power rather than remain merely a European one, Germany needed to acquire the kind of global political and military authority, the secure outlets for trade and capital, and the control of the institutions of finance and commerce which Britain had built up during the previous two centuries – and still enjoyed. This is why Marxist theorists spoke of the need to 'redivide' the world after 1900: world power relations had to change drastically to bring them into line with changes in the world economy wrought by the uneven development of capitalism.

When Hilferding and his fellow Marxists wrote about the need for redivision they were not making a simple identification between imperialism and colonialism, or concentrating on the struggle for colonies and spheres of interest in 'backward' parts of the world. The new phase of imperialism was the result of a change in capitalism as a whole and had global implications: it was a battle for hegemony between the great powers which involved a very wide spectrum of economic and political relationships, both formal and informal, within Europe itself as well as in Africa, Asia or Latin America.[16] The scramble was not a matter of overwhelming importance: African partition was a minor part of the process, occurring in the final stages of free capitalism rather than as a result of mature finance capital and, as such, was part of the original division of the world which had now to be destroyed.

Hilferding – whose understanding of these matters was subtler than that of his more politically embattled comrades, Bukharin and Lenin – recognised that, though Britain might be sliding into industrial backwardness by 1900, the way in which the economy had evolved internationally had helped to slow down her decline as a world power. The rapidity of internal development in the United States and Germany limited the capital resources they could devote to overseas expansion. Britain, still lodged at an earlier stage of development and with finance and industry still separated, could use the

16. See particularly Hilferding, *Finance Capital*, pp. 329–30; Bukharin, *Imperialism and World Economy*, pp. 120–1; and Lenin, 'Imperialism, the Highest Stage of Capitalism', pp. 268–9. There is also a clear recognition of 'informal empire' in Lenin, 'Imperialism', pp. 263–4.

resources of the City to create a world-wide service network, to support her industrial exporters and to fend off the competition of rivals abroad for longer than would otherwise have been possible.[17]

For Bukharin and Lenin, writing in 1915 and 1916, the war in progress was evidently the result of the uneven development of capitalism, with the Anglo-German conflict at the centre of the struggle.[18] Other radicals, and even some Marxists, doubted whether war was an inevitable outcome of the transformation of capitalism. Hobson, for example, felt that, in the longer run, the contending capitalist powers might be forced, simply by the growing internation-alisation of capital, to replace war by 'inter-imperialism', a joint exploitation of the world's resources by the leading economic powers.[19] Kautsky, the leading German Marxist thinker, also believed that the costs of colonialism and militarism were becoming prohibi-tive and that the great colonial powers might renounce the arms race. The result would be a 'cartelisation of foreign policy' or 'holy alliance of the imperialists' and a peaceful division of the globe resulting from economic domination.[20] Neither Bukharin nor Lenin could accept this analysis. Temporary agreements for sharing out the spoils there

17. Hilferding, *Finance Capital*, pp. 324–5, 331.

18. V.I. Lenin, *British Labour and British Imperialism* (1969), pp. 135–6. The analysis presented in this chapter does not imply that Marxist theories of imperialism are unassailable. This is particularly true of the Leninist approach, which limits imperialism to the finance-capitalist stage of development and ignores the importance of capital export before the turn of the century. Lenin was also woefully out of touch with reality when he suggested that finance capitalism was the last stage of capitalism and that the imperialist powers had lost their economic dynamism and were becoming parasitic upon the backward nations of the world. It is noticeable that Hilferding avoided these traps and that the subtitle of his book describes finance capital as being the *latest* stage of capitalist development. For a good critique of Marxist theories of imperialism see Anthony Brewer, *Marxist Theories of Imperialism: A Critical Survey* (2nd edn 1989), which is especially severe on Lenin's numerous errors of fact and logic, as is Bill Warren, *Imperialism: Pioneer of Capitalism* (1980), Chs. 3 and 4, which castigate Lenin for his assumption that capitalism had lost its dynamic and had reached its highest stage. In assuming that the imperialist states had become parasitic and decaying, and that their industry was already in decline as a result of the export of capital, Lenin (in *Imperialism*, pp. 276–85) relied heavily on British material and on Hobson. The influence of Hobson on Lenin's views is discussed in Peter Cain, 'J.A. Hobson, Financial Capitalism and Imperialism in Late Victorian and Edwardian England', *Jour. Imp. and Comm. Hist*. XIII (1985), pp. 10–11. For other critiques of aspects of Marxist theories of imperialism see V.G. Kiernan, *Marxism and Imperialism* (1975), Ch. 1; and Roger Owen and Bob Sutcliffe, eds. *Studies in the Theory of Imperialism* (Oxford, 1972), Chs. I and II.

19. J.A. Hobson, *Imperialism: A Study* (1988 edn), pp. 311–12. On this important aspect of Hobson's thought see P.J. Cain, 'International Trade and Economic Devel-opment in the Work of J.A. Hobson before 1914', *History of Political Economy*, XI (1979), pp. 410ff.

20. Karl Kautsky, 'Ultra-Imperialism', *New Left Review*, 59 (1970).

might be; but, in an unevenly developing world, the fastest growing entities would always have an incentive to break those agreements and take what they wanted by force.[21]

But if the Hobson–Kautsky assumption of a global division of the world bringing permanent peace in its train seems far-fetched, there is no need to go as far as Lenin did and claim that the economic differences between Britain and Germany made war inevitable. What we can say, following Hilferding, is that they probably made fundamental conflict inevitable and, by doing so, drastically narrowed the scope for political and military agreement.[22] It was also the case that, should war break out for any other reasons, the conflict would inevitably become a battle between Britain and Germany for the controlling voice in the management of the world economy and a struggle for empire. The essence of this conflict was expressed with remarkable bluntness in 1907 by Viscount Esher, an important member of the Committee of Imperial Defence:

> Meanwhile the Germans proceed unabashed on their way, and have their objectives clearly in view. The German prestige, rising steadily on the continent of Europe, is more formidable to us than Napoleon at his *apogée*. Germany is going to contest with us the Command of the Sea, and our commercial position. She wants sea-power and the carrying trade of the world. Her geographical grievance has got to be redressed. She must obtain control of the ports at the mouths of the great rivers which tap the middle of Europe. She must get a coastline from which she can draw sailors to her fleets, naval and mercantile. She must have an outlet for her teeming population, and vast acres where Germans can live and remain Germans. These acres only exist within the confines of our Empire. Therefore, 'L'Ennemi c'est L'Allemagne.'[23]

ANGLO-GERMAN RIVALRY AND ITS EFFECTS

Even as late as the 1890s, Britain's most serious confrontations were with Russia and France rather than with Germany. Britain was at loggerheads with the French over imperial acquisitions in Africa and Asia, the contest culminating in the tense dispute at Fashoda in 1898. Fear of Russian ambitions was, if anything, greater: Britain con-

---

21. Lenin, 'Imperialism, the Highest Stage of Capitalism', pp. 275–6, 295; Bukharin, *Imperialism and World Economy*, pp. 141–2.

22. Hilferding, *Finance Capital*, pp. 331–2.

23. M.V. Brett, ed. *Journals and Letters of Reginald Viscount Esher* (1934), II, p. 267, quoted in Court, *British Economic History*, p. 471.

fronted Russia in Turkey, Persia and Afghanistan where, directly or indirectly, Tsarist forces appeared to menace the stability of the Indian empire and the routes to the East. The accommodation between France and Russia in the 1890s was regarded with deep anxiety in Britain because it meant a conjunction of naval forces in the Mediterranean, and effectively ended her predominance there. It was this agreement, together with the expansion of the navies of other powers, which made the 1889 decision on the Two Power Standard – a determination to maintain a navy of greater strength than the combined forces of the next two largest naval powers – almost impossible to implement, even though it was not formally abandoned until 1912.[24]

Conflicts between Britain, France and Russia over imperial territory and imperial strategy meant that, in Salisbury's time, Britain tended to lean towards friendly relations with the Triple Alliance powers led by Germany. Under Bismarck, Germany was not an ambitious power outside Europe, despite her interest in colonies during the 1880s; the recognition that Bismarck was reasonably satisfied with the European status quo after 1870 also helped to keep relations between Britain and Germany cordial. Between 1898 and 1901, Chamberlain made several attempts to persuade his colleagues, and the Germans themselves, of the virtues of a close accommodation between the two powers, despite the Kaiser's open support for the South African republics during the Boer War.[25]

Germany's decision to build a large navy made an alliance or agreement with Britain impossible because an understanding could have been reached only if the Germans had been willing to accept permanent naval inferiority. German *Weltpolitik* was exceedingly tortuous in that it was reckoned to take at least 15 to 20 years to build a navy equivalent to Britain's, and this had to be done, if possible, without provoking too much British antagonism. The Germans feared obsessively that Britain might be tempted to thwart them by making a pre-emptive strike upon their naval force before it became a serious threat to the empire.[26] In the event, the British became convinced that Germany was planning to challenge their power and

24. Arthur J. Marder, *The Anatomy of British Sea Power: A History of British Naval Policy in the Pre-Dreadnought Era* (New York, 1940), Ch. VII and pp. 509–14.
25. J.A.S. Grenville, *Lord Salisbury and Foreign Policy: The End of the Nineteenth Century* (1964), Ch. VII; Monger, *The End of Isolation*, Ch. 2.
26. Jonathan Steinberg, 'The Copenhagen Complex', *Jour. Contemp. Hist.*, I (1966).

were also worried, as were France and Russia, about the possibility of a bid to establish German hegemony on the continent.[27]

Britain's sensitivity on the naval issue clearly indicated the connection between her diplomatic and military stance and her economic power. The navy was not only the key to the defence of Britain herself, but also the crucial safeguard for the enormously complex chain of economic interests which Britain had built up over centuries and without which she was just an offshore island of Europe rather than a great world power. It was for this reason that Grey, as Foreign Secretary, insisted that naval agreements with Germany could be made only on 'the basis of superiority of the British navy', since the German navy 'is not a matter of life and death to them as it is to us'. If Germany were to maintain a navy as large as Britain's, together with her enormous army, 'for us it would not be a question of defeat. Our independence, our very existence would be at stake'.[28]

In 1912, the Admiralty made almost exactly the same claims but expanded the argument, linking it with a possible bid for continental hegemony by Germany:

> There is practically no limit to the ambitions which might be indulged by Germany, or to the brilliant prospects open to her in every quarter of the globe, if the British Navy were out of the way. The combination of the strongest Navy with that of the strongest Army would afford wider possibilities of influence and action than have yet been possessed by any Empire in Modern times.[29]

Indeed, the extent of Germany's economic power, its overseas ramifications and the apparent attempt to combine her formidable military strength with a navy as powerful as Britain's, were felt to be a threat greater than anything Britain had faced in over a century. It was the clearest sign possible of Britain's own loss of industrial leadership, something which France and Russia, for all the difficulties they had caused on her imperial frontiers, had ineffectively challenged. The changes in diplomatic alignments following from this were a direct result of Germany's rise as an industrial power – political reactions to the consequences of uneven development.[30]

27. For the importance of the naval issue in aligning Britain against Germany see P.M. Kennedy, 'German World Policy and the Alliance Negotiations with England, 1897–1900', *Journal of Modern History*, XLV (1973), and idem, *The Rise of the Anglo-German Antagonism*, pp. 415–16, 420–1, 423.

28. See Grey's speech in the House of Commons, 29 March 1909, printed in Sir Edward Grey, *Speeches on Foreign Affairs, 1904–14* (1931), p. 133.

29. Lowe and Dockrill, *The Mirage of Power*, III, p. 459.

30. This seems to be the drift also of Kennedy's argument in *The Rise of the Anglo-German Antagonism*, pp. 464–6. See also the interesting essay by C.A. Fisher, 'The Changing Dimensions of Europe', *Jour. Contemp. Hist.*, 1 (1966).

The agreements of 1904 and 1907, made with France and Russia respectively, indicated clearly that they and Britain had a common and growing fear of German ambitions. The French, already ineradicably hostile to Germany on account of Alsace and Lorraine, were becoming increasingly anxious about Germany's colonial designs, especially in relation to Morocco. The agreement with Britain took the form of an attempt to clear up colonial conflicts and eliminate sources of friction. Britain, for instance, recognised France as the predominant power in Morocco in return for a French promise not to hinder British policy in Egypt – which had long been a source of dispute.[31]

Once the agreement had been reached, the French became anxious to see a similar settlement between their own ally, Russia, and Britain. During the Russian-Japanese War, the commitments made by France and Britain could have resulted in a conflict between them in support of their alliance partners. Russia herself had an interest in reaching agreement with Britain, partly because of her exhausted state after defeat by Japan and partly because of her own nervousness over German and Austrian ambitions in the Balkans. With the British keen to use Russia's temporary weakness to push her into agreement, the Anglo-Russian Convention of 1907 delimited the spheres of the respective powers in Persia and Afghanistan, and temporarily relieved Britain's fears about India. This was of particular importance to Britain since, once the Trans-Siberian Railway had been completed and before the defeat of Russia by Japan, the British had become increasingly gloomy about their ability to forestall a strong advance by Russia on the buffer states around the Indian Empire.[32]

There was very little positive commitment to joint action in these agreements and the British in particular were extremely wary of any formal alliance binding them to fight on the side of France and Russia in a European war. Indeed, given the strong Cobdenite element in the Liberal Cabinet after 1906, no formal commitment to fight could have been made without destroying the government. Nevertheless, Britain's support for France and Russia was stiffened considerably during the years 1906 to 1914 as a result of the naval conflict with Germany and because of the latter's clumsy and counter-productive

31. P. Guillen, 'The Entente of 1904 as a Colonial Settlement', in Prosser Gifford and W. Roger Louis, eds. *France and Britain in Africa* (New Haven, Conn., 1971).
32. Monger, *The End of Isolation*, Chs. 6, 7, 11; Steiner, *Britain and the Origins of the First World War*, Ch. 4.

attempts, particularly in the Moroccan crises of 1906 and 1911, to undermine the Anglo-French colonial settlement.[33]

Although this picture of the inevitability of conflict (rather than the inevitability of war) between Britain and Germany fits in reasonably well with the work of many prominent diplomatic historians, it is not unassailable. Starting from the premiss that the most pressing necessity of British policy around the turn of the century was the security of her Indian and Asiatic interests, it could be inferred that the essential route to this, given a shortage of resources, was an accord with Russia. But that accord could be reached only by way of agreement with Russia's ally, France; the result of this would, inevitably, have put Britain in opposition to Germany. From this perspective, the Anglo-German conflict was a simple by-product of an attempt to safeguard British imperial interests: paradoxically, Germany became the enemy precisely because she was the power least likely to pose a direct threat to the eastern empire.[34] It is true that the British reaction to the German navy in the early days was fairly mild and that the French and Russian ententes were also sought as ways of curbing mounting defence costs independently of any supposed provocation by Germany. Even so, this reading of the creation of the Entente does not really account for the intensity and the widespread nature of Britain's hostility to Germany in the years immediately before the outbreak of war. As the builder of a navy only a few hundred miles from Britain's shores, the Germans were bound to appear more directly threatening than either France or Russia.

German penetration of British and empire markets also contributed to the conflict. British alarm at German 'dumping' of manufactures in her market was much greater in the depressed mid–1890s than afterwards, when the problem was alleviated to some degree by the rapid growth of world trade.[35] Nonetheless, after 1900 Britain's fear

33. S.L. Mayer, 'Anglo-German Rivalry at the Algeciras Conference', in Prosser Gifford and W. Roger Louis, eds. *Britain and Germany in Africa* (New Haven, Conn., 1967); J.S. Mortimer, 'Commercial Interests and German Diplomacy in the Agadir Crisis', *Hist. Jour.*, X (1967); Monger, *The End of Isolation*, Chs. 8 and 10.

34. For this argument see Keith Wilson, *The Policy of the Entente: Essays on the Determinants of British Foreign Policy* (1985); and idem, *Empire and Continent: Studies in British Foreign Policy from the 1880s to the First World War* (1987).

35. The *locus classicus* for the argument over German infiltration of the British domestic market for manufactures is E.E. Williams, *Made in Germany* (Brighton, 1973), first published in 1895. The standard scholarly account is R.J.S. Hoffman, *Great Britain and the German Trade Rivalry, 1875–1914* (1933). For more recent work see H. Neuberger and H.H. Stokes, 'The Anglo-German Trade Rivalry, 1887–1913; a Counterfactual Outcome and Its Implications', *Social Science History*, III (1979);

of German penetration of her domestic market – and imperial ones – was never far below the surface; this antagonism emerged, unashamedly, into the light of day during the brief industrial slump of 1908–9.[36] Like the Fair Traders before them, the Tariff Reformers always gained adherents in depression, and elements within the movement were quite outspokenly anti-German. It is plain that the 'strategic' reasons for free trade espoused by the Foreign Office fitted in neatly enough with the interests of cotton barons and shipbuilders and those who believed that Britain's invisible earnings (which depended to a large degree on the level of world trade in general) were a crucial element in her defence strategy because of the command they gave over vital resources overseas. But, as we have seen, this did not make much impression upon those who felt that the same policy that encouraged the growth of invisibles also eroded the industrial base.

The protectionists and imperialists had no hope of persuading the Liberals to adopt their cause and they failed to win over the Conservatives; but, under the stress of acute depression, the mild revenue tariffs proposed by Conservatives just before the war could have hardened into a protectionist, anti-German weapon under some future government of the Right. Germany was intensely nervous of a possible British tariff and of imperial preference, and some high-ranking officials clearly felt that the introduction of protection by Britain would be a deliberately hostile, even warlike, act.[37] Any settlement of differences between Britain and Germany would have had to include guarantees for maintaining easy entry for German goods into British and imperial markets; there is some sense in Hoffman's claim of 50 years ago that 'the pressure of German business in British markets drove Great Britain towards protection and imperial preference while the drift towards Tariff Reform stimulated German navalism and imperialism'.[38] After 1900, hostility to Germany on the industrial front and the tariff question both became entangled with a wider, right-of-centre, political movement which sought to implement 'social imperialist' policies and to make Britain

Christoph Bucheim, 'Aspects of Nineteenth-Century Anglo-German Trade Rivalry Reconsidered', *Jour. Eur. Econ. Hist.*, X (1981); Steiner, *Britain and the Origins of the First World War*, pp. 29–32; and Kennedy, *The Rise of the Anglo-German Antagonism*, Chs. 15 and 16.

36. Hoffman, *The Anglo-German Trade Rivalry*, pp. 286–9.
37. Ibid. pp. 290–1.
38. Ibid. p. 285.

capable of meeting the challenge of German military and economic competition.[39]

Economic rivalry was fundamental to the dispute between Great Britain and Germany, and was muted only by the rapid growth of international trade just before 1914. It was also a rivalry which was global in scope. The occasional discussions over purely colonial matters and the desultory negotiations about sharing out the Dutch and Portuguese empires should they collapse, were of marginal significance, as contemporaries themselves were well aware.[40]

Once the war had begun, Britain had no real choice but to join in on the side of France and Russia, despite the lack of any formal commitments to give armed support and despite the pacifist inclinations of the majority of the Liberal government. The radical element in the party had been strong enough to prevent any categorical military pledge to Britain's allies and had helped to steer her away from any drastic measures, such as conscription, which would have given Britain's forces great weight in a continental battle.[41] They could not, however, prevent Britain from entering the war against Germany, and this can be explained in a number of ways. In the first place, the Liberal government knew that, had it resigned rather than face a declaration of war, an incoming Conservative government would have opted for belligerency anyway. In the circumstances the Liberals calculated that it was better to stay in power in the hope of retaining influence over the course of the war.[42] Next, although it is probably wrong to infer, as Mayer has done, the existence of a direct link between the various social crises which rent Britain between 1906 and 1914 and the decision to fight,[43] it is now clear that there was a

39. G.R. Searle, *The Quest for National Efficiency, 1899–1914: A Study in British Politics and Political Thought* (Oxford, 1971); idem, 'Critics of Edwardian Society: the Case of the Radical Right', in Alan O'Day, ed. *Edwardian England* (1979); Robert J. Scally, *The Origins of the Lloyd George Coalition: The Politics of Social Imperialism, 1900–16* (Princeton, NJ, 1975).

40. On the Portuguese negotiations see Grenville, *Lord Salisbury's Foreign Policy*, Ch. VII; Richard Langhorne, 'Anglo-German Negotiations Concerning the Future of the Portuguese Colonies, 1911–14', *Hist. Jour.*, XVI (1973); and J.D. Vincent Smith, 'Anglo-German Negotiations Over the Portuguese Colonies in Africa, 1911–14', ibid. XVII (1974).

41. On the Radical influence on foreign policy see A.J.A. Morris, *Radicalism Against War, 1906–1914* (1972); Howard Weinroth, 'The British Radicals and the Balance of Power, 1902–14', *Hist. Jour.*, XXII (1974). For their enemies see A.J.A. Morris, *The Scaremongers: The Advocacy of War and Rearmament, 1896–1914* (1986).

42. K.M. Wilson, 'The British Cabinet's Decision for War, 2 August, 1914', *Brit. Jour. Internat. Stud.*, I (1975).

43. This is a part of Mayer's more general thesis on the relationship between the old aristocratic order and the coming of the war. See Arno J. Mayer, *The Persistence of*

strong, though not very articulate, popular feeling that Germany was the enemy and that Britain had to conquer to survive.[44] This grass-roots conviction, based partly on the alarm and anxieties provoked by German industrial competition, had a significant influence upon Grey's thinking in July and August 1914.

Britain was also committed in a different way. Any continental war from which Britain stood aside and which ended in a victory for Germany would have given the latter just that degree of superiority in Europe which it was the aim of British foreign policy to prevent. On the other hand, although a victory for France and Russia, unaided by Britain, might have been less immediately disastrous, it might still have brought a set of solutions for world problems which drastically reduced Britain's power.

Exactly how the British might fight the war was a more contentious matter, and it divided opinion even after hostilities began. 'Navalists', who felt that Britain's survival depended upon sea-power, went beyond the argument that the fleet was vital to keep open the channels of trade and to maintain supplies of cheap food for the masses lest they reject both the war and the social structures from whence it sprang. They believed, too, that naval predominance offered Britain a chance to contribute to an Allied victory by denying the enemy supplies, rather than by committing herself heavily to fighting on land. Navalist strategies were congenial to the Liberal Party with its abhorrence of conscription, and struck a chord with all those who were fearful of wholesale military slaughter. They also appealed because, if Britain stayed on the periphery of the battle in Europe, there was a greater chance that the existing social and economic structure would survive. Opinion in the army, and in the Foreign Office, was different. There, it was felt that a blockade of Germany would incur the wrath of neutral countries, particularly the United States, without bringing the Germans to heel. Only a massive military commitment in Europe would bring victory. The 'continentalists' won in the end, one reason being that the enormous, and unexpected, enthusiasm for the war shown by the bulk of the

---

the *Old Regime: Europe to the Great War* (1981), esp. Ch. V. Also important in this context are Mayer's 'Domestic Causes of the First World War', in Leonard Kreiger and Fritz Stern, eds. *The Responsibility of Power* (New York, 1967); Donald Lammers, 'Arno Mayer and the British Decision for War', *Jour. Brit. Stud.*, XII (1973); and Michael R. Gordon, 'Domestic Conflict and the Origins of the First World War: the British and German Cases', *Jour. Mod. Hist.*, XLVI (1974).

44. Colin Nicholson, 'Edwardian England and the Coming of the First World War', in O'Day, *Edwardian England*.

population meant that a mass army was raised quickly and that the British could make a major impact on the European mainland.[45]

However hesitantly Britain entered the war, the conflict seemed to offer an ideal opportunity to destroy Germany's burgeoning overseas power, at least temporarily, and to preserve Britain's economic dominance overseas – a dominance without which she was of little account in the world.[46] In the event, the economic strain of war and the destruction of the international economy weakened the basis of Britain's world position: when the war ended, the United States was emerging to challenge Britain for the place in the world for which Germany had fought in vain.

Britain's eventual fate had been briefly foreshadowed during the Boer War. With the usual supplies of gold from the Transvaal cut off, the sharp rise in government spending pushed up interest rates rapidly and threatened a heavy drain of gold. In response, the Conservative government of the day decided that funds would have to be raised in New York as well as London. This aroused the 'intense jealousy'[47] of the City, not least because of the boost it gave to the prestige of the great Anglo-American merchant bank, Morgans. The longer-term significance of the episode was not lost on officialdom in Britain. Borrowing in the United States would be useful in a crisis but ought to be kept carefully in check for fear of the consequences. As a senior Treasury man put it in 1901: 'Our commercial supremacy has to go sooner or later; of that I feel no doubt; but we don't want to accelerate its departure across the Atlantic'.[48] That acceleration began in earnest in World War I: it is little wonder that the City was reluctant to go into battle in 1914.[49]

Nonetheless, despite her many problems, Britain was still formidably strong when war broke out. She had been overhauled as an industrial power and technological leadership had passed to others; but she had compensated by extending her commercial and financial influence across the world over the previous half-century. While remembering the pressures and difficulties presented by the spread of industrialisation, it is important not to forget how much Britain's power had grown and how much more she had to defend in 1914

45. Avner Offer, *The First World War: An Agrarian Interpretation* (Oxford, 1989), esp. Chs. 15–21.

46. Hoffman, *The Anglo-German Trade Rivalry, 1875–1914*, pp. 325–9. This subject is pursued further in the case studies which follow in Volume II of the present study.

47. Kathleen Burk, *Morgan Grenfell: The Biography of a Merchant Bank, 1838–1988* (Cambridge, 1989), p. 118.

48. Ibid. p. 119.

49. Kennedy, *The Realities Behind Diplomacy*, p. 137.

compared with 1850. Moreover, although the war inevitably weakened Britain in the face of the challenge of the United States, its impact was not great enough to ensure American dominance of the world economy after 1918. Britain's service economy, and the gentlemanly elites who managed it, survived the war and subsequently renewed their bid for leadership with much ingenuity and some success. If Britain's inability to retain her position as an industrial leader proved, in the very long run, to be her undoing as an imperial power of the first rank, Hilferding was right to believe that her empire, her enormous accumulation of financial assets spread across the globe, and the banking and commercial skills of the City would be critical in keeping her at the centre of the world economic stage well into the twentieth century.

CHAPTER FIFTEEN
Conclusion

Our first and most general conclusion is that the character and purpose of Britain's presence on the moving frontiers of empire can be fully understood only by linking events in diverse parts of the world to causes that can be traced back to the metropole itself.[1] This claim may seem to be self-evident to readers who are not themselves working underground in one of the many deep shafts of historical research, but specialists will probably be willing to acknowledge that a process of continental drift has taken place in the course of the last thirty years and that the various subdivisions created by detailed research, for all their merits, have not provided an accessible route to an understanding of the larger issues that also demand our attention. The process of reunification poses formidable problems. It is necessary, on the domestic front, to penetrate far below the level of diplomatic exchanges and other direct representations of Britain's international interests; at the same time, it is now impossible to discuss events on the periphery with any pretence at adequacy without incorporating the results of the abundant new research produced in the period since decolonisation. In terms of scholarly output, the burdens of empire are heavier today than they have ever been. Once lifted, however, they become an indispensable asset, and one that future interpretations of imperialism must surely mobilise if they are to achieve credibility.

Our own interpretation attempts to connect metropole and periphery by linking innovations in the finance and service sector to the priorities that shaped both national policy and Britain's unofficial

---

1. Readers should note that a fuller statement, summarising the conclusions of both volumes of this study, can be found in Volume II, Chapter 12.

presence abroad. These innovations, symbolised by the foundation of the Bank of England, the creation of the national debt and the rise of associated gentlemanly activities centred on London, are far more important to an understanding of the economic history of modern Britain than is generally allowed. They were also translated, through wealth made in approved ways, into social status and, by a further transformation, into political authority. Beyond this, they entered into the notion of a wider British mission, one that was Christian, civilised and civilising. These developments took concrete shape in the alliance cemented in the eighteenth century between the landed interest, headed by the aristocracy, and the new 'moneyed men' of the City, who had a common interest in the national debt, in forms of mercantile enterprise that gathered or generated revenue, and in the political system later known as Old Corruption. This coalition was reshaped in the nineteenth century, beginning after the defeat of France in 1815, when the leaders of the landed interest started to dismantle the system of political economy put in place following the Revolution of 1688 and to move towards cheap government and free trade. The transition gathered speed in the second half of the nineteenth century, when the balance of the coalition changed to give greater prominence to financial interests, the leading beneficiaries of economic reform, and when a social merger was effected by extending gentlemanly status to the higher ranks of the new urban middle class, who were coopted into the defence of property and order. Taken together, these realignments were designed to manage a distinctive form of conservative progress, one that safeguarded tradition and privilege while also upholding the rights of 'free-born Englishmen' and offering prospects of material improvement.

This compromise was inspired initially by the need to save the polity from an unacceptable choice between tyranny and anarchy. It was kept alive subsequently by fear of subversion from within, whether by Jacobites or, later, by the menacing forces of industrialisation and their offshoot, socialism, and by perceived threats from abroad, ranging from French republicanism to the dangers posed by new, expansive states, whether democratic, like the United States, or centralised, like Germany. However, the link between domestic developments and Britain's international policy and presence was not simply a defensive one: finance and services were expansive from the outset because the productivity gains derived from innovations in credit, shipping and commercial organisation could be fully realised only by increasing their international scope. The configuration of wealth, status and power that materialised in gentlemanly forms of enterprise was therefore outward-bound as well as inward-looking: in the most general terms, it can be said that the overseas empire and Britain's influence beyond it were extensions abroad of the forces first installed by the Revolution of 1688 and transmuted subsequently by the reforms of the nineteenth century.

In the eighteenth century these forces made their mark both on the colonies of white settlement, where deliberate attempts were made to reproduce and hence to reinforce British landed society, and on India, where efforts were made to raise up a class of indigenous land-holders and where the East India Company, one of the principal manifestations of the new commercial order, extended its sway. The subsequent history of the loss of the American colonies and the acquisition of India was closely bound up with the extension of commercial credit, the search for revenue, and the centralising tendencies of the British state. After 1815, and especially after 1850, City finance and associated services performed a vital, indeed historic, function of integrating countries that lacked adequate capital markets of their own. By funding export development overseas, the City enabled newly incorporated regions to raise and service an increasing volume of foreign loans; by generating a massive invisible income from these activities, the City made a crucial contribution to Britain's balance of payments. In this way, the City and sterling acquired a world role, and London became the centre of a system of global payments that continued to expand right down to the outbreak of war in 1914.

Our argument at this point emphasised the fact that the impulses drawing Britain overseas merged economic considerations with a wider programme of development that aimed at raising the standard of civilisation as well as the standard of living, and was accompanied, accordingly, by exports of liberal political principles and missionary enterprise. The underlying purpose of the venture was to nurture congenial allies at critical points of entry or passage for British trade and finance, thus tightening Britain's control over the system of multilateral exchanges on which her prosperity increasingly depended and strengthening her ability to ward off threats from old rivals in Europe and new competitors (notably the United States) further afield.

These expansionist impulses were pacific as well as imperialist in character; and the imperialist option was peaceful and informal as well as aggressive and territorially acquisitive. Broadly similar impulses therefore produced a range of outcomes that reflected the strength of British interests, the structure of the society concerned and the international environment at the time. The colonies of white settlement, for example, fell more firmly under British influence in the second half of the nineteenth century. As they increased their formal political independence, so they became reliant on flows of British capital to an extent that limited their freedom of action in crucial respects and tied export interests and their political representatives to policy norms, the rules of the game, set by London. A very similar pattern can be discerned in the case of the South American republics, where British finance was heavily involved in funding the apparatus of government as well as the growth of exports, thereby helping both to build new nation states and to subordinate them to external influences. As Disraeli observed, 'colonies do not cease to be colonies because they are independent'.[2] The subsequent history of the countries of white settlement, especially their response to mounting pressures for debt repayment from the close of the nineteenth century, attests to the continuing validity of this observation. Nor is the conclusion qualified by examples of the growth of manufacturing on some parts of the periphery towards the close of the period under review. This development undoubtedly limited the market for exports of British consumer goods, but it met the needs of the City because it economised on the import bill of the satellites concerned and helped to generate the export surplus required to service external debts.

Elsewhere, the application of Palmerston's test that non-European societies should be 'well kept' and 'always accessible' produced more candidates than successes.[3] As British finance and influence extended their range in the second half of the century, it became clear that indigenous societies were often unwilling to respond to external demands on the terms set by foreign interests, even when they were able to do so. India, of course, had already been incorporated into the empire and was managed by English gentlemen in ways that guaranteed conformity to priorities established in London. There, as we have seen, policy was directed towards ensuring that India's external obligations continued to be met: when a choice had to be made between the claims of finance and those of manufacturing, as was increasingly the case in the late nineteenth century, preference was given to the former. The most spectacular example of territorial annexation, the partition of Africa, offers a detailed illustration of

2. Speaking in the House of Commons, 5 February 1863. *Parliamentary Debates* 3rd Ser. 169, c.81.
3. Quoted in M.E. Chamberlain, *The Scramble for Africa* (1974), p. 36.

how the penetration of British interests produced conditions that caused Palmerston's rules to be broken. In the two key cases, Egypt and South Africa, a preoccupation with finance and its attendant political implications provided powerful incentives for moving inland. The City's interests were also at the forefront of Britain's presence in areas of informal influence. Following the Ottoman default of 1875, the City's representatives became heavily involved in managing the empire's affairs to ensure that debt service was resumed, and at the same time less willing to supply new finance, with the result that the Foreign Office was hard-pressed to uphold Britain's wider interests in the region. The case of China demonstrates the central part played by finance in different circumstances, for China remained credit-worthy, and when gaps finally opened in the Great Wall after her defeat at the hands of Japan in 1895, British banks were the first to enter, and Britain became the dominant foreign influence on the Ch'ing regime thereafter.

This evidence points to the need to revise some of the central features of the historiography of British imperialism during the classic phase of nineteenth-century expansion. We have questioned the widespread and long-standing assumption linking the 'triumph of industry' to imperialist expansion, and have emphasised instead the role of finance and services. These activities, as we have noted, have long been either underestimated or neglected by historians, yet they arose before the Industrial Revolution, continued to expand during the nineteenth century and maintained their dynamic after manufacturing had entered its long period of relative decline. The representatives of British industry were less wealthy than their counterparts in the City, made their money in ways that did not meet the approval of their social superiors, and exercised only limited political influence at national level. Of course, to the extent that British finance and services were funding the distribution of British manufactures, the two had an important interest in common. But the City's activities were not simply an offshoot of industry; still less were they beholden to it. The international order that was erected on the basis of free trade and the gold standard served the purposes of finance and services rather better than it did those of manufacturing: the increasing scale and complexity of multilateral trade relations gave the City opportunities and commitments that extended far beyond the distribution of British manufactures. Moreover, where a choice had to be made, policy invariably favoured finance over manufacturing. The empirical evidence is compelling: the manufacturing lobby always put its case, but it rarely got its way, whereas the City's needs were very much to the fore in all the examples we have examined – in exercising informal influence, in acquiring territory and in formulating the principles of colonial administration.

This argument carries wider implications for assessing the influence of pressure groups on policy-making. Our study suggests that what is usually referred to, generically, as the 'business' lobby needs to be disaggregated to account for differences of the kind we have identified between the City and industry – a distinction, of course, that is itself open to further refinement. When this is done, the contrast commonly drawn between officialdom and business loses much of its validity because it is apparent that an important segment of the non-industrial business elite consisted of gentlemen who moved in the same circles and shared the same values as those who had their hands on the levers of power – and often managed their investments too. Imperial and imperialist policies did not issue from a conspiracy by a covert minority but from the open exercise of authority by a respected elite who enjoyed the deference of those they governed. Like-mindedness was certainly extended abroad, but it began at home.

Shifting the basis of causation has also required us to reconsider some of the standard categories and chronological divisions of imperial history. Linking imperialism to the process of industrialisation has produced a number of well-known landmarks: an informal empire in the mid-Victorian era followed by the defensive imperialism of a declining power is one; the 'new' imperialism generated by the crisis of advanced industrial capitalism in the late nineteenth century is another. The expansionist impulses we have identified suggest a very different picture. In the mid-Victorian period, informal empire was more of an ideal than a reality. This was not because Britain was self-sufficient and lacked incentives to expand; on the contrary, the record of attempted house-breaking attests to Britain's need to open up the world economy. It was rather that British manufactures were only just beginning to penetrate countries overseas, even at a time when foreign competition was still very limited, principally because they awaited lubrication from British finance and commercial services.

It was not until the second half of the century, after investors had diversified out of the national debt and when free trade had been installed, that capital flows began to accelerate and transport improvements started to deliver the benefits of cheap, bulk carriage. It was at that point, and not before, that countries beyond Europe could develop a sizeable export trade and hence generate the purchasing power to buy imported manufactures and the revenues to fund external loans. And it was only in the late Victorian period that these forces began to be felt in earnest. In other words, Britain's informal influence was growing at precisely the time when it is conventionally thought to have been in decline, and it continued to extend its reach right down to 1914. By plotting the relative performance of British manufactures, and by then using this measure as a proxy for Britain's standing as a world power, the hand has deceived the eye: historians have overlooked, where they have not minimised, the process by which Britain moved from being an early lender to becoming a mature creditor with an increasingly heavy stake in protecting cross-border property rights and the complex international trade flows that were essential guarantees of debt service. As our argument suggests, the most important examples of territorial acquisition in the late nineteenth century were overflows from these expansionist tendencies, not rearguard actions fought to delay decline.[4]

It is true that this was also the time when rival powers, especially France and Germany, were beginning to flex their muscles, and their activities on the world stage are usually linked to Britain's weakening industrial performance to support the conventional conclusion that her standing as an international power was on the wane. This argument, though now routine, is profoundly unsatisfactory. In the first place, it fails to give adequate recognition to the vigorous, expansionist forces we have identified, and thus neglects the possibility that foreign rivals were reacting to Britain's assertive and imperialist impulses as well as expressing claims of their own. Secondly, the thesis is overwhelmed by contrary evidence, which shows that rival powers failed to topple Britain from her dominant position in any of the contested areas of importance outside Europe. In the dominions and India there was scarcely a contest: even in Canada, which was wide open to influences from her large southern neighbour, British finance and services remained supreme. Elsewhere, besides swallowing the most valuable parts of Africa, Britain increased her grip on the leading South American republics and on China. If France and Germany made more headway in the Ottoman Empire, it was mainly because the City took an unforgiving view of the Ottoman default and had better opportunities in more attractive

---

4. An extension of our argument at this point would give fuller consideration to questions such as the definition and defence of property rights in an international setting, the applicability of the distinction between management debt and development debt, the exercise of what today would be called conditionality, and the possibility of establishing a more rigorous typology for understanding decisions to intervene and decisions to annex.

parts of the world. Despite the declining competitiveness of her manufactures, Britain's ability to impose her will within and beyond the empire was still unmatched in 1914 because the London capital market remained the largest, most efficient and hence most competitive in the world – as Germany and France were well aware.

On the eve of World War I, Britain remained a dynamic and ambitious power, fearful of the cost and wider implications of large-scale conflict, but nevertheless assertive in pursuit of her own expansionist aims. When war came in 1914, it brought many of the expected adverse consequences. But the conclusion that beckons should be resisted: the period between World War I and the end of empire was not simply a long retreat directed by faltering and increasingly weary Titans. Just as the causes and chronology of British imperialism need to be revised for the era before 1914, so too a different perspective is required for appraising imperialist impulses thereafter. The familiar story of Britain's decline as a world power merits reassessment in the light of evidence of her continuing imperialist aspirations and her underestimated successes. The circumstances of the period were different, but Britain's strategy still lay in the hands of officers and gentlemen whose vision of a world order managed from London remained undimmed. This next episode, being in many respects less familiar to historians of imperialism, contains attractions and hazards of its own: some of the existing boundary stones may need to be moved; others have yet to be put in place.

Maps

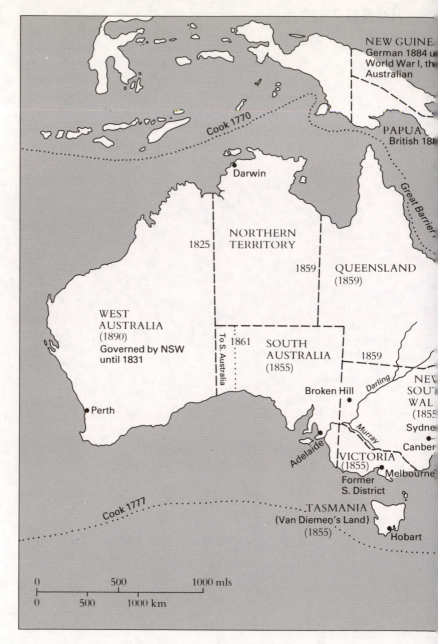

Map 1. Australasia, 1825–1914
After: J.O. Lloyd, *The British Empire, 1558–1933* (Oxford, 1984)

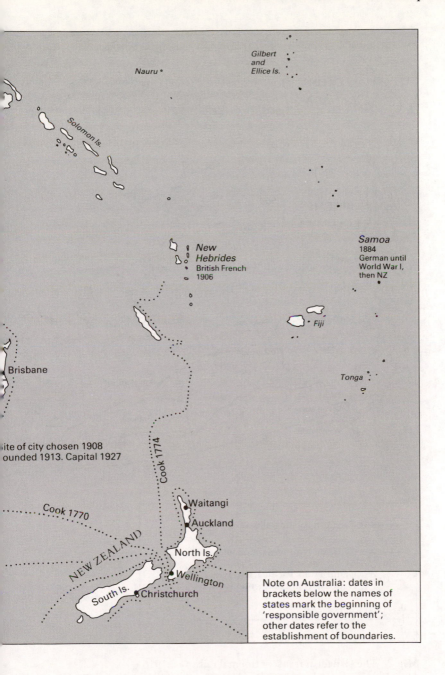

Nauru

Gilbert and Ellice Is.

Solomon Is.

New
Hebrides
British French
1906

Samoa
1884
German until
World War I,
then NZ

Fiji

Brisbane

Tonga

site of city chosen 1908
ounded 1913. Capital 1927

Cook 1774

Cook 1770

Waitangi

Auckland

NEW ZEALAND

North Is.

Wellington

South Is.
Christchurch

Note on Australia: dates in
brackets below the names of
states mark the beginning of
'responsible government';
other dates refer to the
establishment of boundaries.

477

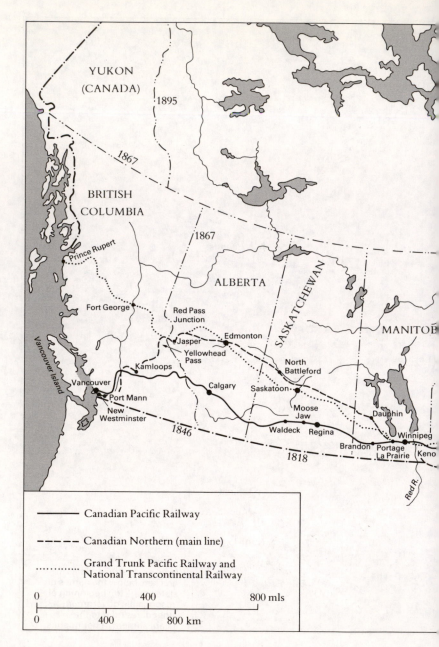

Map 2. The Canadian transcontinental railways, 1916
After: W.J. Easterbrook and H.G.C. Aitkin, *Canadian Economic History* (Toronto, 1956)

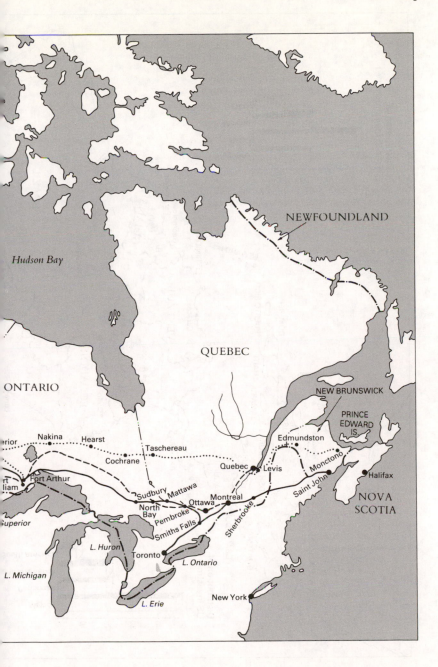

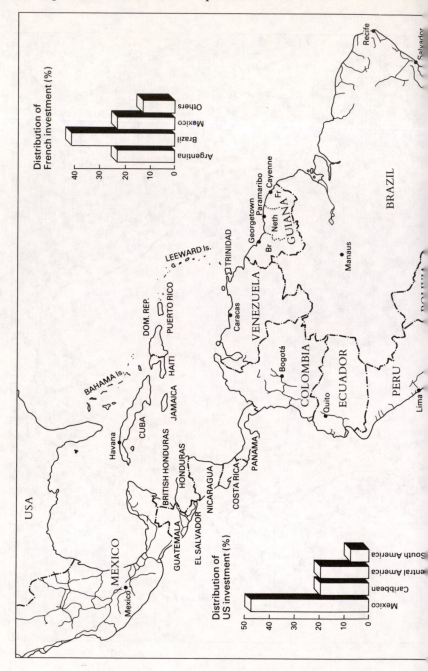

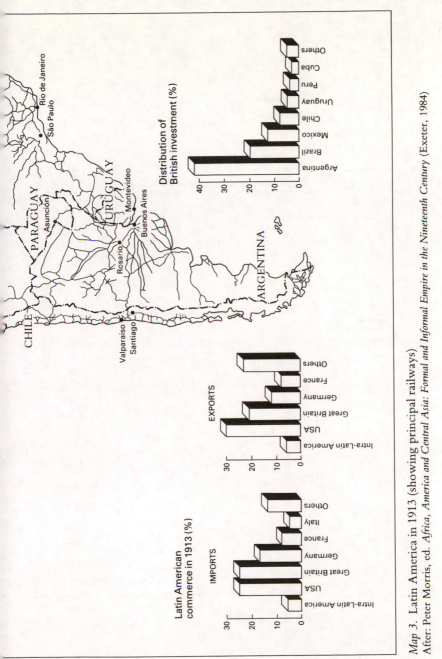

Map 3. Latin America in 1913 (showing principal railways)
After: Peter Morris, ed. *Africa, America and Central Asia: Formal and Informal Empire in the Nineteenth Century* (Exeter, 1984)

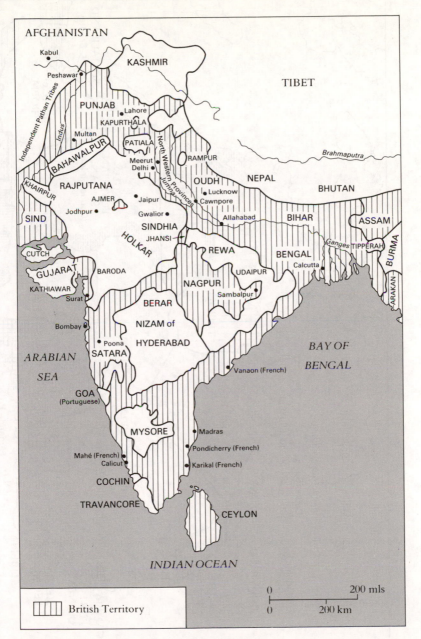

AFGHANISTAN

Kabul

Peshawar

KASHMIR

TIBET

Independent Pathan Tribes

PUNJAB

Lahore

KAPURTHALA

Indus

Multan

BAHAWALPUR

PATIALA

RAMPUR

Brahmaputra

KHAIRPUR

Meerut
Delhi

North Western Provinces

NEPAL

BHUTAN

RAJPUTANA

OUDH

AJMER

Jaipur

Lucknow

Cawnpore

ASSAM

SIND

Jodhpur

Gwalior

Allahabad

BIHAR

Jumna

SINDHIA

Ganges

TIPPERAH

HOLKAR

JHANSI

REWA

BENGAL

BURMA

CUTCH

Calcutta

GUJARAT

BARODA

NAGPUR

UDAIPUR

ARAKAN

KATHIAWAR

Surat

Sambalpur

BERAR

Bombay

NIZAM of

HYDERABAD

BAY OF
BENGAL

Poona

SATARA

ARABIAN
SEA

Vanaon (French)

GOA
(Portuguese)

MYSORE

Madras

Mahé (French)

Pondicherry (French)

Calicut

Karikal (French)

COCHIN

TRAVANCORE

CEYLON

INDIAN OCEAN

0   200 mls

0   200 km

British Territory

Map 4. India on the eve of the Indian Mutiny
After: C.C. Eldridge, *Victorian Imperialism* (1978)

483

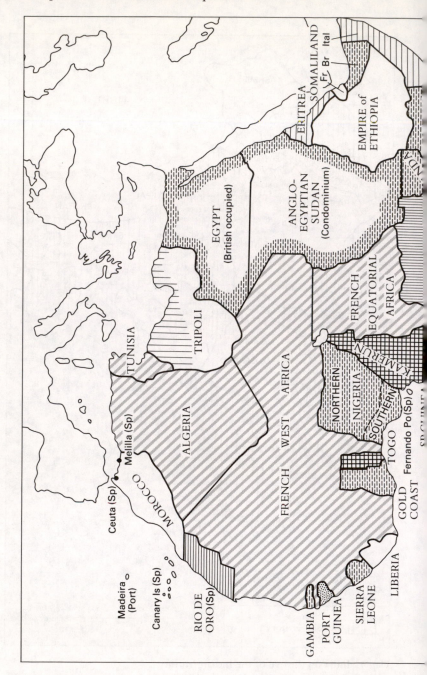

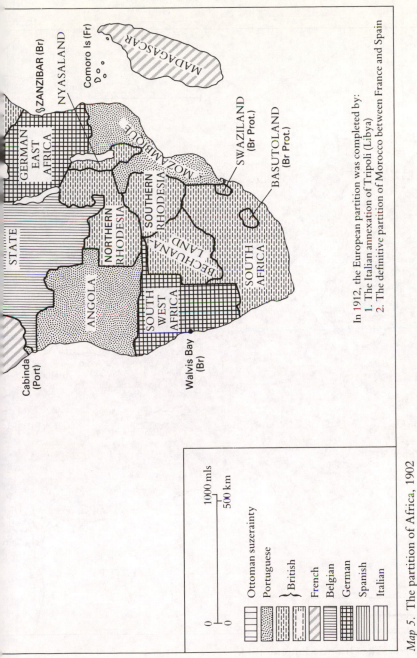

NYASALAND

ZANZIBAR (Br)

Comoro Is (Fr)

MADAGASCAR

GERMAN
EAST
AFRICA

STATE

MOZAMBIQUE

SWAZILAND
(Br Prot.)

BASUTOLAND
(Br Prot.)

NORTHERN
RHODESIA

SOUTHERN
RHODESIA

BECHUANA-
LAND

ANGOLA

SOUTH
AFRICA

SOUTH
WEST
AFRICA

Cabinda
(Port)

Walvis Bay
(Br)

In 1912, the European partition was completed by:
1. The Italian annexation of Tripoli (Libya)
2. The definitive partition of Morocco between France and Spain

1000 mls

500 km

Ottoman suzerainty

Portuguese

} British

French

Belgian

German

Spanish

Italian

Map 5. The partition of Africa, 1902
After: A.D. Roberts, ed. *The Cambridge History of Africa* 6 (Cambridge, 1985)

Map 6. The Ottoman Empire, 1914
After: Marian Kent, ed. *The Great Powers and the End of the Ottoman Empire* (1984)

486

RUSSIA

CASPIAN
SEA

BLACK

SEA

Sinope

Samsun

Batum

Baku

Trebizond

Kars

Aras R.

ARMENIA

Lake
Van

L. Urmia

Kharput

Tehran

Bozanti

Alexandretta

Nisibin

Mosul

PERSIA

Aleppo

Meskene

Dair-az-Zar

Hama

Homs

Euphrates R.

Baghdad

Tripoli

Beirut

LEBANON

Damascus

MESOPOTAMIA
(IRAQ)

Tigris R.

The Shatt-el-Arab

PALESTINE

Jaffa
(Tel Aviv)

Amman

Basra

Jerusalem

Koweit
(Kuwait)

Persian Gulf

TRANS-JORDAN

NEJD

Bahrain

Qatar

HEJAZ

Red Sea

487

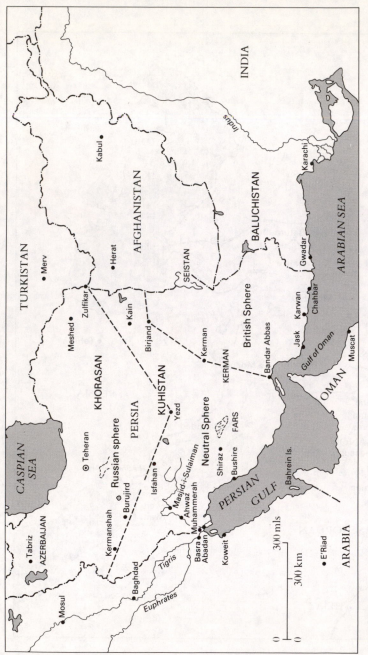

Map 7. Persia, 1914

After: L.C.M. Platt, *Finance, Trade and Politics: British Foreign Policy, 1815–1914* (Oxford, 1968)

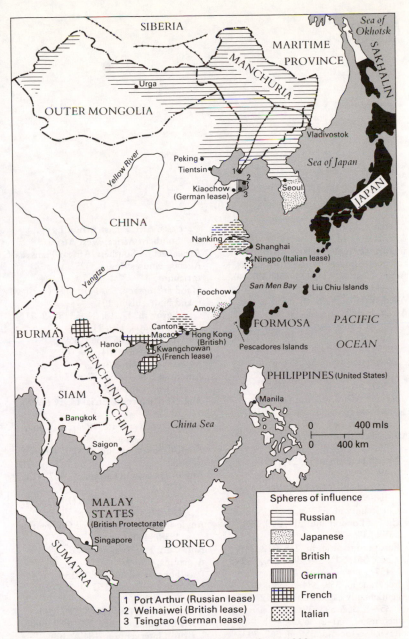

Map 8. Foreign spheres of influence in China about 1900
After: C.C. Eldridge, *Victorian Imperialism* (1978)

Index